Principles behind the Agile Manifesto

We follow these principles:

- Our highest priority is to satisfy the customer through early and continuous delivery of valuable software.

- Welcome changing requirements, even late in development. Agile processes harness change for the customer's competitive advantage.

- Deliver working software frequently, from a couple of weeks to a couple of months, with a preference to the shorter timescale.

- Business people and developers must work together daily throughout the project.

- Build projects around motivated individuals. Give them the environment and support they need, and trust them to get the job done.

- The most efficient and effective method of conveying information to and within a development team is face-to-face conversation.

- Working software is the primary measure of progress.

- Agile processes promote sustainable development. The sponsors, developers, and users should be able to maintain a constant pace indefinitely.

- Continuous attention to technical excellence and good design enhances agility.

- Simplicity—the art of maximizing the amount of work not done—is essential.

- The best architectures, requirements, and designs emerge from self-organizing teams.

- At regular intervals, the team reflects on how to become more effective, then tunes and adjusts its behavior accordingly.

Agile Software Development

Principles, Patterns, and Practices

Robert Cecil Martin

Alan Apt Series

Pearson Education, Inc.
Upper Saddle River, New Jersey 07458

Library of Congress Cataloging-in-Publication Data

Martin, Robert C.
   Agile software development: principles, patterns, and practices / Robert Martin.
      p.   cm.
   Includes bibliographical references and index.
   ISBN 0-13-597444-5
   1. Computer software—Development. 2. eXtreme programming. I. Title.

QA76.76.D47 M362 2002
005.1—dc21   2002070056

Vice President and Editorial Director, ECS: *Marcia J. Horton*
Publisher: *Alan R Apt*
Assistant Editor: *Toni D. Holm*
Editorial Assistant: *Patrick Lindner*
Vice President and Director of Production and Manufacturing, ESM: *David W. Riccardi*
Executive Managing Editor: *Vince O'Brien*
Assistant Managing Editor: *Camille Trentacoste*
Production Editor: *Fran Daniele*
Director of Creative Services: *Paul Belfanti*
Creative Director: *Carole Anson*
Cover Designer: *Bruce Kenselaar*
Art Editor: *Greg Dulles*
Manufacturing Manager: *Trudy Pisciotti*
Manufacturing Buyer: *Lynda Castillo*
Marketing Manager: *Pamela Shaffer*
Assistant Marketing Manager: *Barrie Reinhold*

© 2003 by Pearson Education, Inc.
Pearson Education, Inc.
Upper Saddle River, NJ 07458

ISBN 0-13-597444-5

Pearson Education LTD., *London*
Pearson Education Australia PTY, Limited, *Sydney*
Pearson Education Singapore, Pte. Ltd.
Pearson Education North Asia Ltd., *Hong Kong*
Pearson Education Canada, Ltd., *Toronto*
Pearson Educación de Mexico, S.A. de C.V.
Pearson Education—Japan, *Tokyo*
Pearson Education Malaysia, Pte. Ltd.
Pearson Education, Upper Saddle River, *New Jersey*

Foreword

I'm writing this foreword right after having shipped a major release of the Eclipse open source project. I'm still in recovery mode, and my mind is bleary. But one thing remains clearer than ever: that people, not processes, are the key to shipping a product. Our recipe for success is simple: work with individuals obsessed with shipping software, develop with lightweight processes that are tuned to each team, and adapt constantly.

Double-clicking on developers from our teams reveals individuals who consider programming the focus of development. Not only do they write code; they digest it constantly to maintain an understanding of the system. Validating designs with code provides feedback that's crucial for getting confidence in a design. At the same time, our developers understand the importance of patterns, refactoring, testing, incremental delivery, frequent builds, and other best-practices of XP that have altered the way we view methodologies today.

Skill in this style of development is a prerequisite for success in projects with high technical risk and changing requirements. Agile development is low-key on ceremony and project documentation, but it's intense when it comes to the day-to-day development practices that count. Putting these practices to work is the focus of this book.

Robert is a longtime activist in the object-oriented community, with contributions to C++ practice, design patterns, and object-oriented design principles in general. He was an early and vocal advocate of XP and agile methods. This book builds on these contributions, covering the full spectrum of agile development practice. It's an ambitious effort. Robert makes it more so by demonstrating everything through case studies and lots of code, as befits agile practice. He explains programming and design by actually doing it.

This book is crammed with sensible advice for software development. It's equally good whether you want to become an agile developer or improve the skills you already have. I was looking forward to this book, and I wasn't disappointed.

Erich Gamma
Object Technology International

For Ann Marie, Angela, Micah, Gina, Justin, Angelique, Matt, and Alexis . . .

There is no greater treasure,
Nor any wealthier trove,
Than the company of my family,
And the comfort of their love.

Preface

But Bob, you said you'd be done with the book <u>last</u> year.

—Claudia Frers, *UML World*, 1999

Agile development is the ability to develop software quickly, in the face of rapidly changing requirements. In order to achieve this agility, we need to employ practices that provide the necessary discipline and feedback. We need to employ design principles that keep our software flexible and maintainable, and we need to know the design patterns that have been shown to balance those principles for specific problems. This book is an attempt to knit all three of these concepts together into a functioning whole.

This book describes those principles, patterns, and practices and then demonstrates, how they are applied by walking through dozens of different case studies. More importantly, the case studies are not presented as complete works. Rather, they are designs *in progress*. You will see the designers make mistakes, and you will observe how they identify the mistakes and eventually correct them. You will see them puzzle over conundrums and worry over ambiguities and trade-offs. You will see the *act* of design.

The Devil Is in the Details

This book contains a *lot* of Java and C++ code. I hope you will carefully read that code since, to a large degree, the code is the *point* of the book. The code is the actualization of what this book has to say.

There is a repeating pattern to this book. It consists of a series of case studies of varying sizes. Some are very small, and some require several chapters to describe. Each case study is preceded by material that is meant to prepare you for it. For example, the Payroll case study is preceded by chapters describing the object-oriented design principles and patterns used in the case study.

The book begins with a discussion of development practices and processes. That discussion is punctuated by a number of small case studies and examples. From there, the book moves on to the topic of design and design principles, and then to some design patterns, more design principles that govern packages, and more patterns. All of these topics are accompanied by case studies.

So prepare yourself to read some code and to pore over some UML diagrams. The book you are about to read is *very* technical, and its lessons, like the devil, are in the details.

A Little History

Over six years ago, I wrote a book entitled *Designing Object-Oriented C++ Applications using the Booch Method.* It was something of magnum opus for me, and I was very pleased with the result and with the sales.

This book started out as a second edition to *Designing*, but that's not how it turned out. Very little remains of the original book in these pages. Little more than three chapters have been carried through, and those chapters have been massively changed. The intent, spirit, and many of the lessons of the book are the same. And yet, I've learned a tremendous amount about software design and development in the six years since *Designing* came out. This book reflects that learning.

What a half-decade! *Designing* came out just before the Internet collided with the planet. Since then, the number of abbreviations we have to deal with has doubled. We have Design Patterns, Java, EJB, RMI, J2EE, XML, XSLT, HTML, ASP, JSP, Servlets, Application Servers, ZOPE, SOAP, C#, .NET, etc., etc. Let me tell you, it's been hard to keep the chapters of this book reasonably current!

The Booch Connection

In 1997, I was approached by Grady Booch to help write the third edition of his amazingly successful *Object-Oriented Analysis and Design with Applications.* I had worked with Grady before on some projects, and I had been an avid reader and contributor to his various works, including UML. So I accepted with glee. I asked my good friend Jim Newkirk to help out with the project.

Over the next two years, Jim and I wrote a number of chapters for the Booch book. Of course, that effort meant that I could not put as much effort into this book as I would have liked, but I felt that the Booch book was worth the contribution. Besides, this book was really just a second edition of *Designing* at the time, and my heart wasn't in it. If I was going to say something, I wanted to say something new and different.

Unfortunately, that version of the Booch book was not to be. It is hard to find the time to write a book during normal times. During the heady days of the ".com" bubble, it was nearly impossible. Grady got ever busier with Rational and with new ventures like Catapulse. So the project stalled. Eventually, I asked Grady and Addison–Wesley if I could have the chapters that Jim and I wrote to include in *this* book. They graciously agreed. So several of the case study and UML chapters came from that source.

The Impact of Extreme Programming

In late 1998, XP reared its head and challenged our cherished beliefs about software development. Should we create lots of UML diagrams prior to writing any code, or should we eschew any kind of diagrams and just write lots of code? Should we write lots of narrative documents that describe our design, or should we try to make the *code* narrative and expressive so that ancillary documents aren't necessary? Should we program in pairs? Should we write tests before we write production code? What should we do?

This revolution came at an opportune time for me. During the middle to late 90s, Object Mentor was helping quite a few companies with object-oriented (OO) design and project management issues. We were helping companies get their projects *done*. As part of that help, we instilled our own attitudes and practices into the teams. Unfortunately, these attitudes and practices were not written down. Rather, they were an oral tradition that was passed from us to our customers.

By 1998, I realized that we needed to write down our process and practices so that we could better articulate them to our customers. So, I wrote many articles about process in the *C++ Report*.[1] These articles missed the mark. They were informative, and in some cases entertaining, but instead of codifying the practices and attitudes

---

1. These articles are available in the "publications" section of http://www.objectmentor.com. There are four of them. The first three are entitled "Iterative and Incremental Development" (I, II, III). The last is entitled "C.O.D.E Culled Object Development procEss."

that we actually used in our projects, they were an unwitting compromise to values that had been imposed upon me for decades. It took Kent Beck to show me that.

The Beck Connection

In late 1998, as I was fretting over codifying the Object-Mentor process, I ran into Kent's work on Extreme Programming (XP). The work was scattered through Ward Cunningham's *wiki*[2] and was mixed with the writings of many others. Still, with some work and diligence I was able to get the gist of what Kent was talking about. I was intrigued, but skeptical. Some of the things that XP talked about were exactly on target for my concept of a development process. Other things, however, like the lack of an articulated design step, left me puzzled.

Kent and I could not have come from more disparate software circumstances. He was a recognized Smalltalk consultant, and I was a recognized C++ consultant. Those two worlds found it difficult to communicate with one another. There was an almost Kuhnian[3] paradigm gulf between them.

Under other circumstances, I would never have asked Kent to write an article for the *C++ Report*. But the congruence of our thinking about process was able to breech the language gulf. In February of 1999, I met Kent in Munich at the OOP conference. He was giving a talk on XP in the room across from where I was giving a talk on principles of OOD. Being unable to hear that talk, I sought Kent out at lunch. We talked about XP, and I asked him to write an article for the *C++ Report*. It was a great article about an incident in which Kent and a coworker had been able to make a sweeping design change in a live system in a matter of an hour or so.

Over the next several months, I went through the slow process of sorting out my own fears about XP. My greatest fear was in adopting a process in which there is no explicit up-front design step. I found myself balking at that. Didn't I have an obligation to my clients, and to the industry as a whole, to teach them that design is important enough to spend time on?

Eventually, I realized that I did not really practice such a step myself. Even in all the articles and books I had written about design, Booch diagrams, and UML diagrams, I had always used code as a way to verify that the diagrams were meaningful. In all my customer consulting, I would spend an hour or two helping them to draw diagrams and then I would direct them to explore those diagrams with code. I came to understand that though XP's words about design were foreign (in a Kuhnian[4] sense), the practices behind the words were familiar to me.

My other fears about XP were easier to deal with. I had always been a closet pair programmer. XP gave me a way to come out of the closet and revel in my desire to program with a partner. Refactoring, continuous integration, and customer on-site were all very easy for me to accept. They were very close to the way I already advised my customers to work.

One practice of XP was a revelation for me. Test-first design sounds innocuous when you first hear it. It says to write test cases before you write production code. All production code is written to make failing test cases pass. I was not prepared for the profound ramifications that writing code this way would have. This practice has completely transformed the way I write software, and transformed it for the better. You can see that transformation in this book. Some of the code written in this book was written before 1999. You won't find test cases for that code. On the other hand, all of the code written after 1999 is presented with test cases, and the test cases are typically presented first. I'm sure you'll note the difference.

So, by the fall of 1999 I was convinced that Object Mentor should adopt XP as its process of choice and that I should let go of my desire to write my own process. Kent had done an excellent job of articulating the practices and process of XP, and my own feeble attempts paled in comparison.

---

2.   http://c2.com/cgi/wiki. This website contains a vast number of articles on an immense variety of subjects. Its authors number in the hundreds or thousands. It has been said that only Ward Cunningham could instigate a social revolution using a few lines of Perl.

3.   Any credible intellectual work written between 1995 and 2001 must use the term "Kuhnian." It refers to the book, *The Structure of Scientific Revolutions,* by Thomas S. Kuhn, The University of Chicago Press, 1962.

4.   If you mention Kuhn twice in a paper, you get extra credit.

Organization

This book is organized into six major sections followed by several appendices.

- Section 1: *Agile Development.*
  This section describes the concept of agile development. It starts with the Manifesto of the Agile Alliance, provides an overview of Extreme Programming (XP), and then goes into many small case studies that illuminate some of the individual XP practices—especially those that have an impact upon the way we design and write code.
- Section 2: *Agile Design*
  The chapters in this section talk about object-oriented software design. The first chapter asks the question, *What is Design?* It discusses the problem of, and techniques for, managing complexity. Finally, the section culminates with the *principles of object-oriented class design.*
- Section 3: *The Payroll Case Study*
  This is the largest and most complete case study in the book. It describes the object-oriented design and C++ implementation of a simple batch payroll system. The first few chapters in this section describe the design patterns that the case study encounters. The final two chapters contain the full case study.
- Section 4: *Packaging the Payroll System*
  This section begins by describing the *principles of object-oriented package design.* It then goes on to illustrate those principles by incrementally packaging the classes from the previous section.
- Section 5: *The Weather Station Case Study*
  This section contains one of the case studies that was originally planned for the Booch book. The Weather Station study describes a company that has made a significant business decision and explains how the Java development team responds to it. As usual, the section begins with a description of the design patterns that will be used and then culminates in the description of the design and implementation.
- Section 6: *The ETS Case Study*
  This section contains a description of an actual project that the author participated in. This project has been in production since 1999. It is the automated test system used to deliver and score the registry examination for the National Council of Architectural Registration Boards.
- UML Notation Appendices
  The first two appendices contains several small case studies that are used to describe the UML notation.
- Miscellaneous Appendices

How to Use This Book

If You are a Developer...

Read the book cover to cover. This book was written primarily for developers, and it contains the information you need to develop software in an agile manner. Reading the book cover to cover introduces practices, then principles, then patterns, and then it provides case studies that tie them all together. Integrating all this knowledge will help you get your projects *done.*

If You Are a Manager or Business Analyst...

Read Section 1, *Agile Development.* The chapters in this section provide an in-depth discussion of agile principles and practices. They'll take you from requirements to planning to testing, refactoring, and programming. It will give you guidance on how to build teams and manage projects. It will help you get your projects *done.*

If You Want to Learn UML...

First read Appendix A, *UML Notation I: The CGI Example.* Then read Appendix B, *UML Notation II: The STATMUX.* Then, read all the chapters in Section 3, *The Payroll Case Study.* This course of reading will give you a good grounding in both the syntax and use of UML. It will also help you translate between UML and a programming language like Java or C++.

If You Want to Learn Design Patterns...

To find a particular pattern, use the "List of Design Patterns" on page xxii to find the pattern you are interested in.

To learn about patterns in general, read Section 2, *Agile Design* to first learn about design principles, and then read Section 3, *The Payroll Case Study*; Section 4, *Packaging the Payroll System*; Section 5, *The Weather Station Case Study*; and Section 6, *The ETS Case Study*. These sections define all the patterns and show how to use them in typical situations.

If You Want to Learn about Object-Oriented Design Principles...

Read Section 2, *Agile Design*; Section 3, *The Payroll Case Study*; and Section 4, *Packaging the Payroll System*. These chapters will describe the principles of object-oriented design and will show you how to use them.

If You Want to Learn about Agile Development Methods...

Read Section 1, *Agile Development*. This section describes agile development from requirements to planning, testing, refactoring, and programming.

If You Want a Chuckle or Two...

Read Appendix C, *A Satire of Two Companies*.

Acknowledgments

A heartfelt thanks to:

Lowell Lindstrom, Brian Button, Erik Meade, Mike Hill, Michael Feathers, Jim Newkirk, Micah Martin, Angelique Thouvenin Martin, Susan Rosso, Talisha Jefferson, Ron Jeffries, Kent Beck, Jeff Langr, David Farber, Bob Koss, James Grenning, Lance Welter, Pascal Roy, Martin Fowler, John Goodsen, Alan Apt, Paul Hodgetts, Phil Markgraf, Pete McBreen, H. S. Lahman, Dave Harris, James Kanze, Mark Webster, Chris Biegay, Alan Francis, Fran Daniele, Patrick Lindner, Jake Warde, Amy Todd, Laura Steele, William Pietr, Camille Trentacoste, Vince O'Brien, Gregory Dulles, Lynda Castillo, Craig Larman, Tim Ottinger, Chris Lopez, Phil Goodwin, Charles Toland, Robert Evans, John Roth, Debbie Utley, John Brewer, Russ Ruter, David Vydra, Ian Smith, Eric Evans, everyone in the Silicon Valley Patterns group, Pete Brittingham, Graham Perkins, Phlip, and Richard MacDonald.

The books reviewers:

Pete McBreen / McBreen Consulting
Stephen J. Mellor / Projtech.com
Brian Button / Object Mentor Inc.

Bjarne Stroustrup / AT & T Research
Micah Martin / Object Mentor Inc.
James Grenning / Object Mentor Inc.

A very special thanks to Grady Booch and Paul Becker for allowing me to include chapters that were originally slated for Grady's third edition of *Object Oriented Analysis and Design with Applications*.

A special thanks to Jack Reeves for graciously allowing me to reproduce his "What is Design?" article.

Another special thanks to Erich Gamma, for writing the forward to this book. I hope the fonts are better this time Erich!

The wonderful and sometimes dazzling illustrations at the head of each chapter were drawn by Jennifer Kohnke. The decorative illustrations scattered throughout the midst of the chapters are the lovely product of Angela Dawn Martin Brooks, my daughter, and one of the joys of my life.

Resources

All the source code in this book can be downloaded from www.objectmentor.com/PPP.

About the Authors

Robert C. Martin

Robert C. Martin (Uncle Bob) has been a software professional since 1970 and an international software consultant since 1990. He is founder and president of Object Mentor Inc., a team of experienced consultants who mentor their clients worldwide in the fields of C++, Java, .NET, OO, Patterns, UML, Agile Methodologies, and Extreme Programming. In 1995, Robert authored the best-selling book: *Designing Object Oriented C++ Applications using the Booch Method*, published by Prentice Hall. From 1996 to 1999 he was the editor-in-chief of the C++ Report. In 1997, he was chief editor of the book: *Pattern Languages of Program Design 3*, published by Addison–Wesley. In 1999, he was the editor of *More C++ Gems* published by Cambridge Press. He is co-author, with James Newkirk, of *XP in Practice*, Addision–Wesley, 2001. In 2002, he wrote the long awaited *Agile Software Development: Principles, Patterns, and Practices*, Prentice Hall, 2002. He has published dozens of articles in various trade journals, and is a regular speaker at international conferences and trade shows. And he's as happy as a clam.

James W. Newkirk

James Newkirk is a Software Development Manager/Architect. His eighteen years of experience ranges from programming real-time micro-controllers to web services. He co-wrote *Extreme Programming in Practice*, published by Addison–Wesley, 2001. Since August of 2000 he has been working with the .NET Framework and has contributed to the development of NUnit, a unit-testing tool for .NET.

Robert S. Koss

Robert S. Koss, Ph.D., has been writing software for 29 years. He has applied the principles of Object Oriented Design to many projects where he has served in roles ranging from programmer to senior architect. Dr. Koss has taught hundreds of OOD and programming language courses to thousands of students throughout the world. He is currently employed as a Senior Consultant at Object Mentor, Inc.

Brief Contents

Contents

Chapter 11 **DIP: The Dependency-Inversion Principle**   **127**

> *A. High-level modules should not depend upon low-level modules.*
> *Both should depend on abstractions.*
>
> *B. Abstractions should not depend on details. Details should*
> *depend on abstractions.*

Chapter 12 **ISP: The Interface-Segregation Principle**   **135**

> *Clients should not be forced to depend on methods that they do*
> *not use.*

Section 3 **The Payroll Case Study**   **147**

Chapter 13 **Command and Active Object**   **151**

List of Design Patterns

SECTION 1

Agile Development

"Human Interactions are complicated and never very crisp and clean in their effects, but they matter more than any other aspect of the work."

—Tom DeMarco and Timothy Lister
Peopleware, p. 5

Principles, patterns, and practices are important, but it's the people that make them work. As Alistair Cockburn says,[1] "Process and technology are a second-order effect on the outcome of a project. The first-order effect is the people."

We cannot manage teams of programmers as if they were systems made up of components driven by a process. People are not "plug-compatible programming units."[2] If our projects are to succeed, we are going to have to build collaborative and self-organizing teams.

Those companies that encourage the formation of such teams will have a *huge* competitive advantage over those who hold the view that a software-development organization is nothing more than a pile of twisty little people all alike. A gelled software team is the most powerful software-development force there is.

---

1.   Private communication.
2.   A term coined by Kent Beck.

1

Agile Practices

*The weather-cock on the church spire, though made of iron, would soon be broken
by the storm-wind if it did not understand the noble art of turning to every wind.*

—Heinrich Heine

Many of us have lived through the nightmare of a project with no practices to guide it. The lack of effective practices leads to unpredictability, repeated error, and wasted effort. Customers are disappointed by slipping schedules, growing budgets, and poor quality. Developers are disheartened by working ever longer hours to produce ever poorer software.

Once we have experienced such a fiasco, we become afraid of repeating the experience. Our fears motivate us to create a *process* that constrains our activities and demands certain outputs and artifacts. We draw these constraints and outputs from past experience, choosing things that appeared to work well in previous projects. Our hope is that they will work again and take away our fears.

However, projects are not so simple that a few constraints and artifacts can reliably prevent error. As errors continue to be made, we diagnose those errors and put in place even more constraints and artifacts in order to prevent those errors in the future. After many, projects we may find ourselves overloaded with a huge cumbersome process that greatly impedes our ability to get anything done.

A big cumbersome process can create the very problems that it is designed to prevent. It can slow the team to the extent that schedules slip and budgets bloat. It can reduce responsiveness of the team to the point where they are always creating the wrong product. Unfortunately, this leads many teams to believe that they don't have enough process. So, in a kind of runaway-process inflation, they make their process ever larger.

Runaway-process inflation is a good description of the state of affairs in many software companies circa 2000 A.D. Though there were still many teams operating without a process, the adoption of very large, heavyweight processes is rapidly growing, especially in large corporations. (See Appendix C.)

The Agile Alliance

In early 2001, motivated by the observation that software teams in many corporations were stuck in a quagmire of ever-increasing process, a group of industry experts met to outline the values and principles that would allow software teams to work quickly and respond to change. They called themselves the *Agile Alliance*.[1] Over the next several months, they worked to create a statement of values. The result was *The Manifesto of the Agile Alliance*.

The Manifesto of the Agile Alliance

Manifesto for Agile Software Development

We are uncovering better ways of developing software by doing it and helping others do it. Through this work we have come to value

- Individuals and interactions over processes and tools
- Working software over comprehensive documentation
- Customer collaboration over contract negotiation
- Responding to change over following a plan

That is, while there is value in the items on the right, we value the items on the left more.

Kent Beck	Mike Beedle	Arie van Bennekum	Alistair Cockburn
Ward Cunningham	Martin Fowler	James Grenning	Jim Highsmith
Andrew Hunt	Ron Jeffries	Jon Kern	Brian Marick
Robert C. Martin	Steve Mellor	Ken Schwaber	Jeff Sutherland
Dave Thomas			

Individuals and interactions over processes and tools.   People are the most important ingredient of success. A good process will not save the project from failure if the team doesn't have strong players, but a bad process can make even the strongest of players ineffective. Even a group of strong players can fail badly if they don't work as a team.

A strong player is not necessarily an ace programmer. A strong player may be an average programmer, but someone who works well with others. Working well with others, communicating and interacting, is more important than raw programming talent. A team of average programmers who communicate well are more likely to succeed than a group of superstars who fail to interact as a team.

The right tools can be very important to success. Compilers, IDEs, source-code control systems, etc. are all vital to the proper functioning of a team of developers. However, tools can be overemphasized. An overabundance of big, unwieldy tools is just as bad as a lack of tools.

My advice is to start small. Don't assume you've outgrown a tool until you've tried it and found you can't use it. Instead of buying the top-of-the-line, megaexpensive, source-code control system, find a free one and use it

---

1.   agilealliance.org

until you can demonstrate that you've outgrown it. Before you buy team licenses for the best of all CASE tools, use white boards and graph paper until you can reasonably show that you need more. Before you commit to the top-shelf behemoth database system, try flat files. Don't assume that bigger and better tools will automatically help you do better. Often they hinder more than they help.

Remember, building the team is more important than building the environment. Many teams and managers make the mistake of building the environment first and expecting the team to gel automatically. Instead, work to create the team, and then let the team configure the environment on the basis of need.

Working software over comprehensive documentation. Software without documentation is a disaster. Code is not the ideal medium for communicating the rationale and structure of a system. Rather, the team needs to produce human-readable documents that describe the system and the rationale for their design decisions.

However, too much documentation is worse than too little. Huge software documents take a great deal of time to produce and even more time to keep in sync with the code. If they are not kept in sync, then they turn into large, complicated lies and become a significant source of misdirection.

It is always a good idea for the team to write and maintain a rationale and structure document, but that document needs to be *short* and *salient*. By "short," I mean one or two dozen pages at most. By "salient," I mean it should discuss the overall design rationale and only the highest-level structures in the system.

If all we have is a short rationale and structure document, how do we train new team members to work on the system? We work closely with them. We transfer our knowledge to them by sitting next to them and helping them. We make them part of the team through close training and interaction.

The two documents that are the best at transferring information to new team members are the code and the team. The code does not lie about what it does. It may be hard to extract rationale and intent from the code, but the code is the only unambiguous source of information. The team members hold the ever-changing road map of the system in their heads. There is no faster and more efficient way to transfer that road map to others than human-to-human interaction.

Many teams have gotten hung up in the pursuit of documentation instead of software. This is often a fatal flaw. There is a simple rule called **Martin's first law of documentation** that prevents it:

Produce no document unless its need is immediate and significant.

Customer collaboration over contract negotiation. Software cannot be ordered like a commodity. You cannot write a description of the software you want and then have someone develop it on a fixed schedule for a fixed price. Time and time again, attempts to treat software projects in this manner have failed. Sometimes the failures are spectacular.

It is tempting for the managers of a company to tell their development staff what their needs are, and then expect that staff to go away for a while and return with a system that satisfies those needs. However, this mode of operation leads to poor quality and failure.

Successful projects involve customer feedback on a regular and frequent basis. Rather than depending on a contract or a statement of work, the customer of the software works closely with the development team, providing frequent feedback on their efforts.

A contract that specifies the requirements, schedule, and cost of a project is fundamentally flawed. In most cases, the terms it specifies become meaningless long before the project is complete.[2] The best contracts are those that govern the way the development team and the customer will work together.

As an example of a successful contract, take one I negotiated in 1994 for a large, multiyear, half-million-line project. We, the development team, were paid a relatively low monthly rate. Large payouts were made to us when we delivered certain large blocks of functionality. Those blocks were not specified in detail by the contract. Rather,

---

2. Sometimes long before the contract is signed!

the contract stated that the payout would be made for a block when the block passed the customer's acceptance test. The details of those acceptance tests were not specified in the contract.

During the course of this project, we worked very closely with the customer. We released the software to him almost every Friday. By Monday or Tuesday of the following week, he would have a list of changes for us to put into the software. We would prioritize those changes together and then schedule them into subsequent weeks. The customer worked so closely with us that acceptance tests were never an issue. He knew when a block of functionality satisfied his needs because he watched it evolve from week to week.

The requirements for this project were in a constant state of flux. Major changes were not uncommon. There were whole blocks of functionality that were removed and others that were inserted. Yet the contract, and the project, survived and succeeded. The key to this success was the intense collaboration with the customer and a contract that governed that collaboration rather than trying to specify the details of scope and schedule for a fixed cost.

Responding to change over following a plan.   It is the ability to respond to change that often determines the success or failure of a software project. When we build plans, we need to make sure that our plans are flexible and ready to adapt to changes in the business and technology.

The course of a software project cannot be planned very far into the future. First of all, the business environment is likely to change, causing the requirements to shift. Second, customers are likely to alter the requirements once they see the system start to function. Finally, even if we know the requirements, and we are sure they won't change, we are not very good at estimating how long it will take to develop them.

It is tempting for novice managers to create a nice PERT or Gantt chart of the whole project and tape it to the wall. They may feel that this chart gives them control over the project. They can track the individual tasks and cross them off the chart as they are completed. They can compare the actual dates with the planned dates on the chart and react to any discrepancies.

What *really* happens is that the structure of the chart degrades. As the team gains knowledge about the system, and as the customers gain knowledge about their needs, certain tasks on the chart become unnecessary. Other tasks will be discovered and will need to be added. In short, the plan will undergo changes in *shape*, not just changes in dates.

A better planning strategy is to make detailed plans for the next two weeks, very rough plans for the next three months, and extremely crude plans beyond that. We should know the tasks we will be working on for the next two weeks. We should roughly know the requirements we will be working on for the next three months. And we should have only a vague idea what the system will do after a year.

This decreasing resolution of the plan means that we are only investing in a detailed plan for those tasks that are immediate. Once the detailed plan is made, it is hard to change since the team will have a lot of momentum and commitment. However, since that plan only governs a few weeks' worth of time, the rest of the plan remains flexible.

Principles

The above values inspired the following 12 principles, which are the characteristics that differentiate a set of agile practices from a heavyweight process:

- *Our highest priority is to satisfy the customer through early and continuous delivery of valuable software.*
   The *MIT Sloan Management Review* published an analysis of software development practices that help companies build high-quality products.[3] The article found a number of practices that had a significant impact on the quality of the final system. One practice was a strong correlation between quality and the early deliv-

---

3.   *Product-Development Practices That Work: How Internet Companies Build Software*, MIT Sloan Management Review, Winter 2001, Reprint number 4226.

ery of a partially functioning system. The article reported that *the less functional the initial delivery, the higher the quality in the final delivery.*

Another finding of this article is a strong correlation between final quality and frequent deliveries of increasing functionality. *The more frequent the deliveries, the higher the final quality.*

An agile set of practices delivers early and often. We strive to deliver a rudimentary system within the first few weeks of the start of the project. Then, we strive to continue to deliver systems of increasing functionality every two weeks.

Customers may choose to put these systems into production if they think that they are functional enough. Or they may choose simply to review the existing functionality and report on changes they want made.

- *Welcome changing requirements, even late in development. Agile processes harness change for the customer's competitive advantage.*

    This is a statement of attitude. The participants in an agile process are not afraid of change. They view changes to the requirements as *good* things, because those changes mean that the team has learned more about what it will take to satisfy the market.

    An agile team works very hard to keep the structure of its software flexible so that when requirements change, the impact to the system is minimal. Later in this book we will learn the principles and patterns of object-oriented design that help us to maintain this kind of flexibility.

- *Deliver working software frequently, from a couple of weeks to a couple of months, with a preference to the shorter time scale.*

    We deliver *working* software, and we delivery it early (after the first few weeks) and often (every few weeks thereafter). We are not content with delivering bundles of documents or plans. We don't count those as true deliveries. Our eye is on the goal of delivering software that satisfies the customer's needs.

- *Business people and developers must work together daily throughout the project.*

    In order for a project to be agile, there must be significant and frequent interaction between the customers, developers, and stakeholders. A software project is not like a fire-and-forget weapon. A software project must be continuously guided.

- *Build projects around motivated individuals. Give them the environment and support they need, and trust them to get the job done.*

    An agile project is one in which people are considered the most important factor of success. All other factors—process, environment, management, etc.—are considered to be second order effects, and they are subject to change if they are having an adverse effect upon the people.

    For example, if the office environment is an obstacle to the team, the office environment must be changed. If certain process steps are an obstacle to the team, the process steps must be changed.

- *The most efficient and effective method of conveying information to and within a development team is face-to-face conversation.*

    In an agile project, people *talk* to each other. The primary mode of communication is conversation. Documents may be created, but there is no attempt to capture all project information in writing. An agile project team does not demand written specs, written plans, or written designs. Team members may create them if they perceive an immediate and significant need, but they are not the default. The default is conversation.

- *Working software is the primary measure of progress.*

    Agile projects measure their progress by measuring the amount of software that is currently meeting the customer's need. They don't measure their progress in terms of the phase that they are in or by the volume of documentation that has been produced or by the amount of infrastructure code they have created. They are 30% done when 30% of the necessary functionality is working.

• *Agile processes promote sustainable development. The sponsors, developers, and users should be able to maintain a constant pace indefinitely.*

An agile project is not run like a 50-yard dash; it is run like a marathon. The team does not take off at full speed and try to maintain that speed for the duration. Rather, they run at a fast, but sustainable, pace.

Running too fast leads to burnout, shortcuts, and debacle. Agile teams pace themselves. They don't allow themselves to get too tired. They don't borrow tomorrow's energy to get a bit more done today. They work at a rate that allows them to maintain the highest quality standards for the duration of the project.

• *Continuous attention to technical excellence and good design enhances agility.*

High quality is the key to high speed. The way to go fast is to keep the software as clean and robust as possible. Thus, all agile team members are committed to producing only the highest quality code they can. They do not make messes and then tell themselves they'll clean it up when they have more time. If they make a mess, they clean it up before they finish for the day.

• *Simplicity—the art of maximizing the amount of work not done—is essential.*

Agile teams do not try to build the grand system in the sky. Rather, they always take the simplest path that is consistent with their goals. They don't put a lot of importance on anticipating tomorrow's problems, nor do they try to defend against all of them today. Instead, they do the simplest and highest-quality work today, confident that it will be easy to change if and when tomorrow's problems arise.

• *The best architectures, requirements, and designs emerge from self-organizing teams.*

An agile team is a self-organizing team. Responsibilities are not handed to individual team members from the outside. Responsibilities are communicated to the team as a whole, and the team determines the best way to fulfill them.

Agile team members work together on all aspects of the project. Each is allowed input into the whole. No single team member is responsible for the architecture or the requirements or the tests. The team shares those responsibilities, and each team member has influence over them.

• *At regular intervals, the team reflects on how to become more effective, then tunes and adjusts its behavior accordingly.*

An agile team continually adjusts its organization, rules, conventions, relationships, etc. An agile team knows that its environment is continuously changing and knows that they must change with that environment to remain agile.

Conclusion

The professional goal of every software developer and every development team is to deliver the highest possible value to their employers and customers. And yet our projects fail, or fail to deliver value, at a dismaying rate. Though well intentioned, the upward spiral of process inflation is culpable for at least some of this failure. The principles and values of agile software development were formed as a way to help teams break the cycle of process inflation and to focus on simple techniques for reaching their goals.

At the time of this writing, there were many agile processes to choose from. These include SCRUM,[4] Crystal,[5] Feature Driven Development,[6] Adaptive Software Development (ADP),[7] and most significantly, Extreme Programming.[8]

4.　　www.controlchaos.com

5.　　crystalmethodologies.org

6.　　*Java Modeling In Color With UML: Enterprise Components and Process*, Peter Coad, Eric Lefebvre, and Jeff De Luca, Prentice Hall, 1999.

7.　　[Highsmith2000].

8.　　[Beck1999], [Newkirk2001].

Bibliography

1. Beck, Kent. *Extreme Programming Explained: Embracing Change*. Reading, MA: Addison–Wesley, 1999.
2. Newkirk, James, and Robert C. Martin. *Extreme Programming in Practice*. Upper Saddle River, NJ: Addison–Wesley, 2001.
3. Highsmith, James A. *Adaptive Software Development: A Collaborative Approach to Managing Complex Systems*. New York, NY: Dorset House, 2000.

2

Overview of Extreme Programming

© Jennifer M. Kohnke

As developers we need to remember that XP is not the only game in town.

—Pete McBreen

The previous chapter gave us an outline of what agile software development is about. However, it didn't tell us exactly what to do. It gave us some platitudes and goals, but it gave us little in the way of real direction. This chapter corrects that.

The Practices of Extreme Programming

Extreme programming is the most famous of the agile methods. It is made up of a set of simple, yet interdependent practices. These practices work together to form a whole that is greater than its parts. We shall briefly consider that whole in this chapter, and examine some of the parts in chapters to come.

Customer Team Member

We want the customer and developers to work closely with each other so that they are both aware of each other's problems and are working together to solve those problems.

Who is the customer? The customer of an XP team is the person or group who defines and prioritizes features. Sometimes, the customer is a group of business analysts or marketing specialists working in the same company as the developers. Sometimes, the customer is a user representative commissioned by the body of users. Sometimes the customer is in fact the paying customer. But in an XP project, whoever the customers are, they are members of, and available to, the team.

The best case is for the customer to work in the same room as the developers. Next best is if the customer works in within 100 feet of the developers. The larger the distance, the harder it is for the customer to be a true team member. If the customer is in another building or another state, it is very difficult to integrate him or her into the team.

What do you do if the customer simply cannot be close by? My advice is to find someone who *can* be close by and who is willing and able to stand in for the true customer.

User Stories

In order to plan a project, we must know something about the requirements, but we don't need to know very much. For planning purposes, we only need to know enough about a requirement to estimate it. You may think that in order to estimate a requirement you need to know all its details, but that's not quite true. You have to know that there *are* details, and you have to know roughly the kinds of details there are, but you don't have to know the specifics.

The specific details of a requirement are likely to change with time, especially once the customer begins to see the system come together. There is nothing that focuses requirements better than seeing the nascent system come to life. Therefore, capturing the specific details about a requirement long before it is implemented is likely to result in wasted effort and premature focusing.

When using XP, we get the sense of the details of the requirements by talking them over with the customer, but we do not capture that detail. Rather, the customer writes *a few words* on an index card that we agree will remind us of the conversation. The developers write an estimate on the card at roughly the same time that the customer writes it. They base that estimate on the sense of detail they got during their conversations with the customer.

A user story is a mnemonic token of an ongoing conversation about a requirement. It is a planning tool that the customer uses to schedule the implementation of a requirement based upon its priority and estimated cost.

Short Cycles

An XP project delivers working software every two weeks. Each of these two-week iterations produces working software that addresses some of the needs of the stakeholders. At the end of each iteration, the system is demonstrated to the stakeholders in order to get their feedback.

The Iteration Plan.   An iteration is usually two weeks in length. It represents a minor delivery that may or may not be put into production. It is a collection of user stories selected by the customer according to a budget established by the developers.

The developers set the budget for an iteration by measuring how much they got done in the previous iteration. The customer may select any number of stories for the iteration, so long as the total of their estimates does not exceed that budget.

Once an iteration has been started, the customer agrees not to change the definition or priority of the stories in that iteration. During this time, the developers are free to cut the stories up in to *tasks* and to develop the tasks in the order that makes the most technical and business sense.

The Release Plan.   XP teams often create a release plan that maps out the next six iterations or so. That plan is known as a release plan. A release is usually three months worth of work. It represents a major delivery that can usually be put into production. A release plan consists of prioritized collections of user stories that have been selected by the customer according to a budget given by the developers.

The developers set the budget for the release by measuring how much they got done in the previous release. The customer may select any number of stories for the release so long as the total of the estimates does not exceed that budget. The customer also determines the order in which the stories will be implemented in the release. If the team so desires, they can map out the first few iterations of the release by showing which stories will be completed in which iterations.

Releases are not cast in stone. The customer can change the content at any time. He or she can cancel stories, write new stories, or change the priority of a story.

Acceptance Tests

The details about the user stories are captured in the form of acceptance tests specified by the customer. The acceptance tests for a story are written immediately preceding, or even concurrent with, the implementation of that story. They are written in some kind of scripting language that allows them to be run automatically and repeatedly. Together, they act to verify that the system is behaving as the customers have specified.

The language of the acceptance tests grows and evolves with the system. The customers may recruit the developers to create a simple scripting system, or they may have a separate quality assurance (QA) department that can develop it. Many customers enlist the help of QA in developing the acceptance-testing tool and with writing the acceptance tests themselves.

Once an acceptance test passes, it is added to the body of passing acceptance tests and is never allowed to fail again. This growing body of acceptance tests is run several times per day, every time the system is built. If an acceptance tests fails, the build is declared a failure. Thus, once a requirement is implemented, it is never broken. The system migrates from one working state to another and is never allowed to be inoperative for longer than a few hours.

Pair Programming

All *production* code is written by pairs of programmers working together at the same workstation. One member of each pair drives the keyboard and types the code. The other member of the pair watches the code being typed, looking for errors and improvements.[1] The two interact intensely. Both are completely engaged in the act of writing software.

The roles change frequently. The driver may get tired or stuck, and his pair partner will grab the keyboard and start to drive. The keyboard will move back and forth between them several times in an hour. The resultant code is designed and authored by both members. Neither can take more than half the credit.

Pair membership changes at least once per day so that every programmer works in two different pairs each day. Over the course of an iteration, every member of the team should have worked with every other member of the team, and they should have worked on just about everything that was going on in the iteration.

This dramatically increases the spread of knowledge through the team. While specialties remain and tasks that require certain specialties will usually belong to the appropriate specialists, those specialists will pair with nearly everyone else on the team. This will spread the specialty out through the team such that other team members can fill in for the specialists in a pinch.

Studies by Laurie Williams[2] and Nosek[3] have suggested that pairing does not reduce the efficiency of the programming staff, yet it significantly reduces the defect rate.

---

1. I have seen pairs in which one member controls the keyboard and the other controls the mouse.
2. [Williams2000], [Cockburn2001].
3. [Nosek].

Test-Driven Development

Chapter 4, which is on testing, discusses test-driven development in great detail. The following paragraphs provide a quick overview.

All production code is written in order to make failing unit tests pass. First we write a unit test that fails because the functionality for which it is testing doesn't exist. Then we write the code that makes that test pass.

This iteration between writing test cases and code is very rapid, on the order of a minute or so. The test cases and code evolve together, with the test cases leading the code by a very small fraction. (See "A Programming Episode" in Chapter 6 for an example.)

As a result, a very complete body of test cases grows along with the code. These tests allow the programmers to check whether the program works. If a pair makes a small change, they can run the tests to ensure that they haven't broken anything. This greatly facilitates *refactoring* (discussed later).

When you write code in order to make test cases pass, that code is, by definition, testable. In addition, there is a strong motivation to decouple modules from each other so that they can be independently tested. Thus, the design of code that is written in this fashion tends to be much less coupled. The principles of object-oriented design play a powerful role in helping you with this decoupling.[4]

Collective Ownership

A pair has the right to check out *any* module and improve it. No programmers are individually responsible for any one particular module or technology. Everybody works on the GUI.[5] Everybody works on the middleware. Everybody works on the database. Nobody has more authority over a module or a technology than anybody else.

This doesn't mean that XP denies specialties. If your specialty is the GUI, you are most likely to work on GUI tasks, but you will also be asked to pair on middleware and database tasks. If you decide to learn a second specialty, you can sign up for tasks and work with specialists who will teach it to you. You are not confined to your specialty.

Continuous Integration

The programmers check in their code and integrate several times per day. The rule is simple. The first one to check in wins, everybody else merges.

XP teams use nonblocking source control. This means that programmers are allowed to check any module out at any time, regardless of who else may have it checked out. When the programmer checks the module back in after modifying it, he must be prepared to merge it with any changes made by anyone who checked the module in ahead of him. To avoid long merge sessions, the members of the team check in their modules very frequently.

A *pair* will work for an hour or two on a task. They create test cases and production code. At some convenient breaking point, probably long before the task is complete, the pair decides to check the code back in. They first make sure that all the tests run. They integrate their new code into the existing code base. If there is a merge to do, they do it. If necessary, they consult with the programmers who beat them to the check in. Once their changes are integrated, they build the new system. They run every test in the system, including all currently running acceptance tests. If they broke anything that used to work, they fix it. Once all the tests run, they finish the check in.

Thus, XP teams will build the system many times each day. They build the *whole* system from end to end.[6] If the final result of a system is a CD, they cut the CD. If the final result of the system is an active Web site, they install that Web site, probably on a testing server.

---

4.   See Section II.

5.   I'm not advocating a three-tiered architecture here. I just chose three common partitions of software technology.

6.   Ron Jeffries says, "End to end is farther than you think."

Sustainable Pace

A software project is not a sprint; it is a marathon. A team that leaps off the starting line and starts racing as fast as it can will burn out long before they are close to finishing. In order to finish quickly, the team must run at a sustainable pace; it must conserve its energy and alertness. It must intentionally run at a steady, moderate pace.

The XP rule is that a team is not *allowed* to work overtime. The only exception to that rule is the last week in a release. If the team is within striking distance of its release goal and can sprint to the finish, then overtime is permissible.

Open Workspace

The team works together in an open room. There are tables set up with workstations on them. Each table has two or three such workstations. There are two chairs in front of each workstation for pairs to sit in. The walls are covered with status charts, task breakdowns, UML diagrams, etc.

The sound in this room is a low buzz of conversation. Each pair is within earshot of every other. Each has the opportunity to hear when another is in trouble. Each knows the state of the other. The programmers are in a position to communicate intensely.

One might think that this would be a distracting environment. It would be easy to fear that you'd never get anything done because of the constant noise and distraction. In fact, this doesn't turn out to be the case. Moreover, instead of interfering with productivity, a University of Michigan study suggested that working in a "war room" environment may *increase* productivity by a factor of two.[7]

The Planning Game

The next chapter, "Planning," goes into great detail about the XP planning game. I'll describe it briefly here.

The essence of the planning game is the division of responsibility between business and development. The business people (a.k.a. the customers) decide how important a feature is, and the developers decide how much that feature will cost to implement.

At the beginning of each release and each iteration, the developers give the customers a budget, based on how much they were able to get done in the last iteration or in the last release. The customers choose stories whose costs total up to, but do not exceed that budget.

With these simple rules in place, and with short iterations and frequent releases, it won't be long before the customers and developers get used to the rhythm of the project. The customers will get a sense for how fast the developers are going. Based on that sense, the customers will be able to determine how long their project will take and how much it will cost.

Simple Design

An XP team makes their designs as simple and expressive as they can be. Furthermore, they narrow their focus to consider only the stories that are planned for the current iteration. They don't worry about stories to come. Instead, they migrate the design of the system, from iteration to iteration, to be the best design for the stories that the system currently implements.

This means that an XP team will probably not start with infrastructure. They probably won't select the database first. They probably won't select the middleware first. The team's first act will be to get the first batch of stories working in the *simplest way possible*. The team will only add the infrastructure when a story comes along that forces them to do so.

7.   http://www.sciencedaily.com/releases/2000/12/001206144705.htm

The following three XP mantras guide the developer:

Consider the Simplest Thing That Could Possibly Work.   XP teams always try to find the simplest possible design option for the current batch of stories. If we can make the current stories work with flat files, we might not use a database or EJB. If we can make the current stories work with a simple socket connection, we might not use an ORB or RMI. If we can make the current stories work without multithreading, we might not include mutithreading. We try to consider the simplest way to implement the current stories. Then we choose a solution that is as close to that simplicity as we can *practically* get.

You Aren't Going to Need It.   Yeah, but we *know* we're going to need that database one day. We *know* we're going to need an ORB one day. We *know* we're going to have to support multiple users one day. So we need to put the hooks in for those things *now*, don't we?

An XP team seriously considers what will happen if they resist the temptation to add infrastructure before it is strictly needed. They start from the assumption that they aren't going to need that infrastructure. The team puts in the infrastructure, only if they have proof, or at least very compelling evidence, that putting in the infrastructure now will be more cost effective than waiting.

Once and Only Once.   XPers don't tolerate code duplication. Wherever they find it, they eliminate it.

There are many sources of code duplication. The most obvious are those stretches of code that were captured with a mouse and plopped down in multiple places. When we find those, we eliminate them by creating a function or a base class. Sometimes two or more algorithms may be remarkably similar, and yet they differ in subtle ways. We turn those into functions or employ the TEMPLATE METHOD pattern.[8] Whatever the source of duplication, once discovered, we won't tolerate it.

The best way to eliminate redundancy is to create abstractions. After all, if two things are similar, there must be some abstraction that unifies them. Thus, the act of eliminating redundancy forces the team to create many abstractions and further reduce coupling.

Refactoring[9]

I cover this topic in more detail in Chapter 5. What follows is a brief overview.

Code tends to rot. As we add feature after feature and deal with bug after bug, the structure of the code degrades. Left unchecked, this degradation leads to a tangled, unmaintainable mess.

XP teams reverse this degradation through frequent refactoring. Refactoring is the practice of making a series of tiny transformations that improve the structure of the system without affecting its behavior. Each transformation is trivial, hardly worth doing. But together, they combine into significant transformations of the design and architecture of the system.

After each tiny transformation, we run the unit tests to make sure we haven't broken anything. Then we do the next transformation and the next and the next, running the tests after each. In this manner we keep the system working while transforming its design.

Refactoring is done continuously rather than at the end of the project, the end of the release, the end of the iteration, or even the end of the day. Refactoring is something we do every hour or every half hour. Through refactoring, we continuously keep the code as clean, simple, and expressive as possible.

Metaphor

Metaphor is the least understood of all the practices of XP. XPers are pragmatists at heart, and this lack of concrete definition makes us uncomfortable. Indeed, the proponents of XP have often discussed removing metaphor as a practice. And yet, in some sense, metaphor is one of the most important practices of all.

8.   See Chapter 14, "Template Method & Strategy: Inheritance v. Delegation."

9.   [Fowler99].

Think of a jigsaw puzzle. How do you know how the pieces go together? Clearly, each piece abuts others, and its shape must be perfectly complimentary to the pieces it touches. If you were blind and you had a very good sense of touch, you could put the puzzle together by diligently sifting through each piece and trying it in position after position.

But there is something more powerful than the shape of the pieces binding the puzzle together. There is a picture. The picture is the true guide. The picture is so powerful that if two adjacent pieces of the picture do not have complementary shapes, then you *know* that the puzzle maker made a mistake.

That is the metaphor. It's the big picture that ties the whole system together. It's the vision of the system that makes the location and shape of all the individual modules obvious. If a module's shape is inconsistent with the metaphor, then you know it is the module that is wrong.

Often a metaphor boils down to a system of names. The names provide a vocabulary for elements in the system and help to define their relationships.

For example, I once worked on a system that transmitted text to a screen at 60 characters per second. At that rate, a screen fill could take some time. So we'd allow the program that was generating the text to fill a buffer. When the buffer was full, we'd swap the program out to disk. When the buffer got close to empty, we'd swap the program back in and let it run more.

We spoke about this system in terms of dump trucks hauling garbage. The buffers were little trucks. The display screen was the dump. The program was the garbage producer. The names all fit together and helped us think about the system as a whole.

As another example, I once worked on a system that analyzed network traffic. Every thirty minutes, it would poll dozens of network adapters and pull down the monitoring data from them. Each network adapter gave us a small block of data composed of several individual variables. We called these blocks "slices." The slices were raw data that needed to be analyzed. The analysis program "cooked" the slices, so it was called "The Toaster." We called the individual variables within the slices, "crumbs." All in all, it was a useful and entertaining metaphor.

Conclusion

Extreme programming is a set of simple and concrete practices that combines into an agile development process. That process has been used on many teams with good results.

XP is a good general-purpose method for developing software. Many project teams will be able to adopt it as is. Many others will be able to adapt it by adding or modifying practices.

Bibliography

1. Dahl, Dijkstra. *Structured Programming*. New York: Hoare, Academic Press, 1972.
2. Conner, Daryl R. *Leading at the Edge of Chaos*. Wiley, 1998.
3. Cockburn, Alistair. *The Methodology Space*. Humans and Technology technical report HaT TR.97.03 (dated 97.10.03), http://members.aol.com/acockburn/papers/methyspace/methyspace.htm.
4. Beck, Kent. *Extreme Programming Explained: Embracing Change*. Reading, MA: Addison–Wesley, 1999.
5. Newkirk, James, and Robert C. Martin. *Extreme Programming in Practice*. Upper Saddle River, NJ: Addison–Wesley, 2001.
6. Williams, Laurie, Robert R. Kessler, Ward Cunningham, Ron Jeffries. *Strengthening the Case for Pair Programming*. IEEE Software, July–Aug. 2000.
7. Cockburn, Alistair, and Laurie Williams. *The Costs and Benefits of Pair Programming*. XP2000 Conference in Sardinia, reproduced in *Extreme Programming Examined*, Giancarlo Succi, Michele Marchesi. Addison–Wesley, 2001.
8. Nosek, J. T. *The Case for Collaborative Programming*. Communications of the ACM (1998): 105–108.
9. Fowler, Martin. *Refactoring: Improving the Design of Existing Code*. Reading, MA: Addison–Wesley, 1999.

3

Planning

"When you can measure what you are speaking about, and express it in numbers, you know something about it; but when you cannot measure it, when you cannot express it in numbers, your knowledge is of a meager and unsatisfactory kind."

—Lord Kelvin, 1883

What follows is a description of the planning game from Extreme Programming (XP).[1] It is similar to the way planning is done in several of the other agile[2] methods like SCRUM,[3] Crystal,[4] feature-driven development,[5] and adaptive software development (ADP).[6] However, none of those processes spell it out in as much detail and rigor.

---

1. [Beck99], [Newkirk2001].
2. www.AgileAlliance.org
3. www.controlchaos.com
4. crystalmethodologies.org
5. *Java Modeling In Color With UML: Enterprise Components and Process* by Peter Coad, Eric Lefebvre, and Jeff De Luca, Prentice Hall, 1999.
6. [Highsmith2000].

Initial Exploration

At the start of the project, the developers and customers try to identify all the really significant user stories they can. However, they don't try to identify *all* user stories. As the project proceeds, the customers will continue to write new user stories. The flow of user stories will not shut off until the project is over.

The developers work together to estimate the stories. The estimates are relative, not absolute. We write a number of "points" on a story card to represent the relative cost of the story. We may not be sure just how much time a story point represents, but we do know that a story with eight points will take twice as long as a story with four points.

Spiking, Splitting, and Velocity

Stories that are too large or too small are hard to estimate. Developers tend to underestimate large stories and over-estimate small ones. Any story that is too big should be split into pieces that aren't too big. Any story that is too small should be merged with other small stories.

For example, consider the story, "Users can securely transfer money into, out of, and between their accounts." This is a big story. Estimating will be hard and probably inaccurate. However, we can split it as follow, into many stories that are much easier to estimate:

- Users can log in.
- Users can log out.
- Users can deposit money into their account.
- Users can withdraw money from their account.
- Users can transfer money from their account to another account.

When a story is split or merged, it should be reestimated. It is not wise to simply add or subtract the estimate. The main reason to split or merge a story is to get it to a size where estimation is accurate. It is not surprising to find that a story estimated at five points breaks up into stories that add up to ten! Ten is the more accurate estimate.

Relative estimates don't tell us the absolute size of the stories, so they don't help us determine when to split or merge them. In order to know the true size of a story, we need a factor that we call *velocity*. If we have an accurate velocity, we can multiply the estimate of any story by the velocity to get the actual time estimate for that story. For example, if our velocity is "2 days per story point," and we have a story with a relative estimate of four points, then the story should take eight days to implement.

As the project proceeds, the measure of velocity will become ever more accurate because we'll be able to measure the number of story points completed per iteration. However, the developers will probably not have a very good idea of their velocity at the start. They must create an initial guess by whatever means they feel will give the best results. The need for accuracy at this point is not particularly grave, so they don't need to spend an inordinate amount of time on it. Often, it is sufficient to spend a few days prototyping a story or two to get an idea of the team's velocity. Such a prototype session is called a *spike*.

Release Planning

Given a velocity, the customers can get an idea of the cost of each of the stories. They also know the business value and priority of each story. This allows them to choose the stories they want done first. This choice is not purely a matter of priority. Something that is important, but also expensive, may be delayed in favor of something that is less important but much less expensive. Choices like this are *business* decisions. The business folks decide which stories give them the most bang for the buck.

The developers and customers agree on a date for the first release of the project. This is usually a matter of 2–4 months in the future. The customers pick the stories they want implemented within that release and the rough order in which they want them implemented. The customers cannot choose more stories than will fit according to the current velocity. Since the velocity is initially inaccurate, this selection is crude. But accuracy is not very important at this point in time. The release plan can be adjusted as velocity becomes more accurate.

Iteration Planning

Next, the developers and customers choose an iteration size. This is typically two weeks long. Once again, the customers choose the stories that they want implemented in the first iteration. They cannot choose more stories than will fit according to the current velocity.

The order of the stories within the iteration is a technical decision. The developers implement the stories in the order that makes the most technical sense. They may work on the stories serially, finishing each one after the next, or they may divvy up the stories and work on them all concurrently. It's entirely up to them.

The customers cannot change the stories in the iteration once the iteration has begun. They are free to change or reorder any other story in the project, but not the ones that the developers are currently working on.

The iteration ends on the specified date, *even if all the stories aren't done*. The estimates for all the completed stories are totaled, and the velocity for that iteration is calculated. This measure of velocity is then used to plan the next iteration. The rule is very simple. The planned velocity for each iteration is the measured velocity of the previous iteration. If the team got 31 story points done last iteration, then they should plan to get 31 story points done in the next. Their velocity is 31 points per iteration.

This feedback of velocity helps to keep the planning in sync with the team. If the team gains in expertise and skill, the velocity will rise commensurately. If someone is lost from the team, the velocity will fall. If an architecture evolves that facilitates development, the velocity will rise.

Task Planning

At the start of a new iteration, the developers and customers get together to plan. The developers break the stories down into development tasks. A task is something that one developer can implement in 4–16 hours. The stories are analyzed, with the customers' help, and the tasks are enumerated as completely as possible.

A list of the tasks is created on a flip chart, whiteboard, or some other convenient medium. Then, one by one, the developers sign up for the tasks they want to implement. As each developer signs up for a task, he or she estimates that task in arbitrary task points.[7]

Developers may sign up for any kind of task. Database guys are not constrained to sign up for database tasks. GUI guys can sign up for database tasks if they like. This may seem inefficient, but as you'll see, there is a mechanism that manages this. The benefit is obvious. The more the developers know about the *whole* project, the healthier and more informed the project team is. We want knowledge of the project to spread through the team irrespective of specialty.

Each developer knows how many task points he or she managed to implement in the last iteration. This number is their personal *budget*. No one signs up for more points than they have in their budget.

Task selection continues until either all tasks are assigned or all developers have used their budgets. If there are tasks remaining, then the developers negotiate with each other, trading tasks based on their various skills. If this doesn't make enough room to get all the tasks assigned, then the developers ask the customers to remove tasks or stories from the iteration. If all the tasks are signed up and the developers still have room in their budgets for more work, they ask the customers for more stories.

---

7.   Many developers find it helpful to use "perfect programming hours" as their task points.

The Halfway Point

Halfway through the iteration, the team holds a meeting. At this point, half of the *stories* scheduled for the iteration should be complete. If half the stories aren't complete, then the team tries to reapportion tasks and responsibilities to ensure that all the stories will be complete by the end of the iteration. If the developers cannot find such a reapportionment, then the customers need to be told. The customers may decide to pull a task or story from the iteration. At the very least, they will name the lowest priority tasks and stories so that the developers avoid working on them.

For example, suppose the customers selected eight stories totalling 24 story points for the iteration. Suppose also that these were broken down into 42 tasks. At the halfway point of the iteration, we would expect to have 21 tasks and 12 story points complete. Those 12 story points must represent wholly completed stories. Our goal is to complete stories, not just tasks. The nightmare scenario is to get to the end of the iteration with 90% of the tasks complete, but no stories complete. At the halfway point, we want to see completed stories that represent half the story points for the iteration.

Iterating

Every two weeks, the current iteration ends and the next begins. At the end of each iteration, the current running executable is demonstrated to the customers. The customers are asked to evaluate the look, feel, and performance of the project. They will provide their feedback in terms of new user stories.

The customers see progress frequently. They can measure velocity. They can predict how fast the team is going, and they can schedule high-priority stories early. In short, they have all the data and control they need to manage the project to their liking.

Conclusion

From iteration to iteration and release to release, the project falls into a predictable and comfortable rhythm. Everyone knows what to expect and when to expect it. Stakeholders see progress frequently and substantially. Rather than being shown notebooks full of diagrams and plans, they are shown working software that they can touch, feel, and provide feedback on.

Developers see a reasonable plan based upon their own estimates and controlled by their own measured velocity. They choose the tasks on which they feel comfortable working and keep the quality of their workmanship high.

Managers receive data every iteration. They use this data to control and manage the project. They don't have to resort to pressure, threats, or appeals to loyalty to meet an arbitrary and unrealistic date.

If this sounds like blue sky and apple pie, it's not. The stakeholders won't always be happy with the data that the process produces, especially not at first. Using an agile method does not mean that the stakeholders will get what they want. It simply means that they'll be able to control the team to get the most business value for the least cost.

Bibliography

1. Beck, Kent. *Extreme Programming Explained: Embrace Change*. Reading, MA: Addison–Wesley, 1999.
2. Newkirk, James, and Robert C. Martin. *Extreme Programming in Practice*. Upper Saddle River, NJ: Addison–Wesley, 2001.
3. Highsmith, James A. *Adaptive Software Development: A Collaborative Approach to Managing Complex Systems*. New York: Dorset House, 2000.

4

Testing

© Jennifer M. Kohnke

Fire is the test of gold; adversity, of strong men.

—Seneca (c. 3 B.C.–A.D. 65)

The act of writing a unit test is more an act of design than of verification. It is also more an act of documentation than of verification. The act of writing a unit test closes a remarkable number of feedback loops, the least of which is the one pertaining to verification of function.

Test Driven Development

What if we designed our tests before we designed our programs? What if we refused to implement a function in our programs until there was a test that failed because that function wasn't present? What if we refused to add *even a single line* of code to our programs unless there were a test that was failing because of its absence? What if we incrementally added functionality to our programs by first writing failing tests that asserted the existence of that functionality, and then made the test pass? What effect would this have on the design of the software we were writing? What benefits would we derive from the existence of such a comprehensive bevy of tests?

The first and most obvious effect is that every single function of the program has tests that verify its operation. This suite of tests acts as a backstop for further development. It tells us whenever we inadvertently break some existing functionality. We can add functions to the program, or change the structure of the program, without fear that we will break something important in the process. The tests tell us that the program is still behaving properly. We are thus much freer to make changes and improvement to our program.

A more important, but less obvious, effect is that the act of writing the test first forces us into a different point of view. We must view the program we are about to write from the vantage point of a caller of that program. Thus, we are immediately concerned with the interface of the program as well as its function. By writing the test first, we design the software to be *conveniently callable*.

What's more, by writing the test first, we force ourselves to design the program to be *testable*. Designing the program to be callable and testable is remarkably important. In order to be callable and testable, the software has to be decoupled from its surroundings. Thus, the act of writing tests first *forces us to decouple the software*!

Another important effect of writing tests first is that the tests act as an invaluable form of documentation. If you want to know how to call a function or create an object, there is a test that shows you. The tests act as a suite of examples that help other programmers figure out how to work with the code. This documentation is compileable and executable. It will stay current. It cannot lie.

An Example of Test-First Design

I recently wrote a version of *Hunt the Wumpus*, just for fun. This program is a simple adventure game in which the player moves through a cave trying to kill the Wumpus before the Wumpus eats him. The cave is a set of rooms that are connected to each other by passageways. Each room may have passages to the north, south, east, or west. The player moves about by telling the computer which direction to go.

One of the first tests I wrote for this program was testMove in Listing 4-1. This function creates a new WumpusGame, connects room 4 to room 5 via an east passage, places the player in room 4, issues the command to move east, and then asserts that the player should be in room 5.

Listing 4-1

```
public void testMove()
{
  WumpusGame g = new WumpusGame();
  g.connect(4,5,"E");
  g.setPlayerRoom(4);
  g.east();
  assertEquals(5, g.getPlayerRoom());
}
```

All this code was written before any part of WumpusGame was written. I took Ward Cunningham's advice and wrote the test the way I wanted it to read. I trusted that I could make the test pass by writing the code that conformed to the structure implied by the test. This is called *intentional programming*. You state your intent in a test before you implement it, making your intent as simple and readable as possible. You trust that this simplicity and clarity points to a good structure for the program.

Programming by intent immediately led me to an interesting design decision. The test makes no use of a Room class. The action of *connecting* one room to another communicates my intent. I don't seem to need a Room class to facilitate that communication. Instead, I can just use integers to represent the rooms.

This may seem counter intuitive to you. After all, this program may appear to you to be all about rooms; moving between rooms; finding out what rooms contain; etc. Is the design implied by my intent flawed because it lacks a Room class?

I could argue that the concept of connections is far more central to the Wumpus game than the concept of room. I could argue that this initial test pointed out a good way to solve the problem. Indeed, I think that is the case, but it is not the point I'm trying to make. The point is that the test illuminated a central design issue at a very early stage. *The act of writing tests first is an act of discerning between design decisions.*

Notice that the test tells you how the program works. Most of us could easily write the four named methods of `WumpusGame` from this simple specification. We could also name and write the three other direction commands without much trouble. If later we want to know how to connect two rooms or move in a particular direction, this test will show us how to do it in no uncertain terms. This test acts as a compileable and executable document that describes the program.

Test Isolation

The act of writing tests before production code often exposes areas in the software that ought to be decoupled. For example, Figure 4-1 shows a simple UML diagram[1] of a payroll application. The `Payroll` class uses the `EmployeeDatabase` class to fetch an `Employee` object. It asks the `Employee` to calculate its pay. Then it passes that pay to the `CheckWriter` object to produce a check. Finally, it posts the payment to the `Employee` object and writes the object back to the database.

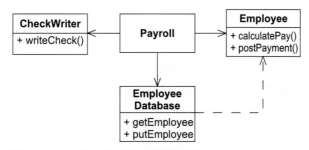

Figure 4-1   Coupled Payroll Model

Presume that we haven't written any of this code yet. So far, this diagram is just sitting on a whiteboard after a quick design session.[2] Now, we need to write the tests that specify the behavior of the `Payroll` object. There are a number of problems associated with writing these tests. First, what database do we use? `Payroll` needs to read from some kind of database. Must we write a fully functioning database before we can test the `Payroll` class? What data do we load into it? Second, how do we verify that the appropriate check got printed? We can't write an automated test that looks on the printer for a check and verifies the amount on it!

The solution to these problems is to use the MOCK OBJECT pattern.[3] We can insert interfaces between all the collaborators of `Payroll` and create test stubs that implement these interfaces.

Figure 4-2 shows the structure. The `Payroll` class now uses interfaces to communicate with the `EmployeeDatabase`, `CheckWriter`, and `Employee`. Three MOCK OBJECTS have been created that implement these interfaces. These MOCK OBJECTS are queried by the `PayrollTest` object to see if the `Payroll` object manages them correctly.

Listing 4-2 shows the intent of the test. It creates the appropriate mock objects, passes them to the `Payroll` object, tells the `Payroll` object to pay all the employees, and then asks the mock objects to verify that all the checks were written correctly and that all the payments were posted correctly.

---

1.   If you don't know UML, there are two appendices that describes it in great detail. See Appendices A and B, starting on page 467.

2.   [Jeffries2001].

3.   [Mackinnon2000].

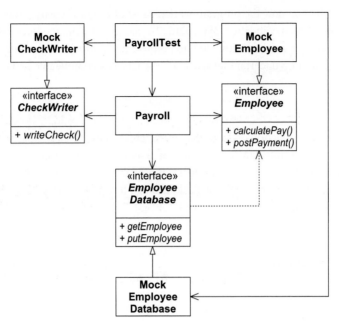

Figure 4-2   Decoupled Payroll using Mock Objects for testing

Listing 4-2

TestPayroll

```
public void testPayroll()
{
  MockEmployeeDatabase db = new MockEmployeeDatabase();
  MockCheckWriter w = new MockCheckWriter();
  Payroll p = new Payroll(db, w);
  p.payEmployees();
  assert(w.checksWereWrittenCorrectly());
  assert(db.paymentsWerePostedCorrectly());
}
```

Of course all this test is checking is that `Payroll` called all the right functions with all the right data. It's not actually checking that checks were written. It's not actually checking that a true database was properly updated. Rather, it is checking that the `Payroll` class is behaving as it should in isolation.

You might wonder what the `MockEmployee` is for. It seems feasible that the real `Employee` class could be used instead of a mock. If that were so, then I would have no compunction about using it. In this case, I presumed that the `Employee` class was more complex than needed to check the function of `Payroll`.

Serendipitous Decoupling

The decoupling of `Payroll` is a good thing. It allows us to swap in different databases and check writers, both for the purpose of testing *and* for extension of the application. I think it is interesting that this decoupling was driven by the need to test. Apparently, the need to isolate the module under test forces us to decouple in ways that are beneficial to the overall structure of the program. *Writing tests before code improves our designs.*

A large part of this book is about design principles for managing dependencies. Those principles give you some guidelines and techniques for decoupling classes and packages. You will find these principles most beneficial if you practice them as part of your unit testing strategy. It is the unit tests that will provide much of the impetus and direction for decoupling.

Acceptance Tests

Unit tests are necessary but insufficient as verification tools. Unit tests verify that the small elements of the system work as they are expected to, but they do not verify that the system works properly as a whole. Unit tests are white-box tests[4] that verify the individual mechanisms of the system. Acceptance tests are black-box tests[5] that verify that the customer requirements are being met.

Acceptance tests are written by folks who do not know the internal mechanisms of the system. They may be written directly by the customer or by some technical people attached to the customer, possibly QA. Acceptance tests are programs and are therefore executable. However, they are usually written in a special scripting language created for customers of the application.

Acceptance tests are the ultimate documentation of a feature. Once the customer has written the acceptance tests, which verify that a feature is correct, the programmers can read those acceptance tests to truly understand the feature. So, just as unit tests serve as compileable and executable documentation for the internals of the system, acceptance tests serve as compileable and executable documentation of the features of the system.

Furthermore, the act of writing acceptance tests first has a profound effect upon the architecture of the system. In order to make the system testable, it has to be decoupled at the high architecture level. For example, the user interface (UI) has to be decoupled from the business rules in such a way that the acceptance tests can gain access to those business rules without going through the UI.

In the early iterations of a project, the temptation is to do acceptance tests manually. This is inadvisable because it deprives those early iterations of the decoupling pressure exerted by the need to automate the acceptance tests. When you start the very first iteration, knowing full well that you must automate the acceptance tests, you make very different architectural trade-offs. And, just as unit tests drive you to make superior design decisions in the small, acceptance tests drive you to make superior architecture decisions in the large.

Creating an acceptance testing framework may seem a daunting task. However, if you take only one iteration's worth of features and create only that part of the framework necessary for those few acceptance tests, you'll find it's not that hard to write. You'll also find that the effort is worth the cost.

Example of Acceptance Testing

Consider, again, the payroll application. In our first iteration, we must be able to add and delete employees to and from the database. We must also be able to create paychecks for the employees currently in the database. Fortunately, we only have to deal with salaried employees. The other kinds of employees have been held back until a later iteration.

We haven't written any code yet, and we haven't invested in any design yet. This is the best time to start thinking about acceptance tests. Once again, intentional programming is a useful tool. We should write the acceptance tests the way we think they should appear, and then we can structure the scripting language and payroll system around that structure.

I want to make the acceptance tests convenient to write and easy to change. I want them to be placed in a configuration-management tool and saved so that I can run them anytime I please. Therefore, it makes sense that the acceptance tests should be written in simple text files.

---

4.   A test that knows and depends on the internal structure of the module being tested.

5.   A test that does not know or depend on the internal structure of the module being tested.

The following is an example of an acceptance-test script:

```
AddEmp 1429 "Robert Martin" 3215.88
Payday
Verify Paycheck EmpId 1429 GrossPay 3215.88
```

In this example, we add employee number 1429 to the database. His name is "Robert Martin," and his monthly pay is $3215.88. Next, we tell the system that it is payday and that it needs to pay all the employees. Finally, we verify that a paycheck was generated for employee 1429 with a `GrossPay` field of $3215.88.

Clearly, this kind of script will be very easy for customers to write. Also, it will be easy to add new functionality to this kind of script. However, think about what it implies about the structure of the system.

The first two lines of the script are functions of the payroll application. We might call these lines payroll transactions. These are functions that payroll users expect. However, the `Verify` line is not a transaction that the users of payroll would expect. This line is a directive that is specific to the acceptance test.

Thus, our acceptance testing framework will have to parse this text file, separating the payroll transactions from the acceptance-testing directives. It must send the payroll transactions to the payroll application and then use the acceptance-testing directives to query the payroll application in order to verify data.

This already puts architectural stress on the payroll program. The payroll program is going to have to accept input directly from users and also from the acceptance-testing framework. We want to bring those two paths of input together as early as possible. So, it looks as if the payroll program will need a transaction processor that can deal with transactions of the form `AddEmp` and `Payday` coming from more than one source. We need to find some common form for those transactions so that the amount of specialized code is kept to a minimum.

One solution would be to feed the transactions into the payroll application in XML. The acceptance-testing framework could certainly generate XML, and it seems likely that the UI of the payroll system could also generate XML. Thus, we might see transactions that looked like the following:

```
<AddEmp PayType=Salaried>
  <EmpId>1429</EmpId>
  <Name>Robert Martin</Name>
  <Salary>3215.88</Salary>
</AddEmp>
```

These transactions might enter the payroll application through a subroutine call, a socket, or even a batch input file. Indeed, it would be a trivial matter to change from one to the other during the course of development. So during the early iterations, we could decide to read transactions from a file, migrating to an API or socket much later.

How does the acceptance-test framework invoke the `Verify` directive? Clearly it must have some way to access the data produced by the payroll application. Once again, we don't want the acceptance-testing framework to have to try to read the writing on a printed check, but we can do the next best thing.

We can have the payroll application produce its paychecks in XML. The acceptance-testing framework can then catch this XML and query it for the appropriate data. The final step of printing the check from the XML may be trivial enough to handle through manual acceptance tests.

Therefore, the payroll application can create an XML document that contains all the paychecks. It might look like this:

```
<Paycheck>
  <EmpId>1429</EmpId>
  <Name>Robert Martin</Name>
  <GrossPay>3215.88</GrossPay>
</Paycheck>
```

Clearly, the acceptance-testing framework can execute the `Verify` directive when supplied with this XML.

Once again, we can spit the XML out through a socket, through an API, or into a file. For the initial iterations, a file is probably easiest. Therefore, the payroll application will begin its life reading XML transactions in from a file and outputting XML paychecks to a file. The acceptance-testing framework will read transactions in text form, translating them to XML and writing them to a file. It will then invoke the payroll program. Finally, it will read the output XML from the payroll program and invoke the `Verify` directives.

Serendipitous Architecture

Notice the pressure that the acceptance tests placed upon the architecture of the payroll system. The very fact that we considered the tests first led us to the notion of XML input and output very quickly. This architecture has decoupled the transaction sources from the payroll application. It has also decoupled the paycheck printing mechanism from the payroll application. These are good architectural decisions.

Conclusion

The simpler it is to run a suite of tests, the more often those tests will be run. The more the tests are run, the faster any deviation from those tests will be found. If we can run all the tests several times a day, then the system will never be broken for more than a few minutes. This is a reasonable goal. We simply don't allow the system to backslide. Once it works to a certain level, it never backslides to a lower level.

Yet verification is just one of the benefits of writing tests. Both unit tests and acceptance tests are a form of documentation. That documentation is compileable and executable; therefore, it is accurate and reliable. Moreover, these tests are written in unambiguous languages that are made to be readable by their audience. Programmers can read unit tests because they are written in their programming language. Customers can read acceptance tests because they are written in a language that they themselves designed.

Possibly the most important benefit of all this testing is the impact it has on architecture and design. To make a module or an application testable, it must also be decoupled. The more testable it is, the more decoupled it is. The act of considering comprehensive acceptance and unit tests has a profoundly positive effect upon the structure of the software.

Bibliography

1. Mackinnon, Tim, Steve Freeman, and Philip Craig. Endo-Testing: Unit Testing with Mock Objects. *Extreme Programming Examined*. Addison–Wesley, 2001.
2. Jeffries, Ron, et al., *Extreme Programming Installed*. Upper Saddle River, NJ: Addison–Wesley, 2001.

5

Refactoring

The only factor becoming scarce in a world of abundance is human attention.

—Kevin Kelly, in *Wired*

This chapter is about human attention. It is about paying attention to what you are doing and making sure you are doing your best. It is about the difference between getting something to work and getting something right. It is about the value we place in the structure of our code.

In his classic book, *Refactoring*, Martin Fowler defines refactoring as "...the process of changing a software system in such a way that it does not alter the external behavior of the code yet improves its internal structure."[1] But why would we want to improve the structure of working code? What about the old saw, "if it's not broken, don't fix it!"?

Every software module has three functions. First, there is the function it performs while executing. This function is the reason for the module's existence. The second function of a module is to afford change. Almost all modules will change in the course of their lives, and it is the responsibility of the developers to make sure that such changes are as simple as possible to make. A module that is hard to change is broken and needs fixing, even though it works. The third function of a module is to communicate to its readers. Developers unfamiliar with the module should be able to read and understand it without undue mental gymnastics. A module that does not communicate is broken and needs to be fixed.

---

1.   [Fowler99], p. xvi.

What does it take to make a module easy to read and easy to change? Much of this book is dedicated to principles and patterns whose primary goal is to help you create modules that are flexible and adaptable. However, it takes something more than just principles and patterns to make a module that is easy to read and change. It takes attention. It takes discipline. It takes a passion for creating beauty.

Generating Primes: A Simple Example of Refactoring[2]

Consider the code in Listing 5–1. This program generates prime numbers. It is one big function with many single letter variables and comments to help us read it.

Listing 5-1

GeneratePrimes.java version 1

```java
/**
 * This class generates prime numbers up to a user-specified
 * maximum.  The algorithm used is the Sieve of Eratosthenes.
 * <p>
 * Eratosthenes of Cyrene, b. c. 276 BC, Cyrene, Libya --
 * d. c. 194, Alexandria.  The first man to calculate the
 * circumference of the Earth.  Also known for working on
 * calendars with leap years, he ran the library at Alexandria.
 * <p>
 * The algorithm is quite simple.  Given an array of integers
 * starting at 2.  Cross out all multiples of 2.  Find the next
 * uncrossed integer, and cross out all of its multiples.
 * Repeat until you have passed the square root of the maximum
 * value.
 *
 * @author Robert C. Martin
 * @version 9 Dec 1999 rcm
 */
import java.util.*;

public class GeneratePrimes
{
  /**
   * @param maxValue is the generation limit.
   */
  public static int[] generatePrimes(int maxValue)
  {
    if (maxValue >= 2) // the only valid case
    {
      // declarations
      int s = maxValue + 1; // size of array
      boolean[] f = new boolean[s];
      int i;

      // initialize array to true.
      for (i = 0; i < s; i++)
        f[i] = true;
```

---

2.   I initially wrote this program for XP Immersion I using tests written by Jim Newkirk. Kent Beck and Jim Newkirk refactored it in front of the students. I have tried to recreate that refactoring here.

```java
    // get rid of known non-primes
    f[0] = f[1] = false;

    // sieve
    int j;
    for (i = 2; i < Math.sqrt(s) + 1; i++)
    {
      if (f[i]) // if i is uncrossed, cross its multiples.
      {
        for (j = 2 * i; j < s; j += i)
          f[j] = false; // multiple is not prime
      }
    }

    // how many primes are there?
    int count = 0;
    for (i = 0; i < s; i++)
    {
      if (f[i])
        count++; // bump count.
    }

    int[] primes = new int[count];

    // move the primes into the result
    for (i = 0, j = 0; i < s; i++)
    {
      if (f[i])                 // if prime
        primes[j++] = i;
    }

    return primes;   // return the primes
  }
  else // maxValue < 2
    return new int[0]; // return null array if bad input.
  }
}
```

The unit test for GeneratePrimes is shown in Listing 5–2. It takes a statistical approach, checking to see if the generator can generate primes up to 0, 2, 3, and 100. In the first case there should be no primes. In the second there should be one prime, and it should be 2. In the third there should be two primes, and they should be 2 and 3. In the last case there should be 25 primes, the last of which is 97. If all these tests pass, then I make the assumption that the generator is working. I doubt this is foolproof, but I can't think of a reasonable scenario where these tests would pass and yet the function would fail.

Listing 5-2

TestGeneratePrimes.java

```java
import junit.framework.*;
import java.util.*;

public class TestGeneratePrimes extends TestCase
{
  public static void main(String args[])
```

```
  {
      junit.swingui.TestRunner.main(
        new String[] {"TestGeneratePrimes"});
  }
  public TestGeneratePrimes(String name)
  {
    super(name);
  }

  public void testPrimes()
  {
    int[] nullArray = GeneratePrimes.generatePrimes(0);
    assertEquals(nullArray.length, 0);

    int[] minArray = GeneratePrimes.generatePrimes(2);
    assertEquals(minArray.length, 1);
    assertEquals(minArray[0], 2);

    int[] threeArray = GeneratePrimes.generatePrimes(3);
    assertEquals(threeArray.length, 2);
    assertEquals(threeArray[0], 2);
    assertEquals(threeArray[1], 3);

    int[] centArray = GeneratePrimes.generatePrimes(100);
    assertEquals(centArray.length, 25);
    assertEquals(centArray[24], 97);
  }
}
```

To help me refactor this program, I am using the *Idea* refactoring browser from *IntelliJ*. This tool makes it trivial to extract methods and rename variables and classes.

It seems pretty clear that the main function wants to be three separate functions. The first initializes all the variables and sets up the sieve. The second actually executes the sieve, and the third loads the sieved results into an integer array. To expose this structure more clearly in Listing 5–3, I extracted those functions into three separate methods. I also removed a few unnecessary comments and changed the name of the class to `PrimeGenerator`. The tests all still ran.

Extracting the three functions forced me to promote some of the variables of the function to static fields of the class. I think this clarifies which variables are local and which have wider influence.

Listing 5-3
`PrimeGenerator.java, version 2`

```
/**
 * This class generates prime numbers up to a user-specified
 * maximum.  The algorithm used is the Sieve of Eratosthenes.
 * Given an array of integers starting at 2:
 * Find the first uncrossed integer, and cross out all its
 * multiples.  Repeat until the first uncrossed integer exceeds
 * the square root of the maximum value.
 */
import java.util.*;
```

```java
public class PrimeGenerator
{
  private static int s;
  private static boolean[] f;
  private static int[] primes;

  public static int[] generatePrimes(int maxValue)
  {
    if (maxValue < 2)
      return new int[0];
    else
    {
      initializeSieve(maxValue);
      sieve();
      loadPrimes();
      return primes;  // return the primes
    }
  }

  private static void loadPrimes()
  {
    int i;
    int j;

    // how many primes are there?
    int count = 0;
    for (i = 0; i < s; i++)
    {
      if (f[i])
        count++; // bump count.
    }

    primes = new int[count];

    // move the primes into the result
    for (i = 0, j = 0; i < s; i++)
    {
      if (f[i])               // if prime
        primes[j++] = i;
    }
  }

  private static void sieve()
  {
    int i;
    int j;
    for (i = 2; i < Math.sqrt(s) + 1; i++)
    {
      if (f[i])  // if i is uncrossed, cross out its multiples.
      {
        for (j = 2 * i; j < s; j += i)
          f[j] = false; // multiple is not prime
      }
    }
  }
```

```java
private static void initializeSieve(int maxValue)
{
  // declarations
  s = maxValue + 1; // size of array
  f = new boolean[s];
  int i;

  // initialize array to true.
  for (i = 0; i < s; i++)
    f[i] = true;

  // get rid of known non-primes
  f[0] = f[1] = false;
}
}
```

The `initializeSieve` function is a little messy, so in Listing 5–4, I cleaned it up considerably. First, I replaced all usages of the `s` variable with `f.length`. Then, I changed the names of the three functions to something a bit more expressive. Finally, I rearranged the innards of `initializeArrayOfIntegers` (née `initializeSieve`) to be a little nicer to read. The tests all still ran.

Listing 5-4

PrimeGenerator.java, version 3 (partial)

```java
public class PrimeGenerator
{
  private static boolean[] f;
  private static int[] result;

  public static int[] generatePrimes(int maxValue)
  {
    if (maxValue < 2)
      return new int[0];
    else
    {
      initializeArrayOfIntegers(maxValue);
      crossOutMultiples();
      putUncrossedIntegersIntoResult();
      return result;
    }
  }

  private static void initializeArrayOfIntegers(int maxValue)
  {
    f = new boolean[maxValue + 1];
    f[0] = f[1] = false;  //neither primes nor multiples.
    for (int i = 2; i < f.length; i++)
      f[i] = true;
  }
```

Next, I looked at `crossOutMultiples`. There were a number of statements in this function, and in others, of the form `if(f[i] == true)`. The intent was to check to see if `i` was uncrossed, so I changed the name of `f` to `unCrossed`. But this lead to ugly statements like `unCrossed[i] = false`. I found the double negative confusing. So I changed the name of the array to `isCrossed` and changed the sense of all the booleans. The tests all still ran.

I got rid of the initialization that set isCrossed[0] and isCrossed[1] to true and just made sure that no part of the function used the isCrossed array for indexes less than 2. I extracted the inner loop of the crossOutMultiples function and called it crossOutMultiplesOf. I also thought that if(isCrossed[i] == false) was confusing, so I created a function called notCrossed and changed the if statement to if (notCrossed(i)). The tests all still ran.

I spent a bit of time writing a comment that tried to explain why you only have to iterate up to the square root of the array size. This led me to extract the calculation into a function, where I could put the explanatory comment. In writing the comment, I realized that the square root is the maximum prime factor of any integer in the array. So I chose that name for the variables and functions that dealt with it. The result of all these refactorings are in Listing 5–5. The tests all still ran.

Listing 5-5

PrimeGenerator.java version 4 (partial)

```java
public class PrimeGenerator
{
  private static boolean[] isCrossed;
  private static int[] result;

  public static int[] generatePrimes(int maxValue)
  {
    if (maxValue < 2)
      return new int[0];
    else
    {
      initializeArrayOfIntegers(maxValue);
      crossOutMultiples();
      putUncrossedIntegersIntoResult();
      return result;
    }
  }

  private static void initializeArrayOfIntegers(int maxValue)
  {
    isCrossed = new boolean[maxValue + 1];
    for (int i = 2; i < isCrossed.length; i++)
      isCrossed[i] = false;
  }

  private static void crossOutMultiples()
  {
    int maxPrimeFactor = calcMaxPrimeFactor();
    for (int i = 2; i <= maxPrimeFactor; i++)
      if (notCrossed(i))
        crossOutMultiplesOf(i);
  }

  private static int calcMaxPrimeFactor()
  {
    // We cross out all multiples of p, where p is prime.
    // Thus, all crossed out multiples have p and q for
    // factors.  If p > sqrt of the size of the array, then
    // q will never be greater than 1.  Thus p is the
    // largest prime factor in the array, and is also
    // the iteration limit.
```

```
    double maxPrimeFactor = Math.sqrt(isCrossed.length) + 1;
    return (int) maxPrimeFactor;
  }

  private static void crossOutMultiplesOf(int i)
  {
    for (int multiple = 2*i;
         multiple < isCrossed.length;
         multiple += i)
      isCrossed[multiple] = true;
  }

  private static boolean notCrossed(int i)
  {
    return isCrossed[i] == false;
  }
```

The last function to refactor is putUncrossedIntegersIntoResult. This method has two parts. The first counts the number of uncrossed integers in the array and creates the result array of that size. The second moves the uncrossed integers into the result array. I extracted the first part into its own function and did some miscellaneous cleanup. The tests all still ran.

Listing 5-6

PrimeGenerator.java, version 5 (partial)

```
private static void putUncrossedIntegersIntoResult()
  {
    result = new int[numberOfUncrossedIntegers()];
    for (int j = 0, i = 2; i < isCrossed.length; i++)
      if (notCrossed(i))
        result[j++] = i;
  }

  private static int numberOfUncrossedIntegers()
  {
    int count = 0;
    for (int i = 2; i < isCrossed.length; i++)
      if (notCrossed(i))
        count++;

    return count;
  }
```

The Final Reread

Next, I made one final pass over the whole program, reading it from beginning to end, rather like one would read a geometric proof. This is an important step. So far, I've been refactoring fragments. Now, I want to see if the whole program hangs together as a *readable* whole.

First, I realize that I don't like the name initializeArrayOf-Integers. What's being initialized is not, in fact, an array of integers, it's an array of booleans. However, initializeArrayOfBooleans is not an improvement. What we are really doing in this method is uncrossing all the relevant integers so that we can then cross out the multiples. So I change the name to uncrossIntegersUpTo. I also realize that I don't like the name isCrossed for the array of booleans. So I change it to crossedOut. The tests all still run.

One might think I'm being frivolous with these name changes, but with a refactoring browser you can afford to do these kinds of tweaks—they cost virtually nothing. Even without a refactoring browser, a simple search and replace is pretty cheap. And the tests strongly mitigate any chance that we might unknowingly break something.

I don't know what I was smoking when I wrote all that `maxPrimeFactor` stuff. Yikes! The square root of the size of the array is not necessarily prime. That method did *not* calculate the maximum prime factor. The explanatory comment was just *wrong*. So I rewrote the comment to better explain the rationale behind the square root and renamed all the variables appropriately.[3] The tests all still run.

What the devil is that +1 doing in there? I think it must have been paranoia. I was afraid that a fractional square root would convert to an integer that was too small to serve as the iteration limit. But that's silly. The true iteration limit is the largest prime less than or equal to the square root of the size of the array. I'll get rid of the +1.

The tests all run, but that last change makes me pretty nervous. I understand the rationale behind the square root, but I've got a nagging feeling that there may be some corner cases that aren't being covered. So I'll write another test to check that there are no multiples in any of the prime lists between 2 and 500. (See the `testExhaustive` function in Listing 5–8.) The new test passes, and my fears are allayed.

The rest of the code reads pretty nicely. So I think we're done. The final version is shown in Listings 5–7 and 5–8.

Listing 5-7

`PrimeGenerator.java` (final)

```java
/**
 * This class generates prime numbers up to a user specified
 * maximum.  The algorithm used is the Sieve of Eratosthenes.
 * Given an array of integers starting at 2:
 * Find the first uncrossed integer, and cross out all its
 * multiples.  Repeat until there are no more multiples
 * in the array.
 */

public class PrimeGenerator
{
  private static boolean[] crossedOut;
  private static int[] result;

  public static int[] generatePrimes(int maxValue)
  {
    if (maxValue < 2)
      return new int[0];
    else
    {
      uncrossIntegersUpTo(maxValue);
      crossOutMultiples();
      putUncrossedIntegersIntoResult();
      return result;
    }
  }

  private static void uncrossIntegersUpTo(int maxValue)
  {
```

---

3.   When Kent Beck and Jim Newkirk refactored this program, they did away with the square root altogether. Kent's rationale was that the square root was hard to understand, and there was no test that failed if you iterated right up to the size of the array. I can't bring myself to give up the efficiency. I guess that shows my assembly-language roots.

```
    crossedOut = new boolean[maxValue + 1];
    for (int i = 2; i < crossedOut.length; i++)
      crossedOut[i] = false;
  }

  private static void crossOutMultiples()
  {
    int limit = determineIterationLimit();
    for (int i = 2; i <= limit; i++)
      if (notCrossed(i))
        crossOutMultiplesOf(i);
  }

  private static int determineIterationLimit()
  {
    // Every multiple in the array has a prime factor that
    // is less than or equal to the sqrt of the array size,
    // so we don't have to cross out multiples of numbers
    // larger than that root.
    double iterationLimit = Math.sqrt(crossedOut.length);
    return (int) iterationLimit;
  }

  private static void crossOutMultiplesOf(int i)
  {
    for (int multiple = 2*i;
         multiple < crossedOut.length;
         multiple += i)
      crossedOut[multiple] = true;
  }

  private static boolean notCrossed(int i)
  {
    return crossedOut[i] == false;
  }

  private static void putUncrossedIntegersIntoResult()
  {
    result = new int[numberOfUncrossedIntegers()];
    for (int j = 0, i = 2; i < crossedOut.length; i++)
      if (notCrossed(i))
        result[j++] = i;
  }

  private static int numberOfUncrossedIntegers()
  {
    int count = 0;
    for (int i = 2; i < crossedOut.length; i++)
      if (notCrossed(i))
        count++;

    return count;
  }
}
```

Listing 5-8

`TestGeneratePrimes.java (final)`

```java
import junit.framework.*;

public class TestGeneratePrimes extends TestCase
{
  public static void main(String args[])
  {
      junit.swingui.TestRunner.main(
        new String[] {"TestGeneratePrimes"});
  }
  public TestGeneratePrimes(String name)
  {
    super(name);
  }

  public void testPrimes()
  {
    int[] nullArray = PrimeGenerator.generatePrimes(0);
    assertEquals(nullArray.length, 0);

    int[] minArray = PrimeGenerator.generatePrimes(2);
    assertEquals(minArray.length, 1);
    assertEquals(minArray[0], 2);

    int[] threeArray = PrimeGenerator.generatePrimes(3);
    assertEquals(threeArray.length, 2);
    assertEquals(threeArray[0], 2);
    assertEquals(threeArray[1], 3);

    int[] centArray = PrimeGenerator.generatePrimes(100);
    assertEquals(centArray.length, 25);
    assertEquals(centArray[24], 97);
  }

  public void testExhaustive()
  {
    for (int i = 2; i<500; i++)
        verifyPrimeList(PrimeGenerator.generatePrimes(i));
  }

  private void verifyPrimeList(int[] list)
  {
    for (int i=0; i<list.length; i++)
        verifyPrime(list[i]);
  }

  private void verifyPrime(int n)
  {
    for (int factor=2; factor<n; factor++)
      assert(n%factor != 0);
  }
}
```

Conclusion

The end result of this program reads much better than it did at the start. The program also works a bit better. I'm pretty pleased with the outcome. The program is much easier to understand and is therefore much easier to change. Also, the structure of the program has isolated its parts from one another. This also makes the program much easier to change.

You might be worried that extracting functions that are only called once might adversely affect performance. I think the increased readability is worth a few extra nanoseconds in most cases. However, there may be deep inner loops where those few nanoseconds will be costly. My advice is to assume that the cost will be negligible and wait to be proven wrong.

Was this worth the time we invested in it? After all, the function worked when we started. I strongly recommend that you *always* practice such refactoring for *every* module you write and for *every* module you maintain. The time investment is very small compared to the effort you'll be saving yourself and others in the near future.

Refactoring is like cleaning up the kitchen after dinner. The first time you skip it, you are done with dinner more quickly. But that lack of clean dishes and clear working space makes dinner take longer to prepare the next day. This makes you want to skip cleaning again. Indeed, you can always finish dinner faster *today* if you skip cleaning, but the mess builds and builds. Eventually you are spending an inordinate amount of time hunting for the right cooking utensils, chiseling the encrusted dried food off the dishes, and scrubbing them down so that they are suitable to cook with. Dinner takes forever. Skipping the cleanup does not really make dinner go faster.

The goal of refactoring, as depicted in this chapter, is to clean your code every day. We don't want the mess to build. We don't want to have to chisel and scrub the encrusted bits that accumulate over time. We want to be able to extend and modify our system with a minimum of effort. The most important enabler of that ability is the cleanliness of the code.

I can't stress this enough. All the principles and patterns in this book come to naught if the code they are employed within is a mess. Before investing in principles and patterns, invest in clean code.

Bibliography

1.   Fowler, Martin. *Refactoring: Improving the Design of Existing Code*. Reading, MA: Addison–Wesley, 1999.

6

A Programming Episode

Design and programming are human activities; forget that and all is lost.

—Bjarne Stroustrup, 1991

In order to demonstrate the XP programming practices, Bob Koss (RSK) and Bob Martin (RCM) will pair program a simple application while you watch like a fly on the wall. We will use test-driven development and a lot of refactoring to create our application. What follows is a pretty faithful reenactment of a programming episode that the two Bobs actually did in a hotel room in late 2000.

We made lots of mistakes while doing this. Some of the mistakes are in code, some are in logic, some are in design, and some are in requirements. As you read, you will see us flail around in all these areas, identifying and then dealing with our errors and misconceptions. The process is messy—as are all human processes. The result … well, it's amazing the order that can arise out of such a messy process.

The program calculates the score of a game of bowling, so it helps if you know the rules. If you don't know the rules of bowling, then check out the accompanying sidebar.

The Bowling Game

RCM: Will you help me write a little application that calculates bowling scores?

RSK: (Reflects to himself, "The XP practice of pair programming says that I can't say, "no," when asked to help. I suppose that's especially true when it is your boss who is asking.") Sure, Bob, I'd be glad to help.

RCM: OK, great! What I'd like to do is write an application that keeps track of a bowling league. It needs to record all the games, determine the ranks of the teams, determine the winners and losers of each weekly match, and accurately score each game.

RSK: Cool. I used to be a pretty good bowler. This will be fun. You rattled off several user stories, which one would you like to start with?

RCM: Let's begin with scoring a single game.

RSK: Okay. What does that mean? What are the inputs and outputs for this story?

RCM: It seems to me that the inputs are simply a sequence of throws. A throw is just an integer that tells how many pins were knocked down by the ball. The output is just the score for each frame.

RSK: I'm assuming you are acting as the customer in this exercise, so what form do you want the inputs and outputs to be in?

RCM: Yes, I'm the customer. We'll need a function to call to add throws and another function that gets the score. Sort of like

```
throwBall(6);
throwBall(3);
assertEquals(9, getScore());
```

RSK: OK, we're going to need some test data. Let me sketch out a little picture of a score card. (See Figure 6-1.)

1	4	4	5	6		5				0	1	7		6			2		6
5		14		29		49		60		61		77		97		117		133	

Figure 6-1   Typical Bowling Score Card

RCM: That guy is pretty erratic.

RSK: Or drunk, but it will serve as a decent acceptance test.

RCM: We'll need others, but let's deal with that later. How should we start? Shall we come up with a design for the system?

RSK: I wouldn't mind a UML diagram showing the problem domain concepts that we might see from the score card. That will give us some candidate objects that we can explore further in code.

RCM: (putting on his powerful object designer hat) OK, clearly a `Game` object consists of a sequence of ten frames. Each `Frame` object contains one, two, or three throws.

RSK: Great minds. That was exactly what I was thinking. Let me quickly draw that. (See Figure 6-2.)

Figure 6-2   UML Diagram of Bowling Score Card

RSK: Well, pick a class … any class. Shall we start at the end of the dependency chain and work backwards? That will make testing easier.

RCM: Sure, why not. Let's create a test case for the `Throw` class.

RSK: (Starts typing.)

```
//TestThrow.java--------------------------------
import junit.framework.*;

public class TestThrow extends TestCase
{
  public TestThrow(String name)
  {
    super(name);
  }

// public void test????
}
```

RSK: Do you have a clue what the behavior of a `Throw` object should be?

RCM: It holds the number of pins knocked down by the player.

RSK: Okay, you just said, in not so many words, that it doesn't really do anything. Maybe we should come back to it and focus on an object that actually has behavior, instead of one that's just a data store.

RCM: Hmm. You mean the `Throw` class might not really exist?

RSK: Well, if it doesn't have any behavior, how important can it be? I don't know if it exists or not yet. I'd just feel more productive if we were working on an object that had more than setters and getters for methods. But if you want to drive … (slides the keyboard to RCM).

RCM: Well, let's move up the dependency chain to `Frame` and see if there are any test cases we can write that will force us to finish `Throw`. (Pushes the keyboard back to RSK.)

RSK: (Wondering if RCM is leading me down a blind alley to educate me or if he is really agreeing with me.) Okay, new file, new test case.

```
//TestFrame.java--------------------------------
import junit.framework.*;
```

```
public class TestFrame extends TestCase
{
  public TestFrame( String name )
  {
    super( name );
  }
  //public void test???
}
```

RCM: OK, that's the second time we've typed that. Now, can you think of any interesting test cases for Frame?

RSK: A Frame might provide its score, the number of pins on each throw, whether there was a strike or a spare . . .

RCM: OK, show me the code.

RSK: (types)

```
//TestFrame.java--------------------------------
import junit.framework.*;

public class TestFrame extends TestCase
{
  public TestFrame( String name )
  {
    super( name );
  }

 public void testScoreNoThrows()
 {
  Frame f = new Frame();
  assertEquals( 0, f.getScore() );
 }
}

//Frame.java-------------------------------------
public class Frame
{
  public int getScore()
  {
    return 0;
  }
}
```

RCM: OK, the test case passes, but getScore is a really stupid function. It will fail if we add a throw to the Frame. So let's write the test case that adds some throws and then checks the score.

```
//TestFrame.java--------------------------------

 public void testAddOneThrow()
 {
   Frame f = new Frame();
   f.add(5);
   assertEquals(5, f.getScore());
 }
```

RCM: That doesn't compile. There's no add method in `Frame`.

RSK: I'll bet if you define the method, it will compile ;-)

RCM:

```
//Frame.java-------------------------------------
public class Frame
{
  public int getScore()
  {
    return 0;
  }

  public void add(Throw t)
  {
  }
}
```

RCM: (thinking out loud) This doesn't compile because we haven't written the `Throw` class.

RSK: Talk to me, Bob. The test is passing an integer, and the method expects a `Throw` object. You can't have it both ways. Before we go down the `Throw` path again, can you describe its behavior?

RCM: Wow! I didn't even notice that I had written `f.add(5)`. I should have written `f.add(new Throw(5))`, but that's ugly as hell. What I *really* want to write is `f.add(5)`.

RSK: Ugly or not, let's leave aesthetics out of it for the time being. Can you describe any behavior of a `Throw` object—binary response, Bob?

RCM: 101101011010100101. I don't know if there is any behavior in `Throw`. I'm beginning to think a `Throw` is just an `int`. However, we don't need to consider that yet since we can write `Frame.add` to take an `int`.

RSK: Then I think we should do that for no other reason than it's simple. When we feel pain, we can do something more sophisticated.

RCM: Agreed.

```
//Frame.java-------------------------------------
public class Frame
{
  public int getScore()
  {
    return 0;
  }

  public void add(int pins)
  {
  }
}
```

RCM: OK, this compiles and fails the test. Now, let's make the test pass.

```
//Frame.java-------------------------------------
public class Frame
{
  public int getScore()
```

```
    {
      return itsScore;
    }

      public void add(int pins)
    {
      itsScore += pins;
    }
    private int itsScore = 0;
  }
```

RCM: This compiles and passes the tests, but it's clearly simplistic. What's the next test case?

RSK: Can we take a break first?

----------------------------Break----------------------------

RCM: That's better.

       Frame.add is a fragile function. What if you call it with an 11?

RSK: It can throw an exception if that happens. But, who is calling it? Is this going to be an application framework that thousands of people will use and we have to protect against such things, or is this going to be used by you and only you? If the latter, just don't call it with an 11 (chuckle).

RCM: Good point, the tests in the rest of the system will catch an invalid argument. If we run into trouble, we can put the check in later.

       So, the add function doesn't currently handle strikes or spares. Let's write a test case that expresses that.

RSK: Hmmmm . . . if we call add(10) to represent a strike, what should getScore() return? I don't know how to write the assertion, so maybe we're asking the wrong question. Or we're asking the right question to the wrong object.

RCM: When you call add(10), or add(3) followed by add(7), then calling getScore on the Frame is meaningless. The Frame would have to look at later Frame instances to calculate its score. If those later Frame instances don't exist, then it would have to return something ugly, like -1. I don't want to return -1.

RSK: Yeah, I hate the -1 idea too. You've introduced the idea of Frames knowing about other Frames. Who is holding these different Frame objects?

RCM: The Game object.

RSK: So Game depends on Frame; and Frame, in turn, depends back on Game. I hate that.

RCM: Frames don't have to depend on Game, they could be arranged in a linked list. Each Frame could hold pointers to its next and previous Frames. To get the score from a Frame, the Frame would look backward to get the score of the previous Frame and forward for any spare or strike balls it needs.

RSK: Okay, I'm feeling kind of dumb because I can't visualize this. Show me some code.

RCM: Right. So we need a test case first.

RSK: For Game or another test for Frame?

RCM: I think we need one for Game, since it's Game that will build the Frames and hook them up to each other.

RSK: Do you want to stop what we're doing on Frame and do a mental longjump to Game, or do you just want to have a MockGame object that does just what we need to get Frame working?

RCM: No, let's stop working on Frame and start working on Game. The test cases in Game should prove that we need the linked list of Frames.

RSK: I'm not sure how they'll show the need for the list. I need code.

RCM: (types)

```java
//TestGame.java-----------------------------------------
import junit.framework.*;

public class TestGame extends TestCase
{
  public TestGame(String name)
  {
    super(name);
  }

  public void testOneThrow()
  {
    Game g = new Game();
    g.add(5);
    assertEquals(5, g.score());
  }

}
```

RCM: Does that look reasonable?

RSK: Sure, but I'm still looking for proof for this list of Frames.

RCM: Me too. Let's keep following these test cases and see where they lead.

```java
//Game.java--------------------------------
public class Game
{
  public int score()
  {
    return 0;
  }

  public void add(int pins)
  {
  }
}
```

RCM: OK, this compiles and fails the test. Now let's make it pass.

```java
//Game.java--------------------------------
public class Game
{
  public int score()
  {
    return itsScore;
  }
```

```
         public void add(int pins)
         {
           itsScore += pins;
         }
         private int itsScore = 0;
       }
```

RCM: This passes. Good.

RSK: I can't disagree with it, but I'm still looking for this great proof of the need for a linked list of
        `Frame` objects. That's what led us to `Game` in the first place.

RCM: Yeah, that's what I'm looking for too. I fully expect that once we start injecting spare and strike test
        cases, we'll have to build `Frames` and tie them together in a linked list. But I don't want to build
        that until the code forces us to.

RSK: Good point. Let's keep going in small steps on `Game`. What about another test that tests two throws
        but with no spare?

RCM: OK, that should pass right now. Let's try it.

```
//TestGame.java-------------------------------------------

  public void testTwoThrowsNoMark()
  {
    Game g = new Game();
    g.add(5);
    g.add(4);
    assertEquals(9, g.score());
  }
```

RCM: Yep, that one passes. Now let's try four balls with no marks.

RSK: Well that will pass, too. I didn't expect this. We can keep adding throws, and we don't ever even
        need a `Frame`. But we haven't done a spare or a strike yet. Maybe that's when we'll have to make
        one.

RCM: That's what I'm counting on. However, consider this test case:

```
//TestGame.java-------------------------------------------
public void testFourThrowsNoMark()
  {
    Game g = new Game();
    g.add(5);
    g.add(4);
    g.add(7);
    g.add(2);
    assertEquals(18, g.score());
    assertEquals(9,  g.scoreForFrame(1));
    assertEquals(18, g.scoreForFrame(2));
  }
```

RCM: Does this look reasonable?

RSK: It sure does. I forgot that we have to be able to show the score in each frame. Ah, our sketch of the
        score card was serving as a coaster for my Diet Coke. Yeah, that's why I forgot.

RCM: (sigh) OK, first let's make this test case fail by adding the `scoreForFrame` method to `Game`.

```
//Game.java---------------------------------

  public int scoreForFrame(int frame)
  {
    return 0;
  }
```

RCM: Great, this compiles and fails. Now, how do we make it pass?

RSK: We can start making `Frame` objects, but is that the simplest thing that will get the test to pass?

RCM: No, actually, we could just create an array of integers in the `Game`. Each call to `add` would append a new integer onto the array. Each call to `scoreForFrame` will just work forward through the array and calculate the score.

```
//Game.java---------------------------------
public class Game
{
  public int score()
  {
    return itsScore;
  }

  public void add(int pins)
  {
    itsThrows[itsCurrentThrow++]=pins;
    itsScore += pins;
  }

  public int scoreForFrame(int frame)
  {
    int score = 0;
    for ( int ball = 0;
      frame > 0 && (ball < itsCurrentThrow);
      ball+=2, frame--)
    {
      score += itsThrows[ball] + itsThrows[ball+1];
    }
    return score;
  }
  private int itsScore = 0;
  private int[] itsThrows = new int[21];
  private int itsCurrentThrow = 0;
}
```

RCM: (very satisfied with himself) There, that works.

RSK: Why the magic number 21?

RCM: That's the maximum possible number of throws in a game.

RSK: Yuck. Let me guess, in your youth you were a Unix hacker and prided yourself on writing an entire application in one statement that nobody else could decipher.

        `scoreForFrame()` needs to be refactored to be more communicative. But before we consider refactoring, let me ask another question. Is `Game` the best place for this method? In my mind, `Game` is violating the Single Responsibility Principle.[1] It is accepting throws *and* it knows how to score for each frame. What would you think about a `Scorer` object?

RCM: (makes a rude oscillating gesture with his hand) I don't know where the functions live now; right now I'm interested in getting the scoring stuff to work. Once we've got that all in place, *then* we can debate the values of the SRP.

However, I see your point about the Unix hacker stuff; let's try to simplify that loop.

```
public int scoreForFrame(int theFrame)
{
  int ball = 0;
  int score=0;
  for (int currentFrame = 0;
       currentFrame < theFrame;
       currentFrame++)
  {
   score += itsThrows[ball++] + itsThrows[ball++];
  }

  return score;
}
```

RCM: That's a little better, but there are side effects in the `score+=` expression. They don't matter here because it doesn't matter which order the two addend expressions are evaluated in. (Or does it? Is it possible that the two increments could be done before either array operation?)

RSK: I suppose we could do an experiment to verify that there aren't any side effects, but that function isn't going to work with spares and strikes. Should we keep trying to make it more readable, or should we push further on its functionality?

RCM: The experiment might only have meaning on certain compilers. Other compilers might use different evaluation orders. I don't know if this is an issue or not, but let's get rid of the potential order dependency and then push on with more test cases.

```
public int scoreForFrame(int theFrame)
{
    int ball = 0;
    int score=0;
    for (int currentFrame = 0;
         currentFrame < theFrame;
         currentFrame++)
    {
      int firstThrow = itsThrows[ball++];
      int secondThrow = itsThrows[ball++];
      score += firstThrow + secondThrow;
    }

    return score;
}
```

RCM: OK, next test case. Let's try a spare.

---

1.   See "SRP: The Single-Responsibility Principle" on page 95.

```
public void testSimpleSpare()
{
  Game g = new Game();
}
```

RCM: I'm tired of writing this. Let's refactor the test and put the creation of the game in a `setUp` function.

```
//TestGame.java----------------------------------------
import junit.framework.*;

public class TestGame extends TestCase
{
  public TestGame(String name)
  {
    super(name);
  }

  private Game g;

  public void setUp()
  {
    g = new Game();
  }

  public void testOneThrow()
  {
    g.add(5);
    assertEquals(5, g.score());
  }

  public void testTwoThrowsNoMark()
  {
    g.add(5);
    g.add(4);
    assertEquals(9, g.score());
  }

  public void testFourThrowsNoMark()
  {
    g.add(5);
    g.add(4);
    g.add(7);
    g.add(2);
    assertEquals(18, g.score());
    assertEquals(9,  g.scoreForFrame(1));
    assertEquals(18, g.scoreForFrame(2));
  }

  public void testSimpleSpare()
  {
  }
}
```

RCM: That's better, now let's write the spare test case.

```
public void testSimpleSpare()
{
  g.add(3);
  g.add(7);
  g.add(3);
  assertEquals(13, g.scoreForFrame(1));
}
```

RCM: OK, that test case fails. Now we need to make it pass.

RSK: I'll drive.

```
public int scoreForFrame(int theFrame)
{
  int ball = 0;
  int score=0;
  for (int currentFrame = 0;
       currentFrame < theFrame;
       currentFrame++)
  {
    int firstThrow = itsThrows[ball++];
    int secondThrow = itsThrows[ball++];

    int frameScore = firstThrow + secondThrow;
    // spare needs next frames first throw
    if ( frameScore == 10 )
      score += frameScore + itsThrows[ball++];
    else
      score += frameScore;
  }

  return score;
}
```

RSK: Yee-HA! That works!

RCM: (grabbing the keyboard) OK, but I think the increment of ball in the `frameScore==10` case shouldn't be there. Here's a test case that proves my point.

```
public void testSimpleFrameAfterSpare()
{
  g.add(3);
  g.add(7);
  g.add(3);
  g.add(2);
  assertEquals(13, g.scoreForFrame(1));
  assertEquals(18, g.score());
}
```

RCM: Ha! See, that fails. Now if we just take out that pesky extra increment …

```
if ( frameScore == 10 )
  score += frameScore + itsThrows[ball];
```

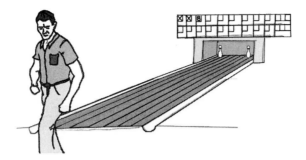

RCM: Uh . . . It still fails . . . Could it be that the `score` method is wrong? I'll test that by changing the test case to use `scoreForFrame(2)`.

```
public void testSimpleFrameAfterSpare()
{
  g.add(3);
  g.add(7);
  g.add(3);
  g.add(2);
  assertEquals(13, g.scoreForFrame(1));
  assertEquals(18, g.scoreForFrame(2));
}
```

RCM: Hmmmm . . . That passes. The `score` method must be messed up. Let's look at it.

```
public int score()
{
  return itsScore;
}

public void add(int pins)
{
  itsThrows[itsCurrentThrow++]=pins;
  itsScore += pins;
}
```

RCM: Yeah, that's wrong. The `score` method is just returning the sum of the pins, not the proper score. What we need `score` to do is call `scoreForFrame()` with the current frame.

RSK: We don't know what the current frame is. Let's add that message to each of our current tests, one at a time, of course.

RCM: Right.

```
//TestGame.java----------------------------------------
  public void testOneThrow()
  {
    g.add(5);
    assertEquals(5, g.score());
    assertEquals(1, g.getCurrentFrame());
  }
```

```
//Game.java--------------------------------
  public int getCurrentFrame()
  {
    return 1;
  }
```

RCM: OK, that works. But it's stupid. Let's do the next test case.

```
public void testTwoThrowsNoMark()
{
  g.add(5);
  g.add(4);
  assertEquals(9, g.score());
  assertEquals(1, g.getCurrentFrame());
}
```

RCM: That one's uninteresting, let's try the next.

```
public void testFourThrowsNoMark()
{
  g.add(5);
  g.add(4);
  g.add(7);
  g.add(2);
  assertEquals(18, g.score());
  assertEquals(9,  g.scoreForFrame(1));
  assertEquals(18, g.scoreForFrame(2));
  assertEquals(2, g.getCurrentFrame());
}
```

RCM: This one fails. Now let's make it pass.

RSK: I think the algorithm is trivial. Just divide the number of throws by two, since there are two throws per frame. Unless we have a strike … but we don't have strikes yet, so let's ignore them here too.

RCM: (flails around adding and subtracting 1 until it works)[2]

```
public int getCurrentFrame()
{
  return 1 + (itsCurrentThrow-1)/2;
}
```

RCM: That isn't very satisfying.

RSK: What if we don't calculate it each time? What if we adjust a currentFrame member variable after each throw?

RCM: OK, let's try that.

```
//Game.java--------------------------------
  public int getCurrentFrame()
  {
    return itsCurrentFrame;
  }
```

2.   Dave Thomas and Andy Hunt call this "programming by coincidence."

```
    public void add(int pins)
    {
      itsThrows[itsCurrentThrow++]=pins;
      itsScore += pins;
      if (firstThrow == true)
      {
        firstThrow = false;
        itsCurrentFrame++;
      }
      else
      {
        firstThrow=true;;
      }
    }

    private int itsCurrentFrame = 0;
    private boolean firstThrow = true;
```

RCM: OK, this works. But it also implies that the current frame is the frame of the last ball thrown, not the frame that the next ball will be thrown into. As long as we remember that, we'll be fine.

RSK: I don't have that good of a memory, so let's make it more readable. But before we go screwing around with it some more, let's pull that code out of add() and put it in a private member function called adjustCurrentFrame() or something.

RCM: OK, that sounds good.

```
    public void add(int pins)
    {
      itsThrows[itsCurrentThrow++]=pins;
      itsScore += pins;
      adjustCurrentFrame();
    }

    private void adjustCurrentFrame()
    {
      if (firstThrow == true)
      {
        firstThrow = false;
        itsCurrentFrame++;
      }
      else
      {
        firstThrow=true;;
      }
    }
```

RCM: Now let's change the variable and function names to be more clear. What should we call itsCurrentFrame?

RSK: I kind of like that name. I don't think we're incrementing it in the right place, though. The current frame, to me, is the frame number that I'm throwing in. So it should get incremented right after the last throw in a frame.

RCM: I agree. Let's change the test cases to reflect that, then we'll fix adjustCurrentFrame.

```
//TestGame.java-------------------------------------------
  public void testTwoThrowsNoMark()
  {
    g.add(5);
    g.add(4);
    assertEquals(9, g.score());
    assertEquals(2, g.getCurrentFrame());
  }

  public void testFourThrowsNoMark()
  {
    g.add(5);
    g.add(4);
    g.add(7);
    g.add(2);
    assertEquals(18, g.score());
    assertEquals(9,  g.scoreForFrame(1));
    assertEquals(18, g.scoreForFrame(2));
    assertEquals(3, g.getCurrentFrame());
  }

//Game.java------------------------------------------------
  private void adjustCurrentFrame()
  {
    if (firstThrow == true)
    {
      firstThrow = false;
    }
    else
    {
      firstThrow=true;
      itsCurrentFrame++;
    }
  }

  private int itsCurrentFrame = 1;
}
```

RCM: OK, that's working. Now let's test getCurrentFrame in the two spare cases.

```
public void testSimpleSpare()
{
  g.add(3);
  g.add(7);
  g.add(3);
  assertEquals(13, g.scoreForFrame(1));
  assertEquals(2, g.getCurrentFrame());
}

public void testSimpleFrameAfterSpare()
{
  g.add(3);
  g.add(7);
  g.add(3);
  g.add(2);
```

```
    assertEquals(13, g.scoreForFrame(1));
    assertEquals(18, g.scoreForFrame(2));
    assertEquals(3, g.getCurrentFrame());
}
```

RCM: This works. Now, back to the original problem. We need `score` to work. We can now write `score` to call `scoreForFrame(getCurrentFrame()-1)`.

```
public void testSimpleFrameAfterSpare()
{
    g.add(3);
    g.add(7);
    g.add(3);
    g.add(2);
    assertEquals(13, g.scoreForFrame(1));
    assertEquals(18, g.scoreForFrame(2));
    assertEquals(18, g.score());
    assertEquals(3, g.getCurrentFrame());
}

//Game.java---------------------------------
    public int score()
    {
        return scoreForFrame(getCurrentFrame()-1);
    }
```

RCM: This fails the `TestOneThrow` test case. Let's look at it.

```
public void testOneThrow()
{
    g.add(5);
    assertEquals(5, g.score());
    assertEquals(1, g.getCurrentFrame());
}
```

RCM: With only one throw, the first frame is incomplete. The score method is calling `scoreForFrame(0)`. This is yucky.

RSK: Maybe, maybe not. Who are we writing this program for, and who is going to be calling `score()`? Is it reasonable to assume that it won't get called on an incomplete frame?

RCM: Yeah, but it bothers me. To get around this, we have take the `score` out of the `testOneThrow` test case. Is that what we want to do?

RSK: We could. We could even eliminate the entire `testOneThrow` test case. It was used to ramp us up to the test cases of interest. Does it really serve a useful purpose now? We still have coverage in all of the other test cases.

RCM: Yeah, I see your point. OK, out it goes. (edits code, runs test, gets green bar) Ahhh, that's better.

Now, we'd better work on the strike test case. After all, we want to see all those `Frame` objects built into a linked list, don't we? (snicker)

```
public void testSimpleStrike()
{
    g.add(10);
```

```
    g.add(3);
    g.add(6);
    assertEquals(19, g.scoreForFrame(1));
    assertEquals(28, g.score());
    assertEquals(3, g.getCurrentFrame());
}
```

RCM: OK, this compiles and fails as predicted. Now we need to make it pass.

```
//Game.java---------------------------------
public class Game
{
  public void add(int pins)
  {
    itsThrows[itsCurrentThrow++]=pins;
    itsScore += pins;
    adjustCurrentFrame(pins);
  }

  private void adjustCurrentFrame(int pins)
  {
    if (firstThrow == true)
    {
      if( pins == 10 ) // strike
        itsCurrentFrame++;
      else
        firstThrow = false;
    }
    else
    {
      firstThrow=true;
      itsCurrentFrame++;
    }
  }

  public int scoreForFrame(int theFrame)
  {
    int ball = 0;
    int score=0;
    for (int currentFrame = 0;
         currentFrame < theFrame;
         currentFrame++)
```

```
      {
        int firstThrow = itsThrows[ball++];
        if (firstThrow == 10)
        {
          score += 10 + itsThrows[ball] + itsThrows[ball+1];
        }
        else
        {
          int secondThrow = itsThrows[ball++];

          int frameScore = firstThrow + secondThrow;
          // spare needs next frames first throw
          if ( frameScore == 10 )
            score += frameScore + itsThrows[ball];
          else
            score += frameScore;
        }

      }

    return score;
  }
  private int itsScore = 0;
  private int[] itsThrows = new int[21];
  private int itsCurrentThrow = 0;
  private int itsCurrentFrame = 1;
  private boolean firstThrow = true;
}
```

RCM: OK, that wasn't too hard. Let's see if it can score a perfect game.

```
public void testPerfectGame()
{
  for (int i=0; i<12; i++)
  {
    g.add(10);
  }
  assertEquals(300, g.score());
  assertEquals(10, g.getCurrentFrame());
}
```

RCM: Urg, it's saying the score is 330. Why would that be?

RSK: Because the current frame is getting incremented all the way to 12.

RCM: Oh! We need to limit it to 10.

```java
private void adjustCurrentFrame(int pins)
{
  if (firstThrow == true)
  {
    if( pins == 10 ) // strike
      itsCurrentFrame++;
    else
      firstThrow = false;
  }
  else
  {
    firstThrow=true;
    itsCurrentFrame++;
  }
  itsCurrentFrame = Math.min(10, itsCurrentFrame);
}
```

RCM: Damn, now it's saying that the score is 270. What's going on?

RSK: Bob, the `score` function is subtracting one from `getCurrentFrame`, so it's giving you the score for frame 9, not 10.

RCM: What? You mean I should limit the current frame to 11 not 10? I'll try it.

```java
itsCurrentFrame = Math.min(11, itsCurrentFrame);
```

RCM: OK, so now it gets the score correct but fails because the current frame is 11 and not 10. Ick! This current frame thing is a pain in the butt. We want the current frame to be the frame the player is throwing into, but what does that mean at the end of the game?

RSK: Maybe we should go back to the idea that the current frame is the frame of the last ball thrown.

RCM: Or maybe we need to come up with the concept of the last *completed* frame? After all, the score of the game at any point in time is the score in the last completed frame.

RSK: A completed frame is a frame that you can write the score into, right?

RCM: Yes, a frame with a spare in it completes after the next ball. A frame with a strike in it completes after the next two balls. A frame with no mark completes after the second ball in the frame.

Wait a minute . . . We are trying to get the `score()` method to work, right? All we need to do is force `score()` to call `scoreForFrame(10)` if the game is complete.

RSK: How do we know if the game is complete?

RCM: If `adjustCurrentFrame` ever tries to increment `itsCurrentFrame` past the tenth frame, then the game is complete.

RSK: Wait. All you are saying is that if `getCurrentFrame` returns 11, the game is complete. That's the way the code works now!

RCM: Hmm. You mean we should change the test case to match the code?

```
public void testPerfectGame()
{
  for (int i=0; i<12; i++)
  {
    g.add(10);
  }
  assertEquals(300, g.score());
  assertEquals(11, g.getCurrentFrame());
}
```

RCM: Well, that works. I suppose it's no worse than `getMonth` returning 0 for January. But I still feel uneasy about it.

RSK: Maybe something will occur to us later. Right now, I think I see a bug. May I?" (grabs keyboard)

```
public void testEndOfArray()
{
  for (int i=0; i<9; i++)
  {
    g.add(0);
    g.add(0);
  }
  g.add(2);
  g.add(8); // 10th frame spare
  g.add(10); // Strike in last position of array.
  assertEquals(20, g.score());
}
```

RSK: Hmm. That doesn't fail. I thought since the 21st position of the array was a strike, the scorer would try to add the 22nd and 23rd positions to the score. But I guess not.

RCM: Hmm, you are still thinking about that scorer object aren't you. Anyway, I see what you were getting at, but since `score` never calls `scoreForFrame` with a number larger than 10, the last strike is not actually counted as a strike. It's just counted as a 10 to complete the last spare. We never walk beyond the end of the array.

RSK: OK, let's pump our original score card into the program.

```
public void testSampleGame()
{
  g.add(1);
  g.add(4);
  g.add(4);
  g.add(5);
  g.add(6);
  g.add(4);
  g.add(5);
  g.add(5);
  g.add(10);
  g.add(0);
  g.add(1);
  g.add(7);
  g.add(3);
  g.add(6);
  g.add(4);
  g.add(10);
```

```
    g.add(2);
    g.add(8);
    g.add(6);
    assertEquals(133, g.score());
}
```

RSK: Well, that works. Are there any other test cases that you can think of?

RCM: Yeah, let's test a few more boundary conditions— how about the poor schmuck who throws 11 strikes and then a final 9?

```
public void testHeartBreak()
{
  for (int i=0; i<11; i++)
   g.add(10);
  g.add(9);
  assertEquals(299, g.score());
}
```

RCM: That works. OK, how about a tenth frame spare?

```
public void testTenthFrameSpare()
{
  for (int i=0; i<9; i++)
    g.add(10);
  g.add(9);
  g.add(1);
  g.add(1);
  assertEquals(270, g.score());
}
```

RCM: (staring happily at the green bar) That works too. I can't think of any more, can you.

RSK: No, I think we've covered them all. Besides, I really want to refactor this mess. I still see the `scorer` object in there somewhere.

RCM: OK, well, the `scoreForFrame` function is pretty messy. Let's consider it.

```
public int scoreForFrame(int theFrame)
{
  int ball = 0;
  int score=0;
```

```
                    for (int currentFrame = 0;
                          currentFrame < theFrame;
                       currentFrame++)
                    {
                      int firstThrow = itsThrows[ball++];
                      if (firstThrow == 10)
                      {
                        score += 10 + itsThrows[ball] + itsThrows[ball+1];
                      }
                      else
                      {
                        int secondThrow = itsThrows[ball++];

                        int frameScore = firstThrow + secondThrow;
                        // spare needs next frames first throw
                        if ( frameScore == 10 )
                          score += frameScore + itsThrows[ball];
                        else
                          score += frameScore;
                      }

                    }

                    return score;
                  }
```

RCM: I'd really like to extract the body of that `else` clause into a separate function named `handleSecondThrow`, but I can't because it uses `ball`, `firstThrow`, and `secondThrow` local variables.

RSK: We could turn those locals into member variables.

RCM: Yeah, that kind of reenforces your notion that we'll be able to pull the scoring out into its own `scorer` object. OK, let's give that a try.

RSK: (grabs keyboard)

```
                  private void adjustCurrentFrame(int pins)
                  {
                    if (firstThrowInFrame == true)
                    {
                      if( pins == 10 ) // strike
                        itsCurrentFrame++;
                      else
                        firstThrowInFrame = false;
                    }
                    else
                    {
                      firstThrowInFrame=true;
                      itsCurrentFrame++;
                    }
                    itsCurrentFrame = Math.min(11, itsCurrentFrame);
                  }
```

```java
public int scoreForFrame(int theFrame)
{
  ball = 0;
  int score=0;
  for (int currentFrame = 0;
       currentFrame < theFrame;
       currentFrame++)
  {
    firstThrow = itsThrows[ball++];
    if (firstThrow == 10)
    {
      score += 10 + itsThrows[ball] + itsThrows[ball+1];
    }
    else
    {
      secondThrow = itsThrows[ball++];

      int frameScore = firstThrow + secondThrow;
      // spare needs next frames first throw
      if ( frameScore == 10 )
        score += frameScore + itsThrows[ball];
      else
        score += frameScore;
    }

  }
  return score;
}
private int ball;
private int firstThrow;
private int secondThrow;

private int itsScore = 0;
private int[] itsThrows = new int[21];
private int itsCurrentThrow = 0;
private int itsCurrentFrame = 1;
private boolean firstThrowInFrame = true;
```

RSK: I hadn't expected the name collision. We already had an instance variable named firstThrow. But it is better named firstThrowInFrame. Anyway, this works now. So we can pull the else clause out into its own function.

```java
public int scoreForFrame(int theFrame)
{
  ball = 0;
  int score=0;
  for (int currentFrame = 0;
       currentFrame < theFrame;
       currentFrame++)
  {
    firstThrow = itsThrows[ball++];
    if (firstThrow == 10)
    {
      score += 10 + itsThrows[ball] + itsThrows[ball+1];
    }
```

```
      else
      {
        score += handleSecondThrow();
      }
    }

    return score;
}

private int handleSecondThrow()
{
    int score = 0;
    secondThrow = itsThrows[ball++];

    int frameScore = firstThrow + secondThrow;
    // spare needs next frames first throw
    if ( frameScore == 10 )
      score += frameScore + itsThrows[ball];
    else
      score += frameScore;
    return score;
}
```

RCM: Look at the structure of scoreForFrame! In pseudocode it looks something like this:

```
if strike
  score += 10 + nextTwoBalls();
else
  handleSecondThrow.
```

RCM: What if we changed it to

```
if strike
  score += 10 + nextTwoBalls();
else if spare
  score += 10 + nextBall();
else
  score += twoBallsInFrame()
```

RSK: Geez! That's pretty much the rules for scoring bowling isn't it? OK, let's see if we can get that structure in the real function. First, let's change the way the ball variable is being incremented, so that the three cases manipulate it independently.

```
public int scoreForFrame(int theFrame)
{
    ball = 0;
    int score=0;
    for (int currentFrame = 0;
         currentFrame < theFrame;
         currentFrame++)
    {
      firstThrow = itsThrows[ball];
      if (firstThrow == 10)
```

```
    {
      ball++;
      score += 10 + itsThrows[ball] + itsThrows[ball+1];
    }
    else
    {
      score += handleSecondThrow();
    }
  }

  return score;
}

private int handleSecondThrow()
{
  int score = 0;
  secondThrow = itsThrows[ball+1];

  int frameScore = firstThrow + secondThrow;
  // spare needs next frames first throw
  if ( frameScore == 10 )
  {
    ball+=2;
    score += frameScore + itsThrows[ball];
  }
  else
  {
    ball+=2;
    score += frameScore;
  }
  return score;
}
```

RCM: (grabs keyboard) OK, now let's get rid of the firstThrow and secondThrow variables and replace them with appropriate functions.

```
public int scoreForFrame(int theFrame)
{
  ball = 0;
  int score=0;
  for (int currentFrame = 0;
       currentFrame < theFrame;
       currentFrame++)
  {
    firstThrow = itsThrows[ball];
    if (strike())
    {
    ball++;
      score += 10 + nextTwoBalls();
    }
    else
    {
      score += handleSecondThrow();
    }
  }
```

```
      return score;
    }

    private boolean strike()
    {
      return itsThrows[ball] == 10;
    }
    private int nextTwoBalls()
    {
      return itsThrows[ball] + itsThrows[ball+1];
    }
```

RCM: That step works, let's keep going.

```
    private int handleSecondThrow()
    {
      int score = 0;
      secondThrow = itsThrows[ball+1];

      int frameScore = firstThrow + secondThrow;
      // spare needs next frames first throw
      if ( spare() )
      {
        ball+=2;
        score += 10 + nextBall();
      }
      else
      {
        ball+=2;
        score += frameScore;
      }
      return score;
    }

    private boolean spare()
    {
      return (itsThrows[ball] + itsThrows[ball+1]) == 10;
    }

    private int nextBall()
    {
      return itsThrows[ball];
    }
```

RCM: OK, that works too. Now let's deal with `frameScore`.

```
    private int handleSecondThrow()
    {
      int score = 0;
      secondThrow = itsThrows[ball+1];

      int frameScore = firstThrow + secondThrow;
      // spare needs next frames first throw
      if ( spare() )
```

```
      {
        ball+=2;
        score += 10 + nextBall();
      }
      else
      {
        score += twoBallsInFrame();
        ball+=2;
      }
      return score;
    }


    private int twoBallsInFrame()
    {
      return itsThrows[ball] + itsThrows[ball+1];
    }
```

RSK: Bob, you aren't incrementing `ball` in a consistent manner. In the spare and strike case, you increment before you calculate the score. In the `twoBallsInFrame` case you increment *after* you calculate the score. And the code *depends* on this order! What's up?

RCM: Sorry, I should have explained. I'm planning on moving the increments into `strike`, `spare`, and `twoBallsInFrame`. That way, they'll disappear from the `scoreForFrame` function, and the function will look just like our pseudocode.

RSK: OK, I'll trust you for a few more steps, but remember, I'm watching.

RCM: OK, now since nobody uses `firstThrow`, `secondThrow`, and `frameScore` anymore, we can get rid of them.

```
    public int scoreForFrame(int theFrame)
    {
      ball = 0;
      int score=0;
      for (int currentFrame = 0;
           currentFrame < theFrame;
           currentFrame++)
      {
        if (strike())
        {
          ball++;
          score += 10 + nextTwoBalls();
        }
        else
        {
          score += handleSecondThrow();
        }
      }

      return score;
    }

    private int handleSecondThrow()
    {
      int score = 0;
      // spare needs next frames first throw
```

```
      if ( spare() )
      {
        ball+=2;
        score += 10 + nextBall();
      }
      else
      {
        score += twoBallsInFrame();
        ball+=2;
      }
      return score;
    }
```

RCM: (The sparkle in his eyes is a reflection of the green bar.) Now, since the only variable that couples the three cases is `ball`, and since `ball` is dealt with independently in each case, we can merge the three cases together.

```
    public int scoreForFrame(int theFrame)
    {
      ball = 0;
      int score=0;
      for (int currentFrame = 0;
           currentFrame < theFrame;
           currentFrame++)
      {
        if (strike())
        {
          ball++;
          score += 10 + nextTwoBalls();
        }
        else if ( spare() )
        {
          ball+=2;
          score += 10 + nextBall();
        }
        else
        {
          score += twoBallsInFrame();
          ball+=2;
        }
      }
      return score;
    }
```

RSK: OK, now we can make the increments consistent and rename the functions to be more explicit. (grabs keyboard)

```
    public int scoreForFrame(int theFrame)
    {
      ball = 0;
      int score=0;
      for (int currentFrame = 0;
           currentFrame < theFrame;
           currentFrame++)
```

```
    {
      if (strike())
      {
        score += 10 + nextTwoBallsForStrike();
        ball++;
      }
      else if ( spare() )
      {
        score += 10 + nextBallForSpare();
        ball+=2;
      }
      else
      {
        score += twoBallsInFrame();
        ball+=2;
      }
    }

    return score;
  }

  private int nextTwoBallsForStrike()
  {
    return itsThrows[ball+1] + itsThrows[ball+2];
  }

  private int nextBallForSpare()
  {
    return itsThrows[ball+2];
  }
```

RCM:　Look at that `scoreForFrame` function! That's the rules of bowling stated about as succinctly as possible.

RSK:　But, Bob, what happened to the linked list of `Frame` objects? (snicker, snicker)

RCM:　(sigh) We were bedevilled by the daemons of diagrammatic overdesign. My God, three little boxes drawn on the back of a napkin, `Game`, `Frame`, and `Throw`, and it was still too complicated and just plain wrong.

RSK:　We made a mistake starting with the `Throw` class. We should have started with the `Game` class first!

RCM:　Indeed! So, next time let's try starting at the highest level and work down.

RSK:　(gasp) Top-down design!??!?!?

RCM:　Correction, top-down, *test-first* design. Frankly, I don't know if this is a good rule or not. It's just what would have helped us in this case. So next time, I'm going to try it and see what happens.

RSK:　Yeah, OK. Anyway, we still have some refactoring to do. The `ball` variable is just a private iterator for `scoreForFrame` and its minions. They should all be moved into a different object.

RCM:　Oh, yes, your `Scorer` object. You were right after all. Let's do it.

RSK:　(grabs keyboard and takes several small steps punctuated by tests to create . . .)

```
//Game.java---------------------------------
public class Game
```

```java
{
  public int score()
  {
    return scoreForFrame(getCurrentFrame()-1);
  }

  public int getCurrentFrame()
  {
    return itsCurrentFrame;
  }

  public void add(int pins)
  {
    itsScorer.addThrow(pins);
    itsScore += pins;
    adjustCurrentFrame(pins);
  }

  private void adjustCurrentFrame(int pins)
  {
    if (firstThrowInFrame == true)
    {
    if( pins == 10 ) // strike
      itsCurrentFrame++;
    else
      firstThrowInFrame = false;
    }
    else
    {
    firstThrowInFrame=true;
    itsCurrentFrame++;
    }
    itsCurrentFrame = Math.min(11, itsCurrentFrame);
  }

public int scoreForFrame(int theFrame)
{
  return itsScorer.scoreForFrame(theFrame);
}

private int itsScore = 0;
private int itsCurrentFrame = 1;
private boolean firstThrowInFrame = true;
private Scorer itsScorer = new Scorer();
}

//Scorer.java---------------------------------
public class Scorer
{
  public void addThrow(int pins)
  {
    itsThrows[itsCurrentThrow++] = pins;
  }

  public int scoreForFrame(int theFrame)
```

```
        {
          ball = 0;
          int score=0;
          for (int currentFrame = 0;
               currentFrame < theFrame;
               currentFrame++)
          {
            if (strike())
            {
              score += 10 + nextTwoBallsForStrike();
                ball++;
            }
            else if ( spare() )
            {
              score += 10 + nextBallForSpare();
              ball+=2;
            }
            else
            {
              score += twoBallsInFrame();
              ball+=2;
            }
          }
          return score;
        }

        private boolean strike()
        {
          return itsThrows[ball] == 10;
        }

        private boolean spare()
        {
          return (itsThrows[ball] + itsThrows[ball+1]) == 10;
        }

        private int nextTwoBallsForStrike()
        {
          return itsThrows[ball+1] + itsThrows[ball+2];
        }

        private int nextBallForSpare()
        {
          return itsThrows[ball+2];
        }

        private int twoBallsInFrame()
        {
          return itsThrows[ball] + itsThrows[ball+1];
        }

        private int ball;
        private int[] itsThrows = new int[21];
        private int itsCurrentThrow = 0;
      }
```

RSK: That's much better. Now, the `Game` just keeps track of frames, and the `Scorer` just calculates the score. The Single Responsibility Principle rocks!

RCM: Whatever. But it is better. Did you notice that the `itsScore` variable is not being used anymore?

RSK: Ha! You're right. Let's kill it. (gleefully starts erasing things)

```
public void add(int pins)
{
  itsScorer.addThrow(pins);
  adjustCurrentFrame(pins);
}
```

RSK: Not bad. Now, should we clean up the `adjustCurrentFrame` stuff?

RCM: OK, let's look at it.

```
private void adjustCurrentFrame(int pins)
{
  if (firstThrowInFrame == true)
  {
    if( pins == 10 ) // strike
      itsCurrentFrame++;
    else
      firstThrowInFrame = false;
  }
  else
  {
    firstThrowInFrame=true;
    itsCurrentFrame++;
  }
  itsCurrentFrame = Math.min(11, itsCurrentFrame);
}
```

RCM: OK, first let's extract the increments into a single function that also restricts the frame to 11. (Brrrr. I still don't like that 11.)

RSK: Bob, 11 means end of game.

RCM: Yeah. Brrrr. (grabs keyboard, makes a couple of changes punctuated by tests)

```
private void adjustCurrentFrame(int pins)
{
  if (firstThrowInFrame == true)
  {
    if( pins == 10 ) // strike
      advanceFrame();
    else
      firstThrowInFrame = false;
  }
  else
  {
    firstThrowInFrame=true;
    advanceFrame();
  }
}
```

```
private void advanceFrame()
{
  itsCurrentFrame = Math.min(11, itsCurrentFrame + 1);
}
```

RCM: OK, that's a little better. Now let's break out the strike case into its own function. (Takes a few small steps and runs tests between each.)

```
private void adjustCurrentFrame(int pins)
{
  if (firstThrowInFrame == true)
  {
    if (adjustFrameForStrike(pins) == false)
      firstThrowInFrame = false;
  }
  else
  {
    firstThrowInFrame=true;
    advanceFrame();
  }
}

private boolean adjustFrameForStrike(int pins)
{
  if (pins == 10)
  {
    advanceFrame();
    return true;
  }
  return false;
}
```

RCM: That's pretty good. Now, about that 11.

RSK: You really hate that don't you.

RCM: Yeah, look at the `score()` function,

```
public int score()
{
  return scoreForFrame(getCurrentFrame()-1);
}
```

RCM: That `-1` is odd. It's the only place we truly use `getCurrentFrame`, and yet we need to adjust what it returns.

RSK: Damn, you're right. How many times have we reversed ourselves on this?

RCM: Too many. But there it is. The code wants `itsCurrentFrame` to represent the frame of the last thrown ball, not the frame we are about to throw into.

RSK: Sheesh, that's going to break lots of test cases.

RCM: Actually, I think we should remove `getCurrentFrame` from all the test cases, and remove the `getCurrentFrame` function itself. Nobody really uses it.

RSK: OK, I get your point. I'll do it. It'll be like putting a lame horse out of its misery. (grabs keyboard)

```
//Game.java----------------------------------
  public int score()
  {
    return scoreForFrame(itsCurrentFrame);
  }
  private void advanceFrame()
  {
    itsCurrentFrame = Math.min(10, itsCurrentFrame + 1);
  }
```

RCM: Oh, for crying out loud. You mean to tell me that we were fretting over *that*. All we did was change the limit from 11 to 10 and remove the -1. Cripes!

RSK: Yeah, Uncle Bob, it really wasn't worth all the angst we gave it.

RCM: I hate the side effect in `adjustFrameForStrike()`. I want to get rid of it. What do you think of this?

```
private void adjustCurrentFrame(int pins)
{
    if ((firstThrowInFrame && pins == 10) ||
        (!firstThrowInFrame))
      advanceFrame();
    else
      firstThrowInFrame = false;
}
```

RSK: I like the idea, and it passes the tests, but I hate the long `if` statement. How about this?

```
private void adjustCurrentFrame(int pins)
{
  if (strike(pins) || !firstThrowInFrame)
    advanceFrame();
  else
    firstThrowInFrame = false;
}

private boolean strike(int pins)
{
  return (firstThrowInFrame && pins == 10);
}
```

RCM: Yeah, that's pretty. We could even go one step further.

```
private void adjustCurrentFrame(int pins)
{
  if (lastBallInFrame(pins))
    advanceFrame();
  else
    firstThrowInFrame = false;
}

private boolean lastBallInFrame(int pins)
{
  return strike(pins) || !firstThrowInFrame;
}
```

RSK: Nice!

RCM: OK, looks like we are done. Let's just read through the whole program and see if it's as simple and communicative as it can be.

```java
//Game.java--------------------------------
public class Game
{
  public int score()
  {
    return scoreForFrame(itsCurrentFrame);
  }

public void add(int pins)
{
  itsScorer.addThrow(pins);
  adjustCurrentFrame(pins);
}

private void adjustCurrentFrame(int pins)
{
  if (lastBallInFrame(pins))
    advanceFrame();
  else
    firstThrowInFrame = false;
}

private boolean lastBallInFrame(int pins)
{
  return strike(pins) || !firstThrowInFrame;
}

private boolean strike(int pins)
{
  return (firstThrowInFrame && pins == 10);
}

private void advanceFrame()
{
  itsCurrentFrame = Math.min(10, itsCurrentFrame + 1);
}

public int scoreForFrame(int theFrame)
{
  return itsScorer.scoreForFrame(theFrame);
}

private int itsCurrentFrame = 0;
private boolean firstThrowInFrame = true;
private Scorer itsScorer = new Scorer();
}

//Scorer.java--------------------------------
public class Scorer
{
  public void addThrow(int pins)
```

```java
      {
        itsThrows[itsCurrentThrow++] = pins;
      }

  public int scoreForFrame(int theFrame)
  {
    ball = 0;
    int score=0;
    for (int currentFrame = 0;
         currentFrame < theFrame;
         currentFrame++)
    {
      if (strike())
      {
        score += 10 + nextTwoBallsForStrike();
         ball++;
      }
      else if ( spare() )
      {
        score += 10 + nextBallForSpare();
        ball+=2;
      }
      else
      {
        score += twoBallsInFrame();
        ball+=2;
      }
    }
    return score;
  }

  private boolean strike()
  {
    return itsThrows[ball] == 10;
  }

  private boolean spare()
  {
    return (itsThrows[ball] + itsThrows[ball+1]) == 10;
  }

  private int nextTwoBallsForStrike()
  {
    return itsThrows[ball+1] + itsThrows[ball+2];
  }

  private int nextBallForSpare()
  {
    return itsThrows[ball+2];
  }

  private int twoBallsInFrame()
  {
    return itsThrows[ball] + itsThrows[ball+1];
  }
```

```
      private int ball;
      private int[] itsThrows = new int[21];
      private int itsCurrentThrow = 0;
    }
```

RCM: OK, that looks pretty good. I can't think of anything else to do.

RSK: Yeah, it's pretty. Let's look over the tests for good measure.

```
    //TestGame.java----------------------------------------
    import junit.framework.*;

    public class TestGame extends TestCase
    {
      public TestGame(String name)
      {
        super(name);
      }

      private Game g;

      public void setUp()
      {
        g = new Game();
      }

      public void testTwoThrowsNoMark()
      {
        g.add(5);
        g.add(4);
        assertEquals(9, g.score());
      }

      public void testFourThrowsNoMark()
      {
        g.add(5);
        g.add(4);
        g.add(7);
        g.add(2);
        assertEquals(18, g.score());
        assertEquals(9,  g.scoreForFrame(1));
        assertEquals(18, g.scoreForFrame(2));
      }

      public void testSimpleSpare()
      {
        g.add(3);
        g.add(7);
        g.add(3);
        assertEquals(13, g.scoreForFrame(1));
      }

      public void testSimpleFrameAfterSpare()
      {
        g.add(3);
        g.add(7);
```

```java
      g.add(3);
      g.add(2);
      assertEquals(13, g.scoreForFrame(1));
      assertEquals(18, g.scoreForFrame(2));
      assertEquals(18, g.score());
    }

    public void testSimpleStrike()
    {
      g.add(10);
      g.add(3);
      g.add(6);
      assertEquals(19, g.scoreForFrame(1));
      assertEquals(28, g.score());
    }

    public void testPerfectGame()
    {
      for (int i=0; i<12; i++)
      {
      g.add(10);
    }
    assertEquals(300, g.score());
  }

public void testEndOfArray()
{
  for (int i=0; i<9; i++)
  {
    g.add(0);
    g.add(0);
  }
  g.add(2);
  g.add(8); // 10th frame spare
  g.add(10); // Strike in last position of array.
  assertEquals(20, g.score());
}

    public void testSampleGame()
    {
      g.add(1);
      g.add(4);
      g.add(4);
      g.add(5);
      g.add(6);
      g.add(4);
      g.add(5);
      g.add(5);
      g.add(10);
      g.add(0);
      g.add(1);
      g.add(7);
      g.add(3);
      g.add(6);
      g.add(4);
```

```
      g.add(10);
      g.add(2);
      g.add(8);
      g.add(6);
      assertEquals(133, g.score());
    }

    public void testHeartBreak()
    {
      for (int i=0; i<11; i++)
        g.add(10);
      g.add(9);
      assertEquals(299, g.score());
    }

    public void testTenthFrameSpare()
    {
      for (int i=0; i<9; i++)
        g.add(10);
      g.add(9);
      g.add(1);
      g.add(1);
      assertEquals(270, g.score());
    }
  }
```

RSK: That pretty much covers it. Can you think of any more meaningful test cases?

RCM: No, I think that's the set. There aren't any there that I'd be comfortable removing at this point.

RSK: Then we're done.

RCM: I'd say so. Thanks a lot for your help.

RSK: No problem, it was fun.

Conclusion

After writing this chapter, I published it on the Object Mentor Web site.[3] Many people read it and gave their comments. Some folks were disturbed that there was almost no object-oriented design involved. I find this response interesting. Must we have object-oriented design in every application and every program? Here is a case where the program simply didn't need much of it. The Scorer class was really the only concession to OO, and even that was more simple partitioning than true OOD.

Other folks thought that there really should be a Frame class. One person went so far as to create a version of the program that contained a Frame class. It was much larger and more complex than what you see above.

Some folks felt that we weren't fair to UML. After all, we didn't do a complete design before we began. The funny little UML diagram on the back of the napkin (Figure 6-2) was not a complete design. It did not include sequence diagrams. I find this argument rather odd. It doesn't seem likely to me that adding sequence diagrams to Figure 6-2 would have caused us to abandon the Throw and Frame classes. Indeed, I think it would have entrenched us in our view that these classes were necessary.

Am I trying to say that diagrams are inappropriate? Of course not. Well, actually, yes, in a way I am. For *this* program, the diagrams didn't help at all. Indeed, they were a distraction. If we had followed them, we would have wound up with a program that was much more complex than necessary. You might contend that we would also

3.   http://www.objectmentor.com

have wound up with a program that was more maintainable, but I disagree. The program we just went through is easy to understand and therefore easy to maintain. There are no mismanaged dependencies within it that make it rigid or fragile.

So, yes, diagrams can be inappropriate at times. When are they inappropriate? When you create them without code to validate them, *and then intend to follow them.* There is nothing wrong with drawing a diagram to explore an idea. However, having produced a diagram, you should not assume that it is the best design for the task. You may find that the best design will evolve as you take tiny little steps, writing tests first.

An Overview of the Rules of Bowling

Bowling is a game that is played by throwing a cantaloupe-sized ball down a narrow alley toward ten wooden pins. The object is to knock down as many pins as possible per throw.

The game is played in ten frames. At the beginning of each frame, all ten pins are set up. The player then gets two tries to knock them all down.

If the player knocks all the pins down on the first try, it is called a "strike," and the frame ends.

If the player fails to knock down all the pins with his first ball, but succeeds with the second ball, it is called a "spare."

After the second ball of the frame, the frame ends even if there are still pins standing.

A strike frame is scored by adding ten, plus the number of pins knocked down by the next two balls, to the score of the previous frame.

A spare frame is scored by adding ten, plus the number of pins knocked down by the next ball, to the score of the previous frame.

Otherwise, a frame is scored by adding the number of pins knocked down by the two balls in the frame to the score of the previous frame.

If a strike is thrown in the tenth frame, then the player may throw two more balls to complete the score of the strike.

Likewise, if a spare is thrown in the tenth frame, the player may throw one more ball to complete the score of the spare.

Thus, the tenth frame may have three balls instead of two.

1	4	4	5	6	◢	5	◢	◼	0	1	7	◢	6	◢	◼	2	◢	6
5		14		29		49		60		61		77		97		117		133	

The score card above shows a typical, if rather poor, game.

In the first frame, the player knocked down 1 pin with his first ball and four more with his second. Thus, his score for the frame is a five.

In the second frame, the player knocked down four pins with his first ball and five more with his second. That makes nine pins total, added to the previous frame makes fourteen.

In the third frame, the player knocked down six pins with his first ball and knocked down the rest with his second for a spare. No score can be calculated for this frame until the next ball is rolled.

In the fourth frame, the player knocked down five pins with his first ball. This lets us complete the scoring of the spare in frame three. The score for frame three is ten, plus the score in frame two (14), plus the first ball of frame four (5), or 29. The final ball of frame four is a spare.

Frame five is a strike. This lets us finish the score of frame four which is $29 + 10 + 10 = 49$.

Frame six is dismal. The first ball went in the gutter and failed to knock down any pins. The second ball knocked down only one pin. The score for the strike in frame five is $49 + 10 + 0 + 1 = 60$.

The rest you can probably figure out for yourself.

SECTION 2

Agile Design

If *agility* is about building software in tiny increments, how can you ever *design* the software? How can you take the time to ensure that the software has a good structure that is flexible, maintainable, and reusable? If you build in tiny increments, aren't you really setting the stage for lots of scrap and rework in the name of refactoring? Aren't you going to miss the big picture?

In an agile team, the big picture evolves along with the software. With each iteration, the team improves the design of the system so that it is as good as it can be for the system as it is *now*. The team does not spend very much time looking ahead to future requirements and needs. Nor do they try to build in today the infrastructure to support the features they think they'll need tomorrow. Rather, they focus on the *current* structure of the system, making it as good as it can be.

Symptoms of Poor Design

How do we know if the design of the software is good? The first chapter in this section enumerates and describes symptoms of poor design. The chapter demonstrates how those symptoms accumulate in a software project and describes how to avoid them.

The symptoms are defined as follows:

1. Rigidity—The design is hard to change.
2. Fragility—The design is easy to break.
3. Immobility—The design is hard to reuse.
4. Viscosity—It is hard to do the right thing.
5. Needless Complexity—Overdesign.
6. Needless Repetition—Mouse abuse.
7. Opacity—Disorganized expression.

These symptoms are similar in nature to code smells,[1] but they are at a higher level. They are smells that pervade the overall structure of the software rather than a small section of code.

---

1.   [Fowler99].

Principles

The rest of the chapters in this section describe principles of object-oriented design that help developers eliminate design smells and build the best designs for the current set of features.

The principles are as follows:

1. SRP—The Single Responsibility Principle
2. OCP—The Open–Closed Principle.
3. LSP—The Liskov Substitution Principle.
4. DIP—The Dependency Inversion Principle.
5. ISP—The Interface Segregation Principle.

These principles are the hard-won product of decades of experience in software engineering. They are not the product of a single mind, but they represent the integration of the thoughts and writings of a large number of software developers and researchers. Although they are presented here as principles of object-oriented design, they are really special cases of long-standing principles of software engineering.

Smells and Principles

A design smell is a symptom, it's something that can be measured, subjectively if not objectively. Often, the smell is caused by the violation of one or more of the principles. For example, the smell of Rigidity is often a result of insufficient attention to The Open–Closed Principle (OCP).

Agile teams apply principles to remove smells. They don't apply principles when there are no smells. It is a mistake to unconditionally conform to a principle just because it is a principle. Principles are not a perfume to be liberally scattered all over the system. Overconformance to the principles leads to the design smell of Needless Complexity.

Bibliography

1. Martin, Fowler. *Refactoring*. Addison–Wesley. 1999.

7

What Is Agile Design?

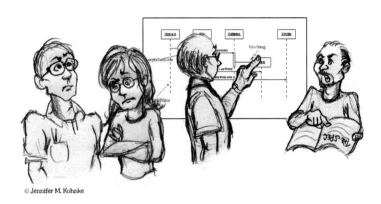

© Jennifer M. Kohnke

"After reviewing the software development life cycle as I understood it, I concluded that the only software documentation that actually seems to satisfy the criteria of an engineering design is the source code listings."

—Jack Reeves

In 1992, Jack Reeves wrote a seminal article in the *C++ Journal* entitled "What is Software Design?"[1] In this article, Reeves argues that the design of a software system is documented primarily by its source code. The diagrams representing the source code are ancillary to the design and are not the design itself. As it turns out, Jack's article was a harbinger of agile development.

In the pages that follow, we will often talk about "The Design." You should not take that to mean a set of UML diagrams separate from the code. A set of UML diagrams may represent parts of a design, but it is not *the* design. The design of a software project is an abstract concept. It has to do with the overall shape and structure of the program as well as the detailed shape and structure of each module, class, and method. It can be represented by many different media, but its final embodiment is source code. In the end, the source code is the design.

What Goes Wrong with Software?

If you are lucky, you start a project with a clear picture of what you want the system to be. The design of the system is a vital image in your mind. If you are luckier still, the clarity of that design makes it to the first release.

Then, something goes wrong. The software starts to rot like a piece of bad meat. As time goes by, the rot spreads and grows. Ugly festering sores and boils accumulate in the code, making it harder and harder to maintain.

---

1. [Reeves92] This is a great paper. I strongly recommend that you read it. I have included it in this book in Appendix D.

Eventually, the sheer effort required to make even the simplest of changes becomes so onerous that the developers and front-line managers cry for a redesign.

Such redesigns rarely succeed. Though the designers start out with good intentions, they find that they are shooting at a moving target. The old system continues to evolve and change, and the new design must keep up. The warts and ulcers accumulate in the new design before it ever makes it to its first release.

Design Smells—The Odors of Rotting Software

You know that the software is rotting when it starts to exhibit any of the following odors:

1. Rigidity—The system is hard to change because every change forces many other changes to other parts of the system.
2. Fragility—Changes cause the system to break in places that have no conceptual relationship to the part that was changed.
3. Immobility—It is hard to disentangle the system into components that can be reused in other systems.
4. Viscosity—Doing things right is harder than doing things wrong.
5. Needless Complexity—The design contains infrastructure that adds no direct benefit.
6. Needless Repetition—The design contains repeating structures that could be unified under a single abstraction.
7. Opacity—It is hard to read and understand. It does not express its intent well.

Rigidity.   Rigidity is the tendency for software to be difficult to change, even in simple ways. A design is rigid if a single change causes a cascade of subsequent changes in dependent modules. The more modules that must be changed, the more rigid the design.

Most developers have faced this situation in one way or another. They are asked to make what appears to be a simple change. They look the change over and make a reasonable estimate of the work required. But later, as they work though the change, they find that there are repercussions to the change that they hadn't anticipated. They find themselves chasing the change through huge portions of the code, modifying far more modules than they had first estimated. In the end, the changes take far longer than the initial estimate. When asked why their estimate was so poor they repeat the traditional software developers' lament, "It was a lot more complicated than I thought!"

Fragility.   Fragility is the tendency of a program to break in many places when a single change is made. Often, the new problems are in areas that have no conceptual relationship with the area that was changed. Fixing those problems leads to even more problems, and the development team begins to resemble a dog chasing its tail.

As the fragility of a module increases, the likelihood that a change will introduce unexpected problems approaches certainty. This seems absurd, but such modules are not at all uncommon. These are the modules that are constantly in need of repair—the ones that are never off the bug list, the ones that the developers know need to be redesigned (but nobody wants to face the spectre of redesigning them), the ones that get *worse* the more you fix them.

Immobility.   A design is immobile when it contains parts that could be useful in other systems, but the effort and risk involved with separating those parts from the original system are too great. This is an unfortunate, but very common, occurrence.

Viscosity.   Viscosity comes in two forms: viscosity of the software and viscosity of the environment.

When faced with a change, developers usually find more than one way to make that change. Some of the ways preserve the design; others do not (i.e., they are hacks.) When the design-preserving methods are harder to employ than the hacks, the viscosity of the design is high. It is easy to do the wrong thing, but hard to do the right thing. We want to design our software such that the changes that preserve the design are easy to make.

Viscosity of environment comes about when the development environment is slow and inefficient. For example, if compile times are very long, developers will be tempted to make changes that don't force large recompiles, even though those changes don't preserve the design. If the source-code control system requires hours to check in just a few files, then developers will be tempted to make changes that require as few check-ins as possible, regardless of whether the design is preserved.

In both cases, a viscous project is a project in which the design of the software is hard to preserve. We want to create systems and project environments that make it easy to preserve the design.

Needless Complexity. A design contains needless complexity when it contains elements that aren't currently useful. This frequently happens when developers anticipate changes to the requirements, and put facilities in the software to deal with those potential changes. At first, this may seem like a good thing to do. After all, preparing for future changes should keep our code flexible and prevent nightmarish changes later.

Unfortunately, the effect is often just the opposite. By preparing for too many contingencies, the design becomes littered with constructs that are never used. Some of those preparations may pay off, but many more do not. Meanwhile the design carries the weight of these unused design elements. This makes the software complex and hard to understand.

Needless Repetition. Cut and paste may be useful text-editing operations, but they can be disastrous code-editing operations. All too often, software systems are built upon dozens or hundreds of repeated code elements. It happens like this:

Ralph needs to write some code that fravles the arvadent. He looks around in other parts of the code where he suspects other arvadent fravling has occurred and finds a suitable stretch of code. He cuts and pastes that code into his module, and he makes the suitable modifications.

Unbeknownst to Ralph, the code he scraped up with his mouse was put there by Todd, who scraped it out of a module written by Lilly. Lilly was the first to fravle an arvadent, but she realized that fravling an arvadent was very similar to fravling a garnatosh. She found some code somewhere that fravled a garnatosh, cut and paste it into her module and modified it as necessary.

When the same code appears over and over again, in slightly different forms, the developers are missing an abstraction. Finding all the repetition and eliminating it with an appropriate abstraction may not be high on their priority list, but it would go a long way toward making the system easier to understand and maintain.

When there is redundant code in the system, the job of changing the system can become arduous. Bugs found in such a repeating unit have to be fixed in every repetition. However, since each repetition is slightly different from every other, the fix is not always the same.

Opacity. Opacity is the tendency of a module to be difficult to understand. Code can be written in a clear and expressive manner, or it can be written in an opaque and convoluted manner. Code that evolves over time tends to become more and more opaque with age. A constant effort to keep the code clear and expressive is required in order to keep opacity to a minimum.

When developers first write a module, the code may seem clear to them. That is because they have immersed themselves within it, and they understand it at an intimate level. Later, after the intimacy has worn off, they may return to that module and wonder how they could have written anything so awful. To prevent this, developers need to put themselves in their readers' shoes and make a concerted effort to refactor their code so that their readers can understand it. They also need to have their code reviewed by others.

What Stimulates the Software to Rot?

In nonagile environments, designs degrade because requirements change in ways that the initial design did not anticipate. Often, these changes need to be made quickly, and they may be made by developers who are not familiar with the original design philosophy. So, though the change to the design works, it somehow violates the original design. Bit by bit, as the changes continue, these violations accumulate, and the design begins to smell.

However, we cannot blame the drifting of the requirements for the degradation of the design. We, as software developers, know full well that requirements change. Indeed, most of us realize that the requirements are the most volatile elements in the project. If our designs are failing due to the constant rain of changing requirements, it is our designs and practices that are at fault. We must somehow find a way to make our designs resilient to such changes and employ practices that protect them from rotting.

Agile Teams Don't Allow the Software to Rot

An agile team thrives on change. The team invests little up front; therefore, it is not vested in an aging initial design. Rather, they keep the design of the system as clean and simple as possible, and back it up with lots of unit tests and acceptance tests. This keeps the design flexible and easy to change. The team takes advantage of that flexibility in order to continuously improve the design so that each iteration ends with a system whose design is as appropriate as it can be for the requirements in that iteration.

The "Copy" Program

Watching a design rot may help illustrate the above points. Let's say your boss comes to you early Monday morning and asks you to write a program that copies characters from the keyboard to the printer. Doing some quick mental exercises in your head, you come to the conclusion that this will be less than ten lines of code. Design and coding time should be a lot less than one hour. What with cross-functional group meetings, quality education meetings, daily group progress meetings, and the three current crises in the field, this program ought to take you about a week to complete—if you stay after hours. However, you always multiply your estimates by three.

"Three weeks," you tell your boss. He harumphs and walks away, leaving you to your task.

The Initial Design.   You have a bit of time right now before that process review meeting begins, so you decide to map out a design for the program. Using structured design you come up with the structure chart in Figure 7-1.

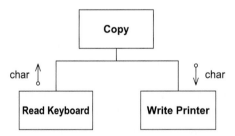

Figure 7-1 Copy Program Structure Chart

There are three modules, or subprograms, in the application. The Copy module calls the other two. The copy program fetches characters from the Read Keyboard module and routes them to the Write Printer module.

You look at your design and see that it is good. You smile and then leave your office to go to that review. At least you'll be able to get a little sleep there.

On Tuesday, you come in a bit early so that you can finish up the Copy program. Unfortunately, one of the crises in the field has warmed up over night, and you have to go to the lab and help debug a problem. On your lunch break, which you finally take at 3 p.m., you manage to type in the code for the Copy program. The result is Listing 7-1.

Listing 7-1

The Copy Program

```
void Copy()
{
  int c;
  while ((c=RdKbd()) != EOF)
    WrtPrt(c);
}
```

You just manage to save the edit, when you realize that you are already late for a quality meeting. You know this is an important one; they are going to be talking about the magnitude of zero defects. So you wolf down your Twinkies and coke and head off to the meeting.

On Wednesday, you come in early again, and this time nothing seems to be amiss. So you pull up the source code for the Copy program and begin to compile it. Lo and behold, it compiles first time with no errors! It's a good thing, too, because your boss calls you into an unscheduled meeting about the need to conserve laser printer toner.

On Thursday, after spending four hours on the phone with a service technician in Rocky Mount, North Carolina, walking him through the remote debugging and error logging commands in one of the more obscure components of the system, you grab a Ho Ho and then test your Copy program. It works, first time! Good thing, too, because your new co-op student has just erased the master source code directory from the server, and you have to go find the latest backup tapes and restore it. Of course the last full backup was taken three months ago, and you have ninety-four incremental backups to restore on top of it.

Friday, is completely unbooked. Good thing too, because it takes all day to get the Copy program successfully loaded into your source code control system.

Of course the program is a raging success, and gets deployed throughout your company. Your reputation as an ace programmer is once again confirmed, and you bask in the glory of your achievements. With luck, you might actually produce thirty lines of code this year!

The Requirements They Are a-Changin'. A few months later, your boss comes to you and says that sometimes they'd like the Copy program to be able to read from the paper tape reader. You gnash your teeth and roll your eyes. You wonder why people are always changing the requirements. Your program wasn't designed for a paper tape reader! You warn your boss that changes like these are going to destroy the elegance of your design. Nevertheless, your boss is adamant. He says the users really need to read characters from the paper tape reader from time to time.

So, you sigh and plan your modifications. You'd like to add a boolean argument to the Copy function. If true, then you'd read from the paper tape reader; if false, you'd read from the keyboard as before. Unfortunately, there are so many other programs using the Copy program now, that you can't change the interface. Changing the interface would cause weeks and weeks of recompiling and retesting. The system test engineers alone would lynch you, not to mention the seven guys in the configuration control group. And the process police would have a field day forcing all kinds of code reviews for every module that called Copy!

No, changing the interface is out. But then, how can you let the Copy program know that it must read from the paper tape reader? You'll use a global of course! You'll also use the best and most useful feature of the C suite of languages, the ?: operator! Listing 7-2 shows the result.

Listing 7-2

First modification of Copy program

```
bool ptFlag = false;
// remember to reset this flag
void Copy()
```

```
{
  int c;
  while ((c=(ptflag ? RdPt() : RdKbd())) != EOF)
    WrtPrt(c);
}
```

Callers of `Copy` who want to read from the paper tape reader must first set the `ptFlag` to true. Then they can call `Copy`, and it will happily read from the paper tape reader. Once `Copy` returns, the caller must reset the `ptFlag`, otherwise the next caller may mistakenly read from the paper tape reader rather than the keyboard. To remind the programmers of their duty to reset this flag, you have added an appropriate comment.

Once again, you release your software to critical acclaim. It is even more successful than before, and hordes of eager programmers are waiting for an opportunity to use it. Life is good.

Give 'em an inch...   Some weeks later, your boss (who is still your boss despite three corporate-wide reorganizations in as many months) tells you that the customers would sometimes like the `Copy` program to output to the paper tape punch.

Customers! They are always ruining your designs. *Writing software would be a lot easier if it weren't for customers*.

You tell your boss that these incessant changes are having a profoundly negative effect upon the elegance of your design. You warn him that if changes continue at this horrid pace, the software will be impossible to maintain before year end. Your boss nods knowingly, and then tells you to make the change anyway.

This design change is similar to the one before it. All we need is another global and another `?:` operator! Listing 7-3 shows the result of your endeavors.

Listing 7-3

```
bool ptFlag = false;
bool punchFlag = false;
// remember to reset these flags
void Copy()
{
  int c;
  while ((c=(ptflag ? RdPt() : RdKbd())) != EOF)
    punchFlag ? WrtPunch(c) : WrtPrt(c);
}
```

You are especially proud of the fact that you remembered to change the comment. Still, you worry that the structure of your program is beginning to topple. Any more changes to the input device will certainly force you to completely restructure the `while`-loop conditional. Perhaps it's time to dust off your resume...

Expect Changes.   I'll leave it to you to determine just how much of the above was satirical exaggeration. The point of the story was to show how the design of a program can rapidly degrade in the presence of change. The original design of the `Copy` program was simple and elegant. Yet after only two changes, it has begun to show the signs of Rigidity, Fragility, Immobility, Complexity, Redundancy, and Opacity. This trend is certainly going to continue, and the program will become a mess.

We might sit back and blame this on the changes. We might complain that the program was well designed for the original spec, and that the subsequent changes to the spec caused the design to degrade. However, this ignores one of the most prominent facts in software development: *requirements always change*!

Remember, the most volatile things in most software projects are the requirements. The requirements are continuously in a state of flux. This is a fact that we, as developers, must accept! *We live in a world of changing requirements, and our job is to make sure that our software can survive those changes.* If the design of our software degrades because the requirements have changed, then we are not being agile.

Agile Design of the Copy Example

An agile development might begin exactly the same way with the code in Listing 7-1.[2] When the boss asked the agile developers to make the program read from the paper tape reader, they would have responded by changing the design to be resilient to that kind of change. The result might have been something like Listing 7-4.

Listing 7-4

Agile version 2 of Copy

```
class Reader
{
  public:
    virtual int read() = 0;
};

class KeyboardReader : public Reader
{
  public:
    virtual int read() {return RdKbd();}
};

KeyboardReader GdefaultReader;

void Copy(Reader& reader = GdefaultReader)
{
  int c;
  while ((c=reader.read()) != EOF)
    WrtPrt(c);
}
```

Instead of trying to patch the design to make the new requirement work, the team siezes the opportunity to improve the design so that it will be resilient to that kind of change in the future. From now on, whenever the boss asks for a new kind of input device, the team will be able to respond in a way that does not cause degradation to the Copy program.

The team has followed the *Open–Closed Principle (OCP)*, which we will be reading about in Chapter 9. This principle directs us to design our modules so that they can be extended without modification. That's exactly what the team has done. Every new input device that the boss asks for can be provided without modifying the Copy program.

Note, however, that the team did not try to anticipate how the program was going to change when they first designed the module. Instead, they wrote it in the simplest way they could. It was only when the requirements did eventually change, that they changed the design of the module to be resilient to that kind of change.

One could argue that they only did half the job. While they were protecting themselves from different input devices, they could also have protected themselves from different output devices. However, the team really has no idea if the output devices will ever change. To add the extra protection now would be work that served no current puprose. It's clear that if such protection is needed, it will be easy to add later. So, there's really no reason to add it now.

---

2.   Actually the practice of test-driven development would very likely force the design to be flexible enough to endure the boss without change. However, in this example, we'll ignore that.

How Did the Agile Developers Know What to Do?

The agile developers in the example above built an abstract class to protect them from changes to the input device. How did they know how to do that? This has to do with one of the fundamental tenets of object-oriented design.

The initial design of the `Copy` program is inflexible because of the *direction* of its dependencies. Look again at Figure 7-1. Notice that the `Copy` module depends directly on the `KeyboardReader` and the `PrinterWriter`. The `Copy` module is a high-level module in this application. It sets the policy of the application. It knows how to copy characters. Unfortunately, it has also been made dependent on the low-level details of the keyboard and printer. Thus, when the low-level details change, the high-level policy is affected.

Once the inflexibility was exposed, the agile developers knew that the dependency from the `Copy` module to the input device needed to be *inverted*[3] so that `Copy` would no longer depend on the input device. They then employed the STRATEGY[4] pattern to create the desired inversion.

So, in short, the agile developers knew what to do because

1. They detected the problem by following agile practices;
2. They diagnosed the problem by applying design principles; and
3. They solved the problem by applying the appropriate design pattern.

The interplay between these three aspects of software development *is* the act of design.

Keeping the Design As Good As It Can Be

Agile developers are dedicated to keeping the design as appropriate and clean as possible. This is not a haphazard or tentative commitment. Agile developers do not "clean up" the design every few weeks. Rather, they keep the software as clean, simple, and expressive as they possibly can, every day, every hour, and even every minute. They never say, "We'll go back and fix that later." They never let the rot begin.

The attitude that agile developers have toward the design of the software is the same attitude that surgeons have toward sterile procedure. Sterile procedure is what makes surgery *possible*. Without it, the risk of infection would be far too high to tolerate. Agile developers feel the same way about their designs. The risk of letting even the tiniest bit of rot begin is too high to tolerate.

The design must remain clean, and since the source code is the most important expression of the design, it must remain clean, too. Professionalism dictates that we, as software developers, cannot tolerate code rot.

Conclusion

So, what is agile design? Agile design is a process, not an event. It's the continous application of principles, patterns, and practices to improve the structure and readability of the software. It is the dedication to keeping the design of the system as simple, clean, and expressive as possible at all times.

During the chapters that follow, we'll be investigating the principles and patterns of software design. As you read them, remember that an agile developer does not apply those principles and patterns to a big, up-front design. Rather, they are applied from iteration to iteration in an attempt to keep the code, and the design it embodies, clean.

Bibliography

1. Reeves, Jack. What Is Software Design? *C++ Journal*, Vol. 2, No. 2. 1992. Available at http://www.bleading-edge.com/Publications/C++Journal/Cpjour2.htm.

3.   See *The Dependency-Inversion Principle (DIP)* in Chapter 11.
4.   We'll learn about STRATEGY in Chapter 14.

8

SRP: The Single-Responsibility Principle

None but Buddha himself must take the responsibility of giving out occult secrets...

—E. Cobham Brewer 1810–1897.
Dictionary of Phrase and Fable. 1898.

This principle was described in the work of Tom DeMarco[1] and Meilir Page-Jones.[2] They called it *cohesion*. They defined cohesion as the functional relatedness of the elements of a module. In this chapter we'll shift that meaning a bit and relate cohesion to the forces that cause a module, or a class, to change.

SRP: The Single-Responsibility Principle

A class should have only one reason to change.

Consider the bowling game from Chapter 6. For most of its development, the Game class was handling two separate responsibilities. It was keeping track of the current frame, and it was calculating the score. In the end, RCM and RSK separated these two responsibilities into two classes. The Game kept the responsibility to keep track of frames, and the Scorer got the responsibility to calculate the score. (See page 78.)

---

1.   [DeMarco79], p. 310.
2.   [Page-Jones88], Chapter 6, p. 82.

Why was it important to separate these two responsibilities into separate classes? Because each responsibility is an axis of change. When the requirements change, that change will be manifest through a change in responsibility amongst the classes. If a class assumes more than one responsibility, then there will be more than one reason for it to change.

If a class has more than one responsibility, then the responsibilities become coupled. Changes to one responsibility may impair or inhibit the ability of the class to meet the others. This kind of coupling leads to fragile designs that break in unexpected ways when changed.

For example, consider the design in Figure 8-1. The Rectangle class has two methods shown. One draws the rectangle on the screen, the other computes the area of the rectangle.

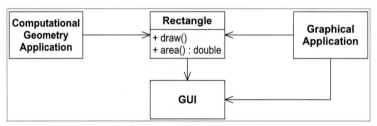

Figure 8-1   More than one responsibility

Two different applications use the Rectangle class. One application does computational geometry. It uses Rectangle to help it with the mathematics of geometric shapes. It never draws the rectangle on the screen. The other application is graphical in nature. It may also do some computational geometry, but it definitely draws the rectangle on the screen.

This design violates the Single-Responsibility Principle (SRP). The Rectangle class has two responsibilities. The first responsibility is to provide a mathematical model of the geometry of a rectangle. The second responsibility is to render the rectangle on a graphical user interface.

This violation of the SRP causes several nasty problems. First, we must include the GUI in the computational geometry application. If this were a C++ application, the GUI would have to be linked in, consuming link time, compile time, and memory footprint. In a Java application, the .class files for the GUI have to be deployed to the target platform.

Second, if a change to the GraphicalApplication causes the Rectangle to change for some reason, that change may force us to rebuild, retest, and redeploy the ComputationalGeometryApplication. If we forget to do this, that application may break in unpredictable ways.

A better design is to separate the two responsibilities into two completely different classes as shown in Figure 8-2. This design moves the computational portions of Rectangle into the GeometricRectangle class. Now changes made to the way rectangles are rendered cannot affect the ComputationalGeometryApplication.

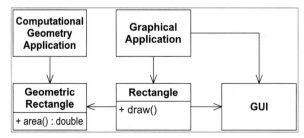

Figure 8-2   Separated Responsibilities

What Is a Responsibility?

In the context of the SRP, we define a responsibility to be "a reason for change." If you can think of more than one motive for changing a class, then that class has more than one responsibility. This is sometimes hard to see. We are accustomed to thinking of responsibility in groups. For example, consider the Modem interface in Listing 8-1. Most of us will agree that this interface looks perfectly reasonable. The four functions it declares are certainly functions belonging to a modem.

Listing 8-1

Modem.java -- SRP Violation

```
interface Modem
{
  public void dial(String pno);
  public void hangup();
  public void send(char c);
  public char recv();
}
```

However, there are two responsibilities being shown here. The first responsibility is connection management. The second is data communication. The dial and hangup functions manage the connection of the modem, while the send and recv functions communicate data.

Should these two responsibilities be separated? That depends on how the application is changing. If the application changes in ways that affect the signature of the connection functions, then the design will smell of Rigidity because the classes that call send and recv will have to be recompiled and redeployed more often than we like. In that case the two responsibilities should be separated as shown in Figure 8-3. This keeps the client applications from coupling the two responsibilities.

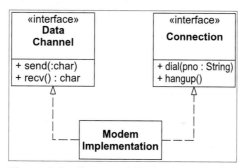

Figure 8-3   Separated Modem Interface

If, on the other hand, the application is not changing in ways that cause the the two responsibilities to change at different times, then there is no need to separate them. Indeed, separating them would smell of Needless Complexity.

There is a corollary here. *An axis of change is an axis of change only if the changes actually occur.* It is not wise to apply the SRP, or any other principle for that matter, if there is no symptom.

Separating Coupled Responsibilities

Notice that in Figure 8-3 I kept both responsibilities coupled in the ModemImplementation class. This is not desirable, but it may be necessary. There are often reasons, having to do with the details of the hardware or OS, that force us to couple things that we'd rather not couple. However, by separating their interfaces we have decoupled the concepts as far as the rest of the application is concerned.

We may view the `ModemImplementation` class as a kludge, or a wart; however, notice that all dependencies flow *away* from it. Nobody needs to depend on this class. Nobody except `main` needs to know that it exists. Thus, we've put the ugly bit behind a fence. Its ugliness need not leak out and pollute the rest of the application.

Persistence

Figure 8-4 shows a common violation of the SRP. The `Employee` class contains business rules and persistence control. These two responsibilities should almost never be mixed. Business rules tend to change frequently, and though persistence may not change as frequently, it changes for completely different reasons. Binding business rules to the persistence subsystem is asking for trouble.

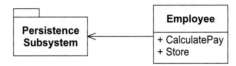

Figure 8-4   Coupled Persistence

Fortunately, as we saw in Chapter 4, the practice of test-driven development will usually force these two responsibilities to be separated long before the design begins to smell. However, in cases where the tests did not force the separation, and the smells of Rigidity and Fragility become strong, the design should be refactored using the FACADE or PROXY patterns to separate the two responsibilities.

Conclusion

The SRP is one of the simplest of the principles, and one of the hardest to get right. Conjoining responsibilities is something that we do naturally. Finding and separating those responsibilities from one another is much of what software design is really about. Indeed, the rest of the principles we will discuss come back to this issue in one way or another.

Bibliography

1. DeMarco, Tom. *Structured Analysis and System Specification.* Yourdon Press Computing Series. Englewood Cliff, NJ: 1979.
2. Page-Jones, Meilir. *The Practical Guide to Structured Systems Design*, 2d ed. Englewood Cliff, NJ: Yourdon Press Computing Series, 1988.

9

OCP: The Open–Closed Principle

Dutch Door—*(Noun) A door divided in two horizontally so that either part can be left open or closed.*

—The American Heritage® Dictionary of the English Language: Fourth Edition. 2000.

As Ivar Jacobson has said, "All systems change during their life cycles. This must be born in mind when developing systems are expected to last longer than the first version."[1] How can we create designs that are stable in the face of change and that will last longer than the first version? Bertrand Meyer gave us guidance as long ago as 1988 when he coined the now famous Open–Closed Principle.[2]

OCP: The Open–Closed Principle

> *Software entities (classes, modules, functions, etc.) should be open for extension, but closed for modification.*

When a single change to a program results in a cascade of changes to dependent modules, the design smells of Rigidity. The OCP advises us to refactor the system so that further changes of that kind will not cause more

1. [Jacobson92], p. 21.
2. [Meyer97], p. 57.

modifications. If the OCP is applied well, then further changes of that kind are achieved by adding new code, not by changing old code that already works.

This may seem like motherhood and apple pie—the golden unachievable ideal—but in fact there are some relatively simple and effective strategies for *approaching* that ideal.

Description

Modules that conform to the Open–Closed Principle have two primary attributes. They are

1. "Open for extension."
   This means that the behavior of the module can be extended. As the requirements of the application change, we are able to extend the module with new behaviors that satisfy those changes. In other words, we are able to change what the module does.
2. "Closed for modification."
   Extending the behavior of a module does not result in changes to the source or binary code of the module. The binary executable version of the module, whether in a linkable library, a DLL, or a Java `.jar`, remains untouched.

It would seem that these two attributes are at odds with each other. The normal way to extend the behavior of a module is to make changes to the source code of that module. A module that cannot be changed is normally thought to have a fixed behavior.

How is it possible that the behaviors of a module can be modified without changing its source code? How can we change what a module does, without changing the module?

Abstraction Is the Key

In C++, Java, or any other OOPL,[3] it is possible to create abstractions that are fixed and yet represent an unbounded group of possible behaviors. The abstractions are abstract base classes, and the unbounded group of possible behaviors is represented by all the possible derivative classes.

It is possible for a module to manipulate an abstraction. Such a module can be closed for modification since it depends upon an abstraction that is fixed. Yet the behavior of that module can be extended by creating new derivatives of the abstraction.

Figure 9–1 shows a simple design that does not conform to the OCP. Both the `Client` and `Server` classes are concrete. The `Client` class *uses* the `Server` class. If we wish for a `Client` object to use a different server object, then the `Client` class must be changed to name the new server class.

Figure 9-1   Client is not open and closed

Figure 9–2 shows the corresponding design that conforms to the OCP. In this case, the `ClientInterface` class is an abstract class with abstract member functions. The `Client` class uses this abstraction; however, objects of the `Client` class will be using objects of the derivative `Server` class. If we want `Client` objects to use a different server class, then a new derivative of the `ClientInterface` class can be created. The `Client` class can remain unchanged.

The `Client` has some work that it needs to get done, and it can describe that work in terms of the abstract interface presented by `ClientInterface`. Subtypes of `ClientInterface` can implement that interface in any

---

3.   Object-oriented programming language.

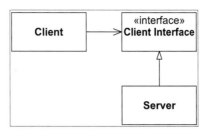

Figure 9-2 STRATEGY pattern: Client is both open and closed

manner they choose. Thus, the behavior specified in Client can be extended and modified by creating new subtypes of ClientInterface.

You may wonder why I named ClientInterface the way I did. Why didn't I call it AbstractServer instead? The reason, as we will see later, is that *abstract classes are more closely associated to their clients than to the classes that implement them.*

Figure 9-3 shows an alternative structure. The Policy class has a set of concrete public functions that implements a policy of some kind. Similar to the functions of the Client in Figure 9-2. As before, those policy functions describe some work that needs to be done in terms of some abstract interfaces. However, in this case, the abstract interfaces are part of the Policy class itself. In C++ they would be pure virtual functions, and in Java they would be abstract methods. Those functions are implemented in the subtypes of Policy. Thus, the behaviors specified within Policy can be extended or modified by creating new derivatives of the Policy class.

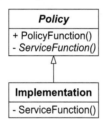

Figure 9-3 Template Method Pattern: Base class is open and closed

These two patterns are the most common ways of satisfying the OCP. They represent a clear separation of generic functionality from the detailed implementation of that functionality.

The Shape Application

The following example has been shown in many books on OOD. It is the infamous "Shape" example. It is normally used to show how polymorphism works. However, this time we will use it to elucidate the OCP.

We have an application that must be able to draw circles and squares on a standard GUI. The circles and squares must be drawn in a particular order. A list of the circles and squares will be created in the appropriate order, and the program must walk the list in that order and draw each circle or square.

Violating the OCP

In C, using procedural techniques that do not conform to the OCP, we might solve this problem as shown in Listing 9-1. Here we see a set of data structures that has the same first element, but is different beyond that. The first element of each is a type code that identifies the data structure as either a circle or a square. The function DrawAllShapes walks an array of pointers to these data structures, examining the type code and then calling the appropriate function (either DrawCircle or DrawSquare).

Listing 9-1

Procedural Solution to the Square/Circle Problem

```
--shape.h-------------------------------------
enum ShapeType {circle, square};

struct Shape
{
  ShapeType itsType;
};

--circle.h------------------------------------
struct Circle
{
  ShapeType itsType;
  double itsRadius;
  Point itsCenter;
};

void DrawCircle(struct Circle*);

--square.h------------------------------------
struct Square
{
  ShapeType itsType;
  double itsSide;
  Point itsTopLeft;
};

void DrawSquare(struct Square*);

--drawAllShapes.cc----------------------------
typedef struct Shape *ShapePointer;

void DrawAllShapes(ShapePointer list[], int n)
{
  int i;
  for (i=0; i<n; i++)
  {
    struct Shape* s = list[i];
    switch (s->itsType)
    {
    case square:
      DrawSquare((struct Square*)s);
    break;

    case circle:
      DrawCircle((struct Circle*)s);
    break;
    }
  }
}
```

The function DrawAllShapes does not conform to the OCP because it cannot be closed against new kinds of shapes. If I wanted to extend this function to be able to draw a list of shapes that included triangles, I would have to modify the function. In fact, I would have to modify the function for any new type of shape that I needed to draw.

Of course this program is only a simple example. In real life, the switch statement in the DrawAllShapes function would be repeated over and over again in various functions all through the application, each one doing something a little different. There might be functions for dragging shapes, stretching shapes, moving shapes, deleting shapes, etc. Adding a new shape to such an application means hunting for every place that such switch statements (or if/else chains) exist and adding the new shape to each.

Moreover, it is very unlikely that all the switch statements and if/else chains would be as nicely structured as the one in DrawAllShapes. It is much more likely that the predicates of the if statements would be combined with logical operators or that the case clauses of the switch statements would be combined so as to "simplify" the local decision making. In some pathological situations, there may be functions that do precisely the same things to Squares that they do to Circles. Such functions would not even have the switch/case statements or if/else chains. Thus, the problem of finding and understanding all the places where the new shape needs to be added can be nontrivial.

Also, consider the kind of changes that would have to be made. We'd have to add a new member to the ShapeType enum. Since all the different shapes depend on the declaration of this enum, we'd have to recompile them all.[4] And we'd also have to recompile all the modules that depend on Shape.

So, not only must we change the source code of all switch/case statements or if/else chains, but we also must alter the binary files (via recompilation) of all the modules that use any of the Shape data structures. Changing the binary files means that any DLLs, shared libraries, or other kinds of binary components must be redeployed. The simple act of adding a new shape to the application causes a cascade of subsequent changes to many source modules and to even more binary modules and binary components. Clearly, the impact of adding a new shape is very large.

Bad Design. Let's run through this again. The solution in Listing 9-1 is Rigid because the addition of Triangle causes Shape, Square, Circle, and DrawAllShapes to be recompiled and redeployed. It is Fragile because there will be many other switch/case or if/else statements that are both hard to find and hard to decipher. It is Immobile because anyone attempting to reuse DrawAllShapes in another program is required to bring along Square and Circle, even if that new program does not need them. Thus, Listing 9-1 exhibits many of the smells of bad design.

Conforming to the OCP

Listing 9-2 shows the code for a solution to the square/circle problem that conforms to the OCP. In this case, we have written an abstract class named Shape. This abstract class has a single abstract method named Draw. Both Circle and Square are derivatives of the Shape class.

Listing 9-2

OOD solution to Square/Circle problem.

```
class Shape
{
  public:
    virtual void Draw() const = 0;
};
```

4.   Changes to enums can cause a change in the size of the variable used to hold the enum. So, great care must be taken if you decide that you don't really need to recompile the other shape declarations.

```
class Square : public Shape
{
  public:
    virtual void Draw() const;
};

class Circle : public Shape
{
  public:
    virtual void Draw() const;
};

void DrawAllShapes(vector<Shape*>& list)
{
  vector<Shape*>::iterator i;
  for (i=list.begin(); i != list.end(); i++)
    (*i)->Draw();
}
```

Note that if we want to extend the behavior of the `DrawAllShapes` function in Listing 9-2 to draw a new kind of shape, all we need do is add a new derivative of the `Shape` class. The `DrawAllShapes` function does not need to change. Thus `DrawAllShapes` conforms to the OCP. Its behavior can be extended without modifying it. Indeed, adding a `Triangle` class has *absolutely no effect* on any of the modules shown here. Clearly some part of the system must change in order to deal with the `Triangle` class, but all of the code shown here is immune to the change.

In a real application, the `Shape` class would have many more methods. Yet adding a new shape to the application is still quite simple since all that is required is to create the new derivative and implement all its functions. There is no need to hunt through all of the application looking for places that require changes. This solution is not **Fragile**.

Nor is the solution **Rigid**. No existing source modules need to be modified, and with one exception, no existing binary modules need to be rebuilt. The module that actually creates instances of the new derivative of `Shape` must be modified. Typically, this is either done by `main`, in some function called by `main`, or in the method of some object created by `main`.[5]

Finally, the solution is not **Immobile**. `DrawAllShapes` can be reused by any application without the need to bring `Square` or `Circle` along for the ride. Thus, the solution exhibits none of the attributes of bad design mentioned previously.

This program conforms to the OCP. *It is changed by adding new code rather than by changing existing code.* Therefore, it does not experience the cascade of changes exhibited by nonconforming programs. The only changes required are the addition of the new module and the change related to `main` that allows the new objects to be instantiated.

OK, I Lied

The previous example was blue sky and apple pie! Consider what would happen to the `DrawAllShapes` function from Listing 9-2 if we decided that *all* `Circles` *should be drawn before any* `Squares`. The `DrawAllShapes` function is not closed against a change like this. To implement that change, we'll have to go into `DrawAllShapes` and scan the list first for `Circles` and then again for `Squares`.

---

5.   Such objects are known as *factories*, and we'll have more to say about them in Chapter 21 on page 269.

Anticipation and "Natural" Structure

Had we anticipated this kind of change, then we could have invented an abstraction that protected us from it. The abstractions we chose in Listing 9-2 are more of a hindrance to this kind of change than a help. You may find this surprising. After all, what could be more natural than a Shape base class with Square and Circle derivatives? Why isn't that natural model the best one to use? Clearly the answer is that the model is *not* natural in a system where ordering is more significant than shape type.

This leads us to a disturbing conclusion. In general, no matter how "closed" a module is, there will always be some kind of change against which it is not closed. *There is no model that is natural to all contexts!*

Since closure cannot be complete, it must be strategic. That is, the designer must choose the kinds of changes against which to close his design. He must guess at the most likely kinds of changes, and then construct abstractions to protect him from those changes.

This takes a certain amount of prescience derived from experience. The experienced designer hopes he knows the users and the industry well enough to judge the probability of different kinds of changes. He then invokes the OCP against the most probable changes.

This is not easy. It amounts to making educated guesses about the likely kinds of changes that the application will suffer over time. When the developers guess right, they win. When they guess wrong, they lose. And they will certainly guess wrong much of the time.

Also, conforming to the OCP is expensive. It takes development time and effort to create the appropriate abstractions. Those abstractions also increase the complexity of the software design. There is a limit to the amount of abstraction that the developers can afford. Clearly, we want to limit the application of the OCP to changes that are likely.

How do we know which changes are likely? We do the appropriate research, we ask the appropriate questions, and we use our experience and common sense. And after all that, *we wait until the changes happen!*

Putting the "Hooks" In

How do we protect ourselves from changes? In the previous century, we had a saying. We'd "put the hooks in" for changes that we thought might take place. We felt that this would make our software flexible.

However, the hooks we put in were often incorrect. Worse, they smelled of Needless Complexity that had to be supported and maintained, even though they weren't used. This is not a good thing. We don't want to load the design with lots of unnecessary abstraction. Rather, we often wait until we actually need the abstraction, and then we put it in.

Fool Me Once...   There is an old saying: "Fool me once, shame on you. Fool me twice, shame on me." This is a powerful attitude in software design. To keep from loading our software with Needless Complexity, we may permit ourselves to be fooled *once*. This means we initially write our code expecting it not to change. When a change occurs, we implement the abstractions that protect us from future changes *of that kind*. In short, we *take the first bullet*, and then we make sure we are protected from any more bullets coming from that gun.

Stimulating Change.   If we decide to take the first bullet, then it is to our advantage to get the bullets flying early and frequently. We want to know what kinds of changes are likely before we are very far down the development path. The longer we wait to find out what kinds of changes are likely, the harder it will be to create the appropriate abstractions.

Therefore, we need to stimulate the changes. We do this through several of the means we discussed in Chapter 2.

- We write tests first. Testing is one kind of usage of the system. By writing tests first we force the system to be testable. Therefore changes in testability will not surprise us later. We will have built the abstractions that make the system testable. We are likely to find that many of these abstractions will protect us from other kinds of changes later.
- We develop using very short cycles—days instead of weeks.
- We develop features before infrastructure and frequently show those features to stakeholders.
- We develop the most important features first.
- We release the software early and often. We get it in front of our customers and users as quickly and as often as possible.

Using Abstraction to Gain Explicit Closure

OK, so we've taken the first bullet. The user wants us to draw all `Circles` before any `Squares`. Now we want to protect ourselves from any future changes of that kind.

How can we close the `DrawAllShapes` function against changes in the ordering of drawing? Remember that closure is based upon abstraction. Thus, in order to close `DrawAllShapes` against ordering, we need some kind of "ordering abstraction." This abstraction would provide an abstract interface through which any possible ordering policy could be expressed.

An ordering policy implies that, given any two objects, it is possible to discover which ought to be drawn first. We can define an abstract method of `Shape` named `Precedes`. This function takes another `Shape` as an argument and returns a `bool` result. The result is `true` if the `Shape` object that receives the message should be drawn before the `Shape` object passed as the argument.

In C++, this function could be represented by an overloaded `operator<` function. Listing 9-3 shows what the `Shape` class might look like with the ordering methods in place.

Now that we have a way to determine the relative ordering of two `Shape` objects, we can sort them and then draw them in order. Listing 9-4 shows the C++ code that does this.

Listing 9-3

Shape with ordering methods

```
class Shape
{
  public:
    virtual void Draw() const = 0;
    virtual bool Precedes(const Shape&) const = 0;

    bool operator<(const Shape& s) {return Precedes(s);}
};
```

Listing 9-4

DrawAllShapes with Ordering

```
template <typename P>
class Lessp // utility for sorting containers of pointers.
{
  public:
    bool operator()(const P p, const P q) {return (*p) < (*q);}
};

void DrawAllShapes(vector<Shape*>& list)
{
    vector<Shape*> orderedList = list;
```

```
sort(orderedList.begin(),
     orderedList.end(),
     Lessp<Shape*>());

vector<Shape*>::const_iterator i;
for (i=orderedList.begin(); i != orderedList.end(); i++)
    (*i)->Draw();
}
```

This gives us a means for ordering Shape objects and for drawing them in the appropriate order. But we still do not have a decent ordering abstraction. As it stands, the individual Shape objects will have to override the Precedes method in order to specify ordering. How would this work? What kind of code would we write in Circle::Precedes to ensure that Circles were drawn before Squares? Consider Listing 9–5.

Listing 9-5

Ordering a Circle

```
bool Circle::Precedes(const Shape& s) const
{
    if (dynamic_cast<Square*>(s))
        return true;
    else
        return false;
}
```

It should be very clear that this function, and all its siblings in the other derivatives of Shape, do not conform to the OCP. There is no way to close them against new derivatives of Shape. Every time a new derivative of Shape is created, all the Precedes() functions will need to be changed.[6]

Of course this doesn't matter if no new derivatives of Shape are ever created. On the other hand, if they are created frequently, this design would cause a significant amount of thrashing. Again, we'd take the first bullet.

Using a "Data-Driven" Approach to Achieve Closure

If we must close the derivatives of Shape from knowledge of each other, we can use a table-driven approach. Listing 9-6 shows one possibility.

Listing 9-6

Table driven type ordering mechanism

```
#include <typeinfo>
#include <string>
#include <iostream>

using namespace std;

class Shape
{
  public:
    virtual void Draw() const = 0;
    bool Precedes(const Shape&) const;
```

---

6.   It is possible to solve this problem by using the ACYCLIC VISITOR pattern described in Chapter 29. Showing that solution now would be getting ahead of ourselves a bit. I'll remind you to come back here at the end of that chapter.

```cpp
    bool operator<(const Shape& s) const
    {return Precedes(s);}
  private:
    static const char* typeOrderTable[];
};

const char* Shape::typeOrderTable[] =
{
    typeid(Circle).name(),
    typeid(Square).name(),
    0
};

// This function searches a table for the class names.
// The table defines the order in which the
// shapes are to be drawn. Shapes that are not
// found always precede shapes that are found.
//
bool Shape::Precedes(const Shape& s) const
{
    const char* thisType = typeid(*this).name();
    const char* argType = typeid(s).name();
    bool done = false;
    int thisOrd = -1;
    int argOrd = -1;
    for (int i=0; !done; i++)
    {
        const char* tableEntry = typeOrderTable[i];
        if (tableEntry != 0)
        {
            if (strcmp(tableEntry, thisType) == 0)
                thisOrd = i;
            if (strcmp(tableEntry, argType) == 0)
                argOrd = i;
            if ((argOrd >= 0) && (thisOrd >= 0))
                done = true;
        }
        else // table entry == 0
            done = true;
    }
    return thisOrd < argOrd;
}
```

By taking this approach, we have successfully closed the DrawAllShapes function against ordering issues in general and each of the Shape derivatives against the creation of new Shape derivatives or a change in policy that reorders the Shape objects by their type. (e.g., changing the ordering so that Squares are drawn first.)

The only item that is not closed against the order of the various Shapes is the table itself. That table can be placed in its own module, separate from all the other modules, so that changes to it do not affect any of the other modules. Indeed, in C++, we can choose which table to use at link time.

Conclusion

In many ways, the OCP is at the heart of object-oriented design. Conformance to this principle is what yields the greatest benefits claimed for object oriented technology (i.e., flexibility, reusability, and maintainability). Yet conformance to this principle is not achieved simply by using an object-oriented programming language. Nor is it a good idea to apply rampant abstraction to every part of the application. Rather, it requires a dedication on the part of the developers to apply abstraction only to those parts of the program that exhibit frequent change. *Resisting premature abstraction is as important as abstraction itself.*

Bibliography

1. Jacobson, Ivar, et al. *Object-Oriented Software Engineering*. Reading, MA: Addison–Wesley, 1992.
2. Meyer, Bertrand. *Object-Oriented Software Construction*, 2d ed. Upper Saddle River, NJ: Prentice Hall, 1997.

10

LSP: The Liskov Substitution Principle

© Jennifer M. Kohnke

The primary mechanisms behind the OCP are abstraction and polymorphism. In statically typed languages like C++ and Java, one of the key mechanisms that supports abstraction and polymorphism is inheritance. It is by using inheritance that we can create derived classes that implement abstract methods in base classes.

What are the design rules that govern this particular use of inheritance? What are the characteristics of the best inheritance hierarchies? What are the traps that will cause us to create hierarchies that do not conform to the OCP? These are the questions that are addressed by the Liskov Substitution Principle (LSP).

LSP: The Liskov Substitution Principle

The LSP can be paraphrased as follows:

SUBTYPES MUST BE SUBSTITUTABLE FOR THEIR BASE TYPES.

Barbara Liskov first wrote this principle in 1988.[1] She said,

> *What is wanted here is something like the following substitution property: If for each object o_1 of type S there is an object o_2 of type T such that for all programs P defined in terms of T, the behavior of P is unchanged when o_1 is substituted for o_2 then S is a subtype of T.*

---

1.   [Liskov88].

The importance of this principle becomes obvious when you consider the consequences of violating it. Presume that we have a function *f* that takes, as its argument, a pointer or reference to some base class *B*. Presume also that there is some derivative *D* of *B* which, when passed to *f* in the guise of *B,* causes *f* to misbehave. Then *D* violates the LSP. Clearly *D* is Fragile in the presence of *f*.

The authors of *f* will be tempted to put in some kind of test for *D* so that *f* can behave properly when a *D* is passed to it. This test violates the OCP because now *f* is not closed to all the various derivatives of *B*. Such tests are a code smell that are the result of inexperienced developers (or, what's worse, developers in a hurry) reacting to LSP violations.

A Simple Example of a Violation of the LSP

Violating the LSP often results in the use of Run-Time Type Information (RTTI) in a manner that grossly violates the OCP. Frequently, an explicit `if` statement or `if/else` chain is used to determine the type of an object so that the behavior appropriate to that type can be selected. Consider Listing 10-1.

Listing 10-1

A violation of LSP causing a violation of OCP.

```
struct Point {double x,y;};

struct Shape {
  enum ShapeType {square, circle} itsType;
  Shape(ShapeType t) : itsType(t) {}
};

struct Circle : public Shape
{
  Circle() : Shape(circle) {};
  void Draw() const;
  Point itsCenter;
  double itsRadius;
};

struct Square : public Shape
{
  Square() : Shape(square) {};
  void Draw() const;
  Point itsTopLeft;
  double itsSide;
};

void DrawShape(const Shape& s)
{
  if (s.itsType == Shape::square)
    static_cast<const Square&>(s).Draw();
  else if (s.itsType == Shape::circle)
    static_cast<const Circle&>(s).Draw();
}
```

Clearly, the `DrawShape` function in Listing 10-1 violates the OCP. It must know about every possible derivative of the `Shape` class, and it must be changed whenever new derivatives of `Shape` are created. Indeed, many rightly view the structure of this function as anathema to good design. What would drive a programmer to write a function like this?

Consider Joe the Engineer. Joe has studied object-oriented technology and has come to the conclusion that the overhead of polymorphism is too high to pay.[2] Therefore, he defined class Shape without any virtual functions. The classes (structs) Square and Circle derive from Shape and have Draw() functions, but they don't override a function in Shape. Since Circle and Square are not substitutable for Shape, DrawShape must inspect its incoming Shape, determine its type, and then call the appropriate Draw function.

The fact that Square and Circle cannot be substituted for Shape is a violation of the LSP. This violation forced the violation of the OCP by DrawShape. Thus, *a violation of LSP is a latent violation of OCP*.

Square and Rectangle, a More Subtle Violation

Of course, there are other, far more subtle, ways of violating the LSP. Consider an application which uses the Rectangle class as described in Listing 10-2.

Listing 10-2

Rectangle class

```
class Rectangle
{
  public:
    void   SetWidth(double w)   {itsWidth=w;}
    void   SetHeight(double h)  {itsHeight=w;}
    double GetHeight() const    {return itsHeight;}
    double GetWidth() const     {return itsWidth;}
  private:
    Point  itsTopLeft;
    double itsWidth;
    double itsHeight;
};
```

Imagine that this application works well and is installed in many sites. As is the case with all successful software, its users demand changes from time to time. One day, the users demand the ability to manipulate *squares* in addition to rectangles.

It is often said that inheritance is the *IS-A* relationship. In other words, if a new kind of object can be said to fulfill the IS-A relationship with an old kind of object, then the class of the new object should be derived from the class of the old object.

For all normal intents and purposes, a square *is a* rectangle. Thus, it is logical to view the Square class as being derived from the Rectangle class. (See Figure 10-1.)

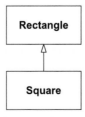

Figure 10-1   Square inherits from Rectangle

This use of the IS-A relationship is sometimes thought to be one of the fundamental techniques of object-oriented analysis:[3] A square is a rectangle, and so the Square class should be derived from the Rectangle class.

2.   On a reasonably fast machine, that overhead is on the order of 1ns per method invocation, so it's hard to see Joe's point.

3.   A term that is frequently used but seldom defined.

However, this kind of thinking can lead to some subtle, yet significant, problems. Generally, these problem are not foreseen until we see them in code.

Our first clue that something has gone wrong might be the fact that a `Square` does not need both `itsHeight` and `itsWidth` member variables. Yet it will inherit them from `Rectangle`. Clearly, this is wasteful. In many cases, such waste is insignificant. But if we must create hundreds of thousands of `Square` objects (e.g., a CAD/ CAE program in which every pin of every component of a complex circuit is drawn as a square), this waste could be significant.

Let's assume, for the moment, that we are not very concerned with memory efficiency. There are other problems that ensue from deriving `Square` from `Rectangle`. `Square` will inherit the `SetWidth` and `SetHeight` functions. These functions are inappropriate for a `Square`, since the width and height of a square are identical. This is a strong indication that there is a problem. However, there is a way to sidestep the problem. We could override `SetWidth` and `SetHeight` as follows:

```
void Square::SetWidth(double w)
{
  Rectangle::SetWidth(w);
  Rectangle::SetHeight(w);
}

void Square::SetHeight(double h)
{
  Rectangle::SetHeight(h);
  Rectangle::SetWidth(h);
}
```

Now, when someone sets the width of a `Square` object, its height will change correspondingly. And when someone sets the height, its width will change with it. Thus, the invariants[4] of the `Square` remain intact. The `Square` object will remain a mathematically proper square.

```
Square s;
s.SetWidth(1); // Fortunately sets the height to 1 too.
s.SetHeight(2); // sets width and height to 2. Good thing.
```

But consider the following function:

```
void f(Rectangle& r)
{
  r.SetWidth(32); // calls Rectangle::SetWidth
}
```

If we pass a reference to a `Square` object into this function, the `Square` object will be corrupted because the height won't be changed. This is a clear violation of LSP. The `f` function does not work for derivatives of its arguments. The reason for the failure is that `SetWidth` and `SetHeight` were not declared `virtual` in `Rectangle`; therefore, they are not polymorphic.

We can fix this easily. However, when the creation of a derived class causes us to make changes to the base class, it often implies that the design is faulty. Certainly it violates the OCP. We might counter this by saying that forgetting to make `SetWidth` and `SetHeight` `virtual` was the real design flaw, and we are just fixing it now. However, this is hard to justify since setting the height and width of a rectangle are exceedingly primitive operations. By what reasoning would we make them `virtual` if we did not anticipate the existence of `Square`.

---

4.   Those properties that must always be true regardless of state.

Still, let's assume that we accept the argument and fix the classes. We wind up with the code in Listing 10-3.

Listing 10-3
Rectangle and Square that are Self-Consistent.

```
class Rectangle
{
  public:
    virtual void SetWidth(double w)   {itsWidth=w;}
    virtual void SetHeight(double h)  {itsHeight=h;}
    double      GetHeight() const    {return itsHeight;}
    double      GetWidth() const     {return itsWidth;}
  private:
    Point   itsTopLeft
    double itsHeight;
    double itsWidth;
};

class Square : public Rectangle
{
  public:
    virtual void SetWidth(double w);
    virtual void SetHeight(double h);
};

void Square::SetWidth(double w)
{
  Rectangle::SetWidth(w);
  Rectangle::SetHeight(w);
}

void Square::SetHeight(double h)
{
  Rectangle::SetHeight(h);
  Rectangle::SetWidth(h);
}
```

The Real Problem

Square and Rectangle now appear to work. No matter what you do to a Square object, it will remain consistent with a mathematical square. And regardless of what you do to a Rectangle object, it will remain a mathematical rectangle. Moreover, you can pass a Square into a function that accepts a pointer or reference to a Rectangle, and the Square will still act like a square and will remain consistent.

Thus, we might conclude that the design is now self-consistent and correct. However, this conclusion would be amiss. A design that is self-consistent is not necessarily consistent with all its users! Consider the following function g:

```
void g(Rectangle& r)
{
  r.SetWidth(5);
  r.SetHeight(4);
  assert(r.Area() == 20);
}
```

This function invokes the `SetWidth` and `SetHeight` members of what it believes to be a `Rectangle`. The function works just fine for a `Rectangle`, but it declares an assertion error if passed a `Square`. So here is the real problem: *The author of* g *assumed that changing the width of a* `Rectangle` *leaves its height unchanged.*

Clearly, it is reasonable to assume that changing the width of a rectangle does not affect its height! However, not all objects that can be passed as `Rectangles` satisfy that assumption. If you pass an instance of a `Square` to a function like g, whose author made that assumption, then that function will malfunction. Function g is **Fragile** with respect to the `Square`/`Rectangle` hierarchy.

Function g shows that there exist functions that take pointers or references to `Rectangle` objects, but that cannot operate properly on `Square` objects. Since, for these functions, `Square` is not substitutable for `Rectangle`, the relationship between `Square` and `Rectangle` violates the LSP.

One might contend that the problem lay in function g—that the author had no right to make the assumption that width and height were independent. The author of g would disagree. The function g takes a `Rectagle` as its argument. There are invariants, statements of truth, that obviously apply to a class named `Rectangle`, and one of those invariants is that height and width are independent. The author of g had every right to assert this invariant. It is the author of `Square` that has violated the invariant.

Interestingly enough, the author of `Square` did not violate an invariant of `Square`. By deriving `Square` from `Rectangle`, the author of `Square` violated an invariant of `Rectangle`!

Validity Is Not Intrinsic

The LSP leads us to a very important conclusion: *A model, viewed in isolation, cannot be meaningfully validated.* The validity of a model can only be expressed in terms of its clients. For example, when we examined the final version of the `Square` and `Rectangle` classes in isolation, we found that they were self-consistent and valid. Yet when we looked at them from the viewpoint of a programmer who made reasonable assumptions about the base class, the model broke down.

When considering whether a particular design is appropriate or not, one cannot simply view the solution in isolation. One must view it in terms of the reasonable assumptions made by the users of that design.[5]

Who knows what reasonable assumptions the users of a design are going to make? Most such assumptions are not easy to anticipate. Indeed, if we tried to anticipate them all, we'd likely wind up imbuing our system with the smell of **Needless Complexity**. Therefore, like all other principles, it is often best to defer all but the most obvious LSP violations until the related **Fragility** has been smelled.

ISA Is about Behavior

So what happened? Why did the apparently reasonable model of the `Square` and `Rectangle` go bad? After all, isn't a `Square` a `Rectangle`? Doesn't the IS-A relationship hold?

Not as far as the author of g is concerned! A square might be a rectangle, but from g's point of view, a `Square` object is definitely *not* a `Rectangle` object. Why? Because the *behavior* of a `Square` object is not consistent with g's expectation of the behavior of a `Rectangle` object. Behaviorally, a `Square` is not a `Rectangle`, and it is *behavior* that software is really all about. The LSP makes it clear that in OOD, the IS-A relationship pertains to *behavior* that can be reasonably assumed and that clients depend on.

5.   Often you will find that those reasonable assumptions are asserted in the unit tests written for the base class. Yet another good reason to practice test-driven development.

Design by Contract

Many developers may feel uncomfortable with the notion of behavior that is "reasonably assumed." How do you know what your clients will really expect? There is a technique for making those reasonable assumptions explicit, thereby enforcing the LSP. The technique is called design by contract (DBC) and is expounded by Bertrand Meyer.[6]

Using DBC, the author of a class explicitly states the contract for that class. The contract informs the author of any client code about the behaviors that can be relied on. The contract is specified by declaring preconditions and postconditions for each method. The preconditions must be true in order for the method to execute. On completion, the method guarantees that the postconditions are true.

We can view the postcondition of `Rectangle::SetWidth(double w)` as follows:

```
assert((itsWidth == w) && (itsHeight == old.itsHeight));
```

In this example, `old` is the value of the `Rectangle` before `SetWidth` is called. Now the rule for preconditions and postconditions of derivatives, as stated by Meyer, is:

> *A routine redeclaration [in a derivative] may only replace the original precondition by one equal or weaker, and the original postcondition by one equal or stronger.*[7]

In other words, when using an object through its base-class interface, the user knows only the preconditions and postconditions of the base class. Thus, derived objects must not expect such users to obey preconditions that are stronger than those required by the base class. That is, they must accept anything that the base class could accept. Also, derived classes must conform to all the postconditions of the base. That is, their behaviors and outputs must not violate any of the constraints established for the base class. Users of the base class must not be confused by the output of the derived class.

Clearly, the postcondition of `Square::SetWidth(double w)` is weaker[8] than the postcondition of `Rectangle::SetWidth(double w)`, since it does not enforce the constraint, `(itsHeight == old.itsHeight)`. Thus, the `SetWidth` method of `Square` violates the contract of the base class.

Certain languages, like Eiffel, have direct support for preconditions and postconditions. You can declare them and have the runtime system verify them for you. Neither C++ nor Java has such a feature. In these languages, we must manually consider the preconditions and postcondition of each method and make sure that Meyer's rule is not violated. Moreover, it can be very helpful to document these preconditions and postconditions in the comments for each method.

Specifying Contracts in Unit Tests

Contracts can also be specified by writing unit tests. By thoroughly testing the behavior of a class, the unit tests make the behavior of the class clear. Authors of client code will want to review the unit tests so that they know what to reasonably assume about the classes they are using.

A Real Example

Enough of squares and rectangles! Does the LSP have a bearing on real software? Let's look at a case study that comes from a project that I worked on a few years ago.

---

6. [Meyer97], Chapter 11, p. 331.

7. [Meyer97], p. 573, Assertion Redeclaration rule (1).

8. The term "weaker" can be confusing. X is weaker than Y if X does not enforce all the constraints of Y. It does not matter how many new constraints X enforces.

Motivation

In the early 1990s, I purchased a third-party class library that had some container classes. The containers were roughly related to the `Bags` and `Sets` of Smalltalk. There were two varieties of `Set` and two similar varieties of `Bag`. The first variety was called "bounded" and was based on an array. The second was called "unbounded" and was based on a linked list.

The constructor for `BoundedSet` specified the maximum number of elements the set could hold. The space for these elements was preallocated as an array within the `BoundedSet`. Thus, if the creation of the `BoundedSet` succeeded, we could be sure that it had enough memory. Since it was based on an array, it was very fast. There were no memory allocations performed during normal operation. And since the memory was preallocated, we could be sure that operating the `BoundedSet` would not exhaust the heap. On the other hand, it was wasteful of memory since it would seldom completely utilize all the space that it had preallocated.

`UnboundedSet`, on the other hand, had no declared limit on the number of elements it could hold. So long as there was heap memory avaliable, the `UnboundedSet` would continue to accept elements. Therefore, it was very flexible. It was also economical in that it only used the memory necessary to hold the elements that it currently contained. It was also slow because it had to allocate and deallocate memory as part of its normal operation. Finally, there was a danger that its normal operation could exhaust the heap.

I was unhappy with the interfaces of these third-party classes. I did not want my application code to be dependent on them because I felt that I would want to replace them with better classes later. Thus, I wrapped the third-party containers in my own abstract interface as shown in Figure 10-2.

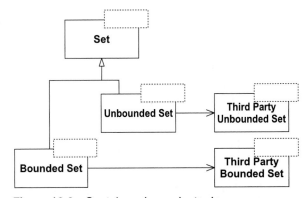

Figure 10-2　Container class adapter layer

I created an abstract class called `Set` that presented pure virtual `Add`, `Delete`, and `IsMember` functions, as shown in Listing 10-4. This structure unified the unbounded and bounded varieties of the two third-party sets and allowed them to be accessed through a common interface. Thus, some client could accept an argument of type `Set<T>&` and would not care whether the actual `Set` it worked on was of the bounded or unbounded variety. (See the `PrintSet` function in Listing 10-5.)

Listing 10-4
Abstract Set Class

```
template <class T>
class Set
{
  public:
    virtual void Add(const T&) = 0;
    virtual void Delete(const T&) = 0;
    virtual bool IsMember(const T&) const = 0;
};
```

Listing 10-5

PrintSet

```
template <class T>
void PrintSet(const Set<T>& s)
{
  for (Iterator<T>i(s); i; i++
    cout << (*i) << endl;
}
```

It is a big advantage not to have to know or care what kind of Set you are using. It means that the programmer can decide which kind of Set is needed in each particular instance, and none of the client functions will be affected by that decision. The programmer may choose an UnboundedSet when memory is tight and speed is not critical, or the programmer may choose an BoundedSet when memory is plentiful and speed is critical. The client functions will manipulate these objects through the interface of the base class Set and will therefore not know or care which kind of Set they are using.

Problem

I wanted to add a PersistentSet to this hierarchy. A persistent set is a set that can be written out to a stream and then read back in later, possibly by a different application. Unfortunately, the only third-party container that I had access to, that also offered persistence, was not a template class. Instead, it accepted objects that were derived from the abstract base class PersistentObject. I created the hierarchy shown in Figure 10-3.

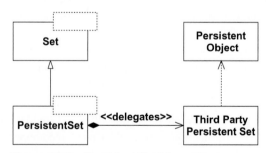

Figure 10-3   Persistent Set Hierarchy

Note that PersistentSet contains an instance of the third-party persistent set, to which it delegates all its methods. Thus, if you call Add on the PersistentSet, it simply delegates that to the appropriate method of the contained third-party persistent set.

On the surface of it, this might look all right. However, there is an ugly implication. Elements that are added to the third-party persistent set must be derived from PersistentObject. Since PersistentSet simply delegates to the third-party persistent set, any element added to PersistentSet must therefore derive from PersistentObject. Yet the interface of Set has no such constraint.

When a client is adding members to the base class Set, that client cannot be sure whether or not the Set might actually be a PersistentSet. Thus, the client has no way of knowing whether or not the elements it adds ought to be derived from PersistentObject.

Consider the code for PersistentSet::Add() in Listing 10-6.

Listing 10-6

```
template <typename T>
void PersistentSet::Add(const T& t)
{
  PersistentObject& p =
    dynamic_cast<PersistentObject&>(t);
  itsThirdPartyPersistentSet.Add(p);
}
```

This code makes it clear that if any client tries to add an object that is not derived from the class `PersistentObject` to my `PersistentSet`, a runtime error will ensue. The `dynamic_cast` will throw `bad_cast`. None of the existing clients of the abstract base class `Set` expects exceptions to be thrown on `Add`. Since these functions will be confused by a derivative of `Set`, this change to the hierarchy violates the LSP.

Is this a problem? Certainly. Functions that never before failed when passed a derivative of `Set` may now cause runtime errors when passed a `PersistentSet`. Debugging this kind of problem is relatively difficult since the runtime error occurs very far away from the actual logic flaw. The logic flaw is either the decision to pass a `PersistentSet` into a function or it is the decision to add an object to the `PersistentSet` that is not derived from `PersistentObject`. In either case, the actual decision might be millions of instructions away from the actual invocation of the `Add` method. Finding it can be a bear. Fixing it can be worse.

A Solution That Does *Not* Conform to the LSP

How do we solve this problem? Several years ago, I solved it by convention. Which is to say that I did not solve it in source code. Rather, I established a convention whereby `PersistentSet` and `PersistentObject` were not known to the application as a whole. They were only known to one particular module. This module was responsible for reading and writing all the containers to and from the persistent store. When a container needed to be written, its contents were copied into appropriate derivatives of `PersistentObject` and then added to `PersistentSet`s, which were then saved on a stream. When a container needed to be read from a stream, the process was inverted. A `PersistentSet` was read from the stream, and then the `PersistentObject`s were removed from the `PersistentSet` and copied into regular (nonpersistent) objects, which were then added to a regular `Set`.

This solution may seem overly restrictive, but it was the only way I could think of to prevent `PersistentSet` objects from appearing at the interface of functions that would want to add nonpersistent objects to them. Moreover, it broke the dependency of the rest of the application on the whole notion of persistence.

Did this solution work? Not really. The convention was violated in several parts of the application by developers who did not understand the necessity for it. That is the problem with conventions—they have to be continually resold to each developer. If the developer has not learned the convention, or does not agree with it, then the convention will be violated. And one violation can compromise the whole structure.

An LSP-Compliant Solution

How would I solve this now? I would acknowledge that a `PersistentSet` does not have an IS-A relationship with `Set`, that it is not a proper derivative of `Set`. Thus, I would separate the hierarchies, but not completely. There are features that `Set` and `PersistentSet` have in common. In fact, it is only the `Add` method that causes the difficulty with LSP. Consequently, I would create a hierarchy in which both `Set` and `PersistentSet` were siblings beneath an abstract interface that allowed for membership testing, iteration, etc. (See Figure 10-4.) This would allow `PersistentSet` objects to be iterated and tested for membership, etc. But it would not afford the ability to add objects that were not derived from `PersistentObject` to a `PersistentSet`.

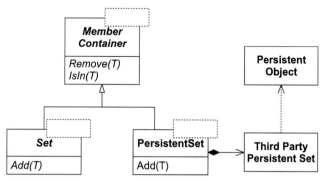

Figure 10-4   A solution that is LSP compliant

Factoring instead of Deriving

Another interesting and puzzling case of inheritance is the case of the `Line` and the `LineSegment`.[9] Consider Listings 10-7 and 10-8. These two classes appear, at first, to be natural candidates for public inheritance. `LineSegment` needs every member variable and every member function declared in `Line`. Moreover, `LineSegment` adds a new member function of its own, `GetLength`, and overrides the meaning of the `IsOn` function. Yet these two classes violate the LSP in a subtle way.

Listing 10-7

geometry/line.h

```
#ifndef GEOMETRY_LINE_H
#define GEOMETRY_LINE_H
#include "geometry/point.h"

class Line
{
  public:
    Line(const Point& p1, const Point& p2);

    double      GetSlope()        const;
    double      GetIntercept()    const; // Y Intercept
    Point       GetP1()           const {return itsP1;};
    Point       GetP2()           const {return itsP2;};
    virtual bool IsOn(const Point&) const;

  private:
    Point itsP1;
    Point itsP2;
};
#endif
```

Listing 10-8

geometry/lineseg.h

```
#ifndef GEOMETRY_LINESEGMENT_H
#define GEOMETRY_LINESEGMENT_H
class LineSegment : public Line
```

<hr>

9.   Despite the similarity that this example has to the Square/Rectangle example, it comes from a real application and was subject to the real problems discussed.

```
{
  public:
    LineSegment(const Point& p1, const Point& p2);
    double      GetLength()        const;
    virtual bool IsOn(const Point&) const;
};
#endif
```

A user of `Line` has a right to expect that all points that are colinear with it are on it. For example, the point returned by the `Intercept` function is the point at which the line intersects the y-axis. Since this point is collinear with the line, users of `Line` have a right to expect that `IsOn(Intercept()) == true`. In many instances of `LineSegment`, however, this statement will fail.

Why is this an important issue? Why not simply derive `LineSegment` from `Line` and live with the subtle problems? This is a judgment call. There are *rare* occasions when it is more expedient to accept a subtle flaw in polymorphic behavior than to attempt to manipulate the design into complete LSP compliance. Accepting compromise instead of pursuing perfection is an engineering trade-off. A good engineer learns when compromise is more *profitable* than perfection. However, conformance to the LSP *should not be surrendered lightly*. The guarantee that a subclass will always work where its base classes are used is a powerful way to manage complexity. Once it is forsaken, we must consider each subclass individually.

In the case of the `Line` and `LineSegment`, there is a simple solution that illustrates an important tool of OOD. If we have access to both the `Line` and `LineSegment` classes, then we can *factor* the common elements of both into an abstract base class. Listings 10-9 through 10-11 show the factoring of `Line` and `LineSegment` into the base class `LinearObject`.

Listing 10-9

geometry/linearobj.h

```
#ifndef GEOMETRY_LINEAR_OBJECT_H
#define GEOMETRY_LINEAR_OBJECT_H

#include "geometry/point.h"

class LinearObject
{
  public:
    LinearObject(const Point& p1, const Point& p2);

    double  GetSlope() const;
    double  GetIntercept() const;

    Point GetP1() const {return itsP1;};
    Point GetP2() const {return itsP2;};
    virtual int    IsOn(const Point&) const = 0; // abstract.

  private:
    Point itsP1;
    Point itsP2;
};
#endif
```

Listing 10-10

`geometry/line.h`

```
#ifndef GEOMETRY_LINE_H
#define GEOMETRY_LINE_H
#include "geometry/linearobj.h"

class Line : public LinearObject
{
  public:
    Line(const Point& p1, const Point& p2);
    virtual bool IsOn(const Point&) const;
};
#endif
```

Listing 10-11

`geometry/lineseg.h`

```
#ifndef GEOMETRY_LINESEGMENT_H
#define GEOMETRY_LINESEGMENT_H
#include "geometry/linearobj.h"

class LineSegment : public LinearObject
{
  public:
    LineSegment(const Point& p1, const Point& p2);

    double      GetLength()        const;
    virtual bool IsOn(const Point&) const;
};
#endif
```

LinearObject represents both Line and LineSegment. It provides most of the functionality and data members for both subclasses, with the exception of the IsOn method, which is pure virtual. Users of LinearObject are not allowed to assume that they understand the extent of the object they are using. Thus, they can accept either a Line or a LineSegment with no problem. Moreover, users of Line will never have to deal with a LineSegment.

Factoring is a design tool that is best applied before there is much code written. Certainly, if there were dozens of clients of the Line class shown in Listing 10-7, we would not have had an easy time of factoring out the LinearObject class. When factoring is possible, however, it is a powerful tool. If qualities can be factored out of two subclasses, there is the distinct possibility that other classes will show up later that need those qualities, too. Of factoring, Rebecca Wirfs–Brock, Brian Wilkerson, and Lauren Wiener say:

> We can state that if a set of classes all support a common responsibility, they should inherit that responsibility from a common superclass.
>
> If a common superclass does not already exist, create one, and move the common responsibilities to it. After all, such a class is demonstrably useful—you have already shown that the responsibilities will be inherited by some classes. Isn't it conceivable that a later extension of your system might add a new subclass that will support those same responsibilities in a new way? This new superclass will probably be an abstract class.[10]

10.   [WirfsBrock90], p. 113.

Listing 10-12 shows how the attributes of `LinearObject` can be used by an unanticipated class, `Ray`. A `Ray` is substitutable for a `LinearObject`, and no user of `LinearObject` would have any trouble dealing with it.

Listing 10-12

`geometry/ray.h`

```
#ifndef GEOMETRY_RAY_H
#define GEOMETRY_RAY_H

class Ray : public LinearObject
{
  public:
    Ray(const Point& p1, const Point& p2);
    virtual bool IsOn(const Point&) const;
};
#endif
```

Heuristics and Conventions

There are some simple heuristics that can give you some clues about LSP violations. They all have to do with derivative classes that somehow *remove* functionality from their base classes. A derivative that does less than its base is usually not substitutable for that base, and therefore violates the LSP.

Degenerate Functions in Derivatives

Consider Listing 10-13. The `f` function in `Base` is implemented. However, in `Derived` it is degenerate. Presumably, the author of `Derived` found that function `f` had no useful purpose in a `Derived`. Unfortunately, the users of `Base` don't know that they shouldn't call `f`, so there is a substitution violation.

Listing 10-13

A degenerate function in a derivative

```
public class Base
{
  public void f() {/*some code*/}
}

public class Derived extends Base
{
  public void f() {}
}
```

The presence of degenerate functions in derivatives is not always indicative of an LSP violation, but it's worth looking at them when they occur.

Throwing Exceptions from Derivatives

Another form of violation is the addition of exceptions to methods of derived classes whose bases don't throw them. If the users of the base classes don't expect exceptions, then adding them to the methods of derivatives is not substitutable. Either the expectations of the users must be altered or the derived classes should not throw the exceptions.

Conclusion

The OCP is at the heart of many of the claims made for OOD. When this principle is in effect, applications are more maintainable, reusable, and robust. The LSP is one of the prime enablers of the OCP. It is the substitutability of subtypes that allows a module, expressed in terms of a base type, to be extensible without modification. That substitutability must be something that developers can depend on implicitly. Thus, the contract of the base type has to be well and prominently understood, if not explicitly enforced, by the code.

The term "IS-A" is too broad to act as a definition of a subtype. The true definition of a subtype is "substitutable," where substitutability is defined by either an explicit or implicit contract.

Bibliography

1. Meyer, Bertrand. *Object-Oriented Software Construction*, 2d ed. Upper Saddle River, NJ: Prentice Hall, 1997.
2. Wirfs–Brock, Rebecca, et al. *Designing Object-Oriented Software*. Englewood Cliffs, NJ: Prentice Hall, 1990.
3. Liskov, Barbara. Data Abstraction and Hierarchy. *SIGPLAN Notices*, 23,5 (May 1988).

11

DIP: The Dependency-Inversion Principle

© Jennifer M. Kohnke

DIP: The Dependency-Inversion Principle

a. High-level modules should not depend on low-level modules. Both should depend on abstractions.
b. Abstractions should not depend on details. Details should depend on abstractions.

Over the years, many have questioned why I use the word "inversion" in the name of this principle. It is because more traditional software development methods, such as Structured Analysis and Design, tend to create software structures in which high-level modules depend on low-level modules, and in which policy depends on detail. Indeed one of the goals of these methods is to define the subprogram hierarchy that describes how the high-level modules make calls to the low-level modules. The initial design of the Copy program in Figure 7-1 on page 90 is a good example of such a hierarchy. The dependency structure of a well-designed, object-oriented program is "inverted" with respect to the dependency structure that normally results from traditional procedural methods.

Consider the implications of high-level modules that depend on low-level modules. It is the high-level modules that contain the important policy decisions and business models of an application. These modules contain the identity of the application. Yet, when these modules depend on the lower level modules, changes to the lower level modules can have direct effects on the higher level modules and can force them to change in turn.

This predicament is absurd! It is the high-level, policy-setting modules that ought to be influencing the low-level, detailed modules. The modules that contain the high-level business rules should take precedence over, and be independent of, the modules that contain the implementation details. High-level modules simply should not depend on low-level modules in any way.

Moreover, it is high-level, policy-setting modules that we want to be able to reuse. We are already quite good at reusing low-level modules in the form of subroutine libraries. When high-level modules depend on low-level modules, it becomes very difficult to reuse those high-level modules in different contexts. However, when the high-level modules are independent of the low-level modules, then the high-level modules can be reused quite simply. This principle is at the very heart of framework design.

Layering

According to Booch, "...all well-structured object-oriented architectures have clearly defined layers, with each layer providing some coherent set of services though a well-defined and controlled interface."[1] A naive interpretation of this statement might lead a designer to produce a structure similar to Figure 11-1. In this diagram, the high-level `Policy` layer uses a lower-level `Mechanism` layer, which in turn uses a detailed-level `Utility` layer. While this may look appropriate, it has the insidious characteristic that the `Policy` layer is sensitive to changes all the way down in the `Utility` layer. *Dependency is transitive*. The `Policy` layer depends on something that depends on the `Utility` layer; thus, the `Policy` layer transitively depends on the `Utility` layer. This is very unfortunate.

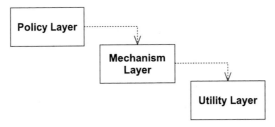

Figure 11-1   Naive layering scheme

Figure 11-2 shows a more appropriate model. Each of the upper-level layers declares an abstract interface for the services that it needs. The lower-level layers are then realized from these abstract interfaces. Each higher-level class uses the next-lowest layer through the abstract interface. Thus, the upper layers do not depend on the lower layers. Instead, the lower layers depend on abstract service interfaces *declared in* the upper layers. Not only is the transitive dependency of `PolicyLayer` on `UtilityLayer` broken, but even the direct dependency of the `PolicyLayer` on `MechanismLayer` is broken.

An Inversion of Ownership

Notice that the inversion here is not just one of dependencies, it is also one of interface ownership. We often think of utility libraries as owning their own interfaces. But when the DIP is applied, we find that the clients tend to own the abstract interfaces and that their servers derive from them.

1.   [Booch96], p. 54.

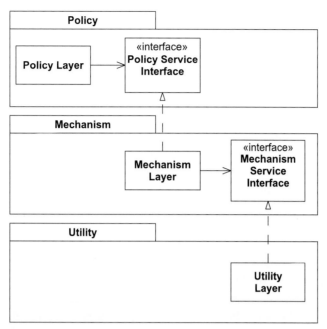

Figure 11-2   Inverted Layers

This is sometimes known as the Hollywood principle: "Don't call us, we'll call you."[2] The lower-level modules provide the implementation for interfaces that are declared within, and called by, the upper-level modules.

Using this inversion of ownership, `PolicyLayer` is unaffected by any changes to `MechanismLayer` or `UtilityLayer`. Moreover, `PolicyLayer` can be reused in any context that defines lower-level modules that conform to the `PolicyServiceInterface`. Thus, by inverting the dependencies, we have created a structure, which is simultaneously more flexible, durable, and mobile.

Depend On Abstractions

A somewhat more naive, yet still very powerful, interpretation of the DIP is the simple heuristic: "Depend on abstractions." Simply stated, this heuristic recommends that you should not depend on a concrete class—that all relationships in a program should terminate on an abstract class or an interface.

According to this heuristic,

- No variable should hold a pointer or reference to a concrete class.
- No class should derive from a concrete class.
- No method should override an implemented method of any of its base classes.

Certainly this heuristic is usually violated at least once in every program. Somebody has to create the instances of the concrete classes, and whatever module does that will depend on them.[3] Moreover, there seems no reason to follow this heuristic for classes that are concrete but nonvolatile. If a concrete class is not going to change very much, and no other similar derivatives are going to be created, then it does very little harm to depend on it.

---

2.   [Sweet85].

3.   Actually, there are ways around this if you can use strings to create classes. Java allows this. So do several other languages. In such languages, the names of the concrete classes can be passed into the program as configuration data.

For example, in most systems the class that describes a string is concrete. In Java, for example, it is the concrete class `String`. This class is not volatile. That is, it does not change very often. Therefore it does no harm to depend directly on it.

However, most concrete classes that *we* write as part of an application program are volatile. It is *those* concrete classes that we do not want to depend directly on. Their volatility can be isolated by keeping them behind an abstract interface.

This is not a complete solution. There are times when the interface of a volatile class must change, and this change must be propagated to the abstract interface that represents the class. Such changes break through the isolation of the abstract interface.

This is the reason that the heuristic is a bit naive. If, on the other hand, we take the longer view that the client classes declare the service interfaces that they need, then the only time the interface will change is when the *client* needs the change. Changes to the classes that implement the abstract interface will not affect the client.

A Simple Example

Dependency inversion can be applied wherever one class sends a message to another. For example, consider the case of the `Button` object and the `Lamp` object.

The `Button` object senses the external environment. On receiving the `Poll` message, it determines whether or not a user has "pressed" it. It doesn't matter what the sensing mechanism is. It could be a button icon on a GUI, a physical button being pressed by a human finger, or even a motion detector in a home security system. The `Button` object detects that a user has either activated or deactivated it.

The `Lamp` object affects the external environment. On receiving a `TurnOn` message, it illuminates a light of some kind. On receiving a `TurnOff` message, it extinguishes that light. The physical mechanism is unimportant. It could be an LED on a computer console, a mercury vapor lamp in a parking lot, or even the laser in a laser printer.

How can we design a system such that the `Button` object controls the `Lamp` object? Figure 11-3 shows a naive design. The `Button` object receives `Poll` messages, determines if the button has been pressed, and then simply sends the `TurnOn` or `TurnOff` message to the `Lamp`.

Figure 11-3   Naive Model of a Button and a Lamp

Why is this naive? Consider the Java code that is implied by this model (Listing 11-1). Note that the `Button` class depends directly on the `Lamp` class. This dependency implies that `Button` will be affected by changes to `Lamp`. Moreover, it will not be possible to reuse `Button` to control a `Motor` object. In this design, `Button` objects control `Lamp` objects, and *only* `Lamp` objects.

Listing 11-1

Button.java

```java
public class Button
{
  private Lamp itsLamp;
  public void poll()
  {
    if (/*some condition*/)
      itsLamp.turnOn();
  }
}
```

This solution violates the DIP. The high-level policy of the application has not been separated from the low-level implementation. The abstractions have not been separated from the details. Without such a separation, the high-level policy automatically depends on the low-level modules, and the abstractions automatically depend on the details.

Finding the Underlying Abstraction

What is the high-level policy? It is the abstraction that underlies the application, the truths that do not vary when the details are changed. It is the system *inside* the system—it is the metaphor. In the Button/Lamp example, the underlying abstraction is to detect an on/off gesture from a user and relay that gesture to a target object. What mechanism is used to detect the user gesture? Irrelevant! What is the target object? Irrelevant! These are details that do not impact the abstraction.

The design in Figure 11-3 can be improved by inverting the dependency on the Lamp object. In Figure 11-4, we see that the Button now holds an association to something called a ButtonServer. ButtonServer provides abstract methods that Button can use to turn something on or off. Lamp implements the ButtonServer interface. Thus, Lamp is now doing the depending, rather than being depended on.

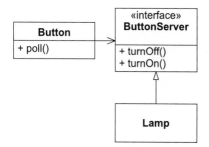

Figure 11-4 Dependency Inversion Applied to the Lamp

The design in Figure 11-4 allows a Button to control any device that is willing to implement the ButtonServer interface. This gives us a great deal of flexibility. It also means that Button objects will be able to control objects that have not yet been invented.

However, this solution also puts a constraint on any object that needs to be controlled by a Button. Such an object *must* implement the ButtonServer interface. This is unfortunate because these objects may also want to be controlled by a Switch object or some object other than a Button.

By inverting the direction of the dependency and making the Lamp do the depending instead of being depended on, we have made Lamp depend on a different detail—Button. Or have we?

Lamp certainly depends on ButtonServer, but ButtonServer does not depend on Button. Any kind of object that knows how to manipulate the ButtonServer interface will be able to control a Lamp. Thus, the dependency is in name only. And we can fix that by changing the name of ButtonServer to something a bit more generic like SwitchableDevice. We can also ensure that Button and SwitchableDevice are kept in separate libraries, so that the use of SwitchableDevice does not imply the use of Button.

In this case, nobody owns the interface. We have the interesting situation where the interface can be used by lots of different clients and implemented by lots of different servers. Thus, the interface needs to stand alone without belonging to either group. In C++, we would put it in a separate namespace and library. In Java we would put it in a separate package.[4]

---

4.   In dynamic languages like Smalltalk, Pyrhon, or Ruby, the interface simply wouldn't exist as an explicit source-code entity.

The Furnace Example

Let's look at a more interesting example. Consider the software that might control the regulator of a furnace. The software can read the current temperature from an IO channel and instruct the furnace to turn on or off by sending commands to a different IO channel. The structure of the algorithm might look something like Listing 11-2.

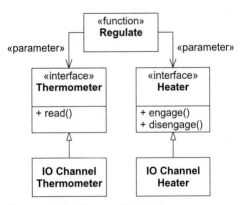

Listing 11-2
Simple algorithm for a thermostat

```
#define TERMOMETER 0x86
#define FURNACE    0x87
#define ENGAGE     1
#define DISENGAGE  0

void Regulate(double minTemp, double maxTemp)
{
  for(;;)
  {
    while (in(THERMOMETER) > minTemp)
      wait(1);
    out(FURNACE,ENGAGE);

    while (in(THERMOMETER) < maxTemp)
      wait(1);
    out(FURNACE,DISENGAGE);
  }
}
```

The high-level intent of the algorithm is clear, but the code is cluttered with lots of low-level details. This code could never be reused with different control hardware.

This may not be much of a loss since the code is very small. But even so, it is a shame to have the algorithm lost for reuse. We'd rather invert the dependencies and see something like Figure 11-5.

```
                        «function»
                         Regulate
       «parameter»                        «parameter»

         «interface»                     «interface»
        Thermometer                         Heater

         + read()                       + engage()
                                        + disengage()

         IO Channel                     IO Channel
        Thermometer                       Heater
```

Figure 11-5   Generic Regulator

This shows that the regulate function takes two arguments that are both interfaces. The Thermometer interface can be read, and the Heater interface can be engaged and disengaged. This is all the Regulate algorithm needs. Now it can be written as shown in Listing 11-3.

Listing 11-3

Generic Regulator

```
void Regulate(Thermometer& t, Heater& h,
              double minTemp, double maxTemp)
{
  for(;;)
  {
    while (t.Read() > minTemp)
      wait(1);
    h.Engage();

    while (t.Read() < maxTemp)
      wait(1);
    h.Disengage();
  }
}
```

This has inverted the dependencies such that the high-level regulation policy does not depend on any of the specific details of the thermometer or the furnace. The algorithm is nicely reusable.

Dynamic v. Static Polymorphism

We have achieved the inversion of the dependencies, and made Regulate generic, through the use of dynamic polymorphism (i.e., abstract classes or interfaces). However, there is another way. We could have used the static form of polymorphism afforded by C++ templates. Consider Listing 11-4.

Listing 11-4

```
template <typename THERMOMETER, typename HEATER>
class Regulate(THERMOMETER& t, HEATER& h,
              double minTemp, double maxTemp)
{
  for(;;)
  {
    while (t.Read() > minTemp)
      wait(1);
    h.Engage();

    while (t.Read() < maxTemp)
      wait(1);
    h.Disengage();
  }
}
```

This achieves the same inversion of dependencies without the overhead (or flexibility) of dynamic polymorphism. In C++, the Read, Engage, and Disengage methods could all be nonvirtual. Moreover, any class that declares these methods can be used by the template. They do not have to inherit from a common base.

As a template, Regulate does not depend on any particular implementation of these functions. All that is required is that the class substituted for HEATER have an Engage and a Disengage method and that the class substituted for THERMOMETER have a Read function. Thus, those classes must implement the interface defined by the template. In other words, both Regulate, and the classes that Regulate uses, must agree on the same interface, and they both depend on that agreement.

Static polymorphism breaks the source-code dependency nicely, but it does not solve as many problems as does dynamic polymorphism. The disadvantages of the template approach are (1) The types of HEATER and THERMOMETER cannot be changed at runtime; and (2) The use of a new kind of HEATER or THERMOMETER will force recompilation and redeployment. So unless you have an extremely stringent requirement for speed, dynamic polymorphism should be preferred.

Conclusion

Traditional procedural programming creates a dependency structure in which policy depends on detail. This is unfortunate since the policies are then vulnerable to changes in the details. Object-oriented programming inverts that dependency structure such that both details and policies depend on abstraction, and service interfaces are often owned by their clients.

Indeed, it is this inversion of dependencies that is the hallmark of good object-oriented design. It doesn't matter what language a program is written in. If its dependencies are inverted, it has an OO design. If its dependencies are not inverted, it has a procedural design.

The principle of dependency inversion is the fundamental low-level mechanism behind many of the benefits claimed for object-oriented technology. Its proper application is necessary for the creation of reusable frameworks. It is also critically important for the construction of code that is resilient to change. Since the abstractions and details are all isolated from each other, the code is much easier to maintain.

Bibliography

1. Booch, Grady. *Object Solutions*. Menlo Park, CA: Addison–Wesley, 1996.
2. Gamma, et al. *Design Patterns*. Reading, MA: Addison–Wesley, 1995.
3. Sweet. Richard E. The Mesa Programming Environment. *SIGPLAN Notices*, 20(7) (July 1985): 216–229.

12

ISP: The Interface-Segregation Principle

This principle deals with the disadvantages of "fat" interfaces. Classes that have "fat" interfaces are classes whose interfaces are not cohesive. In other words, the interfaces of the class can be broken up into groups of methods. Each group serves a different set of clients. Thus, some clients use one group of member functions, and other clients use the other groups.

The ISP acknowledges that there are objects that require noncohesive interfaces; however, it suggests that clients should not know about them as a single class. Instead, clients should know about abstract base classes that have cohesive interfaces.

Interface Pollution

Consider a security system. In this system, there are Door objects that can be locked and unlocked, and which know whether they are open or closed. (See Listing 12-1.)

Listing 12-1
```
Security Door
class Door
{
  public:
    virtual void Lock()   = 0;
    virtual void Unlock() = 0;
    virtual bool IsDoorOpen() = 0;
};
```

This class is abstract so that clients can use objects that conform to the Door interface, without having to depend on particular implementations of Door.

Now consider that one such implementation, TimedDoor, needs to sound an alarm when the door has been left open for too long. In order to do this, the TimedDoor object communicates with another object called a Timer. (See Listing 12-2.)

Listing 12-2
```
class Timer
{
  public:
    void Register(int timeout, TimerClient* client);
};

class TimerClient
{
  public:
    virtual void TimeOut() = 0;
};
```

When an object wishes to be informed about a time-out, it calls the `Register` function of the `Timer`. The arguments of this function are the time of the time-out, and a pointer to a `TimerClient` object whose `TimeOut` function will be called when the time-out expires.

How can we get the `TimerClient` class to communicate with the `TimedDoor` class so that the code in the `TimedDoor` can be notified of the time-out? There are several alternatives. Figure 12-1 shows a naive solution. We force `Door`, and therefore `TimedDoor`, to inherit from `TimerClient`. This ensures that `TimerClient` can register itself with the `Timer` and receive the `TimeOut` message.

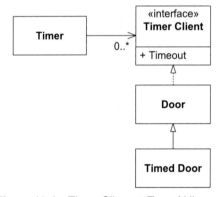

Figure 12-1   Timer Client at Top of Hierarchy

Although this solution is common, it is not without problems. Chief among these is that the `Door` class now depends on `TimerClient`. Not all varieties of `Door` need timing. Indeed, the original `Door` abstraction had nothing whatever to do with timing. If timing-free derivatives of `Door` are created, those derivatives will have to provide degenerate implementations for the `TimeOut` method—a potential violation of the LSP. Moreover, the applications that use those derivatives will have to import the definition of the `TimerClient` class, even though it is not used. That smells of **Needless Complexity** and **Needless Redundancy**.

This is an example of interface pollution, a syndrome that is common in statically typed languages like C++ and Java. The interface of `Door` has been polluted with a method that it does not require. It has been forced to incorporate this method solely for the benefit of one of its subclasses. If this practice is pursued, then every time a derivative needs a new method, that method will be added to the base class. This will further pollute the interface of the base class, making it "fat."

Moreover, each time a new method is added to the base class, that method must be implemented (or allowed to default) in derived classes. Indeed, an associated practice is to add these interfaces to the base class giving them degenerate implementations, specifically so that derived classes are not burdened with the need to implement them. As we learned previously, such a practice can violate the LSP, leading to maintenance and reusability problems.

Separate Clients Mean Separate Interfaces

`Door` and `TimerClient` represent interfaces that are used by completely different clients. `Timer` uses `TimerClient`, and classes that manipulate doors use `Door`. Since the clients are separate, the interfaces should remain separate, too. Why? Because clients exert forces on the interfaces they use.

The Backwards Force Applied by Clients On Interfaces

When we think of forces that cause changes in software, we normally think about how changes to interfaces will affect their users. For example, we would be concerned about the changes to all the users of `TimerClient` if the `TimerClient` interface changed. However, there is a force that operates in the other direction. Sometimes it is the *user* that forces a change to the interface.

For example, some users of `Timer` will register more than one time-out request. Consider the `TimedDoor`. When it detects that the `Door` has been opened, it sends the `Register` message to the `Timer`, requesting a time-out. However, before that time-out expires, the door closes, remains closed for a while, and then opens again. This causes us to register a *new* time-out request before the old one has expired. Finally, the first time-out request expires and the `TimeOut` function of the `TimedDoor` is invoked. The `Door` alarms falsely.

We can correct this situation by using the convention shown in Listing 12-3. We include a unique `timeOutId` code in each time-out registration, and we repeat that code in the `TimeOut` call to the `TimerClient`. This allows each derivative of `TimerClient` to know which time-out request is being responded to.

Listing 12-3
```
Timer with ID
class Timer
{
  public:
    void Register(int timeout,
                  int timeOutId,
                  TimerClient* client);
};

class TimerClient
{
  public:
    virtual void TimeOut(int timeOutId) = 0;
};
```

Clearly this change will affect all the users of `TimerClient`. We accept this since the lack of the `timeOutId` is an oversight that needs correction. However, the design in Figure 12-1 will also cause `Door`, and all clients of `Door` to be affected by this fix! This smells of Rigidity and Viscosity. Why should a bug in `TimerClient` have *any* affect on clients of `Door` derivatives that do not require timing? When a change in one part of the program affects other completely unrelated parts of the program, the cost and repercussions of changes become unpredictable, and the risk of fallout from the change increases dramatically.

ISP: The Interface-Segregation Principle

> *Clients should not be forced to depend on methods that they do not use.*

When clients are forced to depend on methods that they don't use, then those clients are subject to changes to those methods. This results in an inadvertent coupling between all the clients. Said another way, when a client depends on a class that contains methods that the client does not use, but that other clients *do* use, then that client will be affected by the changes that those other clients force upon the class. We would like to avoid such couplings where possible, and so we want to separate the interfaces.

Class Interfaces v. Object Interfaces

Consider the `TimedDoor` again. Here is an object which has two separate interfaces used by two separate clients— `Timer` and the users of `Door`. These two interfaces *must* be implemented in the same object, since the implementation of both interfaces manipulates the same data. So how can we conform to the ISP? How can we separate the interfaces when they must remain together?

The answer to this lies in the fact that clients of an object do not need to access it through the interface of the object. Rather, they can access it through delegation or through a base class of the object.

Separation through Delegation

One solution is to create an object that derives from `TimerClient` and delegates to the `TimedDoor`. Figure 12-2 shows this solution.

When the `TimedDoor` wants to register a time-out request with the `Timer`, it creates a `DoorTimerAdapter` and registers it with the `Timer`. When the `Timer` sends the `TimeOut` message to the `DoorTimerAdapter`, the `DoorTimerAdapter` delegates the message back to the `TimedDoor`.

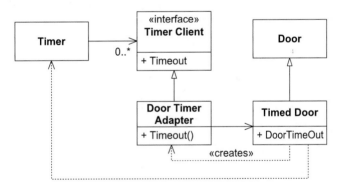

Figure 12-2   Door Timer Adapter

This solution conforms to the ISP and prevents the coupling of `Door` clients to `Timer`. Even if the change to `Timer` shown in Listing 12-3 were to be made, none of the users of `Door` would be affected. Moreover, `TimedDoor` does not have to have the exact same interface as `TimerClient`. The `DoorTimerAdapter` can *translate* the `TimerClient` interface into the `TimedDoor` interface. Thus, this is a very general purpose solution. (See Listing 12-4.)

Listing 12-4

TimedDoor.cpp

```
class TimedDoor : public Door
{
  public:
    virtual void DoorTimeOut(int timeOutId);
};

class DoorTimerAdapter : public TimerClient
{
  public:
    DoorTimerAdapter(TimedDoor& theDoor)
```

refer to the same object! In the future, it may be that the interface objects are separated for some reason. The fact that all interfaces are combined into a single object is information that g does not need to know. Thus, I prefer the polyadic form for such functions.

Grouping Clients.   Clients can often be grouped together by the service methods they call. Such groupings allow segregated interfaces to be created for each group instead of each client. This greatly reduces the number of interfaces that the service has to implement, and it also prevents the service from depending on each client type.

Sometimes, the methods invoked by different groups of clients will overlap. If the overlap is small, then the interfaces for the groups should remain separate. The common functions should be declared in all the overlapping interfaces. The server class will inherit the common functions from each of those interfaces, but it will implement them only once.

Changing Interfaces.   When object-oriented applications are maintained, the interfaces to existing classes and components often change. There are times when these changes have a huge impact and force the recompilation and redeployment of a very large part of the system. This impact can be mitigated by adding new interfaces to existing objects, rather than changing the existing interface. Clients of the old interface that wish to access methods of the new interface can query the object for that interface, as shown in Listing 12-10.

Listing 12-10

```
void Client(Service* s)
{
  if (NewService* ns = dynamic_cast<NewService*>(s))
  {
    // use the new service interface
  }
}
```

As with all principles, care must be taken not to overdo it. The spectre of a class with hundreds of different interfaces, some segregated by client and others segregated by version, would be frightening indeed.

Conclusion

Fat classes cause bizarre and harmful couplings between their clients. When one client forces a change on the fat class, all the other clients are affected. Thus, clients should only have to depend on methods that they actually call. This can be achieved by breaking the interface of the fat class into many client-specific interfaces. Each client-specific interface declares only those functions that its particular client, or client group, invoke. The fat class can then inherit all the client-specific interfaces and implement them. This breaks the dependence of the clients on methods that they don't invoke, and it allows the clients to be independent of each other.

Bibliography

1.   Gamma, et al. *Design Patterns*. Reading, MA: Addison–Wesley, 1995.

SECTION 3

The Payroll Case Study

© Jennifer M. Kohnke

The time has come for our first major case study. We have studied practices and principles. We have discussed the essence of design. We have talked about testing and planning. Now we need to do some real work.

In the next several chapters, we are going to explore the design and implementation of a batch payroll system. A rudimentary specification of that system is included later. As part of that design and implementation, we will find ourselves making use of several different design patterns. Among those patterns are COMMAND, TEMPLATE METHOD, STRATEGY, SINGLETON, NULL OBJECT, FACTORY, and FACADE. These patterns are the topic of the next several chapters. Then, in Chapter 18, we work through the design and implementation of the Payroll problem.

There are several ways to read through this case study:

- Read straight through, first learning the design patterns and then seeing how they are applied to the payroll problem.
- If you know the patterns and are not interested in a review, then go right to Chapter 18.
- Read Chapter 18 first, and then go back and read through the chapters that describe the patterns that were used.
- Read Chapter 18 in bits. When it talks about a pattern with which you are unfamiliar, read through the chapter that describes that pattern, and then return to Chapter 18.
- Indeed, there are no rules. Pick, or invent, the strategy that works best for you.

Rudimentary Specification of the Payroll System

The following are some of the notes we took while conversing with our customer.

This system consists of a database of the employees in the company and their associated data, such as time cards. The system must pay each employee. Employees must be paid the correct amount, on time, by the method that they specify. Also, various deductions must be taken from their pay.

- Some employees work by the hour. They are paid an hourly rate that is one of the fields in their employee record. They submit daily time cards that record the date and the number of hours worked. If they work more than 8 hours per day, they are paid 1.5 times their normal rate for those extra hours. They are paid every Friday.
- Some employees are paid a flat salary. They are paid on the last working day of the month. Their monthly salary is one of the fields in their employee record.
- Some of the salaried employees are also paid a commission based on their sales. They submit sales receipts that record the date and the amount of the sale. Their commission rate is a field in their employee record. They are paid every other Friday.
- Employees can select their method of payment. They may have their paychecks mailed to the postal address of their choice; they may have their paychecks held for pickup by the Paymaster; or they can request that their paychecks be directly deposited into the bank account of their choice.
- Some employees belong to the union. Their employee record has a field for the weekly dues rate. Their dues must be deducted from their pay. Also, the union may assess service charges against individual union members from time to time. These service charges are submitted by the union on a weekly basis and must be deducted from the appropriate employee's next pay amount.
- The payroll application will run once each working day and pay the appropriate employees on that day. The system will be told to what date the employees are to be paid, so it will calculate payments from the last time the employee was paid up to the specified date.

Exercise

Before you continue, you might find it instructive to design the payroll system on your own, now. You might want to sketch some initial UML diagrams. Better yet, you might want to implement the first few use cases test-first. Apply the principles and practices we've learned so far, and try to create a balanced and healthy design.

If you are going to do this, then take a look at the use cases that follow. Otherwise skip them, they'll be presented again in the Payroll chapter.

Use Case 1: Add New Employee

A new employee is added by the receipt of an `AddEmp` transaction. This transaction contains the employee's name, address, and assigned employee number. The transaction has the following three forms:

```
AddEmp <EmpID> "<name>" "<address>" H <hourly-rate>
AddEmp <EmpID> "<name>" "<address>" S <monthly-salary>
AddEmp <EmpID> "<name>" "<address>" C <monthly-salary> <commission-rate>
```

The employee record is created with its fields assigned appropriately.

Alternative:
An error in the transaction structure

If the transaction structure is inappropriate, it is printed out in an error message, and no action is taken.

Use Case 2: Deleting an Employee

Employees are deleted when a `DelEmp` transaction is received. The form of this transaction is as follows:

```
DelEmp <EmpID>
```

When this transaction is received, the appropriate employee record is deleted.

Alternative:
Invalid or unknown EmpID

If the `<EmpID>` field is not structured correctly, or if it does not refer to a valid employee record, then the transaction is printed with an error message, and no other action is taken.

Use Case 3: Post a Time Card

Upon receipt of a `TimeCard` transaction, the system will create a time-card record and associate it with the appropriate employee record.

```
TimeCard <Empld> <date> <hours>
```

Alternative 1:
The selected employee is not hourly

The system will print an appropriate error message and take no further action.

Alternative 2:
An error in the transaction structure

The system will print an appropriate error message and take no further action.

Use Case 4: Posting a Sales Receipt

Upon receipt of the `SalesReceipt` transaction, the system will create a new sales-receipt record and associate it with the appropriate commissioned employee.

```
SalesReceipt <EmpID> <date> <amount>
```

Alternative 1:
The selected employee is not commissioned

The system will print an appropriate error message and take no further action.

Alternative 2:
An error in the transaction structure

The system will print an appropriate error message and take no further action.

Use Case 5: Posting a Union Service Charge

Upon receipt of this transaction, the system will create a service-charge record and associate it with the appropriate union member.

```
ServiceCharge <memberID> <amount>
```

Alternative:
Poorly formed transaction

If the transaction is not well formed or if the `<memberID>` does not refer to an existing union member, then the transaction is printed with an appropriate error message.

Use Case 6: Changing Employee Details

Upon receipt of this transaction, the system will alter one of the details of the appropriate employee record. There are several possible variations to this transaction.

`ChgEmp <EmpID> Name <name>`	Change Employee Name
`ChgEmp <EmpID> Address <address>`	Change Employee Address
`ChgEmp <EmpID> Hourly <hourlyRate>`	Change to Hourly
`ChgEmp <EmpID> Salaried <salary>`	Change to Salaried
`ChgEmp <EmpID> Commissioned <salary> <rate>`	Change to Commissioned
`ChgEmp <EmpID> Hold`	Hold Paycheck
`ChgEmp <EmpID> Direct <bank> <account>`	Direct Deposit
`ChgEmp <EmpID> Mail <address>`	Mail Paycheck
`ChgEmp <EmpID> Member <memberID> Dues <rate>`	Put Employee in Union
`ChgEmp <EmpID> NoMember`	Remove Employee from Union

Alternative:
Transaction Errors

If the structure of the transaction is improper or `<EmpID>` does not refer to a real employee or `<memberID>` already refers to a member, then print a suitable error and take no further action.

Use Case 7: Run the Payroll for Today

Upon receipt of the Payday transaction, the system finds all those employees that should be paid upon the specified date. The system then determines how much they are owed and pays them according to their selected payment method.

```
Payday <date>
```

13

COMMAND and ACTIVE OBJECT

No man has received from nature the right to command his fellow human beings.

—Denis Diderot (1713–1784)

Of all the design patterns that have been described over the years, COMMAND impresses me as one of the simplest and most elegant. As we shall see, the simplicity is deceptive. The range of uses that COMMAND may be put to is probably without bound.

The simplicity of COMMAND, as shown in Figure 13-1, is almost laughable. Listing 13-1 doesn't do much to dampen the levity. It seems absurd that we can have a pattern that consists of nothing more than an interface with one method.

Figure 13-1 COMMAND Pattern

Listing 13-1

Command.java

```java
public interface Command
{
  public void do();
}
```

But, in fact, a very interesting line has been crossed by this pattern. And it is in the crossing of this line that all the interesting complexity lies. Most classes associate a suite of methods with a corresponding set of variables. The COMMAND pattern does not do this. Rather, it encapsulates a function free of any variables.

In strict object-oriented terms, this is anathema—it smacks of functional decomposition. It elevates the role of a function to the level of a class. Blasphemy! Yet, at this boundary where two paradigms clash, interesting things start to occur.

Simple Commands

Several years ago, I consulted for a large firm that made photocopiers. I was helping one of their development teams with the design and implementation of the embedded real-time software that drove the inner workings of a new copier. We stumbled on the idea of using the COMMAND pattern to control the hardware devices. We created a hierarchy that looked something like Figure 13-2.

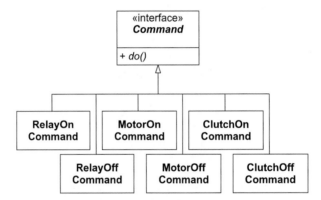

Figure 13-2   Some Simple Commands for the Copier software

The role of these classes should be obvious. When you call do() on a `RelayOnCommand`, it turns some relay on. When you call do() on a `MotorOffCommand`, it turns some motor off. The address of the motor or relay is passed into the object as an argument to its constructor.

With this structure in place, we could now pass `Command` objects around the system and do() them without knowing precisely what kind of `Command` they represented. This led to some interesting simplifications.

The system was event driven. Relays opened or closed, motors started or stopped, and clutches engaged or disengaged based on certain events that took place in the system. Many of those events were detected by sensors. For example, when an optical sensor determined that a sheet of paper had reached a certain point in the paper path, we'd need to engage a certain clutch. We were able to implement this by simply binding the appropriate `ClutchOnCommand` to the object that controlled that particular optical sensor. (See Figure 13-3.)

Figure 13-3   A Command driven by a Sensor

This simple structure has an enormous advantage. The `Sensor` has no idea what it is doing. Whenever it detects an event, it simply calls do() on the `Command` that it is bound to. This means that the `Sensor`s don't have to know about individual clutches or relays. They don't have to know the mechanical structure of the paper path. Their function becomes remarkably simple.

The complexity of determining which relays to close when certain sensors declare events has moved to an initialization function. At some point during the initialization of the system, each `Sensor` is bound to an appropriate `Command`. This puts all the *wiring*[1] in one place and gets it out of the main body of the system. Indeed, it would be possible to create a simple text file that described which `Sensors` were bound to which `Commands`. The initialization program could read this file and build the system appropriately. Thus, the *wiring* of the system could be determined completely outside the program, and it could be adjusted without recompilation.

By encapsulating the *notion* of a command, this pattern allowed us to decouple the logical interconnections of the system from the devices that were being connected. This was a huge benefit.

Transactions

Another common use of the COMMAND pattern, and one that we will find useful in the Payroll problem, is in the creation and execution of transactions. Imagine, for example, that we are writing the software that maintains a database of employees. (See Figure 13-4.) There are a number of operations that users can apply to that database. They can add new employees, delete old employees, or change the attributes of existing employees.

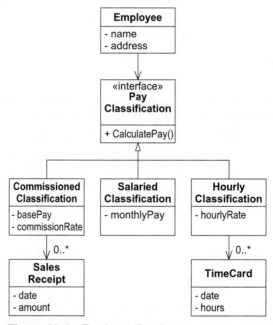

Figure 13-4   Employee Database

When a user decides to add a new employee, that user must specify all the information needed to successfully create the employee record. Before acting on that information, the system needs to verify that the information is syntactically and semantically correct. The COMMAND pattern can help with this job. The `command` object acts as a repository for the unvalidated data, implements the validation methods, and implements the methods that finally execute the transaction.

For example, consider Figure 13-5. The `AddEmployeeTransaction` contains the same data fields that `Employee` contains. It also holds a pointer to a `PayClassification` object. These fields and object are created from the data that the user specifies when directing the system to add a new employee.

The `validate` method looks over all the data and makes sure it makes sense. It checks it for syntactic and semantic correctness. It may even check to ensure that the data in the transaction are consistent with the existing state of the database. For example, it might ensure that no such employee already exists.

---

1.   The logical interconnections between the `Sensors` and `Commands`.

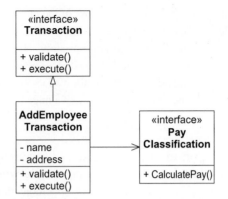

Figure 13-5 `AddEmployee` Transaction

The `execute` method uses the validated data to update the database. In our simple example, a new `Employee` object would be created and loaded with the fields from the `AddEmployeeTransaction` object. The `PayClassification` object would be moved or copied into the `Employee`.

Physical and Temporal Decoupling

The benefit this gives us is in the dramatic decoupling between the code that procures the data from the user, the code that validates and operates on that data, and the business objects themselves. For example, one might expect the data for adding a new employee to be procured from a dialog box in some GUI. It would be a shame if the GUI code contained the validation and execution algorithms for the transaction. Such a coupling would prevent that validation and execution code from being used with other interfaces. By separating the validation and execution code into the `AddEmployeeTransaction` class, we have physically decoupled that code from the procurement interface. What's more, we've separated the code that knows how to manipulate the logistics of the database from the business entities themselves.

Temporal Decoupling

We have also decoupled the validation and execution code in a different way. Once the data have been procured, there is no reason why the validation and execution methods must be called immediately. The transaction objects can be held in a list and validated and executed much later.

Suppose we have a database that must remain unchanged during the day. Changes may only be applied during the hours between midnight and 1 A.M. It would be a shame to have to wait until midnight and then have to rush to type in all the commands before 1 A.M. It would be much more convenient to type in all the commands, have them validated on the spot, and then executed later at midnight. The COMMAND pattern gives us this ability.

UNDO

Figure 13-6 adds the `undo()` method to the COMMAND pattern. It stands to reason that if the `do()` method of a `Command` derivative can be implemented to remember the details of the operation it performs, then the `undo()` method can be implemented to undo that operation and return the system to its original state.

Figure 13-6 Undo variation of the COMMAND Pattern.

Imagine, for example, an application that allows the user to draw geometric shapes on the screen. A toolbar has buttons that allow the user to draw circles, squares, rectangles, etc. Let's say that the user clicks on the *draw circle* button. The system creates a `DrawCircleCommand` and then calls `do()` on that command. The `DrawCircleCommand` object tracks the user's mouse waiting for a click in the drawing window. On receiving that click, it sets the click point as the center of the circle and proceeds to draw an animated circle at that center with a radius that tracks the current mouse position. When the user clicks again, the `DrawCircleCommand` stops animating the circle and adds the appropriate circle object to the list of shapes currently displayed on the canvas. It also stores the ID of the new circle in some private variable of its own. Then it returns from the `do()` method. The system then pushes the expended `DrawCirlceCommand` on the stack of completed commands.

Later, the user clicks the undo button on the toolbar. The system pops the completed commands stack and calls `undo()` on the resulting `Command` object. on receiving the `undo()` message, the `DrawCircleCommand` object deletes the circle matching the saved ID from the list of objects currently displayed on the canvas.

With this technique, you can easily implement the `undo` command in nearly any application. The code that knows how to undo a command is always right next to the code that knows how to perform the command.

ACTIVE OBJECT

One of my favorite uses of the COMMAND pattern is the ACTIVE OBJECT pattern.[2] This is a very old technique for implementing multiple threads of control. It has been used, in one form or another, to provide a simple multitasking nucleus for thousands of industrial systems.

The idea is very simple. Consider Listings 13-2 and 13-3. An `ActiveObjectEngine` object maintains a linked list of `Command` objects. Users can add new commands to the engine, or they can call `run()`. The `run()` function simply walks through the linked list executing and removing each command.

Listing 13-2

ActiveObjectEngine.java

```
import java.util.LinkedList;
import java.util.Iterator;

public class ActiveObjectEngine
{
  LinkedList itsCommands = new LinkedList();

  public void addCommand(Command c)
  {
    itsCommands.add(c);
  }

  public void run()
  {
    while (!itsCommands.isEmpty())
    {
      Command c = (Command) itsCommands.getFirst();
      itsCommands.removeFirst();
      c.execute();
    }
  }
}
```

2.   [Lavender96].

Listing 13-3

Command.java

```
public interface Command
{
  public void execute() throws Exception;
}
```

This may not seem very impressive. But imagine what would happen if one of the Command objects in the linked list cloned itself and then put the clone back on the list. The list would never go empty, and the run() function would never return.

Consider the test case in Listing 13-4. It creates something called a SleepCommand. Among other things, it passes a delay of 1000 ms to the constructor of the SleepCommand. It then puts the SleepCommand into the ActiveObjectEngine. After calling run(), it expects that a certain number of milliseconds has elapsed.

Listing 13-4

TestSleepCommand.java

```
import junit.framework.*;
import junit.swingui.TestRunner;

public class TestSleepCommand extends TestCase
{
  public static void main(String[] args)
  {
    TestRunner.main(new String[]{"TestSleepCommand"});
  }

  public TestSleepCommand(String name)
  {
    super(name);
  }

  private boolean commandExecuted = false;

  public void testSleep() throws Exception
  {
    Command wakeup = new Command()
    {
      public void execute() {commandExecuted = true;}
    };
    ActiveObjectEngine e = new ActiveObjectEngine();
    SleepCommand c = new SleepCommand(1000,e,wakeup);
    e.addCommand(c);
    long start = System.currentTimeMillis();
    e.run();
    long stop = System.currentTimeMillis();
    long sleepTime = (stop-start);
    assert("SleepTime " + sleepTime + " expected > 1000",
           sleepTime > 1000);
    assert("SleepTime " + sleepTime + " expected < 1100",
           sleepTime < 1100);
    assert("Command Executed", commandExecuted);
  }
}
```

Let's look at this test case more closely. The constructor of the `SleepCommand` contains three arguments. The first is the delay time in milliseconds. The second is the `ActiveObjectEngine` that the command will be running in. Finally, there is another command object called `wakeup`. The intent is that the `SleepCommand` will wait for the specified number of milliseconds and will then execute the `wakeup` command.

Listing 13-5 shows the implementation of `SleepCommand`. On execution, `SleepCommand` checks to see if it has been executed previously. If not, then it records the start time. If the delay time has not passed, it puts itself back in the `ActiveObjectEngine`. If the delay time has passed, it puts the `wakeup` command into the `ActiveObjectEngine`.

Listing 13-5

SleepCommand.java

```java
public class SleepCommand implements Command
{
  private Command wakeupCommand = null;
  private ActiveObjectEngine engine = null;
  private long sleepTime = 0;
  private long startTime = 0;
  private boolean started = false;

  public SleepCommand(long milliseconds, ActiveObjectEngine e,
                      Command wakeupCommand)
  {
    sleepTime = milliseconds;
    engine = e;
    this.wakeupCommand = wakeupCommand;
  }

  public void execute() throws Exception
  {
    long currentTime = System.currentTimeMillis();
    if (!started)
    {
      started = true;
      startTime = currentTime;
      engine.addCommand(this);
    }
    else if ((currentTime - startTime) < sleepTime)
    {
      engine.addCommand(this);
    }
    else
    {
      engine.addCommand(wakeupCommand);
    }
  }
}
```

We can draw an analogy between this program and a multithreaded program that is waiting for an event. When a thread in a multithreaded program waits for an event, it usually invokes some operating system call that blocks the thread until the event has occurred. The program in Listing 13-5 does not block. Instead, if the event it is waiting for (`(currentTime - startTime) < sleepTime`) has not occurred, it simply puts itself back into the `ActiveObjectEngine`.

Building multithreaded systems using variations of this technique has been, and will continue to be, a very common practice. Threads of this kind have been known as *run-to-completion* tasks (RTC), because each Command instance runs to completion before the next Command instance can run. The name RTC implies that the Command instances do not block.

The fact that the Command instances all run to completion gives RTC threads the interesting advantage that they all share the same run-time stack. Unlike the threads in a traditional multithreaded system, it is not necessary to define or allocate a separate run-time stack for each RTC thread. This can be a powerful advantage in memory-constrained systems with many threads.

Continuing our example, Listing 13-6 shows a simple program that makes use of SleepCommand and exhibits its multithreaded behavior. This program is called DelayedTyper.

Listing 13-6

DelayedTyper.java

```java
public class DelayedTyper implements Command
{
  private long itsDelay;
  private char itsChar;
  private static ActiveObjectEngine engine =
    new ActiveObjectEngine();
  private static boolean stop = false;

  public static void main(String args[])
  {
    engine.addCommand(new DelayedTyper(100,'1'));
    engine.addCommand(new DelayedTyper(300,'3'));
    engine.addCommand(new DelayedTyper(500,'5'));
    engine.addCommand(new DelayedTyper(700,'7'));

    Command stopCommand = new Command()
    {
      public void execute() {stop=true;}
    };

    engine.addCommand(
      new SleepCommand(20000,engine,stopCommand));
    engine.run();
  }

  public DelayedTyper(long delay, char c)
  {
    itsDelay = delay;
    itsChar = c;
  }

  public void execute() throws Exception
  {
    System.out.print(itsChar);
    if (!stop)
      delayAndRepeat();
  }
```

```
private void delayAndRepeat() throws Exception
{
  engine.addCommand(new SleepCommand(itsDelay,engine,this));
}
}
```

Notice that `DelayedTyper` implements `Command`. The `execute` method simply prints a character that was passed at construction, checks the `stop` flag, and, if not set, invokes `delayAndRepeat`. The `delayAndRepeat` method constructs a `SleepCommand`, using the delay that was passed in at construction. It then inserts the `SleepCommand` into the `ActiveObjectEngine`.

The behavior of this `Command` is easy to predict. In effect, it hangs in a loop repeatedly typing a specified character and waiting for a specified delay. It exits the loop when the `stop` flag is set.

The main program of `DelayedTyper` starts several `DelayedTyper` instances going in the `ActiveObjectEngine`, each with its own character and delay. It then invokes a `SleepCommand` that will set the `stop` flag after a while. Running this program produces a simple string of 1's, 3's, 5's and 7's. Running it again produces a similar, but different string. Here are two typical runs:

```
13571131151137111315113171513111315173111351113711531111357...
13571113151317113151131171351113115173111315113171135111357...
```

These strings are different because the CPU clock and the real-time clock aren't in perfect sync. This kind of nondeterministic behavior is the hallmark of multithreaded systems.

Nondeterministic behavior is also the source of much woe, anguish, and pain. As anyone who has worked on embedded real-time systems knows, it's tough to debug nondeterministic behavior.

Conclusion

The simplicity of the COMMAND pattern belies its versatility. COMMAND can be used for a wonderful variety of purposes ranging from database transactions, to device control, to multithreaded nuclei, to GUI do/undo administration.

It has been suggested that the COMMAND pattern breaks the OO paradigm because it emphasizes functions over classes. That may be true, but in the real world of the software developer, the COMMAND pattern can be very useful.

Bibliography

1. Gamma, et al. *Design Patterns*. Reading, MA: Addison–Wesley, 1995.
2. Lavender, R. G., and D. C. Schmidt. *Active Object: An Object Behavioral Pattern for Concurrent Programming*, in "Pattern Languages of Program Design" (J. O. Coplien, J. Vlissides, and N. Kerth, eds.). Reading, MA: Addison–Wesley, 1996.

14

TEMPLATE METHOD & STRATEGY: Inheritance vs. Delegation

"The best strategy in life is diligence."

—Chinese Proverb

Way, way back in the early 90s—back in the early days of OO—we were all quite taken with the notion of inheritance. The implications of the relationship were profound. With inheritance we could *program by difference*! That is, given some class that did something almost useful to us, we could create a subclass and change only the bits we didn't like. We could reuse code simply by inheriting it! We could establish whole taxonomies of software structures, each level of which reused code from the levels above. It was a brave new world.

Like most brave new worlds, this one turned out to be a bit too starry eyed. By 1995, it was clear that inheritance was very easy to overuse and that overuse of inheritance was very costly. Gamma, Helm, Johnson, and Vlissides went so far as to stress, *"Favor object composition over class inheritance."*[1] So we cut back on our use of inheritance, often replacing it with composition or delegation.

This chapter is the story of two patterns that epitomize the difference between inheritance and delegation. TEMPLATE METHOD and STRATEGY solve similar problems and can often be used interchangeably. However, TEMPLATE METHOD uses inheritance to solve the problem, whereas STRATEGY uses delegation.

TEMPLATE METHOD and STRATEGY both solve the problem of separating a generic algorithm from a detailed context. We see the need for this very frequently in software design. We have an algorithm that is generically applicable. In order to conform to the Dependency-Inversion Principle (DIP), we want to make sure that the

---

1.   [GOF95], p. 20.

generic algorithm does not depend on the detailed implementation. Rather, we want the generic algorithm and the detailed implementation to depend on abstractions.

TEMPLATE METHOD

Consider all the programs you have written. Many probably have this fundamental main-loop structure.

```
Initialize();
while (!done()) // main loop
{
  Idle();         // do something useful.
}
Cleanup();
```

First we initialize the application. Then we enter the main loop. In the main loop we do whatever the program needs us to do. We might process GUI events or perhaps process database records. Finally, once we are done, we exit the main loop and clean up before we exit.

This structure is so common that we can capture it in a class named `Application`. Then we can reuse that class for every new program we want to write. Think of it! We never have to write that loop again![2]

For example, consider Listing 14-1. Here we see all the elements of the standard program. The `InputStreamReader` and `BufferedReader` are initialized. There is a main loop that reads Fahrenheit readings from the `BufferedReader` and prints out Celsius conversions. At the end, an exit message is printed.

Listing 14-1

ftoc raw

```java
import java.io.*;
public class ftocraw
{
  public static void main(String[] args) throws Exception
  {
    InputStreamReader isr = new InputStreamReader(System.in);
    BufferedReader br = new BufferedReader(isr);
    boolean done = false;
    while (!done)
    {
      String fahrString = br.readLine();
      if (fahrString == null || fahrString.length() == 0)
        done = true;
      else
      {
        double fahr = Double.parseDouble(fahrString);
        double celcius = 5.0/9.0*(fahr-32);
        System.out.println("F=" + fahr + ", C=" + celcius);
      }
    }
    System.out.println("ftoc exit");
  }
}
```

This program has all the elements of the main-loop structure. It does a little initialization, does its work in a main loop, and then cleans up and exits.

---

2.   I've also got this bridge I'd like to sell you.

We can separate this fundamental structure from the `ftoc` program by employing the TEMPLATE METHOD pattern. This pattern places all the generic code into an implemented method of an abstract base class. The implemented method captures the generic algorithm, but defers all details to abstract methods of the base class.

So, for example, we can capture the main-loop structure in an abstract base class called `Application`. (See Listing 14-2.)

Listing 14-2

Application.java

```java
public abstract class Application
{
  private boolean isDone = false;

  protected abstract void init();
  protected abstract void idle();
  protected abstract void cleanup();

  protected void setDone()
  {isDone = true;}

  protected boolean done()
  {return isDone;}

  public void run()
  {
    init();
    while (!done())
      idle();
    cleanup();
  }
}
```

This class describes a generic main-loop application. We can see the main loop in the implemented `run` function. We can also see that all the work is being deferred to the abstract methods `init`, `idle`, and `cleanup`. The `init` method takes care of any initialization we need done. The `idle` method does the main work of the program and will be called repeatedly until `setDone` is called. The `cleanup` method does whatever needs to be done before we exit.

We can rewrite the `ftoc` class by inheriting from `Application` and just filling in the abstract methods. Listing 14-3 show what this looks like.

Listing 14-3

ftocTemplateMethod.java

```java
import java.io.*;
public class ftocTemplateMethod extends Application
{
  private InputStreamReader isr;
  private BufferedReader br;

  public static void main(String[] args) throws Exception
  {
    (new ftocTemplateMethod()).run();
  }
```

```java
  protected void init()
  {
    isr = new InputStreamReader(System.in);
    br = new BufferedReader(isr);
  }

  protected void idle()
  {
    String fahrString = readLineAndReturnNullIfError();
    if (fahrString == null || fahrString.length() == 0)
      setDone();
    else
    {
      double fahr = Double.parseDouble(fahrString);
      double celcius = 5.0/9.0*(fahr-32);
      System.out.println("F=" + fahr + ", C=" + celcius);
    }
  }

  protected void cleanup()
  {
    System.out.println("ftoc exit");
  }

  private String readLineAndReturnNullIfError()
  {
    String s;
    try
    {
      s = br.readLine();
    }
    catch(IOException e)
    {
      s = null;
    }
    return s;
  }
}
```

Dealing with the exception made the code get a little longer, but it's easy to see how the old `ftoc` application has been fit into the TEMPLATE METHOD pattern.

Pattern Abuse

By this time you should be thinking, "*Is he serious? Does he really expect me to use this* `Application` *class for all new apps? It hasn't bought me anything, and it's overcomplicated the problem.*"

I chose the example because it was simple and provided a good platform for showing the mechanics of TEMPLATE METHOD. On the other hand, I don't really recommend building `ftoc` like this.

This is a good example of pattern abuse. Using TEMPLATE METHOD for this particular application is ridiculous. It complicates the program and makes its bigger. Encapsulating the main loop of every application in the universe sounded wonderful when we started, but the practical application is fruitless in this case.

Design patterns are wonderful things. They can help you with many design problems. But the fact that they exist does not mean that they should always be used. In this case, while TEMPLATE METHOD was applicable to the problem, its use was not advisable. The cost of the pattern was higher than the benefit it yielded.

So let's look at a slightly more useful example. (See Listing 14-4.)

Bubble Sort[3]

Listing 14-4
BubbleSorter.java

```java
public class BubbleSorter
{
  static int operations = 0;
  public static int sort(int [] array)
  {
    operations = 0;
    if (array.length <= 1)
      return operations;

    for (int nextToLast = array.length-2;
         nextToLast >= 0; nextToLast--)
      for (int index = 0; index <= nextToLast; index++)
        compareAndSwap(array, index);

    return operations;
  }

  private static void swap(int[] array, int index)
  {
    int temp = array[index];
    array[index] = array[index+1];
    array[index+1] = temp;
  }

  private static void compareAndSwap(int[] array, int index)
  {
    if (array[index] > array[index+1])
      swap(array, index);
    operations++;
  }
}
```

The BubbleSorter class knows how to sort an array of integers using the bubble-sort algorithm. The sort method of BubbleSorter contains the algorithm that knows how to do a bubble sort. The two ancillary methods, swap and compareAndSwap, deal with the details of integers and arrays and handle the mechanics that the sort algorithm requires.

3.　Like Application, Bubble Sort is easy to understand and so makes a useful teaching tool. However, no one in their right mind would ever actually use a Bubble Sort if they had any significant amount of sorting to do. There are *much* better algorithms.

Using the TEMPLATE METHOD pattern, we can separate the bubble-sort algorithm out into an abstract base class named `BubbleSorter`. `BubbleSorter` contains an implementation of the `sort` function that calls an abstract method named `outOfOrder` and another called `swap`. The `outOfOrder` method compares two adjacent elements in the array and returns `true` if the elements are out of order. The `swap` method swaps two adjacent cells in the array.

The `sort` method does not know about the array, nor does it care what kind of objects are stored in the array. It just calls `outOfOrder` for various indices into the array and determines whether those indices should be swapped or not. (See Listing 14-5.)

Listing 14-5

BubbleSorter.java

```java
public abstract class BubbleSorter
{
  private int operations = 0;
  protected int length = 0;

  protected int doSort()
  {
    operations = 0;
    if (length <= 1)
      return operations;

    for (int nextToLast = length-2;
         nextToLast >= 0; nextToLast--)
      for (int index = 0; index <= nextToLast; index++)
      {
        if (outOfOrder(index))
          swap(index);
        operations++;
      }

    return operations;
  }

  protected abstract void swap(int index);
  protected abstract boolean outOfOrder(int index);
}
```

Given `BubbleSorter` we can now create simple derivatives that can sort any different kind of object. For example, we could create `IntBubbleSorter`, which sorts arrays of integers, and `DoubleBubbleSorter`, which sorts arrays of doubles. (See Figure 14-1, Listing 14-6, and Listing 14-7.)

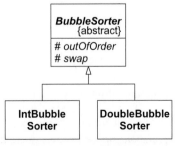

Figure 14-1   Bubble-Sorter Structure

Listing 14-6
IntBubbleSorter.java

```java
public class IntBubbleSorter extends BubbleSorter
{
  private int[] array = null;
  public int sort(int [] theArray)
  {
    array = theArray;
    length = array.length;
    return doSort();
  }

  protected void swap(int index)
  {
    int temp = array[index];
    array[index] = array[index+1];
    array[index+1] = temp;
  }

  protected boolean outOfOrder(int index)
  {
    return (array[index] > array[index+1]);
  }
}
```

Listing 14-7
DoubleBubbleSorter.java

```java
public class DoubleBubbleSorter extends BubbleSorter
{
  private double[] array = null;
  public int sort(double [] theArray)
  {
    array = theArray;
    length = array.length;
    return doSort();
  }

  protected void swap(int index)
  {
    double temp = array[index];
    array[index] = array[index+1];
    array[index+1] = temp;
  }

  protected boolean outOfOrder(int index)
  {
    return (array[index] > array[index+1]);
  }
}
```

The TEMPLATE METHOD pattern shows one of the classic forms of reuse in object-oriented programming. Generic algorithms are placed in the base class and inherited into different detailed contexts. But this technique is not without its costs. Inheritance is a very strong relationship. Derivatives are inextricably bound to their base classes.

For example, the `outOfOrder` and `swap` functions of `IntBubbleSorter` are exactly what are needed for other kinds of sort algorithms. And yet, there is no way to reuse `outOfOrder` and `swap` in those other sort algorithms. By inheriting `BubbleSorter`, we have doomed `IntBubbleSorter` to be bound forever to `BubbleSorter`. The STRATEGY pattern provides another option.

STRATEGY

The STRATEGY pattern solves the problem of inverting the dependencies of the generic algorithm and the detailed implementation in a very different way. Consider, once again, the pattern-abusing `Application` problem.

Rather than placing the generic application algorithm into an abstract base class, we place it into a *concrete* class named `ApplicationRunner`. We define the abstract methods that the generic algorithm must call within an interface named `Application`. We derive `ftocStrategy` from this interface and pass it into the `ApplicationRunner`. `ApplicationRunner` then delegates to this interface. (See Figure 14-2, and Listings 14-8 through 14-10.)

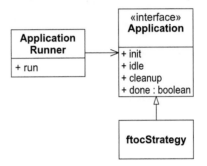

Figure 14-2   Strategy of the Application algorithm

Listing 14-8

ApplicationRunner.java

```java
public class ApplicationRunner
{
  private Application itsApplication = null;

  public ApplicationRunner(Application app)
  {
    itsApplication = app;
  }
  public void run()
  {
    itsApplication.init();
    while (!itsApplication.done())
      itsApplication.idle();
    itsApplication.cleanup();
  }
}
```

Listing 14-9

Application.java

```java
public interface Application
{
  public void init();
  public void idle();
```

```
  public void cleanup();
  public boolean done();
}
```

Listing 14-10

ftocStrategy.java

```java
import java.io.*;
public class ftocStrategy implements Application
{
  private InputStreamReader isr;
  private BufferedReader br;
  private boolean isDone = false;

  public static void main(String[] args) throws Exception
  {
    (new ApplicationRunner(new ftocStrategy())).run();
  }

  public void init()
  {
    isr = new InputStreamReader(System.in);
    br = new BufferedReader(isr);
  }

  public void idle()
  {
    String fahrString = readLineAndReturnNullIfError();
    if (fahrString == null || fahrString.length() == 0)
      isDone = true;
    else
    {
      double fahr = Double.parseDouble(fahrString);
      double celcius = 5.0/9.0*(fahr-32);
      System.out.println("F=" + fahr + ", C=" + celcius);
    }
  }

  public void cleanup()
  {
    System.out.println("ftoc exit");
  }

  public boolean done()
  {
    return isDone;
  }

  private String readLineAndReturnNullIfError()
  {
    String s;
    try
    {
      s = br.readLine();
    }
    catch(IOException e)
```

```
  {
    s = null;
  }
  return s;
}
}
```

It should be clear that this structure has both benefits and costs over the TEMPLATE METHOD structure. STRATEGY involves more total classes and more indirection than TEMPLATE METHOD. The delegation pointer within `ApplicationRunner` incurs a slightly higher cost in terms of run time and data space than inheritance would. On the other hand, if we had many different applications to run, we could reuse the `ApplicationRunner` *instance* and pass in many different implementations of `Application`, thereby reducing the coupling between the generic algorithm and the details it controls.

None of these costs and benefits are overriding. In most cases, none of them matters in the slightest. In the typical case, the most worrisome is the extra class needed by the STRATEGY pattern. However, there is more to consider.

Sorting Again

Consider implementating the bubble sort using the STRATEGY pattern. (See Listings 14-11 through 14-13.)

Listing 14-11

BubbleSorter.java

```java
public class BubbleSorter
{
  private int operations = 0;
  private int length = 0;
  private SortHandle itsSortHandle = null;

  public BubbleSorter(SortHandle handle)
  {
    itsSortHandle = handle;
  }

  public int sort(Object array)
  {
    itsSortHandle.setArray(array);
    length = itsSortHandle.length();
    operations = 0;
    if (length <= 1)
      return operations;

    for (int nextToLast = length-2;
         nextToLast >= 0; nextToLast--)
      for (int index = 0; index <= nextToLast; index++)
      {
        if (itsSortHandle.outOfOrder(index))
          itsSortHandle.swap(index);
        operations++;
      }

    return operations;
  }
}
```

Listing 14-12
`SortHandle.java`

```java
public interface SortHandle
{
  public void swap(int index);
  public boolean outOfOrder(int index);
  public int length();
  public void setArray(Object array);
}
```

Listing 14-13
`IntSortHandle.java`

```java
public class IntSortHandle implements SortHandle
{
  private int[] array = null;

  public void swap(int index)
  {
    int temp = array[index];
    array[index] = array[index+1];
    array[index+1] = temp;
  }

  public void setArray(Object array)
  {
    this.array = (int[])array;
  }

  public int length()
  {
    return array.length;
  }

  public boolean outOfOrder(int index)
  {
    return (array[index] > array[index+1]);
  }
}
```

Notice that the `IntSortHandle` class knows nothing of the `BubbleSorter`. It has no dependency whatever on the bubble-sort implementation. This is not the case with the TEMPLATE METHOD pattern. Look back at Listing 14-6, and you can see that the `IntBubbleSorter` depended directly on `BubbleSorter`, the class that contains the bubble-sort algorithm.

The TEMPLATE METHOD approach partially violates DIP by Implementating the `swap` and `outOfOrder` methods to depend directly on the bubble-sort algorithm. The STRATEGY approach contains no such dependency. Thus, we can use the `IntSortHandle` with `Sorter` implementations other than `BubbleSorter`.

For example, we can create a variation of the bubble sort that terminates early if a pass through the array finds it in order. (See Listing 14-14.) `QuickBubbleSorter` can also use `IntSortHandle` or any other class derived from `SortHandle`.

Listing 14-14

`QuickBubbleSorter.java`

```java
public class QuickBubbleSorter
{
  private int operations = 0;
  private int length = 0;
  private SortHandle itsSortHandle = null;

  public QuickBubbleSorter(SortHandle handle)
  {
    itsSortHandle = handle;
  }

  public int sort(Object array)
  {
    itsSortHandle.setArray(array);
    length = itsSortHandle.length();
    operations = 0;
    if (length <= 1)
      return operations;

    boolean thisPassInOrder = false;
    for (int nextToLast = length-2; nextToLast >= 0 && !thisPassInOrder; nextToLast--)
    {
      thisPassInOrder = true; //potenially.
      for (int index = 0; index <= nextToLast; index++)
      {
        if (itsSortHandle.outOfOrder(index))
        {
          itsSortHandle.swap(index);
          thisPassInOrder = false;
        }
        operations++;
      }
    }

    return operations;
  }
}
```

Thus, the STRATEGY pattern provides one extra benefit over the TEMPLATE METHOD pattern. Whereas the TEMPLATE METHOD pattern allows a generic algorithm to manipulate many possible detailed implementations, the STRATEGY pattern by fully conforming to the DIP allows each detailed implementation to be manipulated by many different generic algorithms.

Conclusion

Both TEMPLATE METHOD and STRATEGY allow you to separate high-level algorithms from low-level details. Both allow the high-level algorithms to be reused independently of the details. At the cost of a little extra complexity, memory, and runtime, STRATEGY also allows the details to be reused independently of the high-level algorithm.

Bibliography

1. Gamma, et al. *Design Patterns*. Reading, MA: Addison–Wesley, 1995.
2. Martin, Robert C., et al. *Pattern Languages of Program Design 3*. Reading, MA: Addison–Wesley, 1998.

15

FACADE and MEDIATOR

© Jennifer M. Kohnke

Symbolism erects a facade of respectability to hide the indecency of dreams.

—Mason Cooley

The two patterns discussed in this chapter have a common purpose. Both impose some kind of policy on another group of objects. FACADE imposes policy from above, and MEDIATOR imposes policy from below. The use of FACADE is visible and constraining, while the use of MEDIATOR is invisible and enabling.

FACADE

The FACADE pattern is used when you want to provide a simple and specific interface onto a group of objects that has a complex and general interface. Consider, for example, DB.java in Listing 26-9 on page 333. This class imposes a very simple interface, specific to ProductData, on the complex and general interfaces of the classes within the java.sql package. Figure 15-1 shows the structure.

Notice that the DB class protects the Application from needing to know the intimacies of the java.sql package. It hides all the generality and complexity of java.sql behind a very simple and specific interface.

A FACADE like DB imposes a lot of policy on the usage of the java.sql package. It knows how to initialize and close the database connection. It knows how to translate the members of ProductData into database fields and back. It knows how to build the appropriate queries and commands to manipulate the database. And it hides all that complexity from its users. From the point of view of the Application, java.sql does not exist; it is hidden behind the FACADE.

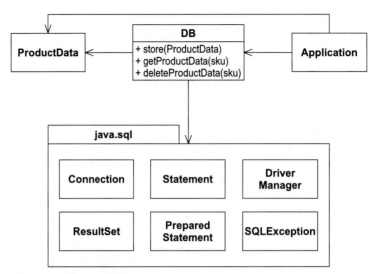

Figure 15-1   The DB FACADE

The use of the FACADE pattern implies that the developers have adopted the convention that all database calls must go through DB. If any part of the Application code goes straight to java.sql rather than through the FACADE, then that convention is violated. As such, the FACADE imposes its polices on the application. By convention, DB has become the sole broker of the facilities of java.sql.

MEDIATOR

The MEDIATOR pattern also imposes policy. However, whereas Facade imposed its policy in a visible and constraining way, MEDIATOR imposes its policies in a hidden and unconstrained way. For example, the QuickEntryMediator class in Listing 15–1 is a class that sits quietly behind the scenes and binds a text-entry field to a list. When you type in the text-entry field, the first element of the list that matches what you have typed is highlighted. This lets you type abbreviations and quickly select a list item.

Listing 15-1

QuickEntryMediator.java

```
package utility;

import javax.swing.*;
import javax.swing.event.*;

/**
QuickEntryMediator.  This class takes a JTextField and a JList.
It assumes that the user will type characters into the
JTextField that are prefixes of entries in the JList.  It
automatically selects the first item in the JList that matches
the current prefix in the JTextField.

If the JTextField is null, or the prefix does not match any
element in the JList, then the JList selection is cleared.

There are no methods to call for this object.  You simply
create it, and forget it.  (But don't let it be garbage
collected...)
```

Example:

```
JTextField t = new JTextField();
JList l = new JList();

QuickEntryMediator qem = new QuickEntryMediator(t, l);
 // that's all folks.

 @author Robert C. Martin, Robert S. Koss
 @date 30 Jun, 1999 2113 (SLAC)
 */

public class QuickEntryMediator {
  public QuickEntryMediator(JTextField t, JList l) {
    itsTextField = t;
    itsList = l;

    itsTextField.getDocument().addDocumentListener(
      new DocumentListener() {
        public void changedUpdate(DocumentEvent e) {
          textFieldChanged();
        }

        public void insertUpdate(DocumentEvent e) {
          textFieldChanged();
        }

        public void removeUpdate(DocumentEvent e) {
          textFieldChanged();
        }
      } // new DocumentListener
    ); // addDocumentListener
  } // QuickEntryMediator()

  private void textFieldChanged() {
    String prefix = itsTextField.getText();

    if (prefix.length() == 0) {
      itsList.clearSelection();
      return;
      }

      ListModel m = itsList.getModel();
      boolean found = false;
      for (int i = 0; found == false && i < m.getSize(); i++) {
      Object o = m.getElementAt(i);
      String s = o.toString();
      if (s.startsWith(prefix)) {
      itsList.setSelectedValue(o, true);
      found = true;
      }
    }

    if (!found) {
      itsList.clearSelection();
      }
  } // textFieldChanged
```

```
    private JTextField itsTextField;
    private JList itsList;
} // class QuickEntryMediator
```

The structure of the `QuickEntryMediator` is shown in Figure 15-2. An instance of `QuickEntry-Mediator` is constructed with a `JList` and a `JTextField`. The `QuickEntryMediator` registers an anonymous `DocumentListener` with the `JTextField`. This listener invokes the `textFieldChanged` method whenever there is a change in the text. This method then finds an element of the `JList` that is prefixed by the text and selects it.

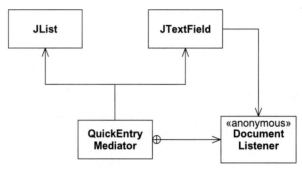

Figure 15-2   QuickEntryMediator

The users of the `JList` and `JTextField` have no idea that this MEDIATOR exists. It sits there quietly, imposing its policy on those objects without their permission or knowledge.

Conclusion

Imposing policy can be done from above using FACADE if that policy needs to be big and visible. On the other hand, if subtlety and discretion are needed, MEDIATOR may be the more appropriate choice. Facades are usually the focal point of a convention. Everyone agrees to use the facade instead of the objects beneath it. Mediator, on the other hand, is hidden from the users. Its policy is a fait accompli rather than a matter of convention.

Bibliography

1.   Gamma, et al. *Design Patterns*. Reading, MA: Addison–Wesley, 1995.

16

SINGLETON and MONOSTATE

"Infinite beatitude of existence! It is; and there is none else beside It."

—The point. Flatland. Edwin A. Abbott

Usually there is a one-to-many relationship between classes and instances. You can create many instances of most classes. The instances are created when they are needed and disposed of when their usefulness ends. They come and go in a flow of memory allocations and deallocations.

However, there are some classes that should have only one instance. That instance should appear to have come into existence when the program started and should be disposed of only when the program ends. Such objects are sometimes the roots of the application. From the roots you can find your way to many other objects in the system. Sometimes they are factories, which you can use to create the other objects in the system. Sometimes these objects are managers, responsible for keeping track of certain other objects and driving them through their paces.

Whatever these objects are, it is a severe logic failure if more than one of them are created. If more than one root are created, then access to objects in the application may depend on a chosen root. Programmers, not knowing that more than one root exist, may find themselves looking at a subset of the application objects without knowing it. If more than one factory exist, clerical control over the created objects may be compromised. If more than one manager exist, activities that were intended to be serial may become concurrent.

It may seem that mechanisms to enforce the singularity of these objects are overkill. After all, when you initialize the application, you can simply create one of each and be done with it. In fact, this is usually the best course of action. Mechanism should be avoided when there is no immediate and significant need. However, we also want our code to communicate our intent. If the mechanism for enforcing singularity is trivial, the benefit of communication may outweigh the cost of the mechanism.

This chapter is about two patterns that enforce singularity. These patterns have very different cost–benefit trade-offs. In many contexts, their cost is low enough to more than balance the benefit of their expressiveness.

SINGLETON[1]

SINGLETON is a very simple pattern. The test case in Listing 16-1 shows how it should work. The first test function shows that the `Singleton` instance is accessed through the public static method `Instance`. It also shows that if `Instance` is called multiple times, a reference to the exact same instance is returned each time. The second test case shows that the `Singleton` class has no public constructors, so there is no way for anyone to create an instance without using the `Instance` method.

Listing 16-1

Singleton Test Case

```
import junit.framework.*;
import java.lang.reflect.Constructor;

public class TestSimpleSingleton extends TestCase
{
  public TestSimpleSingleton(String name)
  {
    super(name);
  }

  public void testCreateSingleton()
  {
    Singleton s = Singleton.Instance();
    Singleton s2 = Singleton.Instance();
    assertSame(s, s2);
  }

  public void testNoPublicConstructors() throws Exception
  {
    Class singleton = Class.forName("Singleton");
    Constructor[] constructors = singleton.getConstructors();
    assertEquals("public constructors.",
                 0, constructors.length);
  }
}
```

This test case is a specification for the SINGLETON pattern. It leads directly to the code shown in Listing 16-2. It should be clear, by inspecting this code, that there can never be more than one instance of the `Singleton` class within the scope of the static variable `Singleton.theInstance`.

---

1.   [GOF95], p. 127.

Listing 16-2
Singleton Implementation

```
public class Singleton
{
  private static Singleton theInstance = null;
  private Singleton() {}

  public static Singleton Instance()
  {
    if (theInstance == null)
      theInstance = new Singleton();
    return theInstance;
  }
}
```

Benefits of the SINGLETON

- **Cross platform.** Using appropriate middleware (e.g., RMI), SINGLETON can be extended to work across many JVMs and many computers.
- **Applicable to any class.** You can change any class into a SINGLETON simply by making its constructors private and by adding the appropriate static functions and variable.
- **Can be created through derivation.** Given a class, you can create a subclass that is a SINGLETON.
- **Lazy evaluation**. If the SINGLETON is never used, it is never created.

Costs of the SINGLETON

- **Destruction is undefined.** There is no good way to destroy or decommission a SINGLETON. If you add a `decommission` method that nulls out `theInstance`, other modules in the system may still be holding a reference to the SINGLETON instance. Subsequent calls to `Instance` will cause another instance to be created, causing two concurrent instances to exist. This problem is particularly acute in C++ where the instance *can be destroyed*, leading to possible dereferencing of a destroyed object.
- **Not inherited.** A class derived from a SINGLETON is not a singleton. If it needs to be a SINGLETON, the static function and variable need to be added to it.
- **Efficiency.** Each call to `Instance` invokes the `if` statement. For most of those calls, the `if` statement is useless.
- **Nontransparent.** Users of a SINGLETON know that they are using a SINGLETON because they must invoke the `Instance` method.

SINGLETON in Action

Assume that we have a Web-based system that allows users to log in to secure areas of a Web server. Such a system will have a database containing user names, passwords, and other user attributes. Assume further that the database is accessed through a third-party API. We could access the database directly in every module that needed to read and write a user. However, this would scatter usage of the third-party API throughout the code, and it would leave us no place to enforce access or structure conventions.

A better solution is to use the FACADE pattern and create a `UserDatabase` class that provides methods for reading and writing `User` objects. These methods access the third-party API of the database, translating between `User` objects and the tables and rows of the database. Within the `UserDatabase`, we can enforce conventions of structure and access. For example, we can guarantee that no `User` record gets written unless it has a nonblank `username`. Or we can serialize access to a `User` record, making sure that two modules cannot simultaneously read and write it.

The code in Listings 16-3 and 16-4 shows a SINGLETON solution. The SINGLETON class is named `UserDatabaseSource`. It implements the `UserDatabase` interface. Notice that the static `instance()` method does not have the traditional `if` statement to protect against multiple creations. Instead, it takes advantage of the Java initialization facility.

Listing 16-3

`UserDatabase Interface`

```
public interface UserDatabase
{
  User readUser(String userName);
  void writeUser(User user);
}
```

Listing 16-4

`UserDatabaseSource Singleton`

```
public class UserDatabaseSource implements UserDatabase
{
  private static UserDatabase theInstance =
    new UserDatabaseSource();

  public static UserDatabase instance()
  {
    return theInstance;
  }

  private UserDatabaseSource()
  {
  }

  public User readUser(String userName)
  {
    // Some Implementation
    return null;  // just to make it compile.
  }

  public void writeUser(User user)
  {
    // Some Implementation
  }
}
```

This is an extremely common use of the SINGLETON pattern. It assures that all database access will be through a single instance of `UserDatabaseSource`. This makes it easy to put checks, counters, and locks in `UserDatabaseSource` that enforce the access and structure conventions mentioned earlier.

MONOSTATE[2]

The MONOSTATE pattern is another way to achieve singularity. It works through a completely different mechanism. We can see how that mechanism works by studying the MONOSTATE test case in Listing 16-5.

The first test function simply describes an object whose x variable can be set and retrieved. But the second test case shows that two instances of the same class behave *as though they were one*. If you set the x variable on

---

2.   [BALL2000].

one instance to a particular value, you can retrieve that value by getting the x variable of a different instance. It's as though the two instances are just different names for the same object.

Listing 16-5

Monostate Test Case

```
import junit.framework.*;

public class TestMonostate extends TestCase
{
  public TestMonostate(String name)
  {
    super(name);
  }

  public void testInstance()
  {
    Monostate m = new Monostate();
    for (int x = 0; x<10; x++)
    {
      m.setX(x);
      assertEquals(x, m.getX());
    }
  }

  public void testInstancesBehaveAsOne()
  {
    Monostate m1 = new Monostate();
    Monostate m2 = new Monostate();

    for (int x = 0; x<10; x++)
    {
      m1.setX(x);
      assertEquals(x, m2.getX());
    }
  }
}
```

If we were to plug the Singleton class into this test case and replace all the new Monostate statements with calls to Singleton.Instance, the test case should still pass. So this test case describes the *behavior* of Singleton without imposing the constraint of a single instance!

How can two instances behave as though they were a single object? Quite simply it means that the two objects must share the same variables. This is easily achieved by making all the variables static. Listing 16-6 shows the implementation of Monostate that passes the above test case. Note that the itsX variable is static. Note also that *none of the methods are static*. This is important as we'll see later.

Listing 16-6

Monostate Implementation

```
public class Monostate
{
  private static int itsX = 0;
  public Monostate() {}

  public void setX(int x)
```

```
  {
    itsX = x;
  }

  public int getX()
  {
    return itsX;
  }
}
```

I find this to be a delightfully twisted pattern. No matter how many instances of `Monostate` you create, they all behave as though they were a *single object*. You can even destroy or decommission all the current instances without losing the data.

Note that the difference between the two patterns is one of behavior vs. structure. The SINGLETON pattern enforces the structure of singularity. It prevents any more than one instance from being created. Whereas MONOSTATE enforces the *behavior* of singularity without imposing structural constraints. To underscore this difference consider that the MONOSTATE test case is valid for the `Singleton` class, but the SINGLETON test case is not even close to being valid for the `Monostate` class.

Benefits of MONOSTATE

- **Transparency**. Users of a MONOSTATE do not behave differently than users of a regular object. The users do not need to know that the object is MONOSTATE.
- **Derivability**. Derivatives of a MONOSTATE are MONOSTATES. Indeed, all the derivatives of a MONOSTATE are part of the *same* MONOSTATE. They all share the same static variables.
- **Polymorphism**. Since the methods of a MONOSTATE are not static, they can be overridden in a derivative. Thus different derivatives can offer different behavior over the same set of static variables.
- **Well-defined creation and destruction.** The variables of a MONOSTATE, being static, have well-defined creation and destruction times.

Costs of MONOSTATE

- **No conversion**. A normal class cannot be converted into a MONOSTATE class through derivation.
- **Efficiency**. A MONOSTATE may go through many creations and destructions because it is a real object. These operations are often costly.
- **Presence**. The variables of a MONOSTATE take up space, even if the MONOSTATE is never used.
- **Platform local.** You can't make a MONOSTATE work across several JVM instances or across several platforms.

MONOSTATE in Action

Consider implementing the simple finite state machine for a subway turnstile shown in Figure 16-1. The turnstile begins its life in the `Locked` state. If a coin is deposited, it transitions to the `Unlocked` state, unlocks the gate, resets any alarm state that might be present, and deposits the coin in its collection bin. If a user passes through the gate at this point, the turnstile transitions back to the `Locked` state and locks the gate.

There are two abnormal conditions. If the user deposits two or more coins before passing through the gate, the coins will be refunded and the gate will remain unlocked. If the user passes through without paying, then an alarm will sound and the gate will remain locked.

The test program that describes this operation is shown in Listing 16-7. Note that the test methods assume that the `Turnstile` is a monostate. It expects to be able to send events and gather queries from different instances. This makes sense if there will never be more than one instance of the `Turnstile`.

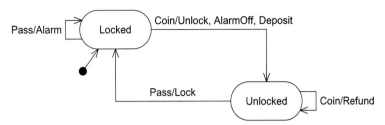

Figure 16-1 Subway Turnstile Finite State Machine

Listing 16-7

TestTurnstile

```java
import junit.framework.*;

public class TestTurnstile extends TestCase
{
  public TestTurnstile(String name)
  {
    super(name);
  }

  public void setUp()
  {
    Turnstile t = new Turnstile();
    t.reset();
  }

  public void testInit()
  {
    Turnstile t = new Turnstile();
    assert(t.locked());
    assert(!t.alarm());
  }

  public void testCoin()
  {
    Turnstile t = new Turnstile();
    t.coin();
    Turnstile t1 = new Turnstile();
    assert(!t1.locked());
    assert(!t1.alarm());
    assertEquals(1, t1.coins());
  }

  public void testCoinAndPass()
  {
    Turnstile t = new Turnstile();
    t.coin();
    t.pass();

    Turnstile t1 = new Turnstile();
    assert(t1.locked());
    assert(!t1.alarm());
    assertEquals("coins", 1, t1.coins());
  }
```

```
public void testTwoCoins()
{
  Turnstile t = new Turnstile();
  t.coin();
  t.coin();

  Turnstile t1 = new Turnstile();
  assert("unlocked", !t1.locked());
  assertEquals("coins",1, t1.coins());
  assertEquals("refunds", 1, t1.refunds());
  assert(!t1.alarm());
}

public void testPass()
{
  Turnstile t = new Turnstile();
  t.pass();
  Turnstile t1 = new Turnstile();
  assert("alarm", t1.alarm());
  assert("locked", t1.locked());
}

public void testCancelAlarm()
{
  Turnstile t = new Turnstile();
  t.pass();
  t.coin();
  Turnstile t1 = new Turnstile();
  assert("alarm", !t1.alarm());
  assert("locked", !t1.locked());
  assertEquals("coin", 1, t1.coins());
  assertEquals("refund", 0, t1.refunds());
}

public void testTwoOperations()
{
  Turnstile t = new Turnstile();
  t.coin();
  t.pass();
  t.coin();
  assert("unlocked", !t.locked());
  assertEquals("coins", 2, t.coins());
  t.pass();
  assert("locked", t.locked());
}
}
```

The implementation of the monostate `Turnstile` is in Listing 16-8. The base `Turnstile` class delegates the two event functions (`coin` and `pass`) to two derivatives of `Turnstile` (`Locked` and `Unlocked`) that represent the states of the finite-state machine.

Listing 16-8
Turnstile

```java
public class Turnstile
{
  private static boolean isLocked = true;
  private static boolean isAlarming = false;
  private static int itsCoins = 0;
  private static int itsRefunds = 0;
  protected final static Turnstile LOCKED = new Locked();
  protected final static Turnstile UNLOCKED = new Unlocked();
  protected static Turnstile itsState = LOCKED;

  public void reset()
  {
    lock(true);
    alarm(false);
    itsCoins = 0;
    itsRefunds = 0;
    itsState = LOCKED;
  }

  public boolean locked()
  {
    return isLocked;
  }

  public boolean alarm()
  {
    return isAlarming;
  }

  public void coin()
  {
    itsState.coin();
  }

  public void pass()
  {
    itsState.pass();
  }

  protected void lock(boolean shouldLock)
  {
    isLocked = shouldLock;
  }

  protected void alarm(boolean shouldAlarm)
  {
    isAlarming = shouldAlarm;
  }

  public int coins()
  {
    return itsCoins;
  }
```

```java
  public int refunds()
  {
    return itsRefunds;
  }

  public void deposit()
  {
    itsCoins++;
  }

  public void refund()
  {
    itsRefunds++;
  }
}

class Locked extends Turnstile
{
  public void coin()
  {
    itsState = UNLOCKED;
    lock(false);
    alarm(false);
    deposit();
  }

  public void pass()
  {
    alarm(true);
  }
}


class Unlocked extends Turnstile
{
  public void coin()
  {
    refund();
  }

  public void pass()
  {
    lock(true);
    itsState = LOCKED;
  }
}
```

This example shows some of the useful features of the MONOSTATE pattern. It takes advantage of the ability for MONOSTATE derivatives to be polymorphic and the fact that MONOSTATE derivatives are themselves MONOSTATES. This example also shows how difficult it can sometimes be to turn a MONOSTATE into a normal class. The structure of this solution depends strongly on the MONOSTATE nature of Turnstile. If we needed to control more than one turnstile with this finite-state machine, the code would require some significant refactoring.

Perhaps you are concerned about the unconventional use of inheritance in this example. Having Unlocked and Locked derived from Turnstile seems a violation of normal OO principles. However, since Turnstile is a MONOSTATE, there are no separate instances of it. Thus, `Unlocked` and `Locked` aren't really separate objects. Instead they are part of the `Turnstile` abstraction. `Unlocked` and `Locked` have access to the same variables and methods that `Turnstile` has access to.

Conclusion

It is often necessary to enforce the constraint that a particular object have only a single instantiation. This chapter has shown two very different techniques. SINGLETON makes use of private constructors, a static variable, and a static function to control and limit instantiation. MONOSTATE simply makes all variables of the object static.

SINGLETON is best used when you have an existing class that you want to constrain through derivation, and you don't mind that everyone will have to call the `instance()` method to gain access. MONOSTATE is best used when you want the singular nature of the class to be transparent to the users or when you want to employ polymorphic derivatives of the single object.

Bibliography

1. Gamma, et al. *Design Patterns*. Reading, MA: Addison–Wesley, 1995.
2. Martin, Robert C., et al. *Pattern Languages of Program Design 3*. Reading, MA: Addison–Wesley, 1998.
3. Ball, Steve, and John Crawford. Monostate Classes: The Power of One. Published in *More C++ Gems*, compiled by Robert C. Martin. Cambridge, UK: Cambridge University Press, 2000, p. 223.

17

NULL OBJECT

Faultily faultless, icily regular, splendidly null, Dead perfection, no more.

—Alfred Tennyson (1809–1892)

Consider the following code:

```
Employee e = DB.getEmployee("Bob");
if (e != null && e.isTimeToPay(today))
  e.pay();
```

We ask the database for an `Employee` object named "Bob." The `DB` object returns `null` if no such object exists. Otherwise, it returns the requested instance of `Employee`. If the employee exists, and if it is time to pay him, then we invoke the `pay` method.

We've all written code like this before. The idiom is common because the first expression of the `&&` is evaluated first in C-based languages, and the second is evaluated only if the first is `true`. Most of us have also been burned by forgetting to test for `null`. Common though the idiom may be, it is ugly and error prone.

We can alleviate the tendency toward error by having `DB.getEmployee` throw an exception instead of returning `null`. However, `try/catch` blocks can be even uglier than checking for `null`. Worse, the use of exceptions forces us to declare them in `throws` clauses. This makes it hard to retrofit exceptions into an existing application.

We can address these issues by using the NULL OBJECT pattern.[1] This pattern often eliminates the need to check for `null`, and it can help to simplify the code.

Figure 17-1 shows the structure. `Employee` becomes an interface that has two implementations. `Employee-Implementation` is the normal implementation. It contains all the methods and variables that you would expect an `Employee` object to have. When `DB.getEmployee` finds an employee in the database, it returns an instance of `EmployeeImplementation`. `NullEmployee` is returned only if `DB.getEmployee` cannot find the employee.

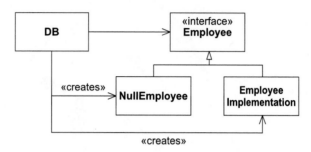

Figure 17-1 NULL OBJECT Pattern

`NullEmployee` implements all the methods of `Employee` to do "nothing." What "nothing" is depends on the method. For example, one would expect that `isTimeToPay` would be implemented to return `false`, since it is never time to pay a `NullEmployee`.

Using this pattern, we can change the original code to look like this:

```
Employee e = DB.getEmployee("Bob");
if (e.isTimeToPay(today))
  e.pay();
```

This is neither error prone nor ugly. There is a nice consistency to it. `DB.getEmployee` *always* returns an instance of `Employee`. That instance is guaranteed to behave appropriately, regardless of whether the employee was found or not.

Of course there will be many cases where we'll still want to know if `DB.getEmployee` failed to find an employee. This can be accomplished by creating a `static final` variable in `Employee` that holds the one and only instance of `NullEmployee`.

Listing 17-1 shows the test case for `NullEmployee`. In this case "Bob" does not exist in the database. Notice that the test case expects `isTimeToPay` to return `false`. Notice also that it expects the employee returned by `DB.getEmployee` to be `Employee.NULL`.

Listing 17-1

TestEmployee.java (Partial)

```
public void testNull() throws Exception
  {
    Employee e = DB.getEmployee("Bob");
```

---

1.   [PLOPD3], p. 5. This delightful article, by Bobby Woolf, is full of wit, irony and practical advice.

```
    if (e.isTimeToPay(new Date()))
      fail();
    assertEquals(Employee.NULL, e);
  }
```

The DB class is shown in Listing 17-2. Notice that, for the purposes of our test, the getEmployee method just returns Employee.NULL.

Listing 17-2

DB.java

```
public class DB
{
  public static Employee getEmployee(String name)
  {
    return Employee.NULL;
  }
}
```

The Employee interface is shown in Listing 17-3. Notice that it has a static variable named NULL that holds an anonymous implementation of Employee. This anonymous implementation is the sole instance of the null employee. It implements isTimeToPay to return false and pay to do nothing.

Listing 17-3

Employee.java

```
import java.util.Date;
public interface Employee
{
  public boolean isTimeToPay(Date payDate);

  public void pay();

  public static final Employee NULL = new Employee()
  {
    public boolean isTimeToPay(Date payDate)
    {
      return false;
    }

    public void pay()
    {
    }
  };
}
```

Making the null employee an anonymous inner class is a way to make sure that there is only a single instance of it. There is no NullEmployee class per se. Nobody else can create other instances of the null employee. This is a good thing because we want to be able to say things like

```
if (e == Employee.NULL)
```

This would be unreliable if it were possible to create many instances of the null employee.

Conclusion

Those of us who have been using C-based languages for a long time have grown accustomed to functions that return null or 0 on some kind of failure. We presume that the return value from such functions needs to be tested. The NULL OBJECT pattern changes this. By using this pattern, we can ensure that functions always return valid objects, even when they fail. Those objects that represent failure do "nothing."

Bibliography

1.   Martin, Robert, Dirk Riehle, and Frank Buschmann. *Pattern Languages of Program Design 3*. Reading, MA: Addison–Wesley, 1998.

18

The Payroll Case Study: Iteration One Begins

© Jennifer M. Kohnke

"Everything which is in any way beautiful is beautiful in itself, and terminates in itself, not having praise as part of itself."

—Marcus Aurelius, circa A.D. 170

Introduction

The following case study describes the first iteration in the development of a simple batch payroll system. You will find the user stories in this case study to be simplistic. For example, taxes are simply not mentioned. This is typical of an early iteration. It will provide only a very small part of the business value the customers need.

In this chapter we will do the kind of quick analysis and design session that often takes place at the start of a normal iteration. The customer has selected the stories for the iteration, and now we have to figure out how we are going to implement them. Such design sessions are short and cursory, just like this chapter. The UML diagrams you see here are no more than hasty sketches on a whiteboard. The real design work will take place in the next chapter, when we work through the unit tests and implementations.

Specification

The following are some notes we took while conversing with our customer about the stories that were selected for the first iteration:

- Some employees work by the hour. They are paid an hourly rate that is one of the fields in their employee record. They submit daily time cards that record the date and the number of hours worked. If they work more than 8 hours per day, they are paid 1.5 times their normal rate for those extra hours. They are paid every Friday.
- Some employees are paid a flat salary. They are paid on the last working day of the month. Their monthly salary is one of the fields in their employee record.
- Some of the salaried employees are also paid a commission based on their sales. They submit sales receipts that record the date and the amount of the sale. Their commission rate is a field in their employee record. They are paid every other Friday.
- Employees can select their method of payment. They may have their paychecks mailed to the postal address of their choice; they may have their paychecks held for pickup by the paymaster; or they can request that their paychecks be directly deposited into the bank account of their choice.
- Some employees belong to the union. Their employee record has a field for the weekly dues rate. Their dues must be deducted from their pay. Also, the union may assess service charges against individual union members from time to time. These service charges are submitted by the union on a weekly basis and must be deducted from the appropriate employee's next pay amount.
- The payroll application will run once each working day and pay the appropriate employees on that day. The system will be told to what date the employees are to be paid, so it will generate payments for records from the last time the employee was paid up to the specified date.

We could begin by generating the database schema. Clearly this problem could use some kind of relational database, and the requirements give us a very good idea of what the tables and fields might be. It would be easy to design a workable schema and then start building some queries. However, this approach will generate an application for which the database is the central concern.

Databases are *implementation details*! Considering the database should be deferred as long as possible. Far too many applications are inextricably tied to their databases because they were designed with the database in mind from the beginning. Remember the definition of abstraction: *the amplification of the essential and the elimination of the irrelevant*. The database is irrelevant at this stage of the project; it is merely a technique used for storing and accessing data, nothing more.

Analysis by Use Cases

Instead of starting with the data of the system, let's start by considering the behavior of the system. After all, it is the system's behavior that we are being paid to create.

One way to capture and analyze the behavior of a system is to create *use cases*. Use cases, as originally described by Jacobson, are very similar to the notion of user stories in XP. A use case is like a user story that has been elaborated with a little more detail. Such elaboration is appropriate once the user story has been selected for implementation in the current iteration.

When we perform use case analysis, we look to the user stories and acceptance tests to find out the kinds of stimuli that the users of this system provide. Then we try to figure out how the system responds to those stimuli.

For example, here are the user stories that our customer has chosen for the next iteration:

1. Add a new employee
2. Delete an employee
3. Post a time card
4. Post a sales receipt
5. Post a union service charge
6. Change employee details (e.g., hourly rate, dues rate.)
7. Run the payroll for today

Let's convert each of these user stories into an elaborated use case. We don't need to go into too much detail—just enough to help us think through the design of the code that fulfills each story.

Adding Employees

Use Case 1
Add New Employee

A new employee is added by the receipt of an `AddEmp` transaction. This transaction contains the employee's name, address, and assigned employee number.   The transaction has three forms:

```
AddEmp <EmpID> "<name>" "<address>" H <hourly-rate>
AddEmp <EmpID> "<name>" "<address>" S <monthly-salary>
AddEmp <EmpID> "<name>" "<address>" C <monthly-salary> <commission-rate>
```

The employee record is created with its fields assigned appropriately.

Alternative 1:
An error in the transaction structure

If the transaction structure is inappropriate, it is printed out in an error message, and no action is taken.

Use case 1 hints at an abstraction. There are three forms of the `AddEmp` transaction, yet all three forms share the `<EmpID>`, `<name>`, and `<address>` fields. We can use the COMMAND pattern to create an `AddEmployee-Transaction` abstract base class with three derivatives: `AddHourlyEmployeeTransaction`, `AddSalaried-EmployeeTransaction` and `AddCommissionedEmployeeTransaction`. (See Figure 18-1.)

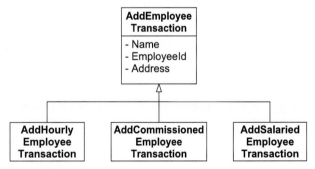

Figure 18-1   `AddEmployeeTransaction` Class Hierarchy

This structure conforms nicely to the Single-Responsibility Principle (SRP) by splitting each job into its own class. The alternative would be to put all these jobs into a single module. While this might reduce the number of classes in the system, and therefore make the system simpler, it would also concentrate all the transaction processing code in one place, creating a large and potentially error-prone module.

Use case 1 specifically talks about an employee record, which implies some sort of database. Again our predisposition to databases may tempt us into thinking about record layouts or the field structure in a relational database table, but we should resist these urges. What the use case is really asking us to do is to create an employee. What is the object model of an employee? A better question might be, What do the three different transactions create? In my view, they create three different kinds of employee objects, mimicking the three different kinds of `AddEmp` transactions. Figure 18-2 shows a possible structure.

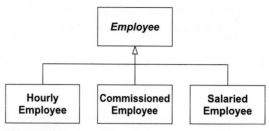

Figure 18-2   Possible `Employee` Class Hierarchy

Deleting Employees

Use Case 2
Deleting an Employee

Employees are deleted when a `DelEmp` transaction is received. The form of this transaction is as follows:

`DelEmp <EmpID>`

When this transaction is received, the appropriate employee record is deleted.

Alternative 1:
Invalid or unknown `EmpID`

If the `<EmpID>` field is not structured correctly, or if it does not refer to a valid employee record, then the transaction is printed with an error message, and no other action is taken.

This use case doesn't give me any design insights at this time, so let's look at the next.

Posting Time Cards

Use Case 3
Post a `Time Card`

On receiving a `TimeCard` transaction, the system will create a time-card record and associate it with the appropriate employee record.

`TimeCard <Empld> <date> <hours>`

Alternative 1:
The selected employee is not hourly

The system will print an appropriate error message and take no further action.

Alternative 2:
An error in the transaction structure

The system will print an appropriate error message and take no further action.

This use case points out that some transactions apply only to certain kinds of employees, strengthening the idea that the different kinds should be represented by different classes. In this case, there is also an association implied between time cards and hourly employees. Figure 18-3 shows a possible static model for this association.

Figure 18-3   Association between `HourlyEmployee` and `TimeCard`

Posting Sales Receipts

Use Case 4
Posting a `Sales Receipt`

Upon receiving the `SalesReceipt` transaction, the system will create a new sales-receipt record and associate it with the appropriate commissioned employee.

```
SalesReceipt <EmpID> <date> <amount>
```

Alternative 1:
The selected employee is not commissioned

The system will print an appropriate error message and take no further action.

Alternative 2:
An error in the transaction structure

The system will print an appropriate error message and take no further action.

This use case is very similar to use case 3. It implies the structure shown in Figure 18-4.

Figure 18-4   Commissioned Employees and Sales Receipts

Posting a Union Service Charge

Use Case 5
Posting a Union Service Charge

Upon receiving this transaction, the system will create a service-charge record and associate it with the appropriate union member.

```
ServiceCharge <memberID> <amount>
```

Alternative 1:
Poorly formed transaction

If the transaction is not well formed or if the `<memberID>` does not refer to an existing union member, then the transaction is printed with an appropriate error message.

This use case shows that union members are not accessed through employee IDs. The union maintains its own identification numbering scheme for union members. Thus, the system must be able to associate union members and employees. There are many different ways to provide this kind of association, so to avoid being arbitrary, let's defer this decision until later. Perhaps constraints from other parts of the system will force our hand one way or another.

One thing is certain. There is a direct association between union members and their service charges. Figure 18-5 shows a possible static model for this association.

Figure 18-5   Union Members and Service Charges

Changing Employee Details

Use Case 6
Changing Employee Details

Upon receiving this transaction, the system will alter one of the details of the appropriate employee record. There are several possible variations to this transaction.

ChgEmp <EmpID> Name <name>	Change Employee Name
ChgEmp <EmpID> Address <address>	Change Employee Address
ChgEmp <EmpID> Hourly <hourlyRate>	Change to Hourly
ChgEmp <EmpID> Salaried <salary>	Change to Salaried
ChgEmp <EmpID> Commissioned <salary> <rate>	Change to Commissioned
ChgEmp <EmpID> Hold	Hold Paycheck
ChgEmp <EmpID> Direct <bank> <account>	Direct Deposit
ChgEmp <EmpID> Mail <address>	Mail Paycheck
ChgEmp <EmpID> Member <memberID> Dues <rate>	Put Employee in Union
ChgEmp <EmpID> NoMember	Remove Employee from Union

Alternative 1:
Transaction Errors

If the structure of the transaction is improper, or <EmpID> does not refer to a real employee, or <memberID> already refers to a member, then print a suitable error and take no further action.

This use case is very revealing. It has told us all the aspects of an employee that must be changeable. The fact that we can change an employee from hourly to salaried means that the diagram in Figure 18-2 is certainly invalid. Instead, it would probably be more appropriate to use the STRATEGY pattern for calculating pay. The Employee class could hold a strategy class named PaymentClassification, as in Figure 18-6. This is an advantage because we can change the PaymentClassification object without changing any other part of the Employee object. When an hourly employee is changed to a salaried employee, the HourlyClassification of the corresponding Employee object is replaced with a SalariedClassification object.

PaymentClassification objects come in three varieties. The HourlyClassification objects maintain the hourly rate and a list of TimeCard objects. The SalariedClassification objects maintain the monthly salary figure. The CommissionedClassification objects maintain a monthly salary, a commission rate, and a list of SalesReceipt objects. I have used composition relationships in these cases because I believe that TimeCards and SalesReceipts should be destroyed when the employee is destroyed.

The method of payment must also be changeable. Figure 18-6 implements this idea by using the STRATEGY pattern and deriving three different kinds of PaymentMethod classes. If an Employee object contains a

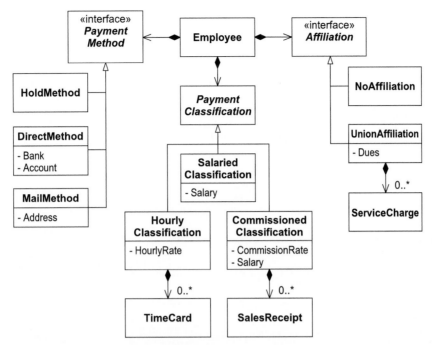

Figure 18-6   Revised Class Diagram for `Payroll -- The Core Model`

`MailMethod` object, the corresponding employee will have his paychecks mailed to him. The address to which the checks are mailed is recorded in the `MailMethod` object. If the `Employee` object contains a `DirectMethod` object, then his pay will be directly deposited into the bank account that is recorded in the `DirectMethod` object. If the `Employee` contains a `HoldMethod` object, his paychecks will be sent to the paymaster to be held for pickup.

Finally, Figure 18-6 applies the NULL OBJECT pattern to union membership. Each `Employee` object contains an `Affiliation` object, which has two forms. If the `Employee` contains a `NoAffiliation` object, then his pay is not adjusted by any organization other than the employer. However, if the `Employee` object contains a `Union-Affiliation` object, that employee must pay the dues and service charges that are recorded in that `UnionAffiliation` object.

This use of these patterns makes this system conform well to the Open-Closed Principle (OCP). The `Employee` class is closed against changes in payment method, payment classification, and union affiliation. New methods, classifications, and affiliations can be added to the system without affecting `Employee`.

Figure 18-6 is becoming our *core model* or architecture. It's at the heart of everything that the payroll system does. There will be many other classes and designs in the payroll application, but they will all be secondary to this fundamental structure. Of course, this structure is not cast in stone: It will be evolving along with everything else.

Payday

Use Case 7
Run the Payroll for Today

> Upon receiving the Payday transaction, the system finds all those employees that should be paid on the specified date. The system then determines how much they are owed and pays them according to their selected payment method.
>
> `Payday <date>`

Although it is easy to understand the intent of this use case, it is not so simple to determine what impact it has on the static structure of Figure 18-6. We need to answer several questions.

First, how does the `Employee` object know how to calculate its pay? Certainly if the employee is hourly, the system must tally up his time cards and multiply by the hourly rate. If the employee is commissioned, the system must tally up his sales receipts, multiply by the commission rate, and add the base salary. But where does this get done? The ideal place seems to be in the `PaymentClassification` derivatives. These objects maintain the records needed to calculate pay, so they should probably have the methods for determining pay. Figure 18-7 shows a collaboration diagram that describes how this might work.

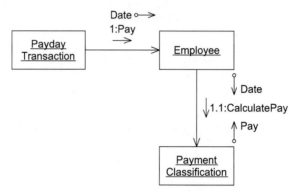

Figure 18-7 Calculating an Employee's Pay

When the `Employee` object is asked to calculate pay, it refers this request to its `PaymentClassification` object. The actual algorithm employed depends on the type of `PaymentClassification` that the `Employee` object contains. Figures 18-8 through 18-10 show the three possible scenarios.

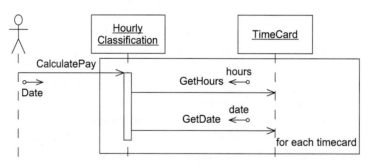

Figure 18-8 Calculating an Hourly Employee's Pay

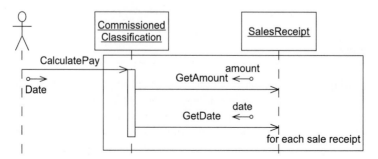

Figure 18-9 Calculating a Commissioned Employee's Pay

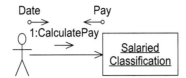

Figure 18-10   Calculating a Salaried Employee's Pay

Reflection: What Have We Learned?

We have learned that a simple use case analysis can provide a wealth of information and insights into the design of a system. Figures 18-6 through 18-10 came about by thinking about the use cases, that is, thinking about behavior.

Finding the Underlying Abstractions

To use the OCP effectively, we must hunt for abstractions and find those that underlie the application. Often these abstractions are not stated or even alluded to by the requirements of the application, or even the use cases. Requirements and use cases may be too steeped in details to express the generalities of the underlying abstractions.

What are the underlying abstractions of the Payroll application? Let's look again at the requirements. We see statements such as "Some employees work by the hour," "Some employees are paid a flat salary," and "Some [...] employees are paid a commission." This hints at the following generalization: "All employees are paid, but they are paid by different schemes." The abstraction here is that "All employees are paid." Our model of the `PaymentClassification` in Figures 18-7 through 18-10 expresses this abstraction nicely. Thus, this abstraction has already been found among our user stories by doing a very simple use-case analysis.

The Schedule Abstraction

Looking for other abstractions, we find "They are paid every Friday," "They are paid on the last working day of the month," and "They are paid every other Friday." This leads us to another generality: "All employees are paid according to some schedule." The abstraction here is the notion of the *schedule*. It should be possible to ask an `Employee` object whether a certain date is its payday. The use cases barely mention this. The requirements associate an employee's schedule with his payment classification. Specifically, hourly employees are paid weekly, salaried employees are paid monthly, and employees receiving commissions are paid biweekly; however, is this association essential? Might not the policy change one day so that employees could select a particular schedule or so that employees belonging to different departments or different divisions could have different schedules? Might not the schedule policy change independently of the payment policy? Certainly, this seems likely.

If, as the requirements imply, we delegated the issue of schedule to the `PaymentClassification` class, then our class could not be closed against issues of change in schedule. When we changed payment policy, we would also have to test schedule. When we changed schedules, we would also have to test payment policy. Both the OCP and the SRP would be violated.

An association between schedule and payment policy could lead to bugs in which a change to a particular payment policy caused incorrect scheduling of certain employees. Bugs like this may make sense to programmers, but they strike fear in the hearts of managers and users. They fear, and rightly so, that if schedules can be broken by a change to payment policy, then *any* change made *anywhere* might cause problems in *any* other unrelated part of the system. They fear that they cannot predict the effects of a change. When effects cannot be predicted, confidence is lost and the program assumes the status of "dangerous and unstable" in the minds of its managers and users.

Despite the essential nature of the schedule abstraction, our use-case analysis failed to give us any direct clues about its existence. To spot it required careful consideration of the requirements and an insight into the wiles of the user community. Overreliance on tools and procedures, and underreliance on intelligence and experience are recipes for disaster.

Figures 18-11 and 18-12 show the static and dynamic models for the schedule abstraction. As you can see, we've employed the STRATEGY pattern yet again. The `Employee` class contains the abstract `PaymentSchedule` class. There are three varieties of `PaymentSchedule` that correspond to the three known schedules by which employees are paid.

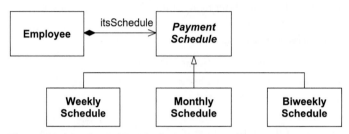

Figure 18-11   Static Model of a `Schedule` Abstraction

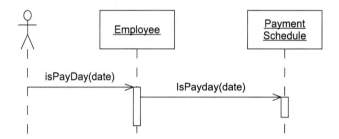

Figure 18-12   Dynamic Model of Schedule Abstraction

Payment Methods

Another generalization that we can make from the requirements is "All employees receive their pay by some method." The abstraction is the `PaymentMethod` class. Interestingly enough, this abstraction is already expressed in Figure 18-6.

Affiliations

The requirements imply that employees may have affiliations with a union; however, the union may not be the only organization that has a claim to some of an employee's pay. Employees might want to make automatic contributions to certain charities or have their dues to professional associations paid automatically. The generalization therefore becomes "The employee may be affiliated with many organizations that should be automatically paid from the employee's paycheck."

The corresponding abstraction is the `Affiliation` class that is shown in Figure 18-6. That figure, however, does not show the `Employee` containing more than one `Affiliation`, and it shows the presence of a `NoAffiliation` class. This design does not quite fit the abstraction we now think we need. Figures 18-13 and 18-14 show the static and dynamic models that represent the `Affiliation` abstraction.

The list of `Affiliation` objects has obviated the need to use the NULL OBJECT pattern for unaffiliated employees. Now, if the employee has no affiliation, his or her list of affiliations will simply be empty.

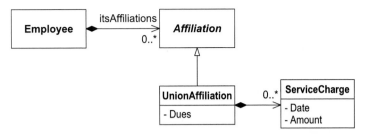

Figure 18-13   Static Structure of `Affiliation` Abstraction

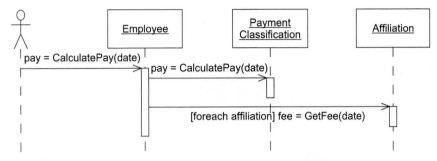

Figure 18-14   Dynamic Structure of `Affiliation` Abstraction

Conclusion

At the beginning of an iteration it is not uncommon to see the team assemble in front of a whiteboard and reason together about the design for the user stories that were selected for that iteration. Such a *quick design session* typically lasts less than an hour. The resulting UML diagrams, if any, may be left on the whiteboard, or erased. They are usually not commited to paper. The purpose of the session is to *start* the thinking process, and give the developers a common mental model to work from. The goal is *not* to nail down the design.

This chapter has been the textual equivalent to such a quick design Session.

Bibliography

1.   Jacobson, Ivar. *Object-Oriented Software Engineering, A Use-Case-Driven Approach*. Wokingham, England: Addison–Wesley, 1992.

19

The Payroll Case Study:
Implementation

© Jennifer M. Kohnke

It's long past time we started writing the code that supports and verifies the designs we've been spinning. I'll be creating that code in very small incremental steps, but I'll show it to you only at convenient points in the text. Don't let the fact that you only see fully formed snapshots of code mislead you into thinking that I wrote it in that form. In fact, between each batch of code you see, there will have been dozens of edits, compiles and test cases, each one making a tiny evolutionary change in the code.

You'll also see quite a bit of UML. Think of this UML as a quick diagram that I sketch on a whiteboard to show you, my pair partner, what I have in mind. UML makes a convenient medium for you and me to communicate by.

Figure 19-1 shows that we represent transactions as an abstract base class named `Transaction`, which has an instance method named `Execute()`. This is, of course, the COMMAND pattern. The implementation of the `Transaction` class is shown in Listing 19-1.

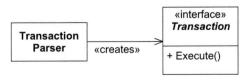

Figure 19-1   Transaction Interface

Listing 19-1

`Transaction.h`

```
#ifndef TRANSACTION_H
#define TRANSACTION_H

class Transaction
{
 public:
  virtual ~Transaction();
  virtual void Execute() = 0;
};

#endif
```

Adding Employees

Figure 19-2 shows a potential structure for the transactions that add employees. Note that it is within these transactions that the employees' payment schedule is associated with their payment classification. This is appropriate, since the transactions are contrivances instead of part of the core model. Thus, the core model is unaware of the association; the association is merely part of one of the contrivances and can be changed at any time. For example, we could easily add a transaction that allows us to change employee schedules.

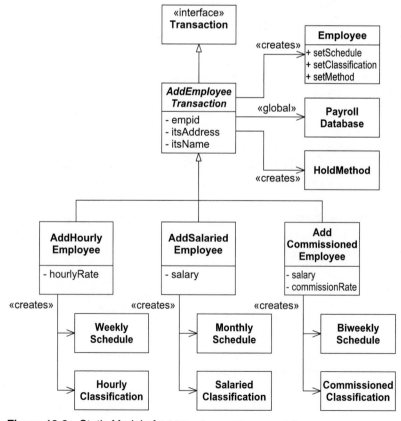

Figure 19-2 Static Model of `AddEmployeeTransaction`

Note, too, that the default payment method is to hold the paycheck with the paymaster. If an employee wants a different payment method, the change must be made with the appropriate ChgEmp transaction.

As usual, we begin writing code by writing tests first. Listing 19-2 is a test case that shows that the AddSalariedTransaction is working correctly. The code to follow will make that test case pass.

Listing 19-2

PayrollTest::TestAddSalariedEmployee

```
void PayrollTest::TestAddSalariedEmployee()
{
  int empId = 1;
  AddSalariedEmployee t(empId, "Bob", "Home", 1000.00);
  t.Execute();

  Employee* e = GpayrollDatabase.GetEmployee(empId);
  assert("Bob" == e->GetName());

  PaymentClassification* pc = e->GetClassification();
  SalariedClassification* sc = dynamic_cast<SalariedClassification*>(pc);
  assert(sc);

  assertEquals(1000.00, sc->GetSalary(), .001);
  PaymentSchedule* ps = e->GetSchedule();
  MonthlySchedule* ms = dynamic_cast<MonthlySchedule*>(ps);
  assert(ms);
  PaymentMethod* pm = e->GetMethod();
  HoldMethod* hm = dynamic_cast<HoldMethod*>(pm);
  assert(hm);
}
```

The Payroll Database

The AddEmployeeTransaction class uses a class called PayrollDatabase. This class maintains all the existing Employee objects in a Dictionary that are keyed by empID. It also maintains a Dictionary that maps union memberIDs to empIDs. The structure for this class appears in Figure 19-3. PayrollDatabase is an example of the FACADE pattern (page 173).

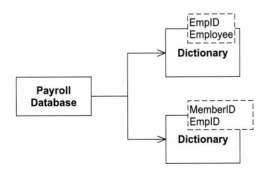

Figure 19-3 Static Structure of PayrollDatabase

Listings 19-3 and 19-4 show a rudimentary implementation of the PayrollDatabase. This implementation is meant to help us with our initial test cases. It does not yet contain the dictionary that maps member IDs to Employee instances.

Listing 19-3

`PayrollDatabase.h`

```
#ifndef PAYROLLDATABASE_H
#define PAYROLLDATABASE_H

#include <map>

class Employee;

class PayrollDatabase
{
 public:
  virtual ~PayrollDatabase();
  Employee* GetEmployee(int empId);
  void AddEmployee(int empid, Employee*);
  void clear() {itsEmployees.clear();}
 private:
  map<int, Employee*> itsEmployees;
};

#endif
```

Listing 19-4

`PayrollDatabase.cpp`

```
#include "PayrollDatabase.h"
#include "Employee.h"

PayrollDatabase GpayrollDatabase;

PayrollDatabase::~PayrollDatabase()
{
}

Employee* PayrollDatabase::GetEmployee(int empid)
{
  return itsEmployees[empid];
}

void PayrollDatabase::AddEmployee(int empid, Employee* e)
{
  itsEmployees[empid] = e;
}
```

In general, I consider database implementations to be details. Decisions about those details should be deferred as long as possible. Whether this particular database will be implemented with an RDBMS, flat files, or an OODBMS is irrelevant at this point. Right now, I'm just interested in creating the API that will provide database services to the rest of the application. I'll find appropriate implementations for the database later.

Deferring details about the database is an uncommon, but very rewarding, practice. Database decisions can usually wait until we have much more knowledge about the software and its needs. By waiting, we avoid the problem of putting too much infrastructure into the database. Rather, we implement just enough database facility for the needs of the application.

Using Template Method to Add Employees

Figure 19-4 shows the dynamic model for adding an employee. Note that the `AddEmployeeTransaction` object sends messages to *itself* in order to get the appropriate `PaymentClassification` and `PaymentSchedule` objects. These messages are implemented in the derivatives of the `AddEmployeeTransaction` class. This is an application of the Template Method pattern.

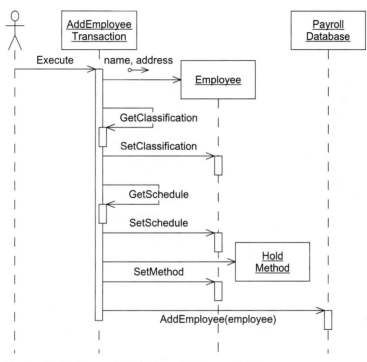

Figure 19-4   Dynamic Model for Adding an Employee

Listings 19-5 and 19-6 show the implementation of the Template Method pattern in the `AddEmployeeTransaction` class. This class implements the `Execute()` method to call two pure virtual functions that will be implemented by derivatives. These functions, `GetSchedule()` and `GetClassification()`, return the `PaymentSchedule` and `PaymentClassification` objects that the newly created `Employee` needs. The `Execute()` method then binds these objects to the `Employee` and saves the `Employee` in the `PayrollDatabase`.

Listing 19-5

AddEmployeeTransaction.h

```
#ifndef ADDEMPLOYEETRANSACTION_H
#define ADDEMPLOYEETRANSACTION_H

#include "Transaction.h"
#include <string>

class PaymentClassification;
class PaymentSchedule;
```

```cpp
class AddEmployeeTransaction : public Transaction
{
 public:
  virtual ~AddEmployeeTransaction();
  AddEmployeeTransaction(int empid, string name, string address);
  virtual PaymentClassification* GetClassification() const = 0;
  virtual PaymentSchedule* GetSchedule() const = 0;
  virtual void Execute();

 private:
  int itsEmpid;
  string itsName;
  string itsAddress;
};
#endif
```

Listing 19-6

AddEmployeeTransaction.cpp

```cpp
#include "AddEmployeeTransaction.h"
#include "HoldMethod.h"
#include "Employee.h"
#include "PayrollDatabase.h"

class PaymentMethod;
class PaymentSchedule;
class PaymentClassification;

extern PayrollDatabase GpayrollDatabase;

AddEmployeeTransaction::~AddEmployeeTransaction()
{
}

AddEmployeeTransaction::
AddEmployeeTransaction(int empid, string name, string address)
  : itsEmpid(empid)
  , itsName(name)
  , itsAddress(address)
{
}

void AddEmployeeTransaction::Execute()
{
  PaymentClassification* pc = GetClassification();
  PaymentSchedule* ps = GetSchedule();
  PaymentMethod* pm = new HoldMethod();
  Employee* e = new Employee(itsEmpid, itsName, itsAddress);
  e->SetClassification(pc);
  e->SetSchedule(ps);
  e->SetMethod(pm);
  GpayrollDatabase.AddEmployee(itsEmpid, e);
}
```

Listings 19-7 and 19-8 show the implementation of the AddSalariedEmployee class. This class derives from AddEmployeeTransaction and implements the GetSchedule() and GetClassification() methods to pass back the appropriate objects to AddEmployeeTransaction::Execute().

Listing 19-7
AddSalariedEmployee.h

```
#ifndef ADDSALARIEDEMPLOYEE_H
#define ADDSALARIEDEMPLOYEE_H

#include "AddEmployeeTransaction.h"

class AddSalariedEmployee : public AddEmployeeTransaction
{
 public:
  virtual ~AddSalariedEmployee();
  AddSalariedEmployee(int empid, string name,
                      string address, double salary);
  PaymentClassification* GetClassification() const;
  PaymentSchedule* GetSchedule() const;

 private:
  double itsSalary;
};
#endif
```

Listing 19-8
AddSalariedEmployee.cpp

```
#include "AddSalariedEmployee.h"
#include "SalariedClassification.h"
#include "MonthlySchedule.h"

AddSalariedEmployee::~AddSalariedEmployee()
{
}

AddSalariedEmployee::
AddSalariedEmployee(int empid, string name,
                    string address, double salary)
  : AddEmployeeTransaction(empid, name, address)
  , itsSalary(salary)
{
}

PaymentClassification*
AddSalariedEmployee::GetClassification() const
{
  return new SalariedClassification(itsSalary);
}

PaymentSchedule* AddSalariedEmployee::GetSchedule() const
{
  return new MonthlySchedule();
}
```

I leave the `AddHourlyEmployee` and `AddCommissionedEmployee` as exercises for the reader. Remember to write your test cases first.

Deleting Employees

Figures 19-5 and 19-6 present the static and dynamic models for the transactions that delete employees.

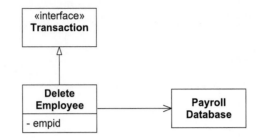

Figure 19-5   Static Model for `DeleteEmployee` Transaction

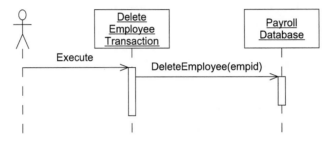

Figure 19-6   Dynamic Model for `DeleteEmployee` Transaction

Listing 19-9 shows the test case for deleting an employee. Listings 19-10 and 19-11 show the implementation of `DeleteEmployeeTransaction`. This is a very typical implementation of the COMMAND pattern. The constructor stores the data that the `Execute()` method eventually operates upon.

Listing 19-9

`PayrollTest::TestDeleteEmployee()`

```
void PayrollTest::TestDeleteEmployee()
{
  cerr << "TestDeleteEmployee" << endl;
  int empId = 3;
  AddCommissionedEmployee t(empId, "Lance", "Home", 2500, 3.2);
  t.Execute();
  {
    Employee* e = GpayrollDatabase.GetEmployee(empId);
    assert(e);
  }
  DeleteEmployeeTransaction dt(empId);
  dt.Execute();
  {
    Employee* e = GpayrollDatabase.GetEmployee(empId);
    assert(e == 0);
  }
}
```

Listing 19-10

`DeleteEmployeeTransaction.h`

```
#ifndef DELETEEMPLOYEETRANSACTION_H
#define DELETEEMPLOYEETRANSACTION_H

#include "Transaction.h"

class DeleteEmployeeTransaction : public Transaction
{
 public:
  virtual ~DeleteEmployeeTransaction();
  DeleteEmployeeTransaction(int empid);
  virtual void Execute();
 private:
  int itsEmpid;
};
#endif
```

Listing 19-11

`DeleteEmployeeTransaction.cpp`

```
#include "DeleteEmployeeTransaction.h"
#include "PayrollDatabase.h"

extern PayrollDatabase GpayrollDatabase;
DeleteEmployeeTransaction::~DeleteEmployeeTransaction()
{
}

DeleteEmployeeTransaction::DeleteEmployeeTransaction(int empid)
  : itsEmpid(empid)
{
}

void DeleteEmployeeTransaction::Execute()
{
  GpayrollDatabase.DeleteEmployee(itsEmpid);
}
```

Global Variables

By now you have noticed the `GpayrollDatabase` global. For decades, textbooks and teachers have been discouraging the use of global variables with good reason. Still, global variables are not intrinsically evil or harmful. This particular situation is an ideal choice for a global variable. There will only ever be one instance of the `PayrollDatabase` class, and it needs to be known by a very wide audience.

You might think that this could be better accomplished by using the SINGLETON or MONOSTATE patterns. It is true that these would serve the purpose. However, they do so by using global variables themselves. A SINGLETON or MONOSTATE is, by definition, a global entity. In this case I felt that a SINGLETON or MONOSTATE would smell of Needless Complexity. It's easier to simply keep the database instance in a global.

Time Cards, Sales Receipts, and Service Charges

Figure 19-7 shows the static structure for the transaction that posts time cards to employees. Figure 19-8 shows the dynamic model. The basic idea is that the transaction gets the Employee object from the PayrollDatabase, asks the Employee for its PaymentClassification object, and then creates and adds a TimeCard object to that PaymentClassification.

Notice that we cannot add TimeCard objects to general PaymentClassification objects; we can only add them to HourlyClassification objects. This implies that we must downcast the Payment-Classification object received from the Employee object to an HourlyClassification object. This is a good use for the dynamic_cast operator in C++, as shown later in Listing 19-15.

Listing 19-12 shows one of the test cases that verifies that time cards can be added to hourly employees. This test code simply creates an hourly employee and adds it to the database. Then it creates a TimeCard-Transaction and invokes Execute(). Then it checks the employee to see if the HourlyClassification contains the appropriate TimeCard.

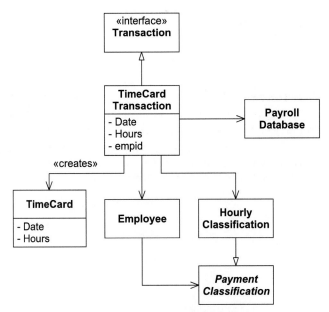

Figure 19-7   Static Structure of TimeCardTransaction

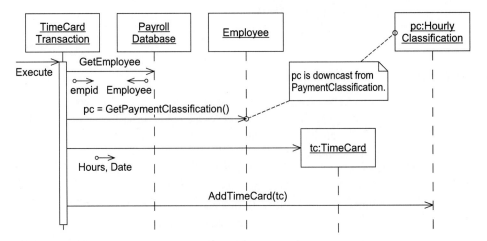

Figure 19-8   Dynamic Model for Posting a TimeCard

Listing 19-12

PayrollTest::TestTimeCardTransaction()

```
void PayrollTest::TestTimeCardTransaction()
{
  cerr << "TestTimeCardTransaction" << endl;
  int empId = 2;
  AddHourlyEmployee t(empId, "Bill", "Home", 15.25);
  t.Execute();
  TimeCardTransaction tct(20011031, 8.0, empId);
  tct.Execute();
  Employee* e = GpayrollDatabase.GetEmployee(empId);
  assert(e);
  PaymentClassification* pc = e->GetClassification();
  HourlyClassification* hc =
    dynamic_cast<HourlyClassification*>(pc);
  assert(hc);
  TimeCard* tc = hc->GetTimeCard(20011031);
  assert(tc);
  assertEquals(8.0, tc->GetHours());
}
```

Listing 19-13 shows the implementation of the TimeCard class. There's not much to this class right now. It's just a data class. Notice that I am using a long integer to represent dates. I'm doing this because I don't have a convenient Date class. I'm probably going to need one pretty soon, but I don't need it now. I don't want to distract myself from the task at hand, which is to get the current test case working. Eventually I will write a test case that will require a true Date class. When that happens, I'll go back and retrofit it into TimeCard.

Listing 19-13

TimeCard.h

```
#ifndef TIMECARD_H
#define TIMECARD_H

class TimeCard
{
 public:
  virtual ~TimeCard();
  TimeCard(long date, double hours);
  long GetDate() {return itsDate;}
  double GetHours() {return itsHours;}
 private:
  long itsDate;
  double itsHours;
};
#endif
```

Listings 19-14 and 19-15 show the implementation of the TimeCardTransaction class. Note the use of simple string exceptions. This is not particularly good long-term practice, but it suffices this early in development. After we get some idea of what the exceptions really ought to be, we can come back and create meaningful exception classes. Note also that the TimeCard instance is created only when we are sure we aren't going to throw an exception, so the throwing of the exception can't leak memory. It's very easy to create code that leaks memory or resources when throwing exceptions, so be careful. [1]

1.   And run, don't walk, to buy *Exceptional C++* and *More Exceptional C++*, by Herb Sutter. These two books will save you much
      anguish, wailing, and gnashing of teeth over exceptions in C++.

Listing 19-14

`TimeCardTransaction.h`

```
#ifndef TIMECARDTRANSACTION_H
#define TIMECARDTRANSACTION_H

#include "Transaction.h"

class TimeCardTransaction : public Transaction
{
 public:
  virtual ~TimeCardTransaction();
  TimeCardTransaction(long date, double hours, int empid);

  virtual void Execute();

 private:
  int itsEmpid;
  long itsDate;
  double itsHours;
};
#endif
```

Listing 19-15

`TimeCardTransaction.cpp`

```
#include "TimeCardTransaction.h"
#include "Employee.h"
#include "PayrollDatabase.h"
#include "HourlyClassification.h"
#include "TimeCard.h"

extern PayrollDatabase GpayrollDatabase;

TimeCardTransaction::~TimeCardTransaction()
{
}

TimeCardTransaction::TimeCardTransaction(long date,
                                         double hours,
                                         int empid)
  : itsDate(date)
  , itsHours(hours)
  , itsEmpid(empid)
{
}

void TimeCardTransaction::Execute()
{
  Employee* e = GpayrollDatabase.GetEmployee(itsEmpid);
  if (e){
    PaymentClassification* pc = e->GetClassification();
    if (HourlyClassification* hc = dynamic_cast<HourlyClassification*>(pc)) {
      hc->AddTimeCard(new TimeCard(itsDate, itsHours));
    } else
```

```
        throw("Tried to add timecard to non-hourly employee");
    } else
        throw("No such employee.");
}
```

Figures 19-9 and 19-10 show a similar design for the transaction that posts sales receipts to a commissioned employee. I've left the implementation of these classes as an exercise.

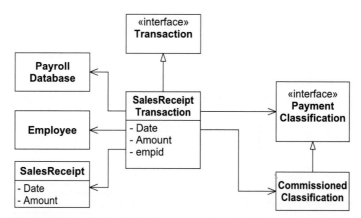

Figure 19-9 Static Model for `SalesReceiptTransaction`

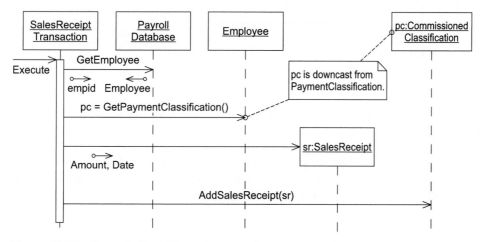

Figure 19-10 Dynamic Model for `SalesReceiptTransaction`

Figures 19-11 and 19-12 show the design for the transaction that posts service charges to union members.

These designs point out a mismatch between the transaction model and the core model that we have created. Our core `Employee` object can be affiliated with many different organizations, but the transaction model assumes that any affiliation must be a union affiliation. Thus, the transaction model provides no way to identify a particular kind of affiliation. Instead, it simply assumes that if we are posting a service charge, then the employee has a union affiliation.

The dynamic model addresses this dilemma by searching the set of `Affiliation` objects contained by the `Employee` object for a `UnionAffiliation` object. It then adds the `ServiceCharge` object to that `UnionAffiliation`.

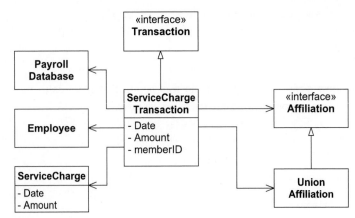

Figure 19-11 Static Model for `ServiceChargeTransaction`

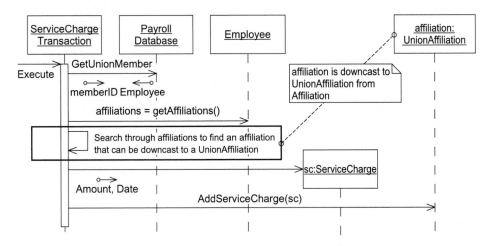

Figure 19-12 Dynamic Model for `ServiceChargeTransaction`

Listing 19-16 shows the test case for the `ServiceChargeTransaction`. It simply creates an hourly employee and adds a `UnionAffiliation` to it. It also makes sure that the appropriate member ID is registered with the `PayrollDatabase`. Then it creates a `ServiceChargeTransaction` and executes it. Finally it makes sure that the appropriate `ServiceCharge` was indeed added to `Employee`'s `UnionAffiliation`.

Listing 19-16

`PayrollTest::TestAddServiceCharge()`

```
void PayrollTest::TestAddServiceCharge()
{
  cerr << "TestAddServiceCharge" << endl;
  int empId = 2;
  AddHourlyEmployee t(empId, "Bill", "Home", 15.25);
  t.Execute();
  Employee* e = GpayrollDatabase.GetEmployee(empId);
  assert(e);
  UnionAffiliation* af = new UnionAffiliation(12.5);
  e->SetAffiliation(af);
  int memberId = 86; // Maxwell Smart
  GpayrollDatabase.AddUnionMember(memberId, e);
  ServiceChargeTransaction sct(memberId, 20011101, 12.95);
```

```
  sct.Execute();
  ServiceCharge* sc = af->GetServiceCharge(20011101);
  assert(sc);
  assertEquals(12.95, sc->GetAmount(), .001);
}
```

Code v. UML. When I drew the UML in Figure 19-12, I thought that replacing NoAffiliation with a list of affiliations was a better design. I thought it was more flexible and less complex. After all, I could add new affiliations any time I wanted, and I didn't have to create the NoAffiliation class. However, when writing the test case in Listing 19-16, I realized that calling SetAffiliation on Employee was better than calling AddAffiliation. After all, the requirements do not ask that an employee have more than one Affiliation, so there is no need to employ dynamic_cast to select between potentially many kinds. Doing so would be more complex than necessary.

This is an example of why doing too much UML without verifying it in code can be dangerous. The code can tell you things about your design that the UML cannot. Here, I was putting structures into the UML that weren't needed. Maybe one day they'd come in handy, but they have to be maintained between now and then. The cost of that maintenance may not be worth the benefit.

In this case, even though the cost of maintaining the dynamic_cast is relatively slight, I'm not going to employ it. Its much simpler to implement without a list of Affiliation objects. So I'll keep the NULL OBJECT pattern in place with the NoAffiliation class.

Listings 19-17 and 19-18 show the implementation of the ServiceChargeTransaction. It is indeed much simpler without the loop looking for UnionAffiliation objects. It simply gets the Employee from the database, downcasts its Affillation to a UnionAffilliation, and adds the ServiceCharge to it.

Listing 19-17

ServiceChargeTransaction.h

```
#ifndef SERVICECHARGETRANSACTION_H
#define SERVICECHARGETRANSACTION_H

#include "Transaction.h"

class ServiceChargeTransaction : public Transaction
{
 public:
  virtual ~ServiceChargeTransaction();
  ServiceChargeTransaction(int memberId, long date, double charge);
  virtual void Execute();

 private:
  int itsMemberId;
  long itsDate;
  double itsCharge;
};
#endif
```

Listing 19-18

ServiceChargeTransaction.cpp

```
#include "ServiceChargeTransaction.h"
#include "Employee.h"
```

```
#include "ServiceCharge.h"
#include "PayrollDatabase.h"
#include "UnionAffiliation.h"

extern PayrollDatabase GpayrollDatabase;

ServiceChargeTransaction::~ServiceChargeTransaction()
{
}

ServiceChargeTransaction::
ServiceChargeTransaction(int memberId, long date, double charge)
:itsMemberId(memberId)
, itsDate(date)
, itsCharge(charge)
{
}

void ServiceChargeTransaction::Execute()
{
  Employee* e = GpayrollDatabase.GetUnionMember(itsMemberId);
  Affiliation* af = e->GetAffiliation();
  if (UnionAffiliation* uaf = dynamic_cast<UnionAffiliation*>(af)) {
    uaf->AddServiceCharge(itsDate, itsCharge);
  }
}
```

Changing Employees

Figures 19-13 and 19-14 show the static structure for the transactions that change the attributes of an employee. This structure is easily derived from Use Case 6. All the transactions take an `EmpID` argument, so we can create a top-level base class called `ChangeEmployeeTransaction`. Below this base class are the classes that change single attributes, such as `ChangeNameTransaction` and `ChangeAddressTransaction`. The transactions that change classifications have a commonality of purpose, in that they all modify the same field of the `Employee` object. Thus, they can be grouped together under the abstract base, `ChangeClassificationTransaction`. The same is true of the transactions that change the payment and the affiliations. This can be seen by the structure of `ChangeMethodTransaction` and `ChangeAffiliationTransaction`.

Figure 19-15 shows the dynamic model for all the change transactions. Again we see the TEMPLATE METHOD pattern in use. In every case, the `Employee` object corresponding to the `EmpID` must be retrieved from the `PayrollDatabase`. Thus, the `Execute` function of `ChangeEmployeeTransaction` implements this behavior and then sends the `Change` message to itself. This method will be declared as virtual and implemented in the derivatives, as shown in Figures 19-16 and 19-17.

Listing 19-19 shows the test case for the `ChangeNameTransaction`. This test case is very simple. It uses the `AddHourlyEmployee` transaction to create an hourly employee named Bill. It then creates and executes a `ChangeNameTransaction` that should change the employee's name to Bob. Finally, it fetches the `Employee` instance from the `PayrollDatabase` and verifies that the name has been changed.

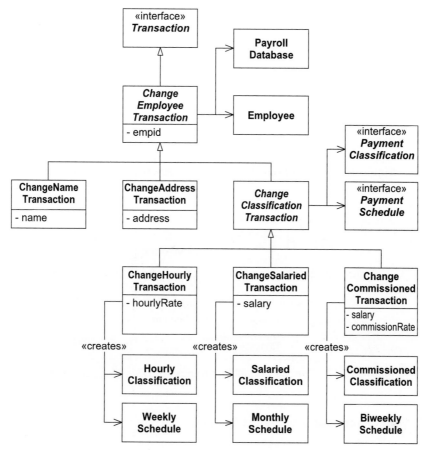

Figure 19-13 Static Model for ChangeEmployeeTransaction

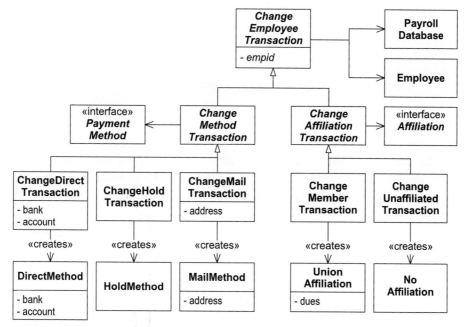

Figure 19-14 Static Model for ChangeEmployeeTransaction (cont.)

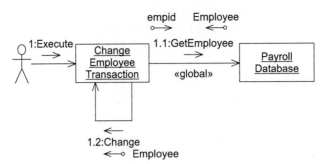

Figure 19-15   Dynamic Model for `ChangeEmployeeTransaction`

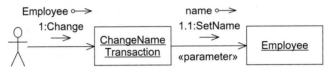

Figure 19-16   Dynamic Model for `ChangeNameTransaction`

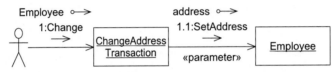

Figure 19-17   Dynamic Model for `ChangeAddressTransaction`

Listing 19-19

`PayrollTest::TestChangeNameTransaction()`

```
void PayrollTest::TestChangeNameTransaction()
{
  cerr << "TestChangeNameTransaction" << endl;
  int empId = 2;
  AddHourlyEmployee t(empId, "Bill", "Home", 15.25);
  t.Execute();
  ChangeNameTransaction cnt(empId, "Bob");
  cnt.Execute();
  Employee* e = GpayrollDatabase.GetEmployee(empId);
  assert(e);
  assert("Bob" == e->GetName());
}
```

Listings 19-20 and 19-21 show the implementation of the abstract base class `ChangeEmployee-Transaction`. The structure of the TEMPLATE METHOD pattern is clearly in evidence. The `Execute()` method simply reads the appropriate `Employee` instance from the `PayrollDatabase` and, if successful, invokes the pure virtual `Change()` function.

Listing 19-20

`ChangeEmployeeTransaction.h`

```
#ifndef CHANGEEMPLOYEETRANSACTION_H
#define CHANGEEMPLOYEETRANSACTION_H

#include "Transaction.h"
#include "Employee.h"
```

```
class ChangeEmployeeTransaction : public Transaction
{
 public:
  ChangeEmployeeTransaction(int empid);
  virtual ~ChangeEmployeeTransaction();
  virtual void Execute();
  virtual void Change(Employee&) = 0;

 private:
  int itsEmpId;
};

#endif
```

Listing 19-21

ChangeEmployeeTransaction.cpp

```
#include "ChangeEmployeeTransaction.h"
#include "Employee.h"
#include "PayrollDatabase.h"

extern PayrollDatabase GpayrollDatabase;

ChangeEmployeeTransaction::~ChangeEmployeeTransaction()
{
}

ChangeEmployeeTransaction::ChangeEmployeeTransaction(int empid)
: itsEmpId(empid)
{
}

void ChangeEmployeeTransaction::Execute()
{
  Employee* e = GpayrollDatabase.GetEmployee(itsEmpId);
  if (e != 0)
    Change(*e);
}
```

Listings 19-22 and 19-23 show the implementation of the ChangeNameTransaction. The second half of the TEMPLATE METHOD can easily be seen. The Change() method is implemented to change the name of the Employee argument. The structure of the ChangeAddressTransaction is very similar and is left as an exercise.

Listing 19-22

ChangeEmployeeTransaction.h

```
#ifndef CHANGENAMETRANSACTION_H
#define CHANGENAMETRANSACTION_H

#include "ChangeEmployeeTransaction.h"
#include <string>
```

```
class ChangeNameTransaction : public ChangeEmployeeTransaction
{
 public:
  virtual ~ChangeNameTransaction();
  ChangeNameTransaction(int empid, string name);
  virtual void Change(Employee&);

 private:
  string itsName;
};

#endif
```

Listing 19-23

ChangeNameTransaction.cpp

```
#include "ChangeNameTransaction.h"

ChangeNameTransaction::~ChangeNameTransaction()
{
}

ChangeNameTransaction::ChangeNameTransaction(int empid,
                                             string name)
: ChangeEmployeeTransaction(empid)
, itsName(name)
{
}

void ChangeNameTransaction::Change(Employee& e)
{
  e.SetName(itsName);
}
```

Changing Classification

Figure 19-18 shows how the dynamic behavior of ChangeClassificationTransaction is envisioned. The TEMPLATE METHOD pattern is used yet again. The transactions must create a new PaymentClassification object and then hand it to the Employee object. This is accomplished by sending the GetClassification mes-

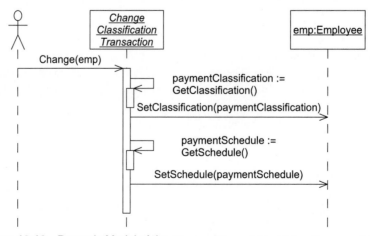

Figure 19-18 Dynamic Model of the ChangeClassificationTransaction

sage to itself. This abstract method is implemented in each of the classes derived from `ChangeClassification-Transaction`, as shown in Figures 19-19 through 19-21.

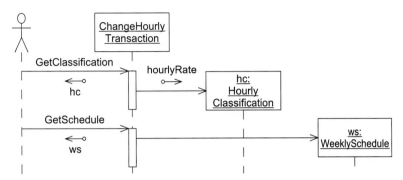

Figure 19-19 Dynamic Model of `ChangeHourlyTransaction`

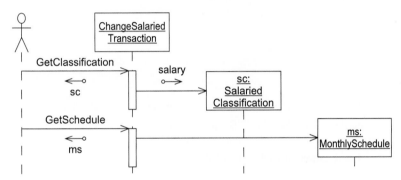

Figure 19-20 Dynamic Model of `ChangeSalariedTransaction`

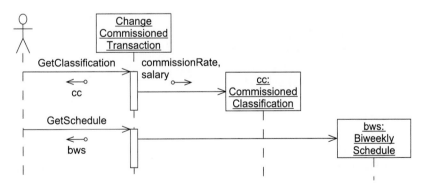

Figure 19-21 Dynamic Model of `ChangeCommissionedTransaction`

Listing 19-24 shows the test case for `ChangeHourlyTransaction`. The test case uses an `AddCommissionedEmployee` transaction to create a commissioned employee. It then creates a `ChangeHourlyTransaction` and executes it. It fetches the changed employee and verifies that its `PaymentClassification` is an `HourlyClassification` with the appropriate hourly rate and that its `PaymentSchedule` is a `WeeklySchedule`.

Listing 19-24

`PayrollTest::TestChangeHourlyTransaction()`

```
void PayrollTest::TestChangeHourlyTransaction()
{
  cerr << "TestChangeHourlyTransaction" << endl;
  int empId = 3;
  AddCommissionedEmployee t(empId, "Lance", "Home", 2500, 3.2);
  t.Execute();
  ChangeHourlyTransaction cht(empId, 27.52);
  cht.Execute();
  Employee* e = GpayrollDatabase.GetEmployee(empId);
  assert(e);
  PaymentClassification* pc = e->GetClassification();
  assert(pc);
  HourlyClassification* hc =
    dynamic_cast<HourlyClassification*>(pc);
  assert(hc);
  assertEquals(27.52, hc->GetRate(), .001);
  PaymentSchedule* ps = e->GetSchedule();
  WeeklySchedule* ws = dynamic_cast<WeeklySchedule*>(ps);
  assert(ws);
}
```

Listings 19-25 and 19-26 show the implementation of the abstract base class `ChangeClassification-Transaction`. Once again, the TEMPLATE METHOD pattern is easy to pick out. The `Change()` method invokes the two pure virtual functions, `GetClassification()` and `GetSchedule()`. It uses the return values from these functions to set the classification and schedule of the `Employee`.

Listing 19-25

`ChangeClassificationTransaction.h`

```
#ifndef CHANGECLASSIFICATIONTRANSACTION_H
#define CHANGECLASSIFICATIONTRANSACTION_H

#include "ChangeEmployeeTransaction.h"

class PaymentClassification;
class PaymentSchedule;

class ChangeClassificationTransaction : public ChangeEmployeeTransaction
{
 public:
  virtual ~ChangeClassificationTransaction();
  ChangeClassificationTransaction(int empid);
  virtual void Change(Employee&);
  virtual PaymentClassification* GetClassification() const = 0;
  virtual PaymentSchedule* GetSchedule() const = 0;
};
#endif
```

Listing 19-26

ChangeClassificationTransaction.cpp

```cpp
#include "ChangeClassificationTransaction.h"

ChangeClassificationTransaction::~ChangeClassificationTransaction()
{
}

ChangeClassificationTransaction::ChangeClassificationTransaction(int empid)
: ChangeEmployeeTransaction(empid)
{
}

void ChangeClassificationTransaction::Change(Employee& e)
{
  e.SetClassification(GetClassification());
  e.SetSchedule(GetSchedule());
}
```

Listings 19-27 and 19-28 show the implementation of the ChangeHourlyTransaction class. This class completes the TEMPLATE METHOD pattern by implementing the GetClassification() and GetSchedule() methods that it inherited from ChangeClassificationTransaction. It implements GetClassification() to return a newly created HourlyClassification. It implements GetSchedule() to return a newly created WeeklySchedule.

Listing 19-27

ChangeHourlyTransaction.h

```cpp
#ifndef CHANGEHOURLYTRANSACTION_H
#define CHANGEHOURLYTRANSACTION_H

#include "ChangeClassificationTransaction.h"

class ChangeHourlyTransaction : public ChangeClassificationTransaction
{
 public:
  virtual ~ChangeHourlyTransaction();
  ChangeHourlyTransaction(int empid, double hourlyRate);
  virtual PaymentSchedule* GetSchedule() const;
  virtual PaymentClassification* GetClassification() const;

 private:
  double itsHourlyRate;
};

#endif
```

Listing 19-28

ChangeHourlyTransaction.cpp

```cpp
#include "ChangeHourlyTransaction.h"
#include "WeeklySchedule.h"
#include "HourlyClassification.h"
```

```
ChangeHourlyTransaction::~ChangeHourlyTransaction()
{
}

ChangeHourlyTransaction::ChangeHourlyTransaction(int empid, double hourlyRate)
: ChangeClassificationTransaction(empid)
, itsHourlyRate(hourlyRate)
{
}

PaymentSchedule* ChangeHourlyTransaction::GetSchedule() const
{
  return new WeeklySchedule();
}

PaymentClassification* ChangeHourlyTransaction::GetClassification() const
{
  return new HourlyClassification(itsHourlyRate);
}
```

As always, the `ChangeSalariedTransaction` and `ChangeCommissionedTransaction` are left to the reader as an exercise.

A similar mechanism is employed for the implementation of `ChangeMethodTransaction`. The abstract `GetMethod` method is used to select the proper derivative of `PaymentMethod`, which is then handed to the `Employee` object. (See Figures 19-22 through 19-25.)

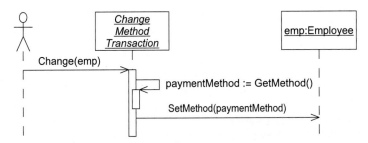

Figure 19-22   Dynamic Model of `ChangeMethodTransaction`

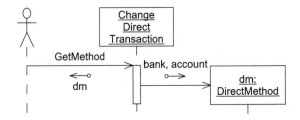

Figure 19-23   Dynamic Model of `ChangeDirectTransaction`

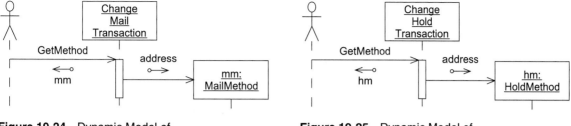

Figure 19-24 Dynamic Model of `ChangeMailTransaction`

Figure 19-25 Dynamic Model of `ChangeHoldTransaction`

The implementation of these classes turned out to be straightforward and unsurprising. They too are left as an exercise.

Figure 19-26 shows the implementation of the `ChangeAffiliationTransaction`. Once again, we use the TEMPLATE METHOD pattern to select the `Affiliation` derivative that should be handed to the `Employee` object. (See Figures 19-27 through 19-29.)

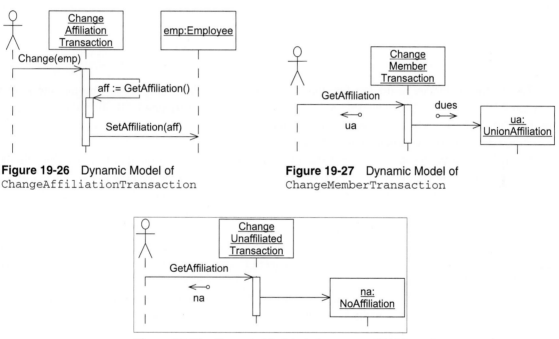

Figure 19-26 Dynamic Model of `ChangeAffiliationTransaction`

Figure 19-27 Dynamic Model of `ChangeMemberTransaction`

Figure 19-28 Dynamic Model of `ChangeUnaffiliatedTransaction`

What Was I Smoking?

I got quite a surprise when I went to implement this design. Look closely at the dynamic diagrams for the affiliation transactions. Can you spot the problem?

I began the implementation, as always, by writing the test case for `ChangeMemberTransaction`. You can see this test case in Listing 19-29. The test case starts out straightforward enough. It creates an hourly employee named Bill and then creates and executes a `ChangeMemberTransaction` to put Bill in the union. Then it checks to see that Bill has a `UnionAffiliation` bound to him and that the `UnionAffiliation` has the right dues rate.

Listing 19-29

PayrollTest::TestChangeMemberTransaction()

```
void PayrollTest::TestChangeMemberTransaction()
{
  cerr << "TestChangeMemberTransaction" << endl;
  int empId = 2;
  int memberId = 7734;
  AddHourlyEmployee t(empId, "Bill", "Home", 15.25);
  t.Execute();
  ChangeMemberTransaction cmt(empId, memberId, 99.42);
  cmt.Execute();
  Employee* e = GpayrollDatabase.GetEmployee(empId);
  assert(e);
  Affiliation* af = e->GetAffiliation();
  assert(af);
  UnionAffiliation* uf = dynamic_cast<UnionAffiliation*>(af);
  assert(uf);
  assertEquals(99.42, uf->GetDues(), .001);
  Employee* member = GpayrollDatabase.GetUnionMember(memberId);
  assert(member);
  assert(e == member);
}
```

The surprise is hidden in the last few lines of the test case. Those lines make sure that the Payroll-Database has recorded Bill's membership in the union. Nothing in the existing UML diagrams makes sure this happens. The UML is only concerned with the appropriate Affiliation derivative being bound to the Employee. I didn't notice the deficit at all. Did you?

I merrily coded the transactions as per the diagrams and then watched the unit test fail. Once the failure occurred, it was obvious what I had neglected. What was not obvious was the solution to the problem. How do I get the membership to be recorded by ChangeMemberTransaction, but erased by ChangeUnaffiliated-Transaction?

The answer was to add another pure virtual function to ChangeAffiliationTransaction named RecordMembership(Employee*). This function is implemented in ChangeMemberTransaction to bind the memberId to the Employee instance. In the ChangeUnaffiliatedTransaction it is implemented to erase the membership record.

Listings 19-30 and 19-31 show the resulting implementation of the abstract base class Change-AffiliationTransaction. Again, the use of the TEMPLATE METHOD pattern is obvious.

Listing 19-30

ChangeAffiliationTransaction.h

```
#ifndef CHANGEAFFILIATIONTRANSACTION_H
#define CHANGEAFFILIATIONTRANSACTION_H

#include "ChangeEmployeeTransaction.h"

class ChangeAffiliationTransaction: public ChangeEmployeeTransaction
{
 public:
  virtual ~ChangeAffiliationTransaction();
```

```
    ChangeAffiliationTransaction(int empid);
    virtual Affiliation* GetAffiliation() const = 0;
    virtual void RecordMembership(Employee*) = 0;
    virtual void Change(Employee&);
};

#endif
```

Listing 19-31

ChangeAffiliationTransaction.cpp

```
#include "ChangeAffiliationTransaction.h"

ChangeAffiliationTransaction::~ChangeAffiliationTransaction()
{
}

ChangeAffiliationTransaction::ChangeAffiliationTransaction(int empid)
: ChangeEmployeeTransaction(empid)
{
}

void ChangeAffiliationTransaction::Change(Employee& e)
{
    RecordMembership(&e);
    e.SetAffiliation(GetAffiliation());
}
```

Listing 19-32 and Listing 19-33 show the implementation of `ChangeMemberTransaction`. This is not particularly complicated or interesting. On the other hand, the implementation of `ChangeUnaffiliated-Transaction` in Listings 19-34 and 19-35 is a bit more substantial. The `RecordMembership` function has to decide whether or not the current employee is a union member. If so, it then gets the `memberId` from the `UnionAffiliation` and erases the membership record.

Listing 19-32

ChangeMemberTransaction.h

```
#ifndef CHANGEMEMBERTRANSACTION_H
#define CHANGEMEMBERTRANSACTION_H

#include "ChangeAffiliationTransaction.h"

class ChangeMemberTransaction : public ChangeAffiliationTransaction
{
 public:
  virtual ~ChangeMemberTransaction();
  ChangeMemberTransaction(int empid, int memberid, double dues);
  virtual Affiliation* GetAffiliation() const;
  virtual void RecordMembership(Employee*);
 private:
  int itsMemberId;
  double itsDues;
};
#endif
```

Listing 19-33

ChangeMemberTransaction.cpp

```cpp
#include "ChangeMemberTransaction.h"
#include "UnionAffiliation.h"
#include "PayrollDatabase.h"

extern PayrollDatabase GpayrollDatabase;

ChangeMemberTransaction::~ChangeMemberTransaction()
{
}

ChangeMemberTransaction::
ChangeMemberTransaction(int empid, int memberid, double dues)
: ChangeAffiliationTransaction(empid)
, itsMemberId(memberid)
, itsDues(dues)
{
}

Affiliation* ChangeMemberTransaction::GetAffiliation() const
{
  return new UnionAffiliation(itsMemberId, itsDues);
}

void ChangeMemberTransaction::RecordMembership(Employee* e)
{
  GpayrollDatabase.AddUnionMember(itsMemberId, e);
}
```

Listing 19-34

ChangeUnaffiliatedTransaction.h

```cpp
#ifndef CHANGEUNAFFILIATEDTRANSACTION_H
#define CHANGEUNAFFILIATEDTRANSACTION_H

#include "ChangeAffiliationTransaction.h"

class ChangeUnaffiliatedTransaction : public ChangeAffiliationTransaction
{
 public:
  virtual ~ChangeUnaffiliatedTransaction();
  ChangeUnaffiliatedTransaction(int empId);
  virtual Affiliation* GetAffiliation() const;
  virtual void RecordMembership(Employee*);
};
#endif
```

Listing 19-35

ChangeUnaffiliatedTransaction.cpp

```cpp
#include "ChangeUnaffiliatedTransaction.h"
#include "NoAffiliation.h"
#include "UnionAffiliation.h"
#include "PayrollDatabase.h"

extern PayrollDatabase GpayrollDatabase;
```

```
ChangeUnaffiliatedTransaction::~ChangeUnaffiliatedTransaction()
{
}

ChangeUnaffiliatedTransaction::ChangeUnaffiliatedTransaction(int empId)
: ChangeAffiliationTransaction(empId)
{
}

Affiliation* ChangeUnaffiliatedTransaction::GetAffiliation() const
{
  return new NoAffiliation();
}

void ChangeUnaffiliatedTransaction::RecordMembership(Employee* e)
{
  Affiliation* af = e->GetAffiliation();
  if (UnionAffiliation* uf = dynamic_cast<UnionAffiliation*>(af))
  {
    int memberId = uf->GetMemberId();
    GpayrollDatabase.RemoveUnionMember(memberId);
  }
}
```

I can't say that I'm very pleased with this design. It bothers me that the ChangeUnaffiliated-Transaction must know about UnionAffiliation. I could solve this by putting RecordMembership and EraseMembership abstract methods in the Affiliation class. However, this would force UnionAffiliation and NoAffiliation to know about the PayrollDatabase. And I'm not very happy about that either.[2]

Still, the implementation as it stands is pretty simple and only slightly violates the OCP. The nice thing is that very few modules in the system know about ChangeUnaffiliatedTransaction, so its extra dependencies aren't doing very much harm.

Paying Employees

Finally, it is time to consider the transaction that is at the root of this application: the transaction that instructs the system to pay the appropriate employees. Figure 19-29 shows the static structure of the PaydayTransaction class. Figures 19-30 through 19-33 describe the dynamic behavior.

These few dynamic models express a great deal of polymorphic behavior. The algorithm employed by the CalculatePay message depends on the kind of PaymentClassification that the employee object contains. The algorithm used to determine if a date is a payday depends on the kind of PaymentSchedule that the Employee contains. The algorithm used to send the payment to the Employee depends on the type of the PaymentMethod object. This high degree of abstraction allows the algorithms to be closed against the addition of new kinds of payment classifications, schedules, affiliations, or payment methods.

---

2.   I could use the VISITOR pattern (page 387) to solve this problem, but that would probably be way overengineered.

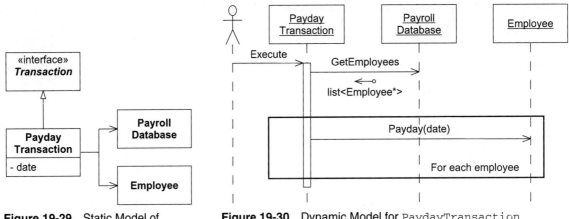

Figure 19-29 Static Model of
`PaydayTransaction`

Figure 19-30 Dynamic Model for `PaydayTransaction`

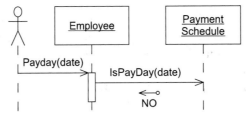

Figure 19-31 Dynamic Model Scenario: "Payday is not today."

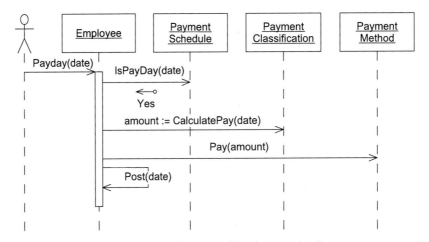

Figure 19-32 Dynamic Model Scenario: "Payday is today."

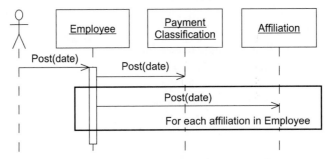

Figure 19-33 Dynamic Model Scenario: Posting Payment

The algorithms depicted in Figure 19-32 and Figure 19-33 introduce the concept of *posting*. After the correct pay amount has been calculated and sent to the Employee, the payment is posted; that is, the records involved in the payment are updated. Thus, we can define the CalculatePay method as calculating the pay from the last posting until the specified date.

Do We Want Developers Making Business Decisions?

Where did this notion of posting come from? It certainly wasn't mentioned in the user stories or use cases. As it happens, I cooked it up as a way to solve a problem that I perceived. I was concerned that the Payday method might be called multiple times with the same date, or with a date in the same pay period, so I wanted to make sure that the employee was not paid more than once. I did this on my own initiative, without asking my customer. It just seemed the right thing to do.

In effect, I have made a business decision. I have decided that multiple runs of the payroll program will produce different results. I should have asked my customer or project manager about this, since they might have very different ideas.

In checking with the customer, I find that the idea of posting goes against his intent.[3] The customer wants to be able to run the payroll system and then review the paychecks. If any of them are wrong, the customer wants to correct the payroll information and run the payroll program again. They tell me that I should never consider time cards or sales receipts for dates outside the current pay period.

So, we have to ditch the posting scheme. It seemed like a good idea at the time, but it was not what the customer wanted.

Paying Salaried Employees

There are two test cases in Listing 19-36. They test whether a salaried employee is being paid appropriately. The first test case makes sure the employee is paid on the last day of the month. The second test case makes sure the employee is not paid if it is not the last day of the month.

Listing 19-36
PayrollTest::TestPaySingleSalariedEmployee & co.

```
void PayrollTest::TestPaySingleSalariedEmployee()
{
  cerr << "TestPaySingleSalariedEmployee" << endl;
  int empId = 1;
  AddSalariedEmployee t(empId, "Bob", "Home", 1000.00);
  t.Execute();
  Date payDate(11,30,2001);
  PaydayTransaction pt(payDate);
  pt.Execute();
  Paycheck* pc = pt.GetPaycheck(empId);
  assert(pc);
  assert(pc->GetPayDate() == payDate);
  assertEquals(1000.00, pc->GetGrossPay(), .001);
  assert("Hold" == pc->GetField("Disposition"));
  assertEquals(0.0, pc->GetDeductions(), .001);
  assertEquals(1000.00, pc->GetNetPay(), .001);
}
```

3.   OK, I am the customer.

```
void PayrollTest::TestPaySingleSalariedEmployeeOnWrongDate()
{
  cerr << "TestPaySingleSalariedEmployeeWrongDate" << endl;
  int empId = 1;
  AddSalariedEmployee t(empId, "Bob", "Home", 1000.00);
  t.Execute();
  Date payDate(11,29,2001);
  PaydayTransaction pt(payDate);
  pt.Execute();
  Paycheck* pc = pt.GetPaycheck(empId);
  assert(pc == 0);
}
```

Remember back in Listing 19-13, when I was implementing the `TimeCard` class, I used a long integer to represent the date? Well, now I have a need for a real `Date` class. These two test cases will not pass unless I can tell whether the pay date is the last day of the month.

It turns out that I wrote a `Date` class about 10 years ago for a C++ class I was teaching. So I dug through my archives and found it on an old sparcstation that I had laying around.[4] I moved it to my development environment and managed to get it to compile in minutes. I found this surprising, since I had written it to work in Linux, but was now using it in Windows 2000. There were a couple of small bugs to fix, and I had to replace my homegrown string class with the STL string class, but in the end the effort was minimal.

Listing 19-37 shows the `Execute()` function of `PaydayTransaction`. It iterates through all the `Employee` objects in the database. It asks each employee if the date on this transaction is its pay date. If so, it creates a new paycheck for the employee and tells the employee to fill in its fields.

Listing 19-37

PaydayTransaction::Execute()

```
void PaydayTransaction::Execute()
{
  list<int> empIds;
  GpayrollDatabase.GetAllEmployeeIds(empIds);

  list<int>::iterator i = empIds.begin();
  for (; i != empIds.end(); i++) {
    int empId = *i;
    if (Employee* e = GpayrollDatabase.GetEmployee(empId)) {
      if (e->IsPayDate(itsPayDate)) {
        Paycheck* pc = new Paycheck(itsPayDate);
        itsPaychecks[empId] = pc;
        e->Payday(*pc);
      }
    }
  }
}
```

Listing 19-38 shows a fragment of `MonthlySchedule.cpp`. Notice that it implements `IsPayDate` to return `true` only if the argument date is the last day of the month. This algorithm points out why I needed the `Date` class. Doing this kind of simple date calculation is very difficult without a good `Date` class.

---

4.   The original oma.com. This was a sparcstation that I purchased for $6,000 from a company that had bought it for a project and then cancelled the project. Back in 1994 that was a real good deal. The fact that the machine is still quietly running on the Object Mentor network is a testimony to how well built it was.

Listing 19-38

MonthlySchedule.cpp (fragment)

```
namespace
{
  bool IsLastDayOfMonth(const Date& date)
  {
    int m1 = date.GetMonth();
    int m2 = (date+1).GetMonth();
    return (m1 != m2);
  }
}

bool MonthlySchedule::IsPayDate(const Date& payDate) const
{
  return IsLastDayOfMonth(payDate);
}
```

Listing 19-39 shows the implementation of `Employee::PayDay()`. This function is the generic algorithm for calculating and dispatching payment for all employees. Notice the rampant use of the STRATEGY pattern. All detailed calculations are deferred to the contained strategy classes: `itsClassification`, `itsAffiliation`, and `itsPaymentMethod`.

Listing 19-39

Employee::PayDay()

```
void Employee::Payday(Paycheck& pc)
{
  double grossPay = itsClassification->CalculatePay(pc);
  double deductions = itsAffiliation->CalculateDeductions(pc);
  double netPay = grossPay - deductions;
  pc.SetGrossPay(grossPay);
  pc.SetDeductions(deductions);
  pc.SetNetPay(netPay);
  itsPaymentMethod->Pay(pc);
}
```

Paying Hourly Employees

Getting the hourly employees paid is a good example of the incrementalism of test-first design. I started with very trivial test cases and worked my way up to ever more complex ones. I'll show the test cases below, and then I'll show you the production code that resulted from them.

Listing 19-40 shows the simplest case. We add an hourly employee to the database and then pay him. Since there aren't any time cards, we expect the paycheck to have a zero value. The utility function `ValidateHourly-Paycheck` represents a refactoring that happened later. At first, that code was simply buried inside the test function. This test case worked without making any changes to the rest of the code.

Listing 19-40

TestPaySingleHourlyEmployeeNoTimeCards

```
void PayrollTest::TestPaySingleHourlyEmployeeNoTimeCards()
{
  cerr << "TestPaySingleHourlyEmployeeNoTimeCards" << endl;
  int empId = 2;
```

```
  AddHourlyEmployee t(empId, "Bill", "Home", 15.25);
  t.Execute();
  Date payDate(11,9,2001); // Friday
  PaydayTransaction pt(payDate);
  pt.Execute();
  ValidateHourlyPaycheck(pt, empId, payDate, 0.0);
}

void PayrollTest::ValidateHourlyPaycheck(PaydayTransaction& pt,
                                         int empid,
                                         const Date& payDate,
                                         double pay)
{
  Paycheck* pc = pt.GetPaycheck(empid);
  assert(pc);
  assert(pc->GetPayDate() == payDate);
  assertEquals(pay, pc->GetGrossPay(), .001);
  assert("Hold" == pc->GetField("Disposition"));
  assertEquals(0.0, pc->GetDeductions(), .001);
  assertEquals(pay, pc->GetNetPay(), .001);
}
```

Listing 19-41 shows two test cases. The first tests whether we can pay an employee after adding a single time card. The second tests whether we can pay overtime for a card that has more than 8 hours on it. Of course, I didn't write these two test cases at the same time. Instead, I wrote the first one and got it working, and then I wrote the second one.

Listing 19-41

Test...OneTimeCard

```
void PayrollTest::TestPaySingleHourlyEmployeeOneTimeCard()
{
  cerr << "TestPaySingleHourlyEmployeeOneTimeCard" << endl;
  int empId = 2;
  AddHourlyEmployee t(empId, "Bill", "Home", 15.25);
  t.Execute();
  Date payDate(11,9,2001); // Friday

  TimeCardTransaction tc(payDate, 2.0, empId);
  tc.Execute();
  PaydayTransaction pt(payDate);
  pt.Execute();
  ValidateHourlyPaycheck(pt, empId, payDate, 30.5);
}

void
PayrollTest::TestPaySingleHourlyEmployeeOvertimeOneTimeCard()
{
  cerr << "TestPaySingleHourlyEmployeeOvertimeOneTimeCard" << endl;
  int empId = 2;
  AddHourlyEmployee t(empId, "Bill", "Home", 15.25);
  t.Execute();
  Date payDate(11,9,2001); // Friday

  TimeCardTransaction tc(payDate, 9.0, empId);
  tc.Execute();
```

```
PaydayTransaction pt(payDate);
pt.Execute();
ValidateHourlyPaycheck(pt, empId, payDate, (8 + 1.5) * 15.25);
}
```

Getting the first test case working was a matter of changing `HourlyClassification::CalculatePay` to loop through the time cards for the employee, add up the hours, and multiply by the pay rate. Getting the second test working forced me to refactor the function to calculate straight and overtime hours.

The test case in Listing 19-42 makes sure that we don't pay hourly employees unless the `Payday-Transaction` is constructed with a Friday.

Listing 19-42

TestPaySingleHourlyEmployeeOnWrongDate

```
void PayrollTest::TestPaySingleHourlyEmployeeOnWrongDate()
{
  cerr << "TestPaySingleHourlyEmployeeOnWrongDate" << endl;
  int empId = 2;
  AddHourlyEmployee t(empId, "Bill", "Home", 15.25);
  t.Execute();
  Date payDate(11,8,2001); // Thursday

  TimeCardTransaction tc(payDate, 9.0, empId);
  tc.Execute();
  PaydayTransaction pt(payDate);
  pt.Execute();

  Paycheck* pc = pt.GetPaycheck(empId);
  assert(pc == 0);
}
```

Listing 19-43 is a test case that makes sure we can calculate the pay for an employee who has more than one time card.

Listing 19-43

TestPaySingleHourlyEmployeeTwoTimeCards

```
void PayrollTest::TestPaySingleHourlyEmployeeTwoTimeCards()
{
  cerr << "TestPaySingleHourlyEmployeeTwoTimeCards" << endl;
  int empId = 2;
  AddHourlyEmployee t(empId, "Bill", "Home", 15.25);
  t.Execute();
  Date payDate(11,9,2001); // Friday

  TimeCardTransaction tc(payDate, 2.0, empId);
  tc.Execute();
  TimeCardTransaction tc2(Date(11,8,2001), 5.0, empId);
  tc2.Execute();
  PaydayTransaction pt(payDate);
  pt.Execute();
  ValidateHourlyPaycheck(pt, empId, payDate, 7*15.25);
}
```

Finally, the test case in Listing 19-44 proves that we will only pay an employee for time cards in the current pay period. Time cards from other pay periods are ignored.

Listing 19-44

`TestPaySingleHourlyEmployeeWithTimeCardsSpanningTwoPayPeriods`

```cpp
void PayrollTest::
TestPaySingleHourlyEmployeeWithTimeCardsSpanningTwoPayPeriods()
{
  cerr << "TestPaySingleHourlyEmployeeWithTimeCards"
          "SpanningTwoPayPeriods" << endl;
  int empId = 2;
  AddHourlyEmployee t(empId, "Bill", "Home", 15.25);
  t.Execute();
  Date payDate(11,9,2001); // Friday
  Date dateInPreviousPayPeriod(11,2,2001);

  TimeCardTransaction tc(payDate, 2.0, empId);
  tc.Execute();
  TimeCardTransaction tc2(dateInPreviousPayPeriod, 5.0, empId);
  tc2.Execute();
  PaydayTransaction pt(payDate);
  pt.Execute();
  ValidateHourlyPaycheck(pt, empId, payDate, 2*15.25);
}
```

The code that makes all this work was grown incrementally, one test case at a time. The structure you see in the code that follows evolved from test case to test case. Listing 19-45 shows the appropriate fragments of `HourlyClassification.cpp`. We simply loop through the time cards. For each time card, we check to see if it is in the pay period. If so, then we calculate the pay it represents.

Listing 19-45

`HourlyClassification.cpp` (Fragment)

```cpp
double HourlyClassification::CalculatePay(Paycheck& pc) const
{
  double totalPay = 0;
  Date payPeriod = pc.GetPayDate();
  map<Date, TimeCard*>::const_iterator i;
  for (i=itsTimeCards.begin(); i != itsTimeCards.end(); i++) {
    TimeCard * tc = (*i).second;
    if (IsInPayPeriod(tc, payPeriod))
      totalPay += CalculatePayForTimeCard(tc);
  }
  return totalPay;
}

bool HourlyClassification::IsInPayPeriod(TimeCard* tc, const Date& payPeriod) const
{
  Date payPeriodEndDate = payPeriod;
  Date payPeriodStartDate = payPeriod - 5;
  Date timeCardDate = tc->GetDate();
  return (timeCardDate >= payPeriodStartDate) &&
         (timeCardDate <= payPeriodEndDate);
}
```

```
double HourlyClassification::
CalculatePayForTimeCard(TimeCard* tc) const
{
    double hours = tc->GetHours();
    double overtime = max(0.0, hours - 8.0);
    double straightTime = hours - overtime;
    return straightTime * itsRate + overtime * itsRate * 1.5;
}
```

Listing 19-46 shows that the WeeklySchedule only pays on Fridays.

Listing 19-46

WeeklySchedule::IsPayDate

```
bool WeeklySchedule::IsPayDate(const Date& theDate) const
{
  return theDate.GetDayOfWeek() == Date::friday;
}
```

I leave calculating the pay for commissioned employees to you. There shouldn't be any big surprises. As a slightly more interesting exercise, allow time cards to be posted on the weekends, and calculate overtime correctly.

Pay Periods: A Design Problem

Now it's time to implement the union dues and service charges. I'm contemplating a test case that will add a salaried employee, convert it into a union member, and then pay the employee and ensure that the dues were subtracted from his pay. I've coded this in Listing 19-47.

Listing 19-47

PayrollTest::TestSalariedUnionMemberDues

```
void PayrollTest::TestSalariedUnionMemberDues()
{
  cerr << "TestSalariedUnionMemberDues" << endl;
  int empId = 1;
  AddSalariedEmployee t(empId, "Bob", "Home", 1000.00);
  t.Execute();
  int memberId = 7734;
  ChangeMemberTransaction cmt(empId, memberId, 9.42);
  cmt.Execute();
  Date payDate(11,30,2001);
  PaydayTransaction pt(payDate);
  pt.Execute();
  ValidatePaycheck(pt, empId, payDate, 1000.0 - ??? );
}
```

Notice the ??? in the last line of the test case. What should I put there? The user stories tell me that union dues are weekly, but salaried employees are paid monthly. How many weeks are in each month? Should I just multiply the dues by four? That's not very accurate. I'll ask the customer what he wants.[5]

The customer tells me that union dues are accrued every Friday. So what I need to do is count the number of Fridays in the pay period and multiply by the weekly dues. There are five Fridays in November, 2001—the month that the test case is written for. So I can modify the test case appropriately.

---

5.   And so Bob talks to himself yet again. Go to www.google.com/groups and look up "Schizophrenic Robert Martin."

Counting the Fridays in a pay period implies that I need to know what the starting and ending dates of the pay period are. I have done this calculation before in the function `IsInPayPeriod` in Listing 19-45 (and you probably wrote a similar one for the `CommissionedClassification`). This function is used by the `CalculatePay` function of the `HourlyClassification` object to ensure that only time cards from the pay period are tallied. Now it seems that the `UnionAffiliation` object must call this function too.

But wait! What is this function doing in the `HourlyClassification` class? We've already determined that the association between the payment schedule and the payment classification is accidental. The function that determines the pay period ought to be in the `PaymentSchedule` class, not in the `PaymentClassification` class!

It is interesting that our UML diagrams didn't help us catch this problem. The problem only surfaced when I started thinking about the test cases for `UnionAffiliation`. This is yet another example of how necessary coding feedback is to any design. Diagrams can be useful, but reliance on them without feedback from the code is risky business.

So how do we get the pay period out of the `PaymentSchedule` hierarchy and into the `PaymentClassification` and `Affiliation` hierarchies? These hierarchies do not know anything about each other. We could put the pay period dates into the `Paycheck` object. Right now, the `Paycheck` just has the end date of the pay period. We ought to be able to get the start date in there, too.

Listing 19-48 shows the change made to `PaydayTransaction::Execute()`. Notice that when the `Paycheck` is created, it is passed both the start and end dates of the pay period. If you jump ahead to Listing 19-55 you will see that it is the `PaymentSchedule` that calculates both. The changes to `Paycheck` should be obvious.

Listing 19-48

`PaydayTransaction::Execute()`

```
void PaydayTransaction::Execute()
{
  list<int> empIds;
  GpayrollDatabase.GetAllEmployeeIds(empIds);

  list<int>::iterator i = empIds.begin();
  for (; i != empIds.end(); i++) {
    int empId = *i;
    if (Employee* e = GpayrollDatabase.GetEmployee(empId)) {
      if (e->IsPayDate(itsPayDate)) {
        Paycheck* pc =
          new Paycheck(e->GetPayPeriodStartDate(itsPayDate), itsPayDate);
        itsPaychecks[empId] = pc;
        e->Payday(*pc);
      }
    }
  }
}
```

The two functions in `HourlyClassification` and `CommissionedClassification` that determined if `TimeCards` and `SalesReceipts` were within the pay period have been merged and moved into the base class `PaymentClassification`. (See Listing 19-49.)

Listing 19-49

`PaymentClassification::IsInPayPeriod(...)`

```
bool PaymentClassification::
IsInPayPeriod(const Date& theDate, const Paycheck& pc) const
```

```
{
  Date payPeriodEndDate = pc.GetPayPeriodEndDate();
  Date payPeriodStartDate = pc.GetPayPeriodStartDate();
  return (theDate >= payPeriodStartDate)
      && (theDate <= payPeriodEndDate);
}
```

Now we are ready to calculate the employee's union dues in `UnionAffilliation::Calculate-`
`Deductions`. The code in Listing 19-50 shows how this is done. The two dates that define the pay period are
extracted from the paycheck and passed to a utility function that counts the number of Fridays between them. This
number is then multiplied by the weekly dues rate to calculate the dues for the pay period.

Listing 19-50

UnionAffiliation::CalculateDeductions()

```
namespace
{
  int NumberOfFridaysInPayPeriod(const Date& payPeriodStart,
                                 const Date& payPeriodEnd)
  {
    int fridays = 0;
    for (Date day = payPeriodStart; day <= payPeriodEnd; day++)
    {
      if (day.GetDayOfWeek() == Date::friday)
        fridays++;
    }
    return fridays;
  }
}

double UnionAffiliation::
CalculateDeductions(Paycheck& pc) const
{
  double totalDues = 0;

  int fridays =
    NumberOfFridaysInPayPeriod(pc.GetPayPeriodStartDate(),
                               pc.GetPayPeriodEndDate());
  totalDues = itsDues * fridays;
  return totalDues;
}
```

The last two test cases have to do with union service charges. The first test case is shown in Listing 19-51. It
makes sure that we deduct service charges appropriately.

Listing 19-51

PayrollTest::TestHourlyUnionMemberServiceCharge

```
void PayrollTest::TestHourlyUnionMemberServiceCharge()
{
  cerr << "TestHourlyUnionMemberServiceCharge" << endl;
  int empId = 1;
  AddHourlyEmployee t(empId, "Bill", "Home", 15.24);
  t.Execute();
```

```
  int memberId = 7734;
  ChangeMemberTransaction cmt(empId, memberId, 9.42);
  cmt.Execute();
  Date payDate(11,9,2001);
  ServiceChargeTransaction sct(memberId, payDate, 19.42);
  sct.Execute();
  TimeCardTransaction tct(payDate, 8.0, empId);
  tct.Execute();
  PaydayTransaction pt(payDate);
  pt.Execute();
  Paycheck* pc = pt.GetPaycheck(empId);
  assert(pc);
  assert(pc->GetPayPeriodEndDate() == payDate);
  assertEquals(8*15.24, pc->GetGrossPay(), .001);
  assert("Hold" == pc->GetField("Disposition"));
  assertEquals(9.42 + 19.42, pc->GetDeductions(), .001);
  assertEquals((8*15.24)-(9.42 + 19.42), pc->GetNetPay(), .001);
}
```

The second test case posed something of a problem for me. You can see it in Listing 19-52. This test case makes sure that service charges dated outside the current pay period are not deducted.

Listing 19-52

PayrollTest::TestServiceChargesSpanningMultiplePayPeriods

```
void PayrollTest::
TestServiceChargesSpanningMultiplePayPeriods()
{
  cerr << "TestServiceChargesSpanningMultiplePayPeriods" << endl;
  int empId = 1;
  AddHourlyEmployee t(empId, "Bill", "Home", 15.24);
  t.Execute();
  int memberId = 7734;
  ChangeMemberTransaction cmt(empId, memberId, 9.42);
  cmt.Execute();
  Date earlyDate(11,2,2001); // previous Friday
  Date payDate(11,9,2001);
  Date lateDate(11,16,2001); // next Friday
  ServiceChargeTransaction sct(memberId, payDate, 19.42);
  sct.Execute();
  ServiceChargeTransaction sctEarly(memberId, earlyDate, 100.00);
  sctEarly.Execute();
  ServiceChargeTransaction sctLate(memberId, lateDate, 200.00);
  sctLate.Execute();
  TimeCardTransaction tct(payDate, 8.0, empId);
  tct.Execute();
  PaydayTransaction pt(payDate);
  pt.Execute();
  Paycheck* pc = pt.GetPaycheck(empId);
  assert(pc);
  assert(pc->GetPayPeriodEndDate() == payDate);
```

```
assertEquals(8*15.24, pc->GetGrossPay(), .001);
assert("Hold" == pc->GetField("Disposition"));
assertEquals(9.42 + 19.42, pc->GetDeductions(), .001);
assertEquals((8*15.24)-(9.42 + 19.42), pc->GetNetPay(), .001);
}
```

To implement this, I wanted `UnionAffiliation::CalculateDeductions` to call `IsInPayPeriod`. Unfortunately, we just put `IsInPayPeriod` in the `PaymentClassification` class. (See Listing 19-49.) It was convenient to put it there while it was the derivatives of `PaymentClassification` that needed to call it. But now other classes need it as well. So I moved the function into the `Date` class. After all, the function is simply determining if a given date is between two other given dates. (See Listing 19-53.)

Listing 19-53

Date::IsBetween

```
static bool IsBetween(const Date& theDate,
                      const Date& startDate,
                      const Date& endDate)
{
  return (theDate >= startDate) && (theDate <= endDate);
}
```

Now, we can finally finish the `UnionAffiliation::CalculateDeductions` function. I leave that as an exercise for you.

Listings 19-54 and 19-55 show the implementation of the `Employee` class.

Listing 19-54

Employee.h

```
#ifndef EMPLOYEE_H
#define EMPLOYEE_H

#include <string>

class PaymentSchedule;
class PaymentClassification;
class PaymentMethod;
class Affiliation;
class Paycheck;
class Date;

class Employee
{
 public:
  virtual ~Employee();
  Employee(int empid, string name, string address);
  void SetName(string name);
  void SetAddress(string address);
  void SetClassification(PaymentClassification*);
  void SetMethod(PaymentMethod*);
  void SetSchedule(PaymentSchedule*);
  void SetAffiliation(Affiliation*);
```

```
  int GetEmpid() const {return itsEmpid;}
  string GetName() const {return itsName;}
  string GetAddress() const {return itsAddress;}
  PaymentMethod* GetMethod() {return itsPaymentMethod;}
  PaymentClassification* GetClassification() {return itsClassification;}
  PaymentSchedule* GetSchedule() {return itsSchedule;}
  Affiliation* GetAffiliation() {return itsAffiliation;}

  void Payday(Paycheck&);
  bool IsPayDate(const Date& payDate) const;
  Date GetPayPeriodStartDate(const Date& payPeriodEndDate) const;

 private:
  int itsEmpid;
  string itsName;
  string itsAddress;
  PaymentClassification* itsClassification;
  PaymentSchedule* itsSchedule;
  PaymentMethod* itsPaymentMethod;
  Affiliation* itsAffiliation;
};


#endif
```

Listing 19-55

Employee.cpp

```
#include "Employee.h"
#include "NoAffiliation.h"
#include "PaymentClassification.h"
#include "PaymentSchedule.h"
#include "PaymentMethod.h"
#include "Paycheck.h"

Employee::~Employee()
{
  delete itsClassification;
  delete itsSchedule;
  delete itsPaymentMethod;
}

Employee::Employee(int empid, string name, string address)
: itsEmpid(empid)
, itsName(name)
, itsAddress(address)
, itsAffiliation(new NoAffiliation())
, itsClassification(0)
, itsSchedule(0)
, itsPaymentMethod(0)
{
}
```

```cpp
void Employee::SetName(string name)
{
  itsName = name;
}

void Employee::SetAddress(string address)
{
  itsAddress = address;
}

void Employee::SetClassification(PaymentClassification* pc)
{
  delete itsClassification;
  itsClassification = pc;
}

void Employee::SetSchedule(PaymentSchedule* ps)
{
  delete itsSchedule;
  itsSchedule = ps;
}

void Employee::SetMethod(PaymentMethod* pm)
{
  delete itsPaymentMethod;
  itsPaymentMethod = pm;
}

void Employee::SetAffiliation(Affiliation* af)
{
  delete itsAffiliation;
  itsAffiliation = af;
}

bool Employee::IsPayDate(const Date& payDate) const
{
  return itsSchedule->IsPayDate(payDate);
}

Date Employee::GetPayPeriodStartDate(const Date& payPeriodEndDate) const
{
  return itsSchedule->GetPayPeriodStartDate(payPeriodEndDate);
}

void Employee::Payday(Paycheck& pc)
{
  Date payDate = pc.GetPayPeriodEndDate();
  double grossPay = itsClassification->CalculatePay(pc);
  double deductions = itsAffiliation->CalculateDeductions(pc);
  double netPay = grossPay - deductions;
  pc.SetGrossPay(grossPay);
  pc.SetDeductions(deductions);
  pc.SetNetPay(netPay);
  itsPaymentMethod->Pay(pc);
}
```

Main Program

The main payroll program can now be expressed as a loop that parses transactions from an input source and then executes them. Figures 19-34 and 19-35 describe the statics and dynamics of the main program. The concept is simple: the `PayrollApplication` sits in a loop, alternately requesting transactions from the `Transaction-Source` and then telling those `Transaction` objects to `Execute`. Note that this is different from the diagram in Figure 19-1, and it represents a shift in our thinking to a more abstract mechanism.

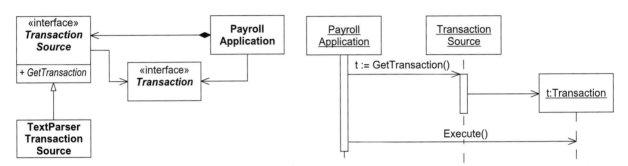

Figure 19-34   Static Model for the Main Program   **Figure 19-35**   Dynamic Model for the Main Program

`TransactionSource` is an abstract class that we can implement in several ways. The static diagram shows the derivative named `TextParserTransactionSource`, which reads an incoming text stream and parses out the transactions as described in the use cases. This object then creates the appropriate `Transaction` objects and sends them along to the `PayrollApplication`.

The separation of interface from implementation in the `TransactionSource` allows the source of the transactions to be abstract; for example, we could easily interface the `PayrollApplication` to a `GUITransactionSource` or a `RemoteTransactionSource`.

The Database

Now that this iteration has been analyzed, designed, and (mostly) implemented, we can consider the role of the database. The class `PayrollDatabase` clearly encapsulates something involving persistence. The objects contained within the `PayrollDatabase` must live longer than any particular run of the application. How should this be implemented? Clearly the transient mechanism used by the test cases is not sufficient for the real system. We have several options.

We could implement `PayrollDatabase` using an object-oriented database management system (OODBMS). This would allow the actual objects to reside within the permanent storage of the database. As designers, we would have little more work to do, since the OODBMS would not add much new to our design. One of the great benefits of OODBMS products is that they have little or no impact on the object model of the applications. As far as the design is concerned, the database barely exists.[6]

Another option would be to use a simple, flat text file to record the data. Upon initialization, the `PayrollDatabase` object could read that file and build the necessary objects in memory. At the end of the program, the `PayrollDatabase` object could write a new version of the text file. Certainly this option would not suffice for a company with hundreds of thousands of employees, or for one that wanted real-time concurrent access to

---

6.   This is optimistic. In a simple application like Payroll, the use of an OODBMS would have very little impact upon the design of the
       program. As applications become more and more complicated, the amount of impact that the OODBMS has upon the application
       increases. Still, the impact is far less than the impact an RDBMS would have.

its payroll database. However, it might suffice for a smaller company, and it could certainly be used as a mechanism for testing the rest of the application classes without investing in a big database system.

Still another option would be to incorporate a relational database management system (RDBMS) into the `PayrollDatabase` object. The implementation of the `PayrollDatabase` object would then make the appropriate queries to the RDMBS to temporarily create the necessary objects in memory.

The point is that, as far as the application is concerned, databases are simply mechanisms for managing storage. They should usually not be considered as a major factor of the design and implementation. As we have shown here, they can be left for last and handled as a detail.[7] By doing so, we leave open a number of interesting options for implementing the needed persistence and for creating mechanisms to test the rest of the application. We also do not tie ourselves to any particular database technology or product. We have the freedom to choose the database we need, based upon the rest of the design, and we maintain the freedom to change or replace that database product in the future as needed.

Summary of Payroll Design

In roughly 50 diagrams, and 3300 lines of code, we have shown the design and implementation of one iteration of the payroll application. The design employs a large amount of abstraction and polymorphism. The result is that large portions of the design are closed against changes of payroll policy. For example, the application could be changed to deal with employees who were paid quarterly based upon a normal salary and a bonus schedule. This change would require *addition* to the design, but little of the existing design and code would change.

During this process, we rarely considered whether we were performing analysis, design, or implementation. Instead, we concentrated upon issues of clarity and closure. We tried to find the underlying abstractions wherever possible. The result is that we have a good starting design for a payroll application, and we have a core of classes that are germane to the problem domain as a whole.

History

The diagrams in this chapter are derived from the Booch diagrams in the corresponding chapter of my 1995 book *Designing Object-Oriented C++ Applications using the Booch Method*. Those diagrams were created in 1994. As I created them, I also wrote some of the code that implemented them, to make sure that the diagrams made sense. However, I did not write anywhere near the amount of code presented here. Therefore, the diagrams did not benefit from significant feedback from the code and tests. This lack of feedback shows.

I wrote the current chapter in the order presented here. In every case, test cases were written before production code. In many cases, those tests were created incrementally, evolving as the production code also evolved. The production code was written to comply with the diagrams so long as that made sense. There were several cases where it did not make sense, and so I changed the design of the code.

One of the first places that this happened was back on page 219 when I decided against multiple `Affiliation` instances in the `Employee` object. Another was on page 229 when I found that I had not considered recording the employee's membership in the union in the `ChangeMemberTransaction`.

This is normal. When you design without feedback, you will necessarily make errors. It was the feedback imposed by the tests cases and running code that found these errors for us.

---

7.   Sometimes the nature of the database is one of the requirements of the application. RDBMSs provide powerful query and reporting systems that may be listed as application requirements. However, even when such requirements are explicit, the designers should still decouple the application design from the database design. The application design should not have to depend on any particular kind of database.

Resources

You can find the final version of this code on the Prentice Hall Web site, or on www.objectmentor.com/PPP.

Bibliography

1. Jacobson, Ivar. *Object-Oriented Software Engineering, A Use-Case-Driven Approach*. Wokingham, UK: Addison–Wesley, 1992.

SECTION 4

Packaging the Payroll System

In this section, we will explore the principles of design that help us split a large software system into packages. The first chapter in this section discusses those principles, the second describes a pattern that we'll use to help improve the packaging structure, and the third shows how the principles and pattern can be applied to the payroll system.

20

Principles of Package Design

Nice Package.

—Anthony

As software applications grow in size and complexity, they require some kind of high-level organization. Classes, while a very convenient unit for organizing small applications, are too finely grained to be used as the sole organizational unit for large applications. Something "larger" than a class is needed to help organize large applications. That something is called a *package*.

This chapter outlines six principles. The first three are principles of *package cohesion*. They help us allocate classes to packages. The last three principles govern *package coupling*. They help us determine how packages should be interrelated. The last two principles also describe a set of *Dependency Management (DM) metrics* that allows developers to measure and characterize the dependency structure of their designs.

Designing with Packages?

In UML, packages can be used as containers for groups of classes. By grouping classes into packages, we can reason about the design at a higher level of abstraction. We can also use the packages to manage the development and distribution of the software. The goal is to partition the classes in an application according to some criteria, and then allocate the classes in those partitions to packages.

But classes often have dependencies on other classes, and these dependencies will very often cross package boundaries. Thus, the packages will have dependency relationships with each other. The relationships between packages express the high-level organization of the application, and they need to be managed.

This begs a large number of questions.

1. What are the principles for allocating classes to packages?
2. What design principles govern the relationships between packages?
3. Should packages be designed before classes (top down)? Or should classes be designed before packages (bottom up)?
4. How are packages physically represented? In C++? In Java? In the development environment?
5. Once created, to what purpose will we put these packages?

This chapter presents six design principles that govern the creation, interrelationship, and use of packages. The first three govern the partitioning of classes into packages. The last three govern the interrelationships between packages.

Granularity: The Principles of Package Cohesion

The three principles of package cohesion help developers decide how to partition classes into packages. They depend on the fact that at least some of the classes and their interrelationships have been discovered. Thus, these principles take a "bottom-up" view of partitioning.

The Reuse–Release Equivalence Principle (REP)

> *The granule of reuse is the granule of release.*

What do you expect from the author of a class library that you are planning to reuse? Certainly you want good documentation, working code, well-specified interfaces, etc. But there are other things you want, too.

First of all, to make it worth your while to reuse this person's code, you want the author to guarantee to maintain it for you. After all, if *you* have to maintain it, you are going to have to invest a tremendous amount of time into it—time that might be better spent designing a smaller and better package for yourself.

Second, you are going to want the author to notify you in advance of any changes he plans to make to the interface and functionality of the code. But notification is not enough. The author must give you the option to refuse to use any new versions. After all, he might introduce a new version while you are in a severe schedule crunch, or he might make changes to the code that are simply incompatible with your system.

In either case, should you decide to reject his version, the author must guarantee to support your use of the old version for a time. Perhaps that time is as short as three months or as long as a year; that is something for the two of you to negotiate. But he can't just cut you loose and refuse to support you. If he won't agree to support your use of his older versions, then you may have to seriously consider whether you want to use his code and be subject to his capricious changes.

This issue is primarily political. It has to do with the clerical and support effort that must be provided if other people are going to reuse code. But those political and clerical issues have a profound effect on the packaging structure of software. In order to provide the guarantees that reusers need, authors must organize their software into reusable packages and then track those packages with release numbers.

The REP states that the granule of reuse (i.e., a package) can be no smaller than the granule of release. Anything that we reuse must also be released and tracked. It is not realistic for a developer to simply write a class and then claim it is reusable. Reusability comes only after there is a tracking system in place that offers the guarantees of notification, safety, and support that the potential reusers will need.

The REP gives us our first hint at how to partition our design into packages. Since reusability must be based on packages, reusable packages must contain reusable classes. So, at least some packages should comprise reusable sets of classes.

It may seem disquieting that a political force would affect the partitioning of our software, but software is not a mathematically pure entity that can be structured according to mathematically pure rules. Software is a human product that supports human endeavors. Software is created and used by humans. And if software is going to be reused, then it must be partitioned in a manner that humans find convenient for that purpose.

So what does this tell us about the internal structure of a package? One must consider the internal contents from the point of view of potential reusers. If a package contains software that should be reused, then it should not also contain software that is not designed for reuse. *Either all of the classes in a package are reusable or none of them are.*

Reusability is not the only criterion; we must also consider who the reuser is. Certainly, a container-class library is reusable, and so is a financial framework. But we would not want them to be part of the same package. There are many people who would like to reuse a container-class library who have no interest in a financial framework. Thus, we want all of the classes in a package to be reusable by the same audience. We do not want an audience to find that a package consists of some classes he needs and others that are wholly inappropriate for him.

The Common-Reuse Principle (CRP)

> *The classes in a package are reused together. If you reuse one of the classes in a package, you reuse them all.*

This principle helps us to decide which classes should be placed into a package. It states that classes that tend to be reused together belong in the same package.

Classes are seldom reused in isolation. Generally, reusable classes collaborate with other classes that are part of the reusable abstraction. The CRP states that these classes belong together in the same package. In such a package, we would expect to see classes that have lots of dependencies on each other.

A simple example might be a container class and its associated iterators. These classes are reused together because they are tightly coupled to each other. Thus, they ought to be in the same package.

But the CRP tells us more than just what classes to put together into a package. It also tells us what classes *not* to put in the package. When one package uses another, a dependency is created between the packages. It may be that the using package only uses one class within the used package. However, that doesn't weaken the dependency at all. The using package still depends on the used package. Every time the used package is released, the using package must be revalidated and rereleased. This is true even if the used package is being released because of changes to a class that the using package doesn't care about.

Moreover, it is common for packages to have physical representations as shared libraries, DLLs, JARs. If the used package is released as a JAR, then the using code depends on the entire JAR. Any modification to that JAR—even if the modification is to a class that the using code does not care about—will still cause a new version of the JAR to be released. The new JAR will still have to be redistributed, and the using code will still have to be revalidated.

Thus, I want to make sure that when I depend on a package, I depend on every class in that package. To say this another way, I want to make sure that the classes that I put into a package are inseparable, that it is impossible to depend on some and not the others. Otherwise, I will be revalidating and redistributing more than is necessary, and I will waste significant effort.

Therefore, the CRP tells us more about what classes shouldn't be together than what classes should be together. The CRP says that classes which are not tightly bound to each other with class relationships should not be in the same package.

The Common-Closure Principle (CCP)

The classes in a package should be closed together against the same kinds of changes. A change that affects a package affects all the classes in that package and no other packages.

This is the Single-Responsibility Principle restated for packages. Just as the SRP says that a class should not contain multiples reasons to change, this principle says that a package should not have multiple reasons to change.

In most applications, maintainability is more important that reusability. If the code in an application must change, you would rather that the changes occur all in one package, rather than being distributed through many packages. If changes are focused into a single package, then we need only release the one changed package. Other packages that don't depend on the changed package do not need to be revalidated or rereleased.

The CCP prompts us to gather together in one place all the classes that are likely to change for the same reasons. If two classes are so tightly bound, either physically or conceptually, that they always change together, then they belong in the same package. This minimizes the workload related to releasing, revalidating, and redistributing the software.

This principle is closely associated with the Open–Closed Principle (OCP). For it is "closure" in the OCP sense of the word that this principle is dealing with. The OCP states that classes should be closed for modification but open for extension. But as we learned, 100% closure is not attainable. Closure must be strategic. We design our systems such that they are closed to the most common kinds of changes that we have experienced.

The CCP amplifies this by grouping together classes that are open to certain types of changes into the same packages. Thus, when a change in requirements comes along, that change has a good chance of being restricted to a minimal number of packages.

Summary of Package Cohesion

In the past, our view of cohesion was much simpler than the last three principles have implied. We used to think that cohesion was simply the attribute of a module to perform one, and only one, function. However, the three principles of package cohesion describe a richer variety of cohesion. In choosing the classes to group together into packages, we must consider the opposing forces involved in reusability and developability. Balancing these forces with the needs of the application is nontrivial. Moreover, the balance is almost always dynamic. That is, the partitioning that is appropriate today might not be appropriate next year. Thus, the composition of the packages will likely jitter and evolve with time as the focus of the project changes from developability to reusability.

Stability: The Principles of Package Coupling

The next three principles deal with the relationships between packages. Here again, we will run into the tension between developability and logical design. The forces that impinge on the architecture of a package structure are technical, political, and volatile.

The Acyclic-Dependencies Principle (ADP)

Allow no cycles in the package-dependency graph.

Have you ever worked all day, gotten some stuff working and then gone home, only to arrive the next morning at to find that your stuff no longer works? Why doesn't it work? Because somebody stayed later than you and changed something you depend on! I call this the "morning-after syndrome."

The morning-after syndrome occurs in development environments where many developers are modifying the same source files. In relatively small projects with just a few developers, it isn't too big a problem. But as the size of the project and the development team grows, the mornings after can get pretty nightmarish. It is not uncommon, in undisciplined teams, for weeks to go by without being able to build a stable version of the project. Instead, everyone keeps on changing and changing their code trying to make it work with the last changes that someone else made.

Over the last several decades, two solutions to this problem have evolved. Both solutions have come from the telecommunications industry. The first is "the weekly build," and the second is the ADP.

The Weekly Build

The weekly build is common in medium-sized projects. It works like this: All the developers ignore each other for the first four days of the week. They all work on private copies of the code and don't worry about integrating with each other. Then, on Friday, they integrate all their changes and build the system.

This has the wonderful advantage of allowing the developers to live in an isolated world for four days out of five. The disadvantage, of course, is the large integration penalty that is paid on Friday.

Unfortunately, as the project grows, it becomes less feasible to finish integrating on Friday. The integration burden grows until it starts to overflow into Saturday. A few such Saturdays are enough to convince the developers that integration should really begin on Thursday. And so the start of integration slowly creeps toward the middle of the week.

As the duty cycle of development vs. integration decreases, the efficiency of the team decreases, too. Eventually this becomes so frustrating that the developers, or the project managers, declare that the schedule should be changed to a biweekly build. This suffices for a time, but the integration time continues to grow with project size.

This eventually leads to a crisis. To maintain efficiency, the build schedule has to be continually lengthened. Yet lengthening the build schedule increases project risks. Integration and testing become harder and harder to do, and the team loses the benefit of rapid feedback.

Eliminating Dependency Cycles

The solution to this problem is to partition the development environment into releasable packages. The packages become units of work, which can be checked out by a developer or a team of developers. When developers get a package working, they release it for use by the other developers. They give it a release number and move it into a directory for other teams to use. They then continue to modify their package in their own private areas. Everyone else uses the released version.

As new releases of a package are made, other teams can decide whether or not to immediately adopt the new release. If they decide not to, they simply continue using the old release. Once they decide that they are ready, they begin to use the new release.

Thus, none of the teams is at the mercy of the others. Changes made to one package do not need to have an immediate effect on other teams. Each team can decide for itself when to adapt its packages to new releases of the packages they use. Moreover, integration happens in small increments. There is no single point in time when all developers must come together and integrate everything they are doing.

This is a very simple and rational process, and it is widely used. However, to make it work you must *manage* the dependency structure of the packages. *There can be no cycles.* If there are cycles in the dependency structure, then the morning-after syndrome cannot be avoided.

Consider the package diagram in Figure 20-1. Here we see a rather typical structure of packages assembled into an application. The function of this application is unimportant for the purpose of this example. What *is* important is the dependency structure of the packages. Notice that this structure is a *directed graph*. The packages are the *nodes*, and the dependency relationships are the *directed edges*.

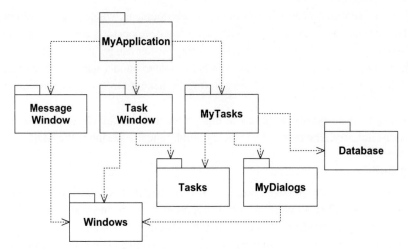

Figure 20-1   Package Structures are a Directed Acyclic Graph

Now notice one more thing. Regardless of the package at which you begin, it is impossible to follow the dependency relationships and wind up back at that package. This structures has no cycles. It is a *directed acyclic graph*. (DAG).

When the team responsible for MyDialogs makes a new release of their package it is easy to find out who is affected; you just follow the dependency arrows backwards. Thus, MyTasks and MyApplication are both going to be affected. The developers currently working on those packages will have to decide when they should integrate with the new release of MyDialogs.

Notice also that when MyDialogs is released, it has utterly no effect on many of the other packages in the system. They don't know about MyDialogs, and they don't care when it changes. This is nice. It means that the impact of releasing MyDialogs is relatively small.

When the developers working on the MyDialogs package would like to run a test of that package, all they need do is compile and link their version of MyDialogs with the version of the Windows package that they are currently using. None of the other packages in the system needs to be involved. This is nice; it means that the developers working on MyDialogs have relatively little work to do to set up a test, and that there are relatively few variables for them to consider.

When it is time to release the whole system, it is done from the bottom up. First the Windows package is compiled, tested, and released. Next are MessageWindow and MyDialogs. These are followed by Task and then TaskWindow and Database. MyTasks is next, and finally MyApplication. This process is very clear and easy to deal with. We know how to build the system because we understand the dependencies between its parts.

The Effect of a Cycle in the Package Dependency Graph

Let us say that the a new requirement forces us to change one of the classes in MyDialogs such that it makes use of a class in MyApplication. This creates a dependency cycle as shown in Figure 20-2.

This cycle creates some immediate problems. For example, the developers working on the MyTasks package know that in order to release, they must be compatible with Task, MyDialogs, Database, and Windows. However, with the cycle in place, they must now also be compatible with MyApplication, TaskWindow, and MessageWindow. That is, MyTasks now depends on *every other package in the system*. This makes MyTasks very difficult to release. MyDialogs suffers the same fate. In fact, the cycle forces MyApplication, MyTasks, and MyDialogs to always be released at the same time. They have, in effect, become one large package. And all the developers who are working in any of those packages will experience the morning-after syndrome once again.

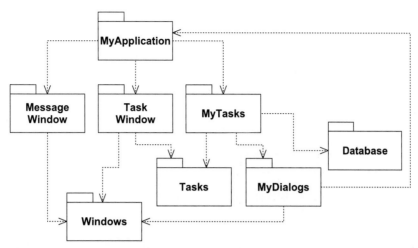

Figure 20-2   A Package Diagram with a Cycle

They will be stepping all over one another since they must all be using exactly the same release of each other's packages.

But this is just part of the trouble. Consider what happens when we want to test the Mydialogs package. We find that we must link in every other package in the system, including the Database package. This means that we have to do a *complete build* just to test MyDialogs. This is intolerable.

If you have ever wondered why you have to link in so many different libraries, and so much of everybody else's stuff, just to run a simple unit test of one of your classes, it is probably because there are cycles in the dependency graph. Such cycles make it very difficult to isolate modules. Unit testing and releasing become very difficult and error prone. And, in C++, compile times grow geometrically with the number of modules.

Moreover, when there are cycles in the dependency graph, it can be very difficult to work out the order in which to build the packages. Indeed, there may be no correct order. This can lead to some very nasty problems in languages like Java that read their declarations from compiled binary files.

Breaking the Cycle

It is always possible to break a cycle of packages and reinstate the dependency graph as a DAG. There are two primary mechanisms.

1. Apply the Dependency-Inversion Principle (DIP). In the case of Figure 20-3, we could create an abstract base class that has the interface that MyDialogs needs. We could then put that abstract base into MyDialogs and inherit it into MyApplication. This inverts the dependency between MyDialogs and MyApplication, thus breaking the cycle. (See Figure 20-3.)

   Notice, once again, that we named the interface after the client rather than the server. This is yet another application of the rule that interfaces belong to clients.
2. Create a new package on which both MyDialogs and MyApplication depend. Move the class(es) that they both depend on into that new package. (See Figure 20-4.)

The "Jitters"

The second solution implies that the package structure is volatile in the presence of changing requirements. Indeed, as the application grows, the package dependency structure jitters and grows. Thus, the dependency structure must always be monitored for cycles. When cycles occur, they must be broken somehow. Sometimes this will mean creating new packages, making the dependency structure grow.

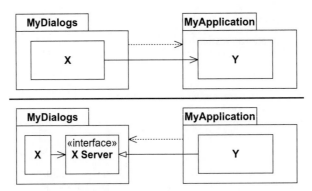

Figure 20-3   Breaking the cycle with dependency inversion

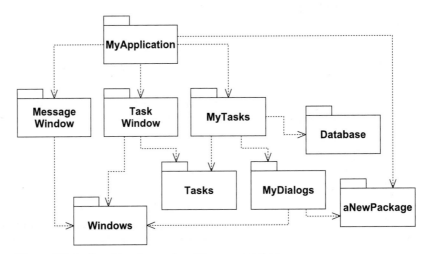

Figure 20-4   Breaking the cycle with a new package

Top-Down Design

The issues we have discussed so far lead to an inescapable conclusion. The package structure cannot be designed from the top down. This means that it is not one of the first things about the system that is designed. Indeed, it seems that it evolves as the system grows and changes.

You may find this to be counterintuitive. We have come to expect that large-grained decompositions, like packages, are also high-level *functional* decompositions. When we see a large-grained grouping like a package dependency structure, we feel that the packages ought to somehow represent the functions of the system. Yet this does not seem to be an attribute of package dependency diagrams.

In fact, package dependency diagrams have very little do to with describing the function of the application. Instead, they are a map to the *buildability* of the application. This is why they aren't designed at the start of the project. There is no software to build, and so there is no need for a build map. But as more and more classes accumulate in the early stages of implementation and design, there is a growing need to manage the dependencies so that the project can be developed without the morning-after syndrome. Moreover, we want to keep changes as localized as possible, so we start paying attention to the SRP and CCP and collocate classes that are likely to change together.

As the application continues to grow, we start becoming concerned about creating reusable elements. Thus, the CRP begins to dictate the composition of the packages. Finally, as cycles appear, the ADP is applied and the package dependency graph jitters and grows.

If we were to try to design the package dependency structure before we had designed any classes, we would likely fail rather badly. We would not know much about common closure, we would be unaware of any reusable elements, and we would almost certainly create packages that produce dependency cycles. Thus, the package dependency structure grows and evolves with the logical design of the system.

The Stable-Dependencies Principle (SDP)

Depend in the direction of stability.

Designs cannot be completely static. Some volatility is necessary if the design is to be maintained. We accomplish this by conforming to the Common-Closure Principle (CCP). Using this principle, we create packages that are sensitive to certain kinds of changes. These packages are *designed* to be volatile. We *expect* them to change.

Any package that we expect to be volatile should not be depended on by a package that is difficult to change! Otherwise the volatile package will also be difficult to change.

It is the perversity of software that a module that you have designed to be easy to change can be made hard to change by someone else simply hanging a dependency on it. Not a line of source code in your module need change, and yet your module will suddenly be hard to change. By conforming to the SDP, we ensure that modules that are intended to be easy to change are not depended on by modules that are harder to change than they are.

Stability

Stand a penny on its side. Is it stable in that position? You'd likely say that it was not. However, unless disturbed, it will remain in that position for a very long time. Thus, stability has nothing directly to do with frequency of change. The penny is not changing, but it is hard to think of it as stable.

Webster says that something is stable if it is "not easily moved."[1] Stability is related to the amount of work required to make a change. The penny is not stable because it requires very little work to topple it. On the other hand, a table is very stable because it takes a considerable amount of effort to turn it over.

How does this relate to software? There are many factors that make a software package hard to change: its size, complexity, clarity, etc. We are going to ignore all those factors and focus on something different. One sure way to make a software package difficult to change is to make lots of other software packages depend on it. A package with lots of incoming dependencies is very stable because it requires a great deal of work to reconcile any changes with all the dependent packages.

Figure 20-5 shows X, a stable package. This package has three packages depending on it; and therefore, it has three good reasons not to change. We say that it is *responsible* to those three packages. On the other hand, X depends on nothing, so it has no external influence to make it change. We say it is *independent*.

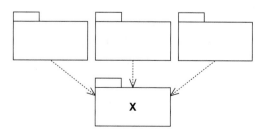

Figure 20-5   X: A Stable Package

---

1.   *Webster's Third New International Dictionary.*

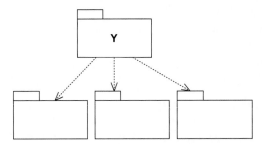

Figure 20-6   Y: An Instable Package

Figure 20-6, on the other hand, shows a very instable package. Y has no other packages depending on it; we say that it is irresponsible. Y also has three packages that it depends on, so changes may come from three external sources. We say that Y is dependent.

Stability Metrics

How can we measure the stability of a package? One way is to count the number of dependencies that enter and leave that package. These counts will allow us to calculate the *positional* stability of the package.

- (C_a) Afferent Couplings: The number of classes outside this package that depend on classes within this package.
- (C_e) Efferent Couplings: The number of classes inside this package that depend on classes outside this package.
- (Instability I)

$$I = \frac{C_e}{C_a + C_e}$$

This metric has the range [0,1]. $I = 0$ indicates a maximally stable package. $I = 1$ indicates a maximally instable package.

The C_a and C_e metrics are calculated by counting the number of *classes* outside the package in question that have dependencies on the classes inside the package in question. Consider the example in Figure 20-7.

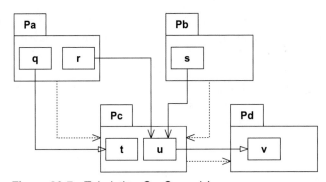

Figure 20-7   Tabulating C_a, C_e, and I.

The dashed arrows between the package represent package dependencies. The relationships between the classes of those packages show how those dependencies are actually implemented. There are inheritance and association relationships.

Now, let's say we want to calculate the stability of the package Pc. We find that there are three classes outside Pc that depend on classes in Pc. Thus $C_a = 3$. Moreover, there is one class outside Pc that classes in Pc depend on. Thus, $C_e = 1$, and $I = 1/4$.

In C++, these dependencies are typically represented by #include statements. Indeed, the I metric is easiest to calculate when you have organized your source code such that there is one class in each source file. In Java, the I metric can be calculated by counting import statements and qualified names.

When the I metric is 1, it means that no other package depends on this package ($C_a = 0$); and this package does depend on other packages ($C_e > 0$). This is as instable as a package can get; it is *irresponsible* and *dependent*. Its lack of dependents gives it no reason *not* to change, and the packages that it depends on may give it ample reason *to* change.

On the other hand, when the I metric is zero it means that the package is depended on by other packages ($C_a > 0$), but does not itself depend on any other packages ($C_e = 0$). It is *responsible* and *independent*. Such a package is as stable as it can get. Its dependents make it hard to change, and it has no dependencies that might force it to change.

The SDP says that the I metric of a package should be larger than the I metrics of the packages that it depends on (i.e., I metrics should decrease in the direction of dependency).

Not All Packages Should Be Stable

If all the packages in a system were maximally stable, the system would be unchangeable. This is not a desirable situation. Indeed, we want to design our package structure so that some packages are instable and some are stable. Figure 20-8 shows an ideal configuration for a system with three packages.

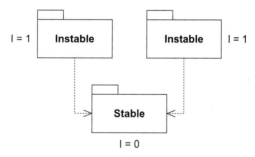

Figure 20-8   Ideal package configuration

The changeable packages are on top and depend on the stable package at the bottom. Putting the instable packages at the top of the diagram is a useful convention since any arrow that points *up* is violating the SDP.

Figure 20-9 shows how the SDP can be violated. Flexible is a package that we intend to be easy to change. We want Flexible to be instable. However, some developer, working in the package named Stable, hung a dependency on Flexible. This violates the SDP since the I metric for Stable is much lower than the I metric for Flexible. As a result, Flexible will no longer be easy to change. A change to Flexible will force us to deal with Stable and all its dependents.

To fix this, we somehow have to break the dependence of Stable on Flexible. Why does this dependency exist? Let's assume that there is a class C within Flexible, that another class U within Stable needs to use. (See Figure 20-10.)

We can fix this by employing the DIP. We create an interface class called IU and put it in a package named UInterface. We make sure that this interface declares all the methods that U needs to use. We then make C inherit from this interface. (See Figure 20-11.) This breaks the dependency of Stable on Flexible and forces both packages to be dependent on UInterface. UInterface is very stable ($I = 0$), and Flexible retains its necessary instability ($I = 1$). All the dependencies now flow in the direction of *decreasing I*.

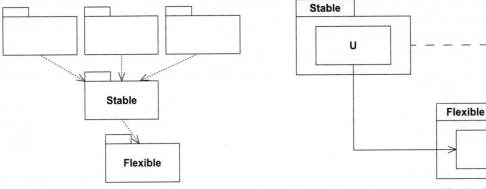

Figure 20-9   Violation of SDP   **Figure 20-10**   The cause of the bad dependency

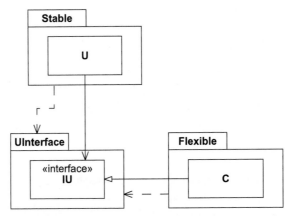

Figure 20-11   Fixing the stability violation using DIP

Where Do We Put the High-level Design?

Some software in the system should not change very often. This software represents the high-level architecture and design decisions. We don't want these architectural decisions to be volatile. Thus, the software that encapsulates the high-level design of the system should be placed into stable packages ($I = 0$). The instable packages ($I = 1$) should only contain the software that is likely to change.

However, if the high-level design is placed into stable packages, then the source code that represents that design will be difficult to change. This could make the design inflexible. How can a package that is maximally stable ($I = 0$) be flexible enough to withstand change? The answer is to be found in the OCP. This principle tells us that it is possible and desirable to create classes that are flexible enough to be extended without requiring modification. What kind of classes conforms to this principle? *Abstract* classes.

The Stable-Abstractions Principle (SAP)

> *A package should be as abstract as it is stable.*

This principle sets up a relationship between stability and abstractness. It says that a stable package should also be abstract so that its stability does not prevent it from being extended. On the other hand, it says that an instable package should be concrete since its instability allows the concrete code within it to be easily changed.

Thus, if a package is to be stable, it should also consist of abstract classes so that it can be extended. Stable packages that are extensible are flexible and do not overly constrain the design.

The SAP and the SDP combined amount to the DIP for packages. This is true because the SDP says that dependencies should run in the direction of stability, and the SAP says that stability implies abstraction. Thus, dependencies run in the direction of abstraction.

However, the DIP is a principle that deals with classes. And with classes there are no shades of grey. Either a class is abstract or it is not. The combination of the SDP and SAP deals with packages and allows that a package can be partially abstract and partially stable.

Measuring Abstraction

The *A* metric is a measure of the abstractness of a package. Its value is simply the ratio of abstract classes in a package to the total number of classes in the package.

N_c—The number of classes in the package.

N_a—The number of abstract classes in the package. Remember, an abstract class is a class with at least one pure interface, and it cannot be instantiated.

A—Abstractness.

$$A = \frac{N_a}{N_c}$$

The *A* metric ranges from 0 to 1. Zero implies that the package has no abstract classes at all. A value of 1 implies that the package contains nothing but abstract classes.

The Main Sequence

We are now in a position to define the relationship between stability (*I*) and abstractness (*A*). We can create a graph with *A* on the vertical axis and *I* on the horizontal axis. If we plot the two "good" kinds of packages on this graph, we will find the packages that are maximally stable and abstract at the upper left at (0,1). The packages that are maximally instable and concrete are at the lower right at (1,0). (See Figure 20-12.)

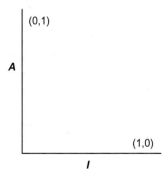

Figure 20-12 The *A–I* Graph

Not all packages can fall into one of these two positions. Packages have degrees of abstraction and stability. For example, it is very common for one abstract class to derive from another abstract class. The derivative is an abstraction that has a dependency. Thus, though it is maximally abstract, it will not be maximally stable. Its dependency will decrease its stability.

Since we cannot enforce that all packages sit at either (0,1) or (1,0), we must assume that there is a locus of points on the *A/I* graph that defines reasonable positions for packages. We can infer what that locus is by finding the areas where packages should *not* be (i.e., zones of *exclusion*). (See Figure 20-13.)

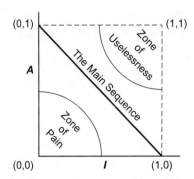

Figure 20-13   Zones of Exclusion

Consider a package in the area of (0,0). This is a highly stable and concrete package. Such a package is not desirable because it is rigid. It cannot be extended because it is not abstract. And it is very difficult to change because of its stability. Thus, we do not normally expect to see well-designed packages sitting near (0,0). The area around (0,0) is a zone of exclusion called the *Zone of Pain*.

It should be noted that there are cases when packages do indeed fall within the Zone of Pain. An example would be a database schema. Database schemas are notoriously volatile, extremely concrete, and highly depended on. This is one of the reasons that the interface between OO applications and databases is so difficult and that schema updates are generally painful.

Another example of a package that sits on (0,0) is a package that holds a concrete utility library. Although such a package has an *I* metric of 1, it may in fact be nonvolatile. Consider a "string" package for example. Even though all the classes within it are concrete, it is nonvolatile. Such packages are harmless in the (0,0) zone since they are not likely to be changed. Indeed, we can consider a third axis of the graph being that of volatility. If so, the graph in Figure 20-13 shows the plane at volatility = 1.

Consider a package near (1,1). This location is undesirable because it is maximally abstract and yet has no dependents. Such packages are useless. Thus, this is called the *Zone of Uselessness*.

It seems clear that we'd like our volatile packages to be as far from both zones of exclusion as possible. The locus of points that is maximally distant from each zone is the line that connects (1,0) and (0,1). This line is known as the *main sequence*.[2]

A package that sits on the main sequence is not "too abstract" for its stability, nor is it "too instable" for its abstractness. It is neither useless, nor particularly painful. It is depended on to the extent that it is abstract, and it depends on others to the extent that it is concrete.

Clearly, the most desirable positions for a package to hold are at one of the two endpoints of the main sequence. However, in my experience less than half the packages in a project can have such ideal characteristics. Those other packages have the best characteristics if they are on or close to the main sequence.

Distance from the Main Sequence

This leads us to our last metric. If it is desirable for packages to be on or close to the main sequence, we can create a metric which measures how far away a package is from this ideal.

D—Distance.

$$D = \frac{|A + I - 1|}{\sqrt{2}}.$$

This metric ranges from [0,~0.707].

2.   The name "main sequence" was adopted because of my interest in astronomy and HR diagrams.

D' —Normalized Distance.

$$D' = |A + I - 1|.$$

This metric is much more convenient than D since it ranges from [0,1]. Zero indicates that the package is directly on the main sequence. One indicates that the package is as far away as possible from the main sequence.

Given this metric, a design can be analyzed for its overall conformance to the main sequence. The D metric for each package can be calculated. Any package that has a D value that is not near zero can be reexamined and restructured. In fact, this kind of analysis has been a great aid to the author in helping to define packages that are more maintainable and less sensitive to change.

Statistical analysis of a design is also possible. One can calculate the mean and variance of all the D metrics for the packages within a design. One would expect a conformant design to have a mean and variance close to zero. The variance can be used to establish "control limits," which can identify packages that are "exceptional" in comparison to all the others. (See Figure 20-14.)

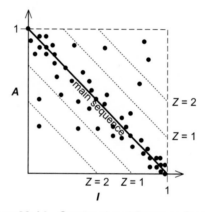

Figure 20-14 Scatter plot of Package D scores

In this scatter plot,[3] we see that the bulk of the packages lies along the main sequence, but some of them are more than one standard deviation ($Z = 1$) away from the mean. These aberrant packages are worth looking at. For some reason, they are either very abstract with few dependents or very concrete with many dependents.

Another way to use the metrics is to plot the D' metric of each package over time. Figure 20-15 shows a mock-up of such a plot. You can see that some strange dependencies have been creeping into the `Payroll` package over the last few releases. The plot shows a control threshold at $D' = 0.1$. The R2.1 point has exceeded this control limit, so it would be worth our while to find out why this package is so far from the main sequence.

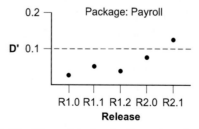

Figure 20-15 Time plot of a single package's D' scores

3. Not based on real data.

Conclusion

The *dependency-management metrics* described in this chapter measure the conformance of a design to a pattern of dependency and abstraction that I think is a "good" pattern. Experience has shown that certain dependencies are good and others are bad. This pattern reflects that experience. However, a metric is not a god; it is merely a measurement against an arbitrary standard. It is certainly possible that the standard chosen in this chapter is appropriate only for certain applications and is not appropriate for others. It may also be that there are far better metrics that can be used to measure the quality of a design.

21

FACTORY

© Jennifer M. Kohnke

The man who builds a factory builds a temple....

—Calvin Coolidge (1872–1933)

The Dependency-Inversion Principle (DIP)[1] tells us that we should prefer dependencies on abstract classes and avoid dependencies on concrete classes, especially when those classes are volatile. Therefore, the following snippet of code violates this principle:

```
Circle c = new Circle(origin, 1);
```

Circle is a concrete class. Therefore, those modules that create instances of Circle must violate DIP. Indeed, any line of code that uses the new keyword violates DIP.

There are times when violating the DIP is mostly harmless.[2] The more likely a concrete class is to change, the more likely depending on it will lead to trouble. But if the concrete class is not volatile, then depending on it is not worrisome.

For example, creating instances of String does not bother me. Depending on String is very safe because String is not likely to change any time soon.

---

1. "DIP: The Dependency-Inversion Principle" on page 127.
2. That's pretty good coverage.

On the other hand, when we are actively developing an application, there are many concrete classes that are very volatile. Depending on them is problematic. We'd rather depend on an abstract interface to shield us from the majority of the changes.

The FACTORY pattern allows us to create instances of concrete objects while depending only on abstract interfaces. Therefore, it can be of great assistance during active development when those concrete classes are highly volatile.

Figure 21-1 shows the problematic scenario. We have a class named SomeApp that depends on the interface Shape. SomeApp uses instances of Shape solely through the Shape interface. It does not use any of the specific methods of Square or Circle. Unfortunately, SomeApp also creates instances of Square and Circle and thus has to depend on the concrete classes.

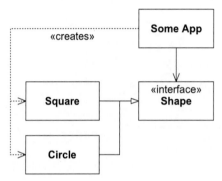

Figure 21-1   An app that violates the DIP to create concrete classes

We can fix this by applying the FACTORY pattern to SomeApp as in Figure 21-2. Here we see the ShapeFactory interface. This interface has two methods: makeSquare and makeCircle. The makeSquare method returns an instance of a Square, and the makeCircle method returns an instance of a Circle. However, the return type of both functions is Shape.

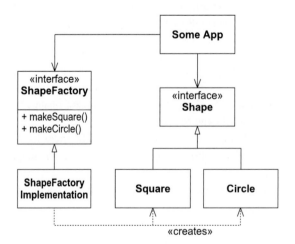

Figure 21-2   Shape Factory

Listing 21-1 shows what the ShapeFactory code looks like, and Listing 21-2 shows ShapeFactory-Implementation.

Listing 21-1

ShapeFactory.java

```java
public interface ShapeFactory
{
  public Shape makeCircle();
  public Shape makeSquare();
}
```

Listing 21-2

ShapeFactoryImplementation.java

```java
public class ShapeFactoryImplementation implements ShapeFactory
{
  public Shape makeCircle()
  {
    return new Circle();
  }

  public Shape makeSquare()
  {
    return new Square();
  }
}
```

Notice that this completely solves the problem of depending on concrete classes. The application code no longer depends on Circle or Square, and yet it still manages to create instances of them. It manipulates those instances through the Shape interface and never invokes methods that are specific to Square or Circle.

The problem of depending on a concrete class has been moved. Someone must create ShapeFactory-Implementation, but nobody else ever needs to create Square or Circle. ShapeFactoryImplementation will most likely be created by main or by an initialization function attached to main.

A Dependency Cycle

Astute readers will recognize that there is a problem with this form of the FACTORY pattern. The class ShapeFactory has a method for each of the derivatives of Shape. This results in a dependency cycle that makes it difficult to add new derivatives to Shape. Every time we add a new Shape derivative, we have to add a method to the ShapeFactory interface. In most cases, this means we'll have to recompile and redeploy all the users of ShapeFactory.[3]

We can get rid of this dependency cycle by sacrificing a little type safety. Instead of giving ShapeFactory one method for every Shape derivative, we can give it just one make function that takes a String. For example, look at Listing 21-3. This technique requires that ShapeFactoryImplementation use an if/else chain on the incoming argument to select which derivative of Shape to instantiate. This is shown in Listings 21-4 and 21-5.

---

3. Again, this isn't exactly necessary in Java. You might get away without recompiling and redeploying clients of a changed interface, but it's a risky business.

Listing 21-3

A snippet that creates a circle

```
public void testCreateCircle() throws Exception
{
  Shape s = factory.make("Circle");
  assert(s instanceof Circle);
}
```

Listing 21-4

ShapeFactory.java

```
public interface ShapeFactory
{
  public Shape make(String shapeName) throws Exception;
}
```

Listing 21-5

ShapeFactoryImplementation.java

```
public class ShapeFactoryImplementation implements ShapeFactory
{
  public Shape make(String shapeName) throws Exception
  {
    if (shapeName.equals("Circle"))
      return new Circle();
    else if (shapeName.equals("Square"))
      return new Square();
    else
      throw new Exception(
        "ShapeFactory cannot create " + shapeName);
  }
}
```

One might argue that this is dangerous because callers who misspell the name of a shape will get a run-time error instead of a compile time error. This is true. However, if you are writing the appropriate number of unit tests and applying test-driven development, then you'll catch these run-time errors long before they become problems.

Substitutable Factories

One of the great benefits of using factories is the ability to substitute one implementation of a factory for another. In this way, you can substitute families of objects within an application.

For example, imagine an application that had to adapt to many different database implementations. In our example, let's assume that the users can either use flat files or they can purchase an Oracle™ adapter. We might use the PROXY[4] pattern to isolate the application from the database implementation. We might also use factories to instantiate the proxies. Figure 21-3 shows the structure.

Notice that there are two implementations of EmployeeFactory. One creates proxies that work with flat files, and the other creates proxies that work with Oracle™. Notice also that the application does not know or care which is being used.

---

4.   We'll study PROXY later on page 327. Right now, all you need to know is that a PROXY is a class that knows how to read particular objects out of particular kinds of databases.

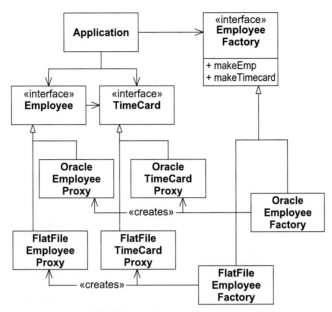

Figure 21-3   Substitutable Factory

Using Factories for Test Fixtures

When writing unit tests, we often want to test the behavior of a module in isolation from the modules it uses. For example, we might have a `Payroll` application that uses a database. (See Figure 21-4.) We may wish to test the function of the `Payroll` module without using the database at all.

We can accomplish this by using an abstract interface for the database. One implementation of this abstract interface uses the real database. Another implementation is test-code written to simulate the behavior of the database and to check that the database calls are being made correctly. Figure 21-5 shows the structure. The `PayrollTest` module tests the `PayrollModule` by making calls to it. It also implements the `Database` interface so that it can trap the calls that `Payroll` makes to the database. This allows `PayrollTest` to ensure that `Payroll` is behaving properly. It also allows `PayrollTest` to simulate many kinds of database failures and problems that are otherwise difficult to create. This is a technique that is sometimes known as *spoofing*.

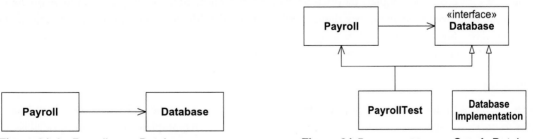

Figure 21-4   Payroll uses Database   **Figure 21-5**   `PayrollTest` Spoofs Database

However, how does `Payroll` get the instance of `PayrollTest` it uses as the `Database`. Certainly `Payroll` isn't going to do the creation of `PayrollTest`. Just as clearly, `Payroll` must somehow get a reference to the `Database` implementation it's going to use.

In some cases, it is perfectly natural for `PayrollTest` to pass the `Database` reference to `Payroll`. In other cases, it may be that `PayrollTest` must set a global variable to refer to the `Database`. In still others, `Payroll` may be fully expecting to create the `Database` instance. In that last case, we can use a `Factory` to fool `Payroll` into creating the test version of the `Database` by passing an alternate factory to `Payroll`.

Figure 21-6 shows a possible structure. The `Payroll` module acquires the factory through a global variable (or a static variable in a global class) named `GdatabaseFactory`. The `PayrollTest` module implements `DatabaseFactory` and sets a reference to itself into that `GdatabaseFactory`. When `Payroll` uses the factory to create a `Database`, the `PayrollTest` module traps the call and passes back a reference to itself. Thus, `Payroll` is convinced that it has created the `PayrollDatabase`, and yet the `PayrollTest` module can fully spoof the `Payroll` module and trap all database calls.

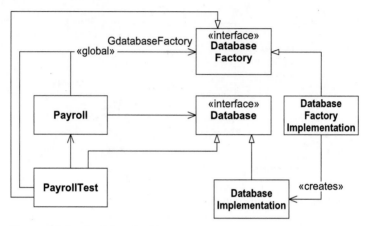

Figure 21-6   Spoofing the Factory

How Important Is It to Use Factories?

A strict interpretation of the DIP would insist on using factories for every volatile class in the system. What's more, the power of the FACTORY pattern is seductive. These two factors can sometimes seduce developers into using factories by default. This is an extreme that I don't recommend.

I don't start out using factories. I only put them into the system when the need for them becomes great enough. For example, if it becomes necessary to use the PROXY pattern, then it will probably become necessary to use a factory to create the persistent objects. Or if, through unit testing, I come across situations where I must spoof the creator of an object, then I will likely use a factory. But I don't start out assuming that factories will be necessary.

Factories are a complexity that can often be avoided, especially in the early phases of an evolving design. When they are employed by default, they dramatically increase the difficulty of extending the design. In order to create a new class, one may have to create as many as four new classes. The four are the two interface classes that represent the new class and its factory and the two concrete classes that implement those interfaces.

Conclusion

Factories are powerful tools. They can be of great benefit in conforming to the DIP. They allow high-level policy modules to create instances of classes without depending on the concrete implementations of those classes. They also make it possible to swap in completely different families of implementations for a group of classes. However, factories are a complexity that can often be avoided. Using them by default is seldom the best course of action.

Bibliography

1.   Gamma, et al. *Design Patterns*. Reading, MA: Addison–Wesley, 1995.

22

The Payroll Case Study (Part 2)

"Rule of thumb: if you think something is clever and sophisticated, beware—
it is probably self-indulgence."

—Donald A. Norman, 1990
(*The Design of Everyday Things*, Donald A. Norman, Doubleday, 1990)

We have done a great deal of analysis, design, and implementation for the Payroll problem. However, we still have many decisions to make. For one thing, the number of programmers who have been working on the problem is— one (me). The current structure of the development environment is consistent with this. All the program files are located in a single directory. There is no higher order structure at all. There are no packages, no subsystems, no releasable units other than the entire application. This will not do going forward.

We must assume that as this program grows, the number of people working on it will grow too. In order to make it convenient for multiple developers, we are going to have to partition the source code into packages that can be conveniently checked out, modified, and tested.

The payroll application currently consists of 3280 lines of code divided into about 50 different classes and 100 different source files. Although this is not a huge number, it does represent an organizational burden. How should we manage these source files?

Along similar lines, how should we divide the work of implementation so that the development can proceed smoothly without the programmers getting in each other's way. We would like to divide the classes into groups that are convenient for individuals or teams to check out and support.

Package Structure and Notation

The diagram in Figure 22-1 shows a possible package structure for the payroll application. We will address the appropriateness of this structure later. For now, we will confine ourselves to how such a structure is documented and used.

See page 481 for a description of the UML notation for packages. By convention, package diagrams are drawn with the dependencies pointing downwards. Packages at the top are dependent. Packages at the bottom are depended on.

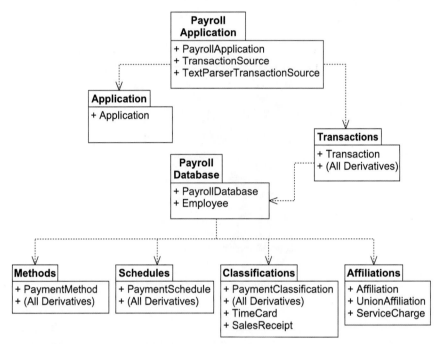

Figure 22-1   Possible Payroll Package Diagram

Figure 22-1 has divided the payroll application into eight packages. The `PayrollApplication` package contains the `PayrollApplication` class and the `TransactionSource` and `TextParserTransactionSource` classes. The `Transactions` package contains the complete `Transaction`-class hierarchy. The constituents of the other packages should be clear by carefully examining the diagram.

The dependencies should also be clear. The `PayrollApplication` package depends on the `Transactions` package because the `PayrollApplication` class calls the `Transaction::Execute` method. The `Transactions` package depends on the `PayrollDatabase` package because each of the many derivatives of `Transaction` communicate directly with the `PayrollDatabase` class. The other dependencies are likewise justifiable.

What criteria did I use to group these classes into packages? I simply stuck the classes that look like they belonged together into the same packages. As we learned in Chapter 20, this is probably not a good idea.

Consider what happens if we make a change to the `Classifications` package. This change will force a recompilation and retest of the `EmployeeDatabase` package, and well it should. But it will also force a recompilation and retest of the `Transactions` package. Certainly the `ChangeClassificationTransaction` and its three derivatives from Figure 19-3 *should* be recompiled and retested, but why should the others be recompiled and retested?

Technically, those other transactions don't need recompilation and retest. However, if they are part of the `Transactions` package, and if the package is going to be rereleased to deal with the changes to the

Classifications package, then it could be viewed as irresponsible not to recompile and retest the package as a whole. Even if all the transactions aren't recompiled and retested, the package itself must be rereleased and re-deployed, and then all of its clients will require revalidation at the very least, and probably recompilation.

The classes in the Transactions package do not share the same closure. Each one is sensitive to its own particular changes. The ServiceChargeTransaction is open to changes to the ServiceCharge class, whereas the TimeCardTransaction is open to changes to the TimeCard class. In fact, as the diagram in Figure 22-1 implies, some portion of the Transactions package is dependent on nearly every other part of the software. Thus, this package suffers a very high rate of release. Every time something is changed anywhere below, the Transactions package will have to be revalidated and rereleased.

The PayrollApplication package is even more sensitive: any change to any part of the system will affect this package, so its release rate must be enormous. You might think that this is inevitable—that as one climbs higher up the package-dependency hierarchy, the release rate must increase. Fortunately, however, this is not true, and avoiding this symptom is one of the major goals of OOD.

Applying the Common-Closure Principle (CCP)

Consider Figure 22-2. This diagram groups the classes of the payroll application together according to their closure. For example, the PayrollApplication package contains the PayrollApplication and Transaction-Source classes. These two classes both depend on the abstract Transaction class, which is in the

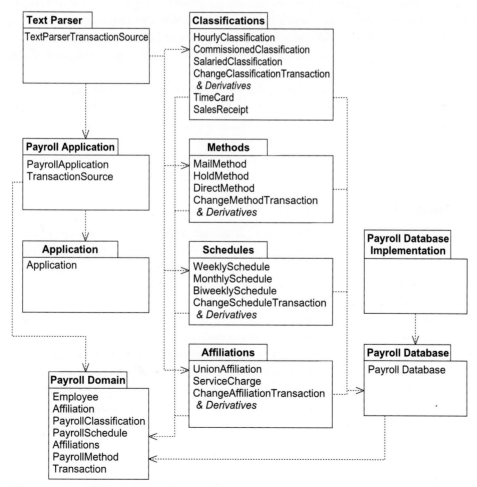

Figure 22-2   A Closed Package Hierarchy for the Payroll Application

`PayrollDomain` package. Note that the `TextParserTransactionSource` class is in another package that depends on the abstract `PayrollApplication` class. This creates an upside-down structure in which the details depend on the generalities, and the generalities are independent. This conforms to the DIP.

The most striking case of generality and independence is the `PayrollDomain` package. This package contains the *essence* of the whole system, yet it depends on nothing! Examine this package carefully. It contains `Employee`, `PaymentClassification`, `PaymentMethod`, `PaymentSchedule`, `Affiliation`, and `Transaction`. This package contains all of the major abstractions in our model, yet it has no dependencies. Why? Because nearly all of the classes it contains are abstract.

Consider the `Classifications` package, which contains the three derivatives of `PaymentClassification`. It also contains the `ChangeClassificationTransaction` class and its three derivatives, along with `TimeCard` and `SalesReceipt`. Notice that any change made to these nine classes is isolated; other than `TextParser`, no other package is affected! Such isolation also holds for the `Methods` package, the `Schedules` package, and the `Affiliations` package. This is quite a bit of isolation.

Notice that the bulk of the executable code is in packages that have few or no dependents. Since almost nothing depends on them, we call them *irresponsible*. The code within those packages is tremendously flexible; it can be changed without affecting many other parts of the project. Notice also that the most general packages of the system contain the least amount of executable code. These packages are heavily depended on, but depend on nothing. Since many packages depend on them, we call them *responsible*, and since they don't depend on anything, we call them *independent*. Thus, the amount of responsible code (i.e., code in which changes would affect lots of other code) is very small. Moreover, that small amount of responsible code is also independent, which means that no other modules will induce it to change. This upside-down structure, with highly independent and responsible generalities at the bottom, and highly irresponsible and dependent details at the top, is the hallmark of object-oriented design.

Contrast Figure 22-1 with Figure 22-2. Notice that the details at the bottom of Figure 22-1 are independent and highly responsible. This is the wrong place for details! Details should depend on the major architectural decisions of the system and should not be depended on. Notice also that the generalities, the packages that define the architecture of the system, are irresponsible and highly dependent. Thus, the packages that define the architectural decisions depend on, and are thus constrained by, the packages that contain the implementation details. This is a violation of the SAP. It would be better if the architecture constrained the details!

Applying the Reuse–Release Equivalency Principle (REP)

What portions of the payroll application can we reuse? If another division of our company wanted to reuse our payroll system, but they had a completely different set of policies, they could not reuse `Classifications`, `Methods`, `Schedules`, or `Affiliations`. However, they could reuse `PayrollDomain`, `Payroll-Application`, `Application`, `PayrollDatabase`, and possibly `PDImplementation`. On the other hand, if another department wanted to write software that analyzed the current employee database, they could reuse `PayrollDomain`, `Classifications`, `Methods`, `Schedules`, `Affiliations`, `PayrollDatabase`, and `PDImplementation`. In each case, the granule of reuse is a package.

Seldom, if ever, would only a single class from a package be reused. The reason is simple: the classes within a package should be cohesive. That means that they depend on one another and cannot be easily or sensibly separated. It would make no sense, for example, to use the `Employee` class without using the `PaymentMethod` class. In fact, in order to do so, you would have to modify the `Employee` class so that it did not contain a `PaymentMethod` class. Certainly we don't want to support the kind of reuse that forces us to modify the reused components. Therefore, the granule of reuse is the package. This gives us another cohesion criterion to employ when trying to group classes into packages: not only should the classes be closed together, they should also be reusable together in conformance with the REP.

Consider again our original package diagram in Figure 22-1. The packages that we might like to reuse, like `Transactions` or `PayrollDatabase`, are not easily reusable because they drag along a lot of extra baggage. The `PayrollApplication` package is horribly dependent (it depends on everything). If we wanted to create a new payroll application that used a different set of schedule, method, affiliation, and classification policies, we would not be able to use this package as a whole. Instead, we would have to take individual classes from `PayrollApplication`, `Transactions`, `Methods`, `Schedules`, `Classifications`, and `Affiliations`. By disassembling the packages in this way, we destroy their release structure. We cannot say that Release 3.2 of `PayrollApplication` is reusable.

Figure 22-1 violates the CRP. Thus, having accepted the reusable fragments of our various packages, the reuser will be faced with a difficult management problem: he will not be able to depend on our release structure. A new release of `Methods` affects him because he is reusing the `PaymentMethod` class. Most of the time, the changes will be to classes that he is not reusing, yet he must still track our new release number and probably recompile and retest his code.

This can be so difficult to manage that the reuser's most likely strategy will be to make a copy of the reusable components and evolve that copy separately from ours. This is not reuse. The two pieces of code will become different and will require independent support, effectively doubling the support burden.

These problems are not exhibited by the structure in Figure 22-2. The packages in that structure are easier to reuse. `PayrollDomain` does not drag along much baggage. It is reusable independently of any of the derivatives of `PaymentMethod`, `PaymentClassification`, `PaymentSchedule`, etc.

The astute reader will notice that the package diagram in Figure 22-2 does not completely conform to the CRP. Specifically, the classes within `PayrollDomain` do not form the smallest reusable unit. The `Transaction` class does not need to be reused with the rest of the package. We could design many applications that access the `Employee` and its fields, but never use a `Transaction`.

This suggests a change to the package diagram, as shown in Figure 22-3. This separates the transactions from the elements that they manipulate. For example, the classes in the `MethodTransactions` package manipulate the classes in the `Methods` package. We have moved the `Transaction` class into a new package named `TransactionApplication`, which also contains `TransactionSource` and a class named `Transaction-Application`. These three form a reusable unit. The `PayrollApplication` class has now become the grand unifier. It contains the main program and also a derivative of `TransactionApplication` called `PayrollApplication`, which ties the `TextParserTransactionSource` to the `TransactionApplication`.

These manipulations have added yet another layer of abstraction to the design. The `Transaction-Application` package can now be reused by any application that obtains `Transactions` from a `TransactionSource` and then `Executes` them. The `PayrollApplication` package is no longer reusable, since it is extremely dependent. However, the `TransactionApplication` package has taken its place, and is more general. Now we can reuse the `PayrollDomain` package without any `Transactions`.

This certainly improves the reusability and maintainability of the project, but at the cost of five extra packages and a more complex dependency architecture. The value of the trade-off depends on the type of reuse that we might expect and the rate at which we expect the application to evolve. If the application remains very stable, and few clients reuse it, then this change is overkill. On the other hand, if many applications will reuse this structure, or we expect the application to experience many changes, then the new structure is superior—it's a judgment call; and it should be driven by data rather then speculation. It is best to start simple and grow the package structure as necessary. Package structures can always be made more elaborate if necessary.

Coupling and Encapsulation

Just as the coupling among classes is managed by encapsulation boundaries in Java and C++, so the couplings among packages can be managed by the export adornments of the UML.

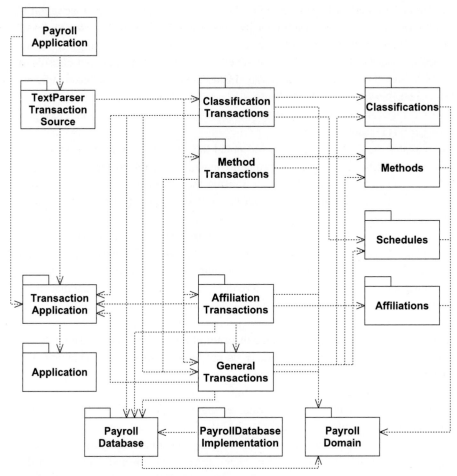

Figure 22-3   Updated Payroll Package Diagram

If a class within one package is to be used by another package, that class must be exported. In UML, classes are exported by default, but we may adorn a package to denote that certain classes should not be exported. Figure 22-4, a blowup of the `Classifications` package, shows that the three derivatives of `PaymentClassification` are exported, but that `TimeCard` and `SalesReceipt` are not. This means that other packages will not be able to use `TimeCard` and `SalesReceipt`; they are private to the `Classifications` package.

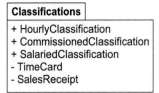

Figure 22-4   Private Classes in Classifications Package

We may want to hide certain classes within a package to prevent afferent couplings. `Classifications` is a very detailed package that contains the implementations of several payment policies. In order to keep this package on the main sequence, we want to limit its afferent couplings, so we hide the classes that other packages don't need to know about.

`TimeCard` and `SalesReceipt` are good choices for private classes. They are implementation details of the mechanisms for calculating an employee's pay. We want to remain free to alter these details, so we need to prevent anyone else from depending on their structure.

A quick glance at Figure 19-7 through Figure 19-10 and Listing 19-15 (page 213 through page 217) shows that the `TimeCardTransaction` and `SalesReceiptTransaction` classes already depend on `TimeCard` and `SalesReceipt`. We can easily resolve this problem, however, as shown in Figure 22-5 and Figure 22-6.

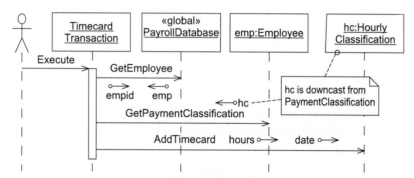

Figure 22-5   Revision to `TimeCardTransaction` to Protect `TimeCard` Privacy

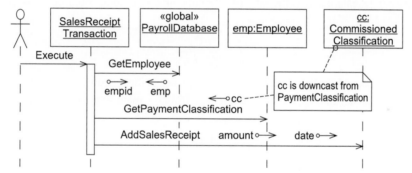

Figure 22-6   Revision to `SalesReceiptTransaction` to Protect `SalesReceipt` Privacy

Metrics

As we showed in Chapter 20, we can quantify the attributes of cohesion, coupling, stability, generality, and conformance to the main sequence with a few simple metrics. But why should we want to? To paraphrase Tom DeMarco: You can't manage what you can't control, and you can't control what you don't measure.[1] To be effective software engineers or software managers, we must be able to control software development practice. If we don't measure it, however, we will never have that control.

By applying the heuristics described below and calculating some fundamental metrics about our object-oriented designs, we can begin to correlate those metrics with measured performance of the software and of the teams that develop it. The more metrics we gather, the more information we will have, and the more control we will eventually be able to exert.

The metrics below have been successfully applied to a number of projects since 1994. There are several automatic tools that will calculate them for you, and they are not hard to calculate by hand. It is also not hard to write a simple shell, python, or ruby script to walk through your source files and calculate them.[2]

---

1.   [DeMarco82], p. 3.

2.   For an example of a shell script, you can download `depend.sh` from the freeware section of `www.objectmentor.com`., or take a look at JDepend at `www.clarkware.com`.

- (*H*) **Relational Cohesion**. One aspect of the cohesion of a package can be represented as the average number of internal relationships per class. Let R be the number of class relationships that are internal to the package (i.e., that do not connect to classes outside the package). Let N be the number of classes within the package. The extra 1 in the formula prevents $H = 0$ when $N = 1$. It represents the relationship that the package has to all its classes.

$$H = \frac{R + 1}{N}$$

- (*C_a*) **Afferent coupling** can be calculated as the number of classes from other packages that depend on the classes within the subject package. These dependencies are class relationships, such as inheritance and association.
- (*C_e*) **Efferent coupling** can be calculated as the number of classes in other packages that the classes in the subject package depend on. As before, these dependencies are class relationships.
- (*A*) **Abstractness** or **Generality** can be calculated as the ratio of the number of abstract classes (or interfaces) in the package to the total number of classes (and interfaces) in the package.[3] This metric ranges from 0 to 1.

$$A = \frac{\text{Abstract Classes}}{\text{Total Classes}}$$

- (*I*) **Instability** can be calculated as the ratio of efferent coupling to total coupling. This metric also ranges from 0 to 1.

$$I = \frac{C_e}{C_e + C_a}$$

- (*D*) **Distance from the Main Sequence.** The main sequence is idealized by the line $A + I = 1$. The formula for D calculates the distance of any particular package from the main sequence. It ranges from ~.7 to 0;[4] the closer to 0, the better.

$$D = \frac{|A + I - 1|}{\sqrt{2}}$$

- (*D'*) **Normalized Distance from the Main Sequence**. This metric represents the D metric normalized to the range [0,1]. It is perhaps a little more convenient to calculate and to interpret. The value 0 represents a package that is coincident with the main sequence. The value 1 represents a package that is as far from the main sequence as is possible.

$$D' = |A + I - 1|$$

Applying the Metrics to the Payroll Application

Table 22-1 shows how the classes in the payroll model have been allocated to packages. Figure 22-7 shows the package diagram for the payroll application with all the metrics calculated. And Table 22-2 shows all of the metrics calculated for each package.

3.   One might think that a better formula for A is the ratio of pure virtual functions to total member functions within the package. However, I have found that this formula weakens the abstraction metric too much. Even one pure virtual function will make a class abstract, and the power of that abstraction is more significant than the fact that the class may have dozens of concrete functions, especially when the DIP is being followed.

4.   It is impossible to plot any package outside the unit square on the graph of A vs. I. This is because neither A nor I can exceed 1. The main sequence bisects this square from (0,1) to (1,0). The points within the square that are farthest from the main sequence are the two corners (0,0) and (1,1). Their distance from the main sequence is

$$\frac{\sqrt{2}}{2} = 0.70710678\ldots$$

Each package dependency in Figure 22-7 is adorned with two numbers. The number closest to the depender package represents the number of classes in that package that depend on the dependee package. The number closest to the dependee package represents the number of classes in that package that the depender package depends on.

Table 22-1

Package	Classes in Package		
Affiliations	ServiceCharge	UnionAffiliation	
AffiliationTransactions	ChangeAffiliationTransaction	ChangeUnaffiliated-Transaction	ChangeMember-Transaction
	ServiceChargeTransaction		
Application	Application		
Classifications	CommissionedClassification	HourlyClassification	SalariedClassification
	SalesReceipt	Timecard	
ClassificationTransaction	ChangeClassification-Transaction	ChangeCommissioned-Transaction	ChangeHourly-Transaction
	ChangeSalariedTransaction	SalesReceiptTransaction	TimecardTransaction
GeneralTransactions	AddCommissionedEmployee	AddEmployeeTransaction	AddHourlyEmployee
	AddSalariedEmployee	ChangeAddressTransaction	ChangeEmployee-Transaction
	ChangeNameTransaction	DeleteEmployeeTransaction	PaydayTransaction
Methods	DirectMethod	HoldMethod	MailMethod
MethodTransactions	ChangeDirectTransaction	ChangeHoldTransaction	ChangeMailTransaction
	ChangeMethodTransaction		
PayrollApplication	PayrollApplication		
PayrollDatabase	PayrollDatabase		
PayrollDatabase-Implementation	PayrollDatabase-Implementation		
PayrollDomain	Affiliation	Employee	PaymentClassification
	PaymentMethod	PaymentSchedule	
Schedules	BiweeklySchedule	MonthlySchedule	WeeklySchedule
TextParserTransaction-Source	TextParserTransactionSource		
TransactionApplication	TransactionApplication	Transaction	TransactionSource

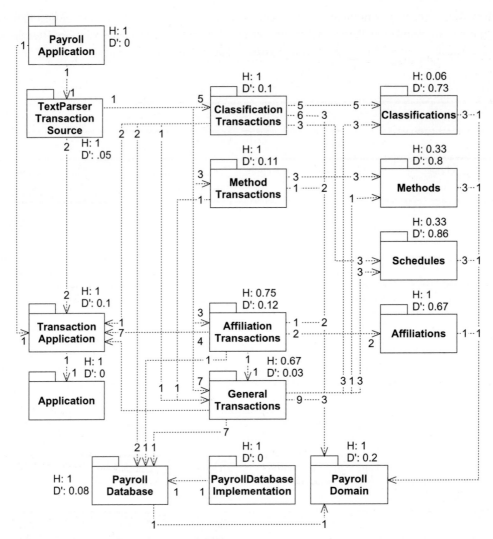

Figure 22-7   Package Diagram with Metrics

Each package in Figure 22-7 is adorned with the metrics that apply to it. Many of these metrics are encouraging. `PayrollApplication`, `PayrollDomain`, and `PayrollDatabase`, for example, have high relational cohesion and are either on or close to the main sequence. However, the `Classifications`, `Methods`, and `Schedules` packages show generally poor relational cohesion and are almost as far from the main sequence as is possible!

These numbers tell us that the partitioning of the classes into packages is weak. If we don't find a way to improve the numbers, then the development environment will be sensitive to change, which may cause unnecessary rerelease and retesting. Specifically, we have low-abstraction packages like `ClassificationTransactions` depending heavily on other low-abstraction packages like `Classifications`. Classes with low abstraction contain most of the detailed code and are therefore likely to change, which will force rerelease of the packages that depend on them. Thus the `ClassificationTransactions` package will have a very high release rate since it is subject to both its own high change rate and that of `Classifications`. As much as possible, we would like to limit the sensitivity of our development environment to change.

Clearly, if we have only two or three developers, they will be able to manage the development environment "in their heads," and the need to maintain packages on the main sequence, for this purpose, will not be great. The

Table 22-2

Package Name	N	A	Ca	Ce	R	H	I	A	D	D′
Affiliations	2	0	2	1	1	1	.33	0	.47	.67
AffiliationTransactions	4	1	1	7	2	.75	.88	.25	.09	.12
Application	1	1	1	0	0	1	0	1	0	0
Classifications	5	0	8	3	2	.06	.27	0	.51	.73
ClassificationTransaction	6	1	1	14	5	1	.93	.17	.07	.10
GeneralTransactions	9	2	4	12	5	.67	.75	.22	.02	.03
Methods	3	0	4	1	0	.33	.20	0	.57	.80
MethodTransactions	4	1	1	6	3	1	.86	.25	.08	.11
PayrollApplication	1	0	0	2	0	1	1	0	0	0
PayrollDatabase	1	1	11	1	0	1	.08	1	.06	.08
PayrollDatabaseImpl...	1	0	0	1	0	1	1	0	0	0
PayrollDomain	5	4	26	0	4	1	0	.80	.14	.20
Schedules	3	0	6	1	0	.33	.14	0	.61	.86
TextParserTransactionSource	1	0	1	20	0	1	.95	0	.03	.05
TransactionApplication	3	3	9	1	2	1	.1	1	.07	.10

more developers there are, however, the more difficult it is to keep the development environment sane. Moreover, the work required to obtain these metrics is minimal compared to the work required to do even a single retest and rerelease.[5] Therefore, it is a judgment call as to whether the work of computing these metrics will be a short-term loss or gain.

Object Factories

Classifications and ClassificationTransactions are so heavily depended on because the classes within them must be instantiated. For example, the TextParserTransactionSource class must be able to create AddHourlyEmployeeTransaction objects; thus, there is an afferent coupling from the TextParser-TransactionSource package to the ClassificationTransactions package. Also, the ChangeHourly-Transaction class must be able to create HourlyClassification objects, so there is an afferent coupling from the ClassificationTransactions package to the Classification package.

Almost every other use of the objects within these packages is through their abstract interface. Were it not for the need to create each concrete object, the afferent couplings on these packages would not exist. For example, if TextParserTransactionSource did not need to create the different transactions, it would not depend on the four packages containing the transaction implementations.

This problem can be significantly mitigated by using the FACTORY pattern. Each package provides an object factory that is responsible for creating all the public objects within that package.

---

5. I spent about two hours compiling by hand the statistics and computing the metrics for the payroll example. Had I used one of the commonly available tools, it would have taken virtually no time at all.

The Object Factory for `TransactionImplementation`

Figure 22-8 shows how to build an object factory for the `TransactionImplementation` package. The `TransactionFactory` package contains the abstract base class, which defines the pure virtual functions that represent the constructors for the concrete transaction objects. The `TransactionImplementation` package contains the concrete derivative of the `TransactionFactory` class and uses all the concrete transactions in order to create them.

The `TransactionFactory` class has a static member declared as a `TransactionFactory` pointer. This member must be initialized by the main program to point to an instance of the concrete `Transaction-FactoryImplementation` object.

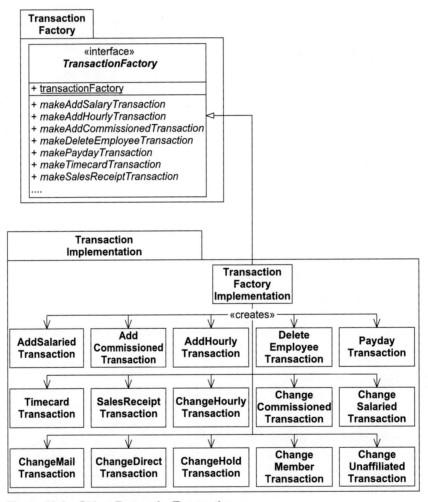

Figure 22-8   Object Factory for Transactions

Initializing the Factories

In order to create objects using the object factories, the static members of the abstract object factories must be initialized to point to the appropriate concrete factory. This must be done before any user attempts to use the factory. The best place to do this is usually the main program, which means that the main program depends on all the factories *and* on all the concrete packages. Thus, each concrete package will have at least one afferent coupling from the main program. This will force the concrete package off the main sequence a bit, but it cannot be helped.[6] It means that we must rerelease the main program every time we change any of the concrete packages. Of course we should probably rerelease the main program for each change anyway, since it will need to be tested regardless.

Figures 22-9 and 22-10 show the static and dynamic structure of the main program in relation to the object factories.

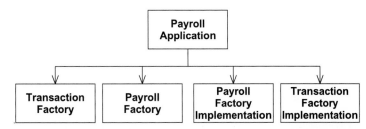

Figure 22-9   Static Structure of Main Program and Object Factories

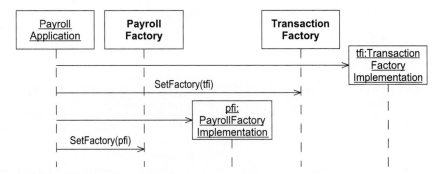

Figure 22-10   Dynamic Structure of Main Program and Object Factories

Rethinking the Cohesion Boundaries

We initially separated `Classifications`, `Methods`, `Schedules`, and `Affiliations` in Figure 22-1. At the time, it seemed like a reasonable partitioning. After all, other users may want to reuse our schedule classes without reusing our affiliation classes. This partitioning was maintained after we split out the transactions into their own packages, creating a dual hierarchy. Perhaps this was too much. The diagram in Figure 22-7 is very tangled.

A tangled package diagram makes the management of releases difficult if it is done by hand. Although package diagrams would work well with an automated project-planning tool, most of us don't have that luxury. Thus, we need to keep our package diagrams as simple as is practical.

In my view, the transaction partitioning is more important than the functional partitioning. Thus, we will merge the transactions into a single `TransactionImplementation` package in Figure 22-11. We will also merge the `Classifications`, `Schedules`, `Methods`, and `Affiliations` packages into a single `Payroll-Implementation` package.

The Final Package Structure

Table 22-3 shows the final allocation of classes to class package. Table 22-4 contains the metrics spreadsheet. Figure 22-11 shows the final package structure, which employs object factories to bring the concrete packages near the main sequence

---

6.   As a practical solution, I usually ignore couplings from the main program.

Table 22-3

Packages	Classes in Packages		
AbstractTransactions	AddEmployeeTransaction	ChangeAffiliationTransaction	ChangeEmployee-Transaction
	ChangeClassification-Transaction	ChangeMethodTransaction	
Application	Application		
PayrollApplication	PayrollApplication		
PayrollDatabase	PayrollDatabase		
PayrollDatabaseImple-mentation	PayrollDatabase-Implementation		
PayrollDomain	Affiliation	Employee	PaymentClassification
	PaymentMethod	PaymentSchedule	
PayrollFactory	PayrollFactory		
PayrollImplementation	BiweeklySchedule	CommissionedClassification	DirectMethod
	HoldMethod	HourlyClassification	MailMethod
	MonthlySchedule	PayrollFactory-Implementation	SalariedClassification
	SalesReceipt	ServiceCharge	Timecard
	UnionAffiliation	WeeklySchedule	
TextParser-TransactionSource	TextParserTransactionSource		
Transaction-Application	Transaction	TransactionApplication	TransactionSource
TransactionFactory	TransactionFactory		
Transaction-Implementation	AddCommissionedEmployee	AddHourlyEmployee	AddSalariedEmployee
	ChangeAddressTransaction	ChangeCommissioned-Transaction	ChangeDirectTransaction
	ChangeHoldTransaction	ChangeHourlyTransaction	ChangeMailTransaction
	ChangeMemberTransaction	ChangeNameTransaction	ChangeSalariedTransaction
	ChangeUnaffiliatedTransaction	DeleteEmployee	PaydayTransaction
	SalesReceiptTransaction	ServiceChargeTransaction	TimecardTransaction
	TransactionFactory-Implementation		

Table 22-4

Package Name	N	A	Ca	Ce	R	H	I	A	D	D′
AbstractTransactions	5	5	13	1	0	.20	.07	1	.05	.07
Application	1	1	1	0	0	1	0	1	0	0
PayrollApplication	1	0	0	5	0	1	1	0	0	0
PayrollDatabase	1	1	19	5	0	1	.21	1	.15	.21
PayrollDatabaseImpl...	1	0	0	1	0	1	1	0	0	0
PayrollDomain	5	4	30	0	4	1	0	.80	.14	.20
PayrollFactory	1	1	12	4	0	1	.25	1	.18	.25
PayrollImplementation	14	0	1	5	3	.29	.83	0	.12	.17
TextParserTransactionSource	1	0	1	3	0	1	.75	0	.18	.25
TransactionApplication	3	3	14	1	3	1.33	.07	1	.05	.07
TransactionFactory	1	1	3	1	0	1	.25	1	.18	.25
TransactionImplementation	19	0	1	14	0	.05	.93	0	.05	.07

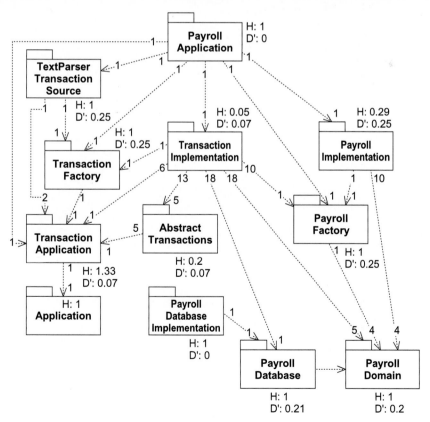

Figure 22-11 Final Payroll Package Structure

The metrics on this diagram are heartening. The relational cohesions are all very high (thanks in part to the relationships of the concrete factories to the objects that they create), and there are no significant deviations from the main sequence. Thus, the couplings between our packages are appropriate to a sane development environment. Our abstract packages are closed, reusable, and heavily depended on, while having few dependencies of their own. Our concrete packages are segregated on the basis of reuse, are heavily dependent on the abstract packages, and are not heavily depended on themselves.

Conclusion

The need to manage package structures is a function of the size of the program and the size of the development team. Even small teams need to partition the source code so that they can stay out of each other's way. Large programs can become opaque masses of source files without some kind of partitioning structure.

Bibliography

1. Benjamin/Cummings. *Object-Oriented Analysis and Design with Applications*, 2d ed.,1994.
2. DeMarco, Tom. *Controlling Software Projects*. Yourdon Press, 1982.

SECTION 5

The Weather Station Case Study

The following chapters contain an in-depth case study of a simple weather monitoring system. Although this case study is fictitious, it has nevertheless been constructed with a high degree of realism. We will encounter the problems of time pressure, legacy code, poor and mutating specifications, new untried technologies, etc. Our goal is to demonstrate how the principles, patterns, and practices that we have learned are used in the real world of software engineering.

As before, we will be encountering several useful design patterns while exploring the development of the weather station. The chapters leading up to the case study will describe those patterns.

23

COMPOSITE

The COMPOSITE pattern is a very simple pattern that has significant implications. The fundamental structure of the COMPOSITE pattern is shown in Figure 23-1. Here we see a hierarchy based on shapes. The `Shape` base class has two derivative shapes named `Circle` and `Square`. The third derivative is the composite. `CompositeShape` keeps a list of many `Shape` instances. When `draw()` is called on `CompositeShape`, it delegates that method to all the `Shape` instances in the list.

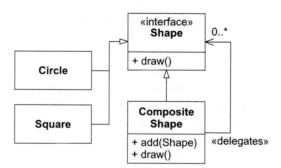

Figure 23-1   Composite Pattern

Thus, an instance of `CompositeShape` appears to the system to be a single `Shape`. It can be passed to any function or object that takes a `Shape`, and it will behave like a `Shape`. However, it is really a proxy[1] for a group of `Shape` instances.

Listing 23-1 and Listing 23-2 show one possible implementation of `CompositeShape`.

Listing 23-1

`Shape.java`

```
public interface Shape
{
  public void draw();
}
```

Listing 23-2

`CompositeShape.java`

```
import java.util.Vector;

public class CompositeShape implements Shape
{
  private Vector itsShapes = new Vector();
  public void add(Shape s)
  {
    itsShapes.add(s);
  }

  public void draw()
  {
    for (int i = 0; i < itsShapes.size(); i++)
    {
      Shape shape = (Shape) itsShapes.elementAt(i);
      shape.draw();
    }
  }
}
```

Example: Composite Commands

Consider the discussion of `Sensors` and `Command` objects we had back on page 152. Figure 13-3 showed a `Sensor` class using a `Command` class. When the `Sensor` detected its stimulus, it called `do()` on the `Command`.

What I failed to mention in that discussion was that there were often cases when a `Sensor` had to execute more than one `Command`. For example, when the paper reached a certain point in the paper path, it would trip an optical sensor. That sensor then stopped a motor, started another, and engaged a particular clutch.

At first we took this to mean that every `Sensor` class would have to maintain a list of `Command` objects. (See Figure 23-2.) However, we soon recognized that whenever a `Sensor` needed to execute more than one `Command`, it always treated those `Command` objects identically. That is, it just iterated over the list and called `do()` on each `Command`. This was ideal for the COMPOSITE pattern.

Figure 23-2   Sensor containing many Commands

---

1.   Notice the similarity in structure to the PROXY pattern.

So we left the `Sensor` class alone and created a `CompositeCommand` as shown in Figure 23-3.

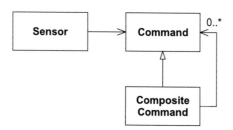

Figure 23-3   Composite Command

This meant that we didn't have to change the `Sensor` or the `Command`. We were able to add the plurality of `Commands` to a `Sensor` without changing either. This is an application of the OCP.

Multiplicity or Not Multiplicity

This leads to an interesting issue. We were able to make our `Sensors` behave as though they contained many `Commands`, without having to modify the `Sensors`. There must be many other situations like this in normal software design. There must be times when you could use COMPOSITE rather than building a list or vector of objects.

Let me say this a different way. The association between `Sensor` and `Command` is one-to-one. We were tempted to change that association to one to many. But instead we found a way to get one-to-many behavior, without a one-to-many relationship. A one-to-one relationship is much easier to understand, code, and maintain than a one-to-many relationship is; so this was clearly the right design trade-off. How many of the one-to-many relationships in your current project could be one-to-one if you used COMPOSITE?

Of course, not all one-to-many relationships can be reverted to one-to-one by using COMPOSITE. Only those in which every object in the list is treated identically are candidates. For example, if you maintained a list of employees and searched through that list for employees whose pay date is today, you probably shouldn't use the COMPOSITE pattern because you wouldn't be treating all the employees identically.

Still, there are quite a few one-to-many relationships that qualify for conversion to COMPOSITE. And the advantages are significant. Instead of duplicating the list management and iteration code in each of the clients, that code appears only once in the composite class.

24

OBSERVER—Backing into a Pattern

© Jennifer M. Kohnke

This chapter serves a special purpose. In it, I will describe the OBSERVER[1] pattern, but that is a minor objective. The primary objective of this chapter is to give you a demonstration of how your design and code can evolve to use a pattern.

In the preceding chapters, we have made use of many patterns. Often we presented them as a *fait accompli*, without showing how the code evolved to use the pattern. This might give you the idea that patterns are simply something you insert into your code and designs in completed form. This is not what I advise. Rather, I prefer to evolve the code I am working on in the direction of its needs. As I refactor it to resolve issues of coupling, simplicity, and expressiveness, I may find that the code has come close to a particular pattern. When that happens, I change the names of the classes and variables to use the name of the pattern, and change the structure of the code to use the pattern in a more regular form. Thus the code *backs into the pattern*.

This chapter sets up a simple problem and then shows how the design and code evolve to solve that problem. The result of the evolution winds up being the OBSERVER pattern. At each stage of the evolution, I will describe the issues I'm trying to resolve, and then show the steps that resolve them.

The Digital Clock

We have a clock object. This object catches millisecond interrupts (known as tics) from the operating system and turns them into the time of day. This object knows how to calculate seconds from milliseconds, minutes from seconds, hours from minutes, days from hours, etc. It knows how many days are in a month, and how many months are in a year. It knows all about leap years, when to have them, and when not. It knows about time. (See Figure 24-1.)

1.   [GOF95], p. 293.

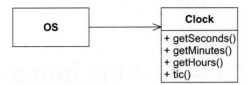

Figure 24-1 Clock

We'd like to create a digital clock that sits on our desktop and continuously displays the time of day. What is the simplest way to accomplish this? We could write the following code:

```
public void DisplayTime
{
  while(1)
  {
    int sec = clock.getSeconds();
    int min = clock.getMinutes();
    int hour = clock.getHours();
    showTime(hour,min,sec);
  }
}
```

Clearly this is suboptimal. It consumes all available CPU cycles to repeatedly display the time. Most of those displays will be wasted because the time will not have changed. It may be that this solution would be adequate in a digital watch or a digital wall clock since conserving CPU cycles is not very important in those systems. However, we don't want this CPU hog running on our desktop.

The fundamental problem is how to efficiently get data from the `Clock` to the `DigitalClock`. I'm going to assume that the `Clock` object and the `DigitalClock` object both exist. My interest is in how to connect them. I can test that connection simply by making sure that the data I get from the `Clock` are the same data I send to the `DigitalClock`.

A simple way to write this test is to create one interface that pretends to be the `Clock` and another that pretends to be the `DigitalClock`. Then I can write special test objects that implement those interfaces and verify that the connection between them works as expected. (See Figure 24-2.)

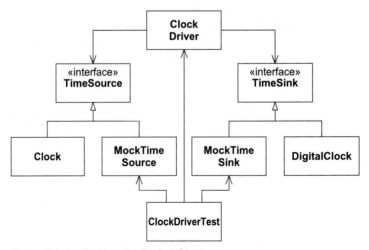

Figure 24-2 Testing the Digital Clock

The ClockDriverTest object will connect the ClockDriver to the two mock objects through the TimeSource and TimeSink interfaces. It will then check each of the mock objects to ensure that the ClockDriver manages to move the time from the source to the sink. If necessary, the ClockDriverTest will also ensure that efficiency is being conserved.

I think it's interesting that we have added interfaces to the design simply as a result of considering how to test it. In order to test a module, you have to be able to isolate it from the other modules in the system, just as we have isolated the ClockDriver from the Clock and DigitalClock. Considering tests first helps us to minimize the coupling in our designs.

OK, how does the ClockDriver work? Clearly, in order to be efficient, the ClockDriver must detect when the time in the TimeSource object has changed. Then, and only then, should it move the time to the TimeSink object. How can the ClockDriver know when the time has changed? It could poll the TimeSource, but that simply recreates the CPU hog problem.

The simplest way for the ClockDriver to know when the time has changed is for the Clock object to tell it. We could pass the ClockDriver to the Clock through the TimeSource interface and then, when the time changes, the Clock can update the ClockDriver. The ClockDriver will, in turn, set the time on the ClockSink. (See Figure 24-3.)

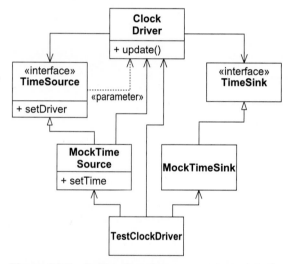

Figure 24-3 Getting the TimeSource to update the ClockDriver

Notice the dependency from the TimeSource to the ClockDriver. It is there because the argument to the setDriver method is a ClockDriver. I'm not very happy with this, since it implies that TimeSource objects must use ClockDriver objects in every case. However, I'll defer doing anything about the dependency until I get this program working.

Listing 24-1 shows the test case for the ClockDriver. Notice that it creates a ClockDriver and binds a MockTimeSource and a MockTimeSink to it. Then it sets the time in the source and expects the time to magically arrive at the sink. The rest of the code is shown in Listings 24-2 through 24-6.

Listing 24-1

ClockDriverTest.java

```
import junit.framework.*;

public class ClockDriverTest extends TestCase
{
  public ClockDriverTest(String name)
```

```
  {
    super(name);
  }

  public void testTimeChange()
  {
    MockTimeSource source = new MockTimeSource();
    MockTimeSink sink = new MockTimeSink();
    ClockDriver driver = new ClockDriver(source,sink);
    source.setTime(3,4,5);
    assertEquals(3, sink.getHours());
    assertEquals(4, sink.getMinutes());
    assertEquals(5, sink.getSeconds());

    source.setTime(7,8,9);
    assertEquals(7, sink.getHours());
    assertEquals(8, sink.getMinutes());
    assertEquals(9, sink.getSeconds());
  }
}
```

Listing 24-2

TimeSource.java

```
public interface TimeSource
{
  public void setDriver(ClockDriver driver);
}
```

Listing 24-3

TimeSink.java

```
public interface TimeSink
{
  public void setTime(int hours, int minutes, int seconds);
}
```

Listing 24-4

ClockDriver.java

```
public class ClockDriver
{
  private TimeSink itsSink;

  public ClockDriver(TimeSource source, TimeSink sink)
  {
    source.setDriver(this);
    itsSink = sink;
  }

  public void update(int hours, int minutes, int seconds)
  {
    itsSink.setTime(hours, minutes, seconds);
  }
}
```

Listing 24-5

MockTimeSource.java

```java
public class MockTimeSource implements TimeSource
{
  private ClockDriver itsDriver;

  public void setTime(int hours, int minutes, int seconds)
  {
    itsDriver.update(hours, minutes, seconds);
  }

  public void setDriver(ClockDriver driver)
  {
    itsDriver = driver;
  }
}
```

Listing 24-6

MockTimeSink.java

```java
public class MockTimeSink implements TimeSink
{
  private int itsHours;
  private int itsMinutes;
  private int itsSeconds;

  public int getSeconds()
  {
    return itsSeconds;
  }

  public int getMinutes()
  {
    return itsMinutes;
  }

  public int getHours()
  {
    return itsHours;
  }

  public void setTime(int hours, int minutes, int seconds)
  {
    itsHours = hours;
    itsMinutes = minutes;
    itsSeconds = seconds;
  }
}
```

OK, now that it works, I can think about cleaning it up. I don't like the dependency from TimeSource to ClockDriver because I want the TimeSource interface to be usable by anybody, not just ClockDriver objects. We can fix this by creating an interface that TimeSource can use and that ClockDriver can implement. We'll call this interface ClockObserver. See Listings 24-7 through 24-10. The code in **bold** has changed.

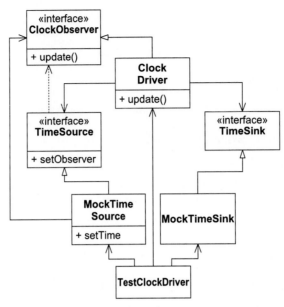

Figure 24-4   Breaking the depency of `TimeSource` upon `ClockDriver`

Listing 24-7

ClockObserver.java

```java
public interface ClockObserver
{
  public void update(int hours, int minutes, int seconds);
}
```

Listing 24-8

ClockDriver.java

```java
public class ClockDriver implements ClockObserver
{
  private TimeSink itsSink;

  public ClockDriver(TimeSource source, TimeSink sink)
  {
    source.setObserver(this);
    itsSink = sink;
  }

  public void update(int hours, int minutes, int seconds)
  {
    itsSink.setTime(hours, minutes, seconds);
  }
}
```

Listing 24-9

TimeSource.java

```java
public interface TimeSource
{
  public void setObserver(ClockObserver observer);
}
```

Listing 24-10

MockTimeSource.java

```java
public class MockTimeSource implements TimeSource
{
  private ClockObserver itsObserver;

  public void setTime(int hours, int minutes, int seconds)
  {
    itsObserver.update(hours, minutes, seconds);
  }

  public void setObserver(ClockObserver observer)
  {
    itsObserver = observer;
  }
}
```

This is better. Now anybody can make use of TimeSource. All they have to do is implement ClockObserver and call SetObserver, passing themselves in as the argument.

I'd like to be able to have more than one TimeSink getting the time. One might implement a digital clock. Another might be used to supply the time to a reminder service. Still another might start my nightly backup. In short, I'd like a single TimeSource to be able to supply the time to multiple TimeSink objects.

So I'll change the constructor of the ClockDriver to take just the TimeSource and then add a method named addTimeSink that allows you to add TimeSink instances any time you want.

The thing I don't like about this is that I now have two indirections. I have to tell the TimeSource who the ClockObserver is by calling setObserver, and I also have to tell the ClockDriver who the TimeSink instances are. Is this double indirection really necessary?

Looking at ClockObserver and TimeSink, I see that they both have the setTime method. It looks like TimeSink could implement ClockObserver. If I did this, then my test program could create a MockTimeSink and call setObserver on the TimeSource. I could get rid of the ClockDriver (and TimeSink) altogether! Listing 24-11 shows the changes to ClockDriverTest.

Listing 24-11

ClockDriverTest.java

```java
import junit.framework.*;

public class ClockDriverTest extends TestCase
{
  public ClockDriverTest(String name)
  {
    super(name);
  }

  public void testTimeChange()
  {
    MockTimeSource source = new MockTimeSource();
    MockTimeSink sink = new MockTimeSink();
    source.setObserver(sink);

    source.setTime(3,4,5);
    assertEquals(3, sink.getHours());
```

```
        assertEquals(4, sink.getMinutes());
        assertEquals(5, sink.getSeconds());

        source.setTime(7,8,9);
        assertEquals(7, sink.getHours());
        assertEquals(8, sink.getMinutes());
        assertEquals(9, sink.getSeconds());
    }
}
```

This means that `MockTimeSink` should implement `ClockObserver` rather than `TimeSink`. See Listing 24-12. These changes work fine. Why did I think I needed a `ClockDriver` in the first place? Figure 24-5 shows the UML.

Listing 24-12

MockTimeSink.java

```java
public class MockTimeSink implements ClockObserver
{
  private int itsHours;
  private int itsMinutes;
  private int itsSeconds;

  public int getSeconds()
  {
    return itsSeconds;
  }

  public int getMinutes()
  {
    return itsMinutes;
  }

  public int getHours()
  {
    return itsHours;
  }

  public void update(int hours, int minutes, int seconds)
  {
    itsHours = hours;
    itsMinutes = minutes;
    itsSeconds = seconds;
  }
}
```

Clearly this is much simpler.

OK, now we can handle multiple `TimeSink` objects by changing the `setObserver` function to `register-Observer` and by making sure that all the registered `ClockObserver` instances are held in a list and updated appropriately. This requires another change to the test program. Listing 24-13 shows the changes. I also did a little refactoring of the test program to make it smaller and easier to read.

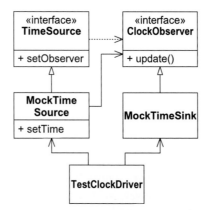

Figure 24-5   Removing `ClockDriver` and `TimeSink`

Listing 24-13
`ClockDriverTest.java`

```java
import junit.framework.*;

public class ClockDriverTest extends TestCase
{
  private MockTimeSource source;
  private MockTimeSink sink;

  public ClockDriverTest(String name)
  {
    super(name);
  }

  public void setUp()
  {
    source = new MockTimeSource();
    sink = new  MockTimeSink();
    source.registerObserver(sink);
  }

    private void assertSinkEquals(
    MockTimeSink sink, int hours, int minutes, int seconds)
  {
    assertEquals(hours, sink.getHours());
    assertEquals(minutes, sink.getMinutes());
    assertEquals(seconds, sink.getSeconds());
  }

  public void testTimeChange()
  {
    source.setTime(3,4,5);
    assertSinkEquals(sink, 3,4,5);

    source.setTime(7,8,9);
    assertSinkEquals(sink, 7,8,9);
  }
```

```java
  public void testMultipleSinks()
  {
    MockTimeSink sink2 = new MockTimeSink();
    source.registerObserver(sink2);

    source.setTime(12,13,14);
    assertSinkEquals(sink, 12,13,14);
    assertSinkEquals(sink2, 12,13,14);
  }
}
```

The change needed to make this work is pretty simple. We change MockTimeSource to hold all registered observers in a Vector. Then, when the time changes, we iterate through the Vector and call update on all the registered ClockObservers. Listings 24-14 and 24-15 show the changes. Figure 24-6 shows the corresponding UML.

Listing 24-14

TimeSource.java

```java
public interface TimeSource
{
  public void registerObserver(ClockObserver observer);
}
```

Listing 24-15

MockTimeSource.java

```java
import java.util.*;

public class MockTimeSource implements TimeSource
{
  private Vector itsObservers = new Vector();

  public void setTime(int hours, int minutes, int seconds)
  {
    Iterator i = itsObservers.iterator();
    while (i.hasNext())
    {
      ClockObserver observer = (ClockObserver) i.next();
      observer.update(hours, minutes, seconds);
    }
  }

  public void registerObserver(ClockObserver observer)
  {
    itsObservers.add(observer);
  }
}
```

This is pretty nice, but I don't like the fact that the MockTimeSource has to deal with the registration and update. It implies that the Clock and every other derivative of TimeSource will have to duplicate that registration and update code. I don't think Clock should have to deal with registration and update. I also don't like the idea of duplicate code. So I'd like to move all that stuff into the TimeSource. Of course, this means that TimeSource

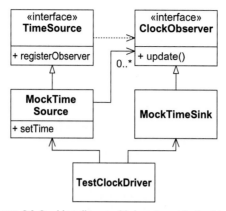

Figure 24-6   Handing multiple `TimeSink` objects

will have to change from an interface to a class. It also means that `MockTimeSource` will shrink to near nothing. Listings 24-16 and 24-17 and Figure 24-7 show the changes.

Listing 24-16

TimeSource.java

```java
import java.util.*;

public class TimeSource
{
  private Vector itsObservers = new Vector();

  protected void notify(int hours, int minutes, int seconds)
  {
    Iterator i = itsObservers.iterator();
    while (i.hasNext())
    {
      ClockObserver observer = (ClockObserver) i.next();
      observer.update(hours, minutes, seconds);
    }
  }

  public void registerObserver(ClockObserver observer)
  {
    itsObservers.add(observer);
  }
}
```

Listing 24-17

MockTimeSource.java

```java
public class MockTimeSource extends TimeSource
{
  public void setTime(int hours, int minutes, int seconds)
  {
    notify(hours, minutes, seconds);
  }
}
```

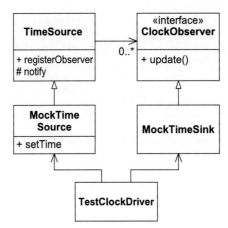

Figure 24-7   Moving registration and update into TimeSource

This is pretty cool. Now, anybody can derive from `TimeSource`. All they have to do to get the observers updated is to call `notify`. But there is still something I don't like about it. `MockTimeSource` inherits directly from `TimeSource`. This means that `Clock` must also derive from `TimeSource`. Why should `Clock` have to depend upon registration and update? `Clock` is just a class that knows about time. Making it depend upon `Time-Source` seems necessary and undesirable.

I know how I'd solve this in C++. I'd create a subclass of both `TimeSource` and `Clock` called `ObservableClock`. I'd override `tic` and `setTime` in `ObservableClock` to call `tic` or `setTime` in `Clock` and then call `notify` in `TimeSource`. See Listing 24-18 and Figure 24-8.

Listing 24-18

ObservableClock.cc (C++)

```
class ObservableClock : public Clock, public TimeSource
{
  public:
    virtual void tic()
    {
      Clock::tic();
      TimeSource::notify(getHours(), getMinutes(), getSeconds());
    }

    virtual void setTime(int hours, int minutes, int seconds)
    {
      Clock::setTime(hours, minutes, seconds);
      TimeSource::notify(hours, minutes, seconds);
    }
};
```

Unfortunately, we don't have this option in Java because the language can't deal with multiple inheritance of classes. So, in Java we either have to leave things as they are or use a delegation hack. The delegation hack is shown in Listings 24-19 through 24-21 and Figure 24-9.

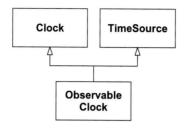

Figure 24-8 Using multiple inheritance in C++ to separate Clock from TimeSource

Listing 24-19

TimeSource.java

```java
public interface TimeSource
{
  public void registerObserver(ClockObserver observer);
}
```

Listing 24-20

TimeSourceImplementation.java

```java
import java.util.*;

public class TimeSourceImplementation
{
  private Vector itsObservers = new Vector();

  public void notify(int hours, int minutes, int seconds)
  {
    Iterator i = itsObservers.iterator();
    while (i.hasNext())
    {
      ClockObserver observer = (ClockObserver) i.next();
      observer.update(hours, minutes, seconds);
    }
  }

  public void registerObserver(ClockObserver observer)
  {
    itsObservers.add(observer);
  }
}
```

Listing 24-21

MockTimeSource.java

```java
public class MockTimeSource implements TimeSource
{
  TimeSourceImplementation tsImp =
    new TimeSourceImplementation();

  public void registerObserver(ClockObserver observer)
  {
    tsImp.registerObserver(observer);
  }
```

```
public void setTime(int hours, int minutes, int seconds)
{
  tsImp.notify(hours, minutes, seconds);
}
}
```

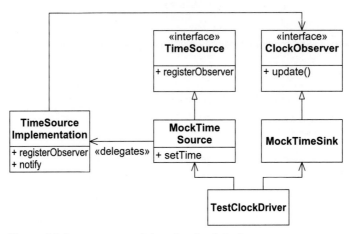

Figure 24-9   `Observer` delegation hack in Java

Notice that the `MockTimeSource` class implements `TimeSource` and contains a reference to an instance of `TimeSourceImplementation`. Notice also that all calls to the `registerObserver` method of `MockTime-Source` are delegated to that `TimeSourceImplementation` object. So too, `MockTimeSource.setTime` invokes `notify` on the `TimeSourceImplementation` instance.

This is ugly, but it has the advantage that `MockTimeSource` does not extend a class. This means that if we were to create `ObservableClock`, it could extend `Clock`, implement `TimeSource`, and delegate to `TimeSourceImplementation`. (See Figure 24-10.) This solves the problem of `Clock` depending upon the registration and update stuff, but at a nontrivial price.

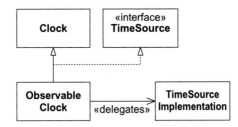

Figure 24-10   The delegation hack for `ObservableClock`

So, let's go back to the way things were in Figure 24-7, before we went down this rathole. We'll simply live with the fact that `Clock` has to depend upon all the registration and update stuff.

`TimeSource` is a stupid name for what the class does. It started out good, back in the days when we had a `ClockDriver`. But things have changed an awful lot since then. We should change the name to something that suggests registration and update. The OBSERVER pattern calls this class `Subject`. Ours seems to be specific to time, so we could call it `TimeSubject`, but that's not a very intuitive name. We could use the old Java moniker `Observable`, but that doesn't ring my chimes either. `TimeObservable`?—No.

Perhaps it is the specificity of the "push-model" observer that is the problem.[2] If we change to a "pull model" we could make the class generic. Then we could change the name of `TimeSource` to `Subject`, and everybody familiar with the OBSERVER pattern would know what it meant.

This is not a bad option. Rather than pass the time in the `notify` and `update` methods, we can have the `TimeSink` ask the `MockTimeSource` for the time. We don't want the `MockTimeSink` to know about the `MockTimeSource`, so we'll create an interface that the `MockTimeSink` can use to get the time. The `MockTimeSource` (and the `Clock`) will implement this interface. We'll call this interface—er—`TimeSource`.

The final state of the code and UML are in Figure 24-11 and Listings 24-22 through 24-27.

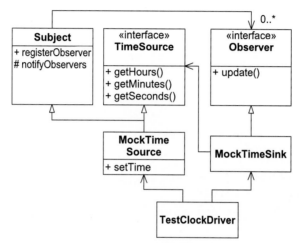

Figure 24-11   Final version of the `Observer` applied to `MockTimeSource` and `MockTimeSink`

Listing 24-22
ObserverTest.java

```java
import junit.framework.*;

public class ObserverTest extends TestCase
{
  private MockTimeSource source;
  private MockTimeSink sink;

  public ObserverTest(String name)
  {
    super(name);
  }

  public void setUp()
  {
    source = new MockTimeSource();
    sink = new  MockTimeSink(source);
    source.registerObserver(sinkprivate void assertSinkEquals(
  }
```

```java
  private void assertSinkEquals(
    MockTimeSink sink, int hours, int minutes, int seconds)
  {
    assertEquals(hours, sink.getHours());
    assertEquals(minutes, sink.getMinutes());
    assertEquals(seconds, sink.getSeconds());
  }

  public void testTimeChange()
  {
    source.setTime(3,4,5);
    assertSinkEquals(sink, 3,4,5);

    source.setTime(7,8,9);
    assertSinkEquals(sink, 7,8,9);
  }

  public void testMultipleSinks()
  {
    MockTimeSink sink2 = new MockTimeSink(source);
    source.registerObserver(sink2);

    source.setTime(12,13,14);
    assertSinkEquals(sink, 12,13,14);
    assertSinkEquals(sink2, 12,13,14);
  }
}
```

Listing 24-23

Observer.java

```java
public interface Observer
{
  public void update();
}
```

Listing 24-24

Subject.java

```java
import java.util.*;

public class Subject
{
  private Vector itsObservers = new Vector();

  protected void notifyObservers()
  {
    Iterator i = itsObservers.iterator();
    while (i.hasNext())
    {
      Observer observer = (Observer) i.next();
      observer.update();
    }
  }
```

```
  public void registerObserver(Observer observer)
  {
    itsObservers.add(observer);
  }
}
```

Listing 24-25
TimeSource.java

```
public interface TimeSource
{
  public int getHours();
  public int getMinutes();
  public int getSeconds();
}
```

Listing 24-26
MockTimeSource.java

```
public class MockTimeSource extends Subject
                            implements TimeSource
{
  private int itsHours;
  private int itsMinutes;
  private int itsSeconds;

  public void setTime(int hours, int minutes, int seconds)
  {
    itsHours = hours;
    itsMinutes = minutes;
    itsSeconds = seconds;
    notifyObservers();
  }

  public int getHours()
  {
    return itsHours;
  }

  public int getMinutes()
  {
    return itsMinutes;
  }

  public int getSeconds()
  {
    return itsSeconds;
  }
}
```

Listing 24-27
MockTimeSink.java

```
public class MockTimeSink implements Observer
{
  private int itsHours;
```

```
    private int itsMinutes;
    private int itsSeconds;
    private TimeSource itsSource;

  public MockTimeSink(TimeSource source)
  {
    itsSource = source;
  }

  public int getSeconds()
  {
    return itsSeconds;
  }

  public int getMinutes()
  {
    return itsMinutes;
  }

  public int getHours()
  {
    return itsHours;
  }

  public void update()
  {
    itsHours = itsSource.getHours();
    itsMinutes = itsSource.getMinutes();
    itsSeconds = itsSource.getSeconds();
  }
}
```

Conclusion

So, we made it. We started with a design problem and, through reasonable evolution, wound up at the canonical OBSERVER pattern. You might complain that since I knew that I wanted to arrive at the OBSERVER I simply arranged it so that I would. I won't deny it. But that's not really the issue.

If you are familiar with design patterns, then when faced with a design problem, a pattern will very likely pop into your mind. The question then is whether or not to implement that pattern directly, or to continue to evolve the code through a series of small steps. This chapter showed what the second option is like. Rather than simply leaping to the conclusion that the OBSERVER pattern was the best choice for the problem at hand, I continued to resolve the issues one by one. Eventually it was pretty clear that the code was heading in the direction of OBSERVER, so I changed the names and put the code into canonical form.

At any point during that evolution, I could have found that my problem was solved and stopped evolving. Or, I might have found that I could solve the problem by changing course and going in a different direction.

The Use of Diagrams in this Chapter

Some of the diagrams I drew for your benefit. I thought it would be easier for you to follow what I was doing by showing you an overview in a diagram. Had I not been trying to expose and expound, I would not have created them. However, *a few* of the diagrams were created for *my* benefit. There were times when I just needed to stare at the structure that I had created so I could see where to go next.

Had I not been writing a book, I would have drawn these diagrams by hand on a scrap of paper or a whiteboard. I would not have taken the time to use a drawing tool. There are no circumstances that I know of where using a drawing tool is faster than a napkin.

Having used the diagrams to help me evolve the code, I would not have kept the diagrams. In every case, the ones I drew for myself were intermediate steps.

Is there value in keeping diagrams at this level of detail? Clearly, if you are trying to expose your reasoning, as I am doing in this book, they come in pretty handy. But usually we are not trying to document the evolutionary path of a few hours of coding. Usually, these diagrams are transient and are better thrown away. At *this* level of detail, the code is generally good enough to act as its own documentation. At higher levels, that is not always true.

The OBSERVER Pattern

OK, so now that we've been through the example and evolved our code to the OBSERVER pattern, it might be interesting to study just what the OBSERVER pattern is. The canonical form of OBSERVER is shown in Figure 24-12. In this example, Clock is being observed by DigitalClock. DigitalClock registers with the Subject interface of Clock. Clock calls the notify method of Subject whenever the time changes for any reason. The notify method of Subject invokes the update method of each registered Observer. Thus, DigitalClock will receive an update message whenever the time changes. It uses that opportunity to ask Clock for the time and then display it.

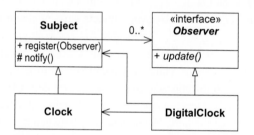

Figure 24-12   Canonical Pull-Model OBSERVER

OBSERVER is one of those patterns that, once you understand it, you see uses for it everywhere. The indirection is very cool. You can register observers with all kinds of objects rather than writing those objects to explicitly call you. While this indirection is a useful way to manage dependencies, it can easily be taken to extremes. Overuse of OBSERVER tends to make systems very difficult to understand and trace.

Push-me-pull-u.   There are two primary models of the OBSERVER pattern. Figure 24-13 shows the *pull model* OBSERVER. It gets its name from the fact that the DigitalClock must pull the time information from the Clock object after receiving the update message.

The advantage of the pull model is its simplicity of implementation and the fact that the Subject and Observer classes can be standard reusable elements in a library. However, imagine that you are observing an employee record with a thousand fields and that you have just received an update message. Which of the thousand fields changed?

When update is called on the ClockObserver, the response is obvious. The ClockObserver needs to pull the time from the Clock and display it. But when update is called on the EmployeeObserver, the response is not so obvious. We don't know what happened. We don't know what to do. Perhaps the employee's name changed, or maybe it was his salary. Maybe he got a new boss. Or maybe his bank account changed. We need help.

This help can be given in the push-model form of the OBSERVER pattern. The structure of the push-model observer is shown in Figure 24-13. Notice that the notify and update methods both take an argument. The argument is a hint, passed from Employee to SalaryObserver through the notify and update methods. That hint tells SalaryObserver the kind of change the Employee record experienced.

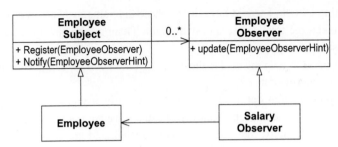

Figure 24-13 Push-Model OBSERVER

The EmployeeObserverHint argument of notify and update might be an enumeration of some kind, a string, or a more complex data structure that contains the old and new values of some field. Whatever it is, its value is being pushed toward the observer.

Choosing between the two different OBSERVER models is simply a matter of the complexity of the observed object. If the observed object is complex, and the observer needs a hint, then the push model is appropriate. If the observed object is simple, then a pull model will do fine.

How OBSERVER Manages the Principles of OOD

The principle that most drives the OBSERVER pattern is the Open–Closed Principle (OCP). The motivation for using the pattern is so that you can add new observing objects without changing the observed object. Thus the observed object stays closed.

Looking back on Figure 24-12, it should be clear that Clock is substitutable for Subject and that DigitalClock is substitutable for Observer. Thus, the Liskov Substitution Principle (LSP) is applied.

Observer is an abstract class, and the concrete DigitialClock depends upon it. The concrete methods of Subject also depend upon it. Hence, the Dependency-Inversion Principle (DIP) is applied in this case. You might think that since Subject has no abstract methods, the dependency between Clock and Subject violates the DIP. However, Subject is a class that ought never to be instantiated. It only makes sense in the context of a derived class. Thus, Subject is *logically* abstract, even though it has no abstract methods. We can enforce the abstractness of Subject by giving it a pure virtual destructor in C++ or by making its constructors protected.

There are hints of the Interface-Segregation Principle (ISP) in Figure 24-11. The Subject and TimeSource classes segregate the clients of the MockTimeSource, providing specialized interfaces for each of those clients.

Bibliography

1. Gamma, et al. *Design Patterns*. Addison–Wesley, 1995.
2. Martin, Robert C., et al. *Pattern Languages of Program Design 3*, Addison–Wesley, 1998.

25

ABSTRACT SERVER, ADAPTER, and BRIDGE

Politicians are the same all over.
They promise to build a bridge even where there is no river.

—Nikita Khrushchev

In the mid-1990s, I was deeply involved with the discussions that coursed through the `comp.object` newsgroup. Those of us who posted messages on that newsgroup argued furiously about different strategies of analysis and design. At one point, we decided that a concrete example would help us evaluate each other's position. So we chose a very simple design problem and proceeded to present our favorite solutions.

The design problem was extraordinarily simple. We chose to design the software that ran inside a simple table lamp. The table lamp has a switch and a light. You could ask the switch whether it was on or off, and you could tell the light to turn on or off. A nice, simple problem.

The debate raged for months. Each person demanded that his own particular style of design was superior to all the others. Some used a simple approach of just a switch and light object. Others thought there ought to be a lamp object that contained the switch and the light. Still others thought that electricity should be an object. One person actually suggested a power-cord object.

Despite the absurdity of most of those arguments, the design model is actually interesting to explore. Consider Figure 25-1. We can certainly make this design work. The `Switch` object can poll the state of the actual switch and can send appropriate `turnOn` an `turnOff` messages to the `Light`.

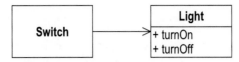

Figure 25-1   Simple table lamp

What don't we like about this design?

Two of our design principles are being violated by this design: the Dependency-Inversion Principle (DIP) and the Open-Closed Principle (OCP). The violation of the DIP is easy to see, the dependency from `Switch` to `Light` is a dependency upon a concrete class. DIP tells us to prefer dependencies on abstract classes. The violation of OCP is a little less direct, but is more to the point. We don't like this design because it forces us to drag a `Light` along everywhere we need a `Switch`. `Switch` cannot be easily extended to control objects other than `Light`.

ABSTRACT SERVER

You might be thinking that you could inherit a subclass from `Switch` that would control something other than a light as in Figure 25-3. But this doesn't solve the problem because `FanSwitch` still inherits the dependency upon `Light`. Wherever you take a `FanSwitch`, you'll have to bring `Light` along. In any case, that particular inheritance relationship also violates the DIP.

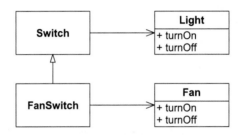

Figure 25-2   A bad way to extended `Switch`

To solve the problem, we invoke one of the simplest of all design patterns: ABSTRACT SERVER. (See Figure 25-2.) By introducing an interface between the `Switch` and the `Light`, we have made it possible for `Switch` to control anything that implements that interface. This immediately satisfies both the DIP and the OCP.

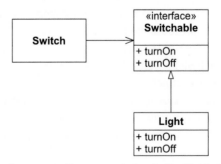

Figure 25-3   ABSTRACT SERVER solution to the Table Lamp problem

Who Owns the Interface?

As an interesting aside, notice that the interface is named for its client. It is called `Switchable` rather than `ILight`. We've talked about this before, and we'll probably notice it again. Interfaces belong to the client, not to the derivative. The logical binding between the client and the interface is stronger than the logical binding between the interface and its derivatives. It is so strong that it makes no sense to deploy `Switch` without `Switchable`; yet it makes perfect sense to deploy `Switchable` without `Light`. The strength of the logical bonds is at odds with the strength of the physical bonds. Inheritance is a much stronger physical bond than association.

In the early 1990s, we used to think that the physical bond ruled. There were very reputable books that recommended that inheritance hierarchies be placed together in the same physical package. This seemed to make sense because inheritance is such a strong physical bond. But over the last decade, we have learned that the physical strength of inheritance is misleading and that inheritance hierarchies should usually not be packaged together. Rather, clients tend to be packaged with the interfaces they control.

This misalignment of the strength of logical and physical bonds is an artifact of statically typed languages like C++ and Java. Dynamically typed languages, like Smalltalk, Python, and Ruby, don't have the misalignment because they don't use inheritance to achieve polymorphic behavior.

Adapter

There is a problem with the design in Figure 25-3. There is a potential violation of the Single-Responsibility Principle (SRP). We have bound together two things, `Light` and `Switchable`, that may not change for the same reasons. What if we can't add the inheritance relationship to `Light`? What if we purchased `Light` from a third party and we don't have the source code. Or what if there is some other class that we want a `Switch` to control but that we can't derive from `Switchable`? Enter the ADAPTER.[1]

Figure 25-4 shows how the `Adapter` pattern can be employed to solve the problem. The adapter derives from `Switchable` and delegates to `Light`. This solves the problem neatly. Now we can have any object that can be turned on or off controlled by a `Switch`. All we need to do is create the appropriate adapter. Indeed, the object need not even have the same `turnOn` and `turnOff` methods that `Switchable` has. The adapter can be *adapted* to the interface of the object.

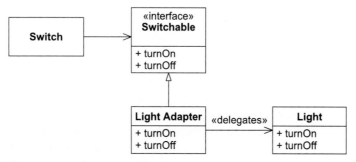

Figure 25-4   Solving the Table Lamp with ADAPTER

TANSTAAFL.   Adapters don't come cheap. You need to write the new class, and you need to instantiate the adapter and bind the adapted object to it. Then, every time you invoke the adapter, you have to pay for the time and space required for the delegation. So clearly, you don't want to use adapters all the time. The ABSTRACT SERVER solution is quite appropriate for most situations. In fact, even the initial solution in Figure 25-1 is pretty good unless you happen to *know* that there are other objects for `Switch` to control.

The Class Form of ADAPTER

The `LightAdapter` class in Figure 25-4 is known as an *object form adapter*. There is another approach known as the *class form adapter,* which is shown in Figure 25-5. In this form, the adapter object inherits from both the `Switchable` interface and the `Light` class. This form is a tiny bit more efficient than the object form and is a bit easier to use, but at the expense of using the high coupling of inheritance.

---

1.   We've seen the ADAPTER before, back in Figures 10-2 and 10-3 starting on page 118.

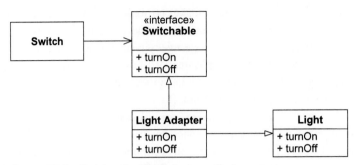

Figure 25-5   Solving the Table Lamp with ADAPTER

The Modem Problem, ADAPTERs and LSP

Consider the situation in Figure 25-6. We have a large number of modem clients all making use of the Modem interface. The Modem interface is implemented by several derivatives, including HayesModem, USRoboticsModem, and EarniesModem. This is a pretty common situation. It conforms nicely to the OCP, LSP, and DIP. Modem clients are unaffected when there are new kinds of modems to deal with. Suppose this situation were to continue for several years. Suppose that there were hundreds of modem clients all making happy use of the Modem interface.

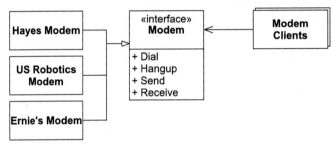

Figure 25-6   Modem Problem

Now suppose that our customers have given us a new requirement. There are certain kinds of modems that don't dial. These are called dedicated modems because they sit at both ends of a dedicated connection.[2] There are several new applications that use these dedicated modems and don't bother to dial. We'll call these the DedUsers. However, our customers want all the current modem clients to be able to use these dedicated modems. They tell us that they don't want to have to modify the hundreds of modem client applications, so those modem clients will simply be told to dial dummy phone numbers.

If we had our druthers, we might want to alter the design of our system as shown in Figure 25-7. We'd make use of the ISP to split the dialling and communications functions into two separate interfaces. The old modems would implement both interfaces, and the modem clients would use both interfaces. The DedUsers would use nothing but the Modem interface, and the DedicatedModem would implement just the Modem interface. Unfortunately this requires us to make changes to all the modem clients—something that our customers forbade.

So what do we do? We can't separate the interfaces as we'd like, yet we must provide a way for all the modem clients to use DedicatedModem. One possible solution is to derive DedicatedModem from Modem and to implement the dial and hangup functions to do nothing, as follows:

---

2.   All modems used to be dedicated. It is only in recent geological epochs that modems took on the ability to dial. In the early Jurassic period, you rented a breadbox-sized modem from the phone company and connected it to another modem through dedicated lines that you also rented from the phone company (life was good for the phone company in the Jurassic). If you wanted to dial, you rented another bread-box-sized unit called an auto dialer.

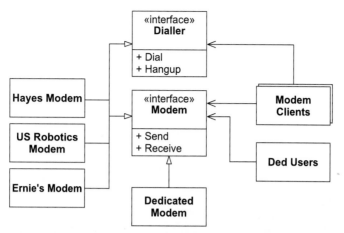

Figure 25-7 Ideal solution to the Modem Problem

```
class DedicatedModem public : Modem
{
  public:
    virtual void dial(char phoneNumber[10]) {}
    virtual void hangup() {}
    virtual void send(char c)
    {...}
    virtual char receive()
    {...}
};
```

Degenerate functions are a sign that we may be violating the LSP. The users of the base class may be expecting `dial` and `hangup` to significantly change the state of the modem. The degenerate implementations in `DedicatedModem` may violate those expectations.

Let's presume that the modem clients were written to expect their modems to be dormant until `dial` is called and to return to dormancy when `hangup` is called. In other words, they don't expect any characters to be coming out of modems that aren't dialled. `DedicatedModem` violates this expectation. It will return characters before `dial` has been called, and it will continue to return them after `hangup` has been called. Thus, `Dedicated-Modem` may crash some of the modem clients.

Now you might suggest that the problem is with the modem clients. They aren't written very well if they crash on unexpected input. I'd agree with that. But it's going to be hard to convince the folks who have to maintain the modem clients to make changes to their software because we are adding a new kind of modem. Not only does this violate the OCP, it's also just plain frustrating. And besides, our customer has explicitly forbidden us from changing the modem clients.

We Can Fix this with a Kludge.   We can simulate a connection status in the `dial` and `hangup` methods of `DedicatedModem`. We can refuse to return characters if `dial` has not been called, or after `hangup` has been called. If we make this change, then all the modem clients will be happy and won't have to change. *All we have to do is convince the* `DedUsers` *to call* `dial` *and* `hangup`. (See Figure 25-8.)

You might imagine that the folks who are building the `DedUsers` find this pretty frustrating. They are explicitly using `DedicatedModem`. *Why should they have to call* `dial` *and* `hangup`? However, they haven't written their software yet, so it's easier to get them to do what we want.

A Tangled Web of Dependencies.   Months later, when there are hundreds of `DedUsers`, our customers present us with a new change. It seems that all these years our programs have not had to dial international phone

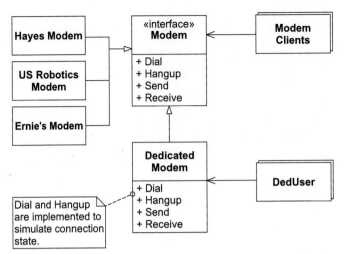

Figure 25-8   Solving the Modem Problem by kluding DedicateModem to simulate connection state

numbers. That's why they got away with the `char[10]` in `dial`. Now, however, our customers want us to be able to dial phone numbers of arbitrary length. They have a need to make international calls, credit-card calls, PIN-identified calls, etc.

Clearly all the modem clients must be changed. They were written to expect `char[10]` for the phone number. Our customers authorize this because they have no choice, and hordes of programmers are put to the task. Just as clearly, the classes in the modem hierarchy must change to accommodate the new phone number size. Our little team can deal with that. *Unfortunately, we now have to go to the authors of the* `DedUsers` *and tell them that they have to change their code!* You might imagine how happy they'll be about that. They aren't calling `dial` because they need to. They are calling `dial` because we told them they have to. And now they are going through an expensive maintenance job because they did what we told them to do.

This is the kind of nasty dependency tangle that many projects find themselves in. A kludge in one part of the system creates a nasty thread of dependency that eventually causes problems in what ought to be a completely unrelated part of the system.

ADAPTER to the Rescue.   We could have prevented this fiasco by using an ADAPTER to solve the initial problem as shown in Figure 25-9. In this case, `DedicatedModem` does not inherit from `Modem`. The modem clients use `DedicatedModem` indirectly through the `DedicatedModemAdapter`. This adapter implements `dial` and `hangup` to simulate the connection state. It delegates `send` and `recieve` calls to the `DedicatedModem`.

Note that this eliminates all the difficulties we had before. `Modem` clients are seeing the connection behavior that they expect, and `DedUsers` don't have to fiddle with `dial` or `hangup`. When the phone number requirement changes, the `DedUsers` will be unaffected. Thus, we have fixed both the LSP and OCP violations by putting the adapter in place.

Note that the kludge still exists. The adapter is still simulating connection state. You may think this is ugly, and I'd certainly agree with you. However, notice that all the dependencies point *away* from the adapter. The kludge is isolated from the system, tucked away in an adapter that barely anybody knows about. The only hard dependency upon that adapter will likely be in the implementation of some factory somewhere.[3]

BRIDGE

There is another way to look at this problem. The need for a dedicated modem has added a new degree of freedom to the `Modem` type hierarchy. When the `Modem` type was initially conceived, it was simply an interface for a set of

---

3.   See Chapter 21, FACTORY.

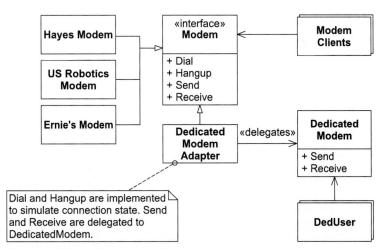

Figure 25-9 Solving the Modem Problem with the ADAPTER

different hardware devices. Thus we had `HayesModem`, `USRModem`, and `ErniesModem` deriving from the base `Modem` class. Now, however, it appears that there is another way to cut at the `Modem` hierarchy. We could have `DialModem` and `DedicatedModem` deriving from `Modem`.

Merging these two independent hierarchies can be done as shown in Figure 25-10. Each of the leaves of the type hierarchy puts either a dialup or dedicated behavior onto the hardware it controls. A `DedicatedHayesModem` object controls a Hayes modem in a dedicated context.

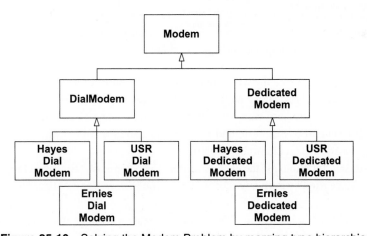

Figure 25-10 Solving the Modem Problem by merging type hierarchies

This is not an ideal structure. Every time we add a new piece of hardware, we must create *two* new classes—one for the dedicated case and one for the dialup case. Every time we add a new connection type, we have to create *three* new classes, one for each of the different pieces of hardware. If these two degrees of freedom are at all volatile, we could wind up with a large number of derived classes before too long.

The BRIDGE pattern often helps in situations where a type hierarchy has more than one degree of freedom. Rather than merge the hierarchies, we can separate them and tie them together with a bridge.

Figure 25-11 shows the structure. We split the modem hierarchy into two hierarchies. One represents the connection method, and the other represents the hardware.

`Modem` users continue to use the `Modem` interface. `ModemConnectionController` implements the `Modem` interface. The derivatives of `ModemConnectionController` control the connection mechanism.

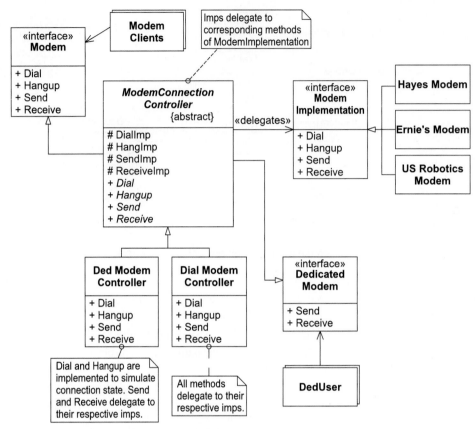

Figure 25-11   BRIDGE solution to the Modem Problem

DialModemController simply passes the dial and hangup method to dialImp and hangImp in the Modem-
ConnectionController base class. Those methods then delegate to the ModemImplementation class where
they are deployed to the appropriate hardware controller. DedModemController implements dial and hangup
to simulate the connection state. It passes send and receive to sendImp and receiveImp, which are then delegated to the ModemImplementation hierarchy as before.

Note that the four imp functions in the ModemConnectionController base class are protected. This is
because they are strictly to be used by derivatives of ModemConnectionController. No one else should be calling them.

This structure is complex, but interesting. We are able to create it without affecting the modem users, and yet
it allows us to completely separate the connection policies from the hardware implementation. Each derivative of
ModemConnectionController represents a new connection policy. That policy can use sendImp, receiveImp,
dialImp, and hangImp to implement that policy. New imp functions could be created without affecting the
users. The ISP could be employed to add new interfaces to the connection controller classes. This could create a
migration path that the modem clients could slowly follow toward an API that is higher level than dial and
hangup.

Conclusion

One might be tempted to suggest that the real problem with the Modem scenario is that the original designers got
the design wrong. They should have known that connection and communication were separate concepts. Had they
done a little more analysis, they would have found this and corrected it. So it is tempting to blame the problem on
insufficient analysis.

Poppycock! There is no such thing as *enough* analysis. No matter how much time you spend trying to figure out the perfect software structure, you will always find that the customer will introduce a change that violates that structure.

There is no escape from this. There are no perfect structures. There are only structures that try to balance the current costs and benefits. Over time those structures must change as the requirements of the system change. The trick to managing that change is to keep the system as simple and flexible as possible.

The ADAPTER solution is simple and direct. It keeps all the dependencies pointing in the right direction, and it's very simple to implement. The BRIDGE solution is quite a bit more complex. I would not suggest embarking down that road until you had very strong evidence that you needed to completely separate the connection and communication policies and that you needed to add new connection policies.

The lesson here, as always, is that a pattern is something that comes with both costs and benefits. You should find yourself using the ones that best fit the problem at hand.

Bibliography

1. Gamma, et al. *Design Patterns*, Reading, MA: Addison–Wesley, 1995.

26

PROXY and STAIRWAY TO HEAVEN: Managing Third Party APIs

© Jennifer M. Kohnke

Does anybody remember laughter?

—Robert Plant, *The Song Remains the Same*

There are many barriers in software systems. When we move data from our program into the database, we are crossing the database barrier. When we send a message from one computer to another, we are crossing the network barrier.

Crossing these barriers can be complicated. If we aren't careful, our software will be more about the barriers than about the problem to be solved. The patterns in this chapter help us cross such barriers while keeping the program centered on the problem to be solved.

PROXY

Imagine that we are writing a shopping-cart system for a Web site. Such a system might have objects for the customer, the order (the cart), and the products in the order. Figure 26-1 shows a possible structure. This structure is simplistic, but will serve for our purposes.

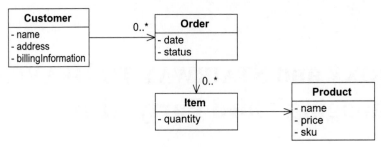

Figure 26-1   Simple shopping cart object model

If we consider the problem of adding a new item to an order, we might come up with the code in Listing 26-1. The `addItem` method of class `Order` simply creates a new `Item` holding the appropriate `Product` and quantity. It then adds that `Item` to its internal `Vector` of `Items`.

Listing 26-1

Adding an item to the Object Model.

```
public class Order
{
  private Vector itsItems = new Vector();
  public void addItem(Product p, int qty)
  {
    Item item = new Item(p, qty);
    itsItems.add(item);
  }
}
```

Now imagine that these objects represent data that are kept in a relational database. Figure 26-2 shows the tables and keys that might represent the objects. To find the orders for a given customer, you find all orders that have the customer's `cusid`. To find all the items in a given order, you find the items that have the order's `orderId`. To find the products referenced by the items, you use the product's `sku`.

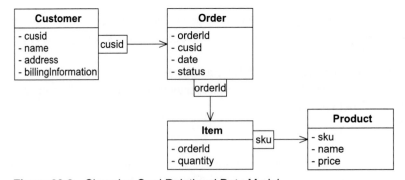

Figure 26-2   Shopping Card Relational Data Model

If we want to add an item row for a particular order, we'd use something like Listing 26-2. This code makes JDBC calls to directly manipulate the relational-data model.

Listing 26-2

Adding an item to the relational model.

```java
public class AddItemTransaction extends Transaction
{
  public void addItem(int orderId, String sku, int qty)
  {
    Statement s = itsConnection.CreateStatement();
    s.executeUpdate("insert into items values(" +
                    orderId + "," + sku + "," +
                    qty + ")");
  }
}
```

These two code snippets are very different, and yet they perform the same logical function. They both connect an item to an order. The first ignores the existence of a database, and the second glories in it.

Clearly the shopping cart program is all about orders, items, and products. Unfortunately, if we use the code in Listing 26-2, we make it about SQL statements, database connections, and piecing together query strings. This is a significant violation of the SRP and possibly the CCP. Listing 26-2 mixes together two concepts that change for different reasons. It mixes the concept of the items and orders with the concept of relational schemas and SQL. If either concept must change for any reason, the other concept will be affected. Listing 26-2 also violates the DIP since the policy of the program depends upon the details of the storage mechanism.

The PROXY pattern is a way to cure these ills. To explore this, let's set up a test program that demonstrates the behavior of creating an order and calculating the total price. The salient part of this program is shown in Listing 26-3.

Listing 26-3

Test program creates order and verifies calculation of price.

```java
public void testOrderPrice()
{
  Order o = new Order("Bob");
  Product toothpaste = new Product("Toothpaste", 129);
  o.addItem(toothpaste, 1);
  assertEquals(129, o.total());
  Product mouthwash = new Product("Mouthwash", 342);
  o.addItem(mouthwash, 2);
  assertEquals(813, o.total());
}
```

The simple code that passes this test is shown in Listings 26-4 through 26-6. It makes use of the simple object model in Figure 26-1. It does not assume that there is a database anywhere. It is also incomplete in many ways. It is just enough code to get the test to pass.

Listing 26-4

order.java

```java
public class Order
{
  private Vector itsItems = new Vector();
```

```java
  public Order(String cusid)
  {
  }

  public void addItem(Product p, int qty)
  {
    Item item = new Item(p,qty);
    itsItems.add(item);
  }

  public int total()
  {
    int total = 0;
    for (int i = 0; i < itsItems.size(); i++)
    {
      Item item = (Item) itsItems.elementAt(i);
      Product p = item.getProduct();
      int qty = item.getQuantity();
      total += p.getPrice() * qty;
    }
    return total;
  }
}
```

Listing 26-5
product.java

```java
public class Product
{
  private int itsPrice;

  public Product(String name, int price)
  {
    itsPrice = price;
  }

  public int getPrice()
  {
    return itsPrice;
  }
}
```

Listing 26-6
item.java

```java
public class Item
{
  private Product itsProduct;
  private int itsQuantity;

  public Item(Product p, int qty)
  {
    itsProduct = p;
    itsQuantity = qty;
  }
```

```
public Product getProduct()
{
  return itsProduct;
}

public int getQuantity()
{
  return itsQuantity;
}
}
```

Figures 26-3 and 26-4 show how the PROXY pattern works. Each object that is to be proxied is split into three parts. The first is an interface that declares all the methods that clients need to invoke. The second is a class that implements those methods without knowledge of the database. The third is the proxy that knows about the database.

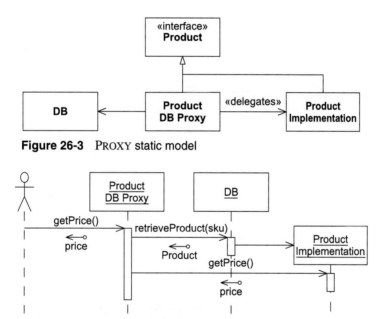

Figure 26-3 PROXY static model

Figure 26-4 PROXY dynamic model

Consider the Product class. We have proxied it by replacing it with an interface. This interface has all the same methods that Product has. The ProductImplementation class implements the interface almost exactly as before. The ProductDBProxy implements all the methods of Product to fetch the product from the database, create an instance of ProductImplementation, and then delegate the message to it.

The sequence diagram in Figure 26-4 shows how this works. The client sends the getPrice message to what it thinks is a Product, but what is really a ProductDBProxy. The ProductDBProxy fetches the Product-Implementation from the database. It then delegates the getPrice method to it.

Neither the client nor the ProductImplementation knows that this has happened. The database has been inserted into the application without either party knowing about it. That's the beauty of the PROXY pattern. In theory, it can be inserted in between two collaborating objects without those objects having to know about it. Thus, it can be used to cross a barrier like a database or a network without either of the participants knowing about it.

In reality, using proxies is nontrivial. To get an idea what some of the problems are, let's try to add the PROXY pattern to the simple shopping cart application.

Proxifying the Shopping Cart

The simplest Proxy to create is for the `Product` class. For our purposes, the product table represents a simple dictionary. It will be loaded in one place with all the products. There is no other manipulation of this table, and that makes the proxies relatively trivial.

To get started, we need a simple database utility that stores and retrieves product data. The proxy will use this interface to manipulate the database. Listing 26-7 shows the test program for what I have in mind. Listings 26-8 and 26-9 make that test pass.

Listing 26-7
DBTest.java

```java
import junit.framework.*;
import junit.swingui.TestRunner;

public class DBTest extends TestCase
{
  public static void main(String[] args)
  {
    TestRunner.main(new String[]{"DBTest"});
  }

  public DBTest(String name)
  {
    super(name);
  }

  public void setUp() throws Exception
  {
    DB.init();
  }

  public void tearDown() throws Exception
  {
    DB.close();
  }

  public void testStoreProduct() throws Exception
  {
    ProductData storedProduct = new ProductData();
    storedProduct.name = "MyProduct";
    storedProduct.price = 1234;
    storedProduct.sku = "999";
    DB.store(storedProduct);
    ProductData retrievedProduct = DB.getProductData("999");
    DB.deleteProductData("999");
    assertEquals(storedProduct, retrievedProduct);
  }
}
```

Listing 26-8
ProductData.java

```java
public class ProductData
{
  public String name;
```

```
  public int price;
  public String sku;

  public ProductData()
  {
  }

  public ProductData(String name, int price, String sku)
  {
    this.name = name;
    this.price = price;
    this.sku = sku;
  }

  public boolean equals(Object o)
  {
    ProductData pd = (ProductData)o;
    return name.equals(pd.name) &&
           sku.equals(pd.sku) &&
           price==pd.price;
  }
}
```

Listing 26-9

DB.java

```
import java.sql.*;

public class DB
{
  private static Connection con;

  public static void init() throws Exception
  {
    Class.forName("sun.jdbc.odbc.JdbcOdbcDriver");
    con = DriverManager.getConnection(
      "jdbc:odbc:PPP Shopping Cart");
  }

  public static void store(ProductData pd) throws Exception
  {
    PreparedStatement s = buildInsertionStatement(pd);
    executeStatement(s);
  }

  private static PreparedStatement
  buildInsertionStatement(ProductData pd) throws SQLException
  {
    PreparedStatement s = con.prepareStatement(
      "INSERT into Products VALUES (?, ?, ?)");
    s.setString(1, pd.sku);
    s.setString(2, pd.name);
    s.setInt(3, pd.price);
    return s;
  }
```

```java
public static ProductData getProductData(String sku) throws Exception
{
  PreparedStatement s = buildProductQueryStatement(sku);
  ResultSet rs = executeQueryStatement(s);
  ProductData pd = extractProductDataFromResultSet(rs);
  rs.close();
  s.close();
  return pd;
}

private static PreparedStatement
buildProductQueryStatement(String sku) throws SQLException
{
  PreparedStatement s = con.prepareStatement(
    "SELECT * FROM Products WHERE sku = ?;");
  s.setString(1, sku);
  return s;
}

private static ProductData
extractProductDataFromResultSet(ResultSet rs) throws SQLException
{
  ProductData pd = new ProductData();
  pd.sku = rs.getString(1);
  pd.name = rs.getString(2);
  pd.price = rs.getInt(3);
  return pd;
}

public static void deleteProductData(String sku) throws Exception
{
  executeStatement(buildProductDeleteStatement(sku));
}

private static PreparedStatement
buildProductDeleteStatement(String sku) throws SQLException
{
  PreparedStatement s = con.prepareStatement(
    "DELETE from Products where sku = ?");
  s.setString(1, sku);
  return s;
}

private static void executeStatement(PreparedStatement s) throws SQLException
{
  s.execute();
  s.close();
}

private static ResultSet
executeQueryStatement(PreparedStatement s)
```

```
  throws SQLException
  {
    ResultSet rs = s.executeQuery();
    rs.next();
    return rs;
  }

  public static void close() throws Exception
  {
    con.close();
  }
}
```

The next step in implementing the proxy is to write a test that shows how it works. This test adds a product to the database. It then creates a `ProductProxy` with the `sku` of the stored product and attempts to use the accessors of `Product` to acquire the data from the proxy. (See Listing 26-10.)

Listing 26-10

ProxyTest.java

```
import junit.framework.*;
import junit.swingui.TestRunner;

public class ProxyTest extends TestCase
{
  public static void main(String[] args)
  {
    TestRunner.main(new String[]{"ProxyTest"});
  }

  public ProxyTest(String name)
  {
    super(name);
  }

  public void setUp() throws Exception
  {
    DB.init();
    ProductData pd = new ProductData();
    pd.sku = "ProxyTest1";
    pd.name = "ProxyTestName1";
    pd.price = 456;
    DB.store(pd);
  }

  public void tearDown() throws Exception
  {
    DB.deleteProductData("ProxyTest1");
    DB.close();
  }

  public void testProductProxy() throws Exception
  {
    Product p = new ProductProxy("ProxyTest1");
    assertEquals(456, p.getPrice());
```

```
      assertEquals("ProxyTestName1", p.getName());
      assertEquals("ProxyTest1", p.getSku());
  }
}
```

In order to make this work, we have to separate the interface of `Product` from its implementation. So I changed `Product` to an interface and created `ProductImp` to implement it. (See Listings 26-11 and 26-12.)

Notice that I have added exceptions to the `Product` interface. This is because I was writing `ProductProxy` (Listing 26-13) at the same time that I was writing `Product`, `ProductImp`, and `ProxyTest`. I implemented them all one accessor at a time. As we will see, the `ProductProxy` class invokes the database, which throws exceptions. I did not want those exceptions to be caught and hidden by the proxy, so I decided to let them escape from the interface.

Listing 26-11

Product.java

```java
public interface Product
{
  public int getPrice() throws Exception;
  public String getName() throws Exception;
  public String getSku() throws Exception;
}
```

Listing 26-12

ProductImp.java

```java
public class ProductImp implements Product
{
  private int itsPrice;
  private String itsName;
  private String itsSku;

  public ProductImp(String sku, String name, int price)
  {
    itsPrice = price;
    itsName = name;
    itsSku = sku;
  }

  public int getPrice()
  {
    return itsPrice;
  }

  public String getName()
  {
    return itsName;
  }

  public String getSku()
  {
    return itsSku;
  }
}
```

Listing 26-13

ProductProxy.java

```java
public class ProductProxy implements Product
{
  private String itsSku;
  public ProductProxy(String sku)
  {
    itsSku = sku;
  }
  public int getPrice() throws Exception
  {
    ProductData pd = DB.getProductData(itsSku);
    return pd.price;
  }

  public String getName() throws Exception
  {
    ProductData pd = DB.getProductData(itsSku);
    return pd.name;
  }

  public String getSku() throws Exception
  {
    return itsSku;
  }
}
```

The implementation of this proxy is trivial. In fact, it doesn't quite match the canonical form of the pattern shown in Figures 26-3 and 26-4. This was an unexpected surprise. My intent was to implement the PROXY pattern. But when the implementation finally materialized, the canonical pattern made no sense.

As shown below, the canonical pattern would have had `ProductProxy` create a `ProductImp` in every method. It would then have delegated that method to the `ProductImp`.

```java
public int getPrice() throws Exception
{
  ProductData pd = DB.getProductData(itsSku);
  ProductImp p = new ProductImp(pd.sku, pd.name, pd.price);
  return p.getPrice();
}
```

The creation of the `ProductImp` is a complete waste of programmer and computer resources. The `ProductProxy` already has the data that the `ProductImp` accessors would return. So there is no need to create, and then delegate to, the `ProductImp`. This is yet another example of how the code may lead you away from the patterns and models you expected.

Notice that the `getSku` method of `ProductProxy` in Listing 26-13 takes this theme one step further. It doesn't even bother to hit the database for the `sku`. Why should it? It already has the `sku`.

You might be thinking that the implementation of `ProductProxy` is very inefficient. It hits the database for each accessor. Wouldn't it be better if it cached the `ProductData` item in order to avoid hitting the database?

This change is trivial, but the only thing driving us to do it is our fear. At this point, we have no data to suggest that this program has a performance problem. And besides, we know that the database engine is doing some caching too. So it's not clear what building our own cache would buy us. We should wait until we see indications of a performance problem before we invent trouble for ourselves.

Proxyifying Relationships.   Our next step is to create the proxy for Order. Each Order instance contains many Item instances. In the relational schema (Figure 26-2), this relationship is captured within the Item table. Each row of the Item table contains the key of the Order that contains it. In the object model, however, the relationship is implemented by a Vector within Order. (See Listing 26-4.) Somehow the proxy is going to have to translate between the two forms.

We begin by posing a test case that the proxy must pass. This test adds a few dummy products to the database. It then obtains proxies to those products, and uses them to invoke addItem on an OrderProxy. Finally, it asks the OrderProxy for the total price. (See Listing 26-14.) The intent of this test case is to show that an OrderProxy behaves just like an Order, but that it obtains its data from the database instead of from in-memory objects.

Listing 26-14
ProxyTest.java

```java
public void testOrderProxyTotal() throws Exception
  {
    DB.store(new ProductData("Wheaties", 349, "wheaties"));
    DB.store(new ProductData("Crest", 258, "crest"));
    ProductProxy wheaties = new ProductProxy("wheaties");
    ProductProxy crest = new ProductProxy("crest");
    OrderData od = DB.newOrder("testOrderProxy");
    OrderProxy order = new OrderProxy(od.orderId);
    order.addItem(crest, 1);
    order.addItem(wheaties, 2);
    assertEquals(956, order.total());
  }
```

In order to make this test case work, we have to implement a few new classes and methods. The first we'll tackle is the newOrder method of DB. It looks like this method returns an instance of something called an OrderData. OrderData is just like ProductData. It is a simple data structure that represents a row of the Order database table. It is shown in Listing 26-15.

Listing 26-15
OrderData.java

```java
public class OrderData
{
  public String customerId;
  public int orderId;

  public OrderData()
  {
  }

  public OrderData(int orderId, String customerId)
  {
    this.orderId = orderId;
    this.customerId = customerId;
  }
}
```

Don't be offended by the use of public data members. This is not an object in the true sense. It is just a container for data. It has no interesting behavior that needs to be encapsulated. Making the data variables private and providing getters and setters would just be a needless complication.

Now we need to write the `newOrder` function of DB. Notice that when we call it in Listing 26-14, we provide the ID of the owning customer, but we do not provide the `orderId`. Each `Order` needs an `orderId` to act as its key. What's more, in the relational schema, each `Item` refers to this `orderId` as a way to show its connection to the `Order`. Clearly the `orderId` must be unique. How does it get created? Let's write a test to show our intent. (See Listing 26-16.)

Listing 26-16
DBTest.java

```java
public void testOrderKeyGeneration() throws Exception
{
  OrderData o1 = DB.newOrder("Bob");
  OrderData o2 = DB.newOrder("Bill");
  int firstOrderId = o1.orderId;
  int secondOrderId = o2.orderId;
  assertEquals(firstOrderId+1, secondOrderId);
}
```

This test shows that we expect the `orderId` to somehow automatically increment every time a new `Order` is created. This is easily implemented by querying the database for the maximum `orderId` currently in use and then adding one to it. (See Listing 26-17.)

Listing 26-17
DB.java

```java
  public static OrderData newOrder(String customerId) throws Exception
  {
    int newMaxOrderId = getMaxOrderId() + 1;
    PreparedStatement s = con.prepareStatement(
      "Insert into Orders(orderId,cusid) Values(?,?);");
    s.setInt(1, newMaxOrderId);
    s.setString(2,customerId);
    executeStatement(s);
    return new OrderData(newMaxOrderId, customerId);
  }

  private static int getMaxOrderId() throws SQLException
  {
    Statement qs = con.createStatement();
    ResultSet rs = qs.executeQuery(
      "Select max(orderId) from Orders;");
    rs.next();
    int maxOrderId = rs.getInt(1);
    rs.close();
    return maxOrderId;
  }
```

Now we can start to write `OrderProxy`. As with `Product`, we need to split `Order` into an interface and an implementation. So `Order` becomes the interface and `OrderImp` becomes the implementation. (See Listings 26-18 and 26-19.)

Listing 26-18

`Order.java`

```java
public interface Order
{
  public String getCustomerId();
  public void addItem(Product p, int quantity);
  public int total();
}
```

Listing 26-19

`OrderImp.java`

```java
import java.util.Vector;

public class OrderImp implements Order
{
  private Vector itsItems = new Vector();
  private String itsCustomerId;

  public String getCustomerId()
  {
    return itsCustomerId;
  }

  public OrderImp(String cusid)
  {
    itsCustomerId = cusid;
  }

  public void addItem(Product p, int qty)
  {
    Item item = new Item(p,qty);
    itsItems.add(item);
  }

  public int total()
  {
    try
    {
      int total = 0;
      for (int i = 0; i < itsItems.size(); i++)
      {
        Item item = (Item) itsItems.elementAt(i);
        Product p = item.getProduct();
        int qty = item.getQuantity();
        total += p.getPrice() * qty;
      }
      return total;
    }
```

```
  catch (Exception e)
  {
    throw new Error(e.toString());
  }
  }
}
```

I had to add some exception processing to OrderImp because the Product interface throws exceptions. I'm getting frustrated with all these exceptions. The implementations of proxies behind an interface should not have an effect on that interface, and yet the proxies are throwing exceptions that propagate out through the interface. So I resolve to change all the Exceptions to Errors so that I don't have to pollute the interfaces with throws clauses and the users of those interfaces with try/catch blocks.

How do I implement addItem in the proxy? Clearly the proxy cannot delegate to OrderImp.addItem! Rather, the proxy is going to have to insert an Item row in the database. On the other hand, I *really want* to delegate OrderProxy.total to OrderImp.total, because I want the business rules (i.e., the policy for creating totals) to be encapsulated in OrderImp. The whole point of building proxies is to separate database implementation from business rules.

In order to delegate the total function, the proxy is going to have to build the complete Order object along with all its contained Items. Thus, in OrderProxy.total, we are going to have to read in all the items from the database, call addItem on an empty OrderImp for each item we find, and then call total on that OrderImp. Thus, the OrderProxy implementation ought to look something like Listing 26-20.

Listing 26-20

OrderProxy.java

```
import java.sql.SQLException;

public class OrderProxy implements Order
{
  private int orderId;

  public OrderProxy(int orderId)
  {
    this.orderId = orderId;
  }

  public int total()
  {
    try
    {
      OrderImp imp = new OrderImp(getCustomerId());
      ItemData[] itemDataArray = DB.getItemsForOrder(orderId);
      for (int i = 0; i < itemDataArray.length; i++)
      {
        ItemData item = itemDataArray[i];
        imp.addItem(new ProductProxy(item.sku), item.qty);
      }
      return imp.total();
    }
    catch (Exception e)
    {
      throw new Error(e.toString());
    }
  }
```

```
  public String getCustomerId()
  {
    try
    {
      OrderData od = DB.getOrderData(orderId);
      return od.customerId;
    }
    catch (SQLException e)
    {
      throw new Error(e.toString());
    }
  }

  public void addItem(Product p, int quantity)
  {
    try
    {
      ItemData id =
        new ItemData(orderId, quantity, p.getSku());
      DB.store(id);
    }
    catch (Exception e)
    {
      throw new Error(e.toString());
    }
  }

  public int getOrderId()
  {
    return orderId;
  }
}
```

This implies the existence of an ItemData class and a few DB functions for manipulating ItemData rows. These are shown in Listings 26-21 through 26-23.

Listing 26-21

ItemData.java

```
public class ItemData
{
  public int orderId;
  public int qty;
  public String sku = "junk";

  public ItemData()
  {
  }

  public ItemData(int orderId, int qty, String sku)
  {
    this.orderId = orderId;
    this.qty = qty;
    this.sku = sku;
  }
```

```
    public boolean equals(Object o)
    {
      ItemData id = (ItemData)o;
      return orderId == id.orderId &&
             qty == id.qty &&
             sku.equals(id.sku);
    }
  }
```

Listing 26-22

DBTest.java

```
  public void testStoreItem() throws Exception
  {
    ItemData storedItem = new ItemData(1, 3, "sku");
    DB.store(storedItem);
    ItemData[] retrievedItems = DB.getItemsForOrder(1);
    assertEquals(1, retrievedItems.length);
    assertEquals(storedItem, retrievedItems[0]);
  }

  public void testNoItems() throws Exception
  {
    ItemData[] id = DB.getItemsForOrder(42);
    assertEquals(0, id.length);
  }
```

Listing 26-23

DB.java

```
  public static void store(ItemData id) throws Exception
  {
    PreparedStatement s = buildItemInsersionStatement(id);
    executeStatement(s);
  }

  private static PreparedStatement
  buildItemInsersionStatement(ItemData id) throws SQLException
  {
    PreparedStatement s = con.prepareStatement(
      "Insert into Items(orderId,quantity,sku) " +
      "VALUES (?, ?, ?);");
    s.setInt(1,id.orderId);
    s.setInt(2,id.qty);
    s.setString(3, id.sku);
    return s;
  }

  public static ItemData[] getItemsForOrder(int orderId)
  throws Exception
  {
    PreparedStatement s =
      buildItemsForOrderQueryStatement(orderId);
    ResultSet rs = s.executeQuery();
    ItemData[] id = extractItemDataFromResultSet(rs);
    rs.close();
```

```
    s.close();
    return id;
}

private static PreparedStatement
buildItemsForOrderQueryStatement(int orderId)
throws SQLException
{
  PreparedStatement s = con.prepareStatement(
    "SELECT * FROM Items WHERE orderid = ?;");
  s.setInt(1, orderId);
  return s;
}

private static ItemData[]    extractItemDataFromResultSet(ResultSet rs)
throws SQLException
{
  LinkedList l = new LinkedList();
  for (int row = 0; rs.next(); row++)
  {
    ItemData id = new ItemData();
    id.orderId = rs.getInt("orderid");
    id.qty = rs.getInt("quantity");
    id.sku = rs.getString("sku");
    l.add(id);
  }
  return (ItemData[]) l.toArray(new ItemData[l.size()]);
}

public static OrderData getOrderData(int orderId)
throws SQLException
{
  PreparedStatement s = con.prepareStatement(
    "Select cusid from orders where orderid = ?;");
  s.setInt(1, orderId);
  ResultSet rs = s.executeQuery();
  OrderData od = null;
  if (rs.next())
    od =  new OrderData(orderId, rs.getString("cusid"));
  rs.close();
  s.close();
  return od;
}
```

Summary of PROXY

This example should have dispelled any false illusions about the elegance and simplicity of using proxies. Proxies are not trivial to use. The simple delegation model implied by the canonical pattern seldom materializes so neatly. Rather, we find ourselves short-circuiting the delegation for trivial getters and setters. For methods that manage 1:N relationships, we find ourselves *delaying* the delegation and moving it into other methods, just as the delegation for addItem was moved into total. Finally, we face the spectre of caching.

We didn't do any caching in this example. The tests all run in less than a second, so there was no need to worry overmuch about performance. But in a real application, the issue of performance and the need for intelligent caching are likely to arise. I do not suggest that you automatically implement a caching strategy because you fear performance will otherwise be too slow. Indeed, I have found that adding caching too early is a very good way to *decrease* performance. If you fear performance may be a problem, I recommend that you conduct some experiments to *prove* that it will be a problem. Once proven, and *only once proven*, you should start considering how to speed things up.

The Benefit of PROXY.   For all the troublesome nature of proxies, they have one very powerful benefit: *the separation of concerns*. In our example, the business rules and the database have been completely separated. OrderImp has no dependence whatever on the database. If we want to change the database schema or change the database engine, we can do so without affecting Order, OrderImp, or any of the other business domain classes.

In those instances where separation of business rules from database implementation is critically important, PROXY can be a good pattern to employ. For that matter, PROXY can be used to separate business rules from *any* kind of implementation issue. It can be used to keep the business rules from being polluted by such things as COM, CORBA, EJB, etc. It is a way to keep the business rule assets of your project separate from the implementation mechanisms that are currently in vogue.

Dealing with Databases, Middleware, and Other Third Party Interfaces

Third party APIs are a fact of life for software engineers. We buy database engines, middleware engines, class libraries, threading libraries, etc. Initially, we use these APIs by making direct calls to them from our application code. (See Figure 26-5.)

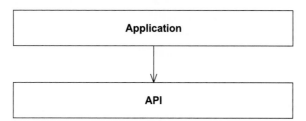

Figure 26-5   Initial relationship between an application and a third party API

Over time, however, we find that our application code becomes more and more polluted with such API calls. In a database application, for example, we may find more and more SQL strings littering the code that also contains the business rules.

This becomes a problem when the third party API changes. For databases it also becomes a problem when the schema changes. As new versions of the API or schema are released, more and more of the application code has to be reworked to align with those changes.

Eventually, the developers decide that they must insulate themselves from these changes. So they invent a layer that separates the application business rules from the third party API. (See Figure 26-6.) They concentrate into this layer all the code that uses the third party API and all of the concepts that are related to the API rather than to the business rules of the application.

Such layers can sometimes be purchased. ODBC or JDBC are such layers. They separate the application code from the actual database engine. Of course, they are also third party APIs in and of themselves; therefore, the application may need to be insulated even from them.

Notice that there is a transitive dependency from the Application to the API. In some applications, that indirect dependence is still enough to cause problems. JDBC, for example, does not insulate the application from the details of the schema.

In order to attain even better insulation, we need to invert the dependency between the application and the layer. (See Figure 26-7.) This keeps the application from knowing anything at all about the third party API, either directly or indirectly. In the case of a database, it keeps the application from direct knowledge of the schema. In the

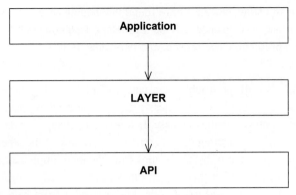

Figure 26-6   Introducing an insulation layer

case of a middleware engine, it keeps the application from knowing anything about the datatypes used by that middleware processor.

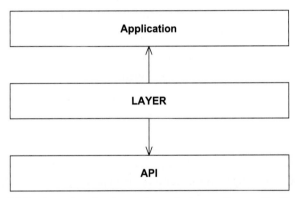

Figure 26-7   Inverting the dependency between the application and Layer

This arrangement of dependencies is precisely what the PROXY pattern achieves. The application does not depend upon the proxies at all. Rather, the proxies depend upon the application and upon the API. This concentrates all knowledge of the mapping between the application and the API into the proxies.

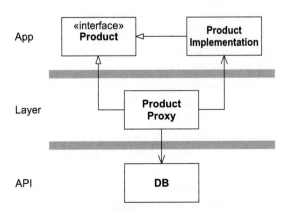

Figure 26-8   How the PROXY inverts the dependency between the application and the Layer

This concentration of knowledge means that the proxies are nightmares. Whenever the API changes, the proxies change. Whenever the application changes, the proxies change. The proxies can become very hard to deal with.

It's good to know where your nightmares live. Without the proxies, the nightmares would be spread throughout the application code.

Most applications don't need proxies. Proxies are a very heavyweight solution. When I see proxy solutions in use, my recommendation in most cases is to take them out and use something simpler. But there are cases when the intense separation between the application and the API afforded by proxies is beneficial. Those cases are almost always in very large systems that undergo frequent schema or API thrashing. Or they are in systems that can ride on top of many different database engines or middleware engines.

STAIRWAY TO HEAVEN[1]

STAIRWAY TO HEAVEN is another pattern that achieves the same dependency inversion as PROXY. It employs a variation on the class form of the ADAPTER pattern. (See Figure 26-9.)

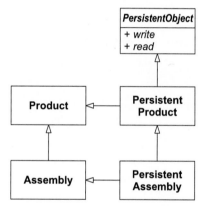

FIGURE 26-9 STAIRWAY TO HEAVEN

PersistentObject is an abstract class that knows about the database. It provides two abstract methods: read and write. It also provides a set of implemented methods that provides the tools needed to implement read and write. PersistentProduct, for example, uses these tools to implement read and write to read and write all the data fields of Product from and to the database. By the same token, PersistentAssembly implements read and write to do the same for the extra fields within Assembly. It inherits the ability to read and write the fields of Product from PersistentProduct and structures the read and write methods so as to take advantage of that fact.

This pattern is only useful in languages that support multiple inheritance. Note that both PersistentProduct and PersistentAssembly inherit from two implemented base classes. What's more, PersistentAssembly finds itself in a *diamond* inheritance relationship with Product. In C++, we use virtual inheritance to prevent two instances of Product from being inherited into PersistentAssembly.

The need for virtual inheritance, or similar relationships in other languages, means that this pattern is somewhat intrusive. It makes itself felt in the Product hierarchy, but the intrusion is minimal.

The benefit of this pattern is that it completely separates knowledge of the database away from the business rules of the application. Those small bits of the application that need to invoke read and write can do so through the following exigency:

1.　[Martin97].

```
PersistentObject* o = dynamic_cast<PersistentObject*>(product);
if (o)
  o->write();
```

In other words, we ask the application object if it conforms to the `PersistentObject` interface, and if so, we invoke either `read` or `write`. This keeps that part of the application that does not need to know about reading and writing completely independent of the `PersistentObject` side of the hierarchy.

Example of STAIRWAY TO HEAVEN

Listings 26-24 through 26-34 show an example of STAIRWAY TO HEAVEN in C++. As usual, it is best to start with the test case. CppUnit[2] is a bit wordy if shown in its entirety, so I have only included the test-case methods in Listing 26-24. The first test-case verifies that a `PersistentProduct` can be passed around the system as a `Product` and then converted to a `PersistentObject` and written at will. We assume that the `PersistentProduct` will write itself in a simple XML format. The second test case verifies the same for `PersistentAssembly`, the only difference being the addition of a second field in the `Assembly` object.

Listing 26-24

`productPersistenceTestCase.cpp {abridged}`

```
void ProductPersistenceTestCase::testWriteProduct()
{
  ostrstream s;
  Product* p = new PersistentProduct("Cheerios");
  PersistentObject* po = dynamic_cast<PersistentObject*>(p);
  assert(po);
  po->write(s);
  char* writtenString = s.str();
  assert(strcmp("<PRODUCT><NAME>Cheerios</NAME></PRODUCT>",
                writtenString) == 0);
}

void ProductPersistenceTestCase::testWriteAssembly()
{
  ostrstream s;
  Assembly* a = new PersistentAssembly("Wheaties", "7734");
  PersistentObject* po = dynamic_cast<PersistentObject*>(a);
  assert(po);
  po->write(s);
  char* writtenString = s.str();
  assert(strcmp("<ASSEMBLY><NAME>Wheaties"
                "</NAME><ASSYCODE>7734</ASSYCODE></ASSEMBLY>",
                writtenString) == 0);

}
```

Next, in Listings 26-25 through 26-28, we see the definitions and implementations of both `Product` and `Assembly`. In the interest of saving space in our example, these classes are nearly degenerate. In a normal application, these classes would contain methods that implemented business rules. Note that there is no hint of persistence in either of these classes. There is no dependence whatever from the business rules to the persistence mechanism. This is the whole point of the pattern.

---

2.   One of the XUnit family of unit test frameworks. See www.junit.org, and www.xprogramming.com for more information.

While the dependency characteristics are good, there is an artifact in Listing 26-27 that is present solely because of the STAIRWAY TO HEAVEN pattern. `Assembly` inherits from `Product` using the `virtual` keyword. This is necessary in order to prevent duplicate inheritance of `Product` in `PersistentAssembly`. If you refer back to Figure 26-9, you'll see that `Product` is the apex of a diamond[3] of inheritance involving `Assembly`, `PersistentProduct`, and `PersistentObject`. To prevent duplicate inheritance of `Product`, it must be inherited virtually.

Listing 26-25
product.h

```
#ifndef STAIRWAYTOHEAVENPRODUCT_H
#define STAIRWAYTOHEAVENPRODUCT_H

#include <string>

class Product
{
 public:
  Product(const string& name);
  virtual ~Product();
  const string& getName() const {return itsName;}
 private:
  string itsName;
};

#endif
```

Listing 26-26
product.cpp

```
#include "product.h"

Product::Product(const string& name)
   : itsName(name)
{
}

Product::~Product()
{
}
```

Listing 26-27
assembly.h

```
#ifndef STAIRWAYTOHEAVENASSEMBLY_H
#define STAIRWAYTOHEAVENASSEMBLY_H

#include <string>
#include "product.h"

class Assembly : public virtual Product
{
 public:
```

3. Sometimes facetiously known as the "deadly diamond of death."

```
  Assembly(const string& name, const string& assyCode);
  virtual ~Assembly();

  const string& getAssyCode() const {return itsAssyCode;}
 private:
  string itsAssyCode;
};

#endif
```

Listing 26-28

assembly.cpp

```
#include "assembly.h"

Assembly::Assembly(const string& name, const string& assyCode)
  :Product(name), itsAssyCode(assyCode)
{
}

Assembly::~Assembly()
{
}
```

Listings 26-29 and 26-30 show the definition and implementation of PersistentObject. Note that while PersistentObject knows nothing of the Product hierarchy, it does seem to know something about how to write XML. At least it understands that objects are written by writing a header, followed by the fields, followed by a footer.

The write method of PersistentObject uses the TEMPLATE METHOD[4] pattern to control the writing of all its derivatives. Thus, the persistent side of the STAIRWAY TO HEAVEN pattern makes use of the facilities of the PersistentObject base class.

Listing 26-29

persistentObject.h

```
#ifndef STAIRWAYTOHEAVENPERSISTENTOBJECT_H
#define STAIRWAYTOHEAVENPERSISTENTOBJECT_H

#include <iostream>

class PersistentObject
{
 public:
  virtual ~PersistentObject();
  virtual void write(ostream&) const;

 protected:
  virtual void writeFields(ostream&) const = 0;

 private:
  virtual void writeHeader(ostream&) const = 0;
  virtual void writeFooter(ostream&) const = 0;
};

#endif
```

---

4.   See Chapter 14: *Template Method & Strategy: Inheritance vs. Delegation*, on page 161.

Listing 26-30

`persistentObject.cpp`

```cpp
#include "persistentObject.h"

PersistentObject::~PersistentObject()
{
}

void PersistentObject::write(ostream& s) const
{
  writeHeader(s);
  writeFields(s);
  writeFooter(s);
  s << ends;
}
```

Listings 26-31 and 26-32 show the implementation of `PersistentProduct`. This class implements the `writeHeader`, `writeFooter`, and `writeField` functions to create the appropriate XML for a `Product`. It inherits the fields and accessors from `Product` and is driven by the write method of its base class `PersistentObject`.

Listing 26-31

`persistentProduct.h`

```cpp
#ifndef STAIRWAYTOHEAVENPERSISTENTPRODUCT_H
#define STAIRWAYTOHEAVENPERSISTENTPRODUCT_H

#include "product.h"
#include "persistentObject.h"

class PersistentProduct : public virtual Product
                        , public PersistentObject
{
 public:
  PersistentProduct(const string& name);
  virtual ~PersistentProduct();

 protected:
  virtual void writeFields(ostream& s) const;

 private:
  virtual void writeHeader(ostream& s) const;
  virtual void writeFooter(ostream& s) const;
};

#endif
```

Listing 26-32

`persistentProduct.cpp`

```cpp
#include "persistentProduct.h"

PersistentProduct::PersistentProduct(const string& name)
:Product(name)
{
}
```

```
PersistentProduct::~PersistentProduct()
{
}

void PersistentProduct::writeHeader(ostream& s) const
{
  s << "<PRODUCT>";
}

void PersistentProduct::writeFooter(ostream& s) const
{
  s << "</PRODUCT>";
}

void PersistentProduct::writeFields(ostream& s) const
{
  s << "<NAME>" << getName() << "</NAME>";
}
```

Finally, Listings 26-33 and 26-34 show how `PersistentAssembly` unifies `Assembly` and `Persistent-Product`. Just like `PersistentProduct`, it overrides `writeHeader`, `writeFooter`, and `writeFields`. However, it implements `writeFields` to invoke `PersistentProduct::writeFields`. Thus, it inherits the ability to write the `Product` part of `Assembly` from `PersistentProduct`, and it inherits the `Product` and `Assembly` fields and accessors from `Assembly`.

Listing 26-33

persistentAssembly.h

```
#ifndef STAIRWAYTOHEAVENPERSISTENTASSEMBLY_H
#define STAIRWAYTOHEAVENPERSISTENTASSEMBLY_H

#include "assembly.h"
#include "persistentProduct.h"

class PersistentAssembly : public Assembly, public PersistentProduct
{
 public:
  PersistentAssembly(const string& name,
                     const string& assyCode);
  virtual ~PersistentAssembly();

 protected:
  virtual void writeFields(ostream& s) const;

 private:
  virtual void writeHeader(ostream& s) const;
  virtual void writeFooter(ostream& s) const;
};

#endif
```

Listing 26-34

persistentAssembly.cpp

```
#include "persistentAssembly.h"

PersistentAssembly::PersistentAssembly(const string& name, const string& assyCode)
: Assembly(name, assyCode)
, PersistentProduct(name)
, Product(name)
{
}

PersistentAssembly::~PersistentAssembly()
{
}

void PersistentAssembly::writeHeader(ostream& s) const
{
  s << "<ASSEMBLY>";
}

void PersistentAssembly::writeFooter(ostream& s) const
{
  s << "</ASSEMBLY>";
}

void PersistentAssembly::writeFields(ostream& s) const
{
  PersistentProduct::writeFields(s);
  s << "<ASSYCODE>" << getAssyCode() << "</ASSYCODE>";
}
```

Conclusion.   I've seen STAIRWAY TO HEAVEN used in many different scenarios with good results. The pattern is relatively easy to set up and has a minimum impact on the objects that contain the business rules. On the other hand, it requires a language, like C++, that supports multiple inheritance of implementation.

Other Patterns That Can Be Used with Databases

Extension Object.   Imagine an extension object[5] that knows how to write the extended object on a database. In order to write such an object, you would ask it for an extension object that matched the "database" key, cast it to a DatabaseWriterExtension, and then invoke the write function.

```
Product p = /* some function that returns a Product */
ExtensionObject e = p.getExtension("Database");
if (e != null)
{
  DatabaseWriterExtension dwe = (DatabaseWriterExtension) e;
  e.write();
}
```

Visitor[6].   Imagine a visitor hierarchy that knows how to write the visited object on a database. You would write an object on the database by creating the appropriate type of visitor, and then calling accept on the object to be written.

5.   See "Extension Object" on page 408

6.   See "Visitor" on page 388

```
Product p = /* some function that returns a Product */
DatabaseWriterVisitor dwv = new DatabaseWriterVisitor();
p.accept(dwv);
```

Decorator[7]. There are two ways to use a decorator to implement databases. You can decorate a business object and give it `read` and `write` methods; or you can decorate a data object that knows how to read and write itself and give it business rules. The latter approach is not uncommon when using object-oriented databases. The business rules are kept out of the OODB schema and added in with decorators.

Facade. This is my favorite starting point. It's simple and effective. On the down side, it couples the business-rule objects with the database. Figure 26-10 shows the structure. The `DatabaseFacade` class simply provides methods for reading and writing all the necessary objects. This couples the objects with the `DatabaseFacade` and vice versa. The objects know about the facade because they are often the ones that call the `read` and `write` functions. The facade knows about the objects because it must use their accessors and mutators to implement the `read` and `write` functions.

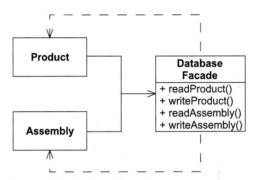

Figure 26-10   Database Facade

This coupling can cause a lot of problems in larger applications; but in smaller apps or in apps that are just starting to grow, it's a pretty effective technique. If you start using a facade and then later decide to change to one of the other patterns to reduce coupling, the facade is pretty easy to refactor.

Conclusion

It is very tempting to anticipate the need for PROXY or STAIRWAY TO HEAVEN long before the need really exists. This is almost never a good idea, especially with PROXY. I recommend starting with FACADE and then refactoring as necessary. You'll save yourself time and trouble if you do.

Bibliography

1. Gamma, et al. *Design Patterns*. Reading, MA: Addison–Wesley, 1995.
2. Martin, Robert C. Design Patterns for Dealing with Dual Inheritance Hierarchies. *C++ Report* (April): 1997.

---

7.   See "Decorator" on page 403

27

Case Study: Weather Station

Written in collaboration with Jim Newkirk

© Jennifer M. Kohnke

The Following Story is fiction, but you may recognize many elements of it from your own exeperience.

The Cloud Company

TCC

The Cloud Company has been the leader in industrial weather monitoring systems (WMS) for the past several years. Their flagship product has been a WMS that keeps track of temperature, humidity, barometric pressure, wind speed and direction, etc. The system displays these readings in real time on a display. It also keeps track of historical information on an hourly and daily basis. This historical data can be pulled up on the display at the request of the user.

The primary customers of Cloud Company products have been the aviation, maritime, agricultural, and broadcast industries. For these industries, WMSs are mission-critical applications. The Cloud Company has a reputation for building highly reliable products that can be installed in relatively uncontrolled environments. This makes the systems somewhat expensive.

The high cost of these systems has cut the Cloud Company off from customers that do not need, and cannot afford, the high-reliability systems that they sell. Cloud Company managers believe that this is a large potential market, and they would like to tap into it.

The Problem.   A competitor named Microburst, Inc., has recently announced a product line that starts at the low end and can be incrementally upgraded to higher reliability. This threatens to cut the Cloud Company off from smaller but growing customers. These customers will already be using Microburst products by the time they grow to a size that would allow them to use Cloud Company products.

More frightening still, the Microburst product boasts the ability to be interconnected at the high end. That is, the high-end upgrades can be networked together into a wide-area weather monitoring system. This threatens to erode the current Cloud Company customer base.

The Strategy.   Although Microburst has successfully demonstrated its low-end units at trade shows, they are not offering production quantity shipments for at least six months. This indicates that there may be engineering or production problems that Microburst has not solved. Moreover, the high-reliability upgrades promised by Microburst as part of the product line are currently not available. It seems that Microburst has announced the product prematurely.

If the Cloud Company can announce a low-end upgradable and connectable product, and begin shipping it *within* six months, then they may be able to capture, or at least stall, customers who would otherwise buy Microburst's products. By stalling the market and thereby depriving Microburst of orders, they might be able to compromise Microburst's ability to solve their engineering and manufacturing problems, a very desirable outcome.

The Dilemma.   A new low-cost and extendable product line requires a significant amount of engineering. The hardware engineers have flatly refused to commit to a six-month development deadline. They believe that it will be twelve months before they could see production-quantity units.

The marketing managers believe that in twelve months, Microburst will be shipping production quantity and will be capturing an irretrievable part of Cloud Company's customers.

The Plan.   Cloud Company managers have decided to announce their new product line immediately and to begin accepting orders that will be shipped before six months have elapsed. They have named the new product Nimbus-LC 1.0. Their plan is to repackage the old, expensive, high-reliability hardware into a new enclosure with a nice LCD touch panel. The high manufacturing cost of these units means that the company will actually lose money on each one that they sell.

Concurrently, the hardware engineers will begin to develop the true low-cost hardware, which will be available in 12 months. This configuration of the product has been called Nimbus-LC 2.0. When production quantities are available, the Nimbus-LC 1.0 will be phased out.

When a Nimbus-LC 1.0 customer wants to upgrade to a higher level of service, his unit will be replaced with a Nimbus-LC 2.0 at no additional cost. Thus, the company is willing to lose money on this product for six months in order to capture, or at least stall, potential Microburst customers.

The WMS-LC Software

The software project for the Nimbus-LC project is complex. The developers must create a software product that can use both the existing hardware as well as the low-cost 2.0 hardware. Prototype units of the 2.0 hardware will not be available for nine months. Moreover, the processor on the 2.0 board is not likely to be the same as the processor on the 1.0 board. Still, the system must operate identically, regardless of which hardware platform it uses.

The hardware engineers will be writing the lowest-level hardware drivers, and they need the application software engineers to design the API for these drivers. This API must be available to the hardware engineers within the next four months. The software must be production ready in 6 months and must be working with the 2.0 hardware in 12 months. They want at least 6 weeks of Q/A for the 1.0 device, so the software engineers really have only 20 weeks to get the software working. Since the hardware platform for the 2.0 version is new, they need 8 to 10 weeks of Q/A. This eats up most of the 3-month period between first prototype and final shipment. Thus the software engineers will have very little time to make the new hardware work.

Software Planning Documents. The developers and marketing folks have written several documents that describe the Nimbus-LC project:

1. "Nimbus-LC Requirements Overview" on page 379
   This document describes the operating requirements of the Nimbus-LC system as they were understood at the time the project was begun.[1]
2. "Nimbus-LC Use Cases" on page 380
   This document describes the actors and use cases derived from the requirements document.
3. "Nimbus-LC Release Plan" on page 381
   This document describes the release plan for the software. This plan tries to address the major risks early in the project life cycle, while assuring that the software will be complete by the necessary deadlines.

Language Selection

The most important constraint upon the language is portability. The short development time, and the even shorter contact that the software engineers will have with the 2.0 hardware demand that both the 1.0 and 2.0 versions use the same software. That is, the source code needs to be identical, or nearly so. If the portability constraint cannot be met by the language, the release of the 2.0 version at the 12-month mark will be in severe jeopardy.

Fortunately, there are few other constraints. The software is not very large, so space is not much of a problem. There are no hard real-time deadlines that are shorter than one second, so speed is not much of an issue. Indeed, the real-time deadlines are so weak that a moderately fast garbage-collecting language would not be inappropriate. The portability constraints, and the lack of any other serious constraints, make the selection of Java quite appropriate.

Nimbus-LC Software Design

According to the release plan, one of the major goals of phase I is to create an architecture that will allow the bulk of the software to be independent of the hardware that it controls. Indeed, we want to separate the abstract behavior of the weather station from its concrete implementation.

For example, the software must be able to display the current temperature regardless of the hardware configuration. This implies the design shown in Figure 27-1.

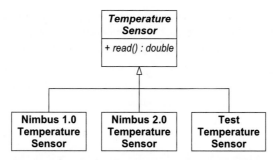

Figure 27-1 Initial Temperature-Sensor Design

An abstract base class named `TemperatureSensor` supplies a polymorphic `read()` function. Derivatives of this base class allow for separate implementations of the `read()` function.

The Test Classes. Notice that there is one derivative for each of the two known hardware platforms. There is also a special derivative named `TestTemperatureSensor`. This class will be used to test the software in a

---

1.   We all know that the requirements document is the most volatile document in any software project.

workstation, which is not connected to Nimbus hardware. This allows the software engineers to write unit tests and acceptance tests for their software even when they don't have access to a Nimbus system.

Also, we have very little time to integrate the Nimbus 2.0 hardware and software together. The Nimbus 2.0 version will be at risk because of this short time frame. By making the Nimbus software work with both the Nimbus 1.0 hardware and with the test class, we will have made the Nimbus software execute on multiple platforms. This lessens the risk of significant portability issues with the Nimbus 2.0.

The test classes also give us the opportunity to test features or conditions that are hard to capture in the software. For example, we can set up the test classes to produce failures that are difficult to simulate with the hardware.

Making Periodic Measurements.   The most common mode of the Nimbus system is when it is displaying current weather-monitoring data. Each of the values are updated at their own particular rate. Temperature is updated once per minute, while barometric pressure is updated once every five minutes. Clearly, we need some kind of scheduler that will trigger these readings and communicate them to the user. Figure 27-2 shows a possible structure.

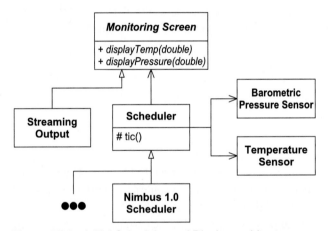

Figure 27-2   Initial Scheduler and Display architecture

We imagine the `Scheduler` to be a base class that has many possible implementations, one for each of the hardware and test platforms. The `Scheduler` has a `tic` function that it expects will be called once every 10 ms. It is the responsibility of the derived class to make this call. (See Figure 27-3.) The `Scheduler` counts the `tic()` calls. Once per minute, it calls the `read()` function of the `TemperatureSensor` and passes the returned temperature to the `MonitoringScreen`. For phase I, we don't need to show the temperature in a GUI, so the derivative of `MonitoringScreen` simply sends the result to an output stream.

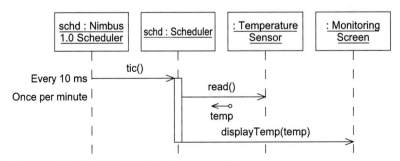

Figure 27-3   Initial Scheduler Sequence Diagram

Barometric Pressure Trend.   The requirements document says that we must report the trend of the baro-metric pressure. This is a value that can have three states: *rising*, *falling*, or *stable*. How do we determine the value of this variable?

According to the Federal Meteorological Handbook,[2] the barometric-pressure trend is calculated as follows:

> *If the pressure is rising or falling at a rate of at least 0.06 inch per hour and the pressure change totals 0.02 inch or more at the time of the observation [to be taken once every three hours], a pressure change remark shall be reported.*

Where do we put this algorithm? If we put it in the `BarometricPressureSensor` class, then that class will need to know the time of each reading, and it will have to keep track of a series of readings going back three hours. Our current design does not allow for this. We could fix this by adding the current time as an argument to the `Read` function of the `BarometricPressureSensor` class and guaranteeing that that function will be called on a regular basis.

However, this couples the trend calculation to the frequency of user updates. It is not inconceivable that a change to the user interface update scheme could affect the pressure-trend algorithm. Also, it is very unfriendly for a sensor to demand that it be read on a regular basis in order to function properly. A better solution needs to be found.

We could have the `Scheduler` keep track of barometric pressure history and calculate trends at need. How-ever, will we then also put temperature and wind speed history in the `Scheduler` class? Every new kind of sensor or history requirement would cause us to change the `Scheduler` class. This has the makings of a maintenance nightmare.

Reconsidering the `Scheduler`.   Take another look at Figure 27-2. Notice that the `Scheduler` is con-nected to each of the sensors and to the user interface. As more sensors are added, and as more user interface screens are added, they will have to be added to the `Scheduler` too. Thus, the `Scheduler` is not closed to the addition of new sensors or user interfaces. This is a violation of the OCP. We would like to design the `Scheduler` so that it is independent of changes and additions to the sensors and user interfaces.

Decoupling the User Interface.   User interfaces are volatile. They are subject to the whims of customers, marketing people, and nearly everyone else who comes in contact with the product. It seems very likely that if any part of the system suffers requirements thrashing, it will be the user interface. Therefore, we should decouple it first.

Figures 27-4 and 27-5 show a new design that uses the OBSERVER pattern. We have made the UI a dependent of the sensor, so that when the sensor reading changes, the UI will be automatically notified. Notice that the depen-

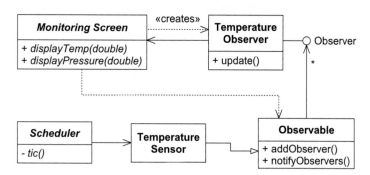

Figure 27-4   Observer decouples UI from Scheduler

2.   *Federal Meteorological Handbook* No. 1, Chapter 11, Section 11.4.6 (http://www.nws.noaa.gov).

dency is indirect. The actual observer is an ADAPTER[3] named `TemperatureObserver`. This object is notified by the `TemperatureSensor` when the temperature reading changes. In response, the `TemperatureObsever` calls the `DisplayTemp` function of the `MonitoringScreen` object.

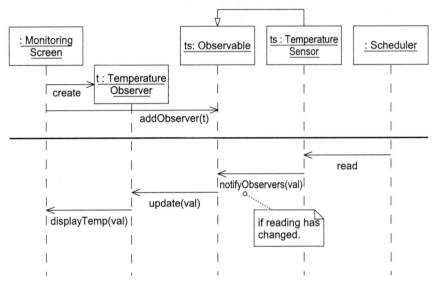

Figure 27-5   Decoupled UI sequence diagram

This design has nicely decoupled the UI from the `Scheduler`. The `Scheduler` now knows nothing of the UI and can focus solely upon telling the sensors when to read. The UI binds itself to the sensors and expects them to report any changes. However, the UI does not know about the sensors themselves. It simply knows about a set of objects that implements the `Observable` interface. This will allow us to add sensors without making significant changes to this part of the UI.

We have also solved the problem of the barometric-pressure trend. This reading can now be calculated by a separate `BarometricPressureTrendSensor` that observes the `BarometricPressureSensor`. (See Figure 27-6.)

Rethinking the Scheduler—Yet Again.   The major role of the `Scheduler` is to tell each of the sensors when they should acquire a new value. However, if future requirements force us to add or remove a sensor, the `Scheduler` will need to be changed. Indeed, the `Scheduler` will have to change, even if we simply want to change the rate of a sensor. This is an unfortunate violation of the OCP. It seems that the knowledge of a sensor's polling rate belongs to the sensor itself and not any other part of the system.

We can decouple the `Scheduler` from the sensors by using the `Listener`[4] paradigm from the Java class library. This is similar to OBSERVER in that you register to be notified of something; but in this case, we want to be notified when a certain event (time) occurs. (See Figure 27-7.)

Sensors create anonymous ADAPTER classes that implement the `AlarmListener` interface. The sensors then register those adapters with the `AlarmClock` (the class we used to call the `Scheduler`). As part of the registration, they tell the `AlarmClock` how often they would like to be woken up (e.g., every second or every fifty milliseconds). When that period expires, the `AlarmClock` sends the `wakeup` message to the adapter, which then sends the `read` message to the sensor.

This has completely changed the nature of the `Scheduler` class. In Figure 27-2 it formed the center of our system and knew about most of the other components. But now it simply sits at the side of the system. It knows

3.   [GOF95], p. 139.

4.   [JAVA98], p. 360.

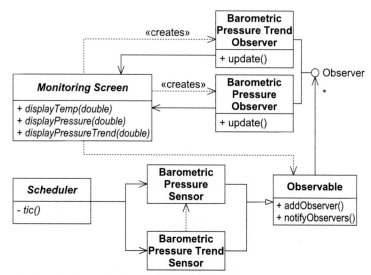

Figure 27-6   Barometric Pressure Observers

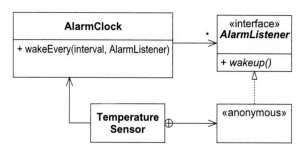

Figure 27-7   Decoupled Alarm clock

nothing about the other components. It conforms to the SRP by doing one job—scheduling—which has nothing whatever to do with weather monitoring. Indeed, it could be reused in many different kinds of applications. In fact, the change is so dramatic that we have changed the name to `AlarmClock`.

   The Structure of the Sensors.   Having decoupled the sensors from the rest of the system, we should look at their internal structure. Sensors now have three separate functions. First, they have to create and register the anonymous derivative of the `AlarmListener`. Second, they have to determine if their readings have changed and invoke the `notifyObservers` method of the `Observable` class. Third, they have to interact with the Nimbus hardware in order to read the appropriate values.

   Figure 27-1 showed how these concerns might be separated. Figure 27-8 integrates that design with the other changes we have made. The `TemperatureSensor` base class deals with the first two concerns, since they are generic. The derivative of `TemperatureSensor` can then deal with the hardware and perform the actual readings.

   Figure 27-8 employs TEMPLATE METHOD in order to achieve the separation between the generic and specific concerns of the `TemperatureSensor`. You can see this pattern in the private `check` and `read` functions of `TemperatureSensor`. When the `AlarmClock` calls `wakeup` on the anonymous class, the anonymous class forwards the call to the `check` function of the `TemperatureSensor`. The `check` function then calls the abstract `read` function of `TemperatureSensor`. This function will be implemented by the derivative to properly interact with the hardware and obtain the sensor reading. The `check` function then determines whether the new reading is different from the previous reading. If a difference is detected, then it notifies the waiting observers.

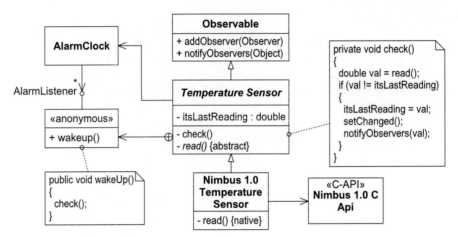

Figure 27-8   Sensor Structure

This nicely accomplishes the separation of concerns that we need. For every new hardware or testing platform, we will be able to create a derivative of `TemperatureSensor` that will work with it. Moreover, that derivative must merely override one very simple function: `read()`. The rest of the functionality of the sensor remains in the base class where it belongs.

Where Is the API?   One of our Release II goals is the creation of a new API for the Nimbus 2.0 hardware. This API should be written in Java, be extensible, and provide simple and direct access to the Nimbus 2.0 hardware. Furthermore, it must serve the Nimbus 1.0 hardware as well. Without that API, all the simple debugging and calibration tools that we write for this project will have to be changed when the new board is introduced. Where is this API within our current design?

It turns out that nothing we have created so far can serve as a simple API. What we are looking for is something like this:

```
public interface TemperatureSensor
{
  public double read();
}
```

We are going to want to write tools that have direct access to this API without having to bother with registering observers. We also don't want sensors at this level to be polling themselves automatically, or interacting with the `AlarmClock`. We want something very simple and isolated that acts as the direct interface to the hardware.

It may seem that we are reversing all our previous arguments. After all, Figure 27-1 shows exactly what we have just asked for. However, the changes we made subsequent to Figure 27-1 were made for sound reasons. What we need is a hybrid that mixes the best of both schemes.

Figure 27-9 employs the BRIDGE pattern to extract the true API from the `TemperatureSensor`. The intent of this pattern is to separate an implementation from an abstraction, so that both may vary independently. In our case, the `TemperatureSensor` is the abstraction, and the `TemperatureSensorImp` is the implementation. Notice that the word "implementation" is being used to describe an abstract interface and that the "implementation" is itself implemented by the `Nimbus1.0TemperatureSensor` class.

Creational Issues.   Look again at Figure 27-9. In order for this to work, a `TemperatureSensor` object must be created and bound to a `Nimbus1.0TemperatureSensor` object. Who takes care of this? Certainly, whatever part of the software is responsible for this will not be platform independent, since it must have explicit knowledge of the platform-dependent `Nimbus1.0TemperatureSensor`.

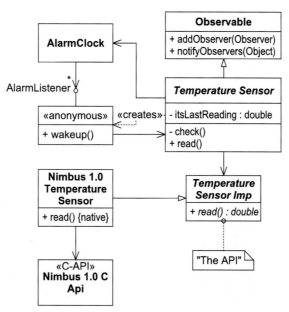

Figure 27-9   Temperature Sensor with API

We could use the main program to do all this. We could write it as shown in Listing 27-1.

Listing 27-1

WeatherStation

```
public class WeatherStation
{
  public static void main(String[] args)
  {
    AlarmClock ac = new AlarmClock(
      new Nimbus1_0AlarmClock;

    TemperatureSensor ts =
      new TemperatureSensor(ac,
        new Nimbus1_0TemperatureSensor);

    BarometricPressureSensor bps =
      new BarometricPressureSensor(ac,
        new Nimbus1_0BarometricPressureSensor);

    BarometricPressureTrend bpt =
      new BarometricPressureTrend(bps)
  }
}
```

This is a workable solution, but requires an awful lot of clerical overhead. Instead, we could use FACTORIES to deal with most of the clerical overhead involved with creation. Figure 27-10 shows the structure.

We have named the factory the `StationToolkit`. This is an interface that presents methods that offer to create instances of the API classes. Each platform will have its own derivative of `StationToolkit`, and that derivative will create the appropriate derivatives of the API classes.

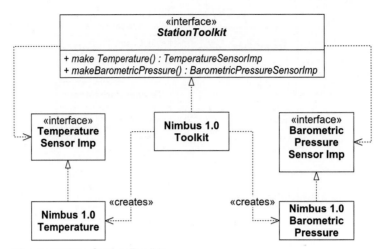

Figure 27-10   Station Toolkit

Now we can rewrite the main function as shown in Listing 27-2. Notice that in order to alter this main program to work with a different platform, all we have to change is the two lines that create the Nimbus1.0AlarmClock and the Nimbus1.0Toolkit. This is a dramatic improvement over Listing 27-1, which required a change for every sensor it created.

Listing 27-2

WeatherStation

```
public class WeatherStation
{
  public static void main(String[] args)
  {
    AlarmClock ac = new AlarmClock(
      new Nimbus1_0AlarmClock;

    StationToolkit st = new Nimbus1_0Toolkit();

    TemperatureSensor ts =
      new TemperatureSensor(ac,st);

    BarometricPressureSensor bps =
      new BarometricPressureSensor(ac,st);

    BarometricPressureTrend bpt =
      new BarometricPressureTrend(bps)
  }
}
```

Notice that the StationToolkit is being passed into each sensor. This allows the sensors to create their own implementations. Listing 27-3 shows the constructor for TemperatureSensor.

Listing 27-3

TemperatureSensor

```
public class TemperatureSensor extends Observable
{
  public TemperatureSensor(AlarmClock ac,
                           StationToolkit st)
```

```
  {
    itsImp = st.makeTemperature();
  }
  private TemperatureSensorImp itsImp;
}
```

Getting the Station Toolkit to Create the AlarmClock.   We can improve matters further by having the `StationToolkit` create the appropriate derivative of the `AlarmClock`. Once again, we will employ the BRIDGE pattern to separate the `AlarmClock` abstraction that is meaningful to the weather-monitoring applications, from the implementation that supports the hardware platform.

Figure 27-11 shows the new `AlarmClock` structure. The `AlarmClock` now receives `tic()` messages through its `ClockListener` interface. These messages are sent from the appropriate derivative of the `AlarmClockImp` class in the API.

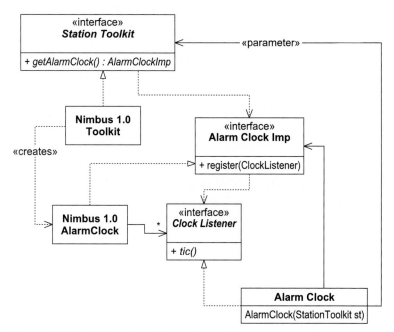

Figure 27-11   Station Toolkit and Alarm Clock

Figure 27-12 shows how the `AlarmClock` gets created. The appropriate `StationToolkit` derivative is passed into the constructor of the `AlarmClock`. The `AlarmClock` directs it to create the appropriate derivative of `AlarmClockImp`. This is passed back to the `AlarmClock`, and the `AlarmClock` registers with it so that it will receive `tic()` messages from it.

Once again, this has an effect upon the main program in Listing 27-4. Notice that now there is only one line that is platform dependent. Change that line, and the entire system will use a different platform.

Listing 27-4

WeatherStation

```
public class WeatherStation
{
  public static void main(String[] args)
  {
    StationToolkit st = new Nimbus1_0Toolkit();
```

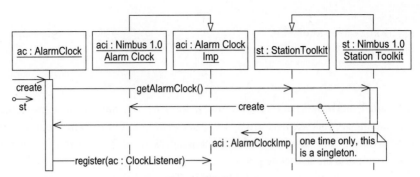

Figure 27-12 Creation of the Alarm Clock

```
    AlarmClock ac = new AlarmClock(st);
    TemperatureSensor ts =
      new TemperatureSensor(ac,st);

    BarometricPressureSensor bps =
      new BarometricPressureSensor(ac,st);

    BarometricPressureTrend bpt =
      new BarometricPressureTrend(bps)
  }
}
```

This is pretty good, but in Java we can do even better. Java allows us to create objects by name. The main program in Listing 27-5 does not need to be changed in order to make it work with a new platform. The name of the `StationToolkit` derivative is simply passed in as a command-line argument. If the name was correctly specified, the appropriate `StationToolkit` will be created, and the rest of the system will behave appropriately.

Listing 27-5

WeatherStation

```
public class WeatherStation
{
  public static void main(String[] args)
  {
    try
    {
      Class tkClass = Class.forName(args[0]);
      StationToolkit st =
        (StationToolkit)tkClass.newInstance();

      AlarmClock ac = new AlarmClock(st);

      TemperatureSensor ts =
        new TemperatureSensor(ac,st);

      BarometricPressureSensor bps =
        new BarometricPressureSensor(ac,st);

      BarometricPressureTrend bpt =
        new BarometricPressureTrend(bps)
    }
```

```
    catch (Exception e)
    {
    }
  }
}
```

Putting the Classes into Packages.   There are several portions of this software that we would like to release and distribute separately. The API and each of its instantiations are reusable without the rest of the application and may be used by the testing and quality assurance teams. The UI and sensors should be separate so that they can vary indepedently. After all, newer products may have better UI's on top of the same system architecture. In fact, Release II will be the first example of this.

Figure 27-13 shows a package structure for Phase I. This package structure nearly falls out of the classes we have designed so far. There is one package for each platform, and the classes in those packages derive from the classes in the API package. The sole client of the API package is the `WeatherMonitoringSystem` package, which holds all the other classes.

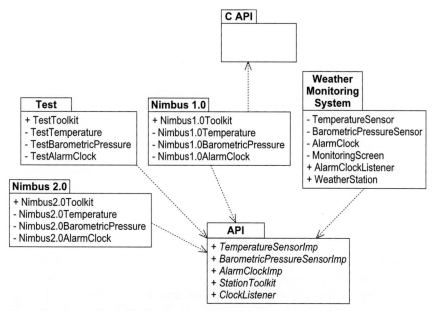

Figure 27-13   Phase I Package Structure

Even though Release I has a very small UI, it is unfortunate that it is mixed in with the `Weather-MonitoringSystem` classes. It would be better to put this class in a separate package. However, we have a problem. As things stand, the `WeatherStation` object creates the `MonitoringScreen` object, but the `MonitoringScreen` object must know about all the sensors in order to add its observers through their `Observable` interface. Thus, if we were to pull the `MonitoringScreen` out into its own package, there would be a cyclic dependency between that package and the `WeatherMonitoringSystem` package. This violates the acyclic-dependencies principle (ADP) and would make the two packages impossible to release independently of each other.

We can fix this by pulling the main program out of the `WeatherStation` class. `WeatherStation` still creates the `StationToolkit` and all the sensors, but it does not create the `MonitoringScreen`. The main program will create the `MonitoringScreen` and the `WeatherStation`. The main program will then pass the `WeatherStation` to the `MonitoringScreen` so that the `MonitoringScreen` can add its observers to the sensors.

How does the `MonitoringScreen` get the sensors from the `WeatherStation`? We need to add some methods to the `WeatherStation` that allow this to take place. See Listing 27-6 to see what this looks like.

Listing 27-6

`WeatherStation`

```
public class WeatherStation
{
  public WeatherStation(String tkName)
  {
    //create station toolkit and sensors as before.
  }

  public void addTempObserver(Observer o)
  {
    itsTS.addObserver(o);
  }

  public void addBPObserver(Observer o)
  {
    itsBPS.addObserver(o);
  }

  public void addBPTrendObserver(Observer o)
  {
    itsBPT.addObserver(o);
  }

// private variables...
  private TemperatuerSensor itsTS;
  private BarometricPressureSensor itsBPS;
  private BarometricPressureTrend itsBPT;
}
```

Now we can redraw the package diagram as shown in Figure 27-14. We have omitted most of the packages that aren't concerned with the `MonitoringScreen`. This looks pretty good. Certainly the `UI` can be varied without affecting the `WeatherMonitoringSystem`. However, the dependency of the `UI` on `WeatherMonitoring-System` will cause problems whenever the `WeatherMonitoringSystem` changes.

Both `UI` and `WeatherMonitoringSystem` are concrete. When one concrete package depends on another, the dependency inversion principle (DIP) is violated. In this case, it would be better if the `UI` depended on something abstract rather than the `WeatherMonitoringSystem`.

We can fix this by creating an interface that the `MonitoringScreen` can use and that the `Weather-Station` derives from. (See Figure 27-15.)

Now, if we put the `WeatherStationComponent` interface into its own package, we will achieve the separation we want. (See Figure 27-16.) Notice that now the `UI` and the `WeatherMonitoringSystem` are completely decoupled. They can both vary independently of each other. This is a good thing.

24-Hour History and Persistence

Points four and five of the Release I deliverables section (see page 382) talk about the need for maintaining a persistent 24-hour history. We know that both the Nimbus 1.0 and Nimbus 2.0 hardware have some kind of nonvolatile memory (NVRAM). On the other hand, the test platform will simulate the nonvolatile memory by using the disk.

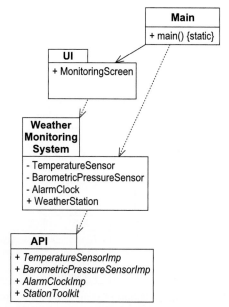

Figure 27-14 Package Diagram with Cycle Broken

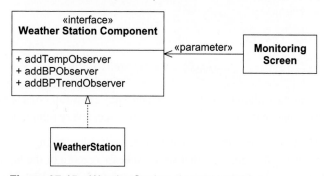

Figure 27-15 WeatherStation abstract interface

We need to create a persistence mechanism that is independent of the individual platforms, while still providing the necessary functionality. We also need to connect this to the mechanisms that maintain the 24-hour historical data.

Clearly, the low-level persistence mechanism should be defined as an interface in the API package. What form should this interface take? The Nimbus I C-API provides calls that allow blocks of bytes to be read and written from particular offsets within the nonvolatile memory. While this is effective, it is also somewhat primitive. Is there a better way?

The Persistent API. The Java environment provides the facilities to allow any object to be immediately converted into an array of bytes. This process is called *serialization*. Such an array of bytes can be reconstituted back into an object through the process of *deserialization*. It would be convenient if our low-level API allowed us to specify an object and a name for that object. Listing 27-7 shows what this might look like.

Listing 27-7

PersistentImp

```
package api;
import java.io.Serializable;
```

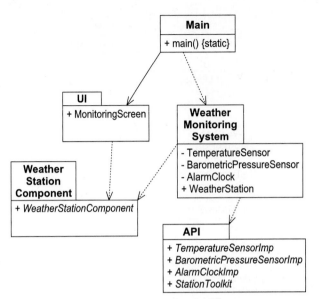

Figure 27-16   Weather Station Component Package Diagram

```
import java.util.AbstractList;
public interface PersistentImp
{
  void store(String name, Serializable obj);
  Object retrieve(String name);
  AbstractList directory(String regExp);
};
```

The `PersistentImp` interface allows you to `store` and `retrieve` full objects by name. The only restriction is that such objects must implement the `Serializable` interface, a very minimal restriction.

24-Hour History.   Having decided on the low-level mechanism for storing persistent data, let's look at the kind of data that will be persistent. Our spec says that we must keep a record of the high and low readings for the previous 24-hour period. Figure 27-23 on page 380 shows a graph with these data. This graph does not seem to make a lot of sense. The high and low readings are painfully redundant. Worse, they come from the last 24-hours on the clock and not from the previous calendar day. Usually, when we want the last 24-hour high and low reading, we want it for the previous calendar day.

Is this a flaw in the spec or a flaw in our interpretation? It will do us no good to implement something according to the spec if the spec is not really what the customer wants.

A quick verification with the stakeholders shows our intuition to be correct. We do indeed want to keep a rolling history of the last 24 hours. However, the historical low and high need to be for the previous calendar day.

The 24-hour High and Low.   The daily high and low values will be based upon real-time readings of the sensors. For example, every time the temperature changes, the 24-hour high and low temperatures will be updated appropriately. Clearly, this is an OBSERVER relationship. Figure 27-17 shows the static structure, and Figure 27-18 shows the relevant dynamic scenarios.

We have chosen to show the OBSERVER pattern using an association marked with the «observes» stereotype. We have created a class called `TemperatureHiLo` that is woken up by the `AlarmClock` every day at midnight. Notice that the `wakeEveryDay` method has been added to `AlarmClock`.

Upon construction of the `TemperatureHiLo` object, it registers with both the `AlarmClock` and with the `TemperatureSensor`. Whenever the temperature changes, the `TemperatureHiLo` object is notified through the OBSERVER pattern. `TemperatureHiLo` then informs the `HiLoData` interface using the `currentReading`

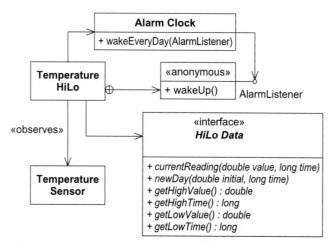

Figure 27-17 `TemperatureHiLo` structure

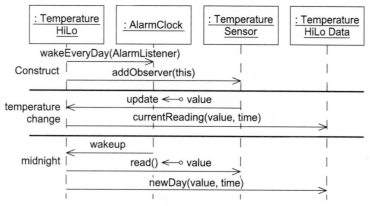

Figure 27-18 HiLo Scenarios

method. HiLoData will have to be implemented with some class that knows how to store the high and low values for the current 24-hour calendar day.

We have separated the TemperatureHiLo class from the HiLoData class for two reasons. First of all, we wanted to separate the knowledge of the TemperatureSensor and AlarmClock from the algorithms that determined the daily highs and lows. Second, and more importantly, the algorithm for determining the daily highs and lows can be reused for barometric pressure, wind speed, dew point, etc. Thus, though we will need BarometricPressureHiLo, DewPointHiLo, WindSpeedHiLo, etc. to observe the appropriate sensors, each will be able to use the HiLoData class to compute and store the data.

At midnight, the AlarmClock sends the wakeup message to the TemperatureHiLo object. TemperatureHiLo responds by fetching the current temperature from the TemperatureSensor and forwarding it to the HiLoData interface. The implementation of HiLoData will have to store the previous calendar day's values using the PersistentImp interface and will also have to create a new calendar day with the initial value.

PersistentImp accesses objects in the persistent store using a string. This string acts as an access key. Our HiLoData objects will be stored and retrieved with strings that have the following format: "<type>+HiLo+<MM><dd><yyyy>." For example, "temperatureHiLo04161998."

Implementing the HiLo Algorithms

How do we implement the HiLoData class? This seems pretty straightforward. Listing 27-8 shows what the Java code for this class looks like.

Listing 27-8

HiLoDataImp

```java
public class HiLoDataImp implements HiLoData,java.io.Serializable
{
  public HiLoDataImp(StationToolkit st, String type,
                     Date theDate, double init,
                     long initTime)
  {
    itsPI = st.getPersistentImp();
    itsType = type;
    itsStorageKey = calculateStorageKey(theDate);
    try
    {
      HiLoData t =(HiLoData)itsPI.retrieve(itsStorageKey);
      itsHighTime =  t.getHighTime();
      itsLowTime =   t.getLowTime();
      itsHighValue = t.getHighValue();
      itsLowValue =  t.getLowValue();
      currentReading(init, initTime);
    }
    catch (RetrieveException re)
    {
      itsHighValue = itsLowValue = init;
      itsHighTime = itsLowTime = initTime;
    }
  }

  public long   getHighTime()  {return itsHighTime;}
  public double getHighValue() {return itsHighValue;}
  public long   getLowTime()   {return itsLowTime;}
  public double getLowValue()  {return itsLowValue;}

  // Determine if a new reading changes the
  // hi and lo and return true if reading changed.
  public void currentReading(double current, long time)
  {
    if (current > itsHighValue)
    {
      itsHighValue = current;
      itsHighTime = time;
      store();
    }
    else if (current < itsLowValue)
    {
      itsLowValue = current;
      itsLowTime = time;
      store();
    }
  }
```

```
public void newDay(double initial, long time)
{
  store();
  // now clear it out and generate a new key.
  itsLowValue = itsHighValue = intial;
  itsLowTime = itsHighTime = time;
  // now calculate a new storage key based on
  // the current date, and store the new record.
  itsStorageKey = calculateStorageKey(new Date());
  store()
}

private store()
{
  try
  {
    itsPI.store(itsStorageKey, this);
  }
  catch (StoreException)
  {
    // log the error somehow.
  }
}

private String calculateStorageKey(Date d)
{
  SimpleDateFormat df = new SimpleDateFormat("MMddyyyy");
  return(itsType + "HiLo" + df.format(d));
}
private double itsLowValue;
private long    itsLowTime;
private double itsHightValue;
private long    itsHighTime;
private String itsType;
// we don't want to store the following.
transient private String itsStorageKey;
transient private api.PersistentImp itsPI;
}
```

Well, maybe it wasn't all *that* straightforward. Let's walk through this code to see what it does.

At the bottom of the class, you'll see the private member variables. The first four variables are expected. They record the high and low values and the times at which those values occurred. The itsType variable remembers the type of readings that this HiLoData is keeping. This variable will have the value "Temp" for temperature, "BP" for barometric pressure, "DP" for dew point, etc. The last two variables are declared transient. This means that they will not be stored in the persistent memory. They record the current storage key and a reference to the PersistentImp.

The constructor takes five arguments. The StationToolkit is needed to gain access to the PersistentImp. The type and Date arguments will be used to build the storage key used for storing and retrieving the object. Finally, the init and initTime arguments are used to initialize the object in the event that PersistentImp cannot find the storage key.

The constructor tries to fetch the data from PersistentImp. If the data are present, it copies the nontransient data into its own member variables. Then it calls currentReading with the initial value and time to make sure that these readings get recorded. Finally, if `currentReading` discovers that there was a change in the high or low data, it returns true, and the `Store` function is invoked to make sure that the persistent memory is updated.

The `currentReading` method is the heart of this class. It compares the old high and low values with the new incoming reading. If the new reading is higher than the old high or lower than the old low, it replaces the appropriate value, records the appropriate time, and stores the changes in persistent memory.

The `newDay` method is invoked at midnight. First, it stores the current `HiLoData` in persistent memory. Then it resets the values of the `HiLoData` for the beginning of a new day. It recomputes the storage key for the new date and then stores the new `HiLoData` in persistent memory.

The `Store` function simply uses the current storage key to write the `HiLoData` object into persistent memory through the `PersistentImp` object.

Finally, the `calculateStorageKey` method builds a storage key from the type of the `HiLoData` and the date argument.

Ugliness.   Certainly the code in Listing 27-8 is not too difficult to understand. However, there is ugliness for another reason. The policy embodied in the functions `currentReading` and `newDay` have to do with managing the high-low data and are independent of persistence. On the other hand, the `store`, and `calculate-StorageKey` methods, the constructor, and the `transient` variables are all specific to persistence and have nothing to do with the management of the highs and lows. This is a violation of the SRP.

In its current commingled state, this class has the makings of a maintenance nightmare. If something fundamental about the persistence mechanism changes, to the extent that the `calculateStorageKey` and `store` functions become inappropriate, then new persistence facilities will have to be grafted into the class. Functions like `newDay` and `currentReading` will have to be altered to invoke the new persistence facilities.

Decoupling Persistence from Policy.   We can avoid these potential problems by decoupling the high-low data-management policy from the persistence mechanism using the PROXY pattern. Look back at Figure 26-7 on page 346. Note the decoupling of the policy layer (application) from the mechanism layer (API).

Figure 27-19 employs the PROXY pattern to effect the necessary decoupling. It differs from Figure 27-17 on page 371 by the addition of the `HiLoDataProxy` class. It is the proxy class to which the `TemperatureHiLo` object actually holds a reference. The proxy, in turn, holds a reference to a `HiLoDataImp` object and delegates calls to it. Listing 27-9 shows the implementing of the critical functions of both `HiLoDataProxy` and `HiLoDataImp`.

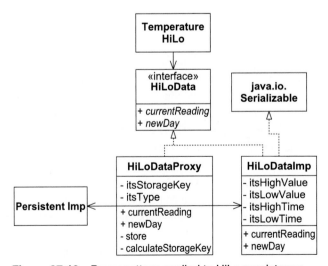

Figure 27-19   Proxy pattern applied to HiLo persistence

Listing 27-9

Snippets of the Proxy solution

```java
class HiLoDataProxy implements HiLoData
{
  public boolean currentReading(double current, long time)
  {
    boolean change;
    change = itsImp.currentReading(current, time);
    if (change)
      store();
    return change;
  }

  public void newDay(double initial, long time)
  {
    store();
    itsImp.newDay(initial, time);
    calculateStorageKey(new Date(time));
    store();
  }

  private HiLoDataImp itsImp;
}

class HiLoDataImp implements HiLoData, java.io.Serializable
{
  public boolean currentReading(double current, long time)
  {
    boolean changed = false;
    if (current > itsHighValue)
    {
      itsHighValue = current;
      itsHighTime = time;
      changed = true;
    }
    else if (current < itsLowValue)
    {
      itsLowValue = current;
      itsLowTime = time;
      changed = true;
    }
    return changed;
  }

  public void newDay(double initial, long time)
  {
    itsHighTime = itsLowTime = time;
    itsHighValue = itsLowValue = initial;
  }
};
```

Notice how the `HiLoDataImp` class has no inkling of persistence. Notice also that the `HiLoDataProxy` class takes care of all the persistence ugliness and then delegates to the `HiLoDataImp`. This is nice. Furthermore, notice how the proxy depends on both `HiLoDataImp` (the policy layer) and `PersistentImp` (the mechanism layer). This is exactly what we were after.

But all is not perfect. The astute reader will have caught the change that we made to the `currentReading` method. We changed it to return a `boolean`. We need this `boolean` in the proxy so that the proxy knows when to call `store`. Why don't we call store every time `currentReading` is called? There are many varieties of NVRAM. Some of them have an upper limit on the number of times you can write to them. Therefore, in order to prolong the life of the NVRAM, we only store into it when the values change. Real life intrudes, yet again.

Factories and Initialization.   Clearly, we don't want `TemperatureHiLo` to know anything about the proxy. It should know only about `HiLoData`. (See Figure 27-19.) Yet somebody is going to have to create the `HiLoDataProxy` for the `TemperatureHiLo` object to use. Also, someone is going to have to create the `HiLoDataImp` to which the proxy delegates.

What we need is a way to create objects without knowing exactly what type of object we are creating. We need a way for `TemperatureHiLo` to create a `HiLoData` without knowing that it is really creating a `HiLoDataProxy` and a `HiLoDataImp`. Again, we fall back on the FACTORY pattern. (See Figure 27-20.)

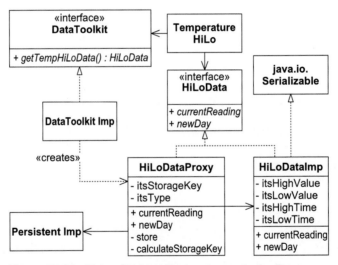

Figure 27-20   Using Abstract Factory to create the Proxy

`TemperatureHiLo` uses the `DataToolkit` interface to create an object that conforms to the `HiLoData` interface. The `getTempHiLoData` method gets deployed to a `DataToolkitImp` object, which creates a `HiLoDataProxy` whose type code is "Temp" and returns it as a `HiLoData`.

This solves the creation problem nicely. `TemperatureHiLo` does not need to depend upon the `HiLoDataProxy` in order to create it. But how does `TemperatureHiLo` gain access to the `DataToolkitImp` object? We don't want `TemperatureHiLo` to know anything about `DataTookitImp` because that would create a dependency from the policy layer to the mechanism layer.

Package Structure.   To answer this question, let's look at the package structure in Figure 27-21. The abbreviation WMS stands for the Weather Monitoring System package that was described in Figure 27-16 on page 370.

Figure 27-21 reenforces our desire for the persistence-interface layer to depend on the policy and mechanism layers. It also shows how we have deployed the classes into the packages. Notice that the abstract factory,

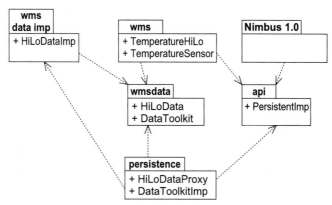

Figure 27-21 PROXY and FACTORY package structure

DataToolkit, is defined in the WMSData package along with HiLoData. HiLoData is implemented in the WMS-DataImp package, whereas DataToolkit is implemented in the persistence package.

Who Creates the Factory? Now, we ask the question once again. How does the instance of wms.TemperatureHiLo gain access to an instance of persistence.DataToolkitImp so that it can call the getTempHiLoData method and create instances of persistence.HiLoDataProxy?

What we need is some statically allocated variable, accessible to the classes in wmsdata, that is declared to hold a wmsdata.DataToolkit, but which is initialized to hold a persistence.DataToolkitImp. Since all variables in Java, including static variables, must be declared in some kind of class, we can create a class named Scope that will have the static variables that we need. We will put this class in the wmsdata package.

Listings 27-10 and 27-11 show how this works. The Scope class in wmsdata declares a static member variable that holds a DataToolkit reference. The Scope class in the persistence package declares an init() function that creates a DataToolkitImp instance and stores it in the wmsdata.Scope.itsDataToolkit variable.

Listing 27-10

wmsdata.Scope

```
package wmsdata;

public class Scope
{
  public static DataToolkit itsDataToolkit;
}
```

Listing 27-11

persistence.Scope

```
package persistence;

public class Scope
{
  public static void init()
  {
    wmsdata.Scope.itsDataToolkit =
                    new DataToolkit();
  }
}
```

There is an interesting symmetry between the packages and the `scope` classes. All the classes in the `wmsdata` package, other than `Scope`, are interfaces that have abstract methods and no variables. But the `wmsdata.Scope` class has a variable and no functions. On the other hand, all the classes in the `persistence` package, other than `Scope`, are concrete classes that have variables. But `persistence.Scope` has a function and no variables.

Figure 27-22 shows how this might be depicted in a class diagram. The `Scope` classes are «utility» classes. All the members of such classes, whether variables or functions, are static—a final element to the symmetry. It would appear that packages which contain abstract interfaces tend to contain utilities that have data and no functions, whereas packages which contain concrete classes tend to contain utilities that have functions and no data.

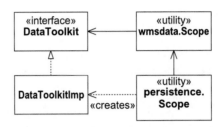

Figure 27-22   Scope Utilities

So, Who Calls `persistence.Scope.init()`?   Probably the `main()` function. The class that holds that main function must be in a package that does not mind a dependency upon `persistence`. We often call the package that contains main the `root` package.

But You Said...   The persistence-implementation layer should not depend on the policy layer. However, a close inspection of Figure 27-21 shows a dependency from the `persistence` to `wmsDataImp`. This dependency can be traced back to Figure 27-20, in which `HiLoDataProxy` depends on `HiLoDataImp`. The reason for this dependency is so `HiLoDataProxy` can create the `HiLoDataImp` that it depends on.

In most cases, the proxy will not have to create the imp because the proxy will be reading the imp from persistent store. That is, the `HiLoDataImp` will be returned to the proxy by a call to `PersistentImp.retrieve`. However, in those rare cases where the retrieve function does not find an object in the persistent store, `HiLoData-Proxy` is going to have to create an empty `HiLoDataImp`.

So, it looks like we need another factory that knows how to create `HiLoDataImp` instances and that the proxy can call. This means more packages and more `Scope` classes, etc.

Is This Really Necessary?   Probably not in this case. We created the factory for the proxy because we wanted `TemperatureHiLo` to be able to work with many different persistence mechanisms. Thus, we had a solid benefit to justify the `DataToolkit` factory. But what benefit would be obtained from interposing a factory between `HiLoDataProxy` and `HiLoDataImp`? If there could be many different implementations of `HiLoDataImp`, and if we wanted the proxy to work with them all, then we might be justified.

However, we don't believe that the requirements are quite that volatile. The `wmsDataImp` package contains weather-monitoring policies and business rules that have remained unchanged for quite a while. It seems unlikely that they will be changing any time in the future. This may sound like famous last words, but you have to draw the line somewhere. In this case, we have decided that the dependency from the proxy to the imp does not represent a big maintenance risk, and we will live without the factory.

Conclusion

Jim Newkirk and I wrote this chapter in early 1998. Jim did the bulk of the coding, and I translated the code into UML diagrams and put words around them. The code is now long-gone. But it was the production of that code that drove the design you see in these pages. Most of the diagrams were produced after the code was complete.

In 1998 neither Jim nor I had heard of Extreme Programming. So the design you see here was not conducted in an environment of Pair-programming and test-driven development. However, Jim and I have always worked in a highly collaborative fashion. Together we would pore over the code he wrote, running it where feasible, making design changes together, and then producing the UML and words in this chapter.

So, although the design here is pre-XP, it was still created in a highly collaborative, code-centric way.

Bibliography

1. Gamma, et al. *Design Patterns*. Reading, MA: Addison–Wesley, 1995.
2. Meyer, Bertrand. *Object-Oriented Software Construction*, 2nd ed. Upper Saddle River, NJ: Prentice Hall, 1997.
3. Arnold, Ken, and James Gosling. *The Java Programming Language*, 2nd ed. Reading, MA: Addison–Wesley, 1998.

Nimbus-LC Requirements Overview

Usage Requirements

This system shall provide automatic monitoring of various weather conditions. Specifically, it must measure the following variables:

- Wind speed and direction
- Temperature
- Barometric pressure
- Relative humidity
- Wind chill
- Dew-point temperature

The system shall also provide an indication of the current trend in the barometric-pressure reading. The three possible values include stable, rising, and falling. For example, the current barometric pressure is 29.95 inches of mercury (IOM) and falling.

The system shall have a display, which continuously indicates all measurements, as well as the current time and date.

24-Hour History

Through the use of a touch screen, the user may direct the system to display the 24-hour history of any of the following measurements:
- Temperature
- Barometric pressure
- Relative humidity

This history shall be presented to the user in the form a line chart. (See Figure 27-23.)

User Setup

The system shall provide the following facilities to the user to allow the station to be configured during installation:

- Setting the current time, date, and time zone.
- Setting the units that will be displayed (English or metric)

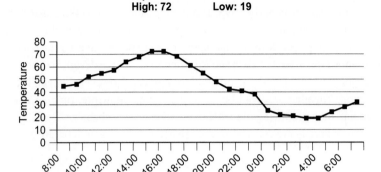

Figure 27-23   Temperature History

Administrative Requirements

The system shall provide a security mechanism for access to the administrative functions of the weather station. These functions include the following:

- Calibrating the sensors against known values
- Resetting the station

Nimbus-LC Use Cases

Actors

In this system, there are two distinct roles played by users.

User.   Users view the real-time weather information that the station is measuring. They also interact with the system to display the historical data associated with the individual sensors.

Administrator.   The administrator manages the security aspects of the system, calibrating the individual sensors, setting the time/date, setting units of measure, and resetting the station when required.

Use Cases

Use Case #1: Monitor Weather Data.   The system will display the current temperature, barometric pressure, relative humidity, wind speed, wind direction, wind chill temperature, dew point, and barometric-pressure trend.

Measurement History

The system will display a line graph depicting the previous 24 hours of readings from the sensors in the system. In addition to the graph, the system will display the current time and date and the highest and lowest readings from the previous 24 hours.

Use Case #2: View Temperature History.

User Case #3: View Barometric Pressure History.

Use Case #4: View Relative Humidity History.

Setup

Use Case #5: Set Units.   The user sets the type of units that will be displayed. The choices are between English and metric values. The default is metric.

Use Case #6: Set Date.   The user will set the current date.

Use Case #7: Set Time.   The user will set the current time and time zone for the system.

Administration

Use Case #8: Reset Weather Station.   The administrator has the ability to reset the station back to its factory default settings. It is important to note that this will erase all of the history that is stored in the station and remove any calibration that may have occurred. As one last check, it will inform the administrator of the consequences and prompt for a go/no go to reset the station.

Use Case #9: Calibrate Temperature Sensor.   The administrator, using a known good source for the temperature, will enter that value into the system. The system shall accept the value and use it internally to calibrate that actual reading with the readings it is currently measuring. For a detailed look at calibrating the sensors, see the hardware description document.

Use Case #10: Calibrate Barometric-Pressure Sensor.

Use Case #11: Calibrate Relative-Humidity Sensor.

Use Case #12: Calibrate Wind-Speed Sensor.

Use Case #13: Calibrate Wind-Direction Sensor.

Use Case #14: Calibrate Dew-Point Sensor.

Use Case #15: Calibration Log.   The system will show the administrator the calibration history of the unit. This history includes the time and date of the calibration, the sensor calibrated, and the value that was used to calibrate the sensor.

Nimbus-LC Release Plan

Introduction

The implementation of the weather station will be done in a series of iterations. Each iteration will build on what has been done previously until we have provided the functionality which is required for release to the customer. This document outlines three releases for this project.

Release I

The release has two goals. The first is to create an architecture that will support the bulk of the application in a manner that is independent of the Nimbus hardware platform. The second goal is to manage the two biggest risks:

1. Getting the old Nimbus 1.0 API to work on the processor board with a new operating system. This is certainly doable, but it is very hard to estimate how long this will take because we cannot anticipate all the incompatibilities.
2. The Java Virtual Machine. We have never used a JVM on an embedded board before. We don't know if it will work with our operating system, or even if it correctly implements all of the Java byte codes properly. Our suppliers assure us that everything will be fine, but we still perceive a significant risk.

The integration of the JVM with the touch screen and graphics subsystem is proceeding in parallel with this release. It is expected to be complete prior to the beginning of the second phase.

Risks

1. Operating system upgrade—We currently use an older version of this OS on our board. In order to use the JVM, we need to upgrade to the latest version of the OS. This also requires us to use the latest version of the development tools.
2. The OS vendor is providing the latest version of the JVM on this version of the OS. In order to stay current, we want to use the 1.2 version of the JVM. However, V1.2 is currently in beta and will change during the construction of the project.
3. Java native interface to the board level "C" API needs to be verified in the new architecture.

Deliverable(s)

1. Our hardware running the new OS along with the latest version of the JVM.
2. A streaming output, which will display the current temperature and barometric-pressure readings. *(Throw away code not used in final release.)*
3. When there is a change in the barometric pressure, the system will inform us as to whether the pressure is rising, falling, or stable.
4. Every hour, the system will display the past 24 hours of measurements for the temperature and barometric pressure. These data will be persistent in that we can cycle the power on the unit and the data will be saved.
5. Every day at 12:00 A.M., the system will display the high and low temperature and barometric pressure for the previous day.
6. All measurements will be in the metric system.

Release II

During this phase of the project, the basis for the user interface is added to the first release. No additional measurements are added. The only change to the measurements themselves is the addition of the calibration mechanism. The primary focus in this phase is on the presentation of the system. The major risk is the software interface to the LCD panel/touch screen. Also, since this is the first release that will display the UI in a form that can be shown to the user, we may begin to have some churn in the requirements. In addition to the software, we will be delivering a specification for the new hardware. This is the main reason for adding of the calibration to this phase of the project. This API will be specified in Java.

Use Cases Implemented

- #2—View Temperature History
- #3—View Barometric-Pressure History
- #5—Set Units
- #6—Set Date
- #7—Set Time/Time Zone
- #9—Calibrate Temperature Sensor
- #10—Calibrate Barometric-Pressure Sensor

Risks

1. The LCD-panel/touch-screen interface to the Java virtual machine needs to be tested on the actual hardware.
2. Requirements changes.
3. Changes in the JVM, along with changes in the Java foundation classes as they proceed from beta to released form.

Deliverable(s)

1. A system that executes and provides all of the functionality specified in the use cases listed above.
2. The temperature, barometric pressure, and time/date portion of Use Case #1 will also be implemented.
3. The GUI portion of the software architecture will be completed as part of this phase.
4. The administrative portion of the software will be implemented to support the temperature and barometric pressure calibrations.
5. A specification for the new hardware API specified in Java instead of "C."

Release III

This is the release prior to customer deployment of the product.

Use Cases Implemented

- #1—Monitor Weather Data
- #4—View Relative-Humidity History
- #8—Reset Weather Station
- #11—Calibrate Relative-Humidity Sensor
- #12—Calibrate Wind-Speed Sensor
- #13—Calibrate Wind-Direction Sensor
- #14—Calibrate Dew-Point Sensor
- #15—Calibration Log

Risks

1. Requirements changes—It is expected that, as more of the product is completed, there may be changes required.
2. Completing the entire product may indicate changes to the hardware API that was specified at the end of Release II.
3. Limits of hardware—As we complete the product, we may run into limitations of the hardware (i.e., memory, CPU, etc.).

Deliverable(s)

1. The new software running on the old hardware platform.
2. A specification for the new hardware that has been validated with this implementation.

SECTION 6

The ETS Case Study

To become a licensed architect in the United States or Canada, you must pass an examination. If you pass, a state licensing board will give you a license to practice architecture. The examination was developed by the Educational Testing Service (ETS) under a charter by the National Council of Architectural Registration Boards (NCARB), and is currently administered by the Chauncey Group International.

In the past, the candidates completed the examination in pencil and paper. These completed examinations were then given to a cadre of jurors for scoring. These jurors were highly experienced architects who would pore over the examinations and decide whether to pass or fail them.

In 1989 NCARB commissioned ETS to research whether or not an automated system could deliver and score portions of the exam. The chapters in this section describe portions of the resulting project. As before, we will encounter a number of useful design patterns in design of this software, so the chapters describing those patterns precede the case study.

28

VISITOR

© Jennifer M. Kohnke

"'T is some visitor," I muttered, "tapping at my chamber door;
Only this and nothing more."

—Edgar Allen Poe, The Raven

Problem: *You need to add a new method to a hierarchy of classes, but the act of adding it will be painful or damaging to the design.*

This is a common problem. For example, suppose you have a hierarchy of `Modem` objects. The base class has the generic methods common to all modems. The derivatives represent the drivers for many different modem manufacturers and types. Suppose also that you have a requirement to add a new method, named `configureForUnix`, to the hierarchy. This method will configure the modem to work with the UNIX operating system. It will do something different in each modem derivative, because each different modem has its own particular idiosyncrasies for setting its configuration and dealing with UNIX.

Unfortunately, adding `configureForUnix` begs a terrible set of questions. What about Windows? What about MacOs? What about Linux? Must we really add a new method to the `Modem` hierarchy for every new operating system that we use? Clearly this is ugly. We'll never be able to close the `Modem` interface. Every time a new operating system comes along, we'll have to change that interface and redeploy all the modem software.

The VISITOR Family of Design Patterns

The VISITOR family allows new methods to be added to existing hierarchies without modifying the hierarchies.

The patterns in this family are as follows:

- VISITOR
- ACYCLIC VISITOR
- DECORATOR
- EXTENSION OBJECT

VISITOR[1]

Consider the `Modem` hierarchy in Figure 28-1. The `Modem` interface contains the generic methods that all modems can implement. There are three derivatives shown—one that drives a Hayes modem, another that drives a Zoom modem, and a third that drives the modem card produced by Ernie, one of our hardware engineers.

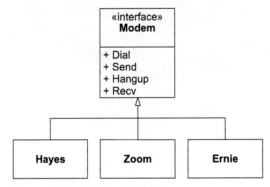

Figure 28-1   Modern Hierarchy

How can we configure these modems for UNIX without putting the `ConfigureForUnix` method in the `Modem` interface? We can use a technique called *dual dispatch*, which is the mechanism at the heart of the VISITOR pattern.

Figure 28-2 shows the VISITOR structure and Listings 28-1 through 28-6 show the corresponding Java code. Listing 28-7 shows the test code that both verifies that the VISITOR works and demonstrates how another programmer should use it.

Listing 28-1

Modem.java

```java
public interface Modem
{
  public void dial(String pno);
  public void hangup();
  public void send(char c);
  public char recv();
  public void accept(ModemVisitor v);
}
```

1.   [GOF95], p. 331.

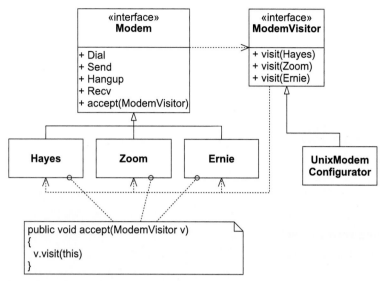

FIGURE 28-2 VISITOR

Listing 28-2

ModemVisitor.java

```java
public interface ModemVisitor
{
  public void visit(HayesModem modem);
  public void visit(ZoomModem modem);
  public void visit(ErnieModem modem);
}
```

Listing 28-3

HayesModem.java

```java
public class HayesModem implements Modem
{
  public void dial(String pno){}
  public void hangup(){}
  public void send(char c){}
  public char recv() {return 0;}
  public void accept(ModemVisitor v) {v.visit(this);}

  String configurationString = null;
}
```

Listing 28-4

ZoomModem.java

```java
public class ZoomModem implements Modem
{
  public void dial(String pno){}
  public void hangup(){}
  public void send(char c){}
  public char recv() {return 0;}
  public void accept(ModemVisitor v) {v.visit(this);}

  int configurationValue = 0;
}
```

Listing 28-5

ErnieModem.java

```java
public class ErnieModem implements Modem
{
  public void dial(String pno){}
  public void hangup(){}
  public void send(char c){}
  public char recv() {return 0;}
  public void accept(ModemVisitor v) {v.visit(this);}

  String internalPattern = null;
}
```

Listing 28-6

UnixModemConfigurator.java

```java
public class UnixModemConfigurator implements ModemVisitor
{
  public void visit(HayesModem m)
  {
    m.configurationString = "&s1=4&D=3";
  }

  public void visit(ZoomModem m)
  {
    m.configurationValue = 42;
  }

  public void visit(ErnieModem m)
  {
    m.internalPattern = "C is too slow";
  }
}
```

Listing 28-7

TestModemVisitor.java

```java
import junit.framework.*;
public class TestModemVisitor extends TestCase
{
  public TestModemVisitor(String name)
  {
    super(name);
  }

  private UnixModemConfigurator v;
  private HayesModem h;
  private ZoomModem z;
  private ErnieModem e;

  public void setUp()
  {
    v = new UnixModemConfigurator();
    h = new HayesModem();
    z = new ZoomModem();
```

```
        e = new ErnieModem();
    }

    public void testHayesForUnix()
    {
        h.accept(v);
        assertEquals("&s1=4&D=3", h.configurationString);
    }

    public void testZoomForUnix()
    {
        z.accept(v);
        assertEquals(42, z.configurationValue);
    }

    public void testErnieForUnix()
    {
        e.accept(v);
        assertEquals("C is too slow", e.internalPattern);
    }
}
```

Notice that there is a method in the visitor hierarchy for every derivative of the visited (Modem) hierarchy. This is a kind of 90° rotation—from derivatives to methods.

The test code shows that to configure a modem for UNIX, a programmer creates an instance of the UnixModemConfigurator class and passes it to the accept function of the Modem. The appropriate Modem derivative will then call visit(this) on ModemVisitor, the base class of UnixModemConfigurator. If that derivative is a Hayes, then visit(this) will call public void visit(Hayes). This will deploy to the public void visit(Hayes) function in UnixModemConfigurator, which then configures the Hayes modem for Unix.

Having built this structure, new operating-system configuration functions can be added by adding new derivatives of ModemVisitor without altering the Modem hierarchy in any way. So the VISITOR pattern substitutes derivatives of ModemVisitor for methods in the Modem hierarchy.

This is called dual dispatch because it involves two polymorphic dispatches. The first is the accept function. This dispatch resolves the type of the object that accept is called upon. The second dispatch is the visit method which resolves to the particular function to be executed. These two dispatches give VISITOR very fast execution speed.

VISITOR Is Like a Matrix

The two dispatches of VISITOR form a matrix of functions. In our modem example, one axis of the matrix is the different types of modems. The other axis is the different types of operating systems. Every cell in this matrix is filled in with a function that describes how to initialize the particular modem for the particular operating system.

ACYCLIC VISITOR

Notice that the base class of the visited (Modem) hierarchy depends on the base class of the visitor hierarchy (ModemVisitor). Notice also that the base class of the visitor hierarchy has a function for each derivative of the visited hierarchy. Thus, there is a cycle of dependencies that ties all the visited derivatives (all the Modems) together. This makes it very difficult to compile the visitor structure incrementally or to add new derivatives to the visited hierarchy.

The VISITOR works very well in programs where the hierarchy to be modified does not need new derivatives very often. If Hayes, Zoom, and Ernie were the only Modem derivatives that were likely to be needed, or if the incidence of new Modem derivatives was expected to be infrequent, then the VISITOR would be very appropriate.

On the other hand, if the visited hierarchy is highly volatile, such that many new derivatives will need to be created, then the Visitor base class (e.g., ModemVisitor) will have to be modified and recompiled along with all its derivatives every time a new derivative is added to the visited hierarchy. In C++, the situation is even worse. The entire visited hierarchy must be recompiled and redeployed whenever any new derivative is added.

To solve these problems, a variation known as ACYCLIC VISITOR can be used.[2] (See Figure 28-3.) This variation breaks the dependency cycle by making the Visitor base class (ModemVisitor) degenerate.[3] The lack of any methods in this class means that it does not depend on the derivatives of the visited hierarchy.

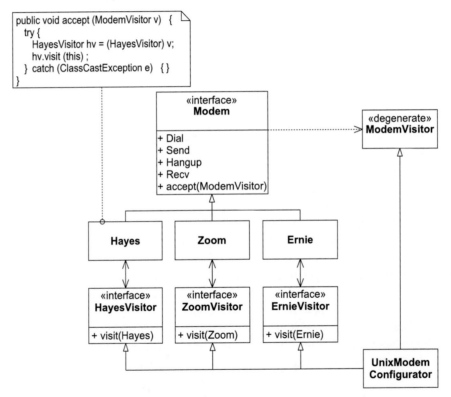

```
public void accept (ModemVisitor v)  {
    try {
        HayesVisitor hv = (HayesVisitor) v;
        hv.visit (this) ;
    } catch (ClassCastException e)  {}
}
```

FIGURE 28-3 ACYCLIC VISITOR

The visitor derivatives also derive from visitor interfaces. There is one visitor interface for each derivative of the visited hierarchy. This is a 180° rotation from derivatives to interfaces. The accept functions in the visited derivatives cast the Visitor base class[4] to the appropriate visitor interface. If the cast succeeds, the method invokes the appropriate visit function. Listings 28-8 through 28-16 show the code.

---

2.   [PLOPD3], p. 93.

3.   A degenerate class is one that has no methods at all. In C++, it would have a pure virtual destructor. In Java, such classes are called "Marker Interfaces."

4.   In C++, we use dynamic_cast.

Listing 28-8

Modem.java

```java
public interface Modem
{
  public void dial(String pno);
  public void hangup();
  public void send(char c);
  public char recv();
  public void accept(ModemVisitor v);
}
```

Listing 28-9

ModemVisitor.java

```java
public interface ModemVisitor
{
}
```

Listing 28-10

ErnieModemVisitor.java

```java
public interface ErnieModemVisitor
{
  public void visit(ErnieModem m);
}
```

Listing 28-11

HayesModemVisitor.java

```java
public interface HayesModemVisitor
{
  public void visit(HayesModem m);
}
```

Listing 28-12

ZoomModemVisitor.java

```java
public interface ZoomModemVisitor
{
  public void visit(ZoomModem m);
}
```

Listing 28-13

ErnieModem.java

```java
public class ErnieModem implements Modem
{
  public void dial(String pno){}
  public void hangup(){}
  public void send(char c){}
  public char recv() {return 0;}
  public void accept(ModemVisitor v)
  {
    try
    {
      ErnieModemVisitor ev = (ErnieModemVisitor)v;
```

```
      ev.visit(this);
    }
    catch (ClassCastException e)
    {
    }
  }

  String internalPattern = null;
}
```

Listing 28-14

HayesModem.java

```
public class HayesModem implements Modem
{
  public void dial(String pno){}
  public void hangup(){}
  public void send(char c){}
  public char recv() {return 0;}
  public void accept(ModemVisitor v)
  {
    try
    {
      HayesModemVisitor hv = (HayesModemVisitor)v;
      hv.visit(this);
    }
    catch (ClassCastException e)
    {
    }
  }

  String configurationString = null;
}
```

Listing 28-15

ZoomModem.java

```
public class ZoomModem implements Modem
{
  public void dial(String pno){}
  public void hangup(){}
  public void send(char c){}
  public char recv() {return 0;}
  public void accept(ModemVisitor v)
  {
    try
    {
      ZoomModemVisitor zv = (ZoomModemVisitor)v;
      zv.visit(this);
    }
    catch(ClassCastException e)
    {
    }
  }

  int configurationValue = 0;
}
```

Listing 28-16

TestModemVisitor.java

```java
import junit.framework.*;
public class TestModemVisitor extends TestCase
{
  public TestModemVisitor(String name)
  {
    super(name);
  }

  private UnixModemConfigurator v;
  private HayesModem h;
  private ZoomModem z;
  private ErnieModem e;

  public void setUp()
  {
    v = new UnixModemConfigurator();
    h = new HayesModem();
    z = new ZoomModem();
    e = new ErnieModem();
  }

  public void testHayesForUnix()
  {
    h.accept(v);
    assertEquals("&s1=4&D=3", h.configurationString);
  }

  public void testZoomForUnix()
  {
    z.accept(v);
    assertEquals(42, z.configurationValue);
  }

  public void testErnieForUnix()
  {
    e.accept(v);
    assertEquals("C is too slow", e.internalPattern);
  }
}
```

This breaks the dependency cycle and makes it easier to add visited derivatives and to do incremental compilations. Unfortunately, it also makes the solution much more complex. Worse still, the timing of the cast can depend on the width and breadth of the visited hierarchy and is therefore hard to characterize.

For hard, real-time systems the large and unpredictable execution time of the cast may make the ACYCLIC VISITOR inappropriate. For other systems, the complexity of the pattern may disqualify it. But for those systems in which the visited hierarchy is volatile, and incremental compilation is important, this pattern can be a good option.

ACYCLIC VISITOR Is Like a Sparse Matrix

Just as the VISITOR pattern created a matrix of functions, with the visited type on one axis and the function to be performed on the other. ACYCLIC VISITOR creates the a *sparse* matrix. The visitor classes do not have to implement `visit` functions for each visited derivative. For example, if `Ernie` modems cannot be configured for UNIX, then the `UnixModemConfigurator` will not implement the `ErnieVisitor` interface. Thus the ACYCLIC VISITOR pattern allows us to ignore certain combinations of derivatives and functions. This can sometimes be a useful advantage.

Using VISITOR in Report Generators

A very common use of the VISITOR pattern is to walk large data structures and generate reports. This keeps the data-structure objects from having any report-generation code. New reports can be added by adding new VISITORs, rather than by changing the code in the data structures. This means that reports can be placed in separate components and individually deployed only to those customers who need them.

Consider a simple data structure that represents a bill of materials. (See Figure 28-4.) There is an unlimited number of reports that we could generate from this data structure. For example, we could generate a report of the total cost of an assembly, or we could generate a report that listed all the piece parts in an assembly.

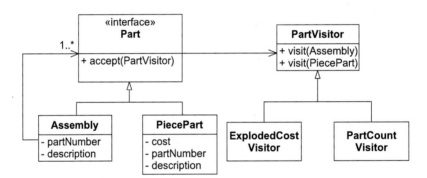

Figure 28-4   Bill-Of-Materials Report-Generator Structure

Each of these reports could be generated by methods in the `Part` class. For example, `getExplodedCost` and `getPieceCount` could be added to the `Part` class. These methods would be implemented in each derivative of `Part`, such that the appropriate reporting was accomplished. Unfortunately, that would mean that every new report that the customers wanted would force us to change the `Part` hierarchy.

The Single Responsibility Principle (SRP) told us that we want to separate code that changes for different reasons. The `Part` hierarchy may change as new kinds of parts are needed. However, it should not change because new kinds of reports are needed. Thus we'd like to separate the reports from the `Part` hierarchy. The VISITOR structure we saw in Figure 28-4 shows how this can be accomplished.

Each new report can be written as a new visitor. We write the `accept` function of `Assembly` to visit the visitor and also call `accept` on all the contained `Part` instances. Thus, the entire tree is traversed. For each node in the tree, the appropriate `visit` function is called on the report. The report accumulates the necessary statistics. The report can then be queried for the interesting data and presented to the user.

This structure allows us to create an unlimited number of reports without affecting the `Part` hierarchy at all. Moreover, each report can be compiled and distributed independently of all the others. This is nice. Listings 28-17 through 28-23 show how this looks in Java.

Listing 28-17

Part.java

```java
public interface Part
{
  public String getPartNumber();
  public String getDescription();
  public void accept(PartVisitor v);
}
```

Listing 28-18

Assembly.java

```java
import java.util.*;

public class Assembly implements Part
{
  public Assembly(String partNumber, String description)
  {
    itsPartNumber = partNumber;
    itsDescription = description;
  }

  public void accept(PartVisitor v)
  {
    v.visit(this);
    Iterator i = getParts();
    while (i.hasNext())
    {
      Part p = (Part)i.next();
      p.accept(v);
    }
  }
  public void add(Part part)
  {
    itsParts.add(part);
  }

  public Iterator getParts()
  {
    return itsParts.iterator();
  }

  public String getPartNumber()
  {
    return itsPartNumber;
  }

  public String getDescription()
  {
    return itsDescription;
  }

  private List itsParts = new LinkedList();
  private String itsPartNumber;
  private String itsDescription;
}
```

Listing 28-19

PiecePart.java

```java
public class PiecePart implements Part
{
  public PiecePart(String partNumber,
                   String description,
                   double cost)
  {
    itsPartNumber = partNumber;
    itsDescription = description;
    itsCost = cost;
  }

  public void accept(PartVisitor v)
  {
    v.visit(this);
  }

  public String getPartNumber()
  {
    return itsPartNumber;
  }

  public String getDescription()
  {
    return itsDescription;
  }

  public double getCost()
  {
    return itsCost;
  }

  private String itsPartNumber;
  private String itsDescription;
  private double itsCost;
}
```

Listing 28-20

PartVisitor.java

```java
public interface PartVisitor
{
  public void visit(PiecePart pp);
  public void visit(Assembly a);
}
```

Listing 28-21

ExplodedCostVisitor.java

```java
public class ExplodedCostVisitor implements PartVisitor
{
  private double cost = 0;
  public double cost() {return cost;}
```

```java
  public void visit(PiecePart p)
  {cost += p.getCost();}

  public void visit(Assembly a) {}

}
```

Listing 28-22

PartCountVisitor.java

```java
import java.util.*;

public class PartCountVisitor implements PartVisitor
{
  public void visit(PiecePart p)
  {
    itsPieceCount++;
    String partNumber = p.getPartNumber();
    int partNumberCount = 0;
    if (itsPieceMap.containsKey(partNumber))
    {
      Integer carrier = (Integer)itsPieceMap.get(partNumber);
      partNumberCount = carrier.intValue();
    }
    partNumberCount++;
    itsPieceMap.put(partNumber, new Integer(partNumberCount));
  }

  public void visit(Assembly a)
  {
  }

  public int getPieceCount() {return itsPieceCount;}
  public int getPartNumberCount() {return itsPieceMap.size();}
  public int getCountForPart(String partNumber)
  {
    int partNumberCount = 0;
    if (itsPieceMap.containsKey(partNumber))
    {
      Integer carrier = (Integer)itsPieceMap.get(partNumber);
      partNumberCount = carrier.intValue();
    }
    return partNumberCount;
  }

  private int itsPieceCount = 0;
  private HashMap itsPieceMap = new HashMap();

}
```

Listing 28-23

TestBOMReport.java

```java
import junit.framework.*;
import java.util.*;
```

```java
public class TestBOMReport extends TestCase
{
  public TestBOMReport(String name)
  {
    super(name);
  }

  private PiecePart p1;
  private PiecePart p2;
  private Assembly a;

  public void setUp()
  {
    p1 = new PiecePart("997624", "MyPart", 3.20);
    p2 = new PiecePart("7734", "Hell", 666);
    a = new Assembly("5879", "MyAssembly");
  }

  public void testCreatePart()
  {
    assertEquals("997624", p1.getPartNumber());
    assertEquals("MyPart", p1.getDescription());
    assertEquals(3.20, p1.getCost(), .01);
  }

  public void testCreateAssembly()
  {
    assertEquals("5879", a.getPartNumber());
    assertEquals("MyAssembly", a.getDescription());
  }

  public void testAssembly()
  {
    a.add(p1);
    a.add(p2);
    Iterator i = a.getParts();
    PiecePart p = (PiecePart)i.next();
    assertEquals(p, p1);
    p = (PiecePart)i.next();
    assertEquals(p, p2);
    assert(i.hasNext() == false);
  }

  public void testAssemblyOfAssemblies()
  {
    Assembly subAssembly = new Assembly("1324", "SubAssembly");
    subAssembly.add(p1);
    a.add(subAssembly);

    Iterator i = a.getParts();
    assertEquals(subAssembly, i.next());
  }

  private boolean p1Found = false;
  private boolean p2Found = false;
  private boolean aFound = false;
```

```
public void testVisitorCoverage()
{
  a.add(p1);
  a.add(p2);
  a.accept(new PartVisitor(){
    public void visit(PiecePart p)
    {
      if (p == p1)
        p1Found = true;
      else if (p == p2)
        p2Found = true;
    }

    public void visit(Assembly assy)
    {
      if (assy == a)
        aFound = true;
    }
  });
  assert(p1Found);
  assert(p2Found);
  assert(aFound);
}


private Assembly cellphone;

void setUpReportDatabase()
{
  cellphone = new Assembly("CP-7734", "Cell Phone");
  PiecePart display = new PiecePart("DS-1428", "LCD Display", 14.37);
  PiecePart speaker = new PiecePart("SP-92", "Speaker", 3.50);
  PiecePart microphone = new PiecePart("MC-28", "Microphone", 5.30);
  PiecePart cellRadio = new PiecePart("CR-56", "Cell Radio", 30);
  PiecePart frontCover = new PiecePart("FC-77", "Front Cover", 1.4);
  PiecePart backCover = new PiecePart("RC-77", "RearCover", 1.2);
  Assembly keypad = new Assembly("KP-62", "Keypad");
  Assembly button = new Assembly("B52", "Button");
  PiecePart buttonCover = new PiecePart("CV-15", "Cover", .5);
  PiecePart buttonContact = new PiecePart("CN-2", "Contact", 1.2);
  button.add(buttonCover);
  button.add(buttonContact);
  for (int i=0; i<15; i++)
    keypad.add(button);
  cellphone.add(display);
  cellphone.add(speaker);
  cellphone.add(microphone);
```

```
      cellphone.add(cellRadio);
      cellphone.add(frontCover);
      cellphone.add(backCover);
      cellphone.add(keypad);
    }


    public void testExplodedCost()
    {
      setUpReportDatabase();
      ExplodedCostVisitor v = new ExplodedCostVisitor();
      cellphone.accept(v);
      assertEquals(81.27, v.cost(), .001);
    }


    public void testPartCount()
    {
      setUpReportDatabase();
      PartCountVisitor v = new PartCountVisitor();
      cellphone.accept(v);
      assertEquals(36, v.getPieceCount());
      assertEquals(8, v.getPartNumberCount());
      assertEquals("DS-1428", 1, v.getCountForPart("DS-1428"));
      assertEquals("SP-92", 1, v.getCountForPart("SP-92"));
      assertEquals("MC-28", 1, v.getCountForPart("MC-28"));
      assertEquals("CR-56", 1, v.getCountForPart("CR-56"));
      assertEquals("RC-77", 1, v.getCountForPart("RC-77"));
      assertEquals("CV-15", 15, v.getCountForPart("CV-15"));
      assertEquals("CN-2", 15, v.getCountForPart("CN-2"));
      assertEquals("Bob", 0, v.getCountForPart("Bob"));
    }
}
```

Other Uses of VISITOR

In general, the Visitor pattern can be used in any application where there is a data structure that needs to be interpreted many different ways. Compilers often create intermediate data structures that represent syntactically correct source code. These data structures are then used to generate compiled code. One could imagine visitors for each different processor or optimization scheme. One could also imagine a visitor that converted the intermediate data structure into a cross-reference listing or even a UML diagram.

Many applications make use of configuration data structures. One could imagine the different subsystems of the application initializing themselves from the configuration data by walking it with their own particular visitors.

In every case where visitors are used, the data structure being used is independent of the uses to which it is being put. New visitors can be created, existing visitors can be changed, and all can be redeployed to installed sites without the recompilation, or redeployment of the existing data structures. This is the power of the VISITOR.

DECORATOR[5]

The visitor gave us a way to add methods to existing hierarchies without changing those hierarchies. Another pattern that accomplishes this is the DECORATOR.

Consider, once again, the `Modem` hierarchy in Figure 28-1. Imagine that we have an application which has many users. Each user, sitting at his computer, can ask the system to call out to another computer using the computer's modem. Some of the users like to hear their modems dial. Others like their modems to be silent.

We could implement this by querying the user preferences at every location in the code where the modem is dialed. If the user wants to hear the modem, we set the speaker volume high. Otherwise, we turn it off.

```
...
Modem m = user.getModem();
if (user.wantsLoudDial())
  m.setVolume(11); // its one more than 10, isn't it?
m.dial(...);
...
```

The spectre of seeing this stretch of code duplicated hundreds of times throughout the application conjures images of 80-hour weeks and heinous debugging sessions. It is something to be avoided.

Another option would be to set a flag in the `modem` object itself and have the `dial` method inspect it and set the volume accordingly.

```
...
public class HayesModem implements Modem
{
  private boolean wantsLoudDial = false;

  public void dial(...)
  {
    if (wantsLoudDial)
    {
      setVolume(11);
    }
    ...
  }
  ...
}
```

This is better, but it must still be duplicated for every derivative of `Modem`. Authors of new derivatives of `Modem` must remember to replicate this code. Depending on programmers memories is pretty risky business.

We could resolve this with the TEMPLATE METHOD[6] pattern by changing `Modem` from an interface to a class, having it hold the `wantsLoudDial` variable, and having it test that variable in the dial function before it calls the `dialForReal` function.

```
...
public abstract class Modem
{
  private boolean wantsLoudDial = false;

  public void dial(...)
```

---

5. [GOF95].

6. See "Template Method" on page 162.

```
  {
    if (wantsLoudDial)
    {
      setVolume(11);
    }
    dialForReal(...)
  }

  public abstract void dialForReal(...);
}
```

This is better still, but why should Modem be affected by the whims of the user in this way? Why should Modem know about loud dialing. Must it then be modified every time the user has some other odd request, like logging out before hangup?

Once again the Common-Closure Principle (CCP) comes into play. We want to separate those things that change for different reasons. We can also invoke the Single-Responsibility Principle (SRP) since the need to dial loudly has nothing to do with the intrinsic functions of Modem and should therefore not be part of Modem.

DECORATOR solves the issue by creating a completely new class named LoudDialModem. LoudDialModem derives from Modem and delegates to a contained instance of Modem. It catches the dial function and sets the volume high before delegating. Figure 28-5 shows the structure.

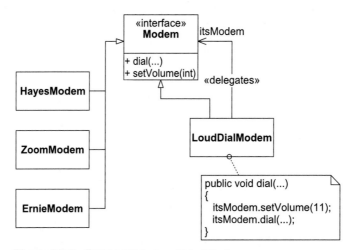

Figure 28-5   DECORATOR: LoudDialModem

Now the decision to dial loudly can be made in one place. At the place in the code where the user sets his preferences, if he requests loud dialing, a LoudDialModem can be created, and the user's modem can be passed into it. LoudDialModem will delegate all calls made to it to the user's modem, so the user won't notice any difference. The dial method, however, will first set the volume high before it delegates to the user's modem. The LoudDialModem can then become the user's modem without anybody else in the system being affected. Listings 28-24 through 28-27 show the code.

Listing 28-24
Modem.java

```
public interface Modem
{
  public void dial(String pno);
```

```java
  public void setSpeakerVolume(int volume);
  public String getPhoneNumber();
  public int getSpeakerVolume();
}
```

Listing 28-25

HayesModem.java

```java
public class HayesModem implements Modem
{
  public void dial(String pno)
  {
    itsPhoneNumber = pno;
  }

  public void setSpeakerVolume(int volume)
  {
    itsSpeakerVolume = volume;
  }

  public String getPhoneNumber()
  {
    return itsPhoneNumber;
  }

  public int getSpeakerVolume()
  {
    return itsSpeakerVolume;
  }

  private String itsPhoneNumber;
  private int itsSpeakerVolume;
}
```

Listing 28-26

LoudDialModem.java

```java
public class LoudDialModem implements Modem
{
  public LoudDialModem(Modem m)
  {
    itsModem = m;
  }

  public void dial(String pno)
  {
    itsModem.setSpeakerVolume(10);
    itsModem.dial(pno);
  }

  public void setSpeakerVolume(int volume)
  {
    itsModem.setSpeakerVolume(volume);
  }
```

```java
  public String getPhoneNumber()
  {
    return itsModem.getPhoneNumber();
  }

  public int getSpeakerVolume()
  {
    return itsModem.getSpeakerVolume();
  }

  private Modem itsModem;
}
```

Listing 28-27

`ModemDecoratorTest.java`

```java
import junit.framework.*;

public class ModemDecoratorTest extends TestCase
{
  public ModemDecoratorTest(String name)
  {
    super(name);
  }

  public void testCreateHayes()
  {
    Modem m = new HayesModem();
    assertEquals(null, m.getPhoneNumber());
    m.dial("5551212");
    assertEquals("5551212", m.getPhoneNumber());
    assertEquals(0, m.getSpeakerVolume());
    m.setSpeakerVolume(10);
    assertEquals(10, m.getSpeakerVolume());
  }

  public void testLoudDialModem()
  {
    Modem m = new HayesModem();
    Modem d = new LoudDialModem(m);
    assertEquals(null, d.getPhoneNumber());
    assertEquals(0, d.getSpeakerVolume());
    d.dial("5551212");
    assertEquals("5551212", d.getPhoneNumber());
    assertEquals(10, d.getSpeakerVolume());

  }
}
```

Multiple Decorators

Sometimes two or more decorators may exist for the same hierarchy. For example, we may wish to decorate the Modem hierarchy with `LogoutExitModem`, which sends the string 'exit' whenever the Hangup method is called. This second decorator will have to duplicate all the delegation code that we have already written in `LoudDialModem`. We can eliminate this duplicate code by creating a new class called `ModemDecorator` that supplies all the delegation code. Then the actual decorators can simply derive from `ModemDecorator` and override only those methods that they need to. Figure 28-6, Listing 28-28, and Listing 28-29 show the structure.

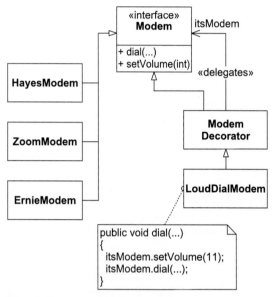

Figure 28-6 `ModemDecorator`

Listing 28-28

ModemDecorator.java

```java
public class ModemDecorator implements Modem
{
  public ModemDecorator(Modem m)
  {
    itsModem = m;
  }

  public void dial(String pno)
  {
    itsModem.dial(pno);
  }

  public void setSpeakerVolume(int volume)
  {
    itsModem.setSpeakerVolume(volume);
  }

  public String getPhoneNumber()
  {
    return itsModem.getPhoneNumber();
  }

  public int getSpeakerVolume()
  {
    return itsModem.getSpeakerVolume();
  }
```

```
  protected Modem getModem()
  {
    return itsModem;
  }

  private Modem itsModem;
}
```

Listing 28-29
```
public class LoudDialModem extends ModemDecorator
{
  public LoudDialModem(Modem m)
  {
    super(m);
  }

  public void dial(String pno)
  {
    getModem().setSpeakerVolume(10);
    getModem().dial(pno);
  }

}
```

EXTENSION OBJECT

Still another way to add functionality to a hierarchy without changing the hierarchy is to employ the EXTENSION OBJECT[7] pattern. This pattern is more complex than the others, but it is also much more powerful and flexible. Each object in the hierarchy maintains a list of special extension objects. Each object also provides a method that allows the extension object to be looked up by name. The extension object provides methods that manipulate the original hierarchy object.

For example, let's assume that we have a bill-of-materials system again. We need to develop the ability for each object in this hierarchy to create an XML representation of itself. We could put toXML methods in the hierarchy, but this would violate the SRP. It may be that we don't want BOM stuff and XML stuff in the same class. We could create XML using a VISITOR, but that doesn't allow us to separate the XML generating code for each type of BOM object. In a VISITOR, all the XML generating code for each BOM class would be in the same VISITOR object. What if we want to separate the XML generation for each different BOM object into its own class?

EXTENSION OBJECT provides a nice way to accomplish this goal. The code in Listings 28-30 through 28-41 shows the BOM hierarchy with two different kinds of extension object. One kind of extension object converts BOM objects into XML. The other kind of extension object converts BOM objects into CSV (comma-separated value) strings. The first kind is accessed by getExtension("XML") and the second by getExtension("CSV"). The structure is shown in Figure 28-7 and was taken from the completed code. The «marker» stereotype denotes a marker interface (i.e., an interface with no methods).

It is very important to understand that I did not simply write this code in Listings 28-30 through 28-41 from scratch. Rather, I evolved the code from test case to test case. The first source file, Listing 28-30, shows all the test cases. They were written in the order shown. Each test case was written before there was any code that could make it pass. Once each test case was written and failing, the code that made it pass was written. The code was never more complicated than necessary to make the *existing* test cases pass. Thus, the code evolved in tiny increments

---

7.   [PLOPD3], p. 79.

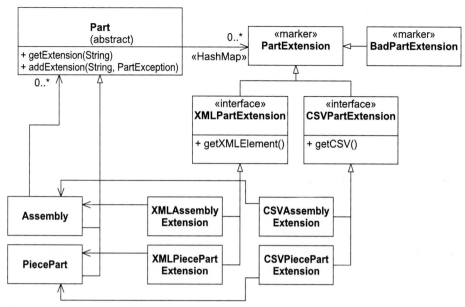

Figure 28-7   Extension Object

from working base to working base. I knew I was trying to build the EXTENSION OBJECT pattern, and I used that to guide the evolution.

Listing 28-30

TestBOMXML.java

```java
import junit.framework.*;
import java.util.*;
import org.jdom.*;

public class TestBOMXML extends TestCase
{
  public TestBOMXML(String name)
  {
    super(name);
  }

  private PiecePart p1;
  private PiecePart p2;
  private Assembly a;

  public void setUp()
  {
    p1 = new PiecePart("997624", "MyPart", 3.20);
    p2 = new PiecePart("7734", "Hell", 666);
    a = new Assembly("5879", "MyAssembly");
  }

  public void testCreatePart()
  {
    assertEquals("997624", p1.getPartNumber());
    assertEquals("MyPart", p1.getDescription());
```

```
    assertEquals(3.20, p1.getCost(), .01);
  }

public void testCreateAssembly()
{
  assertEquals("5879", a.getPartNumber());
  assertEquals("MyAssembly", a.getDescription());
}

public void testAssembly()
{
  a.add(p1);
  a.add(p2);
  Iterator i = a.getParts();
  PiecePart p = (PiecePart)i.next();
  assertEquals(p, p1);
  p = (PiecePart)i.next();
  assertEquals(p, p2);
  assert(i.hasNext() == false);
}

public void testAssemblyOfAssemblies()
{
  Assembly subAssembly = new Assembly("1324", "SubAssembly");
  subAssembly.add(p1);
  a.add(subAssembly);

  Iterator i = a.getParts();
  assertEquals(subAssembly, i.next());
}

public void testPiecePart1XML()
{
  PartExtension e = p1.getExtension("XML");
  XMLPartExtension xe = (XMLPartExtension)e;
  Element xml = xe.getXMLElement();
  assertEquals("PiecePart", xml.getName());
  assertEquals("997624",xml.getChild("PartNumber").getTextTrim());
  assertEquals("MyPart", xml.getChild("Description").getTextTrim());
  assertEquals(3.2, Double.parseDouble(xml.getChild("Cost").getTextTrim()), .01);
}

public void testPiecePart2XML()
{
  PartExtension e = p2.getExtension("XML");
  XMLPartExtension xe = (XMLPartExtension)e;
  Element xml = xe.getXMLElement();
  assertEquals("PiecePart", xml.getName());
  assertEquals("7734", xml.getChild("PartNumber").getTextTrim());
```

```java
    assertEquals("Hell", xml.getChild("Description").getTextTrim());
    assertEquals(666, Double.parseDouble(xml.getChild("Cost").getTextTrim()), .01);
}

public void testSimpleAssemblyXML()
{
    PartExtension e = a.getExtension("XML");
    XMLPartExtension xe = (XMLPartExtension)e;
    Element xml = xe.getXMLElement();
    assertEquals("Assembly", xml.getName());
    assertEquals("5879", xml.getChild("PartNumber").getTextTrim());
    assertEquals("MyAssembly", xml.getChild("Description").getTextTrim());
    Element parts = xml.getChild("Parts");
    List partList = parts.getChildren();
    assertEquals(0, partList.size());
}

public void testAssemblyWithPartsXML()
{
    a.add(p1);
    a.add(p2);
    PartExtension e = a.getExtension("XML");
    XMLPartExtension xe = (XMLPartExtension)e;
    Element xml = xe.getXMLElement();
    assertEquals("Assembly", xml.getName());
    assertEquals("5879", xml.getChild("PartNumber").getTextTrim());
    assertEquals("MyAssembly", xml.getChild("Description").getTextTrim());

    Element parts = xml.getChild("Parts");
    List partList = parts.getChildren();
    assertEquals(2, partList.size());

    Iterator i = partList.iterator();
    Element partElement = (Element)i.next();
    assertEquals("PiecePart", partElement.getName());
    assertEquals("997624", partElement.getChild("PartNumber").getTextTrim());

    partElement = (Element)i.next();
    assertEquals("PiecePart", partElement.getName());
    assertEquals("7734", partElement.getChild("PartNumber").getTextTrim());
}

public void testPiecePart1toCSV()
{
    PartExtension e = p1.getExtension("CSV");
    CSVPartExtension ce = (CSVPartExtension)e;
    String csv = ce.getCSV();
    assertEquals("PiecePart,997624,MyPart,3.2", csv);
}

public void testPiecePart2toCSV()
{
    PartExtension e = p2.getExtension("CSV");
    CSVPartExtension ce = (CSVPartExtension)e;
    String csv = ce.getCSV();
```

```java
      assertEquals("PiecePart,7734,Hell,666.0", csv);
  }

  public void testSimpleAssemblyCSV()
  {
    PartExtension e = a.getExtension("CSV");
    CSVPartExtension ce = (CSVPartExtension)e;
    String csv = ce.getCSV();
    assertEquals("Assembly,5879,MyAssembly", csv);
  }

  public void testAssemblyWithPartsCSV()
  {
    a.add(p1);
    a.add(p2);
    PartExtension e = a.getExtension("CSV");
    CSVPartExtension ce = (CSVPartExtension)e;
    String csv = ce.getCSV();

    assertEquals("Assembly,5879,MyAssembly," +
                 "{PiecePart,997624,MyPart,3.2}," +
                 "{PiecePart,7734,Hell,666.0}"
                 , csv);
  }

  public void testBadExtension()
  {
    PartExtension pe = p1.getExtension("ThisStringDoesn'tMatchAnyException");
    assert(pe instanceof BadPartExtension);
  }

}
```

Listing 28-31
`Part.java`

```java
import java.util.*;

public abstract class Part
{
  HashMap itsExtensions = new HashMap();

  public abstract String getPartNumber();
  public abstract String getDescription();

  public void addExtension(String extensionType, PartExtension extension)
  {
    itsExtensions.put(extensionType, extension);
  }
```

```java
  public  PartExtension getExtension(String extensionType)
  {
    PartExtension pe = (PartExtension) itsExtensions.get(extensionType);
    if (pe == null)
      pe = new BadPartExtension();
    return pe;
  }
}
```

Listing 28-32
PartExtension.java

```java
public interface PartExtension
{
}
```

Listing 28-33
PiecePart.java

```java
public class PiecePart extends Part
{
  public PiecePart(String partNumber, String description, double cost)
  {
    itsPartNumber = partNumber;
    itsDescription = description;
    itsCost = cost;
    addExtension("CSV", new CSVPiecePartExtension(this));
    addExtension("XML", new XMLPiecePartExtension(this));
  }

  public String getPartNumber()
  {
    return itsPartNumber;
  }

  public String getDescription()
  {
    return itsDescription;
  }

  public double getCost()
  {
    return itsCost;
  }

  private String itsPartNumber;
  private String itsDescription;
  private double itsCost;
}
```

Listing 28-34

Assembly.java

```java
import java.util.*;

public class Assembly extends Part
{
  public Assembly(String partNumber, String description)
  {
    itsPartNumber = partNumber;
    itsDescription = description;
    addExtension("CSV", new CSVAssemblyExtension(this));
    addExtension("XML", new XMLAssemblyExtension(this));
  }

  public void add(Part part)
  {
    itsParts.add(part);
  }

  public Iterator getParts()
  {
    return itsParts.iterator();
  }

  public String getPartNumber()
  {
    return itsPartNumber;
  }

  public String getDescription()
  {
    return itsDescription;
  }

  private List itsParts = new LinkedList();
  private String itsPartNumber;
  private String itsDescription;
}
```

Listing 28-35

XMLPartExtension.java

```java
import org.jdom.*;

public interface XMLPartExtension extends PartExtension
{
  public Element getXMLElement();
}
```

Listing 28-36

XMLPiecePartException.java

```java
import org.jdom.*;

public class XMLPiecePartExtension implements XMLPartExtension
{
  public XMLPiecePartExtension(PiecePart part)
  {
    itsPiecePart = part;
  }

  public Element getXMLElement()
  {
    Element e = new Element("PiecePart");
    e.addContent(
      new Element("PartNumber").setText(
        itsPiecePart.getPartNumber()));
    e.addContent(
      new Element("Description").setText(
        itsPiecePart.getDescription()));
    e.addContent(
      new Element("Cost").setText(
        Double.toString(itsPiecePart.getCost())));
    return e;
  }

  private PiecePart itsPiecePart = null;
}
```

Listing 28-37

XMLAssemblyExtension.java

```java
import org.jdom.*;
import java.util.*;

public class XMLAssemblyExtension implements XMLPartExtension
{
  public XMLAssemblyExtension(Assembly assembly)
  {
    itsAssembly = assembly;
  }

  public Element getXMLElement()
  {
    Element e = new Element("Assembly");
    e.addContent(new Element("PartNumber").setText(itsAssembly.getPartNumber()));
    e.addContent(new Element("Description").setText(itsAssembly.getDescription()));
    Element parts = new Element("Parts");
    e.addContent(parts);
    Iterator i = itsAssembly.getParts();
    while (i.hasNext())
    {
      Part p = (Part) i.next();
```

```
      PartExtension pe = p.getExtension("XML");
      XMLPartExtension xpe = (XMLPartExtension)pe;
      parts.addContent(xpe.getXMLElement());
    }
    return e;
  }

  private Assembly itsAssembly = null;
}
```

Listing 28-38

CSVPartExtension.java

```
public interface CSVPartExtension extends PartExtension
{
  public String getCSV();
}
```

Listing 28-39

CSVPiecePartExtension.java

```
public class CSVPiecePartExtension implements CSVPartExtension
{
  private PiecePart itsPiecePart = null;

  public CSVPiecePartExtension(PiecePart part)
  {
    itsPiecePart = part;
  }

  public String getCSV()
  {
    StringBuffer b = new StringBuffer("PiecePart,");
    b.append(itsPiecePart.getPartNumber());
    b.append(",");
    b.append(itsPiecePart.getDescription());
    b.append(",");
    b.append(itsPiecePart.getCost());
    return b.toString();
  }
}
```

Listing 28-40

CSVAssemblyExtension.java

```
import java.util.Iterator;

public class CSVAssemblyExtension implements CSVPartExtension
{
  private Assembly itsAssembly = null;

  public CSVAssemblyExtension(Assembly assy)
  {
    itsAssembly = assy;
  }
```

```
  public String getCSV()
  {
    StringBuffer b = new StringBuffer("Assembly,");
    b.append(itsAssembly.getPartNumber());
    b.append(",");
    b.append(itsAssembly.getDescription());

    Iterator i = itsAssembly.getParts();
    while (i.hasNext())
    {
      Part p = (Part) i.next();
      CSVPartExtension ce = (CSVPartExtension)p.getExtension("CSV");
      b.append(",{");
      b.append(ce.getCSV());
      b.append("}");
    }
    return b.toString();
  }
}
```

Listing 28-41

BadPartExtension.java

```
public class BadPartExtension implements PartExtension
{
}
```

Notice that the extension objects are loaded into each BOM object by that object's constructor. This means that, to some extent, the BOM objects still depend on the XML and CSV classes. If even this tenuous dependency needs to be broken, we could create a FACTORY[8] object that creates the BOM objects and loads their extensions.

The fact that the extension objects can be loaded into the object creates a great deal of flexibility. Certain extension objects can be inserted or deleted from objects depending on the state of the system. It would be very easy to get carried away with this flexibility. For the most part, you probably won't find it necessary. Indeed, the original implementation of `PiecePart.getExtention(String extensionType)` looked like this.

```
public PartExtension getExtension(String extensionType)

{
  if (extensionType.equals("XML"))
    return new XMLPiecePartExtension(this);

  else if (extensionType.equals("CSV"))
    return new XMLAssemblyExtension(this);

  return new BadPartExtension();
}
```

I wasn't particularly thrilled with this because it was virtually identical to the code in `Assembly.get-Extension`. The `HashMap` solution in `Part` avoids this duplication and is just simpler. Anyone reading it will know exactly how extension objects are accessed.

---

8.   See "Factory" on page 269.

Conclusion

The VISITOR family of patterns provides us with a number of ways to modify the behavior of a hierarchy of classes without having to change those classes. Thus, they help us maintain the OCP. They also provide mechanisms for segregating different kinds of functionality, thus keeping classes from getting cluttered with many different functions. As such, they help us maintain the CCP. It should be clear that the SRP, LSP, and DIP are also applied to the structure of the VISITOR family.

The VISITOR patterns are seductive. It is easy to get carried away with them. Use them when they help, but maintain a healthy skepticism about their necessity. Often, something that can be solved with a VISITOR can also be solved by something simpler.

Reminder

Now that you've read this chapter, you may wish to go back to Chapter 9, page 107, and solve the problem of ordering the shapes.

Bibliography

1. Gamma, et al. *Design Patterns*. Reading, MA: Addison–Wesley, 1995.
2. Martin, Robert C., et al. *Pattern Languages of Program Design 3*. Reading, MA: Addison–Wesley, 1998.

29

STATE

A state without the means of some change is without the means of its conservation.

—Edmund Burke (1729–1797)

Finite state automata are among the most useful abstractions in the software arsenal. They provide a simple and elegant way to explore and define the behavior of a complex system. They also provide a powerful implementation strategy that is easy to understand and easy to modify. I use them in all levels of a system, from controlling the high-level GUI[1] to the lowest-level communication protocols. They are almost universally applicable.

Overview of Finite State Automata

A simple *finite state machine* (FSM) can be found in the operation of a subway turnstile. This is the device that controls the gate through which passengers pass to gain access to the subway trains. Figure 29-1 shows the beginnings of the FSM that controls the subway turnstile. This diagram is known as a *state transition diagram,* or STD.[2]

1.　　See "The Taskmaster Architecture" on page 462.
2.　　See "States and Internal Transitions" on page 493, "Transitions between states" on page 494, and "Nested States" on page 494.

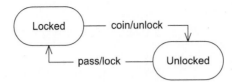

Figure 29-1   Simple Turnstile FSM

STDs are composed of at least four parts. The bubbles are called *states*. Connecting the states are arrows called *transitions*. The transitions are labeled with the name of an *event* followed by the name of an *action*. The STD in Figure 29-1 is read as follows:

- *If* the machine is in the Locked state *and* we get a coin event, *then* we transition to the Unlocked state *and* invoke the unlock action.
- *If* the machine is in the Unlocked state *and* we get a pass event, *then* we transition to the Locked state *and* invoke the lock action.

These two sentences completely describe the diagram in Figure 29-1. Each sentence describes one transition arrow in terms of four elements: the starting state, the event that triggers the transition, the ending state, and the action to be performed. Indeed these transition sentences can be reduced to a simple table called a *state transition table* (STT). It might look like this:

```
Locked    coin    Unlocked    unlock
Unlocked  Pass    Locked      lock
```

How does this machine work? Presume that the FSM begins its life in the Locked state. A passenger walks up to the turnstile and deposits a coin. This causes the software to receive the coin event. The first transition in the STT says that if we are in the Locked state and we get a coin event, then we will transition to the Unlocked state and invoke the unlock action. So the software changes its state to Unlocked and calls the unlock function. The passenger then passes through the gate causing the software to detect a pass event. Since the FSM is now in the Unlocked state, the second transition is invoked, forcing the machine back to the Locked state and causing the lock function to be called.

Clearly the STD and the STT are both simple and elegant descriptions of the behavior of the machine. But they are also very powerful design tools. One of the benefits they convey is the ease with which the designer can detect strange and unhandled conditions. For example, examine each state in Figure 29-1 and apply both known events. Notice that there is no transition to handle a coin event in the Unlocked state, nor is there a transition to handle a pass event in the Locked state.

These omissions are serious logic flaws and are a very common source of programmer error. Programmers often consider the normal course of events more thoroughly than they consider the abnormal possibilities. The STD or STT gives the programmer a way to easily check that the design handles every event in every state.

We can fix the FSM by adding the necessary transitions. The new version is shown in Figure 29-2. Here we can see that if the passenger deposits more coins after the first, the machine remains in the Unlocked state and lights up a little "thank-you" light encouraging the passenger to continue to enter coins.[3] Also, if the passenger manages to pass through the gate while it is locked (perhaps with the aid of a sledge hammer) then the FSM will remain in the Locked state and will sound an alarm.

3.   ;^)

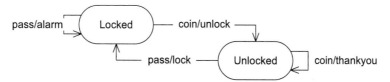

Figure 29-2   Turnstile FSM that covers abnormal events

Implementation Techniques

Nested Switch/Case Statements

There are many different strategies for implementing an FSM. The first, and most direct, is through nested switch/case statements. Listing 29-1 shows one such implementation.

Listing 29-1

Turnstile.java (Nested Switch Case Implementation)

```java
package com.objectmentor.PPP.Patterns.State.turnstile;

public class Turnstile
{
  // States
  public static final int LOCKED = 0;
  public static final int UNLOCKED = 1;

  // Events
  public static final int COIN = 0;
  public static final int PASS = 1;

  /*private*/ int state = LOCKED;

  private TurnstileController turnstileController;

  public Turnstile(TurnstileController action)
  {
    turnstileController = action;
  }

  public void event(int event)
  {
    switch (state)
    {
    case LOCKED:
      switch (event)
      {
      case COIN:
        state = UNLOCKED;
        turnstileController.unlock();
        break;
      case PASS:
        turnstileController.alarm();
        break;
      }
      break;
    case UNLOCKED:
```

```
      switch (event)
      {
      case COIN:
        turnstileController.thankyou();
        break;
      case PASS:
        state = LOCKED;
        turnstileController.lock();
        break;
      }
      break;
    }
  }
}
```

The nested switch/case statement divides the code into four mutually exclusive zones, each corresponding to one of the transitions in the STD. Each zone changes the state as needed and then invokes the appropriate action. Thus, the zone for Locked and Coin changes the state to Unlocked and calls unlock.

There are some interesting aspects to this code that have nothing to do with the nested switch/case statement. In order for them to make sense, you need to see the unit test that I used to check this code. (See Listings 29-2 and 29-3.)

Listing 29-2

TurnstileController.java

```
package com.objectmentor.PPP.Patterns.State.turnstile;

public interface TurnstileController
{
  public void lock();
  public void unlock();
  public void thankyou();
  public void alarm();
}
```

Listing 29-3

TestTurnstile.java

```
package com.objectmentor.PPP.Patterns.State.turnstile;

import junit.framework.*;
import junit.swingui.TestRunner;

public class TestTurnstile extends TestCase
{
  public static void main(String[] args)
  {
    TestRunner.main(new String[]{"TestTurnstile"});
  }

  public TestTurnstile(String name)
  {
    super(name);
  }
```

```java
  private Turnstile t;
  private boolean lockCalled = false;
  private boolean unlockCalled = false;
  private boolean thankyouCalled = false;
  private boolean alarmCalled = false;

  public void setUp()
  {
    TurnstileController controllerSpoof = new TurnstileController()
    {
      public void lock() {lockCalled = true;}
      public void unlock() {unlockCalled = true;}
      public void thankyou() {thankyouCalled = true;}
      public void alarm() {alarmCalled = true;}
    };

    t = new Turnstile(controllerSpoof);
  }

  public void testInitialConditions()
  {
    assertEquals(Turnstile.LOCKED, t.state);
  }

  public void testCoinInLockedState()
  {
    t.state = Turnstile.LOCKED;
    t.event(Turnstile.COIN);
    assertEquals(Turnstile.UNLOCKED, t.state);
    assert(unlockCalled);
  }

  public void testCoinInUnlockedState()
  {
    t.state = Turnstile.UNLOCKED;
    t.event(Turnstile.COIN);
    assertEquals(Turnstile.UNLOCKED, t.state);
    assert(thankyouCalled);
  }

  public void testPassInLockedState()
  {
    t.state = Turnstile.LOCKED;
    t.event(Turnstile.PASS);
    assertEquals(Turnstile.LOCKED, t.state);
    assert(alarmCalled);
  }

  public void testPassInUnlockedState()
  {
    t.state = Turnstile.UNLOCKED;
    t.event(Turnstile.PASS);
    assertEquals(Turnstile.LOCKED, t.state);
    assert(lockCalled);
  }
}
```

The Package Scope State Variable.   Notice the four test functions named `testCoinInLockedState`, `testCoinInUnlockedState`, `testPassInLockedState`, and `testPassInUnlockedState`. These functions test the four transitions of the FSM separately. They do this by forcing the `state` variable of the `Turnstile` to the state they want to check, and then invoking the event they want to verify. In order for the test to access the `state` variable, it cannot be private. Thus, I've made it package scope and added a comment indicating that my intent is that the variable is private.

Object-oriented dogma insists that all instance variables of a class ought to be private. I have blatantly ignored this rule, and by doing so, I have broken the encapsulation of `Turnstile`.

Or have I?

Make no mistake about it, I would rather have kept the `state` variable private. However, to do so would have denied my test code the ability to force its value. I could have created the appropriate `setState` and `getState` methods at package scope, but that seems ridiculous. I was not trying to expose the `state` variable to any class other than `TestTurnstile`, so why should I create a setter and a getter that imply that anyone at package scope can get and set that variable?

One of Java's unfortunate weaknesses is the lack of anything like the C++ `friend` concept. If Java had a `friend` statement, then I could have kept `state` private and declared `TestTurnstile` to be a friend of `Turnstile`. However, as things are, I think that putting `state` at package scope and using the comment to declare my intent is the best option.

Testing the Actions.   Notice the `TurnstileController` interface in Listing 29-2. This was put in place specifically so that the `TestTurnstile` class could ensure that the `Turnstile` class was invoking the right action methods in the right order. Without this interface, it would have been much more difficult to ensure that the state machine was working properly.

This is an example of the impact that testing has upon design. Had I simply written the state machine without thought to testing, it is unlikely that I would have created the `TurnstileController` interface. That would have been unfortunate. The `TurnstileController` interface nicely decouples the logic of the finite state machine from the actions it needs to perform. Another FSM, using very different logic, can use the `TurnstileController` without any impact at all.

The need to create test code that verifies each unit in isolation forces us to decouple the code in ways we might not otherwise think of. Thus, testability is a force that drives the design to a less coupled state.

Costs and Benefits of the Nested Switch/Case Implementation.   For simple state machines, the nested switch/case implementation is both elegant and efficient. All the states and events are visible on one or two pages of code. However, for larger FSMs the situation changes. In a state machine with dozens of states and events, the code devolves into page after page of case statements. There are no convenient locators to help you see where, in the state machine, you are reading. Maintaining long, nested switch/case statements can be a very difficult and error-prone job.

Another cost of the nested switch/case is that there is no good separation between the logic of the finite state machine and the code that implements the actions. That separation is strongly present in Listing 29-1 because the actions are implemented in a derivative of the `TurnstileController`. However, in most nested switch/case FSMs that I have seen, the implementation of the actions is buried in the case statements. Indeed, this is still possible in Listing 29-1.

Interpreting Transition Tables

A very common technique for implementing FSMs is to create a data table that describes the transitions. This table is interpreted by an engine that handles the events. The engine looks up the transition that matches the event, invokes the appropriate action, and changes the state.

Listing 29-4 shows the code that creates the transition table, and Listing 29-5 shows the transition engine. Both of these listings are snippets from the full implementation in Listing 29-12 at the end of this chapter.

Listing 29-4

Building the turnstile transition table

```
public Turnstile(TurnstileController action)
{
  turnstileController = action;
  addTransition(LOCKED,   COIN, UNLOCKED, unlock() );
  addTransition(LOCKED,   PASS, LOCKED,   alarm()  );
  addTransition(UNLOCKED, COIN, UNLOCKED, thankyou());
  addTransition(UNLOCKED, PASS, LOCKED,   lock()   );
}
```

Listing 29-5

The transition engine

```
public void event(int event)
{
  for (int i = 0; i < transitions.size(); i++)
  {
    Transition transition = (Transition) transitions.elementAt(i);
    if (state == transition.currentState && event == transition.event)
    {
      state = transition.newState;
      transition.action.execute();
    }
  }
}
```

Costs and Benefits of Interpreting a Transition Table. One powerful benefit is that the code that builds the transition table reads like a canonical state transition table. The four addTransaction lines can be very easily understood. The logic of the state machine is all in one place and is not contaminated with the implementation of the actions.

Maintaining a finite state machine like this is very easy compared to the nested switch/case implementation. To add a new transition, one simply adds a new addTransition line to the Turnstile constructor.

Another benefit of this approach is that the table can easily be changed at run time. This allows for dynamic alteration of the logic of the state machine. I have used mechanisms like that to allow hot patching of complex finite state machines.

Still another benefit is that multiple tables can be created, each representing a different FSM logic. These tables can be selected at run time based upon starting conditions.

The cost of the approach is primarily speed. It takes time to search through the transition table. For large state machines, that time may become significant. Another cost is the volume of code that must be written to support the table. If you examine Listing 29-12 closely, you'll see a rather large number of small support functions whose aim is to allow the simple expression of the state transition table in Listing 29-4.

The STATE[4] Pattern

Still another technique for implementing finite state machines is the STATE pattern. This pattern combines the efficiency of the nested switch/case statement with the flexibility of interpreting a transition table.

Figure 29-3 shows the structure of the solution. The Turnstile class has public methods for the events and protected methods for the actions. It holds a reference to an interface called TurnstileState. The two derivatives of TurnstileState represent the two states of the FSM.

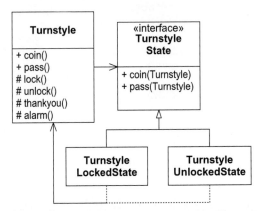

Figure 29-3   The STATE Pattern for the Turnstile

When one of the two event methods of Turnstile is invoked, it delegates that event to the Turnstile-State object. The methods of TurnstileLockedState implement the appropriate actions for the LOCKED state. The methods of TurnstileUnlockedState implement the appropriate actions for the UNLOCKED state. To change the state of the FSM, the reference in the Turnstile object is assigned to an instance of one of these derivatives.

Listing 29-6 shows the TurnstileState interface and its two derivatives. The state machine is easily visible in the four methods of those derivatives. For example, the coin method of LockedTurnstileState tells the Turnstile object to change state to the unlocked state, and then it invokes the unlock action function of Turnstile.

Listing 29-6

TurnstileState.java

```
interface TurnstileState
{
  void coin(Turnstile t);
  void pass(Turnstile t);
}

class LockedTurnstileState implements TurnstileState
{
  public void coin(Turnstile t)
  {
    t.setUnlocked();
    t.unlock();
  }
```

4.   [GOF95], p. 305.

```
  public void pass(Turnstile t)
  {
    t.alarm();
  }
}

class UnlockedTurnstileState implements TurnstileState
{
  public void coin(Turnstile t)
  {
    t.thankyou();
  }

  public void pass(Turnstile t)
  {
    t.setLocked();
    t.lock();
  }
}
```

The `Turnstile` class is shown in Listing 29-7. Notice the static variables that hold the derivatives of `TurnstileState`. These classes have no variables and therefore never need to have more than one instance. Holding the derivative instances of the `TurnstileState` derivatives in variables obviates the need to create a new instance every time the state changes. Making those variables static obviates the need to create new instances of the derivatives in the event that we need more than one instance of `Turnstile`.

Listing 29-7

Turnstile.java

```
public class Turnstile
{
  private static TurnstileState lockedState = new LockedTurnstileState();
  private static TurnstileState unlockedState = new UnlockedTurnstileState();

  private TurnstileController turnstileController;
  private TurnstileState state = lockedState;

  public Turnstile(TurnstileController action)
  {
    turnstileController = action;
  }

  public void coin()
  {
    state.coin(this);
  }

  public void pass()
  {
    state.pass(this);
  }
```

```
public void setLocked()
{
  state = lockedState;
}

public void setUnlocked()
{
  state = unlockedState;
}

public boolean isLocked()
{
  return state == lockedState;
}

public boolean isUnlocked()
{
  return state == unlockedState;
}

void thankyou()
{
  turnstileController.thankyou();
}

void alarm()
{
  turnstileController.alarm();
}

void lock()
{
  turnstileController.lock();
}

void unlock()
{
  turnstileController.unlock();
}
}
```

STATE VS. STRATEGY.   The diagram in Figure 29-3 is strongly reminiscent of the STRATEGY[5] pattern. Both have a context class; both delegate to a polymorphic base class that has several derivatives. The difference (see Figure 29-4) is that, in STATE, the derivatives hold a reference back to the context class. The primary function of the derivatives is to select and invoke methods of the context class through that reference. In the STRATEGY pattern, no such constraint or intent exists. The derivatives of a STRATEGY are not required to hold a reference to the context, and they are not required to call methods on the context. Thus, all instances of the STATE pattern are also instances of the STRATEGY pattern, but not all instances of STRATEGY are STATE.

Costs and Benefits of the STATE Pattern.   The STATE pattern provides a very strong separation between the actions and the logic of the state machine. The actions are implemented in the `Context` class, and the logic is distributed through the derivatives of the `State` class. This makes it very simple to change one without affecting the other. For example, it would be very easy to reuse the actions of the `Context` class with a different state logic

---

5.   See "Strategy" on page 168.

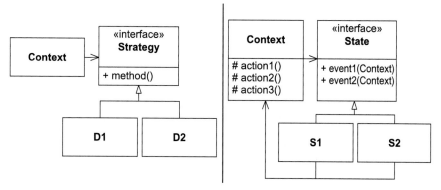

FIGURE 29-4 STATE V. STRATEGY

by simply using different derivatives of the `State` class. Alternatively we could create subclasses of `Context` that modify or replace the actions without affecting the logic of the `State` derivatives.

Another benefit of the this technique is that it is very efficient. It is probably just as efficient as the nested switch/case implementation. Thus, we have the flexibility of the table-driven approach with the efficiency of the nested switch/case approach.

The cost of this technique is twofold. First, the writing of the `State` derivatives is tedious at best. Writing a state machine with 20 states can be mind numbing. Second, the logic is distributed. There is no single place to go to see it all. This makes the code hard to maintain. This is reminiscent of the obscurity of the nested switch/case approach.

SMC—The State-Machine Compiler

The tedium of writing the derivatives of state and the need to have a single place to express the logic of the state machine led me to write a compiler that translates a textual state transition table into the classes necessary to implement the STATE pattern. This compiler is free and can be downloaded from `http://www.objectmentor.com`.

The input to the compiler is shown in Listing 29-8. The syntax is as follows:

```
currentState
{
  event newState action
  . . .
}
```

The four lines at the top describe the name of the state machine, the name of the context class, the initial state, and the name of the exception that will be thrown in the event of an illegal event.

Listing 29-8
Turnstile.sm

```
FSMName Turnstile
Context TurnstileActions
Initial Locked
Exception FSMError
{
    Locked
    {
        coin    Unlocked    unlock
        pass    Locked      alarm
    }
```

```
    Unlocked
    {
        coin      Unlocked      thankyou
        pass      Locked        lock
    }
}
```

In order to use this compiler, you must write a class that declares the action functions. The name of this class is specified in the Context line. I called it TurnstileActions. (See Listing 29-9.)

Listing 29-9

TurntstyleActions.java

```java
public abstract class TurnstileActions
{
  public void lock() {}
  public void unlock() {}
  public void thankyou() {}
  public void alarm() {}
}
```

The compiler generates a class that derives from the context. The name of the generated class is specified in the FSMName line. I called it Turnstile.

I could have implemented the action functions in TurnstileActions. However, I am more inclined to write another class that derives from the generated class and implements the action functions there. This is shown in Listing 29-10.

Listing 29-10

TurnstileFSM.java

```java
public class TurnstileFSM  extends Turnstile
{
  private TurnstileController controller;
  public TurnstileFSM(TurnstileController controller)
  {
    this.controller = controller;
  }

  public void lock()
  {
    controller.lock();
  }

  public void unlock()
  {
    controller.unlock();
  }

  public void thankyou()
  {
    controller.thankyou();
  }
```

```
  public void alarm()
  {
    controller.alarm();
  }
}
```

That's all we have to write. SMC generates the rest. The resulting structure is shown in Figure 29-5. We call this a THREE-LEVEL FINITE STATE MACHINE.[6]

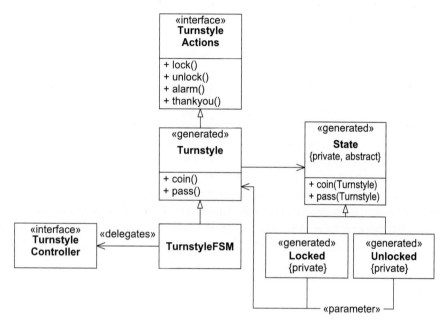

Figure 29-5 Three-Level FSM

The three levels provide the maximum in flexibility at a very low cost. We can create many different finite state machines simply by deriving them from `TurnstileActions`. We can also implement the actions in many different ways simply by deriving from `Turnstile`.

Notice that the generated code is completely isolated from the code that you have to write. You never have to modify the generated code. You don't even have to look at it. You can pay it the same level of attention that you pay to binary code.

You can see the generated code, as well as the other support code for this example, in Listing 29-13 through Listing 29-15 in the Listings section at the end of the chapter.

Costs and Benefits of the SMC Approach to the STATE Pattern. Clearly we have managed to maximize the benefits of the various approaches. The description of the finite state machine is contained all in one place and is very easy to maintain. The logic of the finite state machine is strongly isolated from the implementation of the actions, enabling both to be changed without impact upon the other. The solution is efficient, elegant, and requires a minimum of coding.

The cost is in the use of SMC. You have to have, and to learn how to use, another tool. In this case, however, the tool is remarkably simple to install and use. (See Listing 29-16 and the preceding paragraphs.) And it's free!

6.   [PLoPD1], p. 383.

Where Should State Machines Be Used?

I use state machines (and SMC) for several different classes of applications.

High-Level Application Policies for GUIs

One of the goals of the graphical revolution in the 1980s was to create *stateless* interfaces for humans to use. At the time, computer interfaces were dominated by textual approaches using hierarchical menus. It was easy to get lost in the menu structure, not knowing what *state* the screen was in. GUIs helped mitigate that problem by minimizing the number of state changes that the screen went through. In modern GUIs, a great deal of work is put in to keeping common features on the screen at all times and making sure the user does not get confused by hidden states.

It is ironic, then, that the code implementing these "stateless" GUIs, is strongly state driven. In such GUIs, the code must figure out which menu items and buttons to grey out, which subwindows should appear, which tab should be activated, where the focus ought to be put, etc. All these decisions relate to the state of the interface.

I learned a very long time ago that controlling these factors is a nightmare unless you organize them into a single control structure. That control structure is best characterized as an FSM. Since those days, I have been writing almost all my GUIs using FSMs generated by SMC (or its predecessors).

Consider the state machine in Listing 29-11. This machine controls the GUI for the login portion of an application. Upon getting a start event, the machine puts up a login screen. Once the user hits the enter key, the machine checks the password. If the password is good, it goes to the `loggedIn` state and starts the user process (not shown). If the password is bad, it displays a screen informing the user that his password is bad. If the user wants to try again, he hits the OK button; otherwise he hits the cancel button. If a bad password is entered three times in a row (`thirdBadPassword` event), the machine locks the screen until the administrator password is entered.

Listing 29-11

`login.sm`

```
Initial init
{
  init
  {
    start logginIn displayLoginScreen
  }

  logginIn
  {
    enter checkingPassword checkPassword
    cancel init clearScreen
  }

  checkingPassword
  {
    passwordGood loggedIn startUserProcess
    passwordBad notifyingPasswordBad displayBadPasswordScreen
    thirdBadPassword screenLocked displayLockScreen
  }

  notifyingPasswordBad
  {
    OK checkingPassword displayLoginScreen
    cancel init clearScreen
  }
```

```
  screenLocked
  {
    enter checkingAdminPassword checkAdminPassword
  }

  checkingAdminPassword
  {
    passwordGood init clearScreen
    passwordBad screenLocked displayLockScreen
  }
}
```

What we've done here is to capture the high-level policy of the application in a state machine. This high-level policy lives in one place and is easy to maintain. It vastly simplifies the rest of the code in the system because that code is not mixed with the policy code.

Clearly this approach can be used for interfaces other than GUIs. Indeed, I have used similar approaches for textual and machine–machine interfaces as well. But GUIs tend to be more complex than those others, so the need for them and the volume of them are greater.

GUI Interaction Controllers

Imagine you want to allow your users to draw rectangles on the screen. The gestures they use are as follows: First they click on the rectangle icon in the pallet window. Then they position the mouse in the canvas window at one corner of the rectangle. Then they press the mouse button and drag the mouse toward the desired second corner. While the user drags, an animated image of the potential rectangle appears on the screen. The user manipulates the rectangle to the desired shape by continuing to hold the mouse button down while dragging the mouse. When the rectangle is right, the user releases the mouse button. The program then stops the animation and draws a fixed rectangle on the screen.

Of course, the user can abort this at any time by clicking on a different pallet icon. If the user drags the mouse out of the canvas window, the animation disappears. If the mouse returns to the canvas window, the animation reappears.

Finally, having finished drawing a rectangle, the user can draw another simply by clicking and dragging again in the canvas window. There is no need to click on the rectangle icon in the pallet.

What I have described here is a finite state machine. The state transition diagram appears in Figure 29-6. The solid circle with the arrow denotes the starting state of the state machine.[7] The solid circle with the open circle around it is the final state of the machine.

GUI interactions are rife with finite state machines. They are driven by the incoming events from the user. Those events cause changes in the state of the interaction.

Distributed Processing

Distributed processing is yet another situation in which the state of the system changes based upon incoming events. For example, suppose you had to transfer a large block of information from one node on a network to another. Suppose also that network response time is precious, so you need to chop up the block and send it as a group of small packets.

The state machine depicting this scenario is shown in Figure 29-7. It starts by requesting a transmission session, proceeds by sending each packet and waiting for an acknowledgment, and finishes by terminating the session.

---

7.   See "States and Internal Transitions" on page 493.

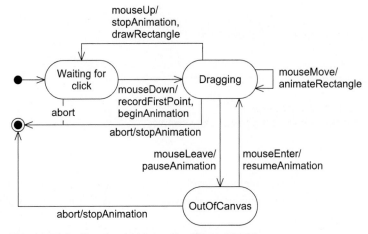

Figure 29-6   Rectangle Interaction State Machine

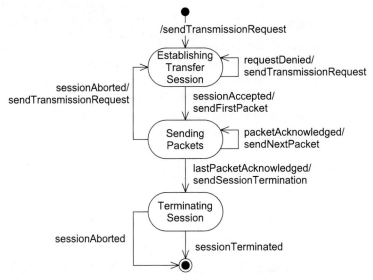

Figure 29-7   Sending large block using many packets

Conclusion

Finite state machines are underutilized. There are many scenarios in which their use would help to create clearer, simpler, more flexible, and more accurate code. Making use of the STATE pattern and simple tools for generating the code from state transition tables can be of great assistance.

Listings

`Turnstile.java` Using Table Interpretation

This listing shows how a finite state machine can be implemented by interpreting a vector of transition data structures. It is completely compatible with the `TurnstileController` in Listing 29-2 and the `TurnstileTest` in Listing 29-3.

Listing 29-12
Turnstile.java using table interpretation

```java
import java.util.Vector;

public class Turnstile
{
  // States
  public static final int LOCKED = 0;
  public static final int UNLOCKED = 1;

  // Events
  public static final int COIN = 0;
  public static final int PASS = 1;

  /*private*/ int state = LOCKED;
  private TurnstileController turnstileController;
  private Vector transitions = new Vector();

  private interface Action
  {
    void execute();
  }

  private class Transition
  {
    public Transition(int currentState, int event,
                      int newState, Action action)
    {
      this.currentState = currentState;
      this.event = event;
      this.newState = newState;
      this.action = action;
    }

    int currentState;
    int event;
    int newState;
    Action action;
  }

  public Turnstile(TurnstileController action)
  {
    turnstileController = action;
    addTransition(LOCKED,   COIN, UNLOCKED, unlock()  );
    addTransition(LOCKED,   PASS, LOCKED,   alarm()   );
    addTransition(UNLOCKED, COIN, UNLOCKED, thankyou());
    addTransition(UNLOCKED, PASS, LOCKED,   lock()    );
  }

  private void addTransition(int currentState, int event,
                             int newState, Action action)
  {
    transitions.add(
      new Transition(currentState, event, newState, action));
  }
```

```java
  private Action lock()
  {
    return new Action(){public void execute(){doLock();}};
  }

  private Action thankyou()
  {
    return new Action(){public void execute(){doThankyou();}};
  }

  private Action alarm()
  {
    return new Action(){public void execute(){doAlarm();}};
  }

  private Action unlock()
  {
    return new Action(){public void execute(){doUnlock();}};
  }

  private void doUnlock()
  {
    turnstileController.unlock();
  }

  private void doLock()
  {
    turnstileController.lock();
  }

  private void doAlarm()
  {
    turnstileController.alarm();
  }

  private void doThankyou()
  {
    turnstileController.thankyou();
  }

  public void event(int event)
  {
    for (int i = 0; i < transitions.size(); i++)
    {
      Transition transition = (Transition) transitions.elementAt(i);
      if (state == transition.currentState && event == transition.event)
      {
        state = transition.newState;
        transition.action.execute();
      }
    }
  }
}
```

`Turnstile.java` Generated by SMC, and Other Support Files

Listings 31-13 through 31-16 complete the code for the SMC example of the turnstile. Turnstile.java was generated by SMC. The generator creates a bit of cruft, but the code is not bad.

Listing 29-13

`Turnstile.java` (generated by SMC)

```
//----------------------------------------------
//
// FSM:        Turnstile
// Context:    TurnstileActions
// Exception: FSMError
// Version:
// Generated: Thursday 09/06/2001 at 12:23:59 CDT
//
//----------------------------------------------


//----------------------------------------------
//
// class Turnstile
//     This is the Finite State Machine class
//
public class Turnstile extends TurnstileActions
{
  private State itsState;
  private static String itsVersion = "";

  // instance variables for each state
  private static Locked itsLockedState;
  private static Unlocked itsUnlockedState;

  // constructor
  public Turnstile()
  {
    itsLockedState = new Locked();
    itsUnlockedState = new Unlocked();

    itsState = itsLockedState;

    // Entry functions for: Locked
  }

  // accessor functions

  public String getVersion()
  {
    return itsVersion;
  }

  public String getCurrentStateName()
  {
    return itsState.stateName();
  }

  // event functions - forward to the current State
```

```
public void pass() throws FSMError
{
  itsState.pass();
}

public void coin() throws FSMError
{
  itsState.coin();
}

//---------------------------------------
//
// private class State
//    This is the base State class
//
private abstract class State
{
  public abstract String stateName();

  // default event functions

  public void pass() throws FSMError
  {
    throw new FSMError( "pass", itsState.stateName());
  }

  public void coin() throws FSMError
  {
    throw new FSMError( "coin", itsState.stateName());
  }

}

//---------------------------------------
//
// class Locked
//    handles the Locked State and its events
//
private class Locked extends State
{
  public String stateName()
    { return "Locked"; }

  //
  // responds to coin event
  //
  public void coin()
  {
    unlock();

    // change the state
    itsState = itsUnlockedState;
  }
```

```
    //
    // responds to pass event
    //
    public void pass()
    {
      alarm();

      // change the state
      itsState = itsLockedState;
    }
  }

  //---------------------------------------------
  //
  // class Unlocked
  //    handles the Unlocked State and its events
  //
  private class Unlocked extends State
  {
    public String stateName()
      { return "Unlocked"; }
    //
    // responds to pass event
    //
    public void pass()
    {
      lock();

      // change the state
      itsState = itsLockedState;
    }

    //
    // responds to coin event
    //
    public void coin()
    {
      thankyou();

      // change the state
      itsState = itsUnlockedState;
    }
  }
}
```

FSMError is the exception that we told SMC to throw if there were ever an illegal event. The turnstile example is so simple that there can't be an illegal event, so the exception is useless. However, in larger state machines, there are events that should not occur in certain states. Those transitions are never mentioned in the input to SMC. Thus, if such an event were ever to occur, the generated code would throw the exception.

Listing 29-14

FSMError.java

```
public class FSMError extends Exception
{
  public FSMError(String event, String state)
```

```
  {
    super("Invalid event:" + event + " in state:" + state);
  }
}
```

The test code for the SMC generated state machine is very similar to all the other test programs we've written in this chapter. There are some minor differences.

Listing 29-15

SMCTurnstileTest.java

```java
import junit.framework.*;
import junit.swingui.TestRunner;

public class SMCTurnstileTest extends TestCase
{
  public static void main(String[] args)
  {
    TestRunner.main(new String[]{"SMCTurnstileTest"});
  }

  public SMCTurnstileTest(String name)
  {
    super(name);
  }

  private TurnstileFSM t;
  private boolean lockCalled = false;
  private boolean unlockCalled = false;
  private boolean thankyouCalled = false;
  private boolean alarmCalled = false;

  public void setUp()
  {
    TurnstileController controllerSpoof =
      new TurnstileController()
    {
      public void lock() {lockCalled = true;}
      public void unlock() {unlockCalled = true;}
      public void thankyou() {thankyouCalled = true;}
      public void alarm() {alarmCalled = true;}
    };

    t = new TurnstileFSM(controllerSpoof);
  }

  public void testInitialConditions()
  {
    assertEquals("Locked", t.getCurrentStateName());
  }

  public void testCoinInLockedState() throws Exception
  {
    t.coin();
    assertEquals("Unlocked", t.getCurrentStateName());
    assert(unlockCalled);
  }
```

```
public void testCoinInUnlockedState() throws Exception
{
  t.coin(); // put in Unlocked state
  t.coin();
  assertEquals("Unlocked", t.getCurrentStateName());
  assert(thankyouCalled);
}

public void testPassInLockedState() throws Exception
{
  t.pass();
  assertEquals("Locked", t.getCurrentStateName());
  assert(alarmCalled);
}

public void testPassInUnlockedState() throws Exception
{
  t.coin(); // unlock
  t.pass();
  assertEquals("Locked", t.getCurrentStateName());
  assert(lockCalled);
}
}
```

The `TurnstileController` class is identical to all the others that appeared in this chapter. You can see it in Listing 29-2.

The `ant` file used to generate the `Turnstile.java` code is shown in Listing 29-16. Note that it's not a very big deal. Indeed, if you wanted to simply type the build command in a DOS window, you could type:

```
java smc.Smc -f TurnstileFSM.sm
```

Listing 29-16

build.xml

```xml
<project name="SMCTurnstile" default="TestSMCTurnstile" basedir=".">

  <property environment="env" />

  <path id="classpath">
    <pathelement path="${env.CLASSPATH}"/>
  </path>

  <target name="TurnstileFSM">
    <java classname="smc.Smc">
      <arg value="-f TurnstileFSM.sm"/>
      <classpath refid="classpath" />
    </java>
  </target>

</project>
```

Bibliography

1. Gamma, et al. *Design Patterns*. Reading, MA: Addison–Wesley, 1995.
2. Coplien and Schmidt. *Pattern Languages of Program Design*. Reading, MA: Addison–Wesley, 1995.

30

The ETS Framework

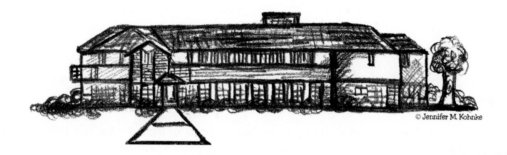

© Jennifer M. Kohnke

By Robert C. Martin and James Newkirk

This chapter describes a significant software project that was developed from March 1993 until late 1997. The software was commissioned by the Educational Testing Service (ETS) and was developed by the two of us and several other developers at Object Mentor, Inc.

Our focus in this chapter is on the techniques, both technical and managerial, for producing a reusable framework. The creation of such a framework was an essential step in the success of the project, and the design and history of its development should prove educational.

No software project is developed in a perfect environment, and this one was no exception. In order to understand the technical aspects of the design, it is important to consider the environmental issues as well. Therefore, before we dive into the software engineering aspects of the project, we are going to give you a bit of background on the project and the environment in which it was developed.

Introduction

Project Overview

To become a licensed architect in the United States or Canada, you must pass an examination. If you pass, a state licensing board will give you a license to practice architecture. The examination was developed by the Educational Testing Service (ETS) under a charter by the National Council of Architectural Registration Boards (NCARB), and it is currently administered by the Chauncey Group International.

The test consists of nine divisions and is taken over a period of several days. In the three graphical divisions of the examination, candidates are asked to create solutions in a CAD-like environment by drawing or placing objects. For example, they might be asked to do the following:

- Design the floor plan of a certain kind of building
- Design a roof to fit on top of an existing building
- Place a proposed building on a parcel of land and design the parking area, road system, and walkway system to serve the building

In the past, the candidates' solutions to these problems were drawn using pencil and paper. These documents were then given to a cadre of jurors for scoring. The jurors were highly experienced architects who would pore over the candidates' solutions and decide whether to pass or fail them.

In 1989, NCARB commissioned ETS to research whether or not an automated system for delivering and scoring the graphical portions of the examination could be developed. By 1992, the ETS and the NCARB had agreed that such a system was indeed possible. Furthermore, they felt that an object-oriented approach would be appropriate due to the constantly changing requirements. So they contacted Object Mentor, Inc. (OMI) to help with the design.

In March 1993, OMI was granted a contract to produce a portion of the test. One year later, after successfully completing that portion, OMI was granted a second contract to produce the bulk of the remainder.

Program Structure.   The structure that ETS decided on was quite elegant. The graphics examination would be broken into 15 different problems, called vignettes. Each vignette tested a particular area of knowledge. One might test the candidate's understanding of roof design, and another might test their understanding of how to design floor plans.

Each vignette was further subdivided into two sections. The "delivery" section was to be a graphical user interface upon which the candidate would "draw" the solution to the problem at hand. The "scoring" section was to read the solution created by the delivery section and score it. Delivery would be conducted at a location convenient to the candidate. The solutions would then be transmitted to a central location where they would be scored.

Scripts.   Although there were only 15 vignettes, each would have many possible "scripts." A script would specify the exact nature of the problem that the candidate would solve. For example, the floor-plan vignette might have one script that asked the candidate to design a library, and another that asked the candidate to design a grocery store. Thus, the vignette programs had to be written in a generic fashion. They had to be delivered and scored in a way that was governed by the script.

Platform.   Both the delivery and scoring programs were to run under Windows 3.1 (later upgraded to W95/NT). The programs were to be written in C++ using object-oriented techniques.

First Contract.   In March 1993, OMI was granted a contract to develop the delivery and scoring of the most complex of all the vignettes: "Building Design." This decision was motivated by Booch's recommendation to develop the highest-risk elements first as a way to manage risk and calibrate the estimation process of the team.

Building Design.   Building Design was to test the candidate's ability to design the floor plan of a relatively simple two-story building. The candidate would be given a building to design, complete with requirements and constraints. The candidate would then use the delivery program to place rooms, doors, windows, corridors, stairs, and elevators into their solution.

The scoring program would then check the solution against a large number of "features" that would assess the candidate's knowledge. The nature of these features is confidential, but in general terms, they would assess things such as the following:

- Does the building meet the requirements of the client?
- Is the building code compliant?
- Has the candidate demonstrated design logic?
- Are the building and its rooms oriented correctly on the site?

Early History 1993–1994

At this early stage, two of us (Martin and Newkirk) were the sole developers working on this project. Our contract with ETS said that we were to produce both the delivery and scoring programs for Building Design. However, we also wanted to develop a reusable framework in conjunction with Building Design.

By 1997, there had to be 15 vignette delivery and scoring programs operational. That gave us four years. We felt that a reusable framework would give us a big advantage toward that goal. Such a framework would also go a long way toward helping us manage the consistency and quality of the vignettes. After all, we didn't want similar features in different vignettes to operate in subtly different ways.

So, in March 1993, we set out to produce the two components of Building Design and also a framework that could be reused by the remaining fourteen vignettes.

Success. In September 1993, the first versions of the delivery and scoring programs were complete, and we demonstrated these programs to representatives of NCARB and ETS. These demonstrations were well received, and a field trial was scheduled for January 1994.

As with most projects, once users see the program actually operating, they realize that what they asked for was not really what they wanted. We had been sending interim versions of the vignette to ETS every week throughout 1993, and there had been a large number of changes and enhancements made right up to that September demonstration.

After the demonstration, the looming field trial caused the rate of changes and enhancements to reach deluge proportions. The two of us were kept busy, full time, making and testing these changes and preparing the programs for the field trial.

This churning of the specification for Building Design was accelerated still further by the results of the field trial, keeping us even busier through the first quarter of 1994.

In December 1993, negotiations were begun for a contract to build the rest of the vignettes. These negotiations would take three months to close. In March 1994, ETS granted OMI a contract to produce a framework and 10 more vignettes. ETS's own engineers would produce the remaining five vignettes based upon our framework.

Framework?

Late in 1993, at the height of the churn in Building Design, one of us (Newkirk) spent a week with one of the engineers at ETS to prepare him for his part in the upcoming contract. The objective was to demonstrate how the code within the 60,000-line, reusable C++ framework could be reused to build other vignettes. However, things did not go well. By the end of the week, it was clear that the only way to reuse the framework was to cut and paste bits and pieces of its source code into the new vignettes. Clearly this was not a good option.

In hindsight, there were two reasons for our failure to create a workable framework. First, we had been focusing on Building Design to the exclusion of all the other vignettes. Second, we went through months of churning requirements and schedule pressure. These two things together allowed concepts that were specific to Building Design to infiltrate the framework.

To a certain extent, we naively took the benefits of object-oriented technology for granted. We felt that by using C++ and by doing a careful object-oriented design, a reusable framework would be easy to create. We were wrong. We discovered what had been known for years—building reusable frameworks is *hard*.

Framework!

In March 1994, after the new contract was signed, we added two more engineers to the project and began developing the new vignettes. We still believed we needed a framework and were convinced that what we had would not serve that function. It was clear we needed to change our strategy.

The 1994 Team

- Robert C. Martin, architect and lead designer, 20+ years experience
- James W. Newkirk, designer and project leader, 15+ years experience
- Bhama Rao, designer and programmer, 12+ years experience
- William Mitchell, designer and programmer, 15+ years experience

The Deadline

The deadline was set by the fact that the test was to go into production in 1997. Candidates would be tested in February and scored in May. This was an absolute requirement.

The Strategy

To make that schedule and to ensure that the quality and consistency of the program could be managed, we adopted a new strategy for the construction of the framework. Portions of the original 60,000-line framework were preserved, *but the majority was scrapped.*

A Rejected Alternative.   One option would have been to try to redesign the framework up front and complete it before any of the vignettes were begun. Indeed, many people would identify this with an architecture-driven approach. However, we chose not to pursue this option, because it would have caused us to produce large amounts of framework code that could not be tested inside working vignettes. We did not trust our ability to completely anticipate the needs of the vignettes. In short, we felt that the architecture needed almost immediate verification by being used in working vignettes. We did not want to guess.

Rebecca Wirfs–Brock once said, "You have to build at least three or more applications against a framework (and then throw them away) before you can be reasonably confident that you have built the right architecture for that domain."[2] After failing to produce a framework, we felt similarly. Thus, we decided that we would develop the framework concurrently with the development of several new vignettes. This would allow us to compare similar features of the vignettes and design those features in a generic and reusable way.

Four vignettes were begun in parallel. As they were being developed, certain portions were found to be similar. These were then refactored into more generic form and refit into all three vignettes. Thus, nothing entered the framework unless it had been successfully reused in at least four vignettes.

Also, portions of Building Design were excised and refactored in a similar fashion. Once these portions were working in all three vignettes, they were placed in the framework.

Among the common features that were added to the framework were the following:

- The structure of the UI screen–Message windows, drawing windows, button palettes, etc.
- Creating, moving, adjusting, identifying, and deleting graphic elements

2.   [BOOCH-OS], p. 275.

- Zooming and scrolling
- Drawing simple sketch elements such as lines, circles, and polylines
- Vignette timing and automatic abort
- Saving and restoring solution files, including error recovery
- Mathematical models of many geometric elements: line, ray, segment, point, box, circle, arc, triangle, polygon, etc. These models include methods such as Intersection, Area, `IsPointIn`, `IsPointOn`, etc.
- Evaluation and weighting of individual scoring features.

Over the next eight months, the framework grew to some 60,000 lines of C++ code, representing somewhat more than one man–year of direct effort. But this framework was being reused by four different vignettes.

Results

Throwing One Away.   What were we to do with the old Building Design? As the framework grew and the new vignettes were successfully reusing it, Building Design stood more and more as an outsider. It was unlike all the other vignettes and would have to be maintained and evolved through separate means. Even though Building Design represented over a man–year of effort, we decided to be ruthless and discard the old version completely. We committed ourselves to redesign and reimplement it later in the project cycle.

Long Initial Development Time.   A negative result of our framework strategy was the relatively long development time for the first vignettes. The first four vignette delivery programs required nearly four man–years to develop.

Reuse Efficiency.   Upon completion of the initial vignettes, the framework was richly endowed with 60,000 lines of C++ code, and the vignette delivery programs were remarkably small. Each program had approximately 4,000 lines of boiler-plate code (i.e., code that is the same for each vignette). Each program also had an average of 6,000 lines of application-specific code. The smallest vignette had as few as 500 lines of application-specific code, and the largest had as many as 12,000. We felt that it was remarkable that, on average, nearly five-sixths of the code in each vignette was pulled from the framework. Only one-tenth of the code within these programs was unique.

Development Productivity.   After the first four vignettes, development time drastically decreased. Seven more delivery programs (including a rewrite of Building Design) were completed within 18 man–months. The line-count ratios of these new vignettes remained roughly the same as the first four.

Moreover, the Building Design program, which took us over one man–year to write the first time, took only 2.5 man–months to rewrite from scratch with the framework in place. This is nearly a 6:1 increase in productivity.

Another way to look at these results is that the first five vignettes, including Building Design, required one man–year of effort apiece. Subsequent vignettes, however, required 2.6 man–months apiece—an increase of nearly 400 percent.

Weekly Delivery.   From the outset of the project, and throughtout its active development, we shipped interim versions to ETS every week. ETS would test and evaluate these versions and then send us a list of changes. We would estimate these changes, and then work with ETS to schedule the week in which they'd be delivered. Difficult changes, or changes of low importance, were often delayed in preference to high priority changes. Thus, ETS kept control of the project and schedule throughout.

A Robust and Flexible Design.   One of the most satisfying aspects of the project is the way that the architecture and framework have weathered the intense flux of requirements changes. During the peak of development, nary a week went by without a long list of changes and fixes being identified. Some of these changes were in response to bugs, but many more were due to changes in the actual requirements. Yet, with all the modifications, fiddling, and tweaking in the midst of heavy development, "the design of the software didn't unravel."[3]

Final Outcome.   By February 1997, architectural candidates began using the delivery programs to take their registration exams. By May 1997, their results began to be scored. The system has been up and running since that time, and it has worked well. Every architect candidate in North America now takes this exam using this software.

Framework Design

The Common Requirements of the Scoring Applications

Consider the problem of how to test someone's knowledge and skill. The scheme that was adopted by ETS for the NCARB programs is quite elaborate. We can illustrate it here by exploring a simple, fictitious example — a test for basic math.

In our basic math test, students are presented with 100 math problems ranging from simple addition and subtraction problems to large multiplication and long-division problems. We will examine their responses to these problems to ascertain their competency and skill in basic math. Our goal is to give them a pass/fail grade. "Pass" means that we are certain that they have acquired the fundamental knowledge and skill needed for basic math. "Fail" means that we are sure that they have not acquired this knowledge and skill. In those cases where we are unsure, we will return a score of "indeterminate."

However, we have another goal, too. We want to be able to enumerate the strengths and weaknesses of the student. We want to partition the topic of basic math into subtopics and then evaluate the student for each of those subtopics.

Consider, for example, the problem of a person who has learned an improper multiplication fact. Perhaps they always mistake 7×8 for 42. This person will get a large percentage of the multiplication and division problems wrong. Certainly that student deserves to fail the test. On the other hand, consider that the student did *everything* else correctly! The student correctly created the partial products in long multiplication and correctly structured the long-division problems. Indeed, the *only* mistake that the student made was $7 \times 8 = 42$. Certainly we'd like to know that. Indeed, since the corrective action for such a student is so simple, we might very well want to give the student a passing grade along with some corrective guidance.

So how can we structure the scoring of the test to determine the areas of basic math in which the student has gained expertise and those areas in which he or she has not? Consider the diagram in Figure 30-1. The rectangles on this diagram show areas of expertise that we want to test for. The lines show a hierarchical dependency. Thus, knowledge of basic math depends on knowledge of terms and factors. Knowledge of terms depends on knowledge of addition facts plus the mechanics of addition and subtraction. Knowledge of addition depends upon knowledge of the commutative and associative properties of addition and the mechanics of carrying.

The leaf rectangles are called "features." Features are units of knowledge that can be evaluated and given acceptable (A), unacceptable (U), or indeterminate (I) values. Thus, given our 100 problems and the student's answers, we want to apply each feature to every problem and determine a score. In the case of the "Carry" feature, we would look at every addition problem and compare it to the student's answer. If the student got all the addition problems correct, the result of the "Carry" feature would, of course, be 'A.' However, for each addition problem that the student got wrong, we would try to determine if the error made was an error in carrying. We might try different combinations of carrying errors to see if one of those errors would lead to the answer that the student gave. If we could determine, with a high degree of probability, that a carry error was made, we would adjust the score of the carry feature accordingly. In the end, the score returned by the carry feature would be a statistical result based upon the total number of wrong answers that could be traced to errors in carrying.

---

3.   Pete Brittingham, NCARB Project Manager, ETS.

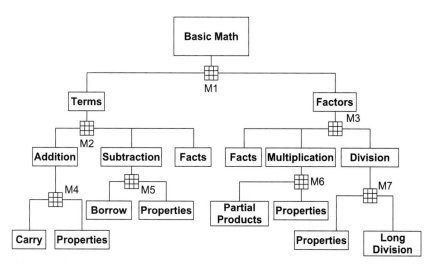

Figure 30-1 Feature Hierarchy for Basic Math

If, for example, the student got half the addition problems wrong, and most of them could be traced to carry errors, we would certainly return a 'U' for the carry feature. If, on the other hand, only a quarter of the errors could be traced to carry errors, we might return an 'I.'

In the end, all the features are evaluated in this manner. Each feature examining the test answers to develop a score for that particular feature. The scores of the various features represent an analysis of the student's knowledge of basic math.

The next step is to derive a final grade from that analysis. To do this, we merge the scores of the features up the hierarchy through the use of weights and matrices. Notice on Figure 30-1 that there are matrix icons at the junctures between the levels of the hierarchy. The matrix associates a weighting factor with the score from each feature and then provides a map for the score for that level in the hierarchy. For example, the matrix just below the Addition node would establish the weights to be applied to the Carry and Properties scores, and would then describe the mapping that would generate the overall score for Addition.

Figure 30-2 shows the form of one of these matrices. The input from Carry is considered more important that the input from Properties, so it is given twice the weight. The weighted scores are then added together, and the result is applied to the matrix.

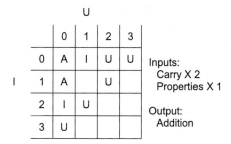

Figure 30-2 The Addition Matrix

For example, let's presume a score of 'I' from Carry, and a score of 'A' from Properties. There are no 'U' scores, so we use the left-most column of the matrix. The weighted 'I' score is 2, so we use the third row of the matrix, giving a result of 'I.' Notice that there are holes in the matrix. These are impossible conditions. Given the current weightings, there is no combination of scores that will select the empty cells in the matrix.

This scheme of weights and matrices is repeated at each level of the hierarchy until a final score is derived. Thus, the final score is a merging and remerging of the various feature scores. The structure of the hierarchy lends itself to very precise tuning on the part of the psychometricians at ETS.

The Design of the Scoring Framework

Figure 30-3 shows the static structure of the scoring framework. The structure can be divided into two major sections. The three classes on the right, shown in distinctive font, are not part of the framework. They represent the classes that must be written for each specific scoring application. The rest of the classes in Figure 30-3 are framework classes, which are common to all scoring applications.

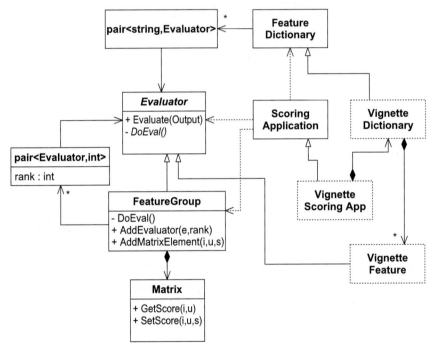

Figure 30-3   Scoring Framework

The most important class in the scoring framework is `Evaluator`. This class is an abstract class that represents both the leaf nodes and the matrix nodes of the scoring tree. The `Evaluate(ostream&)` function is called when the score of a node in the scoring tree is desired. This function makes use of the TEMPLATE METHOD[4] pattern in order to provide a standard method for logging scores to an output device.

Listing 30-1

Evaluator

```
class Evaluator
{
  public:
    enum Score {A,I,U,F,X};
    Evaluator();
    virtual ~Evaluator();

    Score Evaluate(ostream& scoreOutput);
```

4.   [GOF95], p. 325.

```
    void SetName(const String& theName) {itsName = theName;}
    const String& GetName() {return itsName;}

  private:
    virtual Score DoEval() = 0;

    String itsName;
};
```

See Listings 30-1 and 30-2. The `Evaluate()` function calls a private, pure virtual function called `DoEval()`. This function will be overridden to perform the actual evaluation of the scoring-tree node. It returns the score and allows `Evaluate()` to output it in the standard form.

Listing 30-2

Evaluator::Evaluate

```
Evaluator::Score Evaluator::Evaluate(ostream& o)
{
    static char scoreName[] = {'A', 'I', 'U', 'F', 'X'};
    o << itsName << ":";
    score = DoEval();
    o << scoreName[score] << endl;
    return score;
}
```

Leaf nodes of the scoring tree are represented by the `VignetteFeature` class in Figure 30-3. Actually, there would be dozens of such classes in each scoring application. Each would override `DoEval()` to calculate the score for its own particular scoring feature.

Matrix nodes of the scoring tree are represented by the `FeatureGroup` class in Figure 30-3. Listing 30-3 shows what this class looks like. There are two functions that assist in creating a `FeatureGroup` object. The first is `AddEvaluator`, and the second is `AddMatrixElement`.

Listing 30-3

FeatureGroup

```
class FeatureGroup : public Evaluator
{
public:
  FeatureGroup(const RWCString& name);
  virtual ~FeatureGroup();

  void AddEvaluator(Evaluator* e , int rank);

  void AddMatrixElement(int i, int u, Score s);
private:
  Evaluator::Score DoEval();
  Matrix itsMatrix;
  vector<pair<Evaluator*,int> > itsEvaluators;
};
```

The `AddEvaluator` function allows child nodes to be added to the `FeatureGroup`. For example, referring back to Figure 30-1, the `Addition` node would be a `FeatureGroup`, and we would call `AddEvaluator` twice to load the `Carry` and `Properties` nodes to it. The `AddEvaluator` function allows the rank of the evaluator to be specified. The rank is the multiplier that gets applied to the score coming out of the evaluator. Thus, when we called `AddEvaluator` to add `Carry` to the `Addition FeatureGroup`, we would have specified a rank of 2 because the `Carry` feature has twice the weight of the `Properties` feature.

The `AddMatrixElement` function adds a cell to the matrix. It must be called for every cell that requires population. For example, the matrix in Figure 30-2 would be created using the sequence of calls in Listing 30-4.

Listing 30-4

Creation of the Addition Matrix

```
addition.AddMatrixElement(0,0,Evaluator::A);
addition.AddMatrixElement(0,1,Evaluator::I);
addition.AddMatrixElement(0,2,Evaluator::U);
addition.AddMatrixElement(0,3,Evaluator::U);
addition.AddMatrixElement(1,0,Evaluator::A);
addition.AddMatrixElement(1,2,Evaluator::U);
addition.AddMatrixElement(2,0,Evaluator::I);
addition.AddMatrixElement(2,1,Evaluator::U);
addition.AddMatrixElement(3,0,Evaluator::U);
```

The `DoEval` function simply iterates through the list of evaluators, multiplying their score by the rank and adding the product to the appropriate accumulators for I and U scores. Once complete, it uses those accumulators as matrix indices to pull out the final score. (See Listing 30-5.)

Listing 30-5

FeatureGroup::DoEval

```
Evaluator::Score FeatureGroup::DoEval()
{
    int sumU, sumI;
    sumU = sumI = 0;
    Evaluator::Score s, rtnScore;
    Vector<Pair<Evaluator*, int> >::iterator ei;
    ei = itsEvaluators.begin()

    for(; ei != itsEvaluators.end(); ei++)
    {
      Evaluator* e = (*ei).first;
      int rank = (*ei).second;

      s = e.Evaluate(outputStream);

      switch(s)
      {
      case I:
        sumI += rank;
      break;
      case U:
        sumU += rank;
      break;
      }
    } // for ei
    rtnScore = itsMatrix.GetScore( sumI, sumU );
    return rtnScore;
}
```

One last issue remains. How does the scoring tree get built? It was quite evident that the psychometricians at ETS would want the ability to change the topology and weighting of the tree without having to change the actual applications. Thus the scoring tree is built up by the `VignetteScoringApp` class. (See Figure 30-3.)

Each scoring application had its own implementation for this class. One of the responsibilities of this class was to build a derivative of the `FeatureDictionary` class. This class contained a mapping of strings to `Evaluator` pointers.

When a scoring application was started, the scoring framework gained control. It invoked the method in the `ScoringApplication` class that caused the appropriate derivative of the `FeatureDictionary` to be created. It then read a special text file that described the topology of the scoring tree and its weights. This text file identified features by using special names. These names were the names that were associated with the appropriate `Evaluator` pointers in the `FeatureDictionary`.

Thus, in its simplest form, a scoring application was nothing more than a set of features and a method that constructed a `FeatureDictionary`. The building and evaluation of the scoring tree was handled by the framework and was therefore common to all the scoring applications.

A Case for TEMPLATE METHOD

One of the vignettes tested the candidates' abilities to lay out the floor plan of a building such as a library or a police station. In this vignette, the candidate had to draw rooms, corridors, doors, windows, wall openings, stairs, elevators, etc. The program converted the drawing into a data structure that the scoring program could interpret. The object model looked something like Figure 30-4.

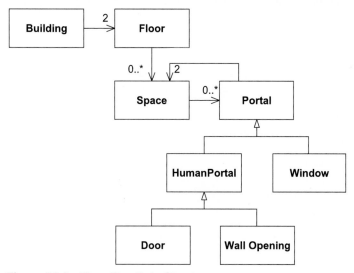

Figure 30-4   Floor Plan Data Structure

Make no mistake about this. The objects in this data structure had very minimal functionality. They were not polymorphic objects in any sense of the word. Rather, they were simple data carriers—A purely representational model.

A building was composed of two floors. Each floor had many spaces. Each space contained many portals, each of which separated two spaces. Portals could be windows or could allow a human to pass through. Human portals were either wall openings or doors.

Scoring was done by testing the solution for a set of *features*. The features were things like the following:

• Did the candidate draw all the required spaces?
• Does each space have an acceptable aspect ratio?

- Does each space have a way in?
- Do external spaces have windows?
- Are the men's and ladies' washrooms connected by a door?
- Does the president's office have a view of the mountains?
- Does the kitchen have easy access to a back alley?
- Does the lunchroom have easy access to the kitchen?
- Can a person navigate the corridor system and get to each room?

The psychometricians at ETS wanted to be able to easily change the shape of the scoring matrix.They wanted to be able to change the weightings, regroup the features into different subhierarchies, etc. They wanted to be able to take out features that they considered worthless or add new features. Most of these manipulations were a matter of changing a single configuration text file.

For performance reasons, we only wanted to calculate the features that were included in the matrix. So we created classes for each feature. Each of these `Feature` classes had an `Evaluate` method that would walk the data structure in Figure 30-4 and calculate a score. This meant that we had dozens and dozens of `Feature` classes that all walked the same data structure. The code duplication was horrendous.

Write a Loop Once

To deal with the code duplication, we started using the TEMPLATE METHOD pattern. This was in 1993 and 1994, long before we knew anything about patterns. We called what we were doing "Write a loop once." (See Listings 30-6 and 30-7.) These are the actual C++ modules from that program.

Listing 30-6

solspcft.h

```
/* $Header: /Space/src_repository/ets/grande/vgfeat/
solspcft.h,v 1.2 1994/04/11 17:02:02 rmartin Exp $ */

#ifndef FEATURES_SOLUTION_SPACE_FEATURE_H
#define FEATURES_SOLUTION_SPACE_FEATURE_H

#include "scoring/eval.h"

template <class T> class Query;

class SolutionSpace;
//-------------------------------------------
// Name
//   SolutionSpaceFeature
//
// Description
//   This class is a base class which provides a loop which
//   scans through the set of solution spaces and then
//   finds all the solution spaces that match it.  Pure virtual
//   functions are provided for when a solution space are found.
//
class SolutionSpaceFeature : public Evaluator
{
  public:
    SolutionSpaceFeature(Query<SolutionSpace*>&);
```

```
    virtual ~SolutionSpaceFeature();
    virtual Evaluator::Score DoEval();
    virtual void NewSolutionSpace(const SolutionSpace&) = 0;
    virtual Evaluator::Score GetScore() = 0;

  private:
    SolutionSpaceFeature(const SolutionSpaceFeature&);
    SolutionSpaceFeature& operator= (const SolutionSpaceFeature&);

    Query<SolutionSpace*>& itsSolutionSpaceQuery;
};
#endif
```

Listing 30-7

solspcft.cpp

```
/* $Header: /Space/src_repository/ets/grande/vgfeat/
solspcft.cpp,v 1.2 1994/04/1 1 17:02:00 rmartin Exp $ */

#include "componen/set.h"

#include "vgsolut/solspc.h"
#include "componen/query.h"
#include "vgsolut/scfilter.h"
#include "vgfeat/solspcft.h"

extern ScoringFilter* GscoreFilter;

SolutionSpaceFeature::SolutionSpaceFeature(Query<SolutionSpace*>& q)
: itsSolutionSpaceQuery(q) {}

SolutionSpaceFeature::~SolutionSpaceFeature() {}

Evaluator::Score SolutionSpaceFeature::DoEval()
{
  Set<SolutionSpace*>& theSet = GscoreFilter->GetSolutionSpaces();
  SelectiveIterator<SolutionSpace*>ai(theSet,itsSolutionSpaceQuery);

  for (; ai; ai++)
  {
    SolutionSpace& as = **ai;
    NewSolutionSpace(as);
  }
  return GetScore();
}
```

As you can see from the comment header, this code was written in 1994. So it'll look a bit strange to those of you who are used to STL. Still, if you ignore the cruft and the bizarre iterators, you'll see the classic TEMPLATE METHOD pattern in there. The DoEval function loops through all the SolutionSpace objects. It then calls the pure virtual NewSolutionSpace function. Derivatives of SolutionSpaceFeature implement NewSolution-Space and measure each space against a particular scoring criterion.

The derivatives of `SolutionSpaceFeature` included features that measured whether the appropriate spaces were placed into the solution, whether the spaces had the appropriate area and aspect ratio, whether elevators stacked properly, etc.

The neat thing about this is that the loop that traverses the data structure is located in one place. All the scoring features inherit it rather than reimplement it.

Some of the features had to measure characteristics of the portals attached to a space. So we reproduced the pattern and created the class `PortalFeature` derived from `SolutionSpaceFeature`. The implementation of `NewSolutionSpace` within `PortalFeature` looped through all the portals in the `SolutionSpace` argument and called the pure virtual function `NewPortal(const Portal&)`. (See Figure 30-5.)

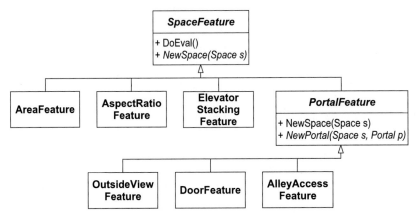

Figure 30-5   TEMPLATE METHOD structure of the scoring features

This structure allowed us to create dozens of different scoring features, each one of which walked the floor-plan data structure, without knowing what the floor-plan data structure looked like. If the details of the floor-plan data structure changed (e.g., we decided to use STL instead of our own iterators), we'd have to change two classes rather than several dozen.

Why did we choose TEMPLATE METHOD over STRATEGY?[5] Consider how much looser the coupling would have been had we used STRATEGY! (See Figure 30-6.)

Using the TEMPLATE METHOD structure, if we had to make a change to the algorithms that walked the data structure, we would have had to change `SpaceFeature` and `PortalFeature`. In all likelihood, this would have forced us to recompile *all* the features. However, using the STRATEGY pattern, the change would have been restricted to the two `Driver` classes. There is virtually no chance that the features would need to be recompiled.

So why did we choose the TEMPLATE METHOD? Because it was simpler. Because the data structure was not something that was going to change frequently. And because recompiling all the features cost just a few minutes.

So, even though the use of inheritance in the TEMPLATE METHOD pattern resulted in a more tightly coupled design, and even though the STRATEGY pattern conforms to the DIP better than the TEMPLATE METHOD pattern does, in the end *it wasn't worth the two extra classes* to implement the STRATEGY.

The Common Requirements of the Delivery Applications

The delivery programs had quite a bit of overlap. For example, the structure of the screen was the same in all vignettes. At the left of the screen was a window that contained nothing but a column of buttons. This window was called the "Command Window." The buttons in the Command Window acted as the controls for the application. They were labeled with terms such as, "Place Item," "Erase," "Move/Adjust," and "Zoom," and "Done." Clicking on these buttons drove the application through the desired behaviors.

---

5.   Clearly, we didn't think of it in those terms. The names of the patterns hadn't been invented at the time we made this decision.

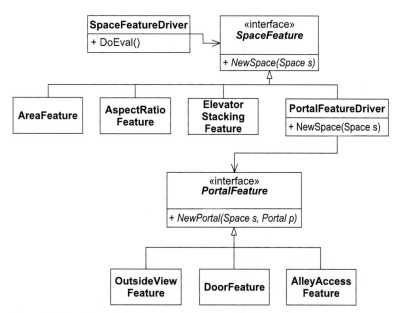

Figure 30-6   Floor-plan scoring structure with STRATEGY

To the right of the Command Window was the Task Window. This was a large scrollable and zoomable area into which the user could draw his solution. Commands initiated in the Command Window were typically used to modify the contents of the Task Window. Indeed, most of the commands that were initiated in the command window required significant interaction within the Task Window.

For example, in order to place a room on a floor plan, the user would click on the Place Item button in the Command Window. A menu of possible rooms would pop up. The user would select the kind of room he wished to place into the floor plan. Then the user would move the mouse into the Task Window and click at the location where he wanted the room to be placed. Depending upon the vignette, this might anchor the upper left corner of the room where the user clicked. The lower left corner of a stretchable room would then follow the motions of the mouse in the Task Window until the user clicked for the second time, anchoring the lower left corner at that position.

These actions were similar, though not identical, in each vignette. Some vignettes did not deal with rooms, but rather dealt with contour lines, property lines, or roofs. Though there were differences, the overall paradigm of operating within the vignettes was quite similar.

This similarity meant that we had a significant opportunity for reuse. We ought to be able to create an object-oriented framework that captured the bulk of the similarities and that allowed the differences to be expressed conveniently. In this we succeeded.

The Design of the Delivery Framework

The ETS framework finally grew to be nearly 75,000 lines of code. Clearly we cannot show all the details of that framework here. Thus, we have chosen two of the most illustrative elements of the framework to explore: the event model and the taskmaster architecture.

The Event Model.   Every action taken by the user caused events to be generated. If the user clicked upon a button, an event named after that button was generated. If the user selected a menu item, an event named for that menu item was generated. Marshalling those events was a significant problem for the framework.

The reason for the problem was the fact that a very large portion of all the events could be handled by the framework, and yet each individual vignette might need to override the way the framework handled a particular event. Thus, we needed to find a way to allow the vignettes the power to override the processing of events if needed.

The problem was complicated by the fact that the list of events was not closed. Each vignette could select its own particular set of buttons in the Command Window and its own particular set of menu items. Thus, the framework needed to marshal the events that were common to all vignettes, while allowing each vignette to override the default processing; and it needed to allow for the vignette to marshal its own vignette-specific events. This was not an easy task to accomplish.

As an example, consider Figure 30-7. This diagram[6] shows a small portion of the finite state machine that would be used to marshal the events that occurred in the Command Window of a vignette. Each vignette had its own special version of this finite state machine.

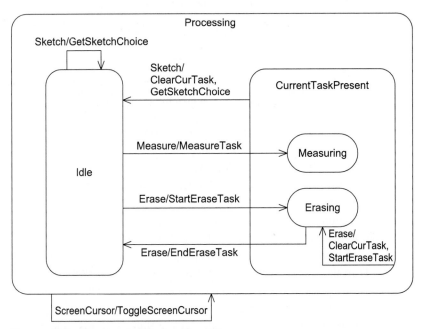

Figure 30-7   Command Window Event Processor

Figure 30-7 shows how three different kinds of events behaved. Let us first consider the simplest case, the ScreenCursor event. This event was generated when the user clicked on the Change Cursor button. Each time the user clicked this button, the cursor in the Task Window would toggle between an arrow and a full-screen cross hair. Thus, although the cursor changed state, no change of state occurred in the event processor.

When a user wants to delete an object he has drawn, he clicks on the Erase button. He then clicks on the item or items in the Task Window that he wants to delete. Finally, he clicks again on the Erase button to commit the deletion. The state machine in Figure 30-7 shows how the Command Window event processor deals with this. The first Erase event causes a transition from the Idle state to the Erasing state and starts up an Erase Task. We'll be talking more about Tasks in the next section. For now, it is sufficient that you know that the Erase Task will deal with any events that take place in the Task Window.

Notice that even in the Erasing state, the ScreenCursor event will still function properly and will not interfere with the erase operation. Notice also that there are two ways out of the Erasing state. If another Erase event occurs, then the Erase Task is ended, committing the erasure, and the state machine transitions back to the idle state. This is the normal way to end the erase operation.

6.   The notation for state diagrams like this is fully described in Appendix B on page 489.

The other way to end the erase operation is to click on some of the other buttons in the Command Window. If, while erasure is in progress, you click on a Command Window button that starts up a different task (e.g., the Sketch button) then the Erase Task is aborted, and the deletion is cancelled.

Figure 30-7 shows how this cancellation works with the Sketch event, but there are many other events not shown that work the same way. If the user hits the Sketch button, either when the system is in the Erasing or Idle state, the system will transition to the Idle state and the GetSketchChoices function will be called. This function puts up the sketch menu, which contains a list of operations that the user can perform. One of those operations is measure.

When the user selects the measure item from the sketch menu, the Measure event occurs. This starts up the Measure Task. When measuring, the user may click on two points in the Task Window. The two points will be marked with tiny little cross hairs, and the distance between them will be reported in a small message window at the bottom of the screen. The user may then click on two more points, and two more, and two more, etc. There is no normal exit from the Measure Task. Instead, the user must click on a button that could start up another task, like Erase or Sketch.

The Event Model Design.   Figure 30-8 shows the static model of the classes that implement the Command Window event processor. The hierarchy on the right represents the CommandWindow, while the hierarchy on the left represents the finite-state machine that translates events into actions.

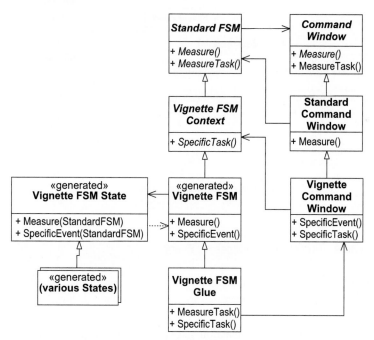

Figure 30-8   Command Window Event Processor Static Model

CommandWindow, StandardCommandWindow, and StandardFSM are framework classes. The rest are specific to the vignette. CommandWindow provides the implementations for standard actions, such as MeasureTask and EraseTask.

Events are received by the VignetteCommandWindow. They are passed to the finite-state machine, which translates them into actions. The actions are then passed back to the CommandWindow hierarchy, which implements them.

The CommandWindow class provides implementations for standard actions such as MeasureTask and EraseTask. A "standard action" is an action that is common to all vignettes. StandardCommandWindow provides for the marshalling of standard events to the finite-state machine. VignetteCommandWindow is specific to the vignette and provides for both the implementation of specific actions and the marshalling of specific events. It also allows the standard implementations and marshalling to be overridden.

Thus, the framework provides default implementations and marshalling for the all the common tasks. But any one of those implementations or marshallings can be overridden by the vignette.

Tracing a Standard Event.   Figure 30-9 shows how a standard event gets marshalled to the finite state machine and translated to a standard action. Message 1 is the Measure event. It comes from the GUI and is passed to the VignetteCommandWindow. The default marshalling for this event is provided by the StandardCommand-Window, so it forwards the event to the StandardFSM in message 1.1.

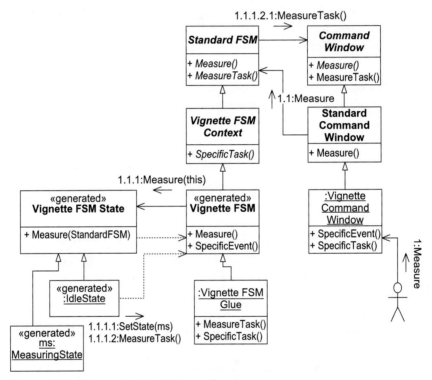

Figure 30-9   Processing the Measure Event

StandardFSM is a framework class that provides an interface for all the incoming standard events and all the outgoing standard actions. None of these functions are implemented at this level. VignetteFSMContext adds interfaces, but no implementations, for vignette-specific events and actions.

The real work of translating an event to an action takes place in the VignetteFSM and VignetteFSMState classes. VignetteFSM contains the implementations for all the event functions. So, the 1.1:Measure message gets deployed down to this level. VignetteFSM responds by sending 1.1.1:Measure(this) to the Vignette-FSMState object.

VignetteFSMState is an abstract class. There are derivatives of this class for each state of the finite-state machine. In Figure 30-9, we presume that the current state of the FSM is Idle. (See Figure 30-7.) Thus the 1.1.1:Measure(this) message gets deployed to the IdleState object. This object responds by sending two messages back to VignetteFSM. The first is 1.1.1.1:SetState(ms), which changes the state of the FSM to the Measuring state. The second message is 1.1.1.2:MeasureTask(), which is the action required by the Measure event in the Idle state.

The `MeasureTask` message is finally implemented in the `VignetteFSMGlue` class, which recognizes the action as a standard action declared in `CommandWindow`, and therefore routes it there in message `1.1.1.2.1:MeasureTask`, thus completing the circuit.

The mechanism employed for converting events to actions is the STATE pattern. We make prodigious use of this pattern in many areas of the framework, as the following sections will show. The «generated» stereotype that appears in the STATE pattern classes indicates that these classes are automatically generated by SMC.

Tracing a Vignette Specific Event.   Figure 30-10 shows what happens when a vignette-specific event occurs. Once again, message `1:SpecificEvent` is caught by the `VignetteCommandWindow`. However, since the marshalling for specific events are implemented at this level, it is the `VignetteCommandWindow` that sends message `1.1:SpecificEvent`. Moreover, it sends it to the `VignetteFSMContext` class where the `SpecificEvent` method was first declared.

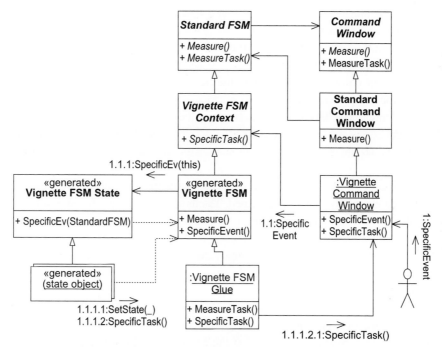

Figure 30-10   Processing a specific event

Once again, the event is deployed to `VignetteFSM`, which, in message `1.1.1:SpecificEv`, negotiates with the current state object to generate the corresponding action. As before, the state object replies with two messages, `1.1.1.1:SetState` and `1.1.1.2:SpecificTask`.

Again, the message is deployed down to `VignetteFSMGlue`. However, this time, it is recognized as a vignette specific action and is therefore routed directly to the `VignetteCommandWindow` where specific actions are implemented.

Generating and Reusing the Command Window State Machine.   At this point, you might be wondering why it requires so many classes to marshal the events and actions in this fashion. Consider, however, that, although there are many classes, there are very few objects. Indeed, the instantiated objects are simply `Vignette-CommandWindow`, `VignetteFSMGlue`, and the various state objects, which are trivial and automatically generated.

Though the flow of messages seems complex, it is really quite simple. The window detects an event, passes it to the FSM for translation to an action, and accepts the action back from the FSM. The rest of the complexity has to do with separating standard actions known to the framework from specific actions known to the vignette.

Another factor impinging on our decision to partition the classes as we did was our use of SMC to automatically generate the finite-state machine classes. Consider the following description, and refer back to Figure 30-7:

```
Idle
{
  Measure  Measuring  MeasureTask
  Erase    Erasing    StartEraseTask
  Sketch   Idle       GetSketchChoice
}
```

Notice that this simple text describes all of the transitions that occur while the state machine is in the `Idle` state. The three lines in the braces identify the event that triggers the transition, the target state of the transition, and the action performed by the transition.

SMC[7] accepts text in this form and generates the classes denoted with «generated». The code generated by SMC requires neither editing nor any inspection.

Using SMC to generate the state machine makes the creation of this part of the event processor for a vignette quite simple. The developer must write the `VignetteCommandWindow` with its corresponding implementations for specific events and actions. The developer must also write the `VignetteFSMContext`, which simply declares interfaces for the specific events and actions. And then the developer needs to write the `VignetteFSMGlue` class, which simply dispatches actions back to `VignetteCommandWindow`. None of these tasks are particularly challenging.

There is one other thing the developer must do. He must write the description of the finite-state machine for SMC. This state machine is actually rather complicated. The diagram in Figure 30-7 doesn't do it justice at all. A real vignette must deal with many dozens of different events, each of which can have remarkably different behaviors.

Fortunately, most of the vignettes behave in roughly the same way. So we were able to use a standard state-machine description as a model and make relatively minor modifications to it for each vignette. Thus, each vignette had its own FSM description.

This approach is somewhat unsatisfying since the FSM description files were very similar. Indeed, there were several occasions when we were forced to change the generic state machine, which meant that we had to make identical or nearly identical changes in each of the FSM description files. This is both tedious and error prone.

We might have invented yet another scheme for separating the generic portion of the FSM description from the specific portion, but in the end we didn't feel it was worth the effort. This is a decision we have chided ourselves for more than once.

The Taskmaster Architecture

We have seen how events get converted into actions and how that conversion is dependent on a relatively complex finite-state machine. Now we are going to look at how the actions themselves are processed. It should come as no surprise that the core of each action is also driven by a finite state machine.

Let's consider the `MeasureTask` that we discussed in the previous section. The user invokes this task when he wants to measure the distance between two points. Once invoked, the user clicks on a point in the `TaskWindow`. A small cross hair will appear at that point. As the user then moves the mouse around, a stretchable line is drawn

---

7.   SMC, the State Machine Compiler, is freeware available from `http://www.objectmentor.com`.

from the click point to the current mouse position. Moreover, the current length of that line is displayed in a separate message window. When the user clicks for the second time, another cross hair is drawn, the stretchable line disappears, and the final distance between the two points is displayed in the message box. If the user then clicks again, the process starts over.

Once the event processor has selected the `MeasureTask`, as shown in Figure 30-9, the `CommandWindow` creates the actual `MeasureTask` object, which then runs the finite-state machine shown in Figure 30-11.

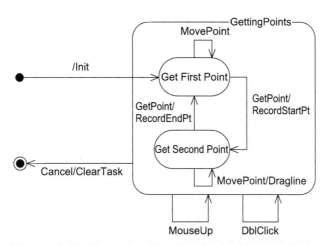

Figure 30-11 Finite-State Machine for the Measure Task.

The `MeasureTask` begins its life by invoking its `init` function and then occupying the `GetFirstPoint` state. GUI events that occur in the `TaskWindow` are routed to the task that is currently executing. Thus, when the user moves the mouse in the `TaskWindow`, the current task receives a `MovePoint` message. Notice that, in the `GetFirstPoint` state, this does nothing (as expected).

When the user finally clicks in the `TaskWindow`, a `GotPoint` event occurs. This causes a transition to the `GetSecondPoint` state and invokes the `RecordStartPt` action. This action will draw the first cross hair and will also remember the location that the mouse was clicked as the starting point.

In the `GetSecondPoint` state, a `MovePoint` event causes the `Dragline` action to be invoked. This action sets XOR mode[8] and draws a line from the remembered starting point to the current mouse location. It also computes the distance between these two points and displays it in the message window.

`MovePoint` events occur frequently whenever the mouse is being moved over the `TaskWindow`, so the motion of the line, and the length displayed in the message window, will appear to continuously update as long as the mouse is in motion.

When the user clicks for the second time, we transition back to the `GetFirstPoint` state and invoke the `RecordEndPt` action. This action turns off XOR mode, erases the line between the first point and the current mouse position, draws a cross hair at the click point, and displays the distance between the starting point and the click point in the message window.

This sequence of events repeats as long as the user desires. It only terminates when the task is cancelled by the `CommandWindow`, probably in response to the user clicking on a command button.

Figure 30-12 shows a somewhat more complex task—that of drawing a "two-point" box. A two-point box is a rectangle that is drawn on the screen with two clicks. The first click anchors one corner of the box. A stretchable box then follows the mouse. When the user clicks for the second time, the box is made permanent.

8.   XOR mode is a mode in which the GUI can be placed. It vastly simplifies the problem of dragging stretchable lines or shapes over existing shapes on the screen. If you don't understand this, don't worry about it.

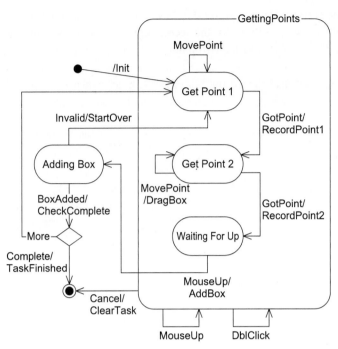

Figure 30-12   Two-Point Box

As before, the task begins in the GetPoint1 state, after invoking Init. In this state, the motion of the mouse is ignored. When the mouse is clicked, we transition to GetPoint2 and invoke the RecordPoint1 action. This action records the click point as the starting point.

In the GetPoint2 state, mouse motion causes the DragBox action to be invoked. This function sets XOR mode and draws the stretchable box from the starting point to the current mouse position.

When the mouse goes down for the second time, we transition to the WaitingForUp state and invoke RecordPoint2. This function simply records the final point for the box. It does not cancel XOR mode, erase the stretchable box, or draw the real box, because we aren't sure if the box is valid yet.

At this point, the mouse is still down, and the user is about to lift his finger off the mouse button. We need to wait for this to occur, otherwise some other task might get the mouse-up event and confuse things. While we are waiting, we ignore any motion of the mouse, leaving the box anchored at the last click point.

Once the mouse comes up, we transition to the AddingBox state and invoke the AddBox function. This function checks to see if the box is valid. There are many reasons why a box might be invalid. It might be degenerate (i.e., its first and final points are the same), or it might conflict with something else on the drawing. Each vignette has the right to reject something that the user has attempted to draw.

If the box is found to be invalid, an Invalid event is generated, and the state machine transitions back to GetPoint1 while invoking the StartOver function. If, however, the box was found to be valid, then the BoxAdded event is generated. This causes the CheckComplete function to be called. This is another vignette-specific function. It determines whether the user should be allowed to continue drawing more boxes or whether the task should be completed.

There are literally dozens of such tasks in the framework. Each is represented by a derivative of the Task class. (See Figure 30-13.) Each task has a finite-state machine within it, and they are substantially more complex than we have been able to show here. Again, each of those state machines was generated by SMC.

Figure 30-13 shows the Taskmaster architecture. This architecture connects the CommandWindow to the TaskWindow, and creates and manages the tasks that the user has selected.

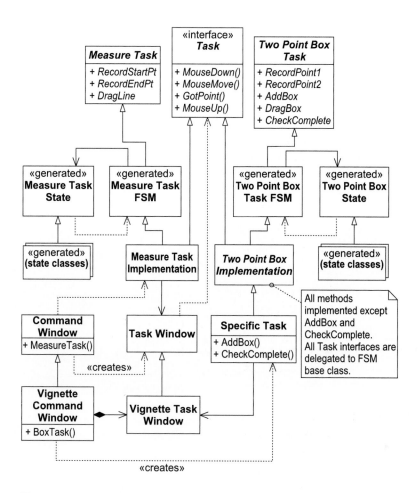

Figure 30-13 Taskmaster Architecture

The diagram shows the two tasks whose FSMs were depicted in Figures 30-11 and 30-12. Notice the use of the SMALL CAPS `STATE` pattern and the classes generated in each of the tasks. All of these classes, down to `Measure-TaskImplementation` and `TwoPointBoxImplementation` are part of the framework. Indeed, the only classes that the developer must write are `VignetteTaskWindow` and the specific derivatives of the task classes.

The classes `MeasureTaskImplementation` and `TwoPointBoxImplementation` represent the many different tasks that are contained in the framework. But note that these classes are abstract. There are a few functions, such as `AddBox` and `CheckComplete`, that are not implemented. Each vignette must implement these functions as needed for their own concerns.

Thus, the tasks contained by the framework govern the bulk of the interactions in all the vignettes. Whenever a developer needs to draw a box, or an object related to a box, that developer can derive a new task from `TwoPointBoxImplementation`. Or whenever he needs to simply place some object on the screen with a single click, he can override `SinglePointPlacementTask`. Or if he needs to draw something based upon a polyline, he can override `PolylineTask`. And these tasks manage the interactions, perform any needed dragging, and give the engineer the hooks needed to validate and create the objects he needs.

Conclusion

Of course there is much more that we could have talked about in this chapter. We could have discussed the elements of the framework that dealt with computational geometry or the bits that dealt with storing and reading the solutions to and from files. We could have discussed the structure of the parameter files that allowed each vignette application to drive many different variations of the same vignette. Unfortunately, neither space nor time permits.

However, we think we covered the aspects of the framework that were most instructional. The strategies we employed in this framework can be employed by others to make their own reusable frameworks.

Bibliography

1. Booch, Grady. *Object-Oriented Design with Applications*. Redwood City, CA: Benjamin Cummings, 1991.
2. Booch, Grady. *Object Solutions*. Menlo Park, CA: Addison–Wesley, 1996.
3. Gamma, et al. *Design Patterns*. Reading, MA: Addison–Wesley, 1995.

APPENDIX A

UML Notation I: The CGI Example

The analysis and design of software comprise a process that cries out for some kind of notation. There have been many attempts at creating such a notation. Flowcharts, data-flow diagrams, entity-relationship diagrams, etc.

The advent of object-oriented programming saw an explosion in notation. There were literally dozens of competing notations for the representation of object-oriented analyses and designs.

The most popular of these notations were the following:

- Booch 94.[1]
- OMT (Object Modeling Technique) as described by Rumbaugh, et al.[2]
- RDD (Responsibility Driven Design) as described by Wirfs-Brock, et al.[3]
- Coad/Yourdon as described by Peter Coad and Ed Yourdon[4]

Of these, Booch 94 and OMT were by far the most important. Booch 94 was hailed as a strong design notation, whereas OMT was considered to be stronger as an analysis notation.

This dichotomy is interesting. In the late 1980s and early 1990s, it was considered one of the advantages of object orientation that analysis and design could be represented by the same notation. Possibly, this was a reaction to the strong separation between the notations for structured analysis and structured design. Crossing the chasm from structured analysis to structured design was well known to be difficult.

When object-oriented notations first exploded upon the scene, it was felt that the same notation would serve both analysis and design. Yet as the decade progressed, analysts and designers began to migrate to their favorite notations. Analysts tended to favor OMT, and designers tended to favor Booch 94. Thus, it appeared that one notation would not really suffice. A notation tuned for analysis was not appropriate for design, and vice versa.

The UML is a single notation, but it has broad applicability. Parts of the notation are usable for analysis; other parts are usable for design. Thus, both analysts and designers can use the UML.

In this chapter, we will be presenting the UML notation from both views. First we will describe an analysis, and then we will go on to describe a design. This description will take place in the form of a miniature case study.

---

1. [BOOCH94].
2. [RUMBAUGH91].
3. [WIRFS90].
4. [COAD91A].

Please note that this ordering of analysis first, and then design, is artificial, and is not intended as a recommendation. Indeed, none of the other case studies in this book makes the distinction between the two. I have presented it this way here simply to illustrate how UML can be used at different levels of abstraction. In a real project all levels of abstraction are produced concurrently—not in sequence.

Course Enrollment System: Problem Description

Suppose that we are working for a company that offers professional training courses in object-oriented analysis and design. The company needs a system that keeps track of the courses being taught and the students that are enrolled. See the "Course Enrollment System" sidebar.

Course Enrollment System

Users must be able to view a menu of the available course offerings and select the course in which they wish to enroll. Once selected, a form should pop up that allows the user to enter the following information:

- Name
- Phone number
- Fax number
- e-mail address

There should be a way for the user to select the manner in which he wants to pay for the course. Those methods may be one of the following:

- Check
- Purchase order
- Credit card

If the user wishes to pay by check, then the form should prompt him for the check number.

If the user wishes to pay by credit card, then the form should prompt him for the credit card number, expiration date, and the name as it appears on the card.

If the user wishes to pay by purchase order, then the form should prompt him for the purchase order number (PO#), the name of the company, and the name and phone number of someone in the accounts payable department.

Once all this information has been filled out, the user will click on a 'submit' button. Another screen will pop up, which summarizes all the information that the user entered. It will instruct the user to print the screen, sign the printed copy, and fax it to the number of the enrollment center.

It should also e-mail an enrollment summary to our enrollments clerk and to the user.

The system will know the maximum number of students for each class, and will automatically mark the class offering as "Sold Out" once that limit has been hit.

The enrollments clerk will be able to e-mail messages to all students enrolled in a given course by bringing up a special form and selecting the course. This form will allow the clerk to type a message and then hit a button that will send it to all students currently enrolled in the selected course.

(continues on next page)

The enrollments clerk will also be able to bring up a form that shows the status of all students for classes that have already been taught. The status will indicate whether or not the student was in attendance and whether or not the student's payment has been received. This form can be brought up on a course-by-course basis. Or the enrollments clerk can ask to see a list of all students who have outstanding balances.

Identifying Actors and Use Cases.   One of the tasks of requirements analysis is to identify the actors and use cases. It should be noted that in a real system, these are not necessarily the first tasks that are appropriate. But for the purposes of this chapter, they are where I choose to begin. In reality, the place you begin is less important than the act of beginning.

Actors

Actors are entities that interact with the system, but are outside the system. Often they are roles played by the users of the system. Sometimes, however, they can be other systems. In this example, all the actors correspond to human users.

Enroller.   This actor enrolls a student in a course. It interacts with the system to select the appropriate course and enter the information about the student and the method of payment.

Enrollment Clerk.   This actor receives e-mail notification of each enrollment. It also sends e-mail notices to students and receives reports about enrollments and payments

Student.   This actor receives e-mail confirmation of enrollment and email notifications from the Enrollment Clerk. The Student attends the courses it is enrolled in.

Use Cases

Having determined the actors, we specify the interactions of these actors with the system. These specifications are called "use cases." A use case describes the interaction between an actor and the system from the actor's point of view. None of the inner workings of the system are discussed, nor is the user interface described in any detail.

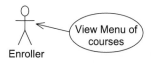

Use Case #1: View Menu of Courses.   The Enroller requests a list of courses that are currently available in the course catalog. The system displays the list of courses. Included in that list are the name, time, place, and cost of the course. The list will also show the number of students allowed in the course and whether or not the course is currently sold out.

Use Case Notation.   The above diagram shows an actor and a use case within a use-case diagram. The actor is the little stick figure, and the use-case is the ellipse. The two are bound together by an association that shows the direction of the data flow.

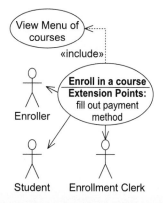

Use Case #2: Enroll in a course.   The Enroller first views the menu of courses (Use Case #1). The Enroller selects a course for enrollment from the menu. The system prompts the Enroller for the name, phone number, fax number, and email address of the student. The system also prompts the Enroller for the preferred payment method.

Extension point: fill out payment method
The Enroller submits the enrollment form. The Student and the Enrollment Clerk are sent email confirming the enrollment. The Enroller is shown a confirmation of the enrollment and is asked to print that confirmation, sign it, and fax it to a specific fax number.

Extending and Using Use Cases.   Use Case #2 has an extension point. This means that other use cases will be extending this use case. The extending use cases are presented below as #2.1, #2.2, and #2.3. Their descriptions are inserted into the previous use case at the extension point. They describe the optional data that need to be entered depending on the selected payment method.

Use Case #2 also has a «include» relationship with Use Case #1, "View Menu of Courses." This means that the description of Use Case #1 is inserted into the appropriate location of Use Case #2.

Note the difference between extending and including. When one use case includes another, the including use case references the included use case. However, when one use case extends another, neither use case refers to the other. Instead, an extending use case is selected based upon context and is inserted into the extended use case at the appropriate point.

We use the «include» relationship when we want to make the structure of the use cases more efficient by collapsing repeated operations into smaller use cases that can be shared among many other use cases. The goal is to manage change and eliminate redundancy. By moving the common parts of many use cases into a single included use case, when the requirements of that common part change, only the single included use case must change.

We use the «extend» relationship when we know that there are many alternatives or options within a use case. We separate the invariant part of the use case from the variable parts. The invariant part becomes the use case that is extended, and the variable parts become the extending use cases. The goal, once again, is change management. In the current example, if new payment options are added, new extending use cases will have to be created, but no existing use cases need to be modified.

Notation for the «include» Relationship.   The diagram for Use Case #2 shows that the "Enroll in a Course" use case is bound to the "View Menu of Courses" use case by a dashed line that terminates in an open arrowhead. The arrowhead points at the included use case and has the stereotype «include».

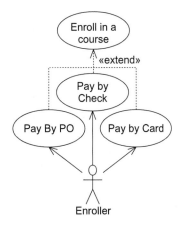

Use Case #2.1: Pay by Purchase Order.   The Enroller is prompted for the PO#, the name of the company, and the name and phone number of someone in the accounts-payable department.

Use Case #2.2: Pay by Check.   The Enroller is prompted for the check number.

Use Case #2.3: Pay by Card.   The Enroller is prompted for the credit card number, expiration date, and the name as it appears on the card.

Notation for Use-Case Extension.   The extending use cases shown above are connected to the extended use case through «extend» relationships. This relationship is drawn as a line that connects the two use cases. Once again, dashed, the line has an open arrowhead. The arrowhead points at the extended use case and has the stereotype «extend».

Use Case #3: Email Messages to Students.   The Enrollment Clerk selects a course and enters the text of a message. The system sends the message to the e-mail addresses of all the students currently enrolled in that class.

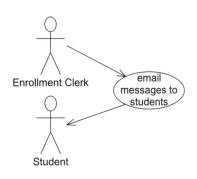

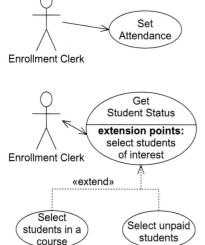

Use Case #4: Set Attendance. The Enrollment Clerk selects a class and a student that is currently enrolled in that class. The system presents the student and shows whether that student was in attendance and whether or not that student's payment has been received. The Enrollment Clerk may then change the attendance or payment status.

Use Case #5: Get Student Status. The Enrollment Clerk selects the students of interest.

Extension Point: 'select students of interest'
The system presents the attendance and payment status of the selected students in a single report.

Extensions There are two use cases that extend Get Student Status.

Use Case #5.1: Select Students in a Course. The system shows a list of all the courses. The Enrollment Clerk selects a course. The system selects all students in that course.

Use Case #5.2: Select Unpaid Students. The Enrollment Clerk indicates that the system should select all unpaid students. The system selects all students who have been marked in attendance and whose payment status indicates that payment has not been received.

Use-Case Reprise. The use cases we have created here describe how the users expect the system to behave. Notice that they do not talk about the details of the user interface. They don't mention icons, menu items, buttons, or scrolling lists. Indeed, even the original specification said more about the user interface than the use cases do. This is intentional. We want the use cases to be lightweight and easy to maintain. As written, these use cases are valid for an extremely large set of possible implementations.

System-Boundary Diagram. The entire set of use cases can be shown in summary by the system-boundary-diagram in Figure A-1. This diagram shows all the use cases in the system surrounded by a rectangle that represents the system boundary. The actors are set outside the system and are connected to the use cases with associations that show the direction that data flows.

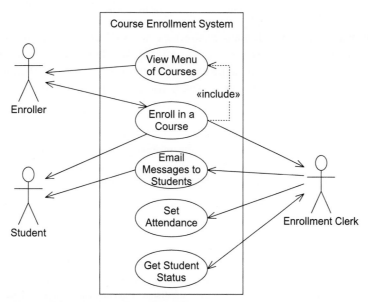

Figure A-1 System-Boundary Diagram

What Do We Use these Diagrams for?   Use-case diagrams, including system-boundary-diagrams, are not software-structure diagrams. They do not give us any information at all about the partitioning of the software elements of the system to be created. These diagrams are used for human communication, primarily between the analysts and the stakeholders. They help to organize the functionality of the system in terms of the different kinds of system users.

Moreover, these diagrams can be quite helpful when presenting the system description to the various kinds of users. Each different kind of user is interested chiefly in his own use cases. The connection of the actors to the use cases serves to focus each different kind of user on the use cases that he or she will be using. In very large systems, you may wish to organize the system boundary diagrams according to actor type so that all different user types can look at the subset of use cases that concerns them.

Finally, remember Martin's first law of documentation: *Produce no document unless its need is immediate and significant.*

These diagrams can be useful, but they are often unnecessary. You should not think of them as required or essential. If you have a need for them, then draw them. Otherwise, wait until you have a need.

The Domain Model

The domain model is a set of diagrams that helps to define the terms that appear in the use cases. These diagrams show the key objects within the problem and their interrelationships. Much pain and suffering have resulted from the tendency to assume that this model is also a model of the software to be built. It is important for both the analyst and the designer to realize that a domain model is a descriptive tool that is used to help humans record their decisions and communicate with each other. The objects in the domain model do not necessarily correspond to the object-oriented design of the software, nor would such a correspondence be a strong benefit.[5]

In Booch 94 and OMT, domain-model diagrams were indistinguishable from diagrams that represented software structure and design. In the worst cases, the domain model diagrams were taken to be high-level design documents and were therefore used to set the high-level structure of the software itself.

To help avoid this kind of mistake, we can take advantage of the features of UML and use a special kind of entity called a «type» in domain models. A «type» represents a role that an object can play. A «type» can have operations and attributes as well as associations with other «type» entities. However, a «type» does not represent a class or object in the design sense. It does not represent an element of software, and it does not map directly to code. It represents a conceptual entity used in the description of the problem.

The Course Catalog.   The first domain abstraction we will consider is the course catalog. This abstraction represents the list of all the courses that are offered. We show this in the domain model (see Figure A-2) for the `Course Catalog` entity by depicting two entities that represent abstractions in the domain: the `CourseCatalog` entity and the `Course` entity. The `CourseCatalog` entity offers many `Course` entities.

Domain-Model Notation.   The notation used in Figure A-2   depicts the two domain abstractions as UML classes with the «type» stereotype. (See sidebar, "Overview of UML Class Notation and Semantics.") This indicates that the classes are conceptual elements of the problem domain and not directly related to software

---

5.   [JACOBSON], p. 133, "We do not believe that the best (most stable) systems are built by *only* using objects that correspond to real-life entities..."

And also on p. 167, "In [other] methods, this [domain] model will also form a base for the actual implementation; that is, the objects are directly mapped onto classes during implementation. However, this is not the case in OOSE, [...]. Our experience with such an approach tells us differently. Instead we develop an analysis model that is more robust and maintainable in the face of future changes rather than using a problem domain model to serve as the base for design and implementation.

[BOOCH96], p. 108, "...there is a tendency in immature projects to consider the domain model resulting from analysis as ready to code [...], thus skipping any further design. Healthy projects recognize that there is still quite some work to do, involving issues such as concurrency, serialization, safety, distributions, and so on, and that the design model may end up looking quite different in a number of subtle ways.

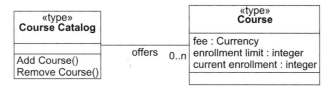

Figure A-2 Domain model for the `Course Catalog` entity

classes. Notice that the `CourseCatalog` entity has two operations: `AddCourse` and `RemoveCourse`. In a «type», operations correspond to *responsibilities*. Thus, the `CourseCatalog` has the responsibility to be able to add and remove courses. Again, these are concepts, not the specifications of member functions within real classes. We use them to communicate with users, not to specify a software structure.

By the same token, the attributes shown in the `Course` entity are concepts. They indicate that the `Course` entity should be responsible to remember its fee, enrollment limit, and current enrollment.

Overview of UML Class Notation and Semantics

In UML, a class is drawn as a rectangle with three compartments. The first compartment specifies the name of the class. The second specifies its attributes and the third its operations.

Within the name compartment, the name can be modified by a stereotype and by properties. The stereotype appears above the name and is enclosed within guillemets (French quotation marks «»). Properties appear below and to the right of the name and are enclosed within braces. (See the following diagram.)

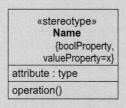

Stereotypes are names that refer to the "kind" of UML class being represented. In UML, a class is simply a named entity that can have attributes and operations. The default stereotype is «implementation class» in which case the UML class corresponds directly to the software notion of a class in a language like C++, Java, Smalltalk, or Eifel. The attributes correspond to member variables, and the operations correspond to member functions.

However, with the stereotype of «type», a UML class does not correspond to a software entity at all. Rather it corresponds to a conceptual entity that exists in the problem domain. The attributes represent the information that logically belongs to that conceptual entity, and the operations represent the responsibilities of that conceptual entity.

There are several other predefined stereotypes that we will be discussing later in this chapter. You are free to create your own stereotypes, too. However, a stereotype is more than just a comment. It specifies the way that all elements of a UML class should be interpreted. So if you make a new stereotype, define it well.

(continues on next page)

Properties are primarily structured comments. Properties are specified in a comma-separated list between braces. Each property is a name = value pair separated by an equal sign (=). If the equal sign is omitted, then the property is assumed boolean and given the value of "true." Otherwise the type of the value is a string.

There are several predefined properties that we will be discussing later in this chapter. However, you are free to add your own at any time. For example, you might create properties like this: {author=Robert C. Martin, date=12/6/97, SPR=4033}

Concept vs. Implementation and the Use of Cloud Icons. I have been placing a lot of stress upon the difference between a class at the conceptual level (i.e., a «type») and a class at the design or implementation level. I feel that this is appropriate because of the danger that conceptual diagrams might be mistaken as specifications for the structure and architecture of the software. Remember, conceptual diagrams are to help communications with the *stakeholders* and are therefore devoid of all the technical issues of software structure.

The use of stereotypes to distinguish between these kinds of diagrams could be overlooked. UML classes for domain models look very much like UML classes for design and implementation. Fortunately, UML allows us to substitute different icons for different stereotypes. Therefore, to further enhance the difference between these kinds of diagrams, we will use a cloud icon to represent «type» classes from now on. This changes the domain model for the Course Catalog entity in Figure A-2 to look like Figure A-3.

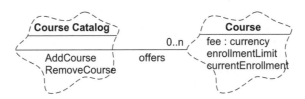

Figure A-3   Domain Model for Course Catalog using Cloud Icons

Completing the Domain Model. So far, the domain model shows a course catalog that contains all the offered courses. But there is a problem here. What do we mean by a course? The same course can be offered at many different times and locations, and it can be taught by many different instructors. Clearly we need two different entities. Let's call the first a Course. It represents the course itself, but not the dates, locations, or instructors. Let's call the second a Session. It represents the date, location, or instructor for a specific course. (See Figure A-4.)

Notation. The lines that connect the entities are called associations. All the associations in Figure A-4 are named, although this is not a rule. Notice that the names are verbs or verb phrases. The little black triangle next to the name points at the predicate of the sentence formed by the two entities and the association. Thus, "Course Catalog offers many Courses," "Session Schedule schedules many Sessions," and "Many students are enrolled in a Session."

I used the word "many" in the previous sentences wherever the "0..*" icon was present on the corresponding relationship. This icon is one of several different *multiplicity* icons that can be placed on the end of an association. They indicate the number of entities that participate in the association. The default multiplicity is "1." (See the sidebar entitled: "Multiplicities.")

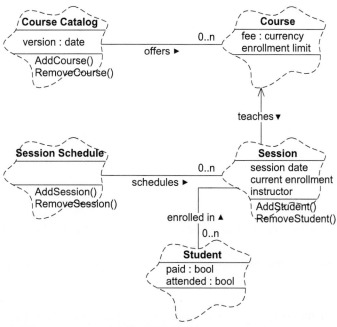

Figure A-4   Courses and Sessions

Multiplicities

There are several multiplicity icons that can be used to adorn associations. They include the following:

- `0..*`   zero to many
- `*`   zero to many
- `1..*`   one to many
- `0..1`   zero or one
- `6`   exactly six
- `3..6`   between three and six
- `3,5`   three or five

Any nonnegative integers can be used between dots or separated by commas.

Associations are assumed to be bidirectional unless there is an arrowhead present. A bidirectional association allows the two entities to know about each other. For example, it is clear that the `CourseCatalog` entity ought to know about its `Courses`, and it seems reasonable that each `Course` entity could know about the `CourseCatalog` it is listed in. The same is true for the `SessionSchedule` and the `Session`.

The presence of an arrowhead restricts the knowledge to the direction indicated. Thus, `Sessions` know about `Courses`, but `Courses` do not know anything about `Sessions`.

Use Case Iterations.   This diagram immediately tells us two things. First, the use cases employ the wrong language in a number of places. Where they talk about course catalogs and courses, they should be talking about session schedules and sessions. Secondly, there are quite a few use cases that were left out. The `CourseCatalog` and the `SessionSchedule` need to be maintained. `Courses` need to be added and removed from the `CourseCatalog`, and `Sessions` need to be added and removed from the `SessionSchedule`.

Thus, by creating a domain model, we better understand the problem at hand. That better understanding helps us to improve and augment the use cases. This iteration between the two is natural and necessary.

If we were pursuing this case study to its conclusion, we would show the changes implied above. But in the interest of efficiently presenting the notation, we will skip the iteration of the use cases.

The Architecture

Now we get down to the business of designing software. The architecture represents the software structures that form the skeleton of the application. The classes and relationships of the architecture map very closely to code.

Deciding the Software Platform.   Before we can begin, however, we must understand the software platform in which this application is going to run. We have a number of choices.

1. A Web-based CGI application. The enrollment and other forms would be accessed by a Web browser. The data would reside at the Web server, and CGI scripts would be invoked by the Web browser to access and manipulate the data.
2. A database application. We could purchase a relational database and use the forms package and 4GL to write the application.
3. Visual XXX. We could purchase a visual programming language. The human interface could be created using the visual construction tools. These tools would invoke the software functions needed to store, retrieve, and manipulate the data.

There are, of course, other options. We could write the whole thing in C without any library or tool support other than the compiler. But this would be silly. The tools are there, and they work. We should use them.

For the purposes of our example, we will assume a Web-based application. This makes sense since then enrollers can be located anywhere in the world; and the enrollment service can be offered on the Internet.

Web Architecture.   We need to decide the overall architecture of the Web applications. How many Web pages will there be, and what CGI programs will they invoke? Figure A-5 shows how we might begin to specify this.

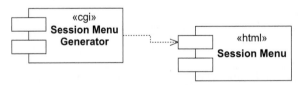

Figure A-5   Session Menu Architecture

Notation.   Figure A-5 is a component diagram. The icons depict physical software components. We have used the stereotype to specify the kind of components. The diagram shows that the Session Menu is displayed as an HTML Web page that is generated by a CGI program called the Session Menu Generator. The dashed arrow between the two components is a dependency relationship. Dependency relationships denote which components have knowledge of other components. In this case, the Session Menu Generator program creates the Session Menu Web page, and therefore has knowledge of it. The Session Menu Web page, on the other hand, has no knowledge of the generator itself.

Custom Icons.   There are two different kinds of components in Figure A-5. To make them visually distinct, we extend UML with two new icons—one for CGI programs and one for HTML pages. Figure A-6 shows the components involved in Use Case #2: Enroll in a course. Web pages are drawn as pages with a 'W' in them. CGI programs are drawn as Circles with "CGI" in them.

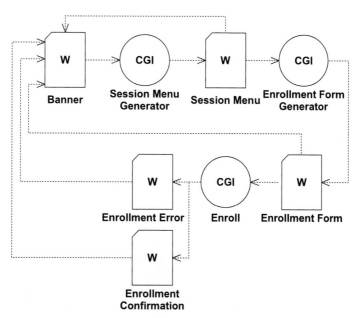

Figure A-6   Enrollment Components

Component Flow.   Figure A-6 introduces two new Web pages and one new CGI program. We have decided that the application should begin with a banner page of some kind. Presumably, this page will have links for the various kinds of operations that users can perform. The Session Menu Generator is invoked by the banner page and generates the Session Menu page. Presumably the Session Menu page has links or buttons that allow the user to enroll in a course. The Session Menu invokes the Enrollment Form Generator CGI to create the form necessary for enrolling in the selected course. Once the user fills out this form, the Enroll CGI is invoked. This program validates and records the information on the form. If the form data are invalid, it generates the Enrollment Error page; otherwise it generates the confirmation page and sends the necessary e-mail messages. (Refer back to Use Case #2.)

Enhancing Flexibility.   The astute reader will have recognized that there is a rather nasty inflexibility built into this component model. The CGI programs generate most of the Web pages. This means that the HTML text within the Web pages must be contained within the CGI programs. This makes modifying the Web pages a matter of modifying and rebuilding the CGI programs. We would rather the bulk of the generated Web pages were created with a nice HTML editor.

Thus, the CGI programs should read in a template of the Web pages that they are going to generate. The template should be marked with special flags, which will be replaced with the HTML that the CGI programs must generate. This means that the CGI programs share something in common. They all read template HTML files and add their own bits of HTML to them.[6]

Figure A-7 shows the resultant component diagram. Notice that I have added a WT icon. This represents an HTML template. It is a text file in HTML format with the special marks that the CGI programs use as insert points for the HTML that they generate. Notice also the direction of the dependency relationships between the CGI programs and the HTML templates. They might appear backwards to you. But remember they are *dependency* relationships, not data flows. The CGI programs know about (depend on) the HTML templates.

---

6.   This chapter was written long before XSLT came on the scene. Nowadays, we'd likely solve the problem by having the CGI scripts (or servlets) generate XML and then invoke an XSLT script to translate that into HTML. On the other hand, generating HTML with XSLT still doesn't give us the ability to design our Web pages with a nice WYSIWYG editor. Sometimes I think the template scheme outlined in this chapter would be better in many instances.

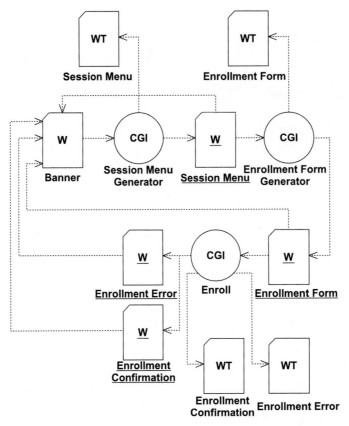

Figure A-7   Adding HTML templates to the Enrollment Component Diagram

The Specification/Instance Dichotomy.   In Figure A-7, the names of the generated Web pages are underlined. This is because these pages only exist at run time. They are instances of the HTML templates. In UML, the convention is that we underline instances. An instance is a software element that is generated from a specification (source document) of some kind. We'll have more to say about this later. For now, simply realize that the elements whose names are not underlined represent elements that must be written by hand and that act as specifications. Elements whose names are underlined are the product of some process that generates them from those specifications.

Using the HTML Templates.   The HTML templates provide a great deal of flexibility to the architecture of this application. How do they work? How do the CGI programs place their generated output in the proper places within the HTML Templates?

We might consider placing a special HTML tag in the HTML template files. Such a tag would mark the position in the generated HTML file where the CGI program would insert its output. However, these generated Web pages may have several sections, each of which might require its own insertion point into which the CGI can insert HTML. Thus, each HTML template could have more than one insertion tag, and the CGI will have to be able to somehow specify which output goes with which tag.

The tag could look like this: `<insert name>` where "name" is an arbitrary string that identifies the insertion point to the CGI. A tag such as `<insert header>` will allow a CGI to specify the name 'header' and then completely replace the tag with generated output.

Clearly each tag is replaced with a string of characters, so each tag represents a kind of named stream of characters. We can imagine the kind of C++ code that might exist in the CGI as follows:

```
HTMLTemplate myPage("mypage.htmp");
myPage.insert("header",
              "<h1> this is a header </h1>\n");
cout << myPage.Generate();
```

This would send HTML to `cout` that was generated from the template `mypage.html` in which the tag `<insert header>` was replaced with the string "`<h1> this is a header </h1>\n`".

Figure A-8 shows how we might design the `HTMLTemplate` class. This class holds the name of the template file as an attribute. It also has methods that allow replacement strings to be inserted for specifically named insertion points. Instances of `HTMLTemplate` will contain a `map` that relates the insertion point name to the replacement string.

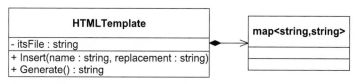

Figure A-8   `HTMLTemplate` design

Notation.   This is our first true class diagram. It shows us two classes related with a *composition* relationship. The icon used for the `HTMLTemplate` class and the `map<string,string>` class is not new to us. It was explained in the sidebar named "Overview of UML Class Notation and Semantics" on page 473. The syntax of the attributes and operations is described below in the sidebar entitled, "Attributes and Operations."

Attributes and Operations

Attributes and operations can be adorned with the following encapsulation specifiers:

+   Public

-        Private

Protected

The type of an attribute can be specified as an identifier that follows the attribute and is separated from it with a colon (e.g., `count : int`).

Similarly, the types of the arguments of a function are specified using the same colon notation (e.g., `SetName (name : string)`).

Finally, the return type of an operation can be specified with an identifier that follows the name and argument list of the operation and is separated from it by a colon (e.g., `Distance(from : Point) : float`).

The arrowhead on the association that connects the two classes in Figure A-8 indicates that `HTMLTemplate` knows about `map<string,string>`, but that the map does not know about the `HTMLTemplate`. The black diamond on the end of the association nearest the `HTMLTemplate` class identifies this as a special case of association called composition. (See the sidebar entitled, "Association, Aggregation, and Composition.") It indicates that `HTMLTemplate` is responsible for the lifetime of the `map` class.

Association, Aggregation, and Composition

An association is a relationship between two classes that allows instances created from those classes to send messages to each other. (i.e., links may exist between objects whose classes are associated). It is denoted by a line that connects the two classes. Associations are most often implemented as instance variables in one class that point or refer to the other.

Association

The navigability of an association can be restricted by adding arrowheads to the associations. When an arrowhead is present, the association can only be navigated in the direction of the arrow. This means that the class to which the arrow points does not know about its associate.

Navigable Association

Aggregation is a special form of association. It is denoted with a white diamond on the aggregate class. Aggregation implies a "whole/part" relationship. The class adjacent to the white diamond is the "whole," and the other class is its "part." The "whole/part" relationship is purely connotative; there is no semantic difference from association[a].

Aggregation

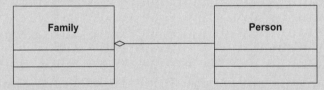

Composition is a special form of aggregation. It is denoted with a black diamond. It implies that the "whole" is responsible for the lifetime of its "part." This responsibility does not imply either creation or deletion responsibility. Rather, it implies that the "whole" must see to it that the "part" is somehow deleted. That can be accomplished by directly deleting the "part," or by passing the "part" to another entity that assumes responsibility for it.

Composition

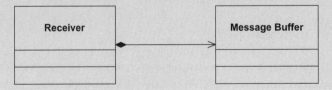

a.   With one exception. Reflexive or cyclic aggregation relationships between *objects* is not allowed. That is, instances cannot participate in a cycle of aggregations. If this rule were not in place, all instances in the cycle would be part of themselves. That is, a part could contain its whole.

Note that this rule does not prevent *classes* from participating in a cycle of aggregations; it simply restricts their instances.

The Database Interface Layer. Each CGI programs must also have access to the data that represent the courses, classes, students, etc. We shall call this the training database. The form of this database is, as yet, undecided. It could be held in a relational database or in a set of flat files. We do not want the architecture of our application to depend on the form in which the data are stored. We would like the bulk of each application to remain unchanged when the form of the database changes. Thus, we will shield the application from the database by interposing a database interface layer (DIL).

In order to be effective, a DIL must have the special dependency characteristics shown in Figure A-9. The DIL depends on the application, and the DIL depends on the database. Neither the application nor the database has any knowledge of each other. This allows us to change the database without necessarily changing the application. It also allows us to change the application without changing the database. We can completely replace the database format or engine without affecting the application.

Figure A-9 Database Interface Layer Dependency Characteristics

Notation. Figure A-9 shows a special kind of class diagram called a "package diagram." The icons denote packages. Their shape is reminiscent of a file folder. Like a file folder, a package is a container. (See the "Packages and Subsystems" sidebar.) The packages in Figure A-9 contain software components such as classes, HTML files, CGI main program files, etc. The dashed arrow that connects the packages represents a *dependency* relationship. The arrowhead points at the target of the dependency. A dependency between packages implies that the dependent package cannot be used without the package on which it depends.

Packages and Subsystems

Packages are drawn as a large rectangle with a smaller rectangular "tab" on the upper left of the large rectangle. Normally, the name of the package is placed in the large rectangle.

Packages can also be drawn with the package name in the "tab" and the contents of the package in the large rectangle. The contents may be classes, files, or other packages. Each can be prefixed with the (-, +, #) encapsulation icons to denote that they are private, public, or protected within the package.

Packages may be connected by one of two different relationships. The dashed dependency arrow is called an *import dependency*. It is a dependency relationship with a stereotype of «import». This

(continues on next page)

stereotype is the default when a dependency is used with a package. The base of the arrow is attached to the importing package, and the arrowhead touches the imported package. An import dependency implies that the importing package has visibility to any of the public elements of the imported package. This means that the elements of the importing package can use any public element of the imported package.

Packages can also be connected with Generalization relationships. The open triangular arrowhead touches the general or abstract package, and the other end of the relationship touches the implementing package. The implementing package has visibility to any public or protected element of the abstract package.

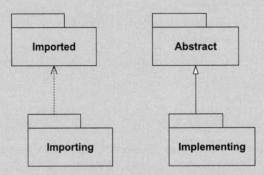

There are several defined stereotypes of package. The default is «package», which denotes a container without any special constraints. It can hold anything that can be modeled in UML. Typically, it is used to denote a physical, *releaseable*, unit. Such a package would be tracked in a configuration management and version control system. It might be represented by subdirectories in a file system or by the module system of a language (e.g., Java packages or JAR files). Packages represent a partitioning of the system that enhances its developability and releasability.

The «subsystem» stereotype for packages denotes a logical element that, in addition to containing model elements, also specifies their behavior. A subsystem can be given operations. Those operations must be supported by use cases or collaborations within the package. Subsystems represent a *behavioral* partitioning of a system or application.

These two kinds of packages are orthogonal to each other. The partitioning that enhances developability and releasability is almost never similar to a partitioning that is based upon behavior. The former is often used by software engineers as the unit of configuration management and version control. The latter is used more often by analysts in order to describe the system in an intuitive fashion and to perform impact analyses when features change or are added.

Database Interface.   The classes within the Training Application package need some way to access the database. This will be accomplished through a set of *interfaces* inside the Training Application package. (See Figure A-10.) These interfaces represent the types in the domain model of Figure A-4 on page 475. The interfaces are implemented by classes in the DIL package. They will be used by the other classes within the Training Application package to access the data in the database. Notice that the direction of the dependencies in Figure A-10 corresponds to the direction of the import relationships between the packages in Figure A-9.

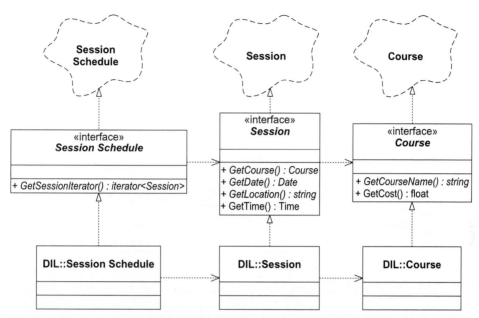

Figure A-10 Database interface classes in the Training Application package

Notation. When the name of a class is written in italics, it indicates that the class is abstract.[7] Since interfaces are completely abstract classes, it is appropriate to italicize their names. The operations are also shown in italics to denote that they are abstract. The classes in the DIL are bound to the interfaces through *realizes* relationships, which are drawn as dashed lines with open triangular arrowheads pointing at the interfaces. In Java, these would represent "`implements`" relationships. In C++, they would represent inheritance.

Interfaces are physical structures. In languages like C++ and Java, they have source code counterparts. Types, on the other hand, are not physical and do not represent something that has a source-code equivalent. In Figure A-10, we have drawn realizes relationships from the interfaces to the types that they represent. This does not represent a physical relationship, nor is there any corresponding source code. In this case, the realizes relationship is showing the correspondence between the physical design entities and the domain model. This correspondence is seldom as clear-cut as depicted here.

The *imports* relationships between the packages in Figure A-9 are shown in Figure A-10 through the use of the double colon. The DIL::Session class is a class named Session that exists in the DIL package and is visible to (has been imported into) the TrainingApplication package. The fact that there are two classes named Session is acceptable since they are in different packages.

The Session Menu Generator. Referring back to Figure A-7, we see that the first CGI program is the SessionMenuGenerator. This program corresponds to the very first use case back on page 469. What does the design of this CGI program look like?

Clearly it must build an HTML representation of the session schedule. Thus, we will need an HTMLTemplate that merges the boiler plate of the session menu with the actual data from the session schedule. Also, the program will use the SessionSchedule interface to access the Session and Course instances in the database in order to get their names, times, locations, and fees. Figure A-11 shows a sequence diagram that describes the process.

---

7. An abstract class has at least one pure (or abstract) method.

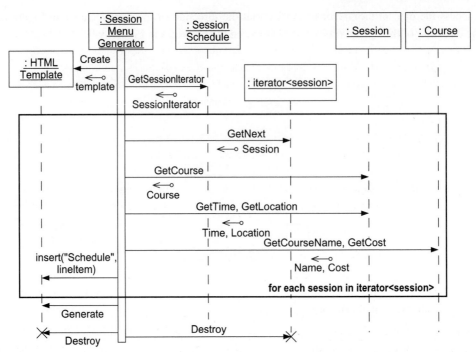

Figure A-11   `SessionMenuGenerator` Sequence Diagram

The `SessionMenuGenerator` object is created by `main` and controls the entire application. It creates an `HTMLTemplate` object passing it the name of the template file. It then fetches an `iterator<Session>`[8] object from the `SessionSchedule` interface. It loops through every `Session` in the `iterator<Session>` asking each `Session` for its `Course`. It fetches the time and location of the course from the `Session` object, and the name and cost of the course from the `Course` object. The last action in the loop is to create a line item from all that information and `Insert` it into the `HTMLTemplate` object at the `Schedule` insertion point. When the loop is completed, the `SessionMenuGenerator` invokes the `Generate` method of the `HTMLTemplate` and then destroys it.

Notation.   The names within the rectangles on the sequence diagram in Figure A-11 are underlined. This indicates that they represent objects rather than classes. Object names are composed of two elements separated by a colon. Prior to the colon is the *simple name* of the object. Following the colon is the name of a class or interface that the object implements. In Figure A-11, the simple names are all omitted, so all the names begin with a colon.

The dashed lines hanging down from the objects are called *lifelines*, and they represent the lifetime of the objects. All the objects in Figure A-11, except `HTMLTemplate` and `iterator<Session>`, show lifelines that start at the top and end at the bottom. By convention, this means that those objects were in existence before the scenario began and remain in existence when the scenario ends. `HTMLTemplate`, on the other hand, is explicitly created and destroyed by `SessionMenuGenerator`. This is evident by the arrow that terminates on `HTMLTemplate`, thus creating it, and the "X" that terminates its lifeline at the bottom. `SessionMenuGenerator` also destroys `Iterator<Session>`; however, it is not clear what object creates it. The creator is probably a derivative of `SessionSchedule`. Thus, while Figure A-11 does not explicitly show the creation of the `Iterator<Session>` object, the position of the start of the object's lifeline implies that it is created at about the time that the `GetSessionIterator` message is sent to the `SessionSchedule` object.

The arrows that connect the lifelines are messages. Time proceeds from top to bottom, so this diagram shows the sequence of messages that are passed between the objects. The messages are named by labels close to the

---

8.   This chapter was written before STL was commonplace. At the time I was using my own container library, which had templated iterators.

arrows. The short arrows with circles on the end are called *data tokens*. They represent data elements that are passed in the context of the message. If they point in the direction of the message, they are parameters of the message. If they point against the direction of the message, they are values returned by the message.

The long, skinny rectangle on the `SessionMenuGenerator` lifeline is called an *activation*. An activation represents the duration of the execution of a method or function. In this case, the message that started the method is not shown. The other lifelines in Figure A-11 do not have activations because the methods are all very short and do not emit other messages.

The bold rectangular box that surrounds some messages in Figure A-11 defines a loop. The completion criterion of the loop is mentioned at the bottom of the box. In this case, the enclosed messages will repeat until all the `Session` objects within `iterator<Session>` have been examined.

Note that two of the message arrows have been overloaded with more than one message. This is just a shorthand to minimize the number of arrows. The messages are sent in the order mentioned, and the return values come back in the same order.

Abstract Classes and Interfaces in Sequence Diagrams

The astute reader will notice that some of the objects in Figure A-11 are instantiated from interfaces. `SessionSchedule`, for example, is one of the database interfaces classes. This may seem to be violating the principle that objects cannot be instantiated from abstract classes or interfaces.

The class name of an object in a sequence diagram does not need to be the name of the actual type of the object. It is sufficient that the object simply conform to the interface of the named class. In a static language like C++, Java, or Eifel, the object should belong either to the class named in the sequence diagram or to a class that derives from the class or interface in the sequence diagram. In dynamic languages like Smalltalk or Objective-C, it is sufficient that the object conform to the interface named in the sequence diagram.[9]

Thus, the `SessionSchedule` object in Figure A-11 refers to an object whose class implements or derives from the `SessionSchedule` interface.

Static Model of the Session Menu Generator.   The dynamic model shown in Figure A-11 implies the static model shown in Figure A-12. Note that the relationships are all either dependencies or stereotyped associations. This is because none of the classes shown in the figure hold instance variables that refer to the others. All the relationships are transient in that they do not outlast the execution of the activation rectangle on the `SessionMenuGenerator` lifeline of Figure A-11.

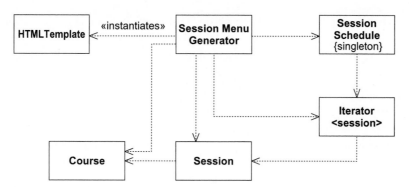

Figure A-12   Static Model of the Session Menu Generator application

9.   If you don't understand this, don't worry about it. In dynamic languages like Smalltalk and Objective-C, you can send any message you like to any object you like. The compiler does not check to see whether the object can accept that message. If, at run time, a message is sent to an object that does not recognize it, a run-time error will occur. Thus, it is possible for two completely different and unrelated objects to accept the same messages. Such objects are said to conform to the same interface.

The relationship between `SessionMenuGenerator` and `SessionSchedule` deserves special mention. Notice that `SessionSchedule` is shown with the `{singleton}` property. This denotes that only one `SessionSchedule` object can exist within the application and that it is accessible at the global scope. (See SINGLETON on page 178.)

The dependency between `SessionMenuGenerator` and `HTMLTemplate` carries the stereotype «creates». This simply indicates that the `SessionMenuGenerator` instantiates `HTMLTemplate` instances.

The associations with «parameter» stereotypes show that the objects find out about each other through method arguments or return values.

How Does the `SessionMenuGenerator` Object Get Control?   The activation rectangle on `Session-MenuGenerator`'s lifeline in Figure A-11 does not show how it was started. Presumably, some higher level entity, like `main()`, called a method on `SessionMenuGenerator`. We might call this method `Run()`. This is interesting because we have several other CGI programs to write, and they will all need to be started by `main()` somehow. Perhaps there is a base class or interface called `CGIProgram` that defines the `Run()` method, and perhaps `SessionMenuGenerator` derives from it.

Getting the User's Input into the CGI Program.   The `CGIProgram` class will help us with another issue. CGI programs are typically invoked by a browser after the user has filled out a form on the browser screen. The data entered by the user are then passed to the `main()` function of the CGI program through standard input. Thus, `main()` could pass a reference to the standard input stream to the `CGIProgram` object, which would in turn make the data conveniently available to its derivatives.

What is the form of the data passed from the browser to the CGI program? It is a set of name-value pairs. Each field in the form that was filled out by the user is given a name. Conceptually, we would like the derivatives of `CGIProgram` to be able to ask for the value of a particular field by simply using its name. For example,

```
string course = GetValue("course");
```

Thus, `main()` creates the `CGIProgram` and primes it with the needed data by passing the standard input stream into its constructor. The `main()` function then calls `Run()` on the `CGIProgram`, allowing it to begin. The `CGIProgram` derivative calls `GetValue(string)` to access the data in the form.

But this leaves us with a dilemma. We'd like to make the `main()` function generic, yet it must create the appropriate derivative of `CGIProgram` and there are many such derivatives. How can we avoid having multiple `main()` functions?

We can solve this by using link-time polymorphism. That is, we implement `main()` in the implementation file of the `CGIProgram` class (i.e., `cgiProgram.cc`). In the body of `main()`, we declare a global function named `CreateCGI`. However, we do not implement the function. Rather, we will implement this function in the implementation file of the derivative of `CGIProgram` (e.g., `sessionMenuGenerator.cc`). (See Figure A-13.)

Authors of CGI programs no longer need to write a `main()` program. Rather, in each derivative of `CGIProgram`, they must supply the implementation for the global function `CreateCGI`. This function returns the derivative back to `main()`, which can then manipulate it as necessary.

Figure A-13 shows how we use components with the «function» stereotype to represent free global functions. The figure also demonstrates the use of properties to show what files the functions are implemented in. Notice that the `CreateCGI` function is annotated with the property `{file=sessionMenuGenerator.cc}`.

Summary

In this chapter, we have walked through a large portion of the UML notation in the context of a simple example. We have shown the various notational conventions used in the different phases of software development. We showed how a problem can be analyzed using use cases and types to form an application domain model. We

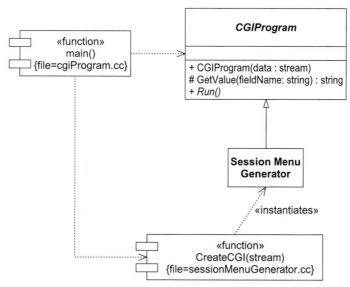

Figure A-13   Architecture of CGI programs

showed how classes, objects, and components can be combined into static and dynamic diagrams to describe the architecture and construction of the software. We showed the UML notation for each of these concepts and demonstrated how the notation can be used. And, by no means of least importance, we showed how all these concepts and notations participate in software-design reasoning.

There is more to learn about UML and software design. The next chapter will use another example to explore more of UML and different analysis and design tradeoffs.

Bibliography

1. Booch, Grady. *Object Oriented Analysis and Design with Applications*, 2nd ed. Benjamin Cummings: 1994.
2. Rumbaugh, et al. *Object Oriented Modeling and Design*. Prentice Hall: 1991.
3. Wirfs-Brock, Rebecca, et al. *Designing Object-Oriented Software*. Prentice Hall: 1990.
4. Coad, Peter, and Ed Yourdon. *Object Oriented Analysis*. Yourdon Press: 1991.
5. Jacobson, Ivar. *Object Oriented Software Engineering a Use Case Driven Approach*. Addison–Wesley, 1992.
6. Cockburn, Alistair. *Structuring Use Cases with Goals*. http://members.aol.com/acockburn/papers/usecass.htm.
7. Kennedy, Edward. *Object Practitioner's Guide*. http://www.zoo.co.uk/~z0001039/PracGuides. November 29, 1997.
8. Booch, Grady. *Object Solutions*. Addison–Wesley, 1995.
9. Gamma, et al. *Design Patterns*. Addison–Wesley, 1995.

APPENDIX B

UML Notation II:
The STATMUX

In this chapter, we continue our exploration of the UML notation, this time focussing on some of its more detail-oriented aspects. As a context for this exploration, we will study the problem of a statistical multiplexor.

The Statistical Multiplexor Definition

A statistical multiplexor is a device that allows multiple serial data streams to be carried over a single telecommunications line. Consider, for example, a device that contains a single 56K modem and has 16 serial ports. When two such devices are connected together over a phone line, characters that are sent into port 1 on one device come out of port 1 on the other device. Such a device can support 16 simultaneous full duplex communications sessions over a single modem.

Figure B-1 shows a typical 1980s application for such a device. In Chicago, we have a mix of ASCII terminals and printers that we want to connect to a VAX in Detroit. We have a leased 56K line that connects the two locations. The statistical multiplexor creates 16 virtual serial channels between the two locations.

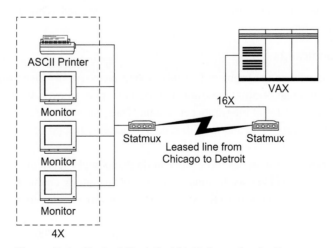

Figure B-1 Typical Statistical Multiplexor Application

Clearly, if all 16 channels are running simultaneously, they will all distribute the 56K throughput between them, yielding an effective bit rate of somewhat less than 3500 bits per second per device. However, most terminals and printers are not busy 100% of the time. Indeed, the duty cycle in many applications is well under 10%. Thus, though the line is shared, statistically each user will perceive near 56K performance.

The problem we are going to study in this chapter is the software inside the statmux. This software controls the modem and serial-port hardware. It also determines the multiplexing protocol used to share the communications line between all the serial ports.

The Software Environment

Figure B-2 is a block diagram[1] that shows where the software fits in the statmux. It sits between the 16 serial ports and the modem.

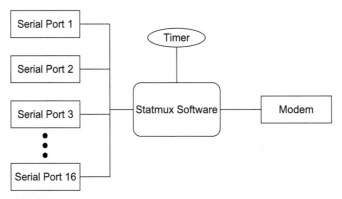

Figure B-2   Statmux system block diagram

Each serial port generates two interrupts to the main processor—one when it is ready to send a character and one when a character has been received. The modem also generates similar interrupts. Thus, there are 34 interrupts coming into the system. The modem interrupts are higher priority than the serial-port interrupts. This ensures that the modem can run at the full 56K speed even if the other serial ports must suffer periods of dormancy.

Finally, there is a timer that generates an interrupt every millisecond. This timer allows the software to schedule events for particular times.

The Real-time Constraints

A little calculation will demonstrate the problem that this system faces. At any given time, 34 interrupts sources may be demanding service at a rate of 5600 interrupts per second—plus an extra thousand interrupts per second from the timer. This amounts to 191,400 interrupts per second. Thus, the software can spend no more than 5.2 μs servicing each interrupt. This is very tight, and we will need a reasonably fast processor to make sure that we don't drop any characters.

To make matters worse, the system has more work to do than simply servicing the interrupts. It also has to manage the communications protocol across the modem, gather the incoming characters from the serial ports, and divvy out the characters that need to be sent to the serial port. All of this is going to require some processing that must somehow fit between the interrupts.

Fortunately, the maximum sustained throughput of the system is only 11,200 characters per second (i.e., the number of characters that can be simultaneously sent and received by the modem). This means that, on average, we have nearly 90 μs between characters.[2]

1.   Block diagrams are a form of Kent Beck's GML (galactic modeling language). GML diagrams are composed of lines, rectangles, circles, ovals, and any other shape necessary to get the point across.

2.   An eternity.

Since our ISRs (interrupt service routines) cannot exceed 5.2 µs in duration, we have at least 94% of the processor still available to us between interrupts. This means we don't need to be overly concerned about efficiency outside of the ISRs.

The Input Interrupt Service Routine

These may have to be written in assembly language. The prime goal of the input ISRs is to get the character from the hardware and store it somewhere where the non-ISR software can deal with it at its leisure. The typical way of dealing with this is to use a ring buffer.

Figure B-3 presents a class diagram that shows the structure of the input ISRs and their ring buffers. We have invented a few new stereotypes and properties to describe the rather unique issues involved with interrupt service routines.

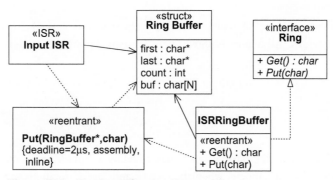

Figure B-3   The Input Service Interrupt Routine

First we have the `InputISR` class. This class has the stereotype «ISR,» which indicates that the class is an interrupt service routine. Such classes are written in assembly language and have only one method. This method has no name and is invoked only when the interrupt occurs.

`InputISR` has an association to its particular `RingBuffer`. The «struct» stereotype on the `RingBuffer` class indicates that this is a class with no methods. It is nothing more than a data structure. We have done this because we expect it to be accessed by assembly language functions that would not otherwise have access to the methods of a class.

The `Put(RingBuffer*, char)` function is shown in a class icon with the stereotype of «reentrant». This stereotype, used in this way, represents a free function that is written to be safe from interrupts.[3] This function adds characters to the ring buffer. It is called by `InputISR` when a character has been received.

The properties on the function indicate that it has a real-time deadline of 2 µs, that it should be written in assembly language, and that it should be coded inline wherever it is invoked. These last two properties are an attempt to meet the first.

The `ISRRingBuffer` class is a regular class whose methods run outside of interrupt service routines. It makes use of the `RingBuffer` struct and provides a class facade for it. Its methods all conform to the «reentrant» stereotype and are therefore interrupt safe.

The `ISRRingBuffer` class realizes the `Ring` interface. This interface allows the clients outside the interrupt service routines to access the characters stored in the ring buffers. This class represents the interface boundary between the interrupts and the rest of the system.

---

3. Reentrancy is a complex topic that is beyond the scope of this chapter. The reader is referred to good texts on real-time and concurrent programming such as Doug Lea's *Concurrent Programming in Java*, Addison–Wesley, 1997.

Stereotypes in List Boxes

When stereotypes appear in the list compartments of classes, they have a special meaning. Those elements that appear below the stereotype conform to that stereotype.

AClass
+ f1()
«mystereotype»
+ f2()
+ f3()

In this example, function f1() has no explicit stereotype. Functions f2() and f3(), however, conform to the «mystereotype» stereotype.

There is no limit on the number of stereotypes that can appear in a list box like this. Each new stereotype overrides the previous. All elements shown between two stereotypes conform to the stereotype above them.

An empty stereotype «» can be used in the midst of a list to show that the following elements have no explicit stereotype.

Ring Buffer Behavior.   The ring buffers can be described by a "simple" state machine as shown in Figure B-4. The state machine shows what happens when the Get() and Put() methods are called on objects of the ISRRingBuffer class.

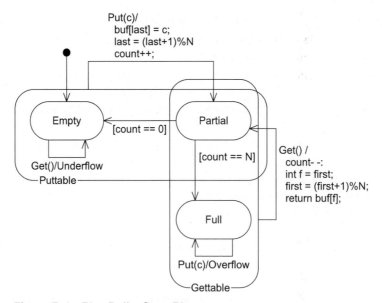

Figure B-4   Ring Buffer State Diagram

The diagram shows the three states that a ring buffer can be in. The machine begins in the Empty state. In the Empty state, the ring buffer has no characters in it. In that state, the Get() method will cause an underflow. We have not here defined what happens during underflow or overflow—those decisions are left for later. The two states

Empty and Partial are substates of the Puttable superstate. The Puttable superstate represents those states in which the Put() method operates without overflowing. Whenever the Put() method is invoked from one of the Puttable states, the incoming character is stored in the buffer, and the counts and indexes are adjusted appropriately. The Partial and Full states are both substates of the Gettable superstate. The Gettable superstate represents those states in which the Get() function operates without underflowing. When Get() is called in those states, the next character is removed from the ring, and is returned to the caller. The counts and indexes are adjusted appropriately. In the Full state, the Put() function results in an Overflow.

The two transitions out of the Partial state are governed by *guard* conditions. The machine transitions from the Partial to the Empty state whenever the count variable goes to zero. Likewise, the machine transitions from the Partial state to the Full state whenever the count variable reaches the size of the buffer (N).

States and Internal Transitions

In UML, a state is represented by a rectangle with rounded corners. This rectangle may have two compartments.

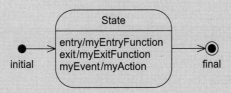

The top compartment simply names the state. If no name is specified, then the state is anonymous. All anonymous states are distinct from one another.

The bottom compartment lists the internal transitions for the state. Internal transitions are denoted as eventName/action. The eventName must be the name of an event that can occur while the machine is in the given state. The machine responds to this event by remaining in the state and executing the specified action.

There are two special events that can be used in internal transitions. They are depicted in the icon above. The entry event occurs when the state is entered. The exit event occurs when the state is exited (even for a transition that returns immediately to that state).

An action may be the name of another finite-state machine that has both an initial and final state. Or an action can be a procedural expression written in some computer language or pseudocode. The procedure may use operations and variables of the object, if any, that contain the state machine. Or, the action can be of the form ^object.message(arg1, arg2, ...), in which case the action causes the named message to be sent to the named object.

There are two special *pseudostate* icons shown in the previous diagram. On the left, we see the black circle that represents the initial pseudostate. On the right, we see the bull's-eye that represents the final pseudostate. When a finite-state machine is initially invoked, it makes a transition from the initial pseudostate to the state to which it is connected. Thus, the initial pseudostate may only have one transition leaving it. When an event causes a transition to the final pseudostate, the state machine shuts down and accepts no more events.

Transitions between States

A finite-state machine is a network of states connected by transitions. Transitions are arrows that connect one state to another. The transition is labeled with the name of the event that triggers it.

Here we see two states connected by a single transition. The transition will be 'fired' if the machine is in `state1` and the `event` occurs. Upon the 'firing' of the transition, `state1` is exited, and any `exit` action is executed. Then the `action` on the transition is executed. Then `state2` is entered, and its `entry` action is executed.

An event on a transition can be qualified with a guard condition. The transition will only fire if the event occurs *and* the guard condition is true. Guard conditions are boolean expressions that appear in square brackets after the event name (e.g., `myEvent[myGuardCondition]`).

Actions on transitions are exactly the same as actions on internal transitions within states. (See "States and Internal Transitions.")

Nested States

When one state icon completely encloses one or more others, the enclosed states are said to be *substates* of the enclosing *superstate*.

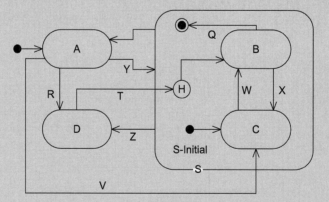

In the diagram above, states B and C are substates of the superstate S. The state machine begins in state A, as shown by the initial pseudostate. If transition V fires, then substate C within superstate S will become active. This will cause the entry functions of both S and C to be invoked.

If transition Y fires while in state A, the machine enters superstate S. A transition into a superstate must result in one of its substates becoming active. If a transition terminates at the edge of a superstate, as transition Y does, then there is a transition from the initial pseudostate within the superstate. Thus, transition Y triggers the transition from the S-Initial pseudostate to substate C.

(continues on next page)

When transition Y is fired, superstate S and substate C are both entered. Any entry actions for S and C are invoked at that time. The superstate's entry actions are invoked before the substate's entry actions. Transitions W and X may now fire, moving the machine between the B and C substates. The exit and entry actions will be performed as usual, but since superstate S is not exited, its exit functions will not be invoked.

Eventually, transition Z will fire. Notice that Z leaves the edge of the superstate. This means that, regardless of whether substate B or C is active, transition Z moves the machine to state D. This is equivalent to two separate transitions, one from C to D and the other from B to D, both labelled Z. When Z fires, the appropriate substate exit action is performed, and then the exit action for superstate S is performed. Then D is entered, and its entry action is performed.

Notice that transition Q terminates on a final pseudostate. If transition Q fires, then superstate S terminates. This will cause the unlabeled transition from S to A to fire. Terminating the superstate also resets any history information, as described later.

Transition T terminates on a special icon within the S superstate. This is called the *history* marker. When transition T fires, the substate that was last active within S becomes active again. Thus, if transition Z had occurred while C was active, then transition T will cause C to become active again.

If transition T fires when the history marker is inactive, then the unlabeled transition from the history marker to substate B fires. This denotes a default when there is no history information available. The history marker is inactive if S has never been entered or just after S has been terminated by transition Q.

Thus the event sequence Y-Z-T will leave the machine in substate C. But both R-T and Y-W-Q-R-T will leave the machine in substate B.

The Output Service Interrupt Routine

The processing for output interrupts is very similar to the processing for input interrupts. However, there are some differences. The noninterrupt parts of the system load up the output ring buffer with characters to be sent. The serial port generates an interrupt whenever it is ready for the next character. The interrupt service routine grabs the next character from the ring buffer and sends it to the serial port.

If there are no characters waiting in the ring buffer when the serial port becomes ready, then the interrupt service routine has nothing to do. The serial port has already signalled its readiness to accept a new character, and it will not do so again until it is given a character to send and finishes sending it. Thus, the flow of interrupts stops. We therefore need a strategy for restarting the output interrupts when new characters arrive. Figure B-5 shows the structure of the output ISR. Its similarity to the input ISR in Figure B-3 is obvious. However, notice the «calls» dependency from the ISRRingBuffer to the OutputISR. This indicates that the ISRRingBuffer object can cause the OutpuISR to execute just as though an interrupt had been received.

Figure B-6 shows the necessary modifications to the finite-state machine of the output ring buffers. Compare this with Figure B4. Notice that the Puttable superstate has been removed and that there are two Put transitions. The first Put transition goes from the Empty state to the Partial state. This will cause the entry action of the Gettable superstate to be executed, which generates an artificial interrupt to the OutputISR.[4] The second Put transition is internal to the Partial state.

---

4. The mechanism for generating an artificial interrupt of this kind is strongly dependent on the platform. On some machines, it is possible to simply call the ISR as though it were a function. Other machines require more elaborate protocols for artificially invoking ISRs.

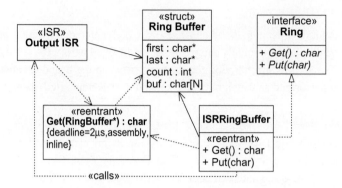

Figure B-5   Output Interrupt Service Routine

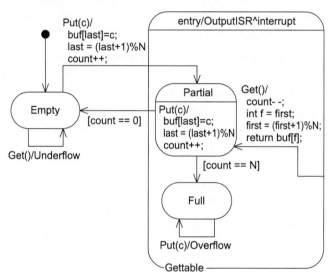

Figure B-6   Output Service Interrupt State machine

The Communications Protocol

Two statmuxes communicate via their modems. Each sends packets to the other over a telecommunications line. We must assume that the line is imperfect and that errors and dropouts can occur. Characters can be lost or garbled during transmission, and spurious characters may be created by electrical discharges or other electromagnetic interference. Therefore, a communications protocol must be put in place between the two modems. This protocol must be able to verify that packets are complete and accurate, and it must be able to retransmit packets that were garbled or lost.

Figure B-7 is an *activity diagram*. (See the "Activity Diagrams" sidebar on page 498.) It shows the communications protocol that our statmuxes will be using. This protocol is a relatively straightforward sliding window protocol with pipelining and piggybacking.[5]

The protocol begins at the initial pseudostate by initializing some variables and then creating three independent threads. The variables will be explained later, in the sections regarding the threads that depend on them. The "timing thread" is used to retransmit packets if no acknowledgment has been received within the allowed time period. It is also used to make sure that acknowledgments of properly received packets are sent in a timely fashion. The "sending thread" is used to send packets that have been queued for transmission. The "receiving thread" is used to receive, validate, and process packets. Let's examine each in turn.

5.   See *Computer Networks*, 2d. ed. Tanenbaum, Prentice Hall, 1988, Sec. 4.4 for more information about this kind of communications protocol.

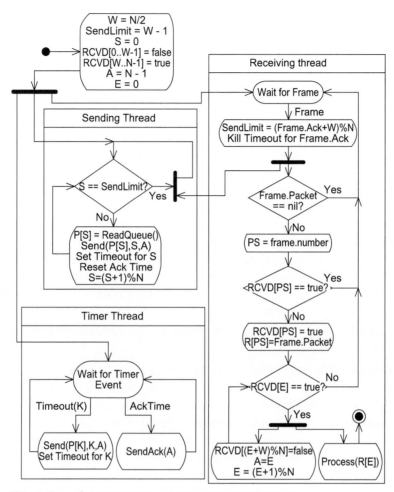

Figure B-7 Communications Protocol Activity Diagram

The Sending Thread.   The S variable contains the serial number that will be stamped on the next outgoing packet. Each packet is numbered with a serial number in the range 0..N. The sending thread will continue to send packets, without waiting for them to be acknowledged, until there are W outstanding unacknowledged packets. W is set to N/2 so that never more than half the serial numbers are in play at any given time. The SendLimit variable normally holds the serial number of the packet that is beyond the window (W), and so it is the smallest serial number that cannot yet be sent.

As the sending thread continues to send packets, it increments S modulo N. When S reaches the SendingLimit, the thread blocks until SendingLimit is changed by the receiving thread. If S has not yet reached the SendingLimit, then a new packet is pulled down from the queue by the ReadQueue() function. The packet is placed in the S position of the P array. We keep the packet in this array in case it needs retransmission. Then the packet is sent along with its serial number (S) and with the piggybacked acknowledgment (A). A is the serial number of the last packet that we received. This variable is updated by the receiving thread.

Having sent the packet, we start a time-out for it. If this time-out occurs before the packet is acknowledged, the timing thread will assume that either the packet or the acknowledgment was lost, and it will retransmit the packet.

At this point, we also reset the Ack timer. When the Ack timer expires, the timer thread assumes that too much time has elapsed since the last time we sent an acknowledgment, so it acknowledges the last-known good packet to be received.

The Receiving Thread.   This thread begins by initializing a few variables. RCVD is an array of boolean flags indexed by serial number. As packets are received, they are marked in RCVD as true. Once a packet is processed, the serial number that is W past that packet is marked false. E is the serial number of the packet we are expecting and is next to be processed; it will always be A+1 modulo N. As part of initialization, we set the last half of RCVD to true to denote the fact that those serial numbers are outside the allowed window. If they were to be received, they would be dropped as duplicate packets.

The receiving thread waits for a frame. A frame may be a packet or just a plain acknowledgment. In either case, it will contain the acknowledgment of the last good packet. We update the SendingLimit and trigger the sending thread. Notice that the SendingLimit is set to W past the last acknowledged frame. Thus, the sender is allowed to use only half the serial number space starting at the last acknowledged packet, so that the sender and receiver have negotiated which half of the serial number space is currently valid.

If the frame contains a packet, then we get the serial number of that packet and check the RCVD array to see if we have already received a packet with this serial number. If so, we drop it as a duplicate. Otherwise, we update the RCVD array to show that the packet has now been received, and we save the packet in the R array.

Although the packets are sent in serial number order, they can be received out of order. This is true simply because packets can get lost and retransmitted. Thus, even though we have just received packet number PS, it may not be the one we were expecting (E). If it is not, we simply wait until E is received. However, if PS == E, then we spawn off a separate thread to process the packet. We also move the allowed serial number window by setting the E+W slot of the RCVD array to false. Finally, we set A to E to signify that E was the last good received serial number, and we increment E.

The Timing Thread.   The timer simply waits for a timer event. There are two kinds of events that can occur. A Timeout(K) event signifies that a packet was sent by the sending thread, but no acknowledgment was ever received. Thus, the timer thread retransmits the K packet and restarts its timer.

The AckTime event is generated by a repeating, retriggerable timer. This timer sends the AckTime event every X milliseconds. However, it can be retriggered to start over at X. The sending thread retriggers this timer every time it sends a packet. This is appropriate because each packet carries a piggyback acknowledgment. If no packet has been sent for X milliseconds, then the AckTime event will occur, and the timer thread will send an acknowledgment frame.

Whew!   You may have found this discussion to be a bit of a struggle to get through. Just imagine what it would have been like without the explanatory text. The diagram may express my intent, but the extra words sure help. Diagrams can seldom stand on their own.

How do we know that the diagram is correct? We don't! It won't surprise me in the slightest if several readers find problem with it. Diagrams can't usually be tested directly the way code can. So we'll have to wait for the code to know if this algorithm is really correct.

These two issues make the utility of such diagrams questionable. They can make good pedagogical tools, but one should not be considered expressive and accurate enough to be the sole specification of a design. Text, code, and tests are also required.

Activity Diagrams

Activity diagrams are a hybrid of state transition diagrams, flowcharts, and petri nets. They are especially good at describing event-driven multithreaded algorithms.

An activity diagram *is* a state diagram. It is still a graph of states connected by transitions. However, in an activity diagram, there are special kinds of states and transitions.

(continues on next page)

Action State

An *action state* is drawn as a rectangle with a flat top and bottom and rounded sides. This icon is distinct from a normal state icon in that the corners are sharp, whereas a state icon has rounded corners. (See "States and Internal Transitions" on page 493.) The inside of the action state contains one or more procedural statements that represent its entry actions. (This is just like a process box in a flowchart)

When an action state is entered, its entry actions are executed immediately. Once those actions are completed, the action state is exited. The outgoing transition must not have an event label, since the "event" is simply the completion of the entry actions. However, there may be several outgoing transitions, each with a mutually exclusive guard condition. The union of all the guard conditions must always be true (i.e., it is impossible to get "stuck" in an action state).

Decisions

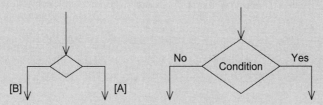

The fact that an action state can have many outgoing guarded transitions means that it can act as a decision step. However, it is often better to specifically denote decisions, for which the diamond icon is traditional.

A transition enters a diamond, and N guarded transitions leave it. Once again, the boolean union of all the outgoing guards must yield truth.

In Figure B-7, we used a variation of the diamond that is more akin to flowcharts. A boolean condition is stated within the diamond, and two outgoing transitions are labeled "Yes" and "No."

Complex Transitions

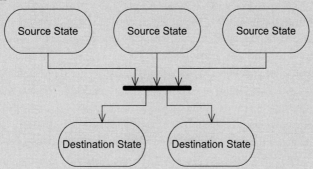

Complex transitions show the splitting and joining of multiple threads of control. They are denoted by the dark bar called an *asynchronization* bar. Arrows connect states to the asynchronization bar. The states that lead to the bar are called *source* states, and the states leading away from the bar are called *destination* states.

(continues on next page)

The entire group of arrows leading to and from the bar form, a *single transition*. The arrows are labeled neither with events nor with guards. The transition fires when all the source states are occupied (i.e., when the three independent threads are in the appropriate states). Moreover, the source states must be true states and not action states (i.e., they must be able to wait).

Upon firing, the source states are all exited, and the destination states are all entered. If there are more destination states than source states, then we have spawned new threads of control. If there are more source states, then some threads have joined.

Each time a source state is entered, the entry is counted. Each time the complex transition fires, the counters in its source states are decremented. A source state is considered to be occupied as long as the counter is nonzero.

As a notational convenience, a true transition or an action state can be used as a source for an asynchronization bar. (See Figure B-7.) In such a case, it is assumed that the transition actually terminates on a true unnamed state, which is a source state of the bar.

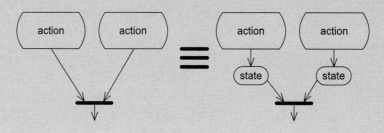

Structure of the Communications Protocol Software.   The three threads of control all share the same variables. Thus, the functions invoked by those threads should probably be methods of the same class. However, most threading systems nowadays equate a thread with an object. That is, each thread has an object that controls it. In UML, these are called *active objects*. (See "Active Objects" on page 502.) So the class that houses the protocol methods will also need to create the active objects that control the threads.

The timer thread will be useful in places other than the protocol, so its thread should probably be created in a different part of the system. This leaves the sending thread and the receiving thread to be created by the protocol object.

Figure B-8 shows an object diagram (see "Object Diagrams" on page 501) that depicts the situation just after the `CommunicationsProtocol` object has been initialized. The `CommunicationsProtocol` has created two `Thread` objects and keeps responsibility for their lifetimes. The `Thread` objects employ the COMMAND[6] pattern in order for the newly created thread of execution to get started. Each `Thread` holds an instance of an object that conforms to the `Runnable` interface. (See "Interface Lollipops" on page 502.) The ADAPTER[7] pattern is then used to bind the `Thread`s to the appropriate methods of the `CommunicationsProtocol` object.

A similar arrangement can be seen between the `Timer` and the `CommunicationsProtocol`. However, in this case the lifetime of the `Timer` object is not controlled by the `CommunicationsProtocol` object.

The «friend» relationships exist because we want the methods invoked by the adapters to be private to `CommunicationsProtocol`. We don't want them to be called by anyone other than the adapters.[8]

---

6.   page 151

7.   page 317

8.   There are several other ways to accomplish this. We could use inner classes in Java.

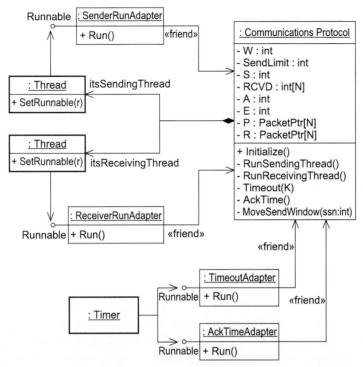

Figure B-8   Object Diagram: Just after protocol object has been initialized

Object Diagrams

Object diagrams depict the static relationships that exist between a set of objects at a particular instance in time. They differ from class diagrams in two ways. First, they depict *objects* instead of *classes* and the *links* between objects rather than the *relationships* between classes. Second, class diagrams show source code relationships and dependencies, whereas object diagrams show only those run-time relationships and dependencies that exist for the instant defined by the object diagram. Thus, the object diagram shows the objects and links that exist when the system is in a particular state.

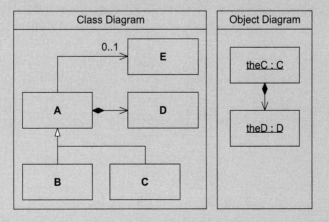

(continues on next page)

In the previous diagram, we see a class diagram and an object diagram that represent one possible state of the objects and links that derive from the classes and relationships in the class diagram. Notice that the objects are drawn in the same manner as they are in a sequence diagram. They are rectangles with underlined, two-component names. Notice also that the relationship on the object diagram is drawn the same way as on the class diagram.

A relationship between two objects is called a link. A link allows messages to flow in the direction of navigability. In this case, messages can flow from `theC` to `theD`. This link exists because there is a composition relationship between class A and class D, and because class C derives from class A. Thus, an instance of class C can have links that are derived from its base classes.

Notice also that the relationship between class A and class E is not represented on the object diagram. This is because the object diagram depicts a particular state of the system during which C objects are not associated with E objects.

Active Objects

Active objects are objects that are responsible for a single thread of execution. The thread of execution does not need to be running inside the methods of the active object. Indeed, the active object typically calls out to other objects. The active object is simply the object in which the thread of execution originates. It is also the object that provides thread management interfaces such as `Terminate` and `Suspend`, and `ChangePriority`.

Active objects are drawn as ordinary objects, but with a bold outline. If the active object also owns other objects that execute within its thread of control, you can draw those objects inside the boundaries of the active object.

Interface Lollipops

Interfaces can be shown as classes with the «interface» stereotype, or they may be shown with a special lollipop icon.

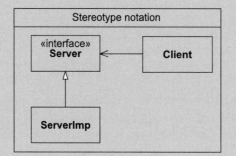
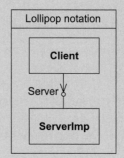

(continues on next page)

Both of the diagrams in this box have exactly the same interpretation. Instances of class `Client` make use of the `Server` interface. The `ServerImp` class implements the `Server` interface.

Either of the two relationships connected to the lollipop can be omitted, as shown in the following diagram:

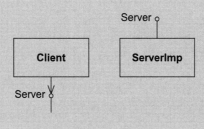

The Initialization Process. The individual processing steps used to initialize the `Communications-Protocol` object are shown in Figure B-9. This is a collaboration diagram. (See "Collaboration Diagram" on page 504.

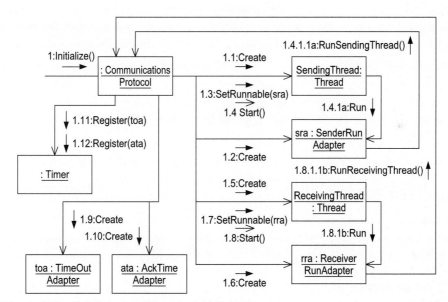

Figure B-9 Collaboration Diagram: Initializing the `CommunicationsProtocol` object

The initialization process begins at message number 1. The `CommunicationsProtocol` receives the `Initialize` message from some unknown source. It responds in messages 1.1 and 1.2 by creating the `SendingThread` object and its associated `SenderRunAdapter`. Then, in messages 1.3 and 1.4, it binds the adapter to the thread and starts the thread.

Notice that message 1.4 is asynchronous, so the initialization process continues with messages 1.5 through 1.8, which simply repeat the procedure for the creation of the `ReceivingThread`. Meanwhile, a separate thread of execution begins in message 1.4.1a, which invokes the `Run` method in the `SenderRunAdapter`. As a result, the adapter sends message 1.4.1.1a:RunSendingThread to the `CommunicationsProtocol` object. This starts the processing of the sending thread. A similar chain of events starts the receiving thread. Finally, messages 1.9 through 1.12 create the timer adapters and register them with the timer.

Collaboration Diagrams

Collaboration diagrams are similar to object diagrams except that they show how the state of the system evolves over time. The messages that are sent between the objects are shown, along with their arguments and return values. Each message is labeled with a sequence number to show the order in relation to the other messages.

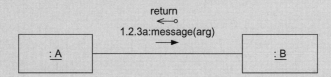

Messages are drawn as small arrows placed near the link between two objects. The arrow points at the object that is receiving the message. The message is labeled with the name and sequence number of the message.

The sequence number is separated from the name of the message by a colon. The message name is followed by parentheses that contain a comma-separated list of the arguments to the message. The sequence number is a dot-separated list of numbers, followed by an optional thread identifier.

The numbers in the sequence number denote both the order of the message and its depth in the calling hierarchy. Message number 1 is the first message to be sent. If the procedure invoked by message 1 invokes two other messages, they will be numbered 1.1 and 1.2, respectively. Once they return and message number 1 completes, the next message will be number 2. By using this scheme of dots, it is possible to completely describe the order and nesting of the messages.

The thread identifier is the name of the thread that the message is executing within. If the thread identifier is omitted, it indicates that the message is executing in the unnamed thread. If message number 1.2 spawns a new thread named "t," the first message of that new thread will be numbered 1.2.1t.

Return values and arguments can be shown by using the data token symbol (the little arrow with the circle on the end). Alternately, return values can be shown using assignment syntax in the message name as follows:

```
1.2.3 : c:=message(a,b)
```

In this case, the return value of "message" will be held in a variable named "c."

A message that uses a filled arrowhead, as shown to the left, represents a synchronous function call. It does not return until all other synchronous messages invoked from its procedure are returned. This is the normal kind of message for C++, Smalltalk, Eiffel, or Java, etc.

The stick arrowhead shown to the left represents an asynchronous message. Such a message spawns a new thread of control to execute the invoked method and then returns immediately. Thus, the message returns before the method is executed. Messages that are sent by the method should have a thread identifier, since they are executing in a thread that differs from the invocation.

Race Conditions within the Protocol. The protocol, as described in Figure B-7, has a number of interesting *race conditions*. A race condition occurs when the order of two separate events cannot be predicted, yet the state of the system is sensitive to that order. The state of the system then depends on which event wins the race.

The programmer attempts to make sure that the system behaves properly regardless of the ordering of the events. However, race conditions are hard to identify. Undiscovered race conditions can lead to transient and difficult-to-diagnose errors.

As an example of a race condition, consider what happens when a packet is sent by the sending thread. (See Figure B-10.) This kind of diagram is called a message sequence chart. (See "Message Sequence Charts" on page 506.) The local sender sends packet S and starts a time-out. The remote receiver receives this packet and lets the remote sender know that S was received OK. The remote sender either sends an explicit ACK or piggybacks an ACK onto the next packet. The local receiver gets this ACK and kills the time-out.

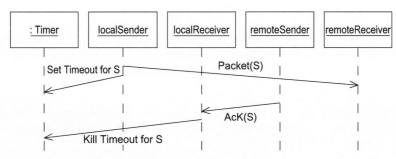

Figure B-10 Acknowledgment of a packet: Normal

Sometimes the ACK doesn't make it back. In that case the time-out expires, and the packet is retransmitted. Figure B-11 shows what happens.

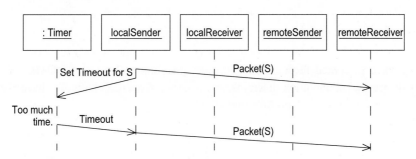

Figure B-11 Acknowledgment lost: Retransmission

A race condition exists between these two extremes. It is possible that the timer will expire just as the ACK is being sent. Figure B-12 shows the scenario. Note the crossed lines. They represent the race. Packet S has been sent and received just fine. Moreover, an ACK was transmitted back. However, the ACK arrived after the time-out had occurred. Thus, the packet gets retransmitted even though the ACK was received.

The logic of Figure B-7 handles this race properly. The remote receiver will realize that the second arrival of packet S is a duplicate and will discard it.

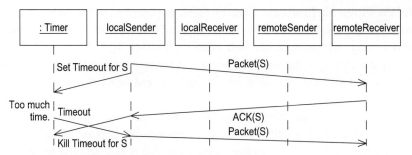

Figure B-12   ACK / Retransmission race condition

Message Sequence Charts

Message sequence charts are a special form of sequence diagrams. The primary difference is that the message arrows are angled downward to show that time can elapse between the sending and the receiving of a message. All the other parts of the sequence diagram may be present, including activations and sequence numbers.

The primary use of message sequence charts is to discover and document race conditions. These charts are very good at showing the relative timings of certain events and how two independent processes can have a different view of the order of events.

Consider Figure B-12. The `Timer` object thinks that the `Timeout` event occurs before the `Kill Timeout` event. However, the `localSender` perceives those two events in the opposite order.

This difference in the perception of the order of events can lead to logic flaws that are extremely sensitive to timing and very hard to reproduce and diagnose. Message sequence charts are a very nice tool for finding these situations before they wreak havoc in the field.

Conclusion

In this chapter, we have presented most of the dynamic modeling techniques of UML. We have seen state machines, activity diagrams, collaboration diagrams, and message sequence charts. We have also seen how these diagrams handle problems of single and multiple threads of control.

Bibliography

1.   Gamma, et al. *Design Patterns*. Reading, MA: Addison–Wesley, 1995.

A Satire of Two Companies

"I've got a good mind to join a club and beat you over the head with it!"

—Rufus T. Firefly

Rufus, Inc.
Project Kickoff

Your name is Bob. The date is January 3, 2001, and your head still aches from the recent millennial revelry. You are sitting in a conference room with several managers and a group of your peers. You are a project team leader. Your boss is there, and he has brought along all of his team leaders. His boss called the meeting.

"We have a new project to develop," says your boss's boss. Call him BB. The points in his hair are so long that they scrape the ceiling. Your boss's points are just starting to grow, but he eagerly awaits the day when he can leave Brylcream stains on the acoustic tiles. BB describes the essence of the new market they have identified and the product they want to develop to exploit this market.

"We must have this new project up and working by fourth quarter, October 1," BB demands. "Nothing is of higher priority; so we are cancelling your current project."

The reaction in the room is stunned silence. Months of work are simply going to be thrown away. Slowly, a murmur of objection begins to circulate around the conference table.

His points give off an evil green glow as BB meets the eyes of everyone in the room. One by one that insidious stare reduces each attendee to quivering lumps of protoplasm. It is clear that he will brook no discussion on this matter.

Once silence has been restored, BB says, "We need to begin immediately. How long will it take you to do the analysis?"

Rupert Industries
Project: ~Alpha~

Your name is Robert. The date is January 3, 2001. The quiet hours spent with your family this holiday have left you refreshed and ready for work. You are sitting in a conference room with your team of professionals. The manager of the division called the meeting.

"We have some ideas for a new project," says the division manager. Call him Russ. He is a high-strung British chap with more energy than a fusion reactor. He is ambitious and driven, but he understands the value of a team.

Russ describes the essence of the new market opportunity the company has identified and introduces you to Jay, the marketing manager who is responsible for defining the products that will address it.

Addressing you, Jay says, "We'd like to start defining our first product offering as soon as possible. When can you and your team meet with me?"

You reply, "We'll be done with the current iteration of our project this Friday. We can spare a few hours for you between now and then. After that, we'll take a few people from the team and dedicate them to you. We'll begin hiring their replacements and the new people for your team immediately."

"Great," says Russ, "But I want you to understand that it is critical that we have something to exhibit at the trade show coming up this

You raise your hand. Your boss tries to stop you, but his spitwad misses you and you are unaware of his efforts.

"Sir, we can't tell you how long the analysis will take until we have some requirements."

"The requirements document won't be ready for three or four weeks," BB says, his points vibrating with frustration. "So, *pretend* that you have the requirements in front of you now. How long will you require for analysis?"

No one breathes. Everyone looks around at everybody else to see if they have some idea.

"If analysis takes any longer than April 1, then we have a problem. Can you finish the analysis by then?"

Your boss visibly gathers his courage, building to the ejaculation, "We'll find a way, Sir!" His points grow 3 mm, and your headache increases by two Tylenols.

"Good." BB smiles. "Now, how long will it take to do the design?"

"Sir," you say. Your boss visibly pales. He is clearly worried that his 3 millimeters are at risk. "Without an analysis, it will not be possible to tell you how long design will take."

BB's expression shifts beyond austere. "PRE-TEND you have the analysis already!" he says, while fixing you with his vacant beady little eyes. "How long will it take you to do the design?"

Two Tylenols are not going to cut it. Your boss, in a desperate attempt to save his new growth, babbles, "Well, sir, with only six months left to complete the project, design had better take no longer than three months."

"I'm glad you agree, Smithers!" BB says, beaming. Your boss relaxes. He knows his points are secure. After a while, he starts lightly humming the Brylcream jingle.

BB continues, "So, analysis will be complete by April 1, design will be complete by July 1, and that gives you three months to implement the project. This meeting is an example of how well our new consensus and empowerment policies are working. Now, get out there and start working. I'll expect to see TQM plans and QIT assignments on my desk by next week. Oh, and don't forget that your cross-functional team meetings and reports will be needed for next month's quality audit."

"Forget the Tylenol," you think to yourself as you return to your cubicle. "I need bourbon."

July. If we can't be there with something significant, we'll lose the opportunity."

"I understand," you reply. "I don't yet know what it is that you have in mind, but I'm sure we can have something by July. I just can't tell you what that something will be right now. In any case, you and Jay are going to have complete control over what we developers do, so you can rest assured that by July you'll have the most important things that can be accomplished in that time ready to exhibit."

Russ nods in satisfaction. He knows how this works. Your team has always kept him advised and allowed him to steer their development. He has the utmost confidence that your team will work on the most important things first and that they will produce a high-quality product.

~ ~ ~

"So Robert," says Jay at the first meeting, "How does your team feel about being split up?"

"We'll miss working with each other," you answer, "but some of us were getting pretty tired of that last project and are looking forward to a change. So, what are you guys cooking up?"

Jay beams. "You know how much trouble our customers currently have..." And he spends a half hour or so describing the problem and possible solution.

"OK, wait a second" you respond. "I need to be clear about this." And so you and Jay talk about how this system might work. Some of Jay's ideas aren't fully formed. You suggest possible solutions. He likes some of them. You continue discussing.

During the discussion, as each new topic is addressed, Jay writes user-story cards. Each card represents something that the new system has to do. The cards accumulate on the table and are spread out in front of you. Both you and Jay point at them, pick them up, and make notes on them as you discuss the stories. The cards are powerful mnemonic devices that you can use to represent complex ideas that are barely formed.

At the end of the meeting you say, "OK, I've got a general idea of what you want. I'm going to talk to the team about it. I imagine there are some experiments they'll want to run with various data-

Visibly excited, your boss comes over to you and says, "Gosh, what a great meeting. I think we're really going to do some world shaking with this project." You nod in agreement, too disgusted to do anything else.

"Oh," your boss continues, "I almost forgot." He hands you a 30-page document. "Remember that the SEI are coming to do an evaluation next week. This is the evaluation guide. You need to read through it, memorize it, and then shred it. It tells you how to answer any questions that the SEI auditors ask you. It also tells you what parts of the building you are allowed to take them to and what parts to avoid. We are determined to be a CMM level 3 organization by June!"

* * *

You and your peers start working on the analysis of the new project. This is difficult because you have no requirements. But, from the 10-minute introduction given by BB on that fateful morning, you have some idea of what the product is supposed to do.

Corporate process demands that you begin by creating a use-case document. You and your team begin enumerating use cases and drawing oval and stick diagrams.

Philosophical debates break out among the team. There is disagreement as to whether certain use cases should be connected with <<extends>> or <<includes>> relationships. Competing models are created, but nobody knows how to evaluate them. The debate continues, effectively paralyzing progress.

After a week, somebody finds the iceberg.com Web site that recommends disposing entirely of <<extends>> and <<includes>> and replacing them with <<precedes>> and <<uses.>> The documents on this Web site, authored by Don Sengroiux, describe a method known as Stalwart analysis, which claims to be a step-by-step method for translating use cases into design diagrams.

More competing use-case models are created using this new scheme; but again, nobody agrees on how to evaluate them. And the thrashing continues.

More and more, the use-case meetings are driven by emotion rather than reason. If it weren't for the fact that you don't have requirements, you'd be pretty upset by the lack of progress you are making.

The requirements document arrives on the 15th of February. And then again on the 20th, 25th, and every week thereafter. Each new version contradicts the previous. Clearly, the marketing folks who are writing the

base structures and presentation formats. Next time we meet, it'll be as a group, and we'll start identifying the most important features of the system.

A week later, your nascent team meets with Jay. They spread the existing user-story cards out on the table and begin to get into some of the details of the system.

The meeting is very dynamic. Jay presents the stories in the order of their importance. There is much discussion about each one. The developers are concerned about keeping the stories small enough to estimate and test. So they continually ask Jay to split one story into several smaller stories. Jay is concerned that each story has a clear business value and priority, so as he splits them, he makes sure this stays true.

The stories accumulate on the table. Jay writes them, but the developers make notes on them as needed. Nobody tries to capture everything that is said. The cards are not meant to capture everything; they are just reminders of the conversation.

As the developers become more comfortable with the stories, they begin writing estimates on them. These estimates are crude and budgetary, but they give Jay an idea of what the story will cost.

At the end of the meeting, it is clear that there are many more stories that could be discussed. It is also clear that the most important stories have been addressed and that they represent several months' worth of work. Jay closes the meeting by taking the cards with him and promising to have a proposal for the first release in the morning.

~ ~ ~

The next morning, you reconvene the meeting. Jay chooses five cards and places them on the table.

"According to your estimates, these cards represent about fifty points worth of work. The last iteration of the previous project managed to get fifty points done in three weeks. If we can get these five stories done in three weeks, we'll be able to demonstrate them to Russ. That will make him feel very comfortable about our progress."

Jay is pushing it. The sheepish look on his face lets you know that he knows it too. You reply,

requirements, empowered though they might be, are not finding consensus.

At the same time, several new competing use-case templates have been proposed by the various team members. Each presents its own particularly creative way of delaying progress. The debates rage on.

On March 1, Percival Putrigence, the process proctor, succeeds in integrating all the competing use-case forms and templates into a single, all-encompassing form. Just the blank form is 15 pages long. He has managed to include every field that appeared on all the competing templates. He also presents a 159-page document describing how to fill out the use-case form. All current use cases must be rewritten according to the new standard.

You marvel to yourself that it now requires 15 pages of fill-in-the-blank and essay questions to answer the question, "What should the system do when the user hits return?"

The corporate process (authored by L. E. Ott, famed author of "Holistic analysis: A progressive dialectic for software engineers") insists that you discover all primary use cases, 87% of all secondary use cases, and 36.274% of all tertiary use cases before you can complete analysis and enter the design phase. You have no idea what a tertiary use case is. So in an attempt to meet this requirement, you try to get your use-case document reviewed by the marketing department. Maybe *they* know what a tertiary use case is.

Unfortunately, the marketing folks are too busy with sales support to talk to you. Indeed, since the project started, you have not been able to get a single meeting with marketing. The best they have been able to do is provide a never-ending stream of changing and contradictory requirements documents.

While one team has been spinning endlessly on the use-case document, another has been working out the domain model. Endless variations of UML documents are pouring out of this team. Every week, the model is reworked. The team members can't decide on whether to use <<interfaces>> or <<types>> in the model. A huge disagreement has been raging on the proper syntax and application of OCL. Others in the team just got back from a five-day class on "catabolism" and have been producing incredibly detailed and arcane diagrams that nobody else can fathom.

On March 27, with one week to go before analysis is to be complete, you have produced a sea of documents

"Jay, this is a new team, working on a new project. It's a bit presumptuous to expect that our velocity will be the same as the previous team's. However, I met with the team yesterday afternoon, and we all agreed that our initial velocity should, in fact, be set to fifty story points for every three weeks. So you've lucked out on this one."

"Just remember," you continue, *"that the story estimates and the velocity are very tentative at this point. We'll learn more when we plan the iteration and even more when we implement it."*

Jay looks over his glasses at you as if to say, "Who's the boss around here anyway?" Then he smiles and says, "Yeah, don't worry, I know the drill by now."

Jay then puts 15 more cards on the table. He says, "If we can get all these cards done by the end of March, we can turn the system over to our beta test customers. And we'll get good feedback from them."

You reply, "OK, so we've got our first iteration defined, and we have the stories for the next three iterations after that. These four iterations will make our first release."

"So," says Jay, "Can you really do these five stories in the next three weeks?"

"I don't know for sure Jay," you reply, "Let's break them down into tasks and see what we get."

*So Jay, you, and your team spend the next several hours taking each of the five stories that Jay chose for the first iteration and breaking it down into small tasks. The developers quickly realize that some of the tasks can be shared between stories and that other tasks have commonalities that can probably be taken advantage of. It is clear that potential designs are popping into the developers' heads. From time to time, they form little discussion knots and scribble **UML** diagrams on some cards.*

Soon, the whiteboard is filled with the tasks that, once completed, will implement the five stories for this iteration. You start the sign-up process by saying, "OK, let's sign up for these tasks."

"I'll take the initial database generation," says Pete, "That's what I did on the last project, and this doesn't look very different. I estimate it at two days."

and diagrams, but you are no closer to a cogent analysis of the problem than you were on January 3.

* * *

And then, a miracle happens.

* * *

On Saturday, April 1, you check your e-mail from home. You see a memo from your boss to BB. It states unequivocally that you are done with the analysis!

You phone your boss and complain, "How could you have told BB that we were done with the analysis?"

"Have you looked at a calendar lately?" he responds, "It's April 1!"

The irony of that date does not escape you. "But we have so much more to think about. So much more to analyze! We haven't even decided whether to use <<extends>> or <<precedes>>!"

"Where is your evidence that you are not done?" inquires your boss impatiently.

"Whaaa...."

But he cuts you off: "Analysis can go on forever, it has to be stopped at some point. And since this is the date it was scheduled to stop, it has been stopped now. On Monday I want you to gather up all existing analysis materials and put them into a public folder. Release that folder to Percival so that he can log it in the CM system by Monday afternoon. Then get busy and start designing."

As you hang up the phone, you begin to consider the benefits of keeping a bottle of bourbon in your bottom desk drawer.

* * *

They threw a party to celebrate the on-time completion of the analysis phase. BB gave a colon stirring speech on empowerment. And your boss, another 3 mm taller, congratulated his team on the incredible show of unity and teamwork. Finally, the CIO takes the stage and tells everyone that the SEI audit went very well, and he thanks everyone for studying and shredding the evaluation guides that were passed out. Level 3 now seems assured and will be awarded by June.

(Scuttlebutt has it that managers at the level of BB and above are to receive significant bonuses once the SEI awards level 3.)

As the weeks flow by, you and your team work on the design of the system. Of course you find that the analysis that the design is supposedly based upon is flawed... no, useless... no, worse than useless. But when you tell your boss that you need to go back and work

"OK, well then I'll take the login screen," says Joe.

"Aw darn," says Elmo, the junior member of the team, "I've never done a GUI, and I kinda wanted to try that one."

"Ah, the impatience of youth," Joe says sagely, with a wink in your direction, "You can assist me with it, young Jedi." To Jay, he says, "I think it'll take me about three days."

One by one, the developers sign up for tasks and estimate them. Both you and Jay know that it is better to let the developers volunteer for tasks than it is to assign the tasks to them. You also know full well that you daren't challenge any of the developers' estimates. You know these guys, and you trust them. You know they are going to do the very best they can.

The developers know that they can't sign up for more than they finished in the last iteration they worked on. Once each developer has filled his schedule for the iteration, he stops signing up for tasks.

Eventually, all the developers have stopped signing up for tasks. But, of course, there are still tasks left on the board.

"I was worried that that might happen," you say. "OK, there's only one thing to do, Jay. We've got too much to do in this iteration. What stories or tasks can we remove."

Jay sighs. He knows that this is the only option. Working overtime at the beginning of a project is insane, and projects where he's tried it have not fared well.

So Jay starts to remove the least important functionality. "Well, we really don't need the login screen just yet. We can simply start the system in the logged-in state."

"Rats!" cries Elmo. "I really wanted to do that."

"Patience, Grasshopper," says Joe. "Those who wait for the bees to leave the hive will not have lips too swollen to relish the honey."

Elmo looks confused.

Everyone looks confused.

"So...," Jay continues, "I think we can also do away with..."

some more on the analysis to shore up its weaker sections, he simply states, "The analysis phase is over. The only allowable activity is design. Now get back to it."

So, you and your team hack the design as best you can, unsure of whether the requirements have been properly analyzed or not. Of course it really doesn't matter much since the requirements document is still thrashing with weekly revisions, and the marketing department still refuses to meet with you.

The design is a nightmare. Your boss recently misread a book named *The Finish Line* in which the author, Mark DeThomaso, blithely suggested that design documents should be taken down to code-level detail.

"If we are going to be working at that level of detail," you ask, "why don't we just write the code instead?"

"Because then you wouldn't be designing, of course. And the only allowable activity in the design phase is design!"

"Besides," he continues, "we have just purchased a company-wide license for Dandelion! This tool enables "round-the-horn engineering!" You are to transfer all design diagrams into this tool. It will automatically generate our code for us! It will also keep the design diagrams in sync with the code!"

Your boss hands you a brightly colored, shrink-wrapped box containing the Dandelion distribution. You accept it numbly and shamble off to your cubicle. Twelve hours, eight crashes, a disk reformatting, and eight shots of 151 later, you finally have the tool installed on your server. You consider the week your team will lose while attending Dandelion training. Then you smile and think, "Any week I'm not here is a good week."

Design diagram after design diagram is created by your team. Dandelion makes it very hard to draw these diagrams. There are dozens and dozens of deeply nested dialog boxes with funny text fields and check boxes that must all be filled in correctly. And then there's the problem of moving classes between packages...

At first, these diagrams are driven from the use cases. But the requirements are changing so often that the use cases rapidly become meaningless.

Debates rage about whether VISITOR or DECORATOR design patterns should be employed. One developer refuses to use VISITOR in any form, claiming that it's not a properly object-oriented construct. Another refuses to use multiple inheritance since it is the spawn of the devil.

And so, bit by bit, the list of tasks shrinks. Developers who lose a task sign up for one of the remaining ones.

The negotiation is not painless. Several times, Jay exhibits obvious frustration and impatience. Once, when tensions are especially high, Elmo volunteers to "Work extra hard to make up some of the missing time." You are about to correct him when, fortunately, Joe looks him in the eye and says, "When once you proceed down the dark path, forever will it dominate your destiny."

In the end, an iteration acceptable to Jay is reached. It's not what Jay wanted. Indeed, it is significantly less. But it's something the team feels that they can achieve in the next three weeks. And, after all, it still addresses the most important things that Jay wanted in the iteration.

"So, Jay," you say when things have quieted down a bit. "When can we expect acceptance tests from you?"

Jay sighs. This is the other side of the coin. For every story the development team implements, Jay must supply a suite of acceptance tests that prove that they work. And the team needs these long before the end of the iteration, since they will certainly point out differences in the way Jay and the developers imagine the system's behavior.

"I'll get you some example test scripts today," Jay promises. "I'll add to them every day after that. You'll have the entire suite by the middle of the iteration."

~ ~ ~

The iteration begins on Monday morning with a flurry of CRC sessions. By midmorning, all the developers have assembled into pairs and are rapidly coding away.

"And now, my young apprentice," Joe says to Elmo, "you shall learn the mysteries of test-first design!"

"Wow, that sounds pretty rad," Elmo replies. "How do you do it?"

Joe beams. It's clear that he has been anticipating this moment. "Laddy-buck, what does the code do right now?"

"Huh?" replies Elmo, "It doesn't do anything at all, there is no code."

Review meetings rapidly degenerate into debates about the meaning of object orientation, the definition of analysis vs. design, or when to use aggregation vs. association.

Midway through the design cycle, the marketing folks announce that they have rethought the focus of the system. Their new requirements document is completely restructured. They have eliminated several major feature areas and replaced them with feature areas that they anticipate customer surveys will show to be more appropriate.

You tell your boss that these changes mean that you need to reanalyze and redesign much of the system. But he says, "The analysis phase is over. The only allowable activity is design. Now get back to it."

You suggest that it might be better to create a simple prototype to show to the marketing folks, and even some potential customers. But your boss says, "The analysis phase is over. The only allowable activity is design. Now get back to it."

Hack, hack, hack, hack. You try to create some kind of a design document that might actually reflect the new requirements documents. However, the revolution of the requirements has not caused them to stop thrashing. Indeed, if anything, the wild oscillations of the requirements document have only increased in frequency and amplitude. You slog your way through them.

On June 15, the Dandelion database gets corrupted. Apparently the corruption has been progressive. Small errors in the database accumulated over the months into bigger and bigger errors. Eventually the CASE tool just stopped working. Of course the slowly encroaching corruption is present on all the backups.

Calls to the Dandelion technical support line go unanswered for several days. Finally you receive a brief e-mail from Dandelion, informing you that this is a known problem, and the solution is to purchase the new version (which they promise will be ready some time next quarter) and then reenter all the diagrams by hand.

* * *

Then, on July 1, another miracle happens! You are done with the design!

Rather than go to your boss and complain, you stock your middle desk drawer with some vodka.

* * *

They threw a party to celebrate the on-time completion of the design phase and their graduation to CMM

"So, consider our task. Can you think of something the code should do?"

"Sure." Elmo says with youthful assurance, "First, it should connect to the database."

"And thereupon, what must needs be required to connecteth the database?"

"You sure talk weird," laughs Elmo. "I think we'd have to get the database object from some registry and call the `Connect()` method."

"Ah. Astute young wizard. Thou perceivest correctly that we requireth an object within which we can cacheth the database object."

"Is 'cacheth' really a word?"

"It is when I say it! So, what test can we write that we know the database registry should pass?"

Elmo sighs. He knows he'll just have to play along. "We should be able to create a database object and pass it to the registry in a `Store()` method. And then we should be able to pull it out of the registry with a `Get()` method and make sure it's the same object."

"Oh, well said, my prepubescent sprite!"

"Hey!"

"So, now, let's write a test function that proves your case."

"But shouldn't we write the database object and registry object first?"

"Ah, you've much to learn my young, impatient one. Just write the test first."

"But it won't even compile!"

"Are you sure? What if it did?"

"Uh..."

"Just write the test, Elmo. Trust me."

And so Joe, Elmo, and all the other developers begin to code their tasks, one test case at a time. The room in which they work is a-buzz with the conversations between the pairs. The murmur is punctuated by an occasional high-five when a pair manages to finish a task or a difficult test case.

As development proceeds, the developers change partners once or twice a day. Each developer gets to see what all the others are doing, and so knowledge of the code spreads generally throughout the team.

Whenever a pair finishes something significant, whether a whole task or just an important

level 3. This time you find BB's speech so stirring that you have to use the restroom before it begins.

There are new banners and plaques all over your workplace. They show pictures of eagles and mountain climbers, and they talk about teamwork and empowerment. They read better after a few scotches. That reminds you that you need to clear out your file cabinet to make room for the brandy.

You and your team begin to code. But you rapidly discover that the design is lacking in some significant areas. Actually it's lacking any significance at all. You convene a design session in one of the conference rooms to try to work through some of the nastier problems. But your boss catches you at it and disbands the meeting saying, "The design phase is over. The only allowable activity is coding. Now get back to it."

The code generated by Dandelion is really hideous. It turns out that you and your team were using association and aggregation the wrong way after all. All the generated code has to be edited to correct these flaws. Editing this code is extremely difficult because it has been instrumented with ugly comment blocks that have special syntax that Dandelion needs in order to keep the diagrams in sync with the code. If you accidentally alter one of these comments, then the diagrams will be regenerated incorrectly. It turns out that "round-the-horn engineering" requires an awful lot of effort.

The more you try to keep the code compatible with Dandelion, the more errors Dandelion generates. In the end, you give up and decide to keep the diagrams up to date manually. A second later, you decide there's no point in keeping the diagrams up to date at all. Besides, who has time?

Your boss hires a consultant to build tools to count the number of lines of code that are being produced. He puts a big thermometer graph on the wall with the number 1,000,000 on the top. Every day he extends the red line to show how many lines have been added.

Three days after the thermometer appears on the wall, your boss stops you in the hall. "That graph isn't growing fast enough. We need to have a million lines done by October 1."

"We aren't even sh-sh-sure that the proshect will require a m-million linezh," you blather.

"We have to have a million lines done by October 1," your boss reiterates. His points have grown again, and

part of a task, they integrate what they have with the rest of the system. Thus, the code base grows daily, and integration difficulties are minimized.

The developers communicate with Jay on a daily basis. They go to him whenever they have a question about the functionality of the system or the interpretation of an acceptance test case.

Jay, good as his word, supplies the team with a steady stream of acceptance-test scripts. The team reads these carefully and thereby gains a much better understanding of what Jay expects the system to do.

By the beginning of the second week, there is enough functionality to demonstrate to Jay. Jay watchs eagerly as the demonstration passes test case after test case.

"This is really cool," Jay says as the demonstration finally ends. "But this doesn't seem like one-third of the tasks. Is your velocity slower than anticipated?"

You grimace. You've been waiting for a good time to mention this to Jay, but now Jay is forcing the issue.

"Yes, unfortunately we are going slower than we had expected. The new application server we are using is turning out to be a pain to configure. Also, it takes forever to reboot, and we have to reboot it whenever we make even the slightest change to its configuration."

Jay eyes you with suspicion. The stress of last Monday's negotiations has still not entirely dissipated. He says, "And what does this mean to our schedule? We can't slip it again, we just can't. Russ will have a fit! He'll haul us all into the woodshed and ream us some new ones."

You look Jay right in the eyes. There's no pleasant way to give someone news like this. So you just blurt out, "Look, if things keep going like their going, then we're not going to be done with everything by next Friday! Now it's possible that we'll figure out a way to go faster. But, frankly, I wouldn't depend on that. You should start thinking about one or two tasks that could be removed from the iteration without ruining the demonstration for Russ. Come hell or high water, we are going to give that demonstration on Friday, and I don't think you want us to choose which tasks to omit."

the Grecian formula he uses on them creates an aura of authority and competence. "Are you sure your comment blocks are big enough?"

Then, in a flash of managerial insight he says, "I have it! I want you to institute a new policy among the engineers. No line of code is to be longer than 20 characters. Any such line must be split into two or more—preferably more. All existing code needs to be reworked to this standard. That'll get our line count up!"

You decide not to tell him that this will require two unscheduled man-months. You decide not to tell him anything at all. You decide that intravenous injections of pure ethanol are the only solution. You make the appropriate arrangements.

Hack, hack, hack, and hack. You and your team madly code away. By August 1, your boss, frowning at the thermometer on the wall institutes a mandatory 50-hour workweek.

Hack, hack, hack, and hack. By September 1, the thermometer is at 1.2 million lines, and your boss asks you to write a report describing why you exceeded the coding budget by 20%. He institutes mandatory Saturdays and demands that the project be brought back down to a million lines. You start a campaign of remerging lines.

Hack, hack, hack, and hack. Tempers are flaring; people are quitting; QA is raining trouble reports down on you. Customers are demanding installation and user manuals; salesmen are demanding advance demonstrations for special customers; the requirements document is still thrashing; the marketing folks are complaining that the product isn't anything like they specified, and the liquor store won't accept your credit card anymore. Something has to give. On September 15, BB calls a meeting.

As he enters the room, his points are emitting clouds of steam. When he speaks, the bass overtones of his carefully manicured voice cause the pit of your stomach to roll over. "The QA manager has told me that this project has less than 50% of the required features implemented. He has also informed me that the system crashes all the time, yields wrong results, and is hideously slow. He has also complained that he cannot keep up with the continuous train of daily releases, each more buggy than the last!"

He stops for a few seconds, visibly trying to compose himself. "The QA manager estimates that, at this

"Aw, for Pete's sake!" Jay barely manages to stifle yelling his last word as he stalks away shaking his head.

Not for the first time, you say to yourself, "Nobody ever promised me project management would be easy." You are pretty sure it won't be the last time either.

~ ~ ~

Actually, things go a bit better than you had hoped. The team does, in fact, have to drop one task from the iteration, but Jay chooses wisely, and the demonstration for Russ goes without a hitch.

Russ is not impressed with the progress, but neither is he dismayed. He simply says, "This is pretty good. But remember, we have to be able to demonstrate this system at the trade show in July, and at this rate it doesn't look like you'll have all that much to show."

Jay, whose attitude has improved dramatically with the completion of the iteration, responds to Russ by saying, "Russ, this team is working hard and well. When July comes around, I am confident that we'll have something significant to demonstrate. It won't be everything, and some of it may be smoke and mirrors, but we'll have something."

Painful though the last iteration was, it calibrated your velocity numbers. The next iteration goes much better. Not because your team gets more done than in the last iteration, but simply because they don't have to remove any tasks or stories in the middle of the iteration.

By the start of the fourth iteration, a natural rhythm is established. Jay, you, and the team know exactly what to expect from each other. The team is running hard, but the pace is sustainable. You are confident that the team can keep up this pace for a year or more.

The number of surprises in the schedule diminishes to near zero; however, the number of surprises in the requirements does not. Jay and Russ frequently look over the growing system and make recommendations or changes to the existing functionality. But all parties realize that these changes take time and must be scheduled. So the changes do not cause anyone's expectations to be violated.

rate of development, we won't be able to ship the product until December!"

Actually, you think it's more like March, but you don't say anything.

"December!" BB roars with such derision that people duck their heads as though he were pointing an assault rifle at them. "December is absolutely out of the question. Team leaders, I want new estimates on my desk in the morning. I am hereby mandating 65-hour work-weeks until this project is complete. And it better be complete by November 1."

As he leaves the conference room, he is heard to mutter, "Empowerment—Bah!"

* * *

Your boss is bald; his points are mounted on BB's wall. The fluorescent lights reflecting off his pate momentarily dazzle you.

"Do you have anything to drink?" he asks. Having just finished your last bottle of Boone's Farm, you pull a bottle of Thunderbird from your bookshelf and pour it into his coffee mug. "What's it going to take to get this project done?" he asks.

"We need to freeze the requirements, analyze them, design them, and then implement them." You say callously.

"By November 1?" your boss exclaims incredulously. "No way! Just get back to coding the damned thing." He storms out, scratching his vacant head.

A few days later, you find that your boss has been transferred to the corporate research division. Turnover has skyrocketed. Customers, informed at the last minute that their orders cannot be fulfilled on time, have begun to cancel their orders. Marketing is reevaluating whether or not this product aligns with the overall goals of the company, etc., etc. Memos fly, heads roll, policies change, and things are, overall, pretty grim.

Finally, by March, after far too many 65-hour weeks, a very shaky version of the software is ready. In the field, bug discovery rates are high, and the technical support staff are at their wit's end trying to cope with the complaints and demands of the irate customers. Nobody is happy.

In April, BB decides to buy his way out of the problem by licensing a product produced by Rupert industries and redistributing it. The customers are mollified, the marketing folks are smug, and you are laid off.

In March, there is a major demonstration of the system to the board of directors. The system is very limited and is not yet in a form good enough to take to the trade show, but progress is steady, and the board is reasonably impressed.

The second release goes even smoother than the first. By now, the team has figured out a way to automate Jay's acceptance-test scripts. They have also refactored the design of the system to the point where it is really easy to add new features and change old ones.

The second release is done by the end of June and is taken to the trade show. It has less in it than Jay and Russ would have liked, but it does demonstrate the most important features of the system. Though customers at the trade show notice that certain features are missing, overall they are very impressed. You, Russ, and Jay all return from the trade show with smiles on your faces. You all feel as though this project is a winner.

Indeed, many months later you are contacted by Rufus, Inc. They had been working on a system like this for their internal operations. They have cancelled the development of that system after a death-march project and are negotiating to license your technology for their environment.

Indeed, things are looking up!

APPENDIX D

The Source Code Is the Design

I can still remember where I was when I had the insight that eventually led to the following article. In the summer of 1986, I was working a temporary consulting assignment at the China Lake Naval Weapons Center in California. While there, I took the opportunity to attend a panel discussion on Ada. At one point, someone in the audience asked the typical question, "Are software developers engineers?" I don't remember the actual answer, but I do recall that it didn't really seem to address the question. So I sat back and started thinking about how I would answer such a question. I am not sure how, but something in the ensuing discussion caused me to recall an article I had read in Datamation *magazine almost 10 years before that. That article had been a rationale for why engineers needed to be good writers (I think that is what it was about—it has been a long time), but the key point I got from the article was the author's contention that the end result of an engineering process was a document. In other words, engineers produced documents, not things. Other people took those documents and produced things. So, my wandering mind asked the question, "Out of all the documentation that software projects normally generate, was there anything that could truly be considered an engineering document?" The answer that came to me was, "Yes, there was such a document, and only one—the source code."*

Looking at the source code as an engineering document—a design—turned my view of my chosen profession upside down. It changed the way I looked at everything. Also, the more I thought about it, the more I felt that it explained an awful lot of the problems that software projects typically encountered. Or rather, I felt that the fact that most people did not understand this distinction, or actively rejected it, explained a lot of things. Several more years went by before the opportunity presented itself for me to make my argument publicly. An article about software design in The C++ Journal *prompted me to write a letter to the editor about the topic. After an exchange of letters, Livleen Singh, the editor, agreed to publish my thoughts on the topic as an article. What follows is the result.*

—Jack Reeves, December, 22, 2001

What Is Software Design?

© *Jack W. Reeves, 1992*

Object-oriented techniques, C++ in particular, seem to be taking the software world by storm. Numerous articles and books have appeared describing how to apply the new techniques. In general, the questions of whether O-O techniques are just hype have been replaced by questions of how to get the benefits with the least amount of pain. Object-oriented techniques have been around for some time, but this exploding popularity seems a bit unusual. Why the sudden interest? All kinds of explanations have been offered. In truth, there is probably no single reason. Probably, a combination of factors has finally reached critical mass, and things are taking off. Nevertheless, it seems that C++ itself is a major factor in this latest phase of the software revolution. Again, there are probably a number of reasons why, but I want to suggest an answer from a slightly different perspective: C++ has become popular because it makes it easier to design software and program at the same time.

If that comment seems a bit unusual, it is deliberate. What I want to do in this article is take a look at the relationship between programming and software design. For almost 10 years, I have felt that the software industry collectively misses a subtle point about the difference between developing a software design and what a software design really is. I think there is a profound lesson in the growing popularity of C++ about what we can do to become better software engineers, if only we see it. This lesson is that programming is not about building software; programming is about designing software.

Years ago, I was attending a seminar where the question came up of whether software development is an engineering discipline or not. While I do not remember the resulting discussion, I do remember how it catalyzed my own thinking that the software industry has created some false parallels with hardware engineering while missing some perfectly valid parallels. In essence, I concluded that we are not software engineers because we do not realize what a software design really is. I am even more convinced of that today.

The final goal of any engineering activity is some type of documentation. When a design effort is complete, the design documentation is turned over to the manufacturing team. This is a completely different group with completely different skills from the design team. If the design documents truly represent a complete design, the manufacturing team can proceed to build the product. In fact, they can proceed to build lots of the product, all without any further intervention from the designers. After reviewing the software development life cycle as I understood it, I concluded that the only software documentation that actually seems to satisfy the criteria of an engineering design is the source-code listings.

There are probably enough arguments both for and against this premise to fill numerous articles. This article assumes that final source code is the real software design and then examines some of the consequences of that assumption. I may not be able to prove that this point of view is correct, but I hope to show that it does explain some of the observed facts of the software industry, including the popularity of C++.

There is one consequence of considering code as software design that completely overwhelms all others. It is so important and so obvious that it is a total blind spot for most software organizations. This is the fact that software is cheap to build. It does not qualify as inexpensive; it is so cheap, it is almost free. If source code is a software design, then actually building software is done by compilers and linkers. We often refer to the process of compiling and linking a complete software system as "doing a build." The capital investment in software construction equipment is low—all it really takes is a computer, an editor, a compiler, and a linker. Once a build environment is available, then actually doing a software build just takes a little time. Compiling a 50,000 line C++ program may seem to take forever, but how long would it take to build a hardware system that had a design of the same complexity as 50,000 lines of C++?

Another consequence of considering source code as software design is the fact that a software design is relatively easy to create, at least in the mechanical sense. Writing (i.e., designing) a typical software module of 50 to 100 lines of code is usually only a couple of day's effort (getting it fully debugged is another story, but more on that later). It is tempting to ask if there is any other engineering discipline that can produce designs of such complexity as software in such a short time, but first we have to figure out how to measure and compare complexity. Nevertheless, it is obvious that software designs get very large rather quickly.

Given that software designs are relatively easy to turn out, and essentially free to build, an unsurprising revelation is that software designs tend to be incredibly large and complex. This may seem obvious, but the magnitude of the problem is often ignored. School projects often end up being several thousand lines of code. There are software products with 10,000-line designs that are given away by their designers. We have long since passed the point where simple software is of much interest. Typical commercial software products have designs that consist of hundreds of thousands of lines. Many software designs run into the millions. Additionally, software designs are almost always constantly evolving. While the current design may only be a few thousand lines of code, many times that may actually have been written over the life of the product.

While there are certainly examples of hardware designs that are arguably as complex as software designs, note two facts about modern hardware. First—complex hardware engineering efforts are not always as free of bugs as software critics would have us believe. Major microprocessors have been shipped with errors in their logic, bridges have collapsed, dams have broken, airliners have fallen out of the sky, and thousands of automobiles and other consumer products have been recalled—all within recent memory and all the result of design errors. Second—complex hardware designs have correspondingly complex and expensive build phases. As a result, the ability to manufacture such systems limits the number of companies that produce truly complex hardware designs. No such limitations exist for software. There are hundreds of software organizations and thousands of very complex software systems in existence. Both the number and the complexity are growing daily. This means that the software industry is not likely to find solutions to its problems by trying to emulate hardware developers. If anything, as CAD and CAM systems have helped hardware designers to create more and more complex designs, hardware engineering is becoming more and more like software development.

Designing software is an exercise in managing complexity. The complexity exists within the software design itself, within the software organization of the company, and within the industry as a whole. Software design is very similar to systems design. It can span multiple technologies and often involves multiple subdisciplines. Software specifications tend to be fluid, changing rapidly and often, usually while the design process is still going on. Software development teams also tend to be fluid, likewise often changing in the middle of the design process. In many ways, software bears more resemblance to complex social or organic systems than to hardware. All of this makes software design a difficult and error-prone process. None of this is original thinking, but almost 30 years after the software engineering revolution began, software development is still seen as an undisciplined art compared to other engineering professions.

The general consensus is that when real engineers get through with a design, no matter how complex, they are pretty sure it will work. They are also pretty sure it can be built using accepted construction techniques. In order for this to happen, hardware engineers spend a considerable amount of time validating and refining their designs. Consider a bridge design, for example. Before such a design is actually built, the engineers do structural analysis—they build computer models and run simulations, they build scale models and test them in wind tunnels or other ways. In short, the designers do everything they can think of to make sure the design is a good design before it is built. The design of a new airliner is even worse; for those, full-scale prototypes must be built and test flown to validate the design predictions.

It seems obvious to most people that software designs do not go through the same rigorous engineering as hardware designs. However, if we consider source code as design, we see that software designers actually do a considerable amount of validating and refining their designs. Software designers do not call it engineering, however, we call it testing and debugging. Most people do not consider testing and debugging as real "engineering"—certainly not in the software business. The reason has more to do with the refusal of the software industry to accept code as design than with any real engineering difference. Mock-ups, prototypes, and breadboards are actually an accepted part of other engineering disciplines. Software designers do not have or use more formal methods of validating their designs because of the simple economics of the software build cycle.

Revelation number one: it is cheaper and simpler to just build the design and test it than to do anything else. We do not care how many builds we do—they cost next to nothing in terms of time, and the resources used can be completely reclaimed later if we discard the build. Note that testing is not just concerned with getting the current design correct, it is part of the process of refining the design. Hardware engineers of complex systems often build models (or at least they visually render their designs using computer graphics). This allows them to get a "feel" for the design that is not possible by just reviewing the design itself. Building such a model is both impossible and unnecessary with a software design. We just build the product itself. Even if formal software proofs were as automatic as a compiler, we would still do build/test cycles. Ergo, formal proofs have never been of much practical interest to the software industry.

This is the reality of the software development process today. Ever more complex software designs are being created by an ever-increasing number of people and organizations. These designs will be coded in some programming language and then validated and refined via the build/test cycle. The process is error prone and not particularly rigorous to begin with. The fact that a great many software developers do not want to believe that this is the way it works compounds the problem enormously.

Most current software development processes try to segregate the different phases of software design into separate pigeonholes. The top-level design must be completed and frozen before any code is written. Testing and debugging are necessary just to weed out the construction mistakes. In between are the programmers, the construction workers of the software industry. Many believe that if we could just get programmers to quit "hacking" and "build" the designs as given to them (and in the process, make fewer errors) then software development might mature into a true engineering discipline. This is not likely to happen as long as the process ignores the engineering and economic realities.

For example, no other modern industry would tolerate a rework rate of over 100% in its manufacturing process. A construction worker who cannot build it right the first time, most of the time, is soon out of a job. In software, even the smallest piece of code is likely to be revised or completely rewritten during testing and debugging. We accept this sort of refinement during a creative process like design, not as part of a manufacturing process. No one expects an engineer to create a perfect design the first time. Even if she does, it must still be put through the refinement process just to prove that it is perfect.

If we learn nothing else from Japanese management techniques, we should learn that it is counterproductive to blame the workers for errors in the process. Instead of continuing to force software development to conform to an incorrect process model, we need to revise the process so that it helps rather than hinders efforts to produce better software. This is the litmus test of "software engineering." Engineering is about how you do the process, not about whether the final design document needs a CAD system to produce it.

The overwhelming problem with software development is that everything is part of the design process. Coding is design, testing and debugging are part of design, and what we typically call software design is still part of design. Software may be cheap to build, but it is incredibly expensive to design. Software is so complex that there are plenty of different design aspects and their resulting design views. The problem is that all the different aspects interrelate (just like they do in hardware engineering). It would be nice if top-level designers could ignore the details of module algorithm design. Likewise, it would be nice if programmers did not have to worry about top-level design issues when designing the internal algorithms of a module. Unfortunately, the aspects of one design layer intrude into the others. The choice of algorithms for a given module can be as important to the overall success of the software system as any of the higher level design aspects. There is no hierarchy of importance among the different aspects of a software design. An incorrect design at the lowest module level can be as fatal as a mistake at the highest level. A software design must be complete and correct in all its aspects, or all software builds based on the design will be erroneous.

In order to deal with the complexity, software is designed in layers. When a programmer is worrying about the detailed design of one module, there are probably hundreds of other modules and thousands of other details that he cannot possibly worry about at the same time. For example, there are important aspects of software design that do not fall cleanly into the categories of data structures and algorithms. Ideally, programmers should not have to worry about these other aspects of a design when designing code.

This is not how it works, however, and the reasons start to make sense. The software design is not complete until it has been coded and tested. Testing is a fundamental part of the design validation and refinement process. The high-level structural design is not a complete software design; it is just a structural framework for the detailed design. We have very limited capabilities for rigorously validating a high-level design. The detailed design will ultimately influence (or should be allowed to influence) the high-level design at least as much as other factors. Refining all the aspects of a design is a process that should be happening throughout the design cycle. If any aspect of the design is frozen out of the refinement process, it is hardly surprising that the final design will be poor or even unworkable.

It would be nice if high-level software design could be a more rigorous engineering process, but the real world of software systems is not rigorous. Software is too complex, and it depends on too many other things. Maybe some hardware does not work quite the way the designers thought it did, or a library routine has an undocumented restriction. These are the kinds of problems that every software project encounters sooner or later. These are the kinds of problems discovered during testing (if we do a good job of testing), for the simple reason that there was no way to discover them earlier. When they are discovered, they force a change in the design. If we are lucky, the design changes are local. More often than not, the changes will ripple through some significant portion of the entire software design (Murphy's law). When part of the effected design cannot change for some reason, then the other parts of the design will have to be weakened to accommodate. This often results is what managers perceive as "hacking," but it is the reality of software development.

For example, I recently worked on a project where a timing dependency was discovered between the internals of module A and another module B. Unfortunately, the internals of module A were hidden behind an abstraction that did not permit any way to incorporate the invocation of module B in its proper sequence. Naturally, by the time the problem was discovered, it was much too late to try to change the abstraction of A. As expected, what happened was an increasingly complex set of "fixes" applied to the internal design of A. Before we finished installing version 1, there was the general feeling that the design was breaking down. Every new fix was likely to break some older fix. This is a normal software development project. Eventually, my colleagues and I argued for a change in the design, but we had to volunteer free overtime in order to get management to agree.

On any software project of typical size, problems like these are guaranteed to come up. Despite all attempts to prevent it, important details will be overlooked. This is the difference between craft and engineering. Experience can lead us in the right direction. This is craft. Experience will only take us so far into uncharted territory. Then we must take what we started with and make it better through a controlled process of refinement. This is engineering.

As just a small point, all programmers know that writing the software design documents after the code instead of before, produces much more accurate documents. The reason is now obvious. The final design, as reflected in code, is the only one refined during the build/test cycle. The probability of the initial design being unchanged during this cycle is inversely related to the number of modules and number of programmers on a project. It rapidly becomes indistinguishable from zero.

In software engineering, we desperately need good design at all levels. In particular, we need good top-level design. The better the early design, the easier detailed design will be. Designers should use anything that helps. Structure charts, Booch diagrams, state tables, PDL, etc.—if it helps, then use it. We must keep in mind, however, that these tools and notations are not a software design. Eventually, we have to create the real software design, and it will be in some programming language. Therefore, we should not be afraid to code our designs as we derive them. We simply must be willing to refine them as necessary.

There is as yet no design notation equally suited for use in both top-level design and detailed design. Ultimately, the design will end up coded in some programming language. This means that top-level design notations have to be translated into the target programming language before detailed design can begin. This translation step takes time and introduces errors. Rather than translate from a notation that may not map cleanly into the programming language of choice, programmers often go back to the requirements and redo the top-level design, coding it as they go. This, too, is part of the reality of software development.

It is probably better to let the original designers write the original code, rather than have someone else translate a language-independent design later. What we need is a unified design notation suitable for all levels of design. In other words, we need a programming language that is also suitable for capturing high-level design concepts.

This is where C++ comes in. C++ is a programming language suitable for real-world projects that is also a more expressive software design language. C++ allows us to directly express high-level information about design components. This makes it easier to produce the design and easier to refine it later. With its stronger type checking, it also helps the process of detecting design errors. This results in a more robust design, in essence a better engineered design.

Ultimately, a software design must be represented in some programming language and then validated and refined via a build/test cycle. Any pretense otherwise is just silliness. Consider what software development tools and techniques have gained popularity. Structured programming was considered a breakthrough in its time. Pascal popularized it and in turn became popular. Object-oriented design is the new rage, and C++ is at the heart of it. Now think about what has not worked. CASE tools? Popular, yes; universal, no. Structure charts? Same thing. Likewise, Warner–Orr diagrams, Booch diagrams, object diagrams, you name it. Each has its strengths, and a single fundamental weakness—it really isn't a software design. In fact, the only software design notation that can be called widespread is PDL, and what does that look like?

This says that the collective subconscious of the software industry instinctively knows that improvements in programming techniques, and real-world programming languages in particular, are overwhelmingly more important than anything else in the software business. It also says that programmers are interested in design. When more expressive programming languages become available, software developers will adopt them.

Also consider how the process of software development is changing. Once upon a time, we had the waterfall process. Now we talk of spiral development and rapid prototyping. While such techniques are often justified with terms like "risk abatement" and "shortened product delivery times," they are really just excuses to start coding earlier in the life cycle. This is good. This allows the build/test cycle to start validating and refining the design earlier. It also means that it is more likely that the software designers who developed the top-level design are still around to do the detailed design.

As noted above, engineering is more about how you do the process than it is about what the final product looks like. We in the software business are close to being engineers, but we need a couple of perceptual changes. Programming and the build/test cycle are central to the process of engineering software. We need to manage them as such. The economics of the build/test cycle, plus the fact that a software system can represent practically anything, makes it very unlikely that we will find any general-purpose methods for validating a software design. We can improve this process, but we cannot escape it.

One final point: the goal of any engineering design project is the production of some documentation. Obviously, the actual design documents are the most important, but they are not the only ones that must be produced. Someone is eventually expected to use the software. It is also likely that the system will have to be modified and enhanced at a later time. This means that auxiliary documentation is as important for a software project as it is for a hardware project. Ignoring for now, user manuals, installation guides, and other documents not directly associated with the design process, there are still two important needs that must be solved with auxiliary design documents.

The first use of auxiliary documentation is to capture important information from the problem space that did not make it directly into the design. Software design involves inventing software concepts to model concepts in a problem space. This process requires developing an understanding of the problem space concepts. Usually, this understanding will include information that does not directly end up being modeled in the software space, but which nevertheless helped the designer determine what the essential concepts were and how best to model them. This information should be captured somewhere in case the model needs to be changed at a later time.

The second important need for auxiliary documentation is to document those aspects of the design that are difficult to extract directly from the design itself. These can include both high-level and low-level aspects. Many of these aspects are best depicted graphically. This makes them hard to include as comments in the source code. This is not an argument for a graphical software design notation instead of a programming language. This is no different from the need for textual descriptions to accompany the graphical design documents of hardware disciplines.

Never forget that the source code determines what the actual design really is, not the auxiliary documentation. Ideally, software tools would be available that postprocessed a source-code design and generated the auxiliary documentation. That may be too much to expect. The next best thing might be some tools that let programmers (or technical writers) extract specific information from the source code that can then be documented in some other way. Undoubtedly, keeping such documentation up to date manually is difficult. This is another argument for the need for more expressive programming languages. It is also an argument for keeping such auxiliary documentation to a minimum and keeping it as informal as possible until as late in the project as possible. Again, we could use some better tools; otherwise we end up falling back on pencil, paper, and chalkboards.

To summarize,

- Real software runs on computers. It is a sequence of ones and zeros that is stored on some magnetic media. It is not a program listing in C++ (or any other programming language).
- A program listing is a document that represents a software design. Compilers and linkers actually build software designs.
- Real software is incredibly cheap to build, and it is getting cheaper all the time as computers get faster.
- Real software is incredibly expensive to design. This is true because software is incredibly complex and because practically all the steps of a software project are part of the design process.
- Programming is a design activity—a good software design process recognizes this and does not hesitate to code when coding makes sense.
- Coding actually makes sense more often than believed. Often, the process of rendering the design in code will reveal oversights and the need for additional design effort. The earlier this occurs, the better will be the design.
- Since software is so cheap to build, formal engineering validation methods are not of much use in real-world software development. It is easier and cheaper to just build the design and test it than to try to prove it.
- Testing and debugging are design activities—they are the software equivalent of the design validation and refinement processes of other engineering disciplines. A good software design process recognizes this and does not try to shortchange the steps.
- There are other design activities—call them top-level design, module design, structural design, architectural design, or whatever. A good software design process recognizes this and deliberately includes the steps.
- All design activities interact. A good software design process recognizes this and allows the design to change, sometimes radically, as various design steps reveal the need.
- Many different software design notations are potentially useful—as auxiliary documentation and as tools to help facilitate the design process. They are not a software design.
- Software development is still more a craft than an engineering discipline. This is primarily because of a lack of rigor in the critical processes of validating and improving a design.
- Ultimately, real advances in software development depend on advances in programming techniques, which in turn mean advances in programming languages. C++ is such an advance. It has exploded in popularity because it is a mainstream programming language that directly supports better software design.
- C++ is a step in the right direction, but still more advances are needed.

Afterword

As I look back on what I wrote almost 10 years ago, I am struck by several points. The first (and most relevant to this book) is that today I am even more convinced of the fundamental truth of the key points that I tried to make than I was then. My conviction is supported by a number of popular developments in the ensuing years that have reinforced many of the points. The most obvious (and perhaps least important) is the popularity of object-oriented programming languages. There are now many OO programming languages besides C++. In addition, there are

OO design notations such as the UML. My contention that OO programming languages have gained popularity because they allow more expressive designs to be captured directly in code seems rather passé now.

The concept of refactoring—restructuring a code base to make it more robust and reusable— also parallels my contention that all aspects of a design should be flexible and allowed to change as the design is validated. Refactoring simply provides a process and a set of guidelines on how to go about improving a design that has demonstrated some weaknesses.

Finally, there is the whole concept of Agile Development. While eXtreme Programming is the best known of these new approaches, they all have in common the recognition that the source code is the most important product of a software-development effort.

On the other hand, there are a number of points—some of which I touched on in the article—that have grown in importance to me in the ensuing years. The first is the importance of architecture, or top-level design. In the article, I made the point that architecture is just one part of design, and it needs to remain fluid as the build/test cycle validates the design. This is fundamentally true, but in retrospect, I think it was a little naïve of me. While the build/test cycle may reveal problems in an architecture, more problems are usually revealed by changing requirements. Designing software "in the large" is tough, and neither new programming languages, like Java or C++, nor graphical notations, such as UML, are of much help to people who do not know how to do it well. Furthermore, once a project has built a significant amount of code around an architecture, fundamentally changing that architecture is often tantamount to scrapping the project and starting over, which means it doesn't happen. Even projects and organizations that fundamentally accept the concept of refactoring are often still reluctant to tackle something that looks like a complete rewrite. This means that getting it right the first time (or at least close) is important, and getting more so as projects get larger. Fortunately, this is the area that software design patterns are helping to address.

One of the other areas that I feel needs more emphasis is auxiliary documentation, especially architecture documentation. While the source code may be the design, trying to figure out the architecture from the source code can be a daunting experience. In the article, I expressed the hope that software tools might emerge to help software developers automatically maintain auxiliary documentation from the source code. I have pretty much given up on that idea. A good object-oriented architecture can usually be described in a few diagrams and a few dozen pages of text. Those diagrams (and text) must concentrate on the key classes and relationships in the design, however. Unfortunately, I see no real hope that software tools are ever going to be smart enough to extract those important aspects from the mass of detail in the source code. That means people are going to have to write and maintain such documentation. I still think it is better to write it after the source code, or at least at the same time, than to try to write it before.

Finally, I remarked at the end of the article that C++ was an advance in programming—and hence software design—art, but that still more advances were needed. Given that I see a total lack of any real advances in programming art in the languages that have risen to challenge C++'s popularity, I feel this is even more true today than it was when I first wrote it.

—Jack Reeves, January, 1, 2002

Index

Practices of eXtreme Programming

Whole Team

All the contributors to an XP project—developers, business analysts, testers, etc.—work together in an open space, members of one team. The walls of this space are littered with big visible charts and other evidences of their progress.

Planning Game

Planning is continuous and progressive. Every two weeks, for the next two weeks, developers estimate the cost of the candidate features, and customers select those features to be implemented based upon cost and business value.

Customer Tests

As part of selecting each desired feature, the customers define automated acceptance tests to show that the feature is working.

Simple Design

The team keeps the design exactly suited for the current functionality of the system. It passes all the tests, contains no duplication, expresses everything the authors want expressed, and contains as little code as possible.

Pair Programming

All production software is built by two programmers, sitting side by side, at the same machine.

Test-Driven Development

The programmers work in very short cycles, adding a failing test, then making it work.

Design Improvement

Don't let the sun set on bad code. Keep the code as clean and expressive as possible.

Continuous Integration

The team keeps the system fully integrated at all times.

Collective Code Ownership

Any pair of programmers can improve any code at any time.

Coding Standard

All the code in the system looks as if it was written by a single—very competent—individual.

Metaphor

The team develops a common vision of how the program works.

Sustainable Pace

The team is in it for the long term. They work hard, at a pace that can be sustained indefinitely. They conserve their energy, treating the project as a marathon rather than a sprint.